D1583159

The Life of Bertrand Russell

by the same author

EINSTEIN: THE LIFE AND TIMES

JBS: THE LIFE AND WORK OF J. B. S. HALDANE

THE HUXLEYS

TIZARD

THE RISE OF THE BOFFINS

THE BIRTH OF THE BOMB

Ronald W. Clark

The Life of Bertrand Russell

JONATHAN CAPE
AND
WEIDENFELD & NICOLSON

FIRST PUBLISHED 1975

JONATHAN CAPE LTD, 30 BEDFORD SQUARE, LONDON WC1
WEIDENFELD & NICOLSON, 11 ST JOHN'S HILL, LONDON SW11

JONATHAN CAPE ISBN 0 224 01165 0
WEIDENFELD & NICOLSON ISBN 0 297 77018 7

PRINTED IN GREAT BRITAIN BY
BUTLER & TANNER LTD
FROME AND LONDON

"When will people learn the robustness of truth? I do not know who my biographer may be, but I should like him to report 'with what flourish his nature will' something like this: 'I was not a solemn stained glass saint, existing only for purposes of edification; I existed from my own centre, many things that I did were regrettable, I did not respect respectable people, and when I pretended to do so it was humbug. I lied and practised hypocrisy, because if I had not I should not have been allowed to do my work; but there is no need to continue the hypocrisy after my death. I hated hypocrisy and lies: I loved life and real people, and wished to get rid of the shams that prevent us from loving real people as they really are. I believed in laughter and spontaneity, and trusted to nature to bring out the genuine good in people, if once genuineness could come to be tolerated.' "

Bertrand Russell to Lady Ottoline Morrell,
27 August 1918

Contents

The Last Attachment

Preface

Men – and women – will be writing about Bertrand Russell as long after his death as they have been writing about Leonardo or Napoleon. His impact on twentieth-century philosophy will be a subject for continuing discussion, and so will the more specific interactions between Russell and Wittgenstein. The effect on the pacifism of the inter-war years of his work for the No-Conscription Fellowship is already being studied. The passage of time will eventually give perspective to the nuclear debate of the post-war decades, and may well provide even more justification for Russell's changes of stance than can be found today. Much the same may well emerge about what has been called his preventive-war phase. Russell's letters to Lucy Donnelly, to Lady Constance Malleson and above all to Lady Ottoline Morrell will, when published in full, reveal the deep emotional complexities of a man for whom no venture was too dangerous, no exploration too unlikely. It will eventually, also, be possible to describe in greater detail some aspects of Russell's later life although it now seems conclusive – at least to the present writer – that these details will not materially alter the picture it is possible to draw today.

All these specialist aspects of one life are different facets of the intellectual diamond which scintillates in the huge quarry of The Bertrand Russell Archives at McMaster University, Hamilton, Ontario. This is the quintessential man, the bundle of contradictions passionately dedicated to intellect, at times carrying the rational argument to irrational extremes; the natural-born emotional adventurer forever hampered by orphaned youth and too-early marriage. This Russell in the round is greater than the sum of his constituent parts, a man of epic proportions, struggling through a lifetime beset with frustration and near-disaster; in youth the constitutional sceptic, in old age the sometimes splendid figure with "courage never to submit or yield".

Marlborough
December 1974

RONALD W. CLARK

Acknowledgments

My first thanks are to The Countess Russell; the Bertrand Russell Estate; McMaster University; and two Canadians and one American. Countess Russell has helped in every possible way, but has made no attempt to restrict complete editorial freedom. Neither she, nor any member of the Bertrand Russell Estate nor of the Bertrand Russell Peace Foundation, has read the manuscript, and there are, indeed, passages in it with which they will probably disagree. However, if a devoted widow and equally devoted colleagues agreed at all points with an objective biographer something would be wrong. A special debt is owed to McMaster University for its permission to quote from Russell's unpublished letters as well as from other material whose copyright it owns. In particular I am grateful to Professor William Ready, who secured Russell's papers, and the copyright in them, for the University; to Kenneth Blackwell, archivist of the University's Bertrand Russell Archives; and to Professor John Slater of the Department of Philosophy, University of Toronto, who owns some 4,000 volumes of Russelliana, the largest collection in the world. Kenneth Blackwell and John Slater have given unqualified advice on many points, and their unrivalled knowledge of Russell's life and work has been invaluable. It is impossible to over-estimate their help, but it must be emphasized that, although they have read the manuscript, the opinions expressed in the biography, and responsibility for the facts given, are mine.

There are many others to whom I am grateful. Lady Constance Malleson, whose undeviating devotion to Russell lasted until his death, more than half a century after their first meeting, was kind enough to lend me her unpublished "Letters to Bertrand Russell from Constance Malleson: 1916–1969", now held by, and the copyright of, McMaster University. Mrs Igor Vinogradoff allowed me to use, at an early stage in my researches, the typed copies of Russell's letters to her mother, Lady Ottoline Morrell, made for her mother in the 1930s, while Xeroxes of the originals were provided through the courtesy of the Humanities Research Center, the University of Texas at Austin, which owns these originals.

Mrs Vinogradoff was helpful in many other ways and allowed me to quote extracts from her mother's diaries and memoirs printed in *Ottoline* and *Ottoline at Garsington*. The Humanities Research Center also co-operated most generously in providing information on other items in its unique collection.

Many who knew Russell well have freely given their help, advice and personal opinions and I am, in addition, grateful to the following for having read parts of the manuscript: Y. R. Chao, Rupert Crawshay-Williams, Mrs Beatrix Dennis, Dr Philip Gaskell, Arthur Goss, Ivor Grattan-Guinness, Mrs Barbara Halpern, the military historian Michael Eliot Howard, Dr Sheila Jones, Adam Roberts, Professor Joseph Rotblat, Boris Uvarov.

I am grateful to the following for permission to use copyright material: George Allen & Unwin for Russell's *Autobiography*, *Portraits from Memory* and *My Philosophical Development*; Lady Allen of Hurtwood; the B.B.C.; the Henry W. and Albert A. Berg Collection, the New York Public Library, the Astor, Lenox and Tilden Foundations for the letters from Bertrand Russell to Gamel Brenan; Professor Norman Birnbaum; the Bodley Head and Henry Regnery for Roy Campbell's *The Georgiad*; Dr Elias Bredsdorff; Gerald Brenan; Mrs Elizabeth Butterworth (Elizabeth Russell); Cambridge University Press for Robert Gittings's *The Forerunner*; Edward Carter; Constable & Co. for George Santayana's *The Letters of George Santayana* and Sir Francis Younghusband's *The Light of Experience*; The Controller of Her Majesty's Stationery Office; Mme Joseph Delteil; Duckworth & Co. for Ralph Schoenman's "Bertrand Russell and the Peace Movement", in George Nakhnikian (ed.), *Bertrand Russell's Philosophy*; Mrs Valerie Eliot; Faber and Faber Ltd and Alfred A. Knopf, Inc., for the extracts from *Ottoline at Garsington* edited by Robert Gathorne–Hardy (copyright © 1974 Julian Vinogradoff); Miss Livia Gollancz; Arthur Goss; Robert Graves; Mrs Barbara Halpern; William Heinemann Ltd, the Strachey Trust and Michael Holroyd (*Lytton Strachey*); Mrs Margaret Adams Kiskadden; Little, Brown & Co. for volumes 1 and 2 of Russell's *Autobiography* (copyright © 1967 and 1968 by George Allen & Unwin); the London School of Economics for extracts from Beatrice Webb's diaries; Executors of the late Kingsley Martin; Julie Medlock; M.I.T. Press for Norbert Wiener's *Ex-Prodigy*; Mrs Dorothy Moore; Mrs Mary Moorman; J. B. Priestley; *Private Eye*; Dr Paul Schilpp for Russell's "My Mental Development"; Charles Scribner's Sons (*The Letters of George Santayana*); Simon and Schuster, Inc., for volume 3 of Russell's *Autobiography* (copyright © 1969 by George Allen & Unwin); the Society of Authors for Katherine Mansfield's *Letters*; *Spectator* (Hamilton, Ontario); Master and Fellows of Trinity College, Cambridge (McTaggart); the Viking Press, Inc. (publishers of *The Collected Letters of D. H. Lawrence* edited by Harry T. Moore. Copyright © 1962 by Angelo Ravagli and C. M. Weekley, Executors of the Estate of Frieda Lawrence Ravagli. All rights reserved), Laurence Pollinger Ltd and the Estate of the late Mrs Frieda Lawrence for selections from letters of D. H. Lawrence; Mrs Harriet E. Whitehead; Executors of the late Ludwig Wittgenstein.

Illustrations

PICTURE CREDITS

The author and publishers would like to thank the following for making photographs available and for giving permission to reproduce illustrations in copyright:

Addresseavisen 46; Associated Press 33, 35, 37, 38, 42, 45; B.B.C. 47, 48, 52; *Boston Globe* 39; Central Press Photos 55; T. E. Corin 29; Cyrus Eaton 50; Fayer & Co. 27; Features International 16, 19, 28; Mrs Barbara Halpern 1, 3, 4, 5, 6, 8, 9; Philippe Halsman 51; Alvin Hunter 40; Imperial College, London 23; Ida Kar 49; Lancashire County Council 12; Mander and Mitcheson 13; Mrs Frances Partridge 36; *The People* 60; Photopress 32; Paul Popper Ltd 26; Press Association 2, 14, 20, 21, 54; Radio Times Hulton Picture Library 24, 25; The Russell Estate 11, 30, 31, 34; Sport & General 10, 57, 58, 59, 62, 63; Trinity College, Cambridge 7; United Press International 18, 41, 43, 44; Mrs Igor Vinogradoff 15.

Plate no. 17 appears by courtesy of Lady Constance Malleson.

In spite of every effort, it has proved impossible to trace the copyright-holders of nos. 22, 53, 56, 61.

The Reason Why

1

The Lodge in the Park

The influence of Bertrand Russell does not spring solely from his intellect, a weapon honed razor-sharp and wielded with impartial relish against both foe and friend. A life-span that only just missed its century also helped; so did ancestry, and so did the genuinely if unexpectedly romantic reasons for which he sometimes marched into battle.

When he was born, the old queen still had three decades to lord it over palm and pine; when he died, men had walked on the moon. When he was young, men still searched with disinterested delight for the logical heart of mathematics; before he died it had been found and had helped to spawn the computer industry. Thus Russell links General Grant's presidency with Nixon's reign, the Zulu wars with the ground-swell of nuclear conscience that floods across frontiers, the vestigial remnants of late nineteenth-century optimism with the dark terror of the times.

This spread of life across four generations provided burden as well as benefit. In education, it is true, his innovations became everyday usage long before his death. To the sexual relationship, a subject never far from intellect or passion, his crusading fervour justified for the masses a freedom previously available only on his own aristocratic and intellectual stamping-grounds. In the politics of peace his record is more contradictory than he would wish and perhaps more successful than his enemies would admit: Pugwash, that little-known international omen of hope which he encouraged into existence, and whose influence surpassed that of C.N.D. of which he became a symbol, may yet be seen to have helped turn men away from the third world war. But in mathematics, where he sought "the true spirit of delight, the exaltation, the sense of being more than man", he was eventually to find sappers working successfully beneath the proud edifice he built. In philosophy he lived long enough to see his revolutionary ideas first abused, then accepted, then become part of history and, as such, vulnerable to dissection and revision. But his spirit survived, buoyed up with an optimism which owed nothing to hope of a next world, unqualified by the wrath to come. After all, he was a Russell.

His long life was begun in a tradition which took it for granted that a man would make his mark on history. On both sides his predecessors had been born to rule, not as a right but a duty, and his radical instincts were based on confidence that to the aristocrat all things are possible. His mother, Kate Stanley, was descended from the French invaders who had landed in 1066, and whose successors had been granted the *pourboire* of an earldom for good work on Bosworth Field. His father, Lord Amberley, son of the 1st Earl Russell who had fought the Reform Bill through Parliament and survived to become Victoria's voice from the past, had been given a comparable though more picturesque background by J. H. Wiffen, librarian to the 1st Earl's father, the 6th Duke of Bedford. Writing the history of the Russells for the duke, Wiffen pressed back regardless, unhampered by mere facts, and unearthed an ancestor who had not only landed, as it were, side by side with the Stanleys near Hastings, but who could claim a link with Olaf the Sharp-eyed, a warrior for whom the dutiful Wiffen found a connection with Scandinavian royalty. In due course of begetting, Olaf produced William, Baron of Briquebec, "the first that took the name of Bertrand". The Baron's son, Hugh Bertrand, crossed the Channel in 1066 and, *vide* Wiffen, the Russells were on their way.

Little of this story was needed. The family could in fact trace a long and distinguished line back to its financial foundation with a plump grant of abbey lands in Tudor times. One incumbent, William, Lord Russell, was executed for alleged complicity in the Rye-House Plot. But, on orders, his chaplain wrote the life of Julian the Apostate which outspokenly argued that resistance to authority may be justified, a belief much favoured by many of the victim's descendants. The accession of William and Mary brought exculpation and a parliamentary bill which claimed that Lord Russell had been wrongly condemned. There was, moreover, family recompense for the miscarriage of justice. The earldom was stepped up to a dukedom. The Stanley "Sans Changer" on their arms might contrast strangely with the Russell "Che Sara Sara", the austere without changing with the happy-go-lucky hedonism of whatever will be, will be; but in mutual self-confidence they were not divided. To Russell, as to all practising members of both families, the fences were there to be taken.

The traditional attitudes had their penalties as certainly as length of life. Leadership demanded that the emotions be kept discreetly from the public gaze. In the world of Russell and his ilk, one did not wince nor cry aloud, a strait-jacketing of the feelings compounded in his case by an intellect which created its own difficulties and traumas. Thus in most of his writings, for most of his friends, an essentially romantic approach to subjects as different as mathematics and the Russian Revolution, the problems of pacifism and of the passions, was concealed by cerebral sparkle. In such circumstances any man might appear more cold-blooded and clinical than he really was. For Russell, whose battened-down youth

The Russell family tree

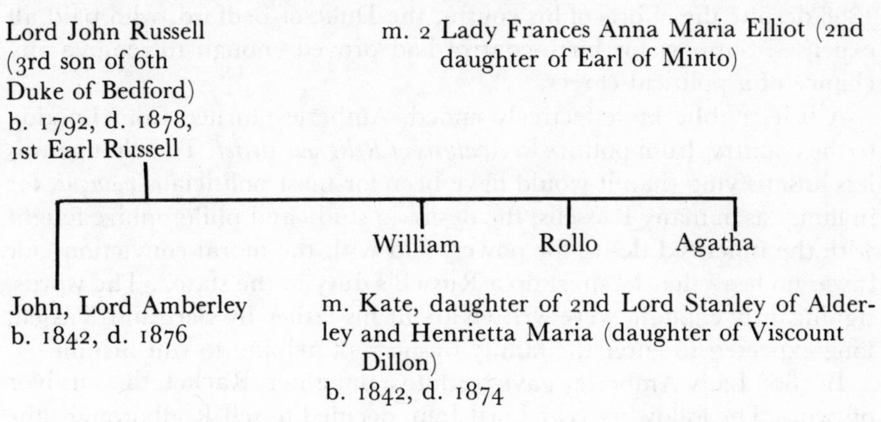

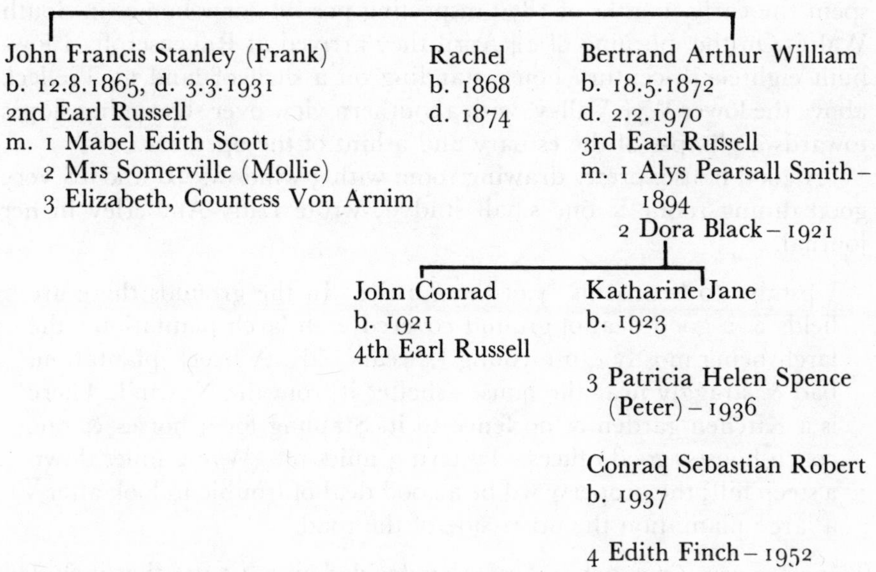

was followed by buttoned-up marriage, two ghosts which gibbered over his shoulder down the years, much emotion demanded much concealment.

Lord Amberley, who suffered from Lord John's fame as much as Russell's own children were to suffer from his, married Kate Stanley on 8 November 1864. He was twenty-one, his wife a few months older. An heir to the title, John Francis Stanley, later known as Frank, was born on 12 August 1865 in, as he put it in his autobiography, "strict accordance with the best English tradition of family duty". Two years later Amberley stood for Nottingham and entered politics. The following year he left them, being unsuccessful in the General Election of 1868 despite the efforts of his cousin, the Duke of Bedford, who paid all expenses. Support for birth-control had proved enough to remove any chance of a political career.

A brief public life effectively ended, Amberley turned from London to the country, from politics to *Analysis of Religious Belief*. The change was less unsatisfying than it would have been for most politicians *manqué*, for in him, "as in many Russells, the desire to study and philosophize fought with the inherited desire for power, and with the moral conviction – for it was no less – that he must do a Russell's duty to the state". The words, significantly enough, were written about his father by Bertrand Russell, long expected to enter the family business of helping to run Britain.

In 1868 Lady Amberley gave birth to a daughter, Rachel, the survivor of twins. The following year Lord John decided to sell Rodborough, the Gloucestershire house in which he had set up his son, and the Amberleys spent the early months of 1870 inspecting possible new homes in South Wales. On the morning of 14 April they arrived at Ravenscroft, a low-built eighteenth-century house standing on a shelf of land at Trelleck above the lower Wye Valley, with a southern view over steepening slopes towards a glimpse of the estuary and a hint of the open sea.

"A good house, pretty drawing room with 3 windows 2E and 1S very good dining room & one small study", wrote Lady Amberley in her journal.

> Upstairs 10 bedrooms, 4 of them attics – In the grounds there are fields & a good deal of ground covered with larch plantations, the larch being mostly quite young (4 years old). A beech plantation, bad & straggly near the house – shelter it from the N. wind. There is a Kitchen garden & no fence to it. Stabling for 3 horses & one coach house – good offices – Tintern 3 miles off – Wye 2 miles down a steep hill; the property wd be a good deal of trouble to look after – a large plantation the other side of the road.

The price was £7,000, but Amberley decided on a £5,000 that included only forty of the estate's eighty-eight acres.

Two months afterwards, the young couple moved in. That evening Amberley took his wife into the surrounding woods she had not yet inspected. "I was quite enchanted with the wildness & beauty of the place", Kate wrote, "so A & I danced round with delight & from that moment I am sure we felt no regret at having left Rodgh. though he had been very unhappy about it before."

Here at Ravenscroft, in what are still almost idyllic surroundings, Bertrand Russell was born two years later: apparently the result, as he eventually learnt, of a misadventure in the unmentionable practice of birth-control, the subject which had already led his father into the political wilderness. So great was Lady Amberley's trust in her husband's efficiency that she refused to admit her pregnancy until five months gone. Lady Russell then offered to take Frank and Rachel into Pembroke Lodge, her Richmond Park home, but Kate declined. Amberley, to judge by his journal, remained sceptical.

The 18th May 1872 was bitterly cold, with a threat of snow. In the afternoon, the weather still lowering, Amberley conducted his wife for a short stroll through the grounds. "At about 3.30 as we were walking along the new avenue (Spruce Avenue) K began to feel labour pains", he wrote that evening.

> We came slowly home. At 3.50 in the study I called out to Williams to tell Richards to harness Fenella. Ten minutes later I went down & ordered Richards to go as fast as possible for the doctor. He was not ready & could not start at once. Soon after this Kate went to bed; pains got more & more severe; she called for chloroform & I gave it in very small quantities. Once only before Audland came she got quiet & near unconsciousness. He arrived at 5.30 & immediately after he sat down the water broke. Almost at once the head was born, & I heard the baby's first scream. She asked what sex – Audland & Lizzie (who was by him) said "We cannot tell yet". In a few minutes Audland said "It's a very fine boy". He was born at 5.45. The pains were awful. Audland remarked that not one child in 30 was as big & fat.

That evening he was found to be 21 ins long, the following morning to be 8 lb. 11½ oz. in weight. "The boy vigorous and strong," Amberley noted in his journal.

Two days later Lord John suggested that the child might be called William. Galahad was next proposed but Lady Stanley implored her daughter not to inflict the name on her child. "Basil", "Ambrose", "Godfrey", "Leo", or "Lionel" were also considered and abandoned. Eventually Wiffen came into his own and, with a cast-back to William, Baron of Briquebec, the boy was christened Bertrand Arthur William – although only the first name appeared on his birth certificate.

Both parents had by this time fallen away from religion and therefore sought a non-religious godparent. Kate Amberley wrote to Helen Taylor, step-daughter and companion of John Stuart Mill, an old friend of Lord Amberley. "We hesitated to ask such a favour of Mr. Mill," she said, "otherwise I wished he too cd. have been a god-father – for there is no one in whose steps I wd. rather see a boy of mine following in ever such a humble way, than in Mr. Mill's." Miss Taylor replied that Mill did not think that it would conflict with his beliefs to become a godfather. In due course he accepted and a second godfather was discovered in

Thomas Cobden-Sanderson. Family friend and an old admirer of Kate Stanley; he was later the founder of the Doves Press, a bookbinder and printer "of admirable taste, fecund and versatile in decorative ideas, impeccable in technique, and scrupulous in finish".

Thus launched, Russell found a grand world prepared to receive him. When he and his sister were staying with their grandparents at Pembroke Lodge in 1874, Queen Victoria drove out with Princess Beatrice to visit Lord John. As the queen noted in her diary, her former Prime Minister was "at the door of the house, which is rather low, but pretty inside, & from which, had it not been so dreadfully foggy, there must be a beautiful view". Her Majesty, who disappointed Rachel by her failure to wear a crown, took tea in the drawing-room. Bertie, reported Lord Amberley's sister, Aunt Agatha, "made a nice little bow – but he was much subdued & did not treat Her Majesty with the utter disrespect I expected". Russell, taking a friend's young son on his knee eighty years later, described how he himself had been taken on Queen Victoria's knee, a tribute either to memory or imagination.

There was another incident which he remembered. "In getting out of a carriage at [Mrs Scott's] door, I fell on the paving stones, and hurt my penis," he wrote. "After this I had to sit twice a day in a hot bath and sponge it carefully. As I had hitherto been taught to ignore it, this puzzled me." Whether his adult life was to be affected, psychologically or physiologically, by this early misfortune is not certain. However, his later admission that he "failed totally" when trying to give his first wife a child, and his second wife's statement that at the beginning of their relationship he was "dubious of ever begetting a child" may be significant. "Gossip", adds this statement, "has put upon his alleged numerous love affairs an entirely false interpretation. I believe that he always hoped that a sufficiently strong attraction to some woman would overcome his disability by spontaneous natural means." The disability, whether due to physical accident or inhibited early upbringing, could certainly be conquered and even its existence was not necessarily a misfortune. With an intellect which could easily have created an unbridgeable gulf separating him from the rest, dedicated to mathematics as much for its detachment from human beings as for anything else, Russell might well have lived his ninety-odd years without much understanding of ordinary men and women; as it was, he shared their physical passion to an abnormal degree.

So, also, did he understand their emotional needs, the result of early multiple bereavement and the move to an environment of almost Grand Guignol darkness. While he and his sister were staying at Pembroke Lodge during the queen's visit in 1874, their elder brother developed diphtheria and the two younger children did not return to Ravenscroft until he had recovered. But the persistence of the bacillus was not at that time realized.

On 12 June 1874, Lady Amberley wrote to her mother that Rachel was also now ill. Russell and his elder brother Frank were quickly packed off to the safety of a farm on the fringe of the estate. Then Lady Amberley herself went down with the infection. In a few days she was dead. Rachel died within the week.

"Of all the children she was the dearest to me," Lord Amberley wrote to Lady Russell, "and so my two greatest treasures in this world are gone almost at one blow." It was not the only one. A few months earlier his brother Rollo had been forced to leave the Foreign Office due to failing sight. Before the year was out his brother Willy had gone mad.

None of this registered on Bertrand's infant memory. Neither did the death-bed scene only eighteen months later when Amberley himself, an old man in his early thirties, lay dying in Ravenscroft. On the morning of 9 January 1876, both sons were brought into the sick room. "Frank remained sobbing & crying, so that his Father's hand was wet with his tears," Maude Stanley wrote. "The Dr. lifted Bertrand up & [Amberley] kissed him gently & softly & said 'Goodbye my little dears for ever'. He then lay perfectly quiet with a smile, never moved or shut his hands, but the breathing at last ceased at 9.30."

The immediate cause of death was bronchitis, Russell wrote, "but he seems to have grown steadily weaker from grief. There are, however, no documents after my mother's death; P[embroke] L[odge] destroyed them to prevent a scandal." For the death of mother, father and sister within less than two years, a sufficiently traumatic experience for a boy of three, was made worse by what followed. Lord Amberley, anxious to protect his sons from a religious upbringing, had appointed as guardians two atheists who were to take over when he died. One was Russell's godfather, Cobden-Sanderson; the second, D. A. Spalding, a young scientist studying animal instincts who in 1873 had been employed by the Amberleys as tutor for Frank.

It is possible that Russell's grandparents would have condoned Cobden-Sanderson's lack of faith, much though they regretted it. Spalding was another matter. It was not only that he came from that limbo between "us" and "them" which was inhabited by governesses, tutors and lesser fry. When first employed by the Amberleys, Spalding had been in an advanced stage of consumption, and to a horrified family Amberley's papers now revealed the sequel that had begun after Russell's birth. "Apparently upon grounds of pure theory," Russell wrote, "my father and mother decided that although [Spalding] ought to remain childless on account of his tuberculosis, it was unfair to expect him to remain celibate. My mother, therefore, allowed him to live with her, though I know of no evidence that she derived any pleasure from doing so." Disclosure of this state of affairs was enough to determine the grandparents. Cobden-Sanderson and Spalding, warned by counsel that they had no chance of defending a case against them, capitulated without a fight and in February 1876 Russell was delivered to his grandparents' home in Richmond Park.

Family silence about the reason for the move was the first instalment of a cover-up that failed; almost forty years later the then Duke of Bedford was still destroying Amberley correspondence. But even though the skeleton was kept in the cupboard for the time being, its presence was intuitively felt by the young Russell; being told so little about his parents, and that little with obvious inhibitions, he "vaguely sensed a dark mystery". Looking back over a youthful shoulder, all he saw was doubt and uncertainty.

It is tempting to speculate on Russell's possible fortunes had he been brought up in the progressive and artistic home of Cobden-Sanderson and his enlightened wife. The strong family feeling which ran in his marrow might have coursed less quickly. He might have been less aware, in day-to-day life, of the public duty of being a Russell. He would certainly have been less emotionally deprived, with all the consequences this would have had for a man more in need of emotional support than he would usually admit. Instead, he came at the age of three to Pembroke Lodge, and to the menage which was so largely to make him the man he became.

Thirty years earlier the house had been granted by the queen to Lord John and his wife for occupation during their lives. A low white building, it stands on a slope dropping from the edge of Richmond Park towards the silver curl of the river. In the distance lies the bushiness of the Royal Parks, Windsor on the skyline and, away to the south, a restraining hand enclosing one side of the Thames Valley, the blue trace of the North Downs. The view itself was to be important to Russell; he grew accustomed to wide horizons with an unimpeded sight of the sunset and was unable to live happily without both.

In the eleven acres surrounding Pembroke Lodge, bluebells carpeted the slopes in spring. The fine trees included beeches, chestnuts and oaks, and gave cover for nightingales, redstarts, woodpeckers, finches and other birds not easily found elsewhere near London. Summer-houses, rose gardens, shaded walks and lawns all contributed to what should have been a happy scene. Beyond, there stretched the magnificence of Richmond Park. Yet even in 1876, both the Lodge and its occupants had an air of being past their prime. Lord John, who was to die two years later, was already a figure from the history books, refighting old battles in his study or being wheeled on bath-chair tours round the grounds. As Russell later remembered it, life at Pembroke Lodge had a ghostly air. "The garden was neglected – big trees lay where they fell and slowly decayed, the bushes choked the paths, & where flowers should have been there was nothing but overgrown box hedges," he wrote. "My grandmother who brought me up had endured one tragedy after another, and I lived wholly in the past. She would call me by mistake by the names of people who were dead." If any doubt remained about dark, looming memories, it was removed by a steep pyramid of earth a few hundred yards from the house: the Henry VIII Mound from whose summit the king had watched for smoke from the Tower, the sign that the executioner had struck Anne Boleyn's head from her pretty neck, making it easier for Henry to regularize his position with the Jane Seymour whom he had married the previous day.

Inside, the Lodge which was to be Russell's home for fourteen impressionable years was equally over-shadowed by things past. Beyond the porch stretched a hall lined with his grandfather's copies of long-forgotten parliamentary debates. Leading from it was the great man's study and the sitting-room which unexpectedly housed a statue symbolizing Italy, presented by a grateful government to Lord John for services rendered. Further back were the sitting-rooms of Lady Russell, of her daughter Agatha, and of her son Rollo.

Into this elderly atmosphere Russell and his brother Frank were now implanted, the latter slightly less vulnerable with his seven additional years, and showing early signs of the stubborn independence that was eventually to drop over the precipice into eccentricity and worse.

Frank had already begun his education at Winchester. His younger brother was to suffer a different fate. "After the dreadful experience she had had with her elder grandson, who would throw her letters unread into the fire, Lady Russell dreaded the fatal influence of schools," commented George Santayana, the philosopher who for years followed the fortunes of both brothers from a ringside seat; "Bertie at least must be preserved pure, religious, and affectionate; he must be fitted to take his grandfather's place as Prime Minister and continue the sacred work of Reform." Bertie, after a brief spell at a local kindergarten, was therefore denied the tempering ordeal of a public school and consigned to a mixed bag of governesses and tutors.

As a result he was for all practical purposes reared by the elderly, by women, in a semi-isolated eyrie. Men died. The sun set. Nothing else seemed certain. The melancholy hovered about him even as he did his best, usually with success, to cope with the task in hand.

Lady Russell's evangelical concern to press her younger grandson into a mould of her own choice stamped him physically, intellectually and emotionally with marks that lasted all his life. A puritan despising comfort, indifferent to food and hating wine, she decreed that the day begin with a cold bath all the year round, followed by half-an-hour's piano practice before family prayers at eight. The availability of sufficient servants in the rambling house did little to ameliorate the spartan conditions, the strictly enforced self-discipline, or the sense of public duty which permeated the household like the smell of hops in a brewery. However, this

Commando existence, which sends a shudder down the modern spine, was in fact no more than the norm in many upper-class nineteenth-century households; if it did nothing to prepare Russell for the life to come, it prepared him well enough for this one. A recruit who had survived Pembroke Lodge could meet with ease the taxing physical demands of a huge literary output and regard imprisonment in his ninetieth year as no more than his own attempt to educate his masters.

If the physical regime of Pembroke Lodge was a well-disguised blessing for a tough, wiry youngster capable of taking the strain, the benefits of the intellectual course plotted by Lady Russell and the succession of governesses and tutors were more questionable. Grandma herself was constantly on the bridge, sparing no one, herself and her grandson least of all. Her aim of putting virtue before everything else was maintained, moreover, with the Jesuitical fervour of the born martyr and the Colonel of the Regiment's unquestioning loyalty. In addition, she had a personality which enabled her to leave some imprint of her beliefs on even such unsuitable material as her younger grandson. On his twelfth birthday he received a Bible; inside the flyleaf were written Lady Russell's favourite texts: "Thou shalt not follow a multitude to do evil", "Be strong, and of a good courage; be not afraid, neither be Thou dismayed; for the Lord Thy God is with thee whithersoever thou goest." These texts profoundly influenced Russell's life, and even kept some meaning after he had ceased to believe in God. Ironically enough, Lady Russell's high fervour did her cause little good. The tough physical regime hardened Russell but at the same time generated a permanent allergy to muscular Christianity; the tempering of his intellectual steel turned it into a bright weapon with which to fight the religion that governed the Orders of the Day at Pembroke Lodge.

Within the framework created by Lady Russell, education was breathed in from the air as well as accepted from the changing staff. The first was probably the more important. The Russells had been part of England's fabric for so long that much knowledge of the external world could be illustrated by reference to some handy ancestor. With Lord John's presence filling every cranny of the place, who needed to be taught about parliamentary reform? Uncle William, otherwise Lord Minto, was a walking epitome of the empire on which the sun never set. Granny could reminisce about friends of Horace Walpole she had known. Russell's Stanley grandmother would describe taking tea in Florence with the widow of Bonnie Prince Charlie, the Young Pretender. Lord John had visited Napoleon on Elba. And much conventional education was almost superfluous when holidays could be spent at the Archbishop of Canterbury's home, when the queen or the Prime Minister might drop in for tea, and when both one's grandmothers could, and did, speak fluent German, French and Italian. Years later, noted one of Russell's friends, when other men spoke of the government as "they", Russell always said "we".

In such a context it was to be expected that Russell's schoolroom should in practice be Lord John's library. His account of it gives a hint of the iconoclasm to come. "There were three huge folio volumes called L'Art de verifier les dates," he has said.

> They were too heavy for me to move, and I speculated as to their contents; I imagined something like the tables for finding Easter in the Prayer Book. At last I became old enough to lift one of the volumes out of the shelf, and I found, to my disgust, that the only "art" involved was that of looking up the date in the book. Then there were "The Annals of Ireland" by the Four Masters, in which I read about the men who went to Ireland before the Flood and were drowned in it; I wondered how the Four Masters knew about them, and read no further. There were also more ordinary books, such as Machiavelli and Gibbon and Swift, and a book in four volumes that I never opened: "The Works of Andrew Marvell Esq. M.P.". It was not till I grew up that I discovered Marvell was a poet rather than a politician. I was not supposed to read any of these books; otherwise I should probably not have read any of them. The net result of them was to stimulate my interest in history. No doubt my interest was increased by the fact that my family had been prominent in English history since the early sixteenth century. I was taught English history as the record of a struggle against the King for constitutional liberty. William Lord Russell, who was executed under Charles II, was held up for special admiration, and the inference was encouraged that rebellion is often praiseworthy.

For relaxation there was his bedroom, its walls covered with Bible prints and the only furniture the bed, a huge cupboard and a stuffed seagull. As reading matter, Coxe's *Pelham Administration*, the *Dispatches of Field Marshal the Duke of Wellington*, Mohan Lal's life of Dost Mohammed, and a set of *The Scottish Nation* whose marks on individual volumes – "Aber–Cust", "Dale–Mac" and "Mac–Zet" – tended to confuse.

Against such facilities for do-it-yourself education, a governess or tutor ran a poor second. Few lasted long, possibly because they failed after apprenticeship to maintain Lady Russell's high standards; more probably because they brought with them a whiff of the unorthodox.

Education by tutors combined with residence in a house that looked out over the world from lofty isolation, and Lady Russell's strong fears of contamination, to limit Russell's contact with other children. Driven into himself, he appeared to concentrate on work with an almost unhealthy single-mindedness, an impression confirmed by his youthful essays, page after page filled with copper-plate writing already showing two of the Russell characteristics: the logical development of one idea into the next, and the pre-writing cerebration which enabled sentence after sentence to be written without correction. There are other indications among his papers that Russell was something of a swot. Even a tutor writes to his charge, "I am quite sure you are much better occupied out of school-hours at football or any other outside exercise, than reading, even if it be Milton or Carlyle." Earnest, lonely, so uncertain of everything that he was already searching out beyond unreliable human relationships towards what he hoped would be the incontrovertible truths of mathematics, Russell was, in the words of his brother, an unendurable little prig. He agreed. "I was", he wrote, "a solitary, shy, priggish youth. I had no experience of the social pleasures of boyhood and did not miss them."

With some boys comparative isolation from other children might not have mattered; for him, with the brakes released before he was ready to take off in life, the lack of close friends compounded the problems of a boy twice-orphaned before he was five. Even Frank, less sensitive, more self-reliant, half-saved by Winchester, suffered from his parents' death and as a result was later wide open to the comforting charms and endless guiles of the redoubtable Lady Scott, that set-piece among predatory mothers-in-law, as well as to the attractions of a surfeit of wives and potential wives. His younger brother, equally driven from emotional pillar to emotional post, yet avoiding the grubby reputation which haunted the 2nd Earl through even his more respectable periods, suffered differently but even more, and the imprint is stamped firm and large on many of his letters. Thus at the age of twelve he writes asking his brother, "What do you think of Auntie's engagement? I can't bear it of course. Auntie says one ought to think of it as one more person to love, but then Auntie will go away."

A few years later the departure of a former governess who had returned to Pembroke Lodge for a few weeks is followed by a diary entry in Russell's hand: "And I am left again to loneliness and reserve." And during the unhappy years of his first marriage, bitterly regretting that his first wife had damaged a miniature of his mother, he explains how he had loved it "with the more intensity because I had not permitted the same sort of love to grow up towards any other possession".

The effects of emotional isolation at Pembroke Lodge can be seen starkly in a private journal, written in Greek characters and disguised as Greek exercises, in which Russell recorded his personal feelings and fears. On 9 March 1888 he writes,

> I read an article in the *Nineteenth Century* today about genius and madness. I was much interested by it. Some few of the characteristics mentioned as denoting genius while showing a tendency to madness I believe I can discern in myself. Such are, sexual passion which I have lately had great difficulty in resisting, and a tinge of melancholy

which I have often had lately and which makes me anxious to go to this tutor as there I shall probably be too much occupied to indulge such thoughts. Also it mentions a desire to commit suicide, which though hitherto very slight, has lately been present more or less with me in particular when up a tree. I should say it is quite possible I may develop more or less peculiarly if I am kept at home much longer. The melancholy in me is I think chiefly caused by the reserve which prompted the writing of this, and which is necessary owing to my opinions.

Lack of an emotional hitching-post was quite clearly a major factor in driving the young Russell out on his quest for an intellectual alternative – for certainty in an uncertain world – a journey which took him first into mathematics and then into philosophy. The expedition had started by 1883 when Frank Russell took his brother's mathematical training in hand. "I gave Bertie his first lesson in Euclid this afternoon," he noted in his diary on 9 August. "He is sure to prove a credit to his teacher. He did very well indeed, and we got half through the Definitions." Here there was to be no difficulty. The trouble came with the Axioms. What was the proof of these, the young pupil asked with naive innocence. Everything apparently rested on them, so it was surely essential that their validity was beyond the slightest doubt. Frank's statement that the Axioms had to be taken for granted was one of Russell's early disillusionments. "At these words my hopes crumbled," he remembered; "... why should I admit these things if they can't be proved?" His brother warned that unless he could accept them it would be impossible to continue. Russell capitulated – provisionally.

The complex attraction which mathematics as a whole was soon exerting combined with Russell's natural ability to prevent him moving on, as he had hoped, from mathematics to science. "It turned out that while not without aptitude for pure mathematics, I was completely destitute of the concrete kinds of skill which are necessary in science," he later recalled. "Moreover, within mathematics it was the most abstract parts which I understood best: I had no difficulty with elliptic functions, but could never succeed in mastering optics. Science was therefore closed to me as a career."

Delight in mathematics continued to grow. It was, Russell has said,

> partly mere pleasure in discovering that I possessed a certain kind of skill, part delight in the power of deductive reasoning, partly the restfulness of mathematical certainty; but more than any of these (while I was still a boy) the belief that nature operates according to mathematical laws, and that human actions, like planetary motions, could be calculated if we had sufficient skill. By the time I was fifteen, I had arrived at a theory very similar to that of the

> Cartesians. The movements of living bodies, I felt convinced, were wholly regulated by the laws of dynamics. But, since I accepted consciousness as an indubitable datum, I could not accept materialism, though I had a certain hankering after it on account of its intellectual simplicity and its rejection of 'non-sense'. I still believed in God, because the First Cause argument seemed irrefutable.

The belief, stuffed into him like forcemeat into a turkey, withered away between the ages of fourteen and eighteen. Sceptical dissent hardened and he began to see religion as an intellectual feather-bed, a too-comforting, barely credible alternative to the attractive austerities of mathematics. For a youth whose intuitive scepticism had shown itself early, this was not surprising.

"They [had] told me when I was an infant that angels watched round my bed while I slept," he remembered. "I'd seen pictures of angels and thought I should very much like to see one, but I supposed that the moment I opened my eyes they fled away. So I thought well, next time I wake up I won't open my eyes and they won't know, and I did so, and I made a grab, thinking I should catch an angel, but I didn't."

As he grew older, the gradual evolution followed a pattern common among contemporary childhoods, in Russell's case aided at first by Mr Ewen, a tutor who was an acquaintance of Marx's daughter, and the man from whom Russell first heard of *Das Kapital* and of non-Euclidean geometry. The tutor was a stout defender of reason, and Russell recalls "poor Ewen getting a whole dinner of argument owing to his running down impulse". He was also an agnostic, and with him Russell discussed his evaporating faith in immortality, an exchange of views which almost certainly led to the tutor getting the sack.

Free will, belief in immortality, then in God, all went overboard one by one. The pilgrimage from faith to doubt left him deeply miserable – "it has taken away cheerfulness, and made it much harder to make bosom friends and, worst of all, it has debarred me from free intercourse with my people, and thus made them strangers to some of my deepest thoughts ..." He read Shelley, and wondered whether anyone like him still existed, then read Carlyle, hoping to find a religion in *Sartor Resartus*, but wrote him off as a rhetorician with no care for truth. This was already the cardinal sin, and if Russell emerged from a profoundly unsatisfactory and profoundly influential childhood carrying any one belief, it was in the need to search for certain truth in an uncertain world.

As for religion, he put on record, two days after his sixteenth birthday, the ideas from which his devout agnosticism was to emerge.

> I should like to believe my people's religion, which was just what I could wish, but alas, it is impossible. I have really no religion, for my God, being a spirit shown merely by reason to exist, his properties

utterly unknown, is no help to my life. I have not the parson's comfortable doctrine, that every good action has its reward, and every sin is forgiven. My whole religion is this: do every duty, and expect no reward for it, either here or hereafter.

Russell's own later accounts of his development at Pembroke Lodge are contradictory. "My childhood was, on the whole, happy and straightforward," he has written, "and I felt affection for most of the grown-ups with whom I was brought in contact." Yet he has also said, "From adolescence onwards I was driven by a desperate misery of loneliness for which I knew that love would be the only cure."

At times, if his reminiscences are to be believed, he was driven almost to breaking-point. One night, he has said, he went to bed determined to commit suicide the following day. But he dreamed that the formidable Benjamin Jowett, Master of Balliol, to which college Frank had by this time gone up, was standing at the foot of his bed. "Don't do it, young man," Jowett was saying. "Don't do it: you will live to regret it." He was dissuaded – at least for a time. But the idea remained only round the corner, and few great men can have left in their records so many reflections that suicide might be the best way out.

Russell's verdicts on his grandmother are conflicting. Some things niggled for years, particularly her habit of squashing any hint of philosophical conversation with the saying, "What is mind? No matter. What is matter? Never mind." After some forty or fifty repetitions, the remark ceased to amuse him. What did amuse him, and what he would gleefully recall after more than eighty years, was the occasion on which she had emitted her own spoonerism, calling to him as "dirty beer". While he was a child, he admitted, she had great affection for him and he responded. But there were other feelings. "My attitude to my grandmother was brutal to a degree," he once wrote, a statement amply justified by the ruthless terms in which, just come of age, he spoke and wrote of dear Granny to his bride-to-be.

Part explanation of these particular contradictions is that up to the age of puberty mere kindliness sufficed. Then the lack of rough-and-tumble contact with other boys compounded what he called the appalling misery of knowing nothing about sex, and Granny was given the blame. Part explanation lies elsewhere, in the influence of exterior circumstance on his judgment. In 1931, when his second marriage was breaking up and gloom both emotional and financial was breaking in, he tended to see Pembroke Lodge as all shadow. Thirty years on, happy with his fourth wife and quite as happy in being at the centre of controversy, he tended to remember the lighter patches and forget the rest. In any case, Pembroke Lodge was no doubt part paradise and part hell.

The first real change came when he was sent to a crammer's school at Old Southgate, North London, to prepare for a scholarship to university. He had looked forward to it. "I feel being where there is some life would do me so much good, leaving me no time to cogitate and get melancholy and morose," he noted. However, most of the other pupils were preparing for the army, and most had the normal sexual rumbustiousness of healthy teenagers. Russell's fastidiousness received a shock for which Pembroke Lodge had not prepared him; there he had at least been alone. He was certainly bullied, not surprisingly considering the exemplary priggishness with which he described his companions: "No mind, no independent thought, no love of good books, nor of the higher refinements of morality; it is really sad that the upper classes of a civilised and (supposedly) moral country can produce nothing better."

Despite its tribulations, however, Southgate was perhaps no worse over all than Pembroke Lodge, whose ghostly quality was relieved only by Uncle Rollo, Lord Amberley's younger brother, an amiable and uncomplaining man who later bore the loss of a leg as philosophically as his partial loss of sight. In Russell's early life, Uncle Rollo has the quality of a *deus ex machina* appearing from the shadows to guide a puzzled youth at a succession of crossroads. An amateur meteorologist, he wrote a respectable paper on the aftermath of the great Krakatoa explosion of 1883 and analysed the information, almost on a man-to-man basis, with his young nephew. It was also Uncle Rollo whom Russell heard discussing his progress with Jowett, and whose revealing "Yes, he's getting on very well indeed" came to the rescue of his confidence at a dangerous moment. "As soon as I realised that I was intelligent," he later noted, "I determined to achieve something of intellectual importance if it should be at all possible, and throughout my youth I let nothing whatever stand in the way of this ambition." However, Rollo Russell was to do something even more important than prick awake his nephew's intellectual ambitions: introduce him to John Tyndall, who aroused the boy's scientific interests, and to Alys Pearsall Smith, who aroused very different feelings and became his first wife.

In 1883 Uncle Rollo moved from Pembroke Lodge to a house on the slopes of Hindhead, the sandy prow of hills forty miles west of London that during the last decades of the nineteenth century became a sub-Alpine retreat for eminent Victorians with a taste for the open. Leslie Stephen criss-crossed the area with his "Sunday Tramps". Frederic Harrison the philosopher lived nearby. So did Edward Whymper the mountaineer, and Conan Doyle who used the surrounding heathlands in his novels. Tennyson, having rented a home among the trees, moved to his "cottage", the neighbouring and comparatively grand Aldworth from which, through the Chanctonbury Gap, he could catch his one blue glimpse of sea. T. H. Huxley and Mrs Humphry Ward had both become inhabitants of a neighbourhood not unlike the Portmeirion peninsula on which Russell ended his days, an area thickly laced with good intentions and high ideals where an intellectual could be found on almost every large stone.

The Hindhead fashion had been started by John Tyndall, the eminent scientist and mountaineer whose lectures at the Royal Institution had been regularly attended by members of the Russell family. His uniquely ugly house was still one of the few in the area when Uncle Rollo moved into nearby Dunrozel. He had already sought Tyndall's advice on how to become a physicist and he now began to take his nephew on regular visits to the great man. By November 1883, Tyndall, a great lover of children, was recording in his diary, "Bertie came to claim a visit to Dunrozel." He and his young wife accepted the invitation brought over by the boy and stayed to supper.

During the next few years, as the inhabitants of Pembroke Lodge made a regular summer migration to the Surrey heights, Russell was often taken to see Tyndall, on one occasion impressing the great man by his efforts to find the centre of gravity when two walking-sticks were hitched together, and on another with the news that he had climbed Piz Palu in the Engadine during a summer holiday. Russell did later record an early ambition to be a physicist, abandoned when he discovered that "laboratories & experiments & mechanisms [baffled him] completely". And a constant refrain in his philosophical work was to be that results could best be achieved by using the scientific methods which Tyndall could rarely be stopped from expounding.

Uncle Rollo's choice of Hindhead was to have a more significant result than friendship with Tyndall. To this Surrey–Sussex border there had also come the Pearsall Smiths, rich Philadelphia Quakers. The father, Robert, had first crossed the Atlantic sixteen years earlier to embark on an evangelical crusade, soon ended by persistent rumours that at his meetings, attended by select groups of spinsters, he had followed too enthusiastically St Paul's injunction to the Romans to "salute one another with a holy kiss". A return to America had been followed by a return to Europe and the Pearsall Smiths had settled into Friday's Hill, an ornate house and farm-estate at Fernhurst, midway between Aldworth and Hindhead.

The family was dominated by Robert's wife Hannah, a woman powered by a mixture of dormant sadism and the religious fervour that had driven her into writing *The Christian's Secret of a Happy Life*, a book which sold more than a quarter of a million copies within a few years of publication. Her son was Logan. Seven years older than Russell, he was to carve himself a small but select literary niche before tottering into euphoric senility. There were two daughters. The elder was by this time Mary Costelloe, a beauty of twenty-five married to a rising young lawyer, a fascinator with burnished gold hair and roving eye almost ready for the arrival at Friday's Hill the following year of the dazzling Bernard Berenson.

The younger daughter was Alys, with blue eyes and nut-brown hair, willowy yet well covered. As reserved as her sister was flamboyant, Alys was resigned to the results. "Thee can get on relying on thy charm," she admitted, "but I have got to be good." A good woman in the worst sense of the word, she turned the other cheek on principle and made perfectly understandable Russell's later commiserations on those who lacked the courage to sin. A picture-book example of American womanhood, devoted to good works, Alys was just twenty-two, recently graduated from the Pennsylvanian women's college of Bryn Mawr. Alys and her family held out more than the attractions of a transatlantic lilt. Whatever their deficiencies, the younger Pearsall Smiths had few taboos, argued about everything, and were willing to consider anything.

Even without Russell's curiosity value as heir to an earldom, he would have been welcomed when Uncle Rollo called with his nephew at Friday's Hill half-way through a long summer's walk, ostensibly on the spur of the moment but more probably for a first look at a remarkable group of near-neighbours. Russell was seventeen. He fell in love with Alys at first sight, a love that trickled away so quietly that after eight years of marriage he was surprised to find it gone. Alys responded more slowly. But by the early 1890s she was as dedicated to Russell as ever woman could be, and remained so for the rest of her life – loved, hated, discarded and ignored; divorced before Russell succeeded his brother as 3rd Earl, platonically reunited with him in her eighties and, as her friends commented, believing to the last that the next telephone-call would be his offer to make an honest countess of her.

Russell's instant obsession with Alys was unfortunate; it was also very much on the cards. The American family had a vigour and a freshness hardly diminished by what Eddie Marsh, one of Russell's Trinity colleagues, described as the "funny grammar they talk to one another", the Quaker "Thee"-ing and "Thou"-ing that Alys retained until her death after the Second World War. "To me, as to Goethe," Russell wrote later, "America seemed a romantic land of freedom, and I found among [the Pearsall Smiths] an absence of many prejudices which hampered me at home. Above all, I enjoyed their emancipation from good taste." They enjoyed Russell, particularly the matriarch, who once admitted "if I *lived* in England, I should want to belong to the aristocracy".

At Friday's Hill, Russell met his brother's friend, George Santayana. "It was strange", wrote Santayana, "to see Bertie, and even his brother, who turned up one day for luncheon, in that American Quaker family, and to hear those young women speak of the elder brother as *Frank*, which I never heard any of his friends or his wives do. But the Russells never knew themselves or their proper place in the world: that was a part of their mixture of genius and folly."

To Friday's Hill came Shaw in his khaki-coloured "health" clothes of Jaeger flannel, and Russell would watch him at work, the names of his characters written on paper and manœuvred on a chess-board to remind him of who was on stage. Graham Wallas, another early member of the Fabian Society, was a frequent visitor. So was Frederic Harrison, who saw all life through the spectacles of Comte's positivism; and Sidney Webb, an ambitious thirty, about to strike out from the Civil Service into the rougher waters of local government. Here also came Beatrice Potter, the most beautiful of the four Potter sisters, a friend and supporter of Alys; she was soon to become Mrs Webb, and quickly put Russell among her "A's" – "aristocratic, anarchic and artistic" – compared with the "B's", among whom she included herself and her future husband, "bourgeois, bureaucratic and benevolent".

The attractions of Friday's Hill for the young Russell, his questioning mind no longer hemmed in by the psychological boundaries of Pembroke Lodge, were strong and obvious. Despite the religiosity, the aggressive propaganda for teetotalism, the relentless seeking about for good causes in need of support, there was a willingness for open discussion, a determination to defend by rational argument, that was entirely new. Only later, as perspectives changed, as personal disenchantment coloured old memories, did he look back on the Friday's Hill menage as not only devout and dedicated, honest and fearless, but also as a small company capable of doing immense harm yet firmly resolved to ignore the catastrophes their actions might cause.

As important as the intellectual stimulation of the Americans in general was the physical stimulation of Alys. Until their first meeting in the summer of 1889, Russell had been coddled in almost monastic seclusion. His sexual education, acquired in the manner of the day by schoolboy gossip and a delving into medical dictionaries, had been purely theoretical; and he was ill-prepared for putting into perspective what he now felt about a luscious Alys. His first visit to Friday's Hill was followed by another and another. Soon he was a regular visitor, quite dazzled by his hosts. The hosts were equally dazzled by him, and during one visit Robert Pearsall Smith took Berenson aside. "Do you see that young man over there?" he asked. "He's Lord John Russell's grandson."

2

Cambridge Chrysalis

At the age of seventeen Russell was slight and precise, an aristocratic sparrow with the trim air of going about his business with the utmost efficiency. None of the fires had yet begun to burn through the neat outer covering; no signs yet showed of the effects which a distinctly exceptional education was to have on a distinctly exceptional pupil. Yet Lady Russell's aggressive idealism had in fact been an unrecognized catalyst inside the extraordinary brain with which the Russells and Stanleys had endowed her grandson. The instruction of tutors, combined with her instinctive knowledge of what she believed to be right, acting together on a boy confidently expected to lead, had resulted in what Santayana called a princely education, but one which was

> a little like cultivating tropical flowers under electric light in a steaming greenhouse. The instruction was well selected, competently given, and absorbed with intense thirst; but it was too good for the outdoor climate. Moreover, there were obstacles that far from being surmounted were built upon as cornerstones of righteousness and sources of superior light. One was the hereditary liberalism and Low Church Piety of the family. Another was Bertie's microscopic intensity that narrowed each of his insights, no matter how varied these insights might be, lost the substance in the visible image, the sense in the logic of the words, and made him, though he might be many-sided, a many-sided fanatic.

None of this was apparent as the family decided on Russell's future. All that came through was a strong line in mathematics. Therefore Cambridge, to which Lord Amberley had gone, was chosen rather than Oxford. A contributing factor may have been the record of Frank, who had spent two years at Balliol before being sent down by Jowett in circumstances that were never satisfactorily explained.

In December 1889, Russell sat for a scholarship to Trinity in mathematics, a subject which had kept him afloat through the worst days at Old Southgate. "There was a footpath leading across fields to New Southgate," he wrote, "and I used to go there alone to watch the sunset and contemplate suicide. I did not, however, commit suicide, because I wished to know more of mathematics." Even at this early stage, there were two elements in the uncontrollable passion for the queen of the sciences which at various times discouraged Russell from jumping under trains, beneath buses, from boats or into rivers. One was the almost mystical importance with which he endowed the subject, a quality which put it on a level with poetry, romantic love, or the splendours of the sea and the mountains which from youth to old age never failed to move him. In direct contrast there was the attraction of a subject totally unimplicated in human feelings and failings. "I like mathematics," he wrote, "because it is *not* human & has nothing particular to do with this planet or with the whole accidental universe – because, like Spinoza's God, it won't love us in return."

Russell's obsession was already visible to the favoured few who, like him, placed mathematics near the centre of the universe. Among them was Alfred North Whitehead, just twenty-nine and, by a turn of the cards that was to affect Russell's entire life, the Trinity examiner. A kindly man already showing a detachment from real life as well as signs of the forgetfulness for which he later became notorious, Whitehead was known in college for his philosophic urge to study out-of-the-way branches of mathematics. His dedication was now illustrated in a slightly irregular way. In the scholarship examination a young man named Bushell gained higher marks than Russell; but Whitehead, feeling intuitively that Russell was the abler man, burned the marks before meeting the other examiners. Then he recommended Russell. "Long afterwards," Russell has recorded, "Whitehead said to me: 'I was justified because you beat him in the Tripos.'"

Having thus backed his fancy, Whitehead took the young man under his wing when in October 1890 Russell settled into rooms in Whewell's Court. The teacher–pupil relationship rapidly changed, first into that of colleagues, then of collaborators – a natural evolution since both men found mathematics leading them towards the narrow postern-gate of philosophy. Together they were to produce *Principia Mathematica*, that landmark in mathematical thinking, and only after a decade of joint work did their contrasting temperaments, aided by external circumstance, force them slowly apart. Perhaps this was inevitable. Whitehead, turning into the metaphysics that Russell believed was a cul-de-sac, saw its principles as truths about the nature of God: Russell had early ruled out even the remote kind of God favoured by Whitehead.

Although their differences rose to the surface in later years, Whitehead's benevolent interest now enabled Russell to settle down to undergraduate life without the emotional manhandling often meted out to sensitive youths, and usually the fate of the man who could accurately be described as a shy prig.

Most of the friendships he formed at Cambridge lasted until death stepped in; many were to play significant parts in his professional or private life. There was Charles Sanger, who had gone up in the same term, also read mathematics, and who accompanied him on walking-tours across the Alps and into Italy during the decade before the First World War. There were Theodore Llewelyn Davies and his brother Crompton. To these close friends there were added the Trevelyan brothers, three great-nephews of Macaulay whose friendship and support was to succour Russell over the years: Charles, who risked his reputation in the House of Commons by defending Russell's activities during the First World War; Robert, whose house under Leith Hill was an ever-open haven in times of trouble; and George, who as Master of Trinity shepherded Russell back to Cambridge from self-imposed wartime exile in 1944. There was Ellis McTaggart, six years Russell's senior, a staunch upholder of Hegelian Idealism, who called himself an atheist but firmly believed in personal immortality – "the bumbling McTaggart chattering about the Absolute", as Palme Dutt percipiently if unkindly called him.

There was also G. E. Moore, pursuing truth "with the tenacity of a bulldog and the integrity of a saint", and already preparing the hammer-blows which, with Russell's, were to bring about the collapse of the reigning Idealism. Moore came up two years after Russell, and the significant effect of each man on the other did not make itself felt until the last few years of the nineteenth century. Then their interactions were to be notable. Russell, checking proofs of his book on the philosophy of Leibniz, commented to Moore, "I have made, however, so many corrections in consequence of your remarks as was possible without radical alteration; & I admit that I was terribly muddled." A few years later, in *The Principles of Mathematics*, he admitted that "on fundamental questions of philosophy [my] position, in all its chief features, [is] derived from Mr. G. E. Moore". And for the first decade or more of the twentieth century the core of his views on ethics – that good and bad, right and wrong, were qualities just as objective and as unimplicated in human affairs as the colour of grass or the hardness of metal – was essentially the view of Moore's *Principia Ethica*.

For his part, Moore always counted Russell among the most important influences of his own philosophical life. Benign even as a young man, he had a nature which Russell described as transparent and crystal as a mountain spring, and it was only by a subterfuge that Russell once tricked him into telling a lie. "Moore," he asked, "do you *always* speak the truth?" "No," answered Moore.

Yet on Moore's side the relationship was one of professional admiration rather than friendship, and when on one occasion Russell remarked, "You don't like me, do you?" Moore thought seriously for a few moments before answering, "No." The conversation then continued, amicably.

The reason for Moore's failure to move from respect to familiarity lay in Russell's apparent ability to quarantine himself from human feelings without undue trouble. He was not, as an acquaintance was to claim, a man without any heart at all; his ruthlessness was often exercised for an intellectual rather than a personal cause. But he could so isolate the heart's demands that the charge of heartlessness stuck easily. "I love to think of the bright shining passionless creation, showing no faintest trace of the agony and bloody sweat out of which it grows," he once wrote. "This is partly why logic and math.'cs. inspire me more than religious writing, because they disdain even to notice suffering." Moore, and others, were allergic to the outlook.

Early in 1893, Russell, by then the established young undergraduate about Cambridge, invited Moore to meet McTaggart for tea in his rooms. "McTaggart, in the course of conversation [was] led to express his well-known view that Time is unreal," said Moore in recalling the occasion. "This must have seemed to me then (as it still does) a perfectly monstrous proposition, and I did my best to argue against it. I don't suppose I argued at all well; but I think I was persistent and found quite a lot of things to say in answer to McTaggart."

Quite a lot was also said in the University Moral Science Club. Russell had joined in February 1891, a few months after coming up, and Moore in his turn joined soon after arriving. Russell was a frequent attender and over the next two decades often used the club as a sounding-board for his ideas, reading before it many papers later refurbished for larger audiences.

His development at Cambridge, where the twentieth century was but a dim threat in the future, followed the expected pattern. Few legends of these days have survived, and even fewer details, but one corner of the veil is lifted by the history of the Magpie and Stump Debating Society. Russell's recorded interventions on the stage of this typical Cambridge group are three, each one an earnest of things to come. On 4 June 1891, at the 533rd meeting, he proposed the motion: "That this house consider it both just and expedient that women should be admitted to equal political rights as men." He argued his case so well that it was necessary for the chairman to decide the motion by casting his vote against it. The following summer, twenty meetings on, Russell proposed that: "The ending or mending of the House of Lords is desirable." As so often in the future, Russell only lost by a short head – in this case by a majority of one.

The third intervention came when the orderly calm of the club was shattered by a palace revolution, by internal schism, and by the election of a new president with George Hamilton-Gordon, later Baron Stanmore, challenging what would now be called the Establishment represented by Robert Erskine Childers, the ill-fated author of *The Riddle of the Sands*.

"Nothing that might influence the small wobbling minority of unprejudiced electors was left undone," says the club's history.

> 'The Court Circular", the official organ of the Legitimist party, made its first and last appearance. Little boys fell gasping in the streets and, as they fell, passed on to willing hands their store of fly-sheets; grown men, with hammer and nails, with scissors and paste, renewed the joys of their youth; and a future knight commander of the British Empire and a budding philosopher took red chalk and ran round the town in a last-minute effort to attract the votes of the fickle electorate.

The future knight commander was Maurice Amos; the philosopher, Russell.

A capacity for friendship, sociability and the frosty glitter with which he could coat the most ordinary subjects, all began to reveal themselves during Russell's undergraduate years. This was acknowledged early in 1892 by his election to the Society. Founded in 1820 as the Cambridge Conversazione Society, and by this time known as the Apostles since membership was limited to a dozen, the Society had been started by a group of young men who had "a common craving for further investigation than was permitted by the opportunities given by the University into higher philosophy". They met in each other's rooms in succession, on Saturday nights, to hear the host read a paper which was afterwards discussed. Meetings usually went on into the small hours and often ended with Sunday breakfast, followed by a long walk during which the argument was continued. For Russell the greatest happiness of his time at Cambridge was connected with the Society; the sense of belonging to an élite, of intellectual comradeship, and of preparing for a role in running the world, began to counteract the effects of Pembroke Lodge.

Although the effects were to remain all his life, and to play havoc with a good deal of it, Cambridge in general and the Society in particular did much to remedy the harm caused by the early death of his parents and the good intentions of Lord and Lady Russell. Some of the earnestness he had breathed in with the air at Richmond was breathed out again with the aid of light-hearted undergraduate humours. Some of the knobbly corners were smoothed away. Some of the almost psychotic isolation from his contemporaries was at least superficially removed.

However, the effect of Cambridge should not be over-estimated. It "brought him out". But it was mainly in the intellectual sphere that the influence worked. The university did its broadening and civilizing job, but in Russell's case it could not entirely compensate for the lack of contact with the ordinary world that had been part and parcel of life at Pembroke Lodge. When he left, he still had a lot to learn the hard way. But if life at Trinity did not entirely prepare him for life outside, it did encourage one dominating factor in his character: not only the spirit of questioning and dissent, but also its extension, the natural and slightly bloody-minded reaction of being perverse for perversity's sake which could be Russell's strength when playing Devil's Advocate, but was dangerously self-damaging when allowed to get out of hand.

At the end of three years Russell was bracketed Seventh Wrangler in the Mathematical Tripos; but he paid a price for success strangely comparable to that paid by Einstein, one of many parallels between the two men's lives. "The coercion [for the examinations] had such a deterring effect," wrote Einstein after graduating from the Zurich Polytechnic, "that after I had passed the final examination I found the consideration of any scientific problems distasteful to me for an entire year." Russell's feelings were much the same. "The attempt to acquire examination technique had led me to think of mathematics as consisting of artful dodges and ingenious devices and as altogether too much like a crossword puzzle," he wrote. "When ... I emerged from my last mathematical examination I swore that I would never look at mathematics again and sold all my mathematical books." The temporary disillusion turned him into the philosophical field where he roamed happily for years.

He was already psychologically prepared for the move since the scepticism which between the ages of fifteen and eighteen had eroded his belief in theological orthodoxy had also been at work on the dogmas of mathematics. When religious belief had affronted his reason and forced him to say farewell to its comforts, he had concentrated with hopeful expectation on mathematics. But the doubts first raised by Euclidean unprovables were increased by work for the Mathematical Tripos. Even some of Euclid's proofs seemed to be shaky, while the existence of non-Euclidean geometry, of whose details he as yet knew nothing, raised disquieting doubts. Elsewhere, he could see, the situation was even worse. "Those who taught me the infinitesimal Calculus did not know the valid proofs of its fundamental theorems and tried to persuade me to accept the official sophistries as an act of faith," he wrote. "I realized that the calculus works in practice but I was at a loss to understand why it should do so." So, disillusioned with mathematics, "presented as a set of clever tricks by which to pile up marks in the Tripos", desiring above everything else "some reason for supposing mathematics true", he turned to philosophy.

In the introduction to the *History of Western Philosophy*, which was to give him a best-seller in his late seventies, Russell provided his own definition of the subject to which he had devoted so much of his life.

> Philosophy, as I shall understand the word, is something intermediate between theology and science. Like theology, it consists of speculations on matters as to which definite knowledge has, so far,

been unascertainable; but, like science, it appeals to human reason rather than to authority, whether that of tradition or that of revelation. All *definite* knowledge – so I should contend – belongs to science; all *dogma* as to what surpasses definite knowledge belongs to theology. But between theology and science there is a No Man's Land, exposed to attack from both sides; this No Man's Land is philosophy.

It was this unmapped area which Russell wished to bring within the territory of definite knowledge by use of his intellect. His primary concern was with finding acceptable proof for things usually taken for granted, and this led him to devote much of his professional life to problems of belief and the theory of knowledge, to the reasoning which led men to separate fact from fiction, dream from waking and reality from illusion. Common sense, after all, did not always prove a sure guide – a lesson pointedly being taught in physics where John Dalton's solid atoms, only recently thought to be the substance of matter, were soon to dissolve first into Rutherford's nuclear atom and later into mere concentrations of electric force.

Russell's sceptical questioning had begun when Uncle Rollo's brother-in-law Harold Joachim, a philosophy don at Merton, had presented the nephew with a reading-list, dealt with at Russell's customary speed. However, the Tripos had ruled out anything more than a temporary devotion to the subject, and it was only now, as he decided to spend a fourth year at Cambridge taking Moral Science, that he plunged into a new world and immediately discovered "all the delight of a new landscape on emerging from a valley".

The plunge came, on the face of it, at a bad time for those short of faith. Until the 1860s the influence of Locke, Berkeley and Hume, the three pillars of British empiricism, had remained comparatively unimpaired, kept alive by Jeremy Bentham, James Mill and John Stuart Mill. Then, with the publication in 1865 of Stirling's *The Secret of Hegel*, the views of Continental metaphysicians, notably the Idealism of Kant and Hegel, began to take over. "In Britain rain comes from Ireland, and Idealism from Germany," Russell observed of the period.

There were many variants of the Idealist belief, but that to which Russell subscribed was the Absolute Idealism derived from Hegel, a philosopher whose views had once been called "the most egregious example of German speculative lunacy". Hegel maintained that ultimate reality consists of mind or spirit rather than matter; that all the objects of external perception will dissolve, when subjected to critical scrutiny, like Prospero's gorgeous palaces and solemn temples. For the Hegelian Idealists, the material world was merely an imperfect or incomplete reality which had no independent existence. It was, moreover, not a world of disconnected parts but one in which each part was connected to every other part, in a way incomprehensible to most men – as Russell once put it, "like a jelly in the fact that, if you touched any one part of it, the whole quivered", but unlike a jelly in that it could not be cut up into pieces. The attraction of Absolute Idealism for Russell was that at the top of ascending tiers of hierarchies, each containing successively more inter-related parts of existence as it was understood, there reigned the Absolute, Hegel's name for God. "In this philosophy I found comfort for a time," he said. " . . . There was a curious pleasure in making oneself believe that time and space are unreal, that matter is an illusion, and that the world really consists of nothing but mind."

He had frequently listened to Hegelian arguments retailed by McTaggart during his first three years at Cambridge, but it was not until his fourth, when he came under the tutelage of George Stout, a man who dedicated his life to unravelling the relationship between mind and matter, that he found it possible to accept them. "He and McTaggart between them caused me to become a Hegelian," Russell has written.

> I remember the precise moment, one day in 1894, as I was walking along Trinity Lane, when I saw in a flash (or thought I saw) that the ontological argument is valid. I had gone out to buy a tin of tobacco; on my way back, I suddenly threw it up in the air, and exclaimed as I caught it: "Great God in boots! the ontological argument is sound."

There was also the infuence of F. H. Bradley, who stares out from Eves's portrait in Merton College with an air of quiet religious certainty. Bradley possessed both a sardonic humour, which could add to Leibniz's "the best of all possible worlds" the comment "and everything in it is a necessary evil", and the single-mindedness to produce *Appearance and Reality*, a distillation of Hegelian ideas which in 1893 began to wrest the philosophical initiative from the Continent.

This was not the first of Bradley which Russell had read. His *Principles of Logic* was on Joachim's reading-list and Russell, who turned to it in September 1893, wrote later that it had influenced him profoundly. The extensive notes which he made at the time show this to be no over-statement. The following spring he tackled *Ethical Studies*; then, in August, *Appearance and Reality*. The effect of Bradley's most important book can be judged from a letter Russell wrote three months later: "My intellectual pleasures during the last years have been growing very rapidly keener . . . I am convinced since reading Bradley that all knowledge is good, and therefore shouldn't need to bother about immediate practical utility . . ."

Just as the *Principles of Logic* had swung the axe accurately and heavily at many accepted ideas, no doubt confirming in Russell's mind a belief that the conventional order of things was there to be felled, *Appearance and Reality* had its own iconoclastic side, avowing in its Preface that "The chief need of English philosophy is, I think, a sceptical study of first principles, and I do not know of any work which seems to meet this need sufficiently. By scepticism is not meant doubt about or disbelief in some tenet or tenets. I understand by it an attempt to become aware of and to doubt all preconceptions." Thus any inhibitions about questioning contemporary dogmas or beliefs which still remained in Russell's mind could now be removed. He might later forget how much he had learned from Bradley's *Logic* and he was certainly to escape from Absolute Idealism with a gasp of relief. But from now on, doubt itself was to be academically respectable.

In Cambridge, as in many other parts of Britain, Idealism was the order of the day, and Russell now found himself in what was to be the unusual situation of swimming with the tide. The majority of his friends accepted the same philosophical beliefs, however much they might argue about everything else, and the last year of his undergraduate life was spent within the body of the intellectual kirk; working, arguing, taking strenuous twenty-mile walks across the Cambridgeshire countryside, and in winter skating with the formal precision of the skilled amateur along the frozen dykes of the nearby fenland, both hearty physical substitutes for the detested team-games.

Thus far, Russell conformed to the accepted pattern. So did his prospects. He was intellectually precocious, the heir to an earldom – although Frank, despite his rackety ways, seemed likely to occupy it for some while – and born with a name that would open most doors. His future, if he really wished to work for a living, seemed to lie in politics or the diplomatic service – after a suitable interval during which he might be expected to play around on the periphery of academic work and pick himself a wife from an assortment of suitable candidates. This would have been the done thing, particularly after the summer of 1894 when he gained an honours degree in the Moral Science Tripos. Russell, foreshadowing the future, almost ostentatiously did something different.

The previous summer he had come of age, and the event had brought him more than legal independence; it had also brought a £20,000 legacy from Lord Amberley's estate, a sum which yielded about £600 a year, and was sufficient to transform Alys Pearsall Smith from a dreamy delight of the future into potential wife. Throughout the spring and summer Russell saw a good deal of her, entertaining her at Cambridge and listening to her theoretical defence of free love. He also listened to her shocked account of how sister Mary had abandoned her husband for Bernard Berenson, an illogical failure to praise practice for following theory which he found disturbing.

In September he proposed. Eventually he was accepted. Reaction was critical. "We are always bad at choosing wives," said Frank, now engaged in the second year of bitter guerrilla warfare with the woman he had married three years previously. In Cambridge, Charles Sanger was warned by Russell that he was about to hear something shocking but on receiving the news took it calmly. "Some hours later," Russell subsequently said, "he came and said that on reflection he found he *was* shocked." However, this reaction to the news that Russell's bride was to be an American woman in her later twenties was mild compared with that of Pembroke Lodge. "They said she was no lady, a baby-snatcher, a low-class adventuress, a designing female taking advantage of my inexperience, a person incapable of all the finer feelings, a woman whose vulgarity would perpetually put me to shame," he has said.

But there was reason for caution on the part of both families. The Russell family looked askance at American manufacturers while the Pearsall Smiths balanced the attractions of a potential 3rd Earl against the gamble of what a twenty-one-year-old might become.

When rumours of an engagement first began to spread, Russell's Aunt Maude sent him a warning. "I hope this is not so," she said, "for if you thought you wd. be too young to enter Parliament before you were 29 I must think it would be a great pity for you to engage yr.self and take such an important step at 21 or 22."

A few months later, he broke the news officially to Pembroke Lodge. Lady Russell went swiftly into action, determined to save her grandson from a marriage she considered would be at least unfortunate and probably disastrous. As it happened, Granny was right. Only her tactics were wrong, since her ensuing succession of subterfuges led Russell to distrust motives honest enough in themselves and to reinforce his determination when it might possibly have weakened.

Lady Russell's opening gambit was made through the family doctor, who disclosed some of the dark facts Russell had already suspected. Uncle Willy was mad. Aunt Agatha had broken off her engagement following insane delusions, and the family appeared to have been perpetually tottering along a narrow path above a mental precipice. Other skeletons may well have been brought out to bolster up the warning that if there were children of the marriage they too could be mad. These revelations, making the most of the instability that can be found in many families if enough effort is made, could well have been reinforced had more then been known of the Pearsall Smiths with their own record of eccentricity and loopiness. As it was, the campaign was sufficient to make Russell gloomily record in his diary the

> solemn and reiterated warnings; the gradual discovery, one by one, of the tragedies, hopeless and unalleviated, which have made up the lives of most of my family; above all, the perpetual gloom which hangs like a fate over P[embroke] L[odge] ... I must for some time

> avoid seeing more than a very little of my people and of P.L., otherwise I shall really begin to fear for my sanity. P.L. is to me like a family vault haunted by the ghosts of maniacs – especially in view of all that I have recently learned from Dr. Anderson.

However, more than this was needed to stop a Russell at the mercy of first love. He and Alys responded with the decision to have no children.

The open avowal to consider contraception, a subject which had already brought poor Amberley to his knees at the start of his career, would have convinced any woman less determined than Lady Russell that she was wasting her time. Instead, she capitalized on her genuinely poor health and the distress that her grandson's marriage would cause, and coaxed from him a promise not to see his betrothed for three months. Granted this, she immediately set about reinforcing success. A useful tool lay to hand in Lord Dufferin and Ava, attaché to Lord John at the Vienna Conference nearly forty years previously. Lord Dufferin was now Ambassador in Paris, and where could a young man more easily be beguiled to forget an infatuation with a North American Quaker? In what might have been a Samsonian act of destruction by surrendering her grandson to the wild delights of man-about-townism, Lady Russell induced Dufferin to initiate him into the sophistications of Paris as his personal attaché.

Russell capitulated. Lord Dufferin made clear to Lady Russell that he appreciated the situation. Her grandson's appointment would of course be honorary and unpaid. "But he will find himself among friends and I will write both to Hardinge and to my son Terence to do everything they can to make his stay agreeable to him," he assured her. To Russell himself he was avuncular: "I am sure you will like it, and the climate is charming at this time of year; and though perhaps there will be a certain amount of work, I hope it will not be too much to prevent you taking advantage of your stay to see all that is to be seen in Paris, for the autumn is the best time for that." He hoped he could tempt him to stay longer than the expected three months, "and to go out a little into Paris society, which would amuse you very much". The following day, as though fearing that he might not be pulling his weight, he wrote again, assuring him that all his companions would be pleasant young men; they had all been told of "the great interest I take in you, and I am sure you will find they will receive you with open arms".

Russell left England early in September. One of his first acts on arrival in Paris was to write to the Ambassador, then in Ireland, explaining that he wished to stay no longer than the three months, thus making it clear that Lady Russell's manœuvre would be stillborn. "I am deeply obliged to you for having given me the appointment," he concluded, "– but as

I do not intend to take up the diplomatic service as my career, it seemed perhaps needless to postpone my wedding."

The letter showed that there was no chance of success for the follow-up on which Lady Russell had embarked. The day that her grandson left Britain, Lord Morley, chief secretary for Ireland, informed her that he needed a new private secretary. "I am not sure, but it might be worth-while for Bertram [*sic*] to try whether he liked the post," he wrote. "Unfortunately, we are not going into our Lodge in the Phoenix Park for a couple of months or more or I should have asked him to come over and stay with us, if he thought it worth while ... The post would be unpaid. The Irish office is not the best school, but it is interesting."

For Lady Russell it was not only interesting but opportune, a chance that might keep her grandson out of matrimonial play for a further spell if he did insist on returning from Paris when the three months were over. His firm "no", in a letter outlining his plans to marry and to try for a Trinity Fellowship, brought a pained response which reveals the fate he was escaping. "I think it a great pity you shd refuse Morley's offer," wrote his grandmother.

> – of course I told him of yr projected marriage, and he answers that it is *not* an obstacle – he mentions that he believes he knows her, but without naming her or makg. any comment – I quite sympathize with yr desire to study economics, and I also see the advantages of a fellowship – but I cannot but strongly feel that for *you*, such employment as J.M. offers and such knowledge and experience as you wd. gain under him in interestg. Ireland, or anywhere, would be better than either. The liberal Ministry will not unfortunately last for ever, and you may never again have such an opening. I *know* yr grandfather and yr father wd. have felt as I do in this matter. Yr. intended marriage prevented you from gog. to Germany last year, whereby if you refuse J.M. it will be an obstacle this year again, in yr. path. I am ambitious for you, my dearest Boy, but even more intensely anxious for what is best for you in the highest sense ...

Odd he might be, yet surely still the stuff of which Prime Ministers were made.

But having beaten a tactical retreat Russell now stood firm and reasserted his intention to marry as soon as possible after returning to England. Nevertheless, given his obedience to her plan, Lady Russell might still have expected it to work. It might have done so had her grandson not been a young man enclosed in his own love; had his grandmother's action not brought a corresponding reaction as inevitable as any in Newtonian physics; or had invincible earnestness not isolated him from those delights of Paris society into which the Ambassador failed to entice him. Even so, he learned a lot during the three months, and not least from his future sister-in-law, later to become Mrs Bernard Berenson, with whom he shared the last week of his stay in Paris on extraordinarily intimate terms.

From the start of the separation from Alys, the Russell of many wives, still forming within the chrysalis of the shy and correct young man, displayed a prodigious capacity for letter-writing. "Last night," he wrote on 30 October, "I counted the letters since our separation and they came to just a hundred": two a day. Through them, as through much of his private correspondence, there runs an almost unbroken link between his physical relationship with women and the intellectual fire of his academic work; only slightly less important are the women friends who are no more than friends but whose stimulation acts as the spur. It is not merely, as he explains to the Alys of their courtship, that "I saw thee worshipped brains, so I thought it wise to make the most of them"; it is not merely, as he writes after dull days at the Embassy, that "My intellect is drying up for want of society . . . it is almost as necessary to my work to see a few chosen people as it is fatal to see many." Reared in comparative seclusion, he had become enraptured with the first personable young woman against whom chance thrust him; now, banished to the Embassy while his mind was bubbling with plans for future work, he began to realize how women were fuel for the Russell machine.

The letters to Alys would have confirmed Lady Russell's worst fears. Discussion of future sexual intercourse, the "when" and "how often" eagerly elaborated, had as much gusto as when, a third of a century later, Russell shocked the United States with his *Marriage and Morals*; in 1894 such talk, even within the context of coming connubial rectitude, had a hint of the "Empire" promenade.

At the Embassy, Russell's colleagues thought him a queer bird. Writing to Alys on the way to France he had asked if he must keep his teetotal pledge. "I had much rather not, as it is awkward for a man to be a teetotaller abroad," he went on, "& I had always meant to drink in Germany, wh. was my reason for not taking the pledge sooner." The ban appears to have been lifted, but Russell was nevertheless a more reserved and less sociable young man than the rest; appalled when disaster threatens after an Assistant Secretary cuts work for the races at Neuilly; distressed when one member of the Embassy staff is caught with a woman on the premises – although overjoyed at the phrase when the culprit is warned to "unfurl a higher standard of morality".

Two things retrieved the popularity of the attaché who would remain on duty during the lunch-hour, busily writing love-letters while the desk opposite him was conveniently empty. One was the ease with which he enciphered and deciphered diplomatic cables, not a particularly difficult operation in the then state of the art but one from which most attachés shrank. Menial tasks, such as copying out "long dispatches attempting to persuade the French Government that a lobster is not a fish," were shared equally with others. But it was Russell who was most frequently called from his bed when a cable had to be put into cipher or taken from it: drudgery for others but almost pleasure for him – "I lay awake a long time morning & evening cyphering in my head," he noted to Alys.

His light-hearted ability on a bicycle was also an accomplishment in an Embassy where the 68-year-old Ambassador was himself an ardent cyclist who sometimes rode up to the Embassy door and wheeled in his own machine. "Coming back", writes Russell of one excursion through the Bois de Boulogne, his colleague "was vastly impressed by my nerve in the traffic – I suppose it is mathematics or something, but I know I'm singularly good at riding through crowded streets! . . . It's nice riding with Dodson, because it makes him mad with envy to see me go without using my hands on the handles."

If it had been Lady Russell's belief that three months in Paris would unlatch her grandson from Alys, Alys herself had in a motherly way expected the experience to widen his worldly knowledge. She was to be disappointed. "As to seeing the world, I stick to my point," Russell wrote to her.

> Since the first week here, I have not had a *scrap* of new experience connected with the Embassy except Phipp's young woman, & I don't know that that was particularly valuable. Where is this vast experience in sitting in a room copying bad English and worse French? *They* show one new possibilities, they are rare types, whereas these are mere common aristocrats, *exactly* like all the rest. It is as tho' thee should recommend a botanist to spend 3 months picking daisies by way of improving his collection.

Russell's "blind fear of the aristocracy and its power", as he put it, was kept well awake at the Embassy, and despite his genial tolerance of the Ambassador, whom he was unable to take very seriously, he regarded "aristocratic acquaintance as a fresh millstone about our necks in toiling up the hill of honesty". But his dislike was personal rather than political, as he makes clear in a warning that an equitable distribution of wealth

> might, if things didn't improve extraordinarily, cut off all the flowers of civilisation. The Shelleys and Darwins and so on, who couldn't have existed at all if they'd had to work for their living, and all the men who spend their youth in voluntary penury over apparently unproductive work & finally produce something great, to everybody's surprise – all these would have been made to do work of generally recognised utility & perhaps ruined by it. And surely one Darwin is more important than 30 million working men & women.

If Embassy life made the occasional demands on his time, it made little on his intellect. To keep that sharpened, he embarked on two papers at which he worked between defining the lobster and writing his twice-daily letters to Alys. One was a dissertation on ethics for the Apostles, the other a paper on space, the predecessor to a Fellowship Thesis on the foundations of geometry. The latter came slowly, and after a particularly dull patch only a visit to American friends of the Pearsall Smiths in Paris got it moving. "The inspiration", he wrote of the visit, "even enabled me to get on with [it] & write several fairly good pages, embodying an entirely original and very bold idea which I got during the month at F[riday's] H[ill] one day when thee was in town. It is *so* bold that it almost terrifies me." When it was finished, he felt that

> it seems to me much too hard to be understood when read aloud, & the crux of the argument, the psychological part, has been treated much too sketchily, for want of the necessary knowledge; but there seems to be a good deal of good reasoning & solid thinking about it. When I'd finished it, I gave a sigh of relief, smoked a pipe & felt like God on the 7th day when he "saw it was good".

Need for stimulation, social or sexual, and the confident satisfaction with work finished, are two characteristics of the twenty-two-year-old Russell revealed in his letters. He is also ambivalent to Frank Russell who, awash with coarse stories, visits him "to see how things were going" and reveals that he plans a domicile in Chicago to get a divorce by Illinois laws. But maybe a peer can be domiciled only in England? And if Frank takes U.S. nationality, what happens to the peerage? Russell, next in line, may well have wondered. "He gives me a sense of perpetual discomfort, like a hair-shirt," he confided to Alys. "I feel the hard rock beneath his soft outside, & it makes me perpetually on tenterhooks for fear of what he will say next."

There is also his dislike of the French, based on what he regards as their sexual hypocrisy compared with his own belief that "falling in love with different people ... is a matter of temperament, & can't be helped", and should therefore be openly accepted as a fact of life. In Paris, he writes,

> everybody is wicked & every time one looks round one sees some blasphemy against love – they make me quiver with disgust, the merest common sights of the street – because the ideal is ever-present & the facts make it so impossible – one feels as if all these people wd. be *so* much better if they could only know the joys of a purer affection, & it makes me *mad* to think all of them condemn themselves & their posterity & everybody to something so *very* different. I should be delighted if the whole French nation were sunk under the sea, & believe the world wd. be vastly the better for it.

Appalled to learn that it was permissible for a Frenchman to make advances to a friend's wife but not to a friend's mistress, shocked at the prostitutes who swarmed round Frank and himself, the young Russell in love felt a Puritan distaste for all things Gallic. More than a vestigial remnant of the feeling showed a decade later in the maturer Russell criticizing Grey's plan to push Britain from the German towards the French end of the military see-saw.

A shadow of Russell's future outspokenness showed in the harsh words with which he laced his love-letters. They were, he later admitted, "full of very severe criticism – I wonder how she stood it". Alys, he pointed out, had no need to struggle for her independence and was thus less angular and pugnacious than most advanced women. But there was, he went on, another reason – "thee is fat". Her English was sometimes brusquely corrected, as when he warned her, "'I didn't use' is an intolerable vulgarism which I've always forgotten to reprove thee for before! One should say: 'I used not'." It was lucky, he conceded, that "thee hasn't got more brains thyself or thee wouldn't have such a respect for mine". But at the prospect of her sister coming to Paris he is more encouraging:

> Logan once told me thee had better taste in pictures than M & yet thee seldom opens thy mouth but leaves all the talking on such subjects to her dogmatising. This is an example of how thee wastes thy mind, not from modesty, but from a combination of laziness & pride, the same pride that kept thee silent so long about thy real opinions.

Turning the other cheek, Alys in London prepared for as simple a wedding as possible. Russell agreed. "The whole fuss of a wedding is so unutterably hateful to me (thee has no conception of how I *loathe* it from the bottom of my soul) that I rejoice in the slightest thing to mitigate it," he wrote. "And it would be lovely to get away directly without being congratulated by a host of silly fools who don't think in their hearts that we are to be congratulated, & if they *did*, would shew better manners in holding their tongues."

It was to be a Quaker ceremony and Alys was relieved to hear that Russell had no special objections. "Don't imagine that I really seriously mind a religious ceremony," he consoled her; "*any* ceremony is disgusting & the mere fact of having to advertise the most intimate thing a little more or less doesn't make much odds. I don't believe it will occur to me to feel shy; like thee I shall be too glad to get the d—d thing over and done with."

In London Lady Russell, faced with fast-diminishing hope that, with two-thirds of the course run, Paris would succeed in its expected task, fell conveniently unwell. The misfortune was counter-productive. "It is sad that my Grandma should be so ill again," Russell wrote to Alys, "but as long as we are able to marry December 14, I wish nothing better for her than a speedy death."

It had long been planned that he should return to England for a brief weekend to address the Apostles early in November, and on the morning of the 3rd he arrived at Newhaven. From here, after going on his knees to kiss English soil again, he pencilled a note to Alys which described how he was now "on English ground once more, my soul brimming with patriotism, enjoying bad tea & bread and butter because they are English". He arrived in Cambridge late in the afternoon, and dined with friends in Edward Marsh's rooms before addressing the Society.

Before returning to London on Sunday he left with Charles Sanger the paper on "Geometrical Axioms" which his friend was to read for him to the Moral Science Club a few days later and which led, in the words of the minutes, "to a very mathematical discussion". He also received advice on his future: safe for a Fellowship, but should stick to his own subjects rather than fly off into economics. Nevertheless, the diplomatic swan among the academic geese now felt that he had the world at his feet. "My visit", he wrote in the train, "... has put me in a very good conceit with myself ..."

As promised, he had not met Alys. However, waiting in London, ready to be convoyed to Paris where she was to study in the Louvre, was Mary Costelloe, between husbands, definitely leaving Frank Costelloe, preparing to join Berenson. It had been agreed with Alys that she would stay at the same hotel where Russell would live for his last ten days in Paris, and it was a sign of sisterly trust that they should share a sitting-room. Here the young Russell could breakfast with Mary each morning; here she would lighten the boredom of his remaining days in Paris, bringing the scent of Alys with her across the Channel.

Before the Cambridge visit, he had been delighted to receive one suggestion from his bride-to-be. "How strange thee should write about Mrchn [Mariechen] giving me a kiss from thee", he replied. "I had thought about it as a thing which was impossible, but would be delightful if it could happen, & I shall not think it as an indecent exhibition of emotion to a sister – how should I? The thought of it is strangely pleasant." When it came, the occasion turned out to be "very pleasant" – although, he added in writing to Alys on the cross-Channel boat, "it made me painfully feel she wasn't thee".

Russell and Mary Costelloe stayed at the Hotel Vouillemont in the Rue Boissy d'Anglais from 4 November until, ten days later, she left on the Orient Express for Munich. Years later he would tell intimate friends of an "*affaire*" with Mary. Considering her current attitude, his later one, and the opportunities offered, it is easy to assume that it was a sexual *affaire*, an assumption not entirely ruled out by his later statement that up until 1911 he had "never had complete relations with any woman except Alys". Always a stickler for the truth, Russell, writing "complete", meant nothing less; and completion was sometimes a problem. However, all the considerable evidence suggests that his experience was less than that, although of only slightly less significance to his future.

"She seems anxious to be 'stimulated' & as I love to stimulate, it works very well," he reported to Alys the day after their arrival at the Vouillemont.

> She has been repeating what she said to thee about thy uselessness & laziness, with assurances that thee is quite capable intellectually if thee chose. Of course one doesn't imagine thee would do any brilliant original thinking, but thee might form a part of the indispensable intelligent audience which involves a lot of exertion and severe thinking in order to get good taste in thought.

Three days later they visited the opera together. But before this, he told Alys, Mary had

> been making me talk about sexual morality & my reasons for preferring chastity to vice, wh. I found rather difficult, but the necessary spirit urged me on. Then she repeated a host of poetry, rather well – & then we discussed the Zeitgeist & my people and God knows what – & finally she discovered to her surprise that it was half-past twelve ... M. is interesting on all sex questions & has told me many things wh. I was glad to know.

Mary was also, twenty-two-year-old Russell poured out to his betrothed, so wise and emotional that she fitted his mood to perfection. "She seems to be enjoying herself very much here & I think grows fonder of me from day to day as I do of her," he wrote after another visit to the opera. This time they sat up until one and when Mary went to bed she proposed "a sisterly kiss" on the forehead. Russell accepted the invitation. The following night "we repeated the ceremony of the evening before, only cheeks instead of forehead. I have a very sisterly affection for M & feel as if I had known her always," he went on. "We have grown so singularly intimate during this week's tête-à-tête & it is nice to give the feeling some expression. I cannot help some psychological interest too in the experience, & the extraordinary difference between almost precisely similar physical sensations according to the psychological accompaniments."

Even before this final touch, the build-up had been too much for Alys, who countered with a long, distressed letter. She had been miserable, crying, and trying to present a good front to the world in the face of such devoted reports about Mary. Reading her letter, realizing that another from him in the same strain was already in the post, Russell sent an impetuous exclamation of concern. Mary had by this time departed and in his sudden isolation he could only think of how he had "been such a fool as to write in an unsympathetic way".

His next reaction was to prepare for Alys a careful 1,400-word document entitled "A Psychological Explanation", an early and revealing example of his ability to charm birds off trees. He started by explaining his life in Paris, "depressed, negative, silent ... with no greater pleasures than warmth and tobacco & solitude", in which he had lost all contact with her world.

> Then M. appeared – fresh from thee and thy world, brimming over with sympathy & friendly frankness, psychological, charming to look at, quite relaxed & as unstrenuous as my mood – also in an odd haunting way reminding me of thee, in her mannerisms, her laugh, her grimaces at disagreeable things, her hair wh. she used to take down in the evening & wh. at other times was done like thine – then she *seemed* honestly & genuinely anxious for thy happiness & for thy best development.

It would have been difficult for any man to have resisted this woman who freely provided "the whole history of her life – from *her* pt. of view – vividly described, with all the little touches that bring conviction – all about her attempts to accommodate herself to [her husband] wh. were intensely pathetic, about her first meeting with Berenson, & how they sat up through a whole night in the starlight out of doors by a campfire ... " Mary had gone on to describe how she

> had last Spring found herself drifting into a physical passion for another, totally uncongenial man & had fled from it & killed it ... Having been utterly starved so long in the way of friendship, finding her frank and psychologically profitable, & in manner as charming as possible – seeing too that I might let myself go completely, & treat her with the same frank affection as if she were a man or I a woman, both of us having our real affections fixed elsewhere – I abandoned myself utterly to the pleasure of her company, thinking *that* a sovereign expedient for making the time pass wh. otherwise wd. have seemed interminable, & feeling justified, after so long a fast, in almost any method of getting a little relief from depression.

Russell admitted that he had "abandoned [himself] too recklessly to M", had been "brutal in [his] way of putting it". "But there can be no joy in friendship if thee hates her," he concluded, "& I suppose thee is right in thy feeling – wh. also is sad. Finally, forgive me – this is an explanation, not an excuse."

On its own, the "Psychological Explanation" suggests that Mary might have seduced him. Taken with the mass of other letters, it suggests that if she tried she failed, but that her ambitions were probably less serious. She tended to collect admirers as a dedicated philatelist collects stamps and Russell, even before he became the equivalent of a Penny Black, was well worth a place in her album. Her gossiping cousins might wonder "whether she deliberately and consciously made young men fall in love with her", but there was no doubt about her delight in arousing the jealousy of Alys. Moreover, beneath her anti-sisterly bitchiness there fluttered a lasting affection which Alys may have feared. More than forty years later, recovering from a critical illness, Mary could write to Russell that "one of the results of illness is to make me understand what things have been precious in my life, and you were one of the most precious". For his part, Russell felt a genuine affection that was never swamped by a searingly accurate judgment of her character.

Bemused with Alys, more shocked than attracted by the sophistication of Mary's beliefs, Russell failed to notice that the magnetism of the latter's quicksilver ways was basically greater than that of the younger sister's moral earnestness. The lesson he learned in Paris was different, and cheap at the price. With his wives, and with his mistresses, Russell was usually to implement the same standard of truth which he sought in his academic work. But from this early example of blithe thoughtlessness he learned that in human relations there were often two ways of presenting the truth, and that one could cause less pain than the other. More than half a century later, staying with a former mistress in Sweden, he was asked by her whether his wife knew they were in the same city, in the same hotel, on the same floor. He was not worried. "I will make little of it," he replied, a method of dealing with highly charged situations that Alys's distraught reaction in 1894 had shown him to be both kinder and more convenient.

It also brought results. Back in England, he was able to make his peace in about ten minutes. The dangerous corner successfully turned, he got on with the job in hand: preparing for his marriage.

3

Marriage in Haste

Russell was married to Alys Pearsall Smith on 13 December 1894 in the Quaker Meeting House in London's St Martin's Lane, with Charles Trevelyan running a book in penny bets on the chances of someone speaking during the Friends' period of silence. None of the Russells was present. The bridegroom had, moreover, received a letter from Lady Russell two days before the ceremony which in effect reproached him for having won the battle. "How thankfully I remember that all through your childhood & boyhood you would always cheerfully give up your own wishes for those of others," he was pointedly told, "never attempt an excuse when you had done wrong, & never fail to receive warning or reproof as gratefully as praise. We trusted you, & you justified our trust, & all was happiness & affection." All that had evaporated; as far as the family was concerned he was now on his own.

The young couple's plans for the future were earnest but modest. The legacy from Lord Amberley meant that even without the safety-net of Pearsall Smith money Russell need not earn a living. Time could therefore be devoted to a leisurely pursuit of satisfying intellectual work. Alys had her good causes: the emancipation of women, teetotalism and a variant of Quakerism which, harking back to its ancestry in Anabaptism, included advocacy of free love. He, for his part, was being drawn towards economics. Its attractions were still over-shadowed by the inner compulsion to find at least some irrefutable truth in the world, but the Idealism he had taken up so enthusiastically had as yet proved of little use; indeed, he was soon to suspect that some of its basic assumptions were incompatible with what he felt, in the marrow of his mind, must be the ultimate truths of mathematics. Therefore it was in mathematics that he would work during the next few years; in mathematics of the most theoretical sort, moreover. As he wrote to Moore a few years later when asked to read a paper to the Apostles, "I can't read on practical things, as I think little about them & cannot prove the few opinions I have in any valid sense." Just how, where and why he would deploy his talents was at the moment immaterial. All life was before him, and for a while he could afford to coast along.

He and Alys had already agreed that immediately after marriage they would travel, and early in 1895 they set off for Berlin. She was to investigate the situation of women in Germany and what the Social Democratic Party intended to do about it. He kept two options open on the future: studying economics at Berlin University and reading steadily for the paper, part philosophical, part mathematical, that he planned to submit as thesis for a Trinity Fellowship.

Russell, approaching twenty-three, still unknown to fame, already had the ability to spark off enthusiasm among those he met. One of them was Hutchins Hapgood, an American whose Berlin address he had been given by Berenson. The two men met for tea at Russell's hotel and the American later recorded "a feeling of intense mental life almost unrivalled in my experience. Ideas simply leaped from him, he bubbled with thick-coming fancies. He excited me like strong drink or a beautiful woman. It was not so much any particular interest that he had at that time – but he couldn't make even an ordinary remark without somehow exciting my intellectual nerves."

Looking ahead to a splendid future, Russell decided to write, as many financially independent men had decided before him.

> I remember a spring morning when I walked in the Tiergarten, and planned to write a series of books in the philosophy of the sciences, growing gradually more concrete as I passed from mathematics to biology; I thought I would also write a series of books on social and political questions, growing gradually more abstract. At last I would achieve a Hegelian synthesis in an encyclopaedic work dealing equally with theory and practice. The scheme was inspired by Hegel, and yet something of it survived the change in my philosophy. The moment had had a certain importance; I can still, in memory, feel the squelching of melting snow beneath my feet, and smell the damp earth that promised the end of winter.

However seriously all this was taken, it had little urgency. He intended to pursue his search for certainty and he meant to develop and air his views of how he thought the world should be run. But this would be his contribution to civilization, not a task carried out to earn a living. Two decades later his attitude was expressed by Aldous Huxley's Mr Scogan, the elderly cynic of *Crome Yellow*, whose creation never ceased to irritate Russell:

> If you're to do anything reasonable in this world, you must have a class of people who are secure, safe from public opinion, safe from poverty, leisured, not compelled to waste their time in the imbecile

routines that go by the name of Honest Work. You must have a class of which the members can think and, within the obvious limits, do what they please. You must have a class in which people who have eccentricities can indulge them and in which eccentricity in general will be tolerated and understood. That's the important thing about an aristocracy.

As a member himself Russell, aged twenty-two, with a new bride by his side, with enough money to travel wherever he wanted, could forgo Honest Work until the spirit moved him, and in the spring he and Alys made for Fiesole. Here in the hills outside Florence, Mary Costelloe had set up home in a small villa next-door to Bernard Berenson's I Tatti. Russell himself later claimed to have had a hand in the romance, as well as in healing the resultant breach with the Pearsall Smiths. "The runaway couple were desperately short of money," he later said. "Mary rushed in with Bernard. It was the first real meeting I had had with Bernard. I was delighted with him. My beautiful and gay 'sister-in-law' asked for £100. It was forthcoming there and then."

Russell's subsequent relationship with Berenson developed with cautious friendliness: Berenson's reaction was much the same. "Bertie I have been seeing a great deal, and I liked him better and better," he wrote to Bob Trevelyan. "His mind is exquisitely active. True it has as yet perhaps not got beyond picking up one moss-grown stone after the other to see what is under it, but that by itself is perfectly delightful. Were I really interested in metaphysics or he in art, we should be superhumanly well joined." Russell, made in a very different mould, faintly suspicious of the other's bright colours, would enthuse about mathematics. "I used to listen with rapture," says Berenson. Of I Tatti, Russell wrote that "The atmosphere of Art and luxury was rather trying ... and at first I couldn't understand why I had liked B.B., but gradually I got to like him again." Artistically, he was difficult to convert, and after his host had once conducted him on a marathon expedition round the Uffizi Russell summed up: "I've looked at everything you wanted me to look at; I've listened to all you've said; but the pictures still don't give me the funny feeling in the stomach they give you." But there was the occasional real contact. When Berenson pointed out the extraordinary beauty of a chance arrangement of pebbles and wood, Russell exclaimed: "But this is out and out mysticism."

Eventually he did suck in some understanding of art, and during a bicycle-tour of Lombardy even influenced Berenson's own views. Russell had just read his host's *Venetian Painters* in manuscript. "I ... felt he was under a misapprehension in following Berkeley's mistaken theory of vision (that we see everything in two dimensions and ourselves supply the third)," he has said. "I put B. B. on to William James's 'Psychology' to dissuade him from his view, and he subsequently modified his view and clarified it greatly."

During the next few years Russell cycled a great deal in Italy – "about as enjoyable as any travelling I have ever done", he wrote to Moore. "Some autumn you must come to Italy with us; it is the most perfect country ever invented. Even small and remote villages are full of absolutely first-rate architecture & the whole plan of life is dignified." He went on foot over the Alps, through the Apennines several times, and to Venice where he and Alys stayed in the Palazzo Capello of Henry James's *Aspern Papers*. "It is perfectly divine here, in Venice. I wish you could be here a while and forget the problems of Ethics in sensuous joys," he wrote to Moore.

> The place is like Heaven, too good for morality. One has only to float lazily through the warm days & nights, & allow every sense to be perpetually clasped in the best things the world can offer. I know no place, not Florence or Rome even, so poetic & so satisfying. We live in a palace with a huge hall, longer than any of our College halls, out of which the rooms open. It has also a garden which is rare in Venice, & the most charming of furniture.

Here was at least a small hint of the inner feeling for art and architecture still largely bottled-up in Russell. It was to remain so for another decade and a half until Lady Ottoline Morrell released it and enabled him to express a whole gamut of appreciations about which he had so long remained inarticulate.

After the first visit to Berenson in 1895 the Russells made for the Adriatic. They travelled in a leisurely progress down the coast through Ravenna, Rimini and Ancona for a few gorgeous weeks of spring and first love, bathing naked off the warm deserted beaches, not thinking very much about the future, let alone worrying. By early summer earnestness began to creep back. The Fellowship Thesis had to be finished by August and Russell's demon took over, upbraiding him for wasted weeks and prodding him home to England.

Here they settled in a small cottage to the north of the village of Fernhurst, not exactly under the eagle eye of Mrs Pearsall Smith but at least in what was for Alys an extension of the family domain. And it was no doubt here that Russell first began to think that "mothers-in-law are a very stubborn part of the Mystery of Evil". Years later, listening to someone else's mother-in-law troubles, he sympathized: "I remember my difficulties at Friday's Hill."

In their new home Russell began writing his thesis. This was for a Fellowship, popularly known as the Prize Fellowship, awarded on the result of an annual competition among college members of a certain age in which all competitors wrote on a subject of their own choice. Russell's was the foundation of geometry, and dealt with the problem raised by Kant's question, "How is Geometry Possible?" At first glance there seemed to be two ways of answering this, and of thus determining the logical relations of the most elementary constituents of space. The answer offered by the Idealists was that no real problem existed since no certain knowledge of the real world was possible independently of existence, and that in some ways geometry was a shining illustration of this. Alternatively, it could be claimed that the workaday truths of geometric axioms were so widespread that they gave the appearance of absolute certainty even though this did not exist. Neither answer satisfied Russell. The first offended his sense of reality, the touchstone of so many beliefs he was to hold. The second, giving only the appearance of certainty, did not give enough. Russell wanted his certainty certain.

His solution, an acceptance of Kant, was to treat space as a form of intuition and then justify the plausibility of geometry on purely logical grounds, the first step in the logicizing of mathematics that he carried on in *The Principles of Mathematics*, and he and Whitehead continued in *Principia Mathematica*. Russell's answer, which he believed had at last "solved all philosophical questions connected with the foundations of geometry", held that projective geometry was wholly *a priori*, dealing with "an object whose properties are logically deduced from its definition, not empirically discovered from data"; but that metrical geometry, "which deals with actually given space, not the mere intellectual construction we have just been discussing – gives results which can only be known empirically and approximately, and can be deduced by no necessity of thought". Whatever validity this answer had, it was to last less than two decades, since it depended on space, whether Euclidean or non-Euclidean, preserving a constant measure of curvature. As Russell himself wrote of the book into which he turned the thesis,

> Einstein's revolution swept away everything at all resembling this point of view. The geometry in Einstein's General Theory of Relativity is such as I had declared to be impossible. The theory of tensors, upon which Einstein based himself, would have been useful to me, but I never heard of it until he used it. Apart from details, I do not think that there is anything valid in this early book.

He submitted his thesis in August and two months later went to Cambridge to hear the result. He arrived a couple of days in advance and called in turn upon Whitehead, referee for the mathematical aspects of the thesis, and upon James Ward who dealt with its philosophical implications. Neither could of course tell him whether he was to be elected, but he hoped to gain some idea of his chances. They appeared to be slim, as he reported that night to Alys. "My darling Rosebud (this is to replace the Little Lark for the future), [Whitehead and Ward] (who are both ultra-empiricists) disagreed with almost every view I advocated; Ward also found my metaphysic and Psychology rather thin – like my chances, I thought, when Whitehead told me. So I don't think I shall be elected tomorrow, and I suspect that I am not much good at Philosophy ... Adieu to sweet dreams." But the following day he was elected, and Whitehead explained to Russell why he, for one, had spoken out: it had been his last chance of criticizing his former pupil.

The Fellowship was for six years and imposed few demands. Russell had neither to reside in college nor to carry out any teaching or research. The election modestly augmented his income, gave him the facilities of Trinity, and at the same time accorded him a status useful to a young man outward bound across the ocean of philosophy. "There is no fear", wrote Uncle Rollo, "of your becoming a cauliflower sort of Fellow, even if you go into residence." But in fact he left England again within a few weeks of election.

The earlier interest of the Russells in the German Social Democrats had by this time hardened into a firm resolution: they would investigate the party in depth, interview its leaders and its members at all levels, attempt to probe beneath the skin in order to understand the status and prospects of the party. As a result Russell's first published book, *German Social Democracy*, the outcome of his Berlin researches and the lectures into which he fashioned them the following year, was political rather than philosophical. In it he vigorously praised the *Communist Manifesto*. However, the praise – a "magnificent work" which "for terse eloquence, for biting wit, and for historical insight ... is, to my mind, one of the best pieces of political literature ever produced" – was for its effectiveness rather than its goals.

In 1895 the German Social Democratic Party, like those of most other European countries, was predominantly Marxist; more than two decades were to pass before the Russian Revolution finally siphoned off the last of its orthodox members, leaving only those prepared to work for the gradual but not the violent overthrow of capitalism. In 1895 they had one special attraction for Russell. At the start of *German Social Democracy* he quotes Engels's belief that German Socialists, descended not only from Saint-Simon, Fourier and Owen but also from Kant, Fichte and Hegel, are in fact the heirs of German classical philosophy. "This haughty claim", says Russell, then in the full flow of his Hegelian enthusiasm,

> expresses the peculiar feature which gives to Social Democracy an interest and a human value beyond that of any ordinary political movement. For Social Democracy is not a mere political party, nor even a mere economic theory; it is a complete self-contained philosophy of the world and of human development; it is, in a word, a religion and an ethic. To judge the work of Marx, or the aims and

beliefs of his followers, from a narrow economic standpoint, is to overlook the whole body and spirit of their greatness.

The view, held before the revisionists so leavened the party's high ideals that it was no longer a threat to authority, was over-romantic, just as his view of the Russian Revolution was to be over-romantic until he had seen its effects in the chaotic aftermath of 1917. The reaction was typical. Beneath Russell's critical analytical intellect there lay the mind of a romantic *manqué*, forever tempted to look out at events through the rosiest of spectacles and see there not the real landscape but a scene of his own imagining. More than sixty years later, explaining his views on nuclear disarmament, he evoked opposition for similar reasons. "I oppose him," said his interviewer, a man unhappy at having to disagree, "because he lays down the law as if the world were peopled by potentially rational, honourable, selfless human beings just waiting to be taught by good example, instead of by fundamentally blind, selfish, deceitful, crafty fools." Much the same optimism powered Russell's interest in the Social Democratic mixture of philosophy, religion and ethics which he and Alys now settled down to study in Berlin.

He himself did not keep a Berlin diary and neither then nor later did he write or say much about the way he and Alys worked. She fills the gap, with a full scrap-book and detailed diary from which it is possible to piece together their working methods. From the start, they had a double advantage. His background gave him immediate entrée to Wilhelm Leibknecht and August Bebel who had founded a party a quarter of a century earlier. Alys, a transatlantic visitor of impeccable references, obvious good intentions and some experience of social work, smoothed the way for investigation of home life, domestic problems and the status of women.

For six weeks the Russells interviewed party members, attended local elections, and saw and spoke with anyone who seemed likely to provide useful information. "Called on Frl. Ottilie Baeden, a seamstress," noted Alys soon after they arrived. "We found her having tea with her old father & 2 little nephews in a small stuffy room with two beds & a sewing-machine." Three days later they visit another party member "in a fairly respectable house, but a very slummy neighbourhood, very noisy and smelly. The woman said her husband was an active *Parteigenosse*, but not in regular work, and this was the first time they had let rooms." They learned that in Berlin University there was a secret Social Democratic Society but that all the members of the Student Corps were conservative.

The investigation gave Russell an early dislike of the military. He wrote to his grandmother,

We know no Prussian officers, & I must say I'm glad we don't. Whenever I think of any particular evil in Germany, I always find, however remote it may seem, that it really springs from militarism and Alsace-Lorraine. I doubt if any historical crime has been more severely punished. But I have got such a hatred of the German Army from it, that I cd. hardly bring myself to be polite even to an individual officer, tho' of course individuals are not to blame. The odd thing is, that even the most cultivated and intelligent opponents of Social Democracy think its internationalism frightfully wicked. We were introduced to a delightful & most gentlemanly man, Professor Sering, but he said as a young man he had been hindered from joining them by the contempt they cast on the glories of the Franco-Prussian war – it never seemed to occur to him that those glories were in reality a bitter shame & disgrace.

Russell returned home with his wife, supplemented his on-the-spot investigations with further background reading, and then, foreshadowing the pattern to come, turned the experience into a talk to the Fabian Society, a course of six lectures at the London School of Economics, and *German Social Democracy*. To the book, Alys contributed an appendix – a pointer to the way in which Russell was to co-opt his wives into his work.

Russell's appearance as one of the first speakers at the London School of Economics, newly formed by the Webbs, gave him a cachet. The mere fact of his election to a Trinity Fellowship showed what a headmaster's report would call "promise", and he had already started the long succession of papers, reviews and review-articles for *Mind*, which continued for half a century. Nevertheless, beyond a small circle, Bertrand Russell was still nothing out of the ordinary, a fact emphasized in the autumn of 1896 when Alys, anxious to display her trophy to the family, took Russell to America.

He was keen to combine social duties with something demanding more mental muscle, and an opportunity arose through that formidable woman, Dr Carey Thomas, president of Bryn Mawr and a cousin of Alys. Her biographer, Edith Finch, was by a strange turn of fate to become Russell's fourth and last wife. Russell, it was agreed in the summer when arrangements for the visit were being organized, should give a short series of lectures at Bryn Mawr based on his Fellowship Thesis, soon to be published as *An Essay on the Foundations of Geometry*.

The president was only the first of the family to rise to the occasion. Her father, Dr James Carey Thomas, was closely connected with Johns Hopkins University in Baltimore and was in England when the Russells' visit was being planned. Telling the Johns Hopkins president that Russell would be lecturing at Bryn Mawr, he added, "as he is a rising man and is said to be quite remarkable I thought it might be a good thing for him to address our Mathematicians . . ." But not everyone had the family enthusiasm of the Carey Thomases. "I never heard of Mr. Bertrand Russell," wrote Simon Newcomb, the astronomer and editor of the *American Journal of Mathematics*, when his opinion was canvassed on the proposed course of six lectures. "If he is going to be in Baltimore on his own account, it might be a graceful act, and one agreeable to the students, to invite him to deliver one, or even two lectures, on the theme you mention. But I cannot imagine that there is anything of real value in the theme that cannot be developed in two lectures, at the outside." Thomas Craig, editor of the *American Journal of Economics*, wondered whether there were "a dozen mathematicians outside of Cambridge who have ever heard [Russell's] name", and regarded the proposed lectures as "a sort of dilettante affair at best". But despite these discouraging opinions, Dr Thomas prevailed: Russell and his wife arrived with a full programme awaiting them in both Bryn Mawr and Baltimore.

At Bryn Mawr, they stayed with Carey Thomas, and from the Deanery Russell sent back to Uncle Rollo his first impressions of the academic world which had produced the women of Friday's Hill. "This College is a very nice place," he began;

> it seems to me much better than Girton & Newnham, especially in the greater freedom it allows to the girls. Also those girls that I have met seem to have more independence of mind, more spirit and more originality, than most of the girls at Cambridge. I give my last lecture today; I have had an extraordinary number of people at them – about 30, I think – many of them teachers and professors, from this and neighbouring colleges. Tomorrow I am giving a lecture wh. I have called "Socialism as the Consummation of Individual Liberty" – I doubt whether I shall convert anybody, as Americans seem very much more opposed to Socialism than English people. Alys, too, has been busy . . .

Alys had indeed been very busy. She had almost inevitably begun with a lecture on temperance, and had travelled on to the history of the Women's Suffrage movement in England and Germany. This was as much as Bryn Mawr would take publicly. It did not deter Mrs Russell from holding private talks with the girls and extending the discussion from political suffrage to free love. She favoured the practice; at least, she favoured it until, some years later, Russell began using her theory for his practice. At Bryn Mawr, she knew she was moving over exceedingly thin ice and after leaving wrote to the president with the hope that it would not break now she had gone. "I do most sincerely hope that it will not get thee into trouble with the Trustees, because thee certainly did not know how I was going to put the thing. I shall never again have such an intelligent audience."

From Bryn Mawr, where Russell renewed his acquaintance with Lucy Donnelly, a contemporary and friend of Alys he had already met at Friday's Hill – and who maintained a half-century's intimate but platonic friendship with him – they travelled to Baltimore. Here they stayed with Carey Thomas's father while Russell gave his lectures on the logic of geometry once again. Almost his only comment on the brief visit referred to Dr Thomas's daughter Helen: deaf, gentle, kind and with astonishingly beautiful red hair. "I was very fond of her for a number of years, culminating in 1900," he remembered. "Once or twice I asked her to kiss me, but she refused."

After a visit to Harvard, the Russells returned to Fernhurst. Before, they had lived in a small house on the fringe of the Friday's Hill estate. Now they moved into Millhanger, a sixteenth-century workman's cottage on the far side of the village, which they hoped would be semi-permanent quarters. Lighting was by oil and the only water came from a well. Even when they had added three more rooms to the tiny house, it was still a two-by-four home compared with Friday's Hill or Pembroke Lodge, a place in which two people, living cheek by jowl, could rasp each other with the minimum of provocation.

Here, throughout 1897, Russell settled down to mathematics, close to the Pearsall Smith base at which he spent a good deal of time, and almost as close to his cousin Lady Mary Howard, married to Gilbert Murray and settled at Churt, just across the Surrey border. He read extensively. He passed his Fellowship Thesis through the press as a book. He travelled frequently to London, usually staying in the Pearsall Smiths' town-house in Belgravia; sometimes to Cambridge where he talked "shop" with Whitehead, Moore, McTaggart and anyone else willing to join in. In Cambridge, also, he worked for a time at the principles of dynamics. "I went to the Cavendish Lab and I studied Clerk Maxwell," he later wrote. "Gradually I found that most of what is philosophically important in the Principles of Dynamics belongs to problems in logic and arithmetic." Occasionally he went to Oxford, hoping on one occasion to see Bradley, and writing to Alys that "it seems the greatest sign of friendship that he can give anyone is to take them to see his dog's grave. There are those who would not sit down among the angels, he says in his book, if their dog were not admitted with them."

But it was only a few years later that he met Bradley – "a black-bearded man with a very intellectual, very sensitive face, beautiful by the beauty of the mind that appears in it," as he wrote in his journal.

> His manners are very courteous and slightly shy. He has the spirituality of those who have worked in spite of great physical pain. I loved the man warmly. We discussed philosophy for some time. I vexed him very much (quite unintentionally) by saying that in philosophical

discussion, so far as I could see, one arrives usually at an ultimate difference as to premisses, where argument is no longer possible. This seemed to him scepticism and an attack upon his life's work. He controlled himself completely, but with difficulty. I was very sorry I had vexed him.

Russell was an unimpressed by Oxford as one might expect a Cambridge man to be. "I enjoyed my stay there," he said after one visit, "bu all the men I met struck me as grossly ignorant. Those who were interestec in physics knew nothing of Clerk Maxwell; those who went in for statistic knew nothing of Karl Pearson."

This lordly dismissal of apparent also-rans was typical of the Russel who still moved almost exclusively in a small, enclosed world, satisfiec with his search for basic truths, and even with a private life whose failing he was to discern only in retrospect. Two events – more accurately, one visit to Paris and one change of philosophical stance – were within a few years to shift the course from that to which Thomas Craig's word, "dilettante", could fairly be applied.

The change of stance was the move from Idealism, arguably the mos significant single step on Russell's philosophical journey, taken in concer with Moore, to whose rooms Russell was a frequent visitor. "The contras between the two men and the two minds was astonishing and fascinating," Leonard Woolf has written of them at this period.

> Russell [had] the quickest mind of anyone I have ever known; like the greatest of chess players he sees in a flash six moves ahead of the ordinary player and one move ahead of all the other Grand Masters. However serious he may be, his conversation scintillates with wit and a kind of puckish humour flickers through his thought. Like most people who possess this kind of mental brilliance, in an argument a slower and duller opponent may ruefully find that Russell is not always entirely scrupulous in taking advantage of his superior skill in the use of weapons. Moore was the exact opposite, and to listen to an argument between the two was like watching a race between the hare and the tortoise. Quite often the tortoise won – and that, of course, was why Russell's thought had been so deeply influenced by Moore and why he still came to Moore's rooms to discuss difficult problems.

As early as December 1897 Russell gave the first hint of what was coming. He was, he then told Moore, writing "a rather scratch sort of paper as I am having what revivalists call 'a dry time'. I have called it 'Seems Madam? Nay, it is': the gist of it being that for all purposes which are not *purely* intellectual, the world of Appearance is the real world – agin McT's notion of getting religion out of philosophy." From this simple elief there was to develop during the coming years his new realism, a hilosophy linked to science in two complementary ways. Its starting-oints were in the realm of mathematics and, later on, in the new physics vith its revolutionary concepts of radioactivity, the quantum theory and elativity. Its method also was essentially that of science since it tried to nalyse complex entities into their parts, and deal with them as a scientist vorking in the laboratory rather than as a theologian forming his ideas f the universe.

There was to be another analogy with the scientific method. Just as cience presents each new theory or discovery as a fresh step towards ltimate truth, rather than ultimate truth itself, so was Russell's philo-ophic journey one of continual reconsideration and reassessment. As the British philosopher Bryan Magee has said, "whereas most great philo-ophers seem to have managed to write one or two masterpieces in which their fully developed views are presented, Russell wrote no such nasterpiece, in my opinion, but, instead, umpteen flawed and super-eded books". So much for his hope of finding certainty: in philosophy, s Whitehead had commented of the new physics, "Certitude was one."

After the "rather scratch sort of paper", the next step came in February 898 when, in Moore's rooms, Russell read to the Moral Science Club paper on "The Constitution of Matter". "Three theoretical con-tructions were expounded, each leading dialectically on to the other," he secretary reported; "firstly the naive scientific atom in a real space – econdly, space the ultimate nature of matter – lastly matter conceived dealistically as a physical monad. The dialectic development was clearly arried out. The discussion was with great difficulty kept anywhere near he point. – so suggestive did the paper seem to be." Sixteen years later Russell recalled how he had "started gaily on the philosophy of matter" nd had been occupying himself ever since in unravelling the necessary reliminaries. "In matters of *work*," he added, "my life has had a very reat continuity and unconscious unity."

From the early attempt to worry out the structure of reality there now leveloped the refutation of Idealism in which Russell and Moore played omplementary parts. Moore, according to Russell's later memory, was nore interested in the rejection of Idealism as such; Russell was more oncerned in refuting its essential monism, which denied any basic dif-erence between mind and matter.

On Russell's part the move away from Idealism was essential if he was o have any hope of completing the major task he had set himself. This vas the building of a new structure of mathematics in which none of the ccepted axioms and concepts need be assumed; only a small number of primitive ideas were required, and from these there could be developed oth the simplest laws of logic and the most abstruse theorems of advanced mathematics. If this were possible, as Russell believed it to be, then logi and mathematics were similar; or, to use his own expression: "They diffe as man and boy; logic is the youth of mathematics and mathematics i the manhood of logic."

Yet Idealist philosophy presented two obstacles. For one thing, Russell' preliminary work seemed to demand admitting external relations, lik "less than" and "greater than", which could be placed between any tw numbers without in any way altering the nature of the numbers. But thi conflicted with the doctrine – Russell called it the "dogma" – of interna relations, according to which "every relation is grounded in the natur of the related terms". Just as important, Idealism by its very natur appeared to make impossible Russell's aim of establishing the objectiv character of mathematical truth. This should, he strongly averred, be in dependent of mathematicians.

During the first half of 1898 he had begun work on his "big book" which, as he described it to friends, would provide a fresh basis for mathe matics. From the first he realized the height of the barriers created b Idealism, and in July reported to Moore that he had only succeeded i finishing the first section of the book "by skating over the difficulties & leaving them to be discussed later", and that it would be at least six month before he was able to make a further attack on it. As it turned out, th greater part of what was to become *The Principles of Mathematics* had t be re-written several times, since though conceived while Russell was stil within the Idealist camp, it was in fact to be a work of his post-Idealis years.

Before the end of 1898 the belief that his views would have to be change if the logical foundation of mathematics was to be well and truly laid wa further strengthened. His colleague McTaggart, planning to visit relative in New Zealand early in 1899, had to supply a stand-in for his Lent Terr lectures. He turned to Russell.

The lectures were to be on Leibniz, Voltaire's Dr Pangloss, the Germa polymath who had waltzed through the second half of the seventeent century as philosopher, scientist, mathematician and diplomat, as muc at ease in the opulent courts of Hanover and Berlin as in the Prussia Royal Academy or London's Royal Society. As a subject, Leibniz pre sented problems since he had created one philosophy to satisfy hi admirers and another which he concealed from the world. Russe appeared to compound the complication by showing in his lectures tha Leibniz had failed to work out the way in which his principles had serve as axioms for his conclusions. Although he rejected Leibniz's attempt t base philosophy on logic, logic in its most formal and mathematical sens was soon to become Russell's chief preoccupation and the mainspring c his own philosophy. But a more immediate result of his reading fo McTaggart's lectures was that it pushed him further from the centre c the Idealist stream: for although Leibniz was an Idealist, he was a monadist and not a monist, as well as being a better logician than all the Absolute Idealists rolled into one, and the logical clarity of his position tended to throw their absurdities into high relief.

The core of Leibniz's philosophy was the monadology, a system suggested by one current scientific advance: the construction of the first microscope, which had revealed to Leeuwenhoek the wriggling forms of spermatozoa and enabled other scientists to show that even a drop of water contained a huge mass of hitherto unsuspected organisms. Extrapolating from science into philosophy, Leibniz conceived the constituent parts of the universe as an infinitely large number of infinitely small parts which he called monads. These constituents he regarded as non-spatio-temporal entities, each self-contained, each mirroring the rest of the universe, and each independent of all other monads. At first glance, this stuck a dagger between the ribs of commonsense, since it seemed clear that whatever else might be in doubt, it was certain that there did exist a causal relationship between different parts of the universe. Shots fired by cannon did kill; thoughts in human minds did lead to action; and, although the mechanism of the event was still unknown, a sharp tap on the knee did produce a reflex movement of the human leg. To Leibniz, such objections were based on a wrong view of the universe. All monads – "veritable Atoms of Nature and, in a word, the very Elements of things" in "Monadology" terms – mirrored the world as it had been created by God, "in the sense that God has so ordained the entire business that all monads independently run their several courses in a gigantic system of craftily devised parallel courses".

After his study of Leibniz, Russell became increasingly convinced that he would have to struggle out of the Idealist morass were he ever to reach the bright fields of mathematical truth.

Moore was meanwhile also struggling to liberate himself from Idealism, and by the start of the twentieth century both men were free. Moore first explained his thoughts in print, in *The Nature of Judgment* in 1899, then in *The Refutation of Idealism* in 1903; Russell in *The Principles of Mathematics*. Yet neither account reveals the tremendous gusto with which both men broke out into their new world. This was left to Russell, more than forty years later. "I felt", he wrote, "... as if I had escaped from a hot-house on to a wind-swept headland ... In the first exuberance of liberation, I became a naive realist and rejoiced in the thought that grass is really green, in spite of the adverse opinion of all philosophers from Locke onwards."

Whatever his contribution to their joint apostasy, it is clear that Russell changed philosophical horses by instinct, adopting the attitude, soon to be followed by Einstein in a different field, of pulling a hypothesis from the air by a process as much artistic as scientific and only then searching about for its justification. This was usually to be his method, spelt out clearly to Bradley years later.

> I don't know how other people philosophise, but what happens with me is, first, a logical instinct that the truth must lie in a certain region, and then an attempt to find its exact whereabouts in that region. I trust the instinct absolutely, though it is blind and dumb; but I know no words vague enough to express it. If I do not hit the exact point in the region, contradictions and difficulties still beset me; but though I know I must be more or less wrong, I don't think I am in the wrong region. The only thing I should ever, in my inmost thoughts, claim for any view of mine, would be that it is in a direction along which one can reach truth – never that it is truth . . .

The search for truth, another way of describing Russell's search for certainty, was to be given an important new turn by his rejection of Idealism. For a basic element of Idealism was that every statement was part of a comprehensive system whose parts were logically related to each other. Any statement that fitted in, or cohered, with the rest of the system was true; any that failed to do so was false. But with this there went a tendency to sit on the fence; the truth of any given proposition was not absolute, and the readiness with which statements hung together in the overall system was merely a measure of their truth, which could have in effect a percentage value attached to it. Russell's objections to this, developed during the first years of the twentieth century, were summed up in the conclusion that "the definition of truth as self-coherence is either meaningless or self-contradictory", and that "the view that truth and falsehood are not absolute opposites but occur in varying degrees, cannot be stated in any form which does not contradict itself".

The move away from the Idealist fold, which demanded the rejection of the coherence theory of truth, could be discerned in the published version of the Leibniz lectures which appeared in 1900. The work which had gone into them was important for other reasons since it confirmed Russell in Leibniz's belief that the task of philosophy was to break down complex ideas into simple ones, an analytical process which would eventually reveal the complete structure of the natural world. This was to be the hard core of Russell's method for the rest of his life, and however much his views developed he continued to use the same path in arriving at them. His two main areas of disagreement with Leibniz were to have equally significant results. He believed that Leibniz's monadology was simply the inevitable result of analysing all statements into the subject–predicate form; and since the monadology was untenable, so was the sovereignty of this form of analysis. In addition, Russell could not accept Leibniz's view that all knowledge was ultimately *a priori*, for he believed that all our knowledge of the world came to us through our senses. These three outcomes of his reading for the Leibniz lectures – an increased trust in the analytical process, suspicion of the subject–predicate form as ubiquitous, and an earthy feeling that our knowledge of the world is based in experience – were to be crucial in Russell's development during the coming decades.

A Critical Exposition of the Philosophy of Leibniz lifted Russell above the well-breeched academic part-timers who in those days doodled in some numbers along the fringes of real work, adding the occasional and useful footnote to their subjects but rarely doing much more. The book came none too early. He was now twenty-eight, and five years of his six-year Fellowship had passed. *German Social Democracy* had of course shown his seriousness, while there could be no doubt that the Hon. Bertrand Russell was an amusing and nimble-witted young man, equipped with all the social graces, extraordinarily attractive to women despite his short stature and almost falsetto laugh ... a man who as unexpectedly as Toulouse-Lautrec would have earned the adjective charismatic had it been in fashion. Yet he was still a lightweight, most frequently referred to as brother of "the wicked earl", poor Frank, soon to be tried by his peers for bigamy.

His comparative slowness in getting off the mark, dangerous in a field where tradition still asserts that a man's best work is likely to be produced before he is forty, contrasts strongly with the Russell of middle and old age, the epitome of Tennyson's aspiring human, "forever seeking something new". The explanation is simple: Alys.

By 1900 he had been married for six years, and as yet there was on the surface no wrinkle to hint that Granny might have been right. In private, as well as in public, Alys and Bertrand Russell were the dutifully loving couple, and if any doubts of their remaining so ever consciously flitted across Bertrand's mind, they were outside the range of Mrs Russell's philosophy. The dire warnings of Lady Russell, who has died early in 1898, appeared to have been unwarranted.

He himself was later to claim that his feelings had evaporated in a moment, on a Cambridgeshire bicycle-ride, an explanation which hardly rang true when he gave it and is now known to have been a gross over-simplification. A more accurate pointer to the real situation is given by a letter written soon after he had parted company with Alys. "My marriage checked growth in one way, even when it was happy; then I had a short time of freedom tho' in pain – then long years of prison – with greater powers of endurance it would not have been prison, but I couldn't make myself rise above it all & live freely in spite of it ..." A little of what this meant in practical terms was revealed in another letter:

> It wasn't Alys that spoilt me; she was not *at all* subservient while I cared for her, quite the reverse – she was constantly away speaking

> on temperance & suffrage – I always encouraged her to go, & even urged her. I used to stay at home waiting to hear her adventures when she returned – I really was not tempestuous & exacting in those days. What spoilt me was that if I didn't struggle for my own happiness, life would grow unbearable – my courage slowly ebbed away. And now still the memory of those years is a recurrent nightmare.

What the nightmare meant to his work was plain. He wrote of life with Alys,

> The first five years were happy indeed – the more peaceful because everything infinite, all the reaching out after the unattainable things, ceased to exist in me. I did a great deal of work, & succeeded in it beyond my hope; but it was entirely technical and dry. Somehow or other the awakening was bound to come. As I look back on the happiness of those years, I feel it to have been not of the best kind. It was associated with hardness & conceit & limitation. It was useful as a rest to nerves; I acquired a background of sanity which has been needed since. Also it wd. have been much harder to acquire knowledge if I had been less satisfied. But it ought not to have been permanent.

There was one other point. "I had been brought up in an aristocratic household but at the time of my first marriage I had cut myself off from aristocratic society." In some ways he was certainly the most democratic of men; but he was also a Russell, and while the world of Friday's Hill was attractive to a youthful visitor from Pembroke Lodge, as a permanent habitation it lacked the necessary little something.

From the mass of personal detail which fills Russell's later correspondence, and from an intimate private journal which he kept intermittently in the early 1900s, two things are quite evident: that despite her good intentions Alys was an intellectual ball-and-chain; and that after the first flush of honeymoon excitement her connubial earnestness, far from satisfying his particular requirements, at first turned him off and eventually evoked distaste.

The situation was transformed during the first years of the twentieth century. Russell's true feelings for his wife burst through the polite covering with which he had so far concealed them even from himself; and at the same time his intellect began to ride up the sky, a fresh star at last scintillating with its long-awaited brilliance. So interrelated were the two processes that it is impossible to say whether the excitement of concentrating on *The Principles of Mathematics* acted as catalyst to his emotional life with Alys or whether the sudden realization of what his marriage had become spurred him on to finish the book he had been working at since 1898.

The event which began the professional transformation and probably prepared the ground for the personal revolution was the International Congress of Philosophy, Logic and the History of Science held in Paris in the summer of 1900. Russell and Whitehead went with their wives, on a mixed professional and private jaunt as common in academic circles then as now – Alys was in fact to read a paper on "L'Éducation des Femmes", which, like her husband's, was to be published in the *Proceedings*. The men would talk shop with their colleagues and the ladies would amuse themselves, visit the art galleries or otherwise enjoy the change of scene. A good time would be had by all.

Russell fitted neatly into the pattern, and his reaction to a family scandal then entertaining England shows how different was the Russell of 1900 from the Russell of later years. Frank had finally tired of the succession of law-suits in which his wife had embroiled him, had journeyed to America, obtained a Reno divorce, married a new wife and returned with her to Britain, a flouting of British law which later brought him to the Bar of the House of Lords. Russell was not amused and failed to acknowledge his brother's return. "From you and Alys at least I was entitled to expect congratulations – not silence," wrote a very huffed 2nd Earl. Russell's reply has not survived, but can be judged from Frank's next letter. "Your suggestion that I should visit you without my wife is not, I hope, meant seriously. You would not expect to have such a proposition made to you in regard to your wife, and I shall prefer to consider it as an inadvertence." Inadvertence or not, in 1900 it was Russell who followed protocol, and his brother who exemplified the aristocratic trait of not giving a damn for anyone.

The journey to Paris and the week's stay in the city brought the Russells and the Whiteheads into closer social contact than before. It was pretty prickly. "Mrs. Whitehead dislikes [Alys]," Russell admitted some years later, "but Whitehead hates her – he has never been able to stand her." Evelyn Whitehead, whose effect on the Russells' lives was to be greater than any of them could have foreseen as they crossed the Channel, was a beautiful and gifted woman who dutifully served her husband for more than half a century. With something like Charles Darwin's need for an illness to keep him going, but frequently at death's door with heart trouble, she was to survive into her nineties. "My wife's background", Whitehead wrote, "is completely different [from my own], namely military and diplomatic. Her vivid life has taught me that beauty, moral and aesthetic, is the aim of existence; and that kindness, and love, and artistic satisfaction are among its modes of attainment." But there was even more to it than this. "By myself," he once said, "I am only one more professor, but with Evelyn I am first-rate." Hers were by no means exceptional characteristics, but they were curiously similar to those of both Lady Ottoline Morrell and Lady Constance Malleson, two women who were later to win Russell's wayward devotion; and they were poles apart from those of Alys, who placed artistic satisfaction several rungs down the ladder from moral fervour.

Whatever unthinkable thoughts Evelyn Whitehead started in Russell's head during this summer week, the effect of the Congress was to be more obvious and more immediate. On the afternoon of 2 August, Russell read his paper – on "L'Idée d'Ordre et la Position Absolue dans l'Espace et le Temps", part reprinted in *Mind* as "Is Position in Time and Space Absolute or Relative?" – before an audience that included Bergson, Poincaré and Couturat. Also present was Giuseppe Peano, the Italian mathematician who had played a key part in the development of symbolic logic.

It had for long been realized that a language of symbolic logic was more convenient for mathematics than the language of everyday life. Leibniz had considered extending symbols for logical operations, but it had been left to George Boole to adopt the idea and, by careful choice of symbols and operations, to create a system which resembled algebra and yet expressed certain logical truths. During the second half of the century this elementary symbolic logic was extended by Gottlob Frege and by Peano among others. Frege took the process a stage further by inventing non-mathematical symbols which could be used where the analogy with mathematics was slight – symbols standing, for instance, for "if – then", "either – or" and "all". Peano had worked independently along comparable lines, in much the same way that Darwin and Wallace worked independently on evolution, and the British and Germans on radar. The outcome was a symbolic notation similar in power to Frege's, although a good deal closer to traditional symbolism than his, and a language in which the signs – for such logical ideas as "the only", "is contained in" and "there exists" – had an unambiguous meaning often lacking in conventional languages; a language, furthermore, in which a sentence demanding many lines in conventional terms could be expressed in a fraction of that space.

But important contributions to the development of symbolic logic were only the first of Peano's achievements. He had also tackled, with some success, a problem that had intrigued mathematicians from the earliest times: that of showing mathematics to be a system of deductions from a single starting-point, or at least from a minimum number. Russell knew of Peano's work before the Paris Congress but had not studied it carefully. Now, listening to the man in person, he realized he had reached a turning-point in his intellectual life. "In discussions at the Congress," he wrote, "I observed that [Peano] was always more precise than anyone else, and that he invariably got the better of any argument upon which he embarked. As the days went by, I decided that this must be owing to his mathematical logic."

Russell approached Peano. "I wish to read all your works," he said.

"Have you got copies with you?" Peano had offprints available and was glad to hand over a set.

The exchange was significant. Whitehead was not only present at the Congress as Russell's colleague; he was roughly half as old again, and two years previously had published his *Treatise on Universal Algebra*. Yet it was Russell, not the older man, who now acted – the first of those occasions when Whitehead, had he been of a more envious nature, might have regarded his colleague as "Always a step ahead of me, / Cool-eyed, confident, lean: / The man I always wish to be, / And never yet have been."

In mid-August they all came home. The Whiteheads returned to the Mill House in Grantchester, where they were bringing up their daughter and two sons, and Whitehead settled down to the second volume of his *Universal Algebra*. The Russells returned to Millhanger. Within a few hours Russell was reporting to Moore, "The Congress was admirable & there was much first-rate discussion of mathematical philosophy. I am persuaded that Peano & his school are the best people of the present time in that line."

In Paris he had seen that Peano's notation and methods led to a new and powerful technique for discovering the truths on which mathematics rested. Now, back in England, he mastered the system and the method, extended them to the logic of relations and incorporated the results in a paper which he sent for publication in the Italian's *Rivista di Matematica*.

He then set about considering the implications of the new tool for "the big book", still on the stocks, still being re-written. The previous summer he had re-drafted Book One, although many difficulties remained. Now, all at once, he saw that Peano's system was not only ideal for his particular job but that it had a utility not even its inventor had appreciated, since it "extended the region of mathematical precision backwards towards regions which had been given over to philosophical vagueness".

The excitement which this realization aroused is not easily understood by those to whom mathematics is merely a working tool, and philosophy a casual cerebration. But each man needs his own stimulant. The spur of matching observed facts with existing theories drove Einstein on to his solution that overturned the physicists' apple-cart. Van Gogh exhausted himself just to make the golden flowers shimmer perceptibly in the heat. Jacques Böell, that immaculate mountaineer of the Dauphiné, describes a mountain-face stimulating a companion "as much as a naked woman". On Russell, a man who could write in his private journal, "Nature is my inspiration, and Mathematics is my purifier," the possibilities opened up by Peano's system had much the same effect.

In the autumn he began using Peano's symbols to worry out some of the points which had been intriguing him for years. As he struggled with them throughout the autumn, the Whiteheads came frequently to Millhanger and the two men discussed the work with mounting enthusiasm. "Every evening the discussion ended with some difficulty," Russell wrote, "and every morning I found that the difficulty of the previous evening had solved itself while I slept. The time was one of intellectual intoxication. My sensations resembled those one has after climbing a mountain in a mist, when, on reaching the summit, the mist suddenly clears, and the country becomes visible for forty miles in every direction."

He worked for three hours in the morning, read after lunch, then worked again after tea. Dinner was usually followed by talks with Alys or by joint reading of the books of the day. Contact with the Pearsall Smiths, way up the hill, was frequent; but with this exception the social round was small and undemanding. Only when they spent a few days in London was work temporarily pushed to the back of the mind.

The Russell who laboured on, nose earnestly to grindstone, still displayed a remarkable priggishness and was frequently burdened with a seriousness unrelieved by the sparkle of his later years. The earnestness shows up prominently in his private journal, where he records taking a fellow-guest on a walk from Gilbert Murray's house through a rain-soaked, bracken-covered landscape that would have delighted Kipling:

> It was an exquisite moment: tender, calm, with melancholy melted into almost joyous resignation and a picture of the old age which the wise may hope to attain. If only, [my companion] remarked, people could learn to view Death as like such a day – a good saying, but she was too young to know the difficulty of doing so, which, though agreeing with her, I attempted to explain ...

Not even the incomparable Gertrude Bell escaped. "She said she would not like to live in a University town, because they know nothing of the great world without," Russell recorded after their meeting at a London gathering. "I replied that they live in a far greater world, the world of ideas and that only with them do I feel really among comrades – very priggish, but appropriate ..."

Appropriate, also, were his views on inequality. Of one fellow-guest at a London dinner-party, he noted,

> But he is too democratic for me – he said his charwoman was more in contact with real things than anybody else he knew. But what can a charwoman know of the spirits of great men or the records of fallen empires or the haunting visions of art & reason? All this and much more I wished to say; but the words stuck in my throat. Let us not delude ourselves with the hope that the best is within the reach of all, or that emotion uninformed by thought can ever attain the highest level. All such opinions seem to me dangerous to civilisation & the outcome of a heart not yet sufficiently mortified.

There is much more in the same vein – the opinions of a young man in his thirties who as an old man in his nineties could still deplore marriage between an upper-class friend and a working-class girl, on the grounds that such things never worked.

At times Russell's poor view of others was equalled only by his good view of himself. Thus after a long evening talk with one friend he reported, "He seemed quite the fool I expected, the more so as he thought it worth while to make up to me. O these worldlings!" A few days later he recorded of a visit to friends, "The talk, the atmosphere of people who care for great things, was balm to me; every moment of the two days I expanded and became a better person ..." Of one friend he confidently notes that "... she begins at once talking of real things, with perfect assurance that I shall answer as she would wish; and it is impossible to withhold from her whatever of good I may have to give ...", while later he finds that "... she is extraordinarily sympathetic to me, and I could not help talking very well ..."

The intellectual brush-off was not reserved for laymen. Richard Haldane, already working his way up towards the Lord Chancellorship and *The Pathway to Reality*, was merely a "sentimental and fluffy-headed old Hegelian", roughly the view which Russell later expressed when preparing to hear Haldane give the presidential address to the Aristotelian Society on "The Methods of Modern Logic and the Conception of Infinity". It was, he wrote to a friend, "a subject on which he knows little and I know a great deal. He is sure to make a fool of himself." He said much the same when reviewing the address in *Mind*; the president, he politely suggested, didn't know what he was talking about.

At Millhanger the social pleasantries were strictly subordinated to work, and to a system that produced a steady ten pages a day. On 31 December 1900, he wrote triumphantly to Helen Thomas of Bryn Mawr announcing that the 200,000-word draft of *The Principles of Mathematics* was finished at last. However, re-writing and revision kept him hard at it for another six months. Then, unexpectedly, he suffered a major setback. This was the discovery of what came to be known as the Russell paradox, a time-bomb ticking away in the heart of mathematics since the days of Epimenides the Cretan who had awkwardly said that all Cretans were liars. Was this statement in fact a lie? The question appeared to have only one answer: if it was it wasn't, and if it wasn't it was. "It is an ancient puzzle and nobody treated that sort of thing as anything but a joke until it was found that it had to do with such important and practical problems as whether there is a greatest cardinal or ordinal number," Russell subsequently explained. "Then at last these contradictions were taken seriously."

The first of the modern paradox problems had been raised by Burali-Forti, who in 1897 showed, not to put too fine a point on it, that the assumption that there is a greatest ordinal number leads immediately to the generation of a greater ordinal number. Two years later Cantor discovered a similar paradox regarding cardinal numbers which, although not published for another thirty years, rapidly became well known within the mathematical community. These and similar paradoxes all raised their awkward questions only in the mathematical stratosphere; their intriguing riddle-me-ree quality, with its hint of a Christmas party-trick, suggested that their importance was probably of significance only to academics. Transformation into something more down-to-earth came when Russell applied Cantor's paradox to "classes", the groups of similar objects which are among the fundamental building-blocks of mathematical philosophy. He later explained,

> This process led me to the consideration of a very peculiar class. Thinking along the lines which had hitherto seemed adequate, it seemed to me that a class sometimes is, and sometimes is not, a member of itself. The class of teaspoons, for example, is not another teaspoon, but the class of things that are not teaspoons, is one of the things that are not teaspoons. There seemed to be instances which are not negative; for example, the class of all classes is a class. The application of Cantor's argument led me to consider the classes that are not members of themselves; and these, it seemed, must form a class. I asked myself whether this class is a member of itself or not. If it is a member of itself, it must possess the defining property of the class, which is to be not a member of itself. If it is not a member of itself, it must not possess the defining property of the class, and therefore must be a member of itself. Thus each alternative leads to its opposite and there is a contradiction.

At first he thought there must be some error in the reasoning. He inspected each step under a logical microscope, but could discover nothing wrong. Neither could Whitehead, who responded to the news by quoting "never glad confident morning again".

However, Russell was not willing to let this paradox destroy his central argument and he spent the rest of the year, and the spring and early summer of 1902, in putting the finishing touches to the book. As far as the contradiction was concerned, he had worked out what he himself well knew was only a crude solution. He put it in an appendix, apologized for its inadequacy, trusted that in due course he would be able to do better, and on 23 May 1902 handed over the manuscript to the publishers.

Then, and only then, did there take place an event which gives the story of mathematics one of its moments of high drama. Russell had read Frege's *Begriffsschrift* in the 1890s but had failed to follow it. Late in 1900 he had bought the first volume of the same author's *Grundgesetze der Arithmetik*, in which Frege had applied his symbolic logic to arithmetic and begun to work out an analysis of arithmetic based entirely on logical operations. Now, reading the book in the quiet of his study at Millhanger, Russell realized that Frege had used, as a cornerstone to his whole philosophy of mathematics, the method of constructing classes which Russell had proved led directly to the paradox.

On 16 June, Russell wrote to Frege. He expressed his appreciation of the *Begriffsschrift*. But, he went on, he had only recently studied the first volume of the *Grundgesetze der Arithmetik*. He agreed with most of it. But, he continued,

> there is just one point where I have encountered a difficulty. You state that a function, too, can act as the indeterminate element. This I formerly believed, but now this view seems doubtful to me because of the following contradiction. Let *w* be the predicate: to be a predicate that cannot be predicated of itself. Can *w* be predicated of itself? From each answer its opposite follows. Therefore we must conclude that *w* is not a predicate. Likewise there is no class (as a totality) of those classes which, each taken as a totality, do not belong to themselves. From this I conclude that under certain circumstances a definable collection does not form a totality.

Frege replied by return. "Your discovery of the contradiction caused me the greatest surprise and, I would almost say, consternation, since it has shaken the basis on which I intended to build arithmetic," he wrote. "... It is all the more serious since, with the loss of my Rule V, not only the foundations of my arithmetic, but also the sole possible foundations of arithmetic, seem to vanish."

Sixty years later, Russell was still impressed by Frege's noble reply. "As I think about acts of integrity and grace, I realise that there is nothing in my knowledge to compare with Frege's dedication to truth," he said.

> His entire life's work was on the verge of completion, much of his work had been ignored to the benefit of men infinitely less capable, his second volume was about to be published, and upon finding that his fundamental assumption was in error, he responded with intellectual pleasure clearly submerging any feelings of personal disappointment. It was almost superhuman, a telling indication of that of which men are capable if their dedication is to creative work and knowledge instead of cruder efforts to dominate and be known.

The verdict tells almost as much about Russell as about Frege.

Russell replied on 24 June and at the same time sent the publishers additional matter for chapter ten which dealt with "The Contradiction". This, however, was only the first repercussion, as Kenneth Blackwell of the Bertrand Russell Archives at McMaster University has recently discovered. When proofs began to arrive weeks later he replaced whole pages – and still further revised the amended material when the new proofs arrived. Finally, in November, he sent to the press two appendices, one giving English readers their first account of Frege's logical and arithmetical doctrines, the other describing the new but only partly successful way in which he now tried to deal with the paradoxes, by means of his latest innovation, the Theory of Types.

Despite the unsolved problem he was moderately pleased. "I am very deep in proofs and Symbolic Logic," he wrote to Gilbert Murray in September, from the Mill House where he was staying with the Whiteheads.

> I created, with all an artist's passion for the perfect, a new treatment of Symbolic Logic, and to my joy Whitehead finds that it has all the beauty and perfection that I hoped. It is an immeasurable comfort to have one department in this smirched and ragged world where one can touch perfection – even if all else one loves has to be abandoned on the threshold of the Temple, as is the case with Mathematics – the very sternest and most austere of all the gods.

The book finally appeared in 1903. Some parts of the 500-page volume, the first comprehensive treatise on the logical foundations of mathematics to be written in English, showed traces of the way in which Russell's beliefs had evolved as the work was written. "For my part," he wrote after publication to Elie Halévy, the French historian, whom he had met at the Whiteheads, "I am very dissatisfied with it & it only remains to hope that Vol. II in which Whitehead and I are collaborating will contain fewer errors and unsolved difficulties."

To Bradley, with whom he was still on friendly terms, he wrote,

> In the book, on the whole, I avoided fundamental questions; as I say in the Preface, my premises are simply assumed. But I hope some day, when the second volume of my present work is finished, to attempt something on the more purely philosophical side of logic. Hitherto I have been hoping Moore would do this better than I could, but I believe he contemplates going into more purely metaphysical questions. In regard to my second chapter, I was in a difficulty. Strictly and logically, it is hardly necessary to master it; but so many of my views are really suggested by Symbolic Logic that I believe, practically, not only it but the second volume are almost indispensable.

Like much that Russell was to accomplish in other fields, *The Principles* burrowed deeply below the accepted order of things, and if the tunnellings seemed at times to run in haphazard directions they were none the less important for that. Whether or not he had justified his thesis was not yet clear. As *Nature* said, the book did not pretend "to say the last word on any subject, and, indeed, bristled with unsolved difficulties, towards the correct solution of which a great step is undoubtedly made by its publication". Russell had explained the few simple concepts which were all his thesis appeared to require, and had described the philosophical processes which could, he claimed, reveal that mathematics was part of logic. The theory hung together. But to be granted proof rather than plausibility it would have to be worked out on the ground, with the purely literary explanation replaced entirely by the special signs of symbolic logic.

This was to be the task of the "second volume" on which he and Whitehead embarked as a joint enterprise. Long before it was completed, Russell himself was to be swept by the personal storm whose aftermath affected the rest of his life. It was to leave him emotionally isolated. It was also to leave him in a mood where immersion in the depths of mathematical logic became not only a pleasure but a consoling defence against personal anguish. Had things been different he might not have pushed on so doggedly and *Principia Mathematica*, as the joint work was to be called, might never have seen the light of day.

4

Repentance at Leisure

The collaboration between Russell and Whitehead which resulted in *Principia Mathematica* began after the autumn of 1900 and before the summer of 1902. The exact date depends partly on definition; partly on the moment, probably unknown to either author, at which each realized that their separate ideas had merged into a single stream. But one thing is certain: before the collaboration had long started Russell's emotional life had been transformed – and in circumstances that he concealed for the rest of his life.

Between February 1901 and February 1902, he experienced what he later called a sudden "conversion", a change of heart which brought with it a love of humanity and a horror of force: he fell out of love with Alys and he fell in love with someone else, a fact which he disclosed only later in letters to Lady Ottoline Morrell, who became his mistress in 1911. There were good reasons for silence, both at the time, and thirty years later when he wrote an autobiographical account of the period. Even to Lady Ottoline he did not confide the name of the woman for whom he "killed passion". She herself, evolving over twenty-five years from mistress to a mother-confessor from whom he was neither anxious nor able to keep many secrets, had no doubts: the love which "died a gradual death for want of nourishment" was in her opinion for Evelyn Whitehead, the wife of Russell's collaborator.

Ottoline's early conjectures were reinforced when Russell wrote to her confessing:

> Much my strongest affection after my love for you is affection for Mrs. Whitehead. This is rooted in years of difficult & very painful cooperation in tasks which both think very important – chiefly keeping Whitehead from knowledge of things which upset his balance. It is not a feeling in which there is anything to cause you jealousy but it is quite indestructible & very deep.

Nothing more than affectionate friendship need necessarily be inferred and the identification of Mrs Whitehead with Russell's Dark Lady is not proved by it. Nevertheless the evidence, though circumstantial, is considerable. It becomes stronger if the course of events is followed chronologically as Russell writes *The Principles of Mathematics* and then, with Whitehead, decides that the planned second volume will become the joint *Principia*; as the lives of the two men, meeting for long, leisurely discussions in Cambridge or Surrey, and wrapt in the most dispassionate academic debate, become entwined in a way that brings intense pain to Russell, but of which Whitehead, oblivious to the storm, appears completely unaware. There are gaps in the story. But there are sufficient exclamations of anguish, let loose at the time, sufficient lookings-in from intelligent outsiders, and above all sufficient hints in the later passionate letters to Ottoline, for the moving picture to emerge.

The initial experience came in February 1901. The Whiteheads and the Russells were both in Cambridge, sharing Professor Maitland's house in Downing College. Alys and Russell went to an evening reading in Newnham by Gilbert Murray of his then unpublished *Hippolytus*. Murray and Russell had been acquaintances for many years. Only now, following the impact of the *Hippolytus*, did they become friends.

Russell returned to Downing College deeply moved. When he and Alys arrived, Mrs Whitehead was in intense pain, apparently the result of a heart-attack. Russell's first account of his reaction was given ten years later in a letter to Lady Ottoline which betrayed no hint of the circumstances or the identity of those involved. "The moment of my first conversion was this way," he said.

> I came to know suddenly (what it was not intended I should know) that a woman whom I liked greatly had a life of utter loneliness, filled with intense tragedy & pain of which she could never speak. I was not free to tell my sympathy, which was so intense as to change my life. I turned to all the ways there might be of alleviating her trouble without seeming to know it & so I went on in thought to loneliness in general, & how only love bridges the chasm – how force is the evil thing, & strife is the root of all evil & gentleness the only balm. I became infinitely gentle for a time. I turned against the S. African war & imperialism (I was an imperialist till then) & I found that I loved children & they loved me. I resolved to bring some good & some hope into her life. All this happened in about five minutes. In spite of many faults & many backslidings I succeeded on the whole in what I undertook then. When I told her of you, she bade me remember that she is permanently better & happier owing to me. But it took me rather more than a year to acquiesce in her pain & to learn to love the cause of it, tho' he deserves much love. It was during that year I learnt whatever wisdom I possessed before meeting you.

As he wrote more than half a century later, "I saw that pain of such intensity completely isolates the sufferer and makes sympathy totally useless. It was frustrated sympathy that gave rise to the experiences I had on that occasion." Another account, identifying Evelyn Whitehead but similar enough to show that the letter to Ottoline referred to the same event, was given by Russell when he wrote his draft autobiography twenty years after telling Ottoline.

The repercussions of this incident were to spread out in widening circles, and at least one aspect of its link with Russell's eventual breach with his wife was described a decade later when he wrote,

> I got on with Alys very well until the Boer war. I felt the Boer war so much that I could not think of anything else, & Alys was jealous of it. She was a foreigner, & in any case couldn't understand feeling so much about anything that didn't touch one personally. Altho' the war was not what actually produced the rupture, it was the real cause. At the beginning of the war I was an imperialist more or less. In the middle of it, for other reasons, I had a sudden "conversion", a change of heart, which brought with it a love of humanity & a horror of force, & incidentally made me a pro-Boer. Alys was puzzled, & disliked it – I remember one day when we were talking with other people she said casually that she wouldn't like to have a child like me.

That the Boer war had not produced any immediate break with Alys is shown by a letter from Sidney to Beatrice Webb, written on 7 March 1900, some five months after the war had started. "Last night, as I sat alone, reading to relieve my loneliness, there came in Bertie Russell and his wife who had seen the windows alight when passing by . . . They asked me to breakfast with them this morning at No. 44, which I did. They were in the best of spirits, keen about the war and eager to get on foot a sane theory of imperialism; anxious to federate the Empire and us all."

However great the change wrought in this attitude by Evelyn Whitehead's pain, it was not only she whom Russell had been observing in the agonies of her heart-attack. There was also her husband, as Russell made clear a few months later when staying at the Mill House. Both the building and its situation had an almost magical quality. The windows, sixteenth-century and hung with flowering creepers, looked out over an old-world garden and yew tree to a mill mentioned by Chaucer. Rupert Brooke had not yet pinned the village into history, but it already had links with Byron and Wordsworth. In the spring there were nightingales; kingfishers haunted the river. It is difficult to believe that Russell, responsive to sense of place as he was, did not react to this atmosphere as he began to realize the unsuspected extent of Mrs Whitehead's problems. He wrote to Alys,

> Evelyn and I had an exceedingly frank talk last night on the subject of Alfred. She saw all that we felt about him when she was ill, in a way that was really uncanny. But at that time she was too much inclined to think herself neglected by him to argue with us. However, I was able to say last night whatever was necessary to her happiness. She was much relieved to have talked it out, & tho' I did not express my whole mind, I completely avoided lying ...

The following day he added a postscript. "All goes well; Evelyn was tired last night, but slept like a top. We have had much talk about Alfred. She has cured herself of the feeling of being neglected, but knows all we felt. I am much relieved at the removal of a secret, & so, it appears, is she ..."

The secret was a double one. First there was Whitehead's mental condition. "Mrs. Whitehead was in perpetual fear that he would go mad," Russell has recorded. "I think in retrospect, that she exaggerated the danger, for she tended to be melodramatic in her outlook. But the danger was certainly real, even if not as great as she believed." In addition there was Whitehead's financial incontinence which led him to run up bills he could not settle. Russell came to the rescue and over the next few years carried on surreptitious financial support. The money was filtered out through Mrs Whitehead with a secrecy he did not lift even for Ottoline, who was later simply told that chance had given him power to relieve solid pain. "What I have been able to do in this way is the most useful thing in my life apart from my work," he wrote of it on one occasion. "Some years back when I had lost self-respect and faith, it was the only thing that kept me from suicide. I knew that my death must ultimately bring disaster."

Although he had quietly slipped into the role of Whitehead's collaborator and of father-confessor to his wife, his emotions were still unrecognized. The Russell who had gone his own way in the face of Granny's warning could not yet think about the unthinkable: the possibility that he had fallen out of love with Alys.

Things went on as before. "The scheme of their joint life is deliberately conceived to attain ends they both believe in, and it is persistently and modestly carried out," Beatrice Webb wrote of the Russells when she stayed at Friday's Hill in July 1901.

> The routine of their daily existence is as carefully planned and executed as our own. They breakfast together in their study at nine o'clock (we breakfast at 8!), then Bertrand works at mathematics until 12.30, then three-quarters-of-an-hour reading together, a quarter-of-an-hour stroll in the garden together. Lunch with us, 1.30; chat in our sitting-room or out of doors, over cigarettes and coffee. Then Bertrand plays croquet with Logan Smith (Alys's brother who

lives here) until tea at 4.30. After that mathematics until 6 o'clock, reading with Alys until 7.30, dine at 8 o'clock, chat and smoke with us until 9.30, another hour's reading aloud with Alys until 10.30 ...

Meanwhile the storm was coming nearer. His Prize Fellowship ran out in the summer of 1901, but he was now invited to lecture for a couple of terms on mathematical logic, and in the autumn the Russells moved in with the Whiteheads at the Mill House. And during the first weeks of 1902, on an afternoon bicycle-ride beneath the huge, open skies of the Cambridgeshire fen-country, he realized that he was no longer in love with Alys. "I had had no idea until this moment that my love for her was even lessening," he stated later. "The problem presented by this discovery was very grave." So grave, in fact, that despite his silence Alys immediately realized something had happened. On 9 February 1902, she questioned him, a weak gambit which merely brought forth an injunction "not to be indiscreet". For the moment she obeyed.

Looking back, Russell suggested that the cause of his emotional *bouleversement* had been simple. "I now believe", he wrote, "that it is not in my nature to remain physically fond of any woman for more than seven or eight years. As I view it now, this was the basis of the matter and the rest was humbug." But he eventually cut these sentences from his autobiography.

At the time it looked different. With the revelation, the emotional obscurities of the past year became clear. To Ottoline he later explained how, before he loved her, he had loved Alys; and how, in between, in 1902, there had been the second woman. "Again I loved," he wrote. "Piercing the prison of flame / Where one stern soul in lonely anguish burned, / Forgetting the earth once more with love I came / Into that hell whence no light hopes returned."

He now knew that he had been seized and overwhelmed, for the first time in his life, by feelings that soared out beyond the orbit of Alys's devotion, a devotion which had rarely evoked passion and no longer evoked love. But his reactions were ambivalent. On the practical intellectual level there was dismay, if not anger, that this could have happened to him, that the convenient apple-cart of existence should have been overturned so suddenly, without warning. There was also an unavoidable anguish; for Russell, certain that he no longer loved Alys, was as certain that the subject of his new desires was not for him. Evelyn Whitehead, who so well fits the picture of the unidentified woman, held him in considerable affection; in different circumstances she might have loved him. But he knew that in the Cambridge of 1902 there were rarely second options for the wives of university dons. Thus the love which he believed would never be quenched could never be admitted – although a curiously moving letter from Mrs Whitehead, written more than a decade later, suggests she may well have known what she dare not discuss. Nothing more can be certain: after Whitehead's death in 1947 Evelyn destroyed Russell's letters; those to her husband and those to herself.

The intensity of feeling mingled with the difficulties of concealment to create a tense and troubled man. Alys realized, as Russell put it in a masterly understatement, that "something was amiss". Thus it was in an atmosphere of cool and diverging personal relationships that in the early spring of 1902, ten weeks after the bicycle-ride, the Russells returned from Cambridge to Fernhurst.

Neither stayed there long and Beatrice Webb, once again at Friday's Hill, noted early in June that Alys had left for a rest-cure and that Russell had been with the Whiteheads for three of the previous eight weeks. Few things escaped Mrs Webb, who after finding Russell less forthcoming than usual recorded in her diary,

> Poor Alys has been too unwell to be here. A consciousness that something is wrong between them has to some extent spoilt our sojourn here, both Sidney and I being completely mystified. We became so concerned about the situation that I suggested that I should take Alys off to Switzerland to complete her cure . . . It is quite clear to me that Bertrand is going through some kind of tragedy of feeling; what is happening to her I suppose I shall answer in the next three or four weeks.

Mrs Webb's curiosity was not to be entirely satisfied. But she carried out her rescue-operation, spending a week with Alys at Monte Generosa, then two in the Engadine. Her only job, she wrote, was to "act as a good companion to Alys Russell and to tide her over a bad time". She appears to have succeeded. "I shall always remember your great kindness to me when I was in great trouble nine years ago," Alys wrote in the summer of 1911, "and I appreciate more than anything else your not speaking about things you must have guessed."

Meanwhile, Russell in England remained emotionally distraught in a mood he has revealed in a significant journal-entry. "I was inspired; my energy was ten times what it usually is. I had a swift insight and sympathy, the sense of new and wonderful wisdom intoxicated me. But I was writing cold letters to Alys, in the deliberate hope of destroying her affection. I was cruel still, and ruthless where I saw no self-denial practised."

The ten-fold energy had carried him along to the final stretch of *The Principles of Mathematics*. He completed it at the Whiteheads', adding the final words in the Mill House with some of Gibbon's exultation as he put down his pen in the garden-room at Lausanne. But there was also desperation. "I finished it in a hurry because the oppression of it grew unendurable," he admitted. He wrote to Lucy Donnelly, telling her the job was done and adding that there was "a thousand times more experience in pain than in pleasure. Artists must have strong passions, but they deceive themselves in fancying it good to indulge their desires. The whole doctrine, too, that writing comes from technique, is quite mistaken; writing is the outlet to feelings which are all but overmastering and are yet mastered."

The following day the Whiteheads, like the rest of Britain, celebrated the end of the Boer War. "And I too felt a great joy that the outer world was not yet such a ruin as the inner," he wrote that night in his journal, "but, yet, the contrast was all but unbearable, and in solitude I sobbed uncontrollably."

Soon, moreover, he had to meet Alys, due home in late June, still in doubt about her husband's affections and escorted from the Continent by Berenson. Without delay, she asked him what his feelings now were. There came, he said,

> the answer that love was dead; and then, in the bedroom her loud heart-rending sobs while I worked at my desk next door. In the evening I walked with Berenson; the beauty of the western twilight, in that strange wood, was disquieting, wonderful, inspiring. I came home and wrote "Monotonous, melancholy, eternal", etc.; a strange, unimaginable, unforgettable day ... Oh the pity of it! How she was crushed and broken! How nearly I relented and said it had been all lies! And how my soul hardened from moment to moment because I left her to sob! In the middle of the night, she came to my door to say she was calmer now, and would hope – poor, poor woman.

But he had still told only half of the story he revealed to Ottoline a decade later – that "Alys never at any time stirred my depths; ten years ago they were stirred, but there was always so much pain that I could never let feeling grow to its full intensity ..."

With the secret burning fiercely inside, he looked to the future. His journal, and an interlocking network of surviving letters, show what it was like: a year of guerrilla warfare that drove Alys to the point of suicide and Russell himself towards the precipice of insanity; a year or two of armed truce during which both sides rested, as much in exhaustion as in defeat; then a longer and apparently recuperative period during which some outward appearances were restored and Alys mistakenly saw acquiescence as acceptance.

In June 1902, the beginning of an awful year, Russell left Fernhurst for a few weeks. He went first to Pembroke Lodge, then to Cambridge. "I sat alone, reading ghostly books," he wrote, "and I worked at Frege, Meinong, and proofs, feeling all work a mere hollow sham." He returned briefly to Fernhurst and then, with Alys, took a cottage at Little Buckland, near Broadway in Worcestershire. He was no doubt wise to seek sanctuary; Mrs Pearsall Smith was probably as aware as Beatrice Webb that "something [was] wrong".

He found little peace as he tried to drown himself in work. All he ever remembered of Little Buckland was that

> in a glass bowl, a gold-fish swam round and round, pressing his nose against the glass, endlessly longing to escape from his prison into the world of light. There I felt that Mrs. Webb had gone over to the other side, and I quarrelled with her. I worked ten hours a day, till I could hardly stand or see for fatigue; I realised that A's love must not be killed, and that her virtue must be my care, probably for ever; and day by day the inspiration left me, and the long task claimed me. But still, after I said cruel things that stabbed her, I felt dimly that only what gives pleasure is wrong, but what gives pain is always either right or at least pardonable.

However hard he struggled at what was to have been volume two of *The Principles of Mathematics*, and was evolving into *Principia Mathematica*, the emotions obstinately stuck spokes in his intellectual wheel. The depth of his despair comes through in a note to Bob Trevelyan who describes a tragedy he had half-completed. "Happy lady in your play who dies at the appropriate moment!" says Russell. "Tragedies are wonderfully cheerful compared to real lives. Give her my congratulations on her happy issue out of all her afflictions."

As for Alys, she cracked under the strain, collapsing and making him realize that he must never leave her for long. The thought of having children by Alys, runs an entry in his journal, "is hell, but so is the fear of her suicide".

They had taken the Little Buckland house only for the autumn. Then they went to Chelsea for six months, hoping that the change of style might provide a solution, that if the personal agonies continued they would at least be diluted by the social demands of London life. There was a lot to be said for the move. "At night, from my study, I see Orion rise and Saturn set, so I have most of the pleasures of the country," Russell wrote to Gilbert Murray. "Though town is a very new departure, I expect to find it interesting, and on the whole not a waste of time ..." But the optimism soon passed and there began "strange months in town, where I learnt to be a social being and not a person of fire and insight; and where she was miserable the whole time, in spite of the pleasure of getting on". Even by November he was writing, "London grows more and more odious to me, and I feel myself again growing rebellious. I must continue not to think of my own happiness – in the early autumn I was in a much better moral state, and poor Alys is suffering for my relapse." The Thames, Whistler's Chelsea Thames of dark currents hurrying to the sea, was a consolation and to his journal Russell confided, "The river is becoming to me a passionate absorbing love. I could drown myself to be one with it." And to Gilbert Murray, "The river shines like burnished bronze under the frosty sun, & the barges float dimly through the brightness like dream-memories of childhood ... Only the river & the gulls are my friends; they are not making money or acquiring power ... "

The move to London was not working. Late in November he and Alys spent four days in Cambridge, two of them at the Mill House where the Whiteheads' children unconsciously rubbed salt in the wounds. "Tiny and North have long observed that I am unhappy," Russell wrote; "Tiny said she used to hope she would be able to lift my unhappiness, but now she was afraid she would never succeed." A fellow-guest remarked that having the Russells dining with the Whiteheads again was quite like old times. "As like as a gibbering spectre is to flesh and blood, I thought," Russell noted. And, a few days later, "When I got home Alys had a crying fit: I know it is my fault, and I must manage better, but it is hard. She too is lonely – good God, what a lonely world it is, though there are so many people in it."

The strain of domestic battle dominated these dreadful months, a continuing wear-and-tear not yet replaced by the comparative relief which followed when he and Alys later agreed on an armistice. "At night, I didn't kiss Alys often enough," he wrote on 25 November, "and she began to cry when I put out the light; but I did nothing to comfort her." When they went to a concert, "she cried visibly the whole time, because I had seemed a little vexed at her lending Murray's book without asking me." And, a few days later, "After the light was out she asked if I remembered the date – I had forgotten it was our wedding-day. Then presently her misery became uncontrollable, and I had to comfort her somehow."

The constant nagging did much to push him into rebellion against the accepted sexual ethic, and later strengthened his advocacy of trial-marriage. The atmosphere is typified by his journal-entry for 28 November 1902:

> At luncheon Alys had just come from seeing the Kinsellas, whose sister Joe had a baby this morning, and nearly died of it, being in fact not yet out of danger. The Kinsellas and Douglas had sat up all night in terrible anxiety. *I*: "It is a terrible position for a man, because he always feels as if he were to blame." *She* (in a tone of evident pleasure): "Yes, and Kate and Louise had been telling him he was." *I*: "That is one of those brutal actions that put people quite out of court. Doesn't thee feel it so?" *She* (feeling my disapproval of her levity): "Yes I do. They didn't tell him so, they only agreed when he said it." I went on for some time trying to make her see why I was shocked at her tone; at last she said: "Yes, I think it just as bad as a husband I knew who abused his wife when for the fourth

time she had a daughter instead of a son." This was to turn the thing into a man-and-woman question, and make out that misogyny was at the bottom of my remarks. Then she began to cry, and I changed the subject ...

At Christmas, almost in desperation, they went to the Berensons outside Florence. Russell's mood is revealed in a letter he wrote to Gilbert Murray as he completed preparations for the trip.

> I have been making myself a shrine, during the last 8 months, where I worship the things of beauty that I have known, & I have learnt to live in this worship even when I am outwardly occupied with things that formerly would have been unendurable to me. A private world, a world of pure contemplation, is a wonderful refuge; but it is very necessary to preserve it from pollution. Strange, the isolation in which we all live; what we call friendship is really the discovery of an isolation like our own, a secret worship of the same gods.

The night before leaving, he and Alys discussed the future, and how much they should tell Mary and her husband. "I urged her being mostly in town, and my being mostly in the country, on account of our work," he wrote. "She said she would be willing if I loved her. Odd woman! She won't leave me unless I don't want her to do so – she is determined that I should suffer somehow. But that is an unjust way of putting it."

The following morning they were off – for "Italy and exile". By what Russell later called a stroke of great good luck, Frank Costelloe had died in 1900. Mary had married Berenson without delay and the couple were now in the first stages of what was to be nearly a half-century of married life. Russell's response to art still lay half-buried in his subconscious "... in my heart, the whole business about Art is external to me – I believe it with my intellect, but in feeling I am a good British Philistine," he admitted to Berenson.

The self-accusation is explained in a letter to Gilbert Murray, written from I Tatti.

> Just behind the house is a hill-side covered with cypress and pine & little oaks that still have autumn leaves; & the air is full of deep-toned Italian bells. The house has been furnished by Berenson with exquisite taste; it has some very good pictures, & a most absorbing library. But the business of existing beautifully, except when it is hereditary, always slightly shocks my Puritan soul – thoughts of the East End, of intelligent women whose lives are sacrificed to the saving of pence, of young men driven to journalism or schoolmastering when they ought to do research, come up perpetually in my mind; but I do not justify the feeling, as some one ought to keep up this ideal

of beautiful houses. But I think one makes great demands on the mental furniture where the outside is so elaborate, & one is shocked by lapses that one would otherwise tolerate.

Here above Florence – "where Alys was very unhappy, though I did my best for her" – Russell began what is arguably his most famous essay, "The Free Man's Worship": "the total result of so much suffering", as it seemed to him in retrospect. "The human surroundings were ideally the worst," he remembered, "but I spent long days alone on the hillsides & in the groves of olive & cypress, with the Arno below & the austere barren country above." The essay, a short but profoundly moving cry of defiance against the human predicament, couched in terms of romantic disillusion, was an attempt to write out the turmoil which the lyrical setting of I Tatti and the ecstatic happiness of Mary and Berenson made even more unbearable. Russell's bleak philosophy of the universe, built "on the firm foundation of unyielding despair", he eventually admitted to be an attempt to rationalize Evelyn Whitehead's suffering, the traumatic experience which had made him "suddenly and vividly aware of the loneliness in which most people live, and passionately desirous of finding ways of diminishing this tragic isolation". Yet the loneliness was not only Evelyn Whitehead's. It was Russell's also. Significantly he starts "The Free Man's Worship" with Mephistopheles' account of the world to Dr Faustus, the necromancer willing to sell his soul in return for a second youth. The essay was, he wrote a decade later, "only for people in great unhappiness".

Russell sets his problem and gives his own answer.

That Man is the product of causes which had no prevision of the end they were achieving; that his origin, his growth, his hopes and fears, his loves and his beliefs, are but the outcome of accidental collocations of atoms; that no fire, no heroism, no intensity of thought and feeling, can preserve an individual life beyond the grave; that all the labours of the ages, all the devotion, all the inspiration, all the noonday brightness of human genius, are destined to extinction in the vast death of the solar system, and that the whole temple of Man's achievement must inevitably be buried beneath the debris of a universe in ruins – all these things, if not quite beyond dispute, are yet so nearly certain, that no philosophy which rejects them can hope to stand.

Faced with this, Russell saw only one reply.

In action, in desire, we must submit perpetually to the tyranny of outside forces; but in thought, in aspiration, we are free, free from our fellow men, free from the petty planet on which our bodies impotently crawl, free even, while we live, from the tyranny of death. Let us learn, then, that energy of faith which enables us to live constantly in the vision of the good; and let us descend, in action, into the world of fact, with that vision always before us.

He completed the essay back in England, adding an appeal for "fellow-sufferers in the same darkness", and imploring that "when their day is over, when their good and their evil have become eternal by the immortality of the past, be it ours to feel that, where they suffered, where they failed, no deed of ours was the cause ..." Alys, reading the typescript, disliked this final charitable addition. "It was", Russell wrote, "written as exhortation to myself to treat her decently. But she has never felt the kind of comradeship in disaster of which I speak – her unhappiness shut her up more than ever in herself."

"The Free Man's Worship" – whose title Russell inexplicably changed to "A Free Man's Worship" between the 1910 and 1918 re-publications – was a *tour de force*, an impassioned example of lyrical prose which retained its power to influence readers whatever Russell himself might eventually think of its style. Thirty years later, it has been remarked, "students of English in Calcutta University would recite the last paragraphs of this essay with the feeling with which they would recite a select page from the 'Areopagitica', 'Unto This Last', or 'Sartor Resartus'". Among the first to see it was Bernard Berenson. "Perhaps the most flattering appreciation to be given of it is that the whole is neither out of tune with, nor unworthy of, the two splendid passages you wrote here," was his verdict. "I see no objection to this essay form. I have no wish of my own with regard to the shape your writing is to take. I am eager that you shall express yourself sooner or later, and meanwhile you must write and write until you begin to feel that you are saying what you want to say, in the way that you wish others to understand it."

Looking back after a decade, Russell had reservations about the essay. "I wrote with passion & force, because I really thought I had a gospel," he said. "... Now I am cynical about the gospel, because it won't stand the test of life. No gospel will, except to do one's work, & trust to luck for the great things – inspiration & fire & passion." Yet if he questioned the interpretation which "The Free Man's Worship" put on the facts of life, he had no doubt about the facts themselves.

A quarter of a century later he wrote,

Fundamentally, my view of man's place in the cosmos remains unchanged. I still believe that the major processes of the universe proceed according to the laws of physics; that they have no reference to our wishes, and are likely to involve the extinction of life on this planet; that there is no good reason for expecting life after death; and that good and evil are ideas which throw no light upon the non-human world. I still believe that, in times of moral difficulty and

> emotional stress, the attitude expressed in this essay is, at any rate for temperaments like my own, the one which gives most help in avoiding moral shipwreck.

Back in England, early in 1903, the prospect of the foreseeable future drove Russell steadily downhill. He went to Cambridge to confer with Whitehead, and Alys joined him for a night but was terribly unhappy. There was good enough reason: he had just told her he refused to live there because she got on his nerves when with Cambridge people. "I am unhappy beyond what I know how to bear," he wrote; "my work is second-rate, and all I care for is gone or going. The fire and inspiration I had have left me, and I cannot believe I shall do any more useful things to make the long pain worthwhile." He long remembered his emotions of this traumatic period, "horribly painful, almost all of them. The country is vast & level, with wide skies & quiet fields stretching away to the horizon – very satisfying when one is happy, but rather a mockery when one is not, because it is so peaceful. It is strange how one lives through things – it makes life seem so long, & as if it was not one life but many."

With the Murrays at Churt, he recorded how Alys "spent the first evening trying to make me appear odious and ridiculous to Gilbert and Mary". His misery continued, but it was misery which now drove him to work. "I am learning not to feel tragic always," he wrote in his journal. "There are many times when existence seems unbearable; but if I see what work to do, and a reasonable prospect of accomplishing it, I can bear misery. It is when my life seems useless that despair comes. But fortunately now-a-days despair puts me to sleep – I sometimes doze most of the day. I am planning to work on the aim and scope of Philosophy."

As his relations with Alys simmered, he determined to make one last effort. "... Yesterday the Whiteheads came, and left this evening: a successful visit, though Alys was unhappy till this morning," he wrote in his journal on 8 March.

> I was throughout in a mood of blank misery; I have been realising that I don't do enough for Alys, but the thought of doing more is unbearable almost. There is only one thing more I can do, and that is children; if medically not inadvisable, that is what I must do. Suppose I have a child full of Carey [Thomas] and Mrs. Smith, and see all its faults being exaggerated.

Four days later he saw his doctor "who said it was my duty to run the risk of conception, the fear of heredity being grossly exaggerated. He says 50% of insane have alcoholic parentage, only 15% insane parentage. This seems to settle the matter." Settle it, that is, until Russell the potential parent was overtaken by Russell the statistician; his footnote in the journal reads: "But he didn't say what proportion of the total population are insane and drunken respectively, so that his argument is formally worthless."

Five days later he records, "Last night for the first time I made the last possible sacrifice. In return I am to have three weeks' liberty. Perhaps that will give me time to recover myself for the moment: till it all begins again." But three weeks later there comes a journal entry. He wrote,

> The last sacrifice to A. was not adequately carried out, and failed totally. She has been very depressed, and explained, with perfect clear-sightedness, why she hated it, and didn't want a repetition at present. I shirked my duty on that occasion: I ought to have been more self-forgetful. But one good effect has resulted: her feelings won my respect, and I liked her better than I have done for a long time. Consequently I have been able to have more pseudo-intimate talks with her and she is much cheered up the last two days. Until then, I was about as miserable as I have ever been, though without any sharp anguish.

Another cause of misery was that his three weeks' liberty had been reduced to a week with George Trevelyan in Devonshire because, as he recorded in his journal, "Moore, to whose reading party I was going, wrote curtly to say he didn't want me. He has never forgiven my homilies, though they produced the reformation I hoped for."

This was in fact only part of the story. Russell had been invited to join the party by Bob Trevelyan, who had issued the invitation off his own bat. Merely as a matter of courtesy, Russell had asked Moore if this would be agreeable. "About the reading party," Moore had replied, "since you ask me to say if your coming would make any difficulty, I think I had better tell you that it would. As this is so, I am very sorry Bob suggested it to you." To Desmond MacCarthy, also to be a member of the party, he wrote,

> Of course, I can't be sure that [Russell] would spoil it for anyone but me; but I do suppose that the others, too, and you yourself, would rather that he would not be there for nearly so long. Don't you feel this yourself? And then I do think that the effect he would have on me would also indirectly make it much more unpleasant for the rest of you; I can't be at my ease while he is there, and I don't know how miserable I might not get.

So Russell had merely a week's respite before finding himself back with Alys. But now the first phase was ending, the reduction in temperature being as much due to exhaustion as to anything else. There is an entry in his journal which reveals the state of affairs.

[Alys] is still miserable; she still says things that make me feel rasped through and through, and still day by day I wonder how another 24 hours of such utter misery can be endured. But there is every reason to expect 40 years of just such torture. In some ways, her illness makes things easier; when she is bouncing and metallic, she is much harder to bear. Poor woman! When she is not present, I am sorry for her; but when I see and hear her, I become all nerves, and can think of nothing but the wish to escape. She is always bumping into furniture, treading on one's toes, and upsetting lamps; and mentally she does just the same sort of thing. She asked me why I won't undress in her presence. The other day she wept, and said she had gone right out of my life: I tried to say gently that I had had to learn to live alone: "I know", she replied, "the ascent to the stars must be made in solitude". N.B. This is flattery, and is designed to please, for it is well known that all *men* like flattery. My work goes badly; new difficulties come up as fast as the old ones are solved. The political views interest me immensely, and if I could get away from her, I could work at the [Free] Trade [Campaign] as well as Mathematics; but I am spending on not being cruel to her as much energy as would make a whole political campaign. And the irony is that we are both wretched, and that she would be quite happy if I were dead, and no longer there to remind her of the wound to her vanity. Oh, it is damnable. My mind is going. I can no longer write. But if I go away, even for two days, I become a different person.

He often went, finding excuses to make long visits to Cambridge, and in the spring and summer making vigorous walking-tours. Sometimes he went alone, sometimes with George Trevelyan. For long he continued to wear, even on such walks, the white, starched collars which were *de rigeur* as gentlemanly attire. Finally he was persuaded by Trevelyan to wear soft collars during the day; but at night, however small the cottage or inn, he changed back into the stiff, high-necked variety. This failure to exhibit the tweediness of the outdoor man outlasted the Edwardian age. The Russell who crossed the Alps on foot before the First World War and climbed the mountains of Snowdonia after the Second did so in clothes nearly as incongruous.

He enjoyed his walking, enhanced by a good eye for scenery. "I came here along the coast today from St. Ives," he wrote on one tour; "parts of my walk wonderfully beautiful, and the whole heightened by the tingling sense of health which comes of many days in the open air. The great moments of a walking-tour are when one reaches some good point of view rather tired, and sits on the ground to enjoy it. The sudden sense of rest blends with the landscape most curiously ..."

On his own, he began to recover. With Alys, all the old agonies were quickly revived by the smother of her good intentions and her preoccupation with the inessential – "I suppose that she will never learn that other people have more important things than clothes and food in their lives" – and by an emotional blindness of elephantine proportions: "She assured me that people come to her rather than me with their troubles . . ." Russell noted. "She also instanced Evelyn on her side. What a strangely unreal world she lives in!"

Nevertheless, he hated hurting her. "I know I am deeply the worse for what I have made Alys suffer; & if I hadn't borne with her so long, I should have been more the worse for it," he wrote. "As it is, there is a core of hardness which I strike against whenever I think of her deserted & lonely."

Outwardly, they kept the united, smiling front that convention demanded, struggling on and foxing even the almost unfoxable Beatrice Webb, who was unable to pin down what she felt was wrong. She found the Russells on holiday in Normandy, riding and reading together but not serenely happy, "a tragic austerity and effort in their relations ... it is strange they cannot enjoy light-hearted happiness in each other's love and comradeship – but there is something that interferes, and friends can only look on with respect and admiration and silent concern." On this occasion Russell minded the Webbs more than usual. "They have a competent way of sizing up a Cathedral, and pronouncing on it with an air of authority and an evident feeling that the L.C.C. would have done it better," he confided to Gilbert Murray. "They take all the colour out of life and make everything one cares for turn to dust and ashes."

As he and Alys grew more resigned, she still believing only that he had fallen out of love, he outwardly letting the anguish drain away without sign of complications, the situation became more bearable. By early 1905 he could write, "I have got over my chief sorrow pretty completely – more completely than is desirable, but that can't be helped. I have learnt a *modus vivendi* with Alys: I never look at her, so that I avoid the pain of her insincere expression and the petty irritation of her awkwardness of movement." For her part, Alys continued to find consolation in good works.

The gradual acceptance of the facts hardened under the routine of daily life. But it was life very different from before and the change could not be concealed from close friends. Bob Trevelyan could write that when he and his wife visited the Russells, host and hostess would sit facing one another across the table; but talking only to the guests. And a letter that Alys wrote to her husband in the autumn of 1905 says revealingly, "It seems odd to be writing to thee upstairs when thee is only downstairs, but as we never talk intimately now, it is easier to write things than to say them ... I had given up hoping to be a help, but I thought I could just live on humbly beside thee, gratefully accepting all I get from thee &, tho able to give nothing in return that thee values, at any rate not interfering with thy work." In years to come she would confide to friends how she hoped that acquiescence in the situation, failure to make a fuss, would give him peace for his work. For his part, Russell was to explain how only the anguish of the situation had screwed him to the necessary pitch of concentration for *Principia Mathematica*.

The ascetic isolation in which he immersed himself more and more came out in letters to intimate friends. "I cannot agree with you", replied Maud Burdett, with whom he had learned to read and write in the Richmond kindergarten, "that 'one would never be unhappy if one could always forget the existence of human beings' ... Bertie, don't, for pity's sake, allow the love of solitude to completely immerse your body, soul and spirit." In fact he well knew that human beings were always there; and, as he admitted, the intellect had to accept the fact – "philosophy in modern times", he was to warn, "has been pursued mainly by retired students, who have forgotten, in their academic cloisters, their function of supplying metaphysics which take account of the needs of the human heart."

Both Russell and Alys survived the second phase. They agreed to keep a composed public face, spend increasing time apart but cover the fact with the excuse that he had to be much in Cambridge. In this climate relations slowly edged back, not towards the normal but towards the bearable. Exploring Italy on foot in summer with the Sangers or the Trevelyans – "I got on very well without any money; philosophers have no need of pelf" – he would send a regular report-card back home. Much away, his business-like letters to Alys reporting gossip, university appointments and the bric-à-brac of social life, he once again signed himself, "thine all, Bertie". It looked as if the dangerous corner had been turned.

As the temperature dropped back to normal they moved to a more permanent home. Since the break in 1902 they had been away from Millhanger quite frequently, renting houses not only in Chelsea and the Cotswolds but in Churt and Tilford, both a few miles from Fernhurst. Now they determined to make a new start. Russell commissioned Henry Fletcher, another Trinity man, to build the first house at Bagley Wood, today a flourishing community on the southern outskirts of Oxford. The location was not accidental. A few years earlier Hannah Pearsall Smith, following the death of her husband, had joined Logan at Court Place, an ample house standing in eight acres of wooded grounds on the Thames below Oxford. Now the Russells moved into Lower Copse, a few miles away.

Even before the move he had begun to dig into the money inherited on his coming of age. The reasons for thus living beyond his income were fourfold, he explained to a friend.

(1) it is interest, & I have no children; therefore there is no sound reason for wishing to keep the capital intact. (2) My wife has expectations of a moderate sort, & when they are realised I shall save. (3) All sorts of objects turn up that I feel bound to give money to; if I give the money now, it does good now, instead of having to wait for it until I am dead. (4) Tho' at present it would interfere with my work to have to earn a living, I think ultimately it will be a good thing for me to take a professorship somewhere, so I have no need to hoard.

Lower Copse was a comfortable, almost cosy background to his intellectual battles and it tended to make less likely any further widening of the chasm which separated him from his wife. However, Alys, believing that the marriage was now dropping back into a bearable rut, would have been sadly disabused by the entries in her husband's journal. In 1905, three years after the apocalyptic bicycle-ride, there comes a long entry symptomatic of the combined sexual and intellectual frustration still bubbling away beneath the surface even after the move to Bagley Wood.

The habit of not speaking to Alys about anything that really interests me, and the instinct of concealing my feelings from her, make it very hard not to be untruthful with her, and not to keep silence about things that I ought to tell her about. I do not always resist this temptation successfully; and what is worse, it is making me generally secretive. But that is not the worst. I foresee that continence will become increasingly difficult, and that I shall be tempted to get into more or less flirtatious relations with women I don't respect. Where I feel respect or real affection, it is fairly easy to behave rightly; the difficulty is where I feel that a slightly wrong behaviour would not do any moral injury to its object. There is no doubt a sexual element in my desire to be intimate with women I respect; but in that I see no harm. It is only to be discovered by inference and general principles, and if duly kept in check, seems rather good than bad. But the other is wholly bad; it not only ought not to be indulged, but it ought not to be felt. The worst of it is that, unless I find some way of dealing with it, it will presumably grow stronger; and some day, in a moment of weakness, I may persuade myself there is no harm in acting upon it. It is rather a mental than a physical feeling: it is a desire for excitement, and for a respite from the incessant checking of every impulse. Another difficulty, connected with this, is the very slight interest I take in my work and in philosophy generally. If this can't be cured, my fertility will cease. A sort of paralysis of impulse has passed from my life into my thinking, and seems to be very serious for my intellectual future.

Persistently worried about his intellectual future, he had already taken steps to deal with the paralysis, although how much was conscious, how much the subconscious reaction to his mood, it is hard to say. The previous year he had met, at the Chelsea home of George Trevelyan and his wife, an intelligent and attractive woman eight years his junior of whom he was to say to her son half a century later, "Hardly a week goes by without my thinking of your mother." She was Miss Ivy Pretious, still only twenty-five, but the extremely competent secretary of the Free Trade Union. Russell lost no time in striking up a friendship with Miss Pretious and it has been suggested that he wished to strike up something less platonic. However, his letters to her – and one to Lucy Donnelly – show him in another light: that of the ever-helpful outsider innocently getting himself more involved than he wished.

The friendship had started while the Russells were still living in Chelsea, and he was able to visit Miss Pretious and make little of it to Alys, whose good works often took her from London. At times there was disappointment, as when he wrote, "My wife has decided to stay in town on the night of the 12th. & I can't well manage to come to dinner. But I will (unless I am prevented by some unforeseen circumstance) come about 6 or 6.15 till seven. I am much disappointed but vexatious things will happen." To Lucy Donnelly he admitted,

> I am now and have been for some time horribly anxious about a girl [Miss Pretious] for whom, though I see her very seldom, I have a great deal of affection, though not, I think, a bit more than she deserves. She is in the gravest danger from a man [R. McKenna, M.P.] who is simply a blackguard, but who has acquired a great influence over her by means of his ability and strength of will. There is nothing I can do, except to exhort her on the rare occasions when the opportunity occurs; and I only know what I know because I guessed her circumstances and got her to confess, and she will not let me speak to him.

At about this point George Trevelyan and his wife, well aware that Russell's marriage was on the rocks, began to fear trouble. What happened next is recounted in a note from their daughter, Mary Moorman, written many years later.

> They . . . agreed that Janet [Trevelyan] should speak to B.R. about his relations with I.P., and in due course [in April 1905] B.R. came at her request and had a long conversation with Janet, who pointed out the difficult position he might be putting I.P. into, especially if she were to begin to feel affection for him. He accepted this caution with perfect agreement, only saying that I.P. had always seemed so capable of judging for herself. As a result of this conversation B.R.

and I.P. soon afterwards agreed not to write to each other or meet for some considerable time.

The next evening B.R. again came to see Janet Trevelyan, this time to discuss the question of his marriage. While they were talking Mrs. Russell unexpectedly called. She enquired affectionately about I.P. [who was ill] and they then both left together. B.R. had told Janet that he hoped for a gradual estrangement and an ultimate parting, but that he dreaded proposing a parting now because she still clung to him although she had completely lost his affection. They had built themselves a house near Oxford and were going there immediately. He also told Janet that his wife knew everything that went on between himself and I.P. because he told her every time he was going to see her and outwardly she maintained an attitude of great interest in their friendship. She too, often called on Ivy herself, and was outwardly affectionate, but her underlying jealousy made her at times tell untrue stories about I.P. to other people.

It was not only Mrs Trevelyan who was worried. Across the bottom of the letter to Lucy Donnelly, which she sent back to him years later, Russell wrote, "Janet Trevelyan & Mrs. Whitehead, not knowing the circumstances, combined to scold me as a philanderer." Miss Pretious was clearly competent to look after herself; in any case, soon after the start of the friendship Russell and Alys were due to leave London for Bagley Wood, a move that reduced the dangers of tête-à-tête dinners. However, his "great deal of affection" could easily have grown into something more, and it was not until rather later in the day that he decided to pull back from the relationship.

Some of the first repercussions of the move to Bagley Wood were described by Russell in a letter to Miss Pretious shortly before his departure for Oxford. "I begin to see possibilities of emancipation from my bondage," he wrote.

I have been thinking of the future, & it strikes me as likely that during the next two years or so I shall be able to free myself to a considerable extent. This prospect has rather cheered me up, when otherwise I should be depressed.

Going to a new place will for a time diminish the complications of my life as well as the pleasures. As soon as I come back from my walk, I shall plunge into work, which is almost as good as drink for producing oblivion, & quite as bad for producing headache. I have had a bad conscience about my work; for several years now I have not been enough interested in it, & I must try seriously to recover some of the zest with which I used to pursue it. You probably can hardly realise what a jealous taskmaster creative work like mine can be. My great difficulty is constant weariness, which is making me prematurely old; & I can't get rid of this except by simplifying my life.

Far from simplifying it, the relationship complicated it still further, and soon after moving to Bagley Wood Russell was having to take evasive action. "I am very sorry to say I do not think I ought to come & see you, although Janet has no objection," he wrote.

> I didn't mean to give the impression that it was because I had promised her that I thought I ought not to come, but because my judgment went with what she said. Yes, of course there is no change in spirit, only a realisation of things I was too much inclined to forget. One reason, which alone now seems to me sufficient, is that my wife is so much less unhappy than in town; & however much one may feel her feelings unreasonable, I still hardly feel justified in giving her so much pain unless it is for some very important & definite purpose . . . I did wrong to let my friendship become anything you would miss, since in any case I should have seen very little of you.

However, the friendship did not entirely peter out and eighteen months later he was fearing that there might be "the same kind of thing to go through as there was a year and a half ago – I don't wish to have to endure that again". He had firmly made up his mind. "I fear that if I go to Argyll Mansions it will revive my wife's animosity, which is now more or less dormant."

In fact, they met again when Russell stood as a Women's Suffrage candidate in the Wimbledon by-election later in the same year. Correspondence was renewed, and so were suspicions; Russell believed that Alys was steaming open Miss Pretious's letters, but comforted her with "luckily there was nothing that it would matter being read".

On that note the relationship ended, the level at which Russell wanted it to end. For most men it would have been important. For Russell, after the storm which had ripped him from the moorings a few years earlier, the whole affair was essentially low-key. This was no bad thing. One mental torment at a time was enough and nothing could take away the shimmering experience which, secret though it was, had for a while made the grass grow greener and the stars blaze more brightly in the skies. Despite the pain, he wanted the romantic ecstasy again. The search for it was to drive him on inexorably, as much as the hope of intellectual satisfaction, as much as the desire for sexual relief, for the next half-century. Only a man of Russell's stamina and intellectual dexterity could have stayed the course.

The emotional agony which began virtually as Russell started work on the *Principia*, and the intellectual demands which that work made upon him, would have been enough to absorb normal energies. Russell, foreshadowing the polymath activities of the years to come, found time for a lot more. His star had risen with the publication of *The Principles of Mathematics*, as he discovered at a Rome Congress on mathematics in 1908 – "I am even being contended for by rival factions, each of which wishes to start a new learned journal for which they want my support" – and he was now a contributor of lengthy review-articles to *Mind* and to mathematical as well as to less specialized journals. During this same period, moreover, he began to show the facility for dropping in the apposite phrase which annoyed the more austere of his colleagues and baffled those who unsuccessfully tried to imitate him. Thus in *Determinism and Morals* he explained,

> Bradshaw consists entirely of predictions as to the actions of engine-drivers; but no-one doubts Bradshaw on the ground that the volitions of engine-drivers are not governed by motives. If we really believed that other people's actions did not have causes, we could never try to influence other people's actions; for such influence can only act if we know, more or less, what causes will produce the actions we desire. If we could never try to influence other people's actions, no man would try to get elected to Parliament, or ask a woman to marry him: argument, exhortation, and command would become mere idle breath.

His approach sent a tremor of semi-envious resentment through many academics, a feeling increased by such statements as, "The reader who will, throughout Dr. Schiller's essay on the ambiguity of truth, substitute 'butter' for 'truth' and 'margarine' for 'falsehood', will find that the point involved is one which has no special relevance to the nature of truth." At times, moreover, he could inject the pun into even his most serious works. Thus in *The Principles of Mathematics*, after commenting that Hegel's followers had tamely repeated the dictum that everything discrete is also continuous and *vice versa*, he added that over the meaning of the two words they had "preserved a discreet and continuous silence".

It was not only Russell's ability to turn the right popular phrase as well as expound the best academic argument with a light touch which at times exasperated his colleagues. There was his cocksureness, a quality suggested in Moore's account of a visit to Bagley Wood. He wrote in his diary,

> Walk with Russell after tea; try to explain to him about objects seeming bigger & smaller, & am amazed because he seems to wish to drop subject . . . After Mrs. R. gone to bed very hot dispute, before [Maurice] Amos, as to means of "knowing"; whether I can "know" Amos' toothache; I get angry & think Russell bad at seeing point, apt to defend himself by bringing in irrelevant points & too arrogant.

> Talk with him all next morning of knowledge of prop[osition]s & self-evidence, after reading him in [The] Edinburgh [Review] on Pragmatism. Santayana, Miss M. Strachey & Ray to lunch. Sant. talks much & seems nicely frank; Logan comes in. Walk with R. after tea & discuss my lectures. We explain about probability to Amos: again I think R. misses points & is too confident of insufficient explanations as to meaning of words ...

Moore's reference to Russell's paper in the *Edinburgh Review* was significant of the growing interest that the author had been taking in Pragmatism, "the genuinely new philosophy" which he tended to see as a brash utilitarian import from the United States. He had first met William James, its latest and most formidable standard-bearer, more than two decades earlier at Friday's Hill, when both had been guests of the Pearsall Smiths. He and Alys had stayed with James at Harvard in 1896 and, if he could never summon up much agreement with the psychologist turned philosopher, there was a good deal of possibly reluctant respect. To James himself Russell had written, "The pragmatic difference that pragmatism makes to me is that it encourages religious beliefs, & that I consider religious belief pernicious." In the *Edinburgh Review* he had followed a reflective and not unkindly review with the verdict that pragmatists just saw no need to trouble about discovering truth; what was thought to be true was all that mattered. "To sum up," he concluded,

> Pragmatism appeals to the temper of mind which finds on the surface of this planet the whole of its imaginative material; which feels confident of progress, and unaware of non-human limitations to human power; which loves battle, with all its attendant risks, because it has no real doubt that it will achieve victory; which desires religion, as it desires railways and electric light, as a comfort and a help in the affairs of this world, not as providing non-human objects to satisfy the hunger for perfection and for something to be worshipped without reserve.

Little of this was of much good to Russell even though he had, by 1909, the year of his article in the *Edinburgh Review*, become almost inured to the essential failure of his personal life. His attitude was still as he had recorded it in an unpublished note headed "Why do men persist in living?" "But for one who does not believe in any 'other world', whether a heaven or a mystical transfiguration of this world," he ended by asking, "is there any way by which he can strengthen his life with the kind of hope or belief that could be called religious?" The reply, he concluded, "is in the negative".

5

Principia Mathematica

During the harrowing years which followed the rupture of his marriage with Alys, Russell produced with Whitehead the main work for which he will always be remembered: *Principia Mathematica*, like *Das Kapital* a book more discussed than read but one which nevertheless offered for the first time a foundation of mathematics.

In general terms, the genesis of the work is clear. In *The Principles of Mathematics*, Russell had tried to show that the objects with which mathematics was concerned could be defined within the language of symbolic logic and that, if they were manipulated according to the principles of logic, then nothing more was needed to prove all mathematical propositions. But *The Principles* stated its case by analysis and discussion, almost without using the special symbols of mathematical logic; it argued that the method should work, but did not test the argument. This was to be the job of Russell's second volume, which he planned to write exclusively for mathematicians and which would demonstrate by example "that all pure mathematics deals exclusively with concepts definable in terms of a very small number of fundamental logical concepts, and that all its propositions are deducible from a very small number of fundamental logical principles".

As he discussed this second volume with Whitehead in the summer of 1901, Whitehead became increasingly interested in the problems which it raised. "The project of deducing mathematics from logic appealed to him, and to my great joy he agreed to collaborate," Russell wrote. "I knew that my mathematical capacity was not equal to accomplishing the task unaided." Whitehead had other but equally good reasons for embarking on a joint enterprise, since he also was already writing the second volume of his *Universal Algebra*. "We ... discovered that our projected volumes were practically on identical topics," he recorded, "so we coalesced to produce a joint work. We hoped that a short period of one year or so would complete the job. Then our horizon extended and, in the course of eight or nine years, 'Principia Mathematica' was produced." Thus Peano's new symbolism merged both with Russell's ambition to discover the nature of mathematical truth, and with Whitehead's interest in widening the field of mathematics itself.

So much is certain. Doubt remains about the precise influence of each man's ideas on the other as the work progressed, as successive difficulties were met and overcome, and as what had initially been conceived as one volume expanded into a three-volume work of nearly 2,000 pages, with a fourth volume on geometry to be written by Whitehead alone – but never completed. There are several reasons for fuzziness about the working details of this unique literary and scientific collaboration. For one thing the two authors were in close personal contact throughout the nine years, visiting each other's homes for weeks at a time and hammering out, in discussion that often removed the need for letters, many important points and problems. Whitehead was, in any case, an incorrigible non-letter-writer and the task of squeezing a written reply from him to even the most urgent request was more difficult than extracting blood from the proverbial stone. Finally, there is the destruction of Russell's letters by Evelyn Whitehead after her husband's death, an act of literary vandalism – apparently carried out on Whitehead's instructions – which has had an effect diametrically opposite from that presumably intended: it has encouraged rather than decreased speculation about Russell's professional and personal relationship with the Whiteheads.

It is thus difficult to be precise about the date at which the great collaboration started, let alone to allocate credit for any particular part of the book in more than general terms. Russell's recollections in old age are at times contradictory; and while he and Whitehead remained friends until the latter's death in 1947, a coolness developed between them as early as 1914. Three years later, Whitehead wrote him a letter suggesting that he was vexed by the use which Russell had made in *Our Knowledge of the External World* of notes which Whitehead had given him. Although Russell felt he had sufficiently acknowledged this help, Whitehead then stopped sending him his work. But professional disagreements were not the only cause of umbrage. "Although it may seem strange," Russell wrote in 1932, "the fact that we took different views of the war made collaboration after 1914 almost impossible." Moreover, after 1925, and thence onwards to the end of his life, Whitehead felt that he had been unfairly saddled with the fresh ideas Russell wrote into the second edition of the *Principia*. All these points play cumulative if small parts in limiting the knowledge of who was responsible for what.

Most of the evidence comes from Russell himself, and the interval of a third of a century must not be forgotten. He has said that

> Broadly speaking, Whitehead left the philosophical problems to me. As for the mathematical problems, Whitehead invented most of the notation, except in so far as it was taken over from Peano;

> I did most of the work concerned with series and Whitehead did most of the rest. But this only applies to first drafts. Every part was done three times over. When one of us had produced a first draft, he would send it to the other, who would usually modify it considerably. After which, the one who had made the first draft would put it into final form.

Later he added that there was "hardly a page in the three volumes which can be attributed to either of us singly", and that "frequently a draft of some portion would go backwards and forwards between us many times before we were satisfied". Years later Whitehead noted that the introductory discussions in volume one were "practically due to Russell". When it came to preparing the manuscript for the press in 1909, Russell virtually took over, since he then had no professional duties, while Whitehead was still teaching at Cambridge.

In practical details, collaboration was complete and harmonious. According to Russell, Whitehead was the more patient, accurate and careful, and often saved him from a hasty and superficial treatment of difficulties that he found uninteresting. He in turn sometimes thought Whitehead's treatment of problems unnecessarily complicated, and tried to simplify the drafts. At times this brought a reproof, as when Whitehead returned the outline of an early section with the protest, "Everything, even the object of the book, has been sacrificed to making proofs look short and neat. It is essential, especially in the early parts, that the proofs be written out fully." A note in Russell's handwriting across Whitehead's comment says, "A criticism of my first draft of the Logic of Propositions for the beginning of Principia Mathematica. Whitehead was entirely right."

Such real differences as there were sprang largely from the two men's contrasted estimates of reality. Russell, fresh from his rebellion against the Hegelian idea that everything was inter-connected in a universe conceived as "more like a pot of treacle than a heap of shot", believed that each separate shot "had hard and precise boundaries". Whitehead, less certain that life was so simple, revealed his opposing view in one illuminating comment to Russell: "You think the world is what it looks like in fine weather at noon-day; I think it is what it seems like in the early morning when one first wakes from deep sleep."

This basic difference of outlook was reinforced by their different approaches to their joint task. Russell wished, as a philosophical exercise, to reconstruct mathematics on a new logical foundation: Whitehead, as a mathematician, was more concerned with giving his existing mathematical beliefs an additional superstructure of logic. In theory, the two approaches were not necessarily conflicting; in practice, they resulted in a difference of emphasis.

The Herculean task was not completed without a dangerous amount of mental wear-and-tear. "At the time I often wondered whether I should ever come out at the other end of the tunnel in which I seemed to be," Russell wrote. "I used to stand on the footbridge at Kennington, near Oxford, watching the trains go by, and determining that tomorrow I would place myself under one of them. But when the morrow came I always found myself hoping that perhaps 'Principia Mathematica' would be finished some day."

Whitehead seems to have taken the task more in his intellectual stride, although Russell was never under any illusion about the part which his collaborator played. "Neither of us alone could have written the book," was his verdict. "Even together, and with the alleviation brought by mutual discussion, the effort was so severe that at the end we both turned aside from mathematical logic with a kind of nausea."

The working materials of the book, hundreds of long sheets covered with line after line of logical symbols written in Russell's neat hand – many annotated with the words "this will not do" – are evidence of the enormity of the task. As to Russell's driving-force, a clue to this was given a few years later when he wrote of the great body of abstract thought embodied in the work:

> What makes it vital, what makes it fruitful, is the absolute unbridled Titanic passion that I have put into it. It is passion that has made my intellect clear, passion that has made me never stop to ask myself if the work was worth doing, passion that has made me not care if no human being ever read a word of it; it is passion that enabled me to sit for years before a blank page, thinking the whole time about one probably trivial point which I could not get right . . .

One is not expected to take too literally the claim that a blank page did really hold his attention for years – he admits elsewhere to "describing things which one finds almost unendurable in such a repulsive manner as to cause others to share one's fury". Nevertheless, there were long periods during which the creative process stood waiting for the lights to go green.

Most of the work was on a plane to which neither Russell nor Whitehead would try to pull up the layman, but an idea of its emotional content has been given by both men. Whitehead, sending a page of quotations to Russell, introduces it with the words: "Dear Bertie, The following seems to me rather beautiful." And Russell, writing when the great job was done, asserts,

> I am *sure* there can be no really great achievement except through pain; it is pain that gives clear sure beauty, the sense of having been

wrought in the fire. Even in my purely mathal. work, the *intensity* of my love for it, the passionate longing for perfect beauty, came out of pain – it is pain that gives love the quality of yearning.

From the start, one of the main problems to be overcome was that of the paradoxes which had so nearly brought him to a halt when writing *The Principles of Mathematics*. Russell had then with a single letter virtually demolished much of the structure that Frege had built over a lifetime. But he had not been able to follow on from that destructive operation, and in the summer of 1902 had been forced to ride rough-shod over the unsolved problem. He continued to wrestle with it, desperately hoping that a way of breaking the deadlock would present itself. What made the situation worse was his own ambivalence. From one standpoint it seemed to him that "the contradictions were trivial, and ... my time was spent in considering matters that seemed unworthy of serious attention". Yet, as he and Whitehead pressed on, it became increasingly clear that failure would mean a broken link in the long chain which they hoped to forge between the first and last pages.

There was at least one false dawn. Thus on 23 May 1903, Russell wrote in his journal: "4 days ago solved Contradiction – the relief of this is unspeakable." He elaborated his solution and wrote to Whitehead who responded by telegram: "Heartiest congratulations aristotle secundus. I am delighted." But across the form Russell later scrawled: "*A propos* of solving the contradiction (but the solution was wrong)."

Another two years passed before a solution began to appear – yet another before it finally emerged. The first stage gave the answer to what was essentially a linguistic problem: subsequently Russell realized it could be used to deal with the mathematical problem arising out of the contradictions.

The beginning was the doctrine described in "On Denoting". Here Russell pointed out that denoting-phrases, in contrast to proper names, could describe nonexistent objects, such as "the round square"; specific objects such as "the present President of the United States"; or unidentifiable and therefore ambiguous objects such as "a man". When writing *The Principles of Mathematics*, he had assumed that every denoting word or phrase referred either to a thing or to a concept. Belief that "whatever may be an object of thought ... has being, i.e., *is* in some sense" led in practice to some odd situations. There was no doubt about the proposition "the golden mountain does not exist" being a true proposition; yet if "the golden mountain" did not exist, surely this made the proposition meaningless? This difficulty had been covered in Russell's mind at the time of *The Principles of Mathematics* by acceptance of the view held by Alexius Meinong, that the logical subject of a statement is "the golden mountain", even though no golden mountain exists. At first Russell agreed; his views having, as he said, "a kind of morning innocence which they lost in the labour and heat of the day". Then, at work on *The Principles of Mathematics*, he began to feel that Meinong's sense of reality was too weak.

However, he could not yet strike free from the belief that whatever could be an object of thought had some existence, however shadowy. He retained it as late as 1904 when his three-part discussion of "Meinong's Theory of Complexes and Assumptions" was published in *Mind*. Only with the theory of descriptions outlined in "On Denoting", did he finally cast Meinong's theory overboard and decide that the problem of granting *is*-ness to round squares and golden mountains was merely a pseudo-problem solved by analysing and then re-defining what one was talking about.

Another kind of problem solved by implementing Russell's proposals was typified by his favourite example. "If *a* is identical with *b*, whatever is true of the one is true of the other, and either may be substituted for the other in any proposition without altering the truth or falsehood of that proposition," he writes in "On Denoting". "Now George IV wished to know whether Scott was the author of *Waverley*; and in fact Scott *was* the author of *Waverley*. Hence we may substitute *Scott* for *the author of Waverley*, and thereby prove that George IV wished to know whether Scott was Scott." This of course was nonsense. As Russell went on, "an interest in the law of identity can hardly be attributed to the first gentleman of Europe".

Russell's solution to these ambiguities, a solution which he claimed cleared up "two millennia of muddle-headedness about 'existence'", and which he always regarded as his most important philosophical achievement, lay in a realization that denoting-phrases were different in one vital way from proper names: they had no significance in isolation and were given significance only by incorporation in a sentence. Confusion between the function of referential denoting-phrases and the function of proper names could be avoided, Russell now proposed, by translating sentences in which they occurred into a form where there was no chance of such confusion. Thus the answer to George IV's inquiry was in Russell's form a conjunction of three statements: "1) At least one person wrote *Waverley*, 2) At most one person wrote *Waverley*, and 3) It is not the case that anyone both wrote *Waverley* and was not identical with Scott."

For everyday use this was obviously over-tortuous. But what it did was to introduce a new precision into areas where precision was needed and help remove the ambiguities which sometimes confuse ordinary speech. Thus it enabled philosophers, as well as lesser mortals, to have a better idea of what they were talking about.

Such was Russell's view of what he had done. There were others, and they grew in numbers through the years. One was voiced more than half a century later by Gilbert Ryle, who saw both the problem and its solution as reflecting a linguistic image of philosophy not only different from Russell's but was one whose existence Russell was to deny with increasing vehemence in his old age.

Writing of the paradox which Russell had discovered in Frege's work, Ryle described it as a major leak in the dry dock which the two men had built for mathematics. "Russell found a patch for the leak," he went on.

> Underlying the familiar distinction between truth and falsehood, there is a more radical distinction between significance and meaninglessness. True and false statements are both significant, but some forms of words, with the vocabulary and constructions of statements, are neither true nor false but nonsensical – and nonsensical not for reasons of wording, or of grammar, but for logical reasons. The self-subverting statements were of this sort, neither true nor false, but nonsensical simulacra of statements. Notice, it is only of such things as complex verbal expressions that we can ask whether they are significant or nonsense. The question could not be asked of mental processes; or of Platonic entities. So logic is from the start concerned, not with these but rather with what can or cannot be significantly said. Its subject-matter is a linguistic one, though its tasks are not at all those of philology.

Thus, in Ryle's view Russell had by his Theory of Descriptions done in one way what Einstein was to do with his revelations that indeterminacy lay at the foundation of the sub-atomic world: started a crusade which he was to regret.

"On Denoting" was sent to Professor Stout, the editor of *Mind*, in 1905. The paper had not long made its appearance before it occurred to Russell that the process which it applied to the linguistic descriptions of everyday life might be applied with equal success to the logical paradoxes, especially those which were basically mathematical. In December 1905, he read a paper to the London Mathematical Society suggesting a number of ways in which the principles of "On Denoting" might be applied to mathematics. In the following May a further paper favoured one of them, the "no classes" theory which attempts to emasculate the paradoxes by eliminating the necessity for recognizing classes. But when, after five months, the society finally decided to publish this second paper, Russell was no longer satisfied. He withdrew it.

Meanwhile he had been developing a solution to the problem of the paradoxes by applying the increased precision of the Theory of Descriptions outlined in "On Denoting" to the makeshift solution included as an appendix to *The Principles of Mathematics*. Surely, he asked himself, the class-symbols of mathematics might, like denoting-phrases, be considered as having significance only when they formed part of the mathematical equivalent of sentences? If this were so, might it not be possible to dissolve the contradiction of the classes that both were, and were not, members of themselves? In fact, could not the concepts of mathematics, as well as the objects of everyday speech, be described more satisfactorily by contextual definition?

The answer to these questions was given in "Mathematical Logic as Based on the Theory of Types", published in the *American Journal of Mathematics* in 1908. Here Russell elaborated into a finished theory the rough sketch which he had included in *The Principles of Mathematics* five years previously. First he outlined the various kinds of contradictions, mathematical and linguistic, and included the saying by Epimenides the Cretan that all Cretans were liars. He continued,

> In the above contradictions (which are merely selections from an indefinite number) there is a common characteristic, which we may describe as self-reference or reflexiveness. The remark of Epimenides must include itself in its own scope. If *all* classes, provided they are not members of themselves, are members of *w*, this must also apply to *w*; and similarly for the analogous relational contradiction. In the cases of names and definitions, the paradoxes result from considering non-nameability and indefinability as elements in names and definitions. In each contradiction something is said about *all* cases of some kind, and from what is said a new case seems to be generated, which both is and is not of the same kind as the cases of which *all* were concerned in what was said.

Having thus analysed the basic cause of all the contradictions, Russell cut the Gordian knot first by suggesting that mathematical propositions, like the semantic propositions of "On Denoting", might be grammatically impeccable yet still meaningless; then avoiding this result by arranging propositions in a hierarchy of types. Statements about objects made sense only when made within the same hierarchical group. But within the group they had their own hierarchy – a case of pecking order within pecking order. Transferred to the realm of mathematics, this concept was to prove a useful new weapon.

Russell toiled away at the implications during the last weeks of 1907. "I work 9 or 10 hours most days," he wrote on 25 December, "so that the rest of the day I am in a mere lethargy. Today, in honour of our Saviour, I have only done 7½ hours. But I get a great deal of pleasure out of my work, & it is far the most satisfactory thing in my life, so I can't complain of it ..." Later he was to explain that he was stuck for two years, adding, "When I got unstuck it took me five years to write it down."

Whitehead was not at first entirely happy with Russell's solution. "I have been studying you on Types," he wrote on 6 January 1908. "As far as I understand, I approve highly – But the points are so subtle that I have grave doubts as to whether all the difficulties that you are dodging are really present to my mind – The following remarks occur to me, and I may as well make them, since they may help to stimulate thought, however beside the point ..." Then, at the end of a long letter, there comes a final admission of his position on this particular issue: "I have no theory one way or the other on this point – all I mean is that I am in a fog as to where you are ..."

As far as Russell was concerned the fog had been dispersed. After the discovery of the Theory of Types, it only remained to write the book out. "The manuscript became more and more vast, and every time that I went out for a walk I used to be afraid that the house would catch fire and the manuscript get burnt up," he later wrote.

Much of it consisted of a tightly knit argument conducted not in everyday language but in the specially invented language of symbolic logic. A curving bar stood for "not", a bold v for "or", a square dot for "and", while other logical constants were indicated by such devices as a U on its side for "implies" and a three-barred "equals" sign for "is equivalent to". A reviewer later said,

> It is easy to picture the dismay of the innocent person who out of curiosity looked into the later part of the book. He would come upon whole pages without a single word of English below the headline; he would see instead, scattered in wild profusion, disconnected Greek and Roman letters of every size interspersed with brackets and dots and inverted commas, with arrows and exclamation marks standing on their heads, and with even more fantastic signs for which he would with difficulty so much as find names.

These not only ruled out a typed version of the manuscript but meant that it was destined to be a printer's nightmare.

Most of the details were worked out between the two authors. Grantchester was usually preferred to Fernhurst, a choice due partly to Evelyn Whitehead's ill-health and consequent dislike of travel. But there is a suggestion, in papers and in the few available reminiscences, that Whitehead, quiet, reflective, almost retiring, shrank from performing in the champagne-like sparkle that Russell tended to create about himself, and that he certainly shrank from discussing his professional work amid such ebullience. The awkwardness which prevented some men from talking about sex in mixed company, or about religion in any, equally inhibited Whitehead from discussing the semi-sacred topics of mathematics or philosophy with those who did not always take them with his own high seriousness.

Russell had no such inhibitions. "Bertie informs me", wrote Lytton Strachey after a weekend with the Russells and the Pearsall Smiths, "that he has now abolished not only 'classes', but 'general propositions' – he thinks they're all merely the fantasies of the human mind. He's come to this conclusion because he finds it's the only way in which to get round the Cretan who said that all Cretans were liars." And to his mother he passed on the information: "Russell is writing a chapter on the Improper Infinitive." To the Webbs also, as innocent of mathematical logic as of original sin, Russell volubly expounded his theories when they stayed for six summer weeks at Bagley Wood. But Beatrice Webb's diary entry, noting that the Russells were working on "their" big book, implies some misunderstanding.

While Russell concentrated on the main task he made time to pursue the stray hare that popped up during the discussions with Whitehead. He wrote an account of recent work in the philosophy of mathematics for the *International Monthly*, acceding to the editor's request to make it "as romantic as possible". He described some of the delights of the subject in "The Study of Mathematics", wrote many articles and reviews dealing with Meinong's work which had led him to develop his Theory of Descriptions, and carried on one running battle with the Scottish logician MacColl, and another with Henri Poincaré.

More important, he was beginning to seek a substitute for the coherence theory of truth which he had thrown overboard with Idealism some years previously. In June 1905 he addressed the Jowett Society in Oxford and the Moral Science Club in Cambridge on "The Nature of Truth". The following year he reviewed Joachim's book of the same name, read a paper on the subject to the Aristotelian Society, and in the last section of it gave a hint of thoughts to come. But these papers and reviews criticized the discarded truth-theory of the Idealists rather than replaced it; Russell was still only groping his way towards a substitute.

A letter to Ivy Pretious, written on the day he became a Fellow of the Royal Society, suggests the *tempo* of his days. First, he tells her, he did an hour and a half's work on *Principia*. Then he left Bagley Wood for London. "In the train up & down I read the proofs of the French translation of my book on Leibniz practically the whole time," he goes on.

> In London I had a Women's Suffrage Committee (it was the day after Asquith's remarks on the subject) & then I had to go to the Royal Society to be admitted as a Fellow. I got home at 8, and after dinner I had to write an article & several letters on Women's Suffrage, & a critical letter to Graham Wallas about a book of his I have been reading in MS. After that I went to bed. I have written about 2,000 pages of the MS of my book since last September; there will be about 6,000 or 8,000 altogether. I have no time to think about anything, which is very pleasant, and it is comforting to have a big continuous job on hand.

But the job would not last for ever. By the spring of 1909 the end was in sight. He spent a short holiday with the Whiteheads in Cornwall and began to face a future without the *Principia*. "That was the only time when

I completely lost faith in myself & thought of myself as a mere cumberer of the earth," he later wrote. "I resolved to commit suicide as soon as I could get rid of certain definite obligations which for the moment made it impossible."

Those obligations – completing *Principia Mathematica* and later seeing it through the press, helping to maintain Whitehead financially – still remained as he returned to Bagley Wood for the final pull that would finish the job. Except for the physical contiguity of Alys he was on his own, just as he had been during the years at Pembroke Lodge. "All the spectres used to come out and gibber at me when I was alone," was the memory that refused to go away. "As long as I live I shall never get over the horror of the years I spent at Bagley Wood." Three years later, as the train passed through Goring Gap on to the Oxfordshire plain, with dreaming spires only a few puffs away to the north, he could still write,

> Now I am in sight of Boar's Hill & Cumnor, which have less pleasant associations. I find time only increases the horror in retrospect of my time at Oxford. I didn't let myself know at the time how much I was suffering. I had the consciousness of steady moral deterioration moving towards some débâcle, with a growing sense that virtue is not worth the spiritual death that it costs ... It was only the big book that made it bearable ...

By the summer of 1909 he was on the last lap, and in the autumn Whitehead began negotiations for publication. "Land in sight at last," he wrote, announcing that he was seeing the Syndics of the Cambridge University Press. "Like the Greek ten thousand we ejaculate 'Printing! Printing!'" The optimism was premature. *Principia Mathematica* presented formidable problems, not the least being the text itself with its characters from the alphabet of symbolic logic, available in no existing printing-fount. In addition, there was its length. "As to cutting down," wrote Whitehead to Russell, after a tentative suggestion from the publishers,

> it seems to me improbable that we could save more than 100 printed pages without very seriously diminishing the value of the work, and even that in the end would be bad commercial policy. We should have diminished the "staying power" or permanence of the work in the various departments of thought in which it deals. I do not mean that anyone again is likely to try and cover the whole field (in this generation, at least) – but short books and tracts might supersede us in every particular department unless we use sufficient amplitude of exposition. Given such an amplitude, the enormous advantage of completeness will (I hope) keep us going – but without it, cheapness and intelligibility over the particular portion in question would make the student take to incomplete short books – Meanwhile I hold that

> there is no need to give the "Press" or the "Royal" the slightest hint that there is any remote chance of the book being published even in incomplete form unless they put it through – they would at once cut down their proposed contribution ...

Russell agreed, and they now prepared their formal "advertisement" as Whitehead called it. The Syndics of the Cambridge University Press were cautious, and deferred making any recommendation until they could have before them a report on the manuscript. A month later they braced themselves and decided to shoulder half of what they expected to be a loss of £600. "Agreed", say the Press minutes, "that the Syndics undertake the publication on the half-profit system of Whitehead and Russell's 'Principia Mathematica' provided that a grant of £300 towards the cost be obtained from the Royal Society or some other source and that in this case a further sum of £300 be granted towards the cost from the Syndics' Cambridge account." The Royal Society obliged, but only with £200. The authors themselves saved the day by delving into their private pockets and the Press agreed to print 750 copies of volume one, and 500 copies each of the other two volumes. "We thus earned minus £50 each by ten years' work," Russell commented. "This beats the record of 'Paradise Lost'."

He still had to dispose of *Principia*. A few weeks later he was able to tell Lucy Donnelly that he had

> arrived at a great moment; tomorrow I go to Cambridge, taking with me the MS of the book for the printers. There is a certain amount at the end which is not yet finished, but over 4,000 pages are ready and the rest can be finished easily. I have been working like a black to get the last bits of revision done in time ... and now the MS is packed in two large crates, and now I feel more or less as people feel at the death of an ill-tempered invalid whom they nursed and hated for years. It is amusing to think how much time and trouble has been spent on small points in obscure corners of the book, which possibly no human being will ever discover. Owing, I imagine, to the near prospect of taking the MS to the Press, I have been lately in a state of strange and unusual excitement, very loud and bristling and argumentative.

Two years earlier he had written that when the book was ready he would "feel such a sense of lightness & freedom from responsibility as I have not felt since I finished the Tripos in 1893". But now there was no lightness. Instead, after the death the release; after the death the emptiness. "I have made a mess of my private life," he continued to Lucy.

> – I have not lived up to my ideals, & I have failed to get or give happiness. And as a natural result, I have tended to grow cynical

about private relations & personal happiness – whether my own or other people's. So all my idealism has become concentrated on my work, which is the one thing in which I have not disappointed myself, & in which I have made none of the compromises which destroy faith.

Principia had become the intellectual sea in which he had gladly immersed himself, as the awfulness of his relationship with Alys, and the agony of his frustrated passion, had for a while made life almost unbearable. But even in his thirties Russell was a man with infinite interests and an equal capacity for satisfying them. His stapling-up of philosophy with homely facts, the quasi-popular papers that he wrote while dealing with the erudite complexities of symbolic logic, foreshadowed much of his later writing. In much the same way his political activities during the first decade of the new century were an augury of things to come. Liberal in sympathies, rational in outlook, and with a vigorous mistrust of all established religion and most political orthodoxies which made him at best a controversial ally and at worst a dangerous one, Russell was tentatively dabbling in politics for most of the years during which *Principia* was coming to birth.

At first glance, "dabbling" looks unfair. Russell stood as a parliamentary candidate for Wimbledon. His friends in Cambridge and in London, as well as the Pearsall Smiths in Surrey, all thought and talked politics as if the mantle of government was theirs for the wearing. He became a relentless political activist during the First World War, and throughout his life was an ardent advocate of parliamentary democracy through the support first of the Liberal Party and then of Labour. Yet on each occasion he stood for Parliament he knew that he had not the slightest chance of being elected, and has made no secret of the fact that success would have shocked him. He has stated that when *Principia Mathematica* was finished he "felt an inclination to go into politics". Yet this cannot have been strong since he rejected invitations to stand for at least two Liberal seats and, although agreeing to address the Liberal Association at Bedford, answered the local selection-committee in terms which he must have known would make inevitable his rejection as a candidate. When he succeeded to the earldom, he showed no wish to take his seat in the House of Lords, waited some years before making his maiden speech, and in the following thirty-five years spoke only on two or three occasions.

His reluctance to use conventional political machinery, not at all what had been expected of him in the Pembroke Lodge days, sprang from a contempt for the compromise and wheeler-dealing which he saw as essential to political life, and from a realization that his own particular powers could best be deployed on extra-parliamentary propaganda. This was sensible as far as it went. Nevertheless, it kept him on the touch-lines rather than in the field.

His early interests were in the problems of Empire, in Tariff Reform, and in the Women's Suffrage movement of which Alys was such an ardent supporter. The first of these was to have long-term repercussions, leading as it did to his suspicion of British policy in 1914, to his opposition to the war, and to his emergence as a public figure. This progression started when he joined "the Co-efficients", a dining and discussion club founded in 1902 by Sidney Webb, anxious that the problems of Empire should be discussed by the right people. Russell was invited to the inaugural meeting, held in Sir Edward Grey's rooms. Here he found himself in the unlikely company of R. B. Haldane, Leo Amery, Halford Mackinder the geographer, and Leo Maxse, who was already, in the words of H. G. Wells, "denouncing the German peril and demanding the Great War". Wells himself and Pember Reeves, a New Zealand progressive settled in England, were the only two with whom Russell felt much sympathy, although after their first meeting he recorded Grey as being very interesting. Lord Milner, Henry Newbolt of "Drake's Drum", Colonel Repington and J. L. Garvin also became members, and Russell soon realized he was a fish very much out of water.

In the summer of 1903 he resigned "because", in his own words written at the time, "the Empire has come to seem to me not worth preserving". Wells, who sympathized but did not resign, noted that Russell "flung out of the club", after saying that "there were a multitude of things he valued before the Empire. He would rather wreck the Empire than sacrifice freedom. So if this devotion was what the club meant——! And out he went ..." Russell, recalling the event thirty years later, remembered a speech by Grey advocating the Anglo-French Entente, negotiations for which were about to start. "I stated my objections to the policy very forcibly, and pointed out the likelihood of its leading to war, but no one agreed with me," he wrote, "so I resigned."

The effects of this debate were to be far-reaching. Russell, not quite innocent of Francophobia, saw war as the inevitable outcome of an Anglo-French alliance. Quite as important, he found it difficult to believe that Grey could see otherwise. No man, in Russell's view, could be as stupid as that if he had reached Grey's position, and the implication was obvious. Thus Grey and the Co-efficients swung Russell towards the conspiracy view of history that was often to warp his future judgments.

His brief flirtation with the Co-efficients denoted a love of argument rather than political ambition. However, his links with the Webbs in particular, and with the Fabians in general, certainly drew him into much political discussion, while he lectured and occasionally wrote in defence of women's suffrage and Free Trade. "I went to Bertie's lecture on Friday," Logan reported to his sister, Mary.

It was very clear & intellectual & even witty, & was successful in every way. He is writing a good deal, & becoming quite a public man. It seems like using a razor to chop wood, but such people are necessary to the State, & a person like Bertie must be haunted by "ancestral voices prophesying war". He is not as yet a party politician, & I don't think that he will stand for Parliament. But he is conscientious, public-spirited & likes excitement, so I suppose he will always be popping out of his cloister into the world.

The popping-out was fairly frequent. "I remember when Tariff Reform began, going about London and looking at the working men & seeing them in my thoughts ground under Trusts & landlords, robbed of half the poor livelihood they had, from being deluded by interested sophists," Russell once recalled. "It seemed to me so terrible that I *had* to do something for Free Trade, little as it was ..."

However, none of this suggested more than the *dilettante*, the non-political animal whose attitude was outlined in two letters to Elie Halévy. He wrote,

Stout's expectation of my going into politics in no way surprises me, tho' I do not intend doing so. I was brought up in the instinctive and unquestioned belief that politics was the only possible career: throughout my undergraduate time, I fully expected to go into Parliament; it was only when I got my Fellowship that I decided to stick to academic work. And since then, at intervals, especially at times of crisis, I have thought seriously of standing as a candidate. But at present my Volume II absolutely absorbs me; I must get that done before my mind is free; & when it is done, I shall be too old & too inelastic to acquire the habits of a practical life. So politics is really out of the question.

He later reaffirmed his position. "It is a great comfort to me that you think I am right to keep out of politics," he told Halévy. "Almost everybody here thinks I ought to stand for Parliament, & I have great difficulty in withstanding this opinion, as it has an echo in my instincts, tho' not in my reason. So any support in sticking to philosophy is very welcome to me."

He continued to stick, even in 1907 when he stood for Parliament without the faintest intention of entering it. Early in May he wrote to Ivy Pretious,

I have to tell you a queer piece of news which will amuse and shock you, & put you in a fix. Don't repeat the news until it is public property, as it probably will be tomorrow. I am most likely going to stand at Wimbledon in the interest of Women's Suffrage; they think it desirable to run someone as a means of propaganda, & tho' I hate it, I can see no adequate reason to refuse, as no one else can be got at such short notice. I should of course in addition profess all my usual opinions. I should not do it if there was a chance of getting in, as I am determined not to go into politics ... It is a howling joke, & amuses me almost as much as it annoys me ...

His agreement to stand was not quite as baseless as he makes out. He sincerely believed both in votes for women and in the tactics of the Suffragists, whose non-violent policy was opposed to that of the Suffragettes, and his public support was itself significant. "The mere fact that a thinker of his intellectual distinction should stand primarily to promote woman's suffrage marks an immense advance in the fortunes of the cause," reported the *Daily Chronicle*.

Wimbledon, south-west of London, had been held for years by the Unionists, and was a safe seat for their candidate, Henry Chaplin. Defeated in Lincolnshire during the recent General Election, he could hardly fail here, but it had been expected that the seat would be uncontested, and Russell's sudden appearance, less than a fortnight before polling day, savoured of disrespect if not of indecency. To make matters worse he appeared not as a Liberal supporting Women's Suffrage, which would have been just tolerable, but as the first candidate of the National Union of Women's Suffrage Societies. He did announce himself as of Liberal beliefs, promised to support the party, but added that he would "give precedence, in every case, to women's suffrage", which as he must have known wrecked any chance of Liberal support. The local organization backed smartly away.

In the twelve days that remained before polling, Russell held a full quota of meetings. Most were packed, the audience often being made up in equal parts of those who came to ridicule votes for women and those who came to inspect the man rash enough to support the idea. Even his opponents found him attractive, and what seems to have been a Liberal ditty admitted, "Although we may oppose the plan / Of giving womenfolk a vote / Still to the ordinary man / Few things are more engaging than / The Russell of the Petticoat."

At least one report was eulogistic: "He is elegant, good-looking, courteous and enthusiastic. Slight in build, dark, and immaculate in dress, he wears a heavy moustache, above a pair of eyes ever ready to twinkle into merriment." Although Russell was not as serious as his supporters believed, his meetings had a worthiness brought out in Alys's letters to her mother. "This campaign is very educating to the Electorate & I believe it is the only way of bringing the question of Suffrage to them," she wrote. "All our speakers are at a very high serious level & force their audiences to rise above jokes."

This was pitching it rather high. At Russell's first meeting, rats were released among the audience, driving most of the ladies on to their chairs where long skirts were clutched tightly round improperly exposed legs; at another, the proceedings were enlivened by the introduction of cayenne pepper. Later still there came the incident of the egg, a lesson in counter-productive effort. Alys had been enthusiastic in her support, as she explained to her mother. "I look as handsome as I can & only speak once or twice," she wrote. " 'Women shd. be modest'! Lion [Phillimore] is lending me her brand new hat with 2 bright blue feathers on it – blue is our colour, & fortunately I have 4 blue dresses." But a campaign egg landed over Alys's eye as she left one meeting. "I am afraid it will swell up," she wrote, "but it will make good election material. B's Committee pretended to be very sorry ... but in reality were delighted, & at once sent word of it to the Press." The following day a spokesman for Mr Chaplin appeared with apologies. "I was very dignified," Alys related, "& said it must be a public apology, as I had not been hit in my private capacity." In an age when ladies were still kept above the rough-and-tumble, the egg helped Russell. Nevertheless, he polled a meagre 3,299 votes against Chaplin's 10,263, figures which more than trebled the previous Unionist majority.

He was not disillusioned by the result, while contact with politics had opened his eyes. "Ten days of standing for Parliament gave me more relations with concrete realities than a lifetime of thought," he wrote to William James.

His foray into the political field was to have another, and momentous, effect on Russell's life. Little as he had relished the prospect, or the experience, it had brought him into contact with Liberal politicians, and it was therefore not remarkable that in the autumn of 1909 Logan, now well settled into Court Place with Mrs Pearsall Smith, should drive across to Bagley Wood with a bosom friend of his Balliol days, Philip Morrell, now Liberal M.P. for South Oxfordshire, and Philip's wife Lady Ottoline.

The visit had overtones from the past as well as significance for the future. A decade earlier Logan had not only been an intimate of Philip, as strikingly handsome as he was politically ambitious; to Philip he had also dedicated his first, innocent book, *The Youth of Parnassus*. When Philip married Ottoline, Logan had been too shattered to attend the wedding. Only later had he relented. "I think I *can* go on seeing you after all," he told Philip. "I find Ottoline very interesting, so I shall be able to keep on coming to see you, not as your friend, but as Ottoline's." Later still, after helping Philip in the campaign which brought him to Parliament in 1906, he expressed a passion for Ottoline as deep as that previously felt for Philip, an ironic quirk in the situation as he drove old friend and wife through the Oxford lanes to meet his beloved sister, Alys, and her husband.

Lady Ottoline Morrell was one of the most striking women in Britain.

In 1909 her golden hair had not yet deepened in colour, her face had not yet developed the lines that Augustus John was to caricature, and the tall figure that later carried a touch of the bizarre radiated a diamantine charm that sparkled without disturbing. A year younger than Russell, half-sister of the Duke of Portland, she had been brought up in aristocratic circles which overlapped those of his youth. Indeed, years earlier they had met when she was visiting a distant relative at Ham House, near Pembroke Lodge, and he was an elegant Cambridge graduate. "I sat looking at this little mathematical wonder as he sat leaning his back against the mantelpiece, his legs crossed – the same position that he stands in today," she recalled. "My aunt made me laugh by reminding him how, when he was a small child, someone gave him a blue Conservative rosette to wear, and he snatched it off, threw it to the ground, and stamped it under his small feet." They had met again when Logan was campaigning for Morrell, an occasion of which Russell later claimed to Ottoline, "I began to wish to [know you] because of what I saw you were making of Philip." But he had resisted the temptation.

Now, aged thirty-seven and seven years celibate, he was a very different animal. "Bertrand Russell is most fascinating," Ottoline wrote on her return from the September meeting. "I don't think I have ever met anyone more attractive, but very alarming, so quick and clear-sighted, and supremely intellectual – cutting false and real asunder. Somebody called him 'The Day of Judgment'." "His notice flattered me very much," she went on, "and though I trembled at the feeling that in half an hour he would see how silly I was and despise me, his great wit and humour gave me courage to talk ..." The phrase, "most fascinating", illustrates Russell's unexpected power to captivate women, a power which until now had lain largely unemployed. His conversation helped. So did the searchlight of his attention which he could focus with all the danger of sunlight concentrated on a dry leaf through a magnifying glass. There was his personality, overflowing with confidence, and his knack of making a woman feel she was the only one in the room, the town or the world. There was also his deep but concealed interest in sex, half satyr-like, half unsophisticated.

During that September afternoon, Russell and Ottoline had a talk on the way to the river that he later admitted was "the beginning – since then I have never consciously lost an opportunity. But only dim instinct knew what was happening – my conscious knowledge was fugitive." The following day Philip's mother drove Ottoline to Court Place to see Mrs Pearsall Smith. Alys was there. "She said that Bertie had enjoyed our visit and would like to come and see us in London," Ottoline wrote. "It would be very delightful, but I really have not the courage for it. In ten minutes he would be disappointed and bored. He makes me feel as if I were as empty as an old drum." But she had been affected. So had Russell.

A few weeks later, *Principia Mathematica* at last delivered, he took a deep breath and began to look around. "I felt somewhat at a loose end," he wrote. "The feeling was delightful, but bewildering, like coming out of prison." But preparations were already in hand for the coming election and he decided to help the Liberals. "I did not want to help the Member for the constituency in which I was living, as he had broken some pledges which I considered important," he wrote. "I therefore decided to help the Member for the neighbouring constituency across the river." This was Philip Morrell.

The New Romantic

6

Ottoline

Russell's decision to canvass for Philip Morrell in the January 1910 election may have been entirely disinterested. Yet it is easy to see how his hunger for personal affection, for draughts of an antidote to the unrelieved earnestness of Alys, could, from the autumn of 1909 – the time from which he "never consciously lost an opportunity" – have thrust him, subconsciously maybe, towards the sparkling world through which Lady Ottoline was wafted with the help of courage, an original mind and a ducal background.

In the Oxfordshire campaign of 1910, as in Wimbledon three years previously, he imposed his personality on hostile audiences even though he had little success in conjuring out their votes. Ancestry counted, particularly in England outside the towns, where touching the forelock was still not only a courtesy but an insurance for keeping a job. Experience counted, giving Lord John's grandson a reflex response to the temper of a meeting and thus a head-start over the pack. Courage helped too, and Lady Ottoline recorded in her diary one occasion which foreshadows the Trafalgar Square rallies of fifty years on.

> At some places we were stoned and booed at. Watlington was particularly violent. Bertie Russell had come with us to speak at a large meeting there. There seemed no chance of anyone being listened to, much less anyone so quiet and remote as Bertie Russell, but undaunted he stood up and began to speak. Catcalls, whistles and yells redoubled, but something in his passionate sincerity and intellectual force arrested them, and in a few moments, much to our surprise, he was being listened to with attention. Very seldom have I seen intellectual integrity triumph over democratic disorder.

But integrity was not enough. Philip Morrell was defeated. However, later in the year he was adopted by the newly created north-country constituency of Burnley. Russell was again asked to help in the campaigning, and although new teaching duties kept him out of this particular fray, his conscious was already taking over from his subconscious. "I have never thrown away any letters of yours since the one when you asked me to come to Burnley for the election in 1910," he wrote to Ottoline years later.

The duties which kept an eager Russell from the Burnley campaign arose from a five-year Trinity lectureship in logic and the principles of mathematics, set up largely on the advocacy of Whitehead, about to leave for London where he was to have a year to himself before taking up a new teaching-post at University College, and anxious that the ideas presented in *Principia Mathematica* would continue to be taught in Cambridge. In addition to a stipend of £210 a year, the lecturer had rooms in college and could dine in hall. Even so, the appointment was not to the permanent staff, and when Whitehead congratulated Russell he pointed out that there was "no implication that the lectureship will be continued after five years".

In the early autumn, a few weeks before the Burnley campaign, Russell moved into rooms in Nevile's Court, Trinity, officially quarters for "the superior class to which unmarried fellows have the first claim". His quarters, he told Lucy Donnelly, included "a fairly large room, looking out on a Renaissance cloistered court, with Wren's Library at one end and the Elizabethan College Hall at the other ... many books, but only one picture (the picture of my mother that used to be at Bagley Wood) and the little Spinoza and Leibniz. In the main it is rather severe."

Here he settled down, back among friends. At Trinity, McTaggart still lectured on the moral sciences. Hardy was already emerging as one of the leading pure mathematicians of his day, while Lytton Strachey, whose family Russell had long known, came up for meetings of the Apostles. There was also Maynard Keynes, hard at work in King's on his *Treatise on Probability* which used logical axioms as the basis for the mathematics of probability much as Russell and Whitehead had used them as foundation for the general body of mathematics. Russell had known Keynes, ten years his junior, since the beginning of the century and had a healthy respect for what he later called the sharpest and clearest intellect he had ever known. "When I argued with him I felt that I took my life in my hands," he wrote; and, asked by Harold Nicolson what he had thought of Keynes, he replied, "Obviously a nice man, but I did not enjoy his company. He made me feel a fool." Moore was soon to return as university lecturer, and for him Russell maintained a professional respect barely qualified by personal disgruntlement. "This morning I went to hear [him] lecture," he wrote soon after Moore's return; "–he was extraordinarily good–very clear, caring passionately about the subject, obviously feeling it quite overwhelmingly important to get at the truth, thinking so hard that whenever he came to a stop he was panting–only just enough aware of his audience to keep him talking, otherwise absorbed in his topics."

Russell's subject at Trinity was still a specialized one, and for some while he had only three in his course on mathematical logic: C. D. Broad, E. H. Neville, and H. T. J. Norton, who was to anticipate some of J. B. S. Haldane's applications of mathematics to the problems of heredity. There was a compensation for the small number. Russell could later claim, "One hundred per cent of my pupils get Fellowships."

Teaching, however, was not the most mentally stimulating of his professional activities, much as he enjoyed training his young men to appreciate the delights of mathematical logic. He still wanted to understand the way the world was built, and by 1910 was already honing up for the task the tools he had fashioned for tackling the more specialized problems of *The Principles of Mathematics* and *Principia Mathematica*. The outcome, to be progressively developed over the years, was the new logical analytic method of philosophy. "The old logic put thought in fetters, . . . the new logic gives it wings," he maintained.

As he settled during the autumn of 1910, a major crisis acrose around *Principia*. Volume one had been greeted with respect and only minor criticism by the extremely small number of men competent to review it. But while volume two was in the press Whitehead discovered that he had made a fundamental mistake when preparing Part III of the second volume which dealt with cardinal arithmetic. Russell had not noticed it, and it was only now, in January 1911, that it was picked up by Whitehead. He wrote to Russell,

> Unless you have all the answers clear in your mind, I am sure that we ought to stop the printing. We shall wreck all our work from an impatience over the last few months of thought. Here is our last chance of making ourselves intelligible. No more non-committal covering-up of our intelligibilities will do – that is to say, unless I have hopelessly misconceived this work. In that case, too, the need of a *very* full explanatory addition at this point is all the more necessary – So please stop the printing and let us think quietly over the matter. At the very least the symbolism is entirely ambiguous and subject to limitations not disclosed anywhere, unless these deductions are true.

The printing was quickly halted, while for nearly five months the authors ironed out the error and its implications.

Russell was now thirty-eight. One great work was almost behind him and he knew that his position was assured. But he faced a bleak future. With rooms in Trinity he need see even less of Alys. He prepared to sell the Bagley Wood home and simultaneously took another, and smaller, house at Van Bridge on the outskirts of Fernhurst. The prospect was to some extent ameliorated by his intense personal involvement with mathematics. It was softened by his deep love of Cambridge. All the same, it was a dispiriting outlook. He might almost have echoed T. H. Huxley at forty-five, "looking towards the end".

Yet the future was in fact to have a quality midway between dream and drama, a future transformed by Lady Ottoline. Their *affaire* began in the spring of 1911 and was concealed from all but a few close friends until it eventually drifted into a relationship more of acolyte and mother-confessor than lover and mistress. It ranks high among well-documented love-affairs since Russell wrote some two thousand letters to Ottoline, frequently three a day during the heat of his excitement. She replied with nearly sixteen hundred. Read as a whole, and with the repetitions ignored, the correspondence has the quality of a work of art.

The story which it tells is an unlikely one. On the one hand Ottoline at the centre of the social roundabout, with successful husband and young daughter, both of whom she adored; on the other, the aristocratic philosopher with little but his wit to support him. Their interactions during the three years before the outbreak of the First World War were personally important for Ottoline but important on a higher level for Russell. It was not only that the dispassionate mathematician, emotionally immobilized by frustrated love, became once more the passionate human being whose ardour was matched only by a determination to get his own way. It was not only that his tentative and half-suppressed feelings for art, architecture and music were formed and then coaxed out into the open. The logician was transformed into the man of the world, and the good intentions of the 1900s given practical muscle that was to serve him well in the coming crusading years. The First World War was to create the decisive watershed in Russell's life. Ottoline prepared him for it.

"Bertie Russell attracted, frightened me," she wrote in her diary of a meeting shortly after the encounter at Bagley Wood, "but everything he said had an intense, piercing, convincing quality. The first time that it dawned on me that he was not so happy in his own life was one evening at dinner. Sitting next to me, he said with intensity, 'There is always a tragedy in everyone's life, if one knows them well enough to find it out.'" Russell himself remembered the same evening. "I was wildly excited that night and couldn't make out why – of course it was you. I could easily have talked the whole night through without an instant's pause, if I could have been listened to so long."

There were further meetings after Philip Morrell's electoral defeat and before he was offered the new constituency of Burnley in December 1910. Nothing came of them. Not until March 1911 did the wheels of chance mesh together and produce the meeting that was to change Russell's life.

He was to give three lectures at the Sorbonne in Paris and arranged to spend the night of Sunday 19 March at the Morrells' home in Bedford Square. On arrival he learned that Philip had been unexpectedly called away. However, he was not – as might be inferred from his autobiography – to have Lady Ottoline to himself for the evening. With an intuition which was half social convention, half the instinctive caution that enabled her to survive the traumatic experience of Russell's worship, his hostess had invited two dinner-guests: Russell's old Cambridge friend, Ralph Hawtrey, and the American Ethel Sands.

It was late before the two guests left and Russell was alone with Lady Ottoline. They sat talking over the fire until four in the morning. Russell, recording the event a few days later, wrote, "I did not know I loved you till I heard myself telling you so – for one instant I thought 'Good God, what have I said?' and then I knew it was the truth." Ottoline's version, confided to her diary shortly afterwards, raises a doubt as to whether the revelation was as unpremeditated as Russell later tried to convince himself. "I was utterly unprepared for the flood of passion which he now poured out on me," she wrote. "My imagination was swept away, but not my heart, although it was very much moved and upset. All Bertie's eloquence was brought to bear on me, urging me as a matter of duty to give up everything for him, and go forth with him into a new life." This she had no intention of doing, and she also had qualifications more considerable than Russell was openly to acknowledge. "For external and accidental reasons," he wrote, "I did not have full relations with Ottoline that evening, but we agreed to become lovers as soon as possible." Their letters of the next few days and weeks tell a different story. Whatever the exact mixture of Ottoline's feelings for Russell, part admiration, part pity, she had not the slightest intention of breaking up her marriage, and was still in two, or even more, minds about becoming Russell's mistress.

On the train to Paris, after meeting Bob Trevelyan, he wrote the first of the impassioned letters which were to continue for years. "Bob Trevy babbled on; every now & then I woke up & wondered who he was talking about just then," he said. "Fortunately *yes* & *quite so* & *ah indeed* were enough for him ... It was altogether extraordinary to me that you should love me – I feel myself so rugged & ruthless, & so removed from the whole aesthetic side of life – a sort of logic machine warranted to destroy any idea that is not very robust."

In Paris, where the beautiful Mrs Halévy beguiled his lonely hours, he found awaiting him a letter from Ottoline who wrote soberly of the hand of fate which held her back. "All my life," Russell replied, "except a short time after my marriage, I have been driven on by restless inward furies, flogging me to activity & never letting me rest, till I feel often so weary that it seems as if no more could be borne. You would change all that if you were willing. You could give me inward joy and expel the demons ..."

But once among the philosophers he began to sober up. "I don't at the moment see how things will work out," he wrote.

> My serious & intended view is that our love would be degraded if we allowed it to be surrounded by the sordid atmosphere of intrigue – prying servants, tattling friends & gradually increasing suspicion. All this is inevitable if we attempt secrecy; we cannot hope to succeed in it ... If you will tell Philip & let me tell Alys, I can acquiesce in your staying with him; then the deceit & sordidness is avoided. And then you can still help him politically. That seems to me the right course, as well as the most likely to minimise scandal. But whatever you say I shan't give up the hope of everything. I have been told, & believe, that your obstinacy is incredible: so is mine.

On Saturday he returned from Paris, where "all the eminent Frenchmen ... passed like phantasms in a mist of sea". He paid a social call at Bedford Square, where Ottoline gave him a private note, then returned to Fernhurst. "It is horrible here," he wrote from his bedroom. "Poor Alys gets on my nerves to such an extent that I don't know how to bear it another moment. I always find her very trying after an absence, but this time naturally it is particularly bad." She was, he now decided, "kind, hard-working, insincere & treacherous".

As he read and re-read the note Ottoline had given him it became clear that she had by no means made up her mind to become his mistress. "I don't quite know why I have to ask for all or nothing," he wrote to her, "but I know I am right. I feel that if you refuse all, I shall be terribly tempted to accept less, but it would be wrong – I should be somehow degraded by it, and that would degrade our love." But it was not only the uncertainty that worried him. Setting the pattern for the future, he off-loaded his practical as well as his emotional troubles. One was the writing of a little book for the Home University Library that was to become a classic, *The Problems of Philosophy*. It would have been difficult enough to fit into the schedule, without this personal upheaval. "Heaven knows how I shall manage," he wrote, "but I must do it as I have signed the contract."

But he was thoroughly depressed and ended his letter convinced that she would decide against him. "If I were less tired," he concluded, "I would be more hopeful, but just now I merely feel that life is one long irony, in which the good things come in glimpses that only make common life harder. I cannot understand the wishes for a future life – it is the chief consolation that in the grave there is rest."

But despite the uncertain future, he now broke the news to Alys. She "took it very well", he wrote, adding later,

> I do not think she is suffering very much. All the real pain was nine years ago, when I told her I no longer loved her. Since then life together has been very difficult, & I am quite certain she will be happier when she has abandoned the struggle, & I think she really

knows she will. It will be a great boon to me, not only because I hardly know how to endure her, but more because she has a subtle bad influence, a weaker form of Balzac's Cousine Bette.

He also wrote to the Whiteheads, by this time living in Chelsea, telling them what had happened. He asked Ottoline whether she would call on Mrs Whitehead. "I do not know what he thought would come of this interview," she wrote years later, "but I obediently went to see her, and I was able to tell her far more plainly than I could tell him what I felt. I have always felt that she was a previous object of his love."

In fact she went not only once but on three successive days, on the last of which she arranged to meet Russell in the Whiteheads' house in Carlyle Square. By this time he had resigned himself to the end of the affair before it had started, and while breaking his journey at the Whiteheads' on his return to Cambridge, wrote a long letter of renunciation ending "Good-bye, goodbye, goodbye".

What happened in Chelsea on the morning of 30 March is not certain. Ottoline, writing in 1931, says, "I had another interview with Bertie at the Whiteheads' house, to say goodbye, and to tell him that it was impossible for me to leave Philip, but he begged me to see him again. His despair weighed on me, and filled me with gloom. I felt it was impossible to cast him off." Russell, on the other hand, writing to her shortly after she had left him at the Whiteheads' for Bedford Square, thanks her for "the dear letter you gave me when you went away today": a letter which suggested it was not at all goodbye.

An explanation of the apparent contradiction lies in the anguished situation of Ottoline, as her letters written during the last days of March make quite clear. She was, she said, tied by eight years of affection and responsibility to Philip even though she and he were only devoted friends; but to cast him off would ruin his life and that of their daughter Julian. Nevertheless it would, she felt passionately, be madness for Russell and herself to let each other go. For the moment, at least, they decided not to part.

From this point on, roughly ten days after the Sunday meeting that had started it all, the *affaire* began to crystallize. Russell's motive in having Mrs Whitehead meet the woman with whom he was now so passionately in love quickly become clear. Once she had talked with Ottoline, Evelyn Whitehead became not only counsellor but one-woman Fifth Column, passing on to Russell whatever information she could glean from her old friend, the unsuspecting Alys.

While Ottoline lived in London, Russell was firmly tied to Cambridge, but he dealt smartly with this particular problem. "I have been cunning," he wrote, "& have arranged, with the full concurrence of the authorities, to give only two lectures a week, supplemented by individual teaching.

The result is that I shall be able to come to London sometimes without having to put off a lecture. This is very desirable." Thus they could meet as frequently as Ottoline could discreetly arrange, and if she had not yet decided to accede "all" she had at least not withdrawn from "perhaps".

Alys soon agreed that she and Russell would continue to keep up appearances by meeting from time to time. Philip also acquiesced, although it is not quite certain exactly how clearly he – or Ottoline, for that matter – yet realized where events were leading. He had no objection if Russell continued to visit Bedford Square, asking only that they did not have to meet.

Only later did awful possibilities arise. Mrs Whitehead warned that Philip might become unhinged and murder them both; Russell feared that Alys would fall back on a threat of suicide. Neither warning nor fear was justified and for Russell, as well as for Ottoline, the problems of the spring and early summer were more conventional ones. Where could they meet without scandal? Who should be let into the secret of their relationship.

There was nothing untoward in their being seen together occasionally, but the occasions would have to be rationed, and tactfully organized, if gossip were not to touch both Ottoline's reputation and Philip's political prospects. Gossip might also, in the climate of the times, endanger Russell's career at Trinity, although in his state of mind that counted for little.

Friends were not slow to rally round. Ethel Sands opened her house to them. Evelyn Whitehead, as well as passing on to Russell all the latest intelligence gained from his wife, offered the Carlyle Square premises as a haven. Her husband agreed to this, although the visits from Alys were less than welcome. Russell has said Whitehead detested Alys, and Whitehead himself exclaimed on one occasion, "She was such an awful liar."

However, in spite of co-operation from the Whiteheads and Ethel Sands, the couple were for many weeks driven to a series of meetings which had a touch of farce. Sometimes they met in the British Museum, Russell having first warned her not to visit any of the remote rooms as he might waste time finding her. More usually they met out of doors. "I think it is better to avoid places like Kensington Gardens, where we should meet all our friends," Russell wrote. "The only plan I can think of is to meet at some Underground station exit, & take a cab to some out-of-the-way place like Putney Heath where we could walk if it was fine." They also went to Richmond Park, to Hampstead Heath and to Wimbledon Common. Luckily, it was a good summer, and after one meeting when the sun had shone Russell noted how it had changed on their return: "Providence has been very kind to us and evidently approves." Both were busy people, but from the first Russell was ready to cancel appointments and re-write his diary as necessary. "I can come day or night or any time," he wrote on one occasion. "I quite agree about the bird in the hand, so the sooner the better."

At times they appear to have taken extraordinary risks, as when Russell wrote, "I could get a room at some other hotel, say Hotel Russell (isn't it?) in Russell Square, and we could go there, if you have not arranged with Miss Sands, otherwise Miss Sands' will do very well." Since Lady Ottoline was already one of London's well-known characters, and Russell was scarcely inconspicuous, the suggestion of booking a room only a few hundred yards from the Morrells' Bedford Square house adds a note of audacity to the situation. It was not the only one. "Your economical soul will be glad to hear that the hotel only charged 2s. 6d. for the room when it found I was not staying the night," he wrote on another occasion.

While the Whiteheads were understanding, there was a strict limitation on the help they felt able to give. Evelyn Whitehead wanted neither her servants nor her children to suspect. The latter were very perceptive, and if they saw Ottoline would guess at once. One day both sons presented a difficulty and Russell had to warn Ottoline, "I find the Whiteheads are coming to London Monday by the same train with me, so you must keep inside the waiting-room if by any chance you arrive before me. They would not wish their children to see us."

Ottoline's spare time in London was limited, Russell's permissible absences from Cambridge were the same, and fitting one to the other demanded good staff-management and split-minute control. "I have never missed a train after leaving you, tho' I have had to get in after they had started," he told her in one of his thrice-daily letters. Hers, which he kept in a special locked metal box, were brought to him by the bedmaker who called him each morning. He was usually awake, waiting for them.

On one occasion she visited him in his Cambridge rooms. "It is obvious my bedmaker is quite unsuspicious," he reported afterwards. "She considers you tall, which is true if not penetrating . . . I don't think she sniffed your scent or thought me a gay dog." There was something special about having Ottoline in his rooms, with their homely air and the sound of birds in the Master's Garden outside his windows. "This place is very much where the civilised half of me belongs," he confided. "I love the courts and the willows, & my rooms, & the feeling that the things of the intellect are respected here. I even have owls at night, so I am very well off."

It was some weeks, and there was much demur, before Ottoline finally agreed to more than clandestine and unsatisfactorily brief meetings. She eventually succumbed at Studland on the Dorset coast, where the Morrells rented Cliff End for some weeks at Easter. Both the place and the occasion were curious since Studland was then a fashionable small resort, well filled with those who knew both Ottoline and Russell. He himself had spent a short holiday there the previous summer, meeting Clive Bell and other members of the embryonic Bloomsbury set. Indeed, those who were to visit the Morrells at Cliff End this Easter included Alys's niece, Ray Costelloe, and Logan, while Philip was to be absent for only a relatively short while after Easter to attend to business at Westminster.

"It would be absolutely useless, so far as [Alys] is concerned, for me not to come to Studland," Russell had written to Ottoline. "If I come after term has begun, as you seemed to think would be best (i.e. after the 21st) she will not know I am away from Cambridge. In any case, unless from detectives, she will know nothing. I told her once for all that I would tell her nothing further." Later the same day he was able to report that the situation was well in hand.

> I have just had a thoroughly satisfactory talk with Alys. I have agreed to preserve appearances by coming to her for occasional week-ends, when we shall have visitors and be seen together. She has agreed to go on taking my money (which was a very vital point), & to stay here, instead of at Iffley, during the next term. I made her understand that if there came to be much scandal it would grow impossible even to keep up appearances. Pride & prudence will combine to keep her silent, & tho' her family will guess that something is up, I feel sure she won't breathe a word, & I don't believe they will think of you. So really our minds may be easy about her. I dislike yielding to threats, but it has been quite effective. I feel *quite sure* she will do nothing harmful now.

A week later he left Fernhurst for Hindhead station and the down line for Southampton and Swanage rather than the up line for London and Cambridge. He lunched on the train, since he did not want to waste the first moments of arrival in eating, changed at Southampton, and here picked up a telegram from Ottoline confirming that Philip had left. It also confirmed their earlier arrangements: he would take a cab from Swanage to Studland – probably Philip's would wait for him – she would walk out to meet him, he would let his bags go on by the cab, and they would follow together on foot.

The previous evening Ottoline had told Philip, leaving for London the next morning, that she was expecting Russell, who had asked if he could see her at Studland. She also told her husband that Russell was now asking her to leave him. At this point emotions crystallized and an approach of tragedy can be sensed. Philip, dearly in love with his wife, put her happiness first, and asked, "Do you want to go? You must if you want to." Ottoline, realizing fully for the first time where her attraction to Russell might lead, was both shocked and hurt.

Nevertheless, she was waiting by the roadside. "He assumed at once that I was his possession, and started to investigate, to explore, to probe," she later wrote. "I shrank back, for it was intolerable to me to have the hands of this psychological surgeon investigating the tangle of thoughts, feelings and emotions which I had never yet allowed anyone to see." However, this was only one side of the coin.

> I felt uplifted and flattered that this remarkable man should carry me up with him into worlds of thought that I had not dreamed of; he talked of his life and work and thoughts, and if only he had been different in his person, I should probably have been entirely carried off my feet, and have flown with him through worlds of thought and sense. But, to my shame, however much I was thrilled with the beauty and transcendence of his thoughts, I could hardly bear the lack of physical attraction, the lack of charm and gentleness and sympathy, that are so essential to me, and yet so rare.

As for Russell, he had thoughts for no one but himself. "What Philip might think or feel", he later wrote," was a matter of indifference to me." The next few days he remembered as "among the few moments when life seemed all that it might be". Easter over, he bid her goodbye on a hillside above the town, then walked into Swanage. Here he went to ground in a teashop, venturing on to the station only after the train from London had been in some time. On it had been Philip Morrell.

Almost as his train drew out, he began a letter, "–absurd ... but I can't do anything else". It had been very hard to leave her.

> I wanted to carry you off with me to some sunny Italian hillside–to live in our love & think of nothing else but beauty. If we had met many years ago–say at the time when we met at Ham–you would have thought my atheism wicked, & I should have thought you lost in ancient error. When at last I did get to know you slightly, I supposed you cared for clothes & bibelots, & that the rest was politeness & making conversation. I was a fool–& so years were wasted.

The days at Studland consolidated their feelings, and soon after he felt confident enough to warn her of what she was in for. "I have a perfectly cold intellect, which insists upon its rights & respects nothing," he wrote.

> It will sometimes hurt you, sometimes seem cynical, sometimes heartless. It is very much more dominant at certain times than at others. You won't much like it. But it belongs with my work–I have deliberately cultivated it, & it is really the main thing that I have put discipline into. In time I believe you will not mind it, but the sudden absolute cessation of feeling when I think must be trying at first. And nothing is sacred to it–it looks at everything quite

impartially, as if it were someone else. Happily I have its approval in all I feel to you – it hasn't found anything to say against you or against my trusting our love. It is not in that way it is a danger, but that some day in some other way it might hurt you, & that its habit of enveloping may vex you. I have preserved my faiths in a very difficult atmosphere – the intellect fights every inch of the ground, & for anyone else it may not be pleasant.

To Ottoline the warning was a challenge. What had started as primarily an emotional relationship rapidly developed into a complementary intellectual partnership in which Russell poured out his hopes and plans and philosophical ambitions without inhibition. He had to be careful how he did it. Ottoline could write letters in the security of her own room. At Cambridge he was at the mercy of unannounced chance visitors and on occasion had difficulty in warding off the helpful offer to post the letter he had been seen completing. In the Athenaeum, Uncle Rollo might suddenly appear. And in railway-carriages it was always a fine point whether other travellers were not also enjoying his letters. Nevertheless he wrote before breakfast most mornings, again during the day and last thing at night. Sometimes a fourth letter was squeezed in.

Soon after Studland, the accommodating relationship which Ottoline had developed with Philip, and which Russell had secured with Alys, was endangered by a violent spasm of protest. Logan, incensed at what he correctly imagined to be the state of play, induced Alys to threaten naming Ottoline in a suit for divorce, an action that would have been disastrous for Ottoline's happiness and Philip's career, to say nothing of Russell's at Trinity. For him it was the most dangerous corner he had yet had to turn. How it was negotiated is described in three letters.

Late in May he warned Ottoline that Alys, "very wild and very miserable", was considering action.

She says, what I find it hard to believe, that she had not understood I was going to Studland, and heard it first from Logan. She is very full of anger against us both. I shall have to see more of her than I intended, I think, at any rate for a while. I cannot endure her misery. She refuses to live with Logan, but is filled with dread of loneliness – & it does seem a very awful prospect. She asked me whether if she had a child I would acknowledge it! I can't imagine who the father would be. Besides it is a thousand to one against its occurring even if that difficulty had been overcome. But it shows how desperate she is – Of course I said I would acknowledge it. The rest of the time she was saying either that the one important thing was to save my work & influence, or that I had become a public danger & ought to be publicly exposed!

Eight days later, after the Whiteheads had suggested that Russell should consider resigning from Trinity, he is able to send reassuring news:

> I gather it is all right. Logan & Alys have been here and have agreed to everything. She now agrees to a complete parting, & nothing legal. So all is well. There need be no further agitations. She has a good side which had come uppermost. For the moment I am too tired to feel much except the stretched cord relaxing.

Later in the day he wrote again,

> We are safer now than ever before. Logan says he doesn't wish to speak to P[hilip] again, so you will get P quite in time. A. absolutely undertakes to do nothing, & we are both to say that we are parting because of incompatibility. Nothing will be done to make my position at Trinity impossible. Having once condoned, they will hold their tongues for their own sakes.

What had happened was that Logan, having written a long letter to Philip, had been invited to discuss his protests with the Morrells at Newington, Ethel Sands's house outside Oxford. Here Philip, cheerful and unmoved as Ottoline described him, had behaved with the tolerant decency he showed throughout the whole affair, calming an irritable Logan and making it clear that his chances of causing trouble were slight.

With Philip's help, Russell had been saved. Only one thing worried him. "I imagine what Logan said to [Philip]", Russell now told Ottoline, "was that people wd say he condoned things for the sake of your money – (it seems to me hardly anybody but the Smiths would think of such a thing – still it is a pity that he hasn't got money of his own). That is what Logan said to Mrs. Whitehead – a poisonous thought to put into a man's mind."

But all was now well. Alys arranged to join Logan and was to spend four decades with him, first in the country, later in Chelsea. Those who suspected something more than a nearly amicable agreement to differ between Russell and his wife usually took care not to ask awkward questions. Philip accepted the situation for Ottoline's sake, turning a blind eye to the liaison as long as it was managed discreetly.

While the situation behind the scenes was thus apparently settled, it was still necessary that the outside world, registering the separation of Russell and his wife, should receive no hint of the reason. At times, Russell thought it "prudent to appear unhappy". At others he was forced to simulate regret, a fact which gave him wry amusement. He confided to Ottoline,

> I hate this injured-martyr business, but it can't be helped. It is funny that the welfare of Philip and Julian should depend upon my

assuming virtues I don't possess – but since it is so, may God give me strength to play the hypocrite – to manage the half-repressed sigh, the sad smile, the praise of Alys which only exhibits my own nobility of soul, & all the rest of the apparatus. When I am bankrupt I can hire myself to a troop of nigger minstrels as the melancholy man who is the foil for the clown. It is rather agreeable to pretend to be cheerful when one is miserable, but pretending to be heart-broken when one is filled with happiness is rather a dirty business. However, as it has to be done I get my fun out of it.

A fair slice of hypocrisy went into the dirty business. Russell had a life-long dedication to the truth and nothing but the truth; however, this was one episode when he made little of things and saw to it that a minimum number of friends knew the whole truth. There was honourable enough reason: Russell the philosopher was too infatuated to care very much what Trinity might think or do to him, much as he loved his life there; if his brother could survive the matrimonial antics which had made him a national figure, and earned him his title of "the wicked Earl", the heir to the earldom had no need to worry about an *affaire* with the half-sister of a duke. However, the point of the issue was the vulnerable position of Philip, whose parliamentary chances could have been destroyed by a proletariat still easily shocked at the idea of the unmentionable being practised. Thus Russell and Ottoline had to be careful, although at times their care was minimal. She, for instance, is told on one occasion, "If you want to see me elsewhere than at Bedford Square, my view is that the safest plan will be for you to come to the station & wait in the first class waiting room on the departure platform, & then go with me in a taxi to some hotel & walk in with me. That involves less risk than in any other plan, & doesn't look odd to the hotel authorities." Russell, one feels, must have maintained a high level of oddness rating.

From the first he was obsessed with meeting her where neither would be reminded of family ties and, an earnest of his essentially romantic nature, in the deep country rather than in towns. In the summer of 1911 she was due to stay with her mother-in-law at Broughton Grange, a house on the outskirts of Banbury. On hearing the news Russell consulted Bradshaw, worked out cross-country railway connections, and decided that if he took rooms in Chipping Norton or Kingham, she could visit him surreptitiously but frequently. "I long to get right away with you, where you won't have your household on your mind," he said in outlining the plan. "I think in the winter it could be done with perfect safety – it makes such a difference to you being free from maids and housekeeping & fuss." As an inducement he offered to shave off his moustache, a feature to which she had first objected after their days at Studland. The moustache survived another five months and only in December could he tell her, "It passed away peacefully last night & will be cremated the next time my bedroom fire is lighted. I hope you will like the result. My mouth turns out to be thin-lipped and rather cynical; I think I look older. I get funny sensations of things touching my upper lip – especially when I blow my nose. But I didn't find it sore." It did make a difference, though. Legend asserts that the moustache-less Russell was at first unrecognized at a meeting of the Aristotelian Society of which he had become president for the first time earlier in 1911.

The Broughton plan fell through for the moment and Russell increased his efforts to find a *pied-à-terre* in London where they could meet. "It will be very nice," he wrote, "& we shall have a great sense of liberty & I can have books there & means of making tea, & even peppermints in some secret recess!" The ever-helpful Evelyn again came to the rescue. "Mrs. W. undertook to find me a place in Chelsea," he wrote. "She thinks a flat safer than a house – says I couldn't leave a house empty & a servant would be a nuisance." However, Chelsea had to be abandoned as a substitute for Putney Heath or the semi-surreptitious hotel room: there was a recurrent rumour that Alys and Logan might move there from the country. A comparable danger ruled out Gray's Inn, suggested by Ottoline. At first Russell was enthusiastic – "you could come there very early – you might be going to consult your lawyer". Two days later the idea was turned down. "I found a charming apartment & was just deciding on it," he wrote, "when I observed that opposite on the same floor were Sidgwick & Uthwatt, who Alys knows & who inherited a parlourmaid of ours."

For a man of Russell's position, a *pied-à-terre* in London would be quite acceptable, and while the search for it went on the real secret was, despite multiple chances of discovery, kept from all but a small number of close friends. The Whiteheads had been told partly because of Russell's continuing work with Alfred, partly because Evelyn Whitehead had long filled the role of confidante from which she now retired to make way for a multi-purpose Ottoline. Others in the secret included Roger Fry, suffering from his own private passion for Ottoline. "He says the Stephens know, but not from him," Russell told Ottoline in June: "... that Virginia is the dominant one among them, & that he impressed upon her, so that she believed it, that she must avoid even the slightest joke or gossip; the argument which he thought impressed her was that it might prevent my doing any more work".

Ethel Sands knew. So did several of Russell's intimate Cambridge friends, including Lowes Dickinson, although most were only aware that for unexplained reasons Russell had finally parted from Alys. She herself told Moore the convenient half-truth. "While I am writing I should like to tell you, in case you have not heard, that Bertie is staying on in College, while I am living here," she said. "Bertie and I have been very unhappy together for many years, but we have done our best to make a possible common life. Now we feel it will be better for both of us to separate for a time, & we hope our friends will stick by us & go on loving us both as much as they can."

Bob Trevelyan was told a similar story, a revelation that brought from his mother the comment, "I am sorry to hear about your friend Mr. Russell. He seemed such a nice young man, but then I expect that she got ideas above her station." Keeping Ottoline off-stage frequently demanded some attention to detail, and when Russell stayed with the Trevelyans he was careful to provide her in advance with self-addressed envelopes for her letters. This was as well. "The whole post was handed to Mrs. Bob while we were at breakfast and she distributed it," he told her, an event which would have caused Ottoline's distinctive handwriting to be identified. Even to Lucy Donnelly, with whom he was usually quite frank, he made singularly little of the separation, and gave no hint of another woman. The servants knew, of course, and so did the hotel-keepers; but then, as Russell himself has written, mankind was still "divided by the bells at the front door into visitors and servants".

If there was a gap in the story it was soon filled by rumour, at least in Cambridge, where it was borne along by Jane Harrison, the formidable Newnham classicist whom Russell had long known through their mutual contacts with Gilbert Murray. "Envied for her power of enduring excess in whisky and cigarettes," as Russell described her in his private journal, she had "heard, on very reliable authority, that the real cause of his leaving Alys was a married woman in Cambridge, name unknown".

The terms in which Russell dealt with this situation, about which so many friends had so few hard facts, are best gauged from the condolences he received from Frank, who with his current wife expressed much regret. "We had, as you say, an idea, but only an idea, that the original devotion had rather passed away, and that you found each other trying, but we hoped nothing so definite as a separation would result," he said. "People of good manners can often manage to get on in the same house, once they have agreed to differ, and I hope for the comfort of both of you, and your friends, that this may still be the case."

The amount of truth in the mutual-agreement theory can be judged by a letter from Alys to Beatrice Webb. She had heard of the death of Sturge Moore, G. E. Moore's elder brother, and regarded his life as a bad failure. She admitted,

> I have been feeling as if mine were too, as I do care so much about Bertie and have tried so much to make him happy. But caring isn't always enough, I know, and we are very different. He wants constant change and new friends, whereas I love my old friends the best and cling to old habits. What you wrote about truthfulness is true also –

I can tell a lie from cowardice or other motives, but I always know it is a lie and regret it, whereas Bertie has to persuade himself first that it is true. But you mustn't be angry with him for not continuing to care for me – that is the law of his nature, and besides I have failed him in many ways, and though I have had a terrible six months, in time I shall settle down to be content with his happiness.

Mary Berenson, who had amiably accepted Russell's falling out of love with her sister and sent him a note stressing "continued friendliness and good wishes", took a different view of his falling in love with Ottoline. She not only wrote what Russell remembered as a "cutting letter", saying she wanted no more to do with him, but added that her husband felt the same. This was untrue. But Russell, who believed it, dropped Berenson so completely that the latter could ask himself in his diary "... did Russell from the beginning feel that I did not belong to his world, glad to get rid of me?" It was not until 1936 that they met again. "It was during this stay in London – our last one – that a kind of *rapprochement* with Bertie Russell took place, engineered I believe by Trevy," Berenson's secretary, Nicky Mariano, has written. "He came to lunch and seemed to me utterly fascinating. B.B. – probably comparing him with former days – found him cool and contemptuous and did not expect any further developments, in which he was right."

This breach with Berenson was one of the few to spring from the *affaire* with Ottoline, which dominated the central years of Russell's life. Through it ran two threads, one sexual, the other intellectual and aesthetic. About the first there was trouble almost from the start. It was not merely that Ottoline was a distinctly reluctant mistress. She simply did not care for Russell as much as he cared for her. "Her feelings were romantic and sentimental rather than passionate, and my feelings seemed to her quite unreasonable," he recorded in old age. "I think she thought of me in terms of troubadours and courtly love, not in terms of everyday earthly passion." And by 1911 Russell was distinctly earthly.

This "yes–no–perhaps" trait brought their relationship to the verge of rupture at regular intervals during the next five years. It was nevertheless more than counter-balanced by two things: the lasting influence of Russell's intellect on a mind that had been waiting for just such a bracing contact; and the impact of Ottoline's aesthetic, social and religious *sensibilia* on Bertrand Russell.

During the next few years, both influences were continuously at work and if the one merely affected Ottoline's life the other dominated Russell's. Throughout these years he worked on at Trinity as Lecturer. Publication of *Principia* reinforced his reputation and the rest followed. Presiding over a section of the International Congress of Mathematicians, contributing to the *Monist*, the *Hibbert Journal*, the *Proceedings of the Aristotelian Society*, he outwardly remained the academic *par excellence*.

But the co-author of *Principia Mathematica* was changing in many ways. The innate priggishness of the Russell who had filled his journal with proper thoughts was dissolving into a more understanding and more human quality. Moreover, Ottoline's pantheistic streak, with its recognition of the gods, as well as God, in the sunset, in the music of Beethoven, and in the consuming flame of literary genius, was arousing in Russell the aesthetic feelings that not even Bernard Berenson's touch had been able to unbutton. "Nowadays," as he wrote in May 1911, "I long to have beautiful things about me – I used to be indifferent or even wish not to have anything nice – my life was so full of discords that it seemed a vain pretence."

The same was true of music. Half a century later one acute observer noted that Russell's liking for music was genuine but not urgent. "I don't think he ever felt an active need for it except when in the company of some woman who loved music herself and whom he loved – or hoped to love," he said. Thus it came about that Russell often declared to Ottoline how much he wished to listen to music with her. "It is so nice hearing it in a Cathedral, where the surroundings are beautiful & there is no applause," he wrote, after listening to Bach's Passion Music at Ely.

> It is the most wonderful music – it really does surpass even the best of poetry. It is broad and calm like nature, not ignoring disturbing things but rising above them. At one moment it gave me an overwhelming conviction of sin – I wanted to proclaim myself a miserable sinner & prostrate myself – not that I thought of any particular sin, but it made one's ordinary world so small. Then I rose into it & became uplifted. I have seldom been so moved by music – it was *very* difficult to keep from tears. But it is too long for human endurance, & before the end I was too tired to hear it ... What Bach gives one is in itself as great as anything in life; but if one gave oneself up to it, one would do very little for mankind. Music doesn't help me to write; it is so complete in itself, & there are no words for the feelings it gives – that is just why it is so important.

There were other and more direct ways in which Ottoline influenced Russell's work. In the early days she had hindered. "I find it so hard to concentrate my mind on work," he wrote. "I suppose that will be easier when I am more used to you & when all the externals are settled. But at present I only give half my mind to work & after I have been at it for a bit I find myself pulling out your letters & reading them over – which is shameful, but I am not ashamed of it." Within a few months, however, another factor was pulling another way. He wrote,

I try to think there will be many years ahead, but so long as we both have our work utterly separate it makes a separation in what is important. I *will* associate you with my work, somehow, in time, even if it means altering the nature of my work. I have done all I ever intended to do in the way of mathematics – when the publication of this big book is finished, I should in any case do no more in that line. I meant anyhow to take to philosophy, & in that I can associate you to a great extent, if you are mostly in the country. It is important to do so – it will make my work much better. Most of what I want to write in philosophy will be more or less popular, & I can work in the sort of things we have talked about. I have never before felt anything in my life as important as my work – now I feel our love is more important than anything. That is partly because I have finished the most difficult & serious piece of work I shall ever have had to do. If I died tomorrow, other people could manage the printing. Until that was done, I was oppressed by the sense of its importance, & by the feeling that I *must* finish it – it has been for many years a constant weight on my mind. Now that weight is off it, & it makes an enormous difference. I am reading Carlyle's letters at the time he was writing the French Revolution, & I know so well all the feelings of oppression he complains of. But this book has been a bigger job than that ...

Nearly three years later the result of this resolution to extend his interests became evident. In February 1914 he wrote,

Dearest, you *have* liberated something very important in me, an imagination, chiefly. Whitehead ... has been telling me that my mind has been improved very greatly the last two or three years, that in fact it has risen to an altogether higher class. He says I used to have great ingenuity in defending rather narrow & limited points of view, but now I have an altogether broader scope, & that if my present work develops as it promises, it will put me among the few great philosophers. Altho' this is so agreeable, I think it is true, & it is really largely due to you.

Not even Russell, master of the objective approach, can always be acquitted of tailoring his words to the moods of a loved one: yet the evidence in his correspondence with Ottoline is overwhelming. Years earlier, the influence of Alys had helped channel his intellectual activities into *German Social Democracy*. The emotional crash with her had brought about "The Free Man's Worship" and had driven him into the wilderness where he had been able to concentrate on *Principia*. Now his change in focus from mathematical logic to philosophy was to be spurred on by the richly musical drawl of Lady Ottoline, a woman whose influence on Russell was to continue for the rest of his life.

The ideal vehicle on which her influence could first be exercised had been quite fortuitously provided by Gilbert Murray. This was the "shilling shocker", *The Problems of Philosophy*, which Russell had been conscripted to write in the autumn of 1910. Murray was one of the three general editors of the Home University Library, a series of hard-back books published at the almost revolutionary price of one shilling "to get the best minds in the country into direct touch with the great masses of people who now read Harmsworth or nothing at all". Would Russell contribute a volume on the principles of mathematics – or at least think it over? When Russell balked, Murray suggested philosophy. "Tell me of another philosopher who is 1. completely alive and original; 2. democratic, so that he wants to communicate his thought to shop assistants; 3. sharp-eyed and not wobbly or sloppy in thought, and then I will cease to persecute you."

Russell agreed. In fact, the invitation to write on philosophy had come at a fortunate moment. Throughout the previous decade he had been immersed in the problems of symbolic deductive reasoning; but his preoccupation had not stopped him from considering the implications to philosophy of the various theories he had put forward to solve the problems dealt with in *Principia Mathematica*. In particular the Theory of Descriptions proposed a new method of tackling a basic problem of philosophy: is there any knowledge in the world so certain that no reasonable man could doubt it? The theory provided a way of replacing things known until then only by description with other things with which we had personal acquaintance. Russell had, right from the time he hit upon the theory, wondered whether it was applicable right across the domain of human knowledge. He had for some while been wanting to discover whether this was so, and Murray's invitation gave him the opportunity.

But he had not got very far when Ottoline appeared on the scene. Delivery date was only six months away, and he was thus forced to concentrate on the job while still in the rosy flush of third love and anxious to initiate Ottoline into the pleasures of philosophy. As a captive audience of one, she was interested enough to listen and intelligent enough to ask the right questions. The outcome was a masterpiece.

At first he planned to break the back of the work during a fortnight at the Whiteheads' country cottage at Lockeridge, near the Wiltshire town of Marlborough. This idea fell through, and the book was finally written partly in his Cambridge rooms; partly on a brief holiday in the Malvern Hills with Alfred Whitehead's son North: and partly at Ipsden, a village in the Chiltern Hills, a few miles from the Morrells' country house at Peppard.

Russell's first visit to Peppard came early in June and it was here that he met Philip for the first time since his liaison with Ottoline. The occasion, passing off without incident, marked the start of an increasingly tolerant relationship between the two men, and before the end of the month Philip seemed pleased that Russell was planning to spend some time near Peppard. "I must try to find more things to say about [my work] without being too technical," he wrote on his return from this first visit. "And I love the thought of reading philosophy with you. There is a great deal that we might read – any quantity of Plato – Berkeley – parts of Descartes – it will all be delightful." Shortly afterwards there arrived in Cambridge a huge bunch of flowers from the Peppard garden. "Leibniz and Spinoza on my mantelpiece look at them in surprise," he told her. "Leibniz with cynical amusement, Spinoza with grave wonder."

Shortly afterwards, in the Malverns with North, he was dogged by further proofs of *Principia*. "I wrote the stuff such ages ago & have quite forgotten it," he wrote as the proofs continued to arrive. "I dare say it is the most important work I shall ever have done, but it is hard to judge. It is very unlikely that I shall ever do any more mathematical work. I feel it would only be more of the same kind, which could just as well be done by someone else."

Coping with proofs in the Malverns, he found it difficult to squeeze in time for the Shilling Shocker, but by the time he returned to Cambridge in mid-month a good part of the work had been done. During the latter part of June he went down to Peppard again more than once, the only problem being in avoiding Ottoline's other visitors who knew him and who might grow suspicious. He was therefore given regular and detailed instructions as to when and how to arrive. When Desmond MacCarthy and Goldsworthy Lowes Dickinson had been visiting the Morrells, for instance, he was told that they would be leaving at 10.45 and that the 9.35 from Paddington, arriving Reading 10.21, would presumably be safe since their respective cabs would cross *en route* to Peppard. Good staff-work with telegrams clinched the arrangements, and when schedules were tight Russell was advised to use one approach to the village while departing guests used another.

By mid-July a good deal of the Shilling Shocker was complete, and the next month Russell went down to Ipsden, a village a few miles from Peppard, to add the finishing touches. Here he would devote mornings to the work, cycle over to Ottoline for lunch, then read chapters to her before cycling back at midnight.

For her, it was an experience that almost removed the remaining doubts about her relationship with Russell. "It was exhausting but delightful for me to have my mind kept in strict order, driven on to the end of a subject, through tangled bushes and swamps, till it reached open grounds," she wrote in her journal.

> I often wriggled and rebelled, and wanted to hide under shady, sentimental willow trees, but this was never allowed. Bertie would take

> me metaphorically by the hand and pull me up and urge me on; or perhaps take me roughly by the shoulder and shake me, telling me that I was not being honest, and that I must face the truth. Together we seemed, as we sat in those beech woods, to be on a journey through tangled and perplexing forest in search of light and truth, tearing down old dusty growths in my mind, and opening dark windows that had been blocked up in the lower depths of my being.

For Russell, the impersonal delights of philosophy were more inextricably twined up with personal affairs. He wrote,

> It was delicious in the woods at Peppard. I think it was a better place than any we have been in yet. Only the time was so short that even I could not imagine it was for ever, as I usually manage to do. I felt too that you were very tired. Please don't give another thought to my wish for children. From the first moment, you told me not to expect them, so I hadn't set my heart on your having a child. It is in every way more convenient that it should not happen & it is by no means vital to me.

Vital or not, it was a subject which Russell, ever hoping for a son, had first raised in April. Then he had learned that an operation after the birth of her daughter had made it most unlikely that Ottoline would again bear children. Nevertheless, he was still discussing the idea, despite Ottoline's sage comment that if it were possible then Alys would be enraged.

For the moment, but only for that, he was ready to pass on to other matters. She sent him a heart-shaped locket holding a tress of her hair. "You needn't be afraid of being sentimental," he commented on receiving it. "I am at least as sentimental as you are." In return he gave her a locket that had belonged to his mother.

At this stage he began to have doubts about continued residence in Trinity. "If I were in the country where I could see you often & other people sometimes, I should get much more new work done," he wrote. "And fundamentally that is the most important thing. Other people can teach it, but the work I have done is chiefly important for its bearings, which no one will discover if I don't point them out. What will help my work most will be if I can see you very often, without a tiring journey & without an earthquake, so that ordinary thoughts can exist in the same day."

To some extent this happened, and *The Problems of Philosophy* was continued as they both settled down, after the preliminary turmoils, into the first stage of what he at least still believed could be a cosy relationship. Russell for his part was anxious to guide his life so that no chance of being with her was lost. He turned down an invitation to lecture in Dublin for a term. He was unable to get to either London or Paris "without very great inconvenience & upsetting many arrangements", he explained to one correspondent. And he rejected an invitation from Professor Ralph Perry to lecture at Harvard the following year, pleading lectures in Cambridge unwilling to let the Atlantic separate him from Ottoline, who agreed that it would be dreadful to be parted for so long.

On her side, she gained a confidence from Russell that she had previously lacked. "... I found my friendship with Bertie Russell was giving me more assurance as I felt that if he could care for me and like to talk to me it meant that I was not so very stupid and dull", she wrote in her diary. "Also my intimacy with him was leading me back into a more natural and serious world of thought than I had drifted into by my attempts to adapt myself to *****, who had been mocking and jealous of my efforts to develop my intellectual side, for he liked to keep intellectual superiority over his female friends. Also ***** was entirely lacking in the instinct of responsibility for the welfare of the nation – an instinct which both Bertie and I have probably inherited, as each of us had come out of many generations of an historical family."

Yet even in these halcyon first few months there were hints of the recurrent disagreements of following years. Thus before summer there was something of a crisis, almost certainly about sex. Some months later Russell would write of it, "I remember now the exact spot in the woods at Peppard where you said Studland seemed very long ago, & I remember just the stab of pain it caused me to realise how you had changed."

During the summer, as their exchange of confidences grew more intimate, Russell revealed how Ottoline was not his second but his third love. As early as April he had said that after Alys he had "loved once again, nine years ago: but that was unhappy, & died a gradual death for want of nourishment". Now he expanded on the situation in a poem.

Thrice have I loved. Once in the morning dew,
Singing with spring-time birds a careless strain,
Forgetting earth, I soared to heaven, and knew
Joys that forget the burden of man's pain.

Again I loved. Piercing the prison of flame,
Where one stern soul in lonely anguish burned,
Forgetting earth once more with love I came
Into that hell whence no light hopes returned.

Once more I love, and married in my love,
Heaven and hell have made this earth divine;
Grief deep as hell, joy vast as heaven above,
Mingle their fires and through man's labours shine.

But he refused to be drawn about details. "The one thing I absolutely must not tell about is what happened 9 years ago. It is possible I may be able to some day. At present I am absolutely bound not to." A few days later, he sent a letter which intrigued Ottoline even more.

First, you must not wish me to make friendships with women. Mrs. Whitehead I have a friendship with which I would not lose for a great deal – indeed could not lose. Lucy Silcox [headmistress of the school to which Ottoline had sent her daughter] I know well and like greatly; but she is not really important to me. Believe me, I *know* I am right in saying it is better I should avoid intimacy with other women. You will make a grave mistake if you go against this knowledge.

The mention of Evelyn Whitehead may have aroused Ottoline's first suspicions. However, Mrs Whitehead was still providing a meeting-place at her Chelsea home, and still passing on from the unwitting Alys a running intelligence-report of what was going on in that enemy camp. Ottoline, wisely, did not press the point.

Throughout June and July he persevered in his attempts to initiate Ottoline into the mysteries of his work. He did not have to start entirely from scratch. At the age of twenty-four she had been interested in philosophy and had attended the course on logic at St Andrews University, taking this subject rather than philosophy itself because David Ritchie, who held the chair of logic and metaphysics, was considered the best professor in the university. A man who "considered that the ultimate value of religion depended on the ideal it set before mankind when represented in its highest form", he had helped mould the Ottoline of fourteen years later.

Russell was, he now wrote to her, anxious to "explain obversion, inversion, reversion, introversion, extroversion, etc. etc. Perhaps by the time you are 60, I shall think the moment come for applying logic to some of the simpler problems of life, such as the proof that business is business or boys will be boys." At times love got its lines crossed with philosophy, as when he wrote that the following was a geometrical proof in the manner of Spinoza of a proposition it was important she should know.

Axiom I. The attraction between one and another person is directly proportional to the merit of the other person & inversely proportional to the square of the distance between us. Axiom II. O is one object of infinite merit. Axiom III. The distance between O and me is zero. The pupil is expected to construct both the proposition & its proof from the above data, remembering that the letter "O" stands for the "object". I have endeavoured to produce belief in the proposition by the intuitive method, which points out the number of facts both explicable by any other hypotheses, but in the end the geometrico-deductive method is the best. It is hoped that this method will produce the desired result in the reader.

Late in July he finished *The Problems of Philosophy*, sent it to the publishers and shortly afterwards posted a second copy to Whitehead. Then, in mid-August, Ottoline left England for Marienbad, leaving Philip at Peppard with their daughter Julian. Russell followed, crossing the Channel second-class to avoid being recognized by fellow-travellers, staying at a hotel near to Ottoline's and visiting her daily until being forbidden to do so by the hotel-manager. Philip arrived soon after Russell's departure and was told by the vindictive manager that a gentleman had come to see his wife every day. Rising to the occasion, Philip said he was very glad to hear she had had company.

Russell returned to Cambridge without having been recognized *en route*, or missed. "I arrived without having seen a soul I knew, which was lucky." Moreover, none of the letters awaiting him had needed an immediate reply, and he believed himself safely out of the wood. He was soon disillusioned. "Alys had guessed or discovered all about Marienbad," he informed Ottoline. "She told Mrs. W. that for the first time you had gone abroad without either P. or your maid, & that I was not to be found at Ipsden. She urged Mrs. W. to write there to see if I answered – couldn't see that that was not a thing to do . . . I don't know how Alys knew you hadn't taken your maid. She knows a lot somehow." However, there were no repercussions and he got down to the work to hand: masses of proofs, an invitation from the Heretics, the Cambridge discussion society, to read what was to be a famous paper on Bergson, and a letter from the former Ivy Pretious, now married to Charles Tennyson.

The letter, begging him not to avoid her, was sent on to Ottoline for advice. "[It] caused me some perplexity," said Russell, apparently fearful of what might happen next, "but I think I must call in London some time – I have really no right not to renew the acquaintance, as the need for philanthropy is past." He dealt with Miss Pretious, got through "mountains" of letters, managed half of his proofs and began to think about the Bergson paper. In fine fettle, he went on: "I have the energy of 20 steam engines and can plough through my work at a great rate."

For one thing, he was beginning to realize how useful the writing of *The Problems of Philosophy* had been to him. Nearing the end of the task he had remarked, "Doing this book has given me a map of the theory of knowledge which I hadn't before. From that point of view it will have been a great help in my own work." Months later, dealing with the proofs after virtually forgetting the book, he added, "I am surprised to find how much of my philosophy comes into the S[hilling] S[hocker] – of course in technical writing all sorts of points wd. have to be gone into, & there wd. have to be controversy; but the essentials are all there."

The essentials were the methods by which it was possible for us to know what the physical world really was. Ever since his jettisoning of Idealism, he had believed that knowledge of the external world could be gained only through the senses. Yet science – and particularly "the new physics" with its revelation of the unexpected natures of radio-activity, the nuclear atom and the relativistic world – showed how unreliable the senses could be. Thus the relation of perception to physics became the nub of the problem and, as he wrote years later, this problem occupied him intermittently from 1910 onwards.

In the tentative solution outlined in *The Problems of Philosophy*, Idealism was replaced by a dualism of physical objects, which cause our sense-data, and by mind, which was rather hazily conceived as being the matrix within which sense-data exist. The existence of matter was justified on the evidence of sense-data and certain principles of inference; the existence of mind on the evidence of immediate experience. The world was further divided on the basis of the philosopher's universals and particulars, entities which consist respectively of abstract general ideas such as whiteness, or goodness, and individuated objects such as the white flag or an act of friendship.

In discussing our knowledge of these entities, Russell reflected the urgent demand of his childhood for certainty, reviving a distinction which had a long history in philosophy but had never been fully exploited – the distinction between knowledge by acquaintance and knowledge by description. His work on definite descriptions and logic generally enabled him to defend the thesis, wholly new to him, that any understandable statement must be composed only of constituents known by acquaintance. A statement which on the face of it reported knowledge by description was translatable, by his logical apparatus, into a statement (or statements) containing only elements known by acquaintance. So statements about a physical object such as a chair are translated into statements about sense-data, such as patches of colour, which are known by acquaintance.

Part of this approach had been outlined by Russell in the spring when he addressed the Moral Science Club in his own rooms on "Knowledge by Acquaintance and Knowledge by Description", a paper later read to the Aristotelian Society. He wrote in old age,

> The distinction is quite simple whatever other people may have tried to make you think. A single word of which you know the meaning through having what it means wordlessly pointed out to you is one designating knowledge by acquaintance. This includes all the commonest nouns, such as eyes, and nose, and cat and dog, and also includes the proper names of people you know. Knowledge by de-

scription, on the other hand, requires a phrase consisting of several words, none of them, separately, pointing to a definite object but, taken altogether, sometimes indicating something. Take, say, "the tallest man in the United States". Probably no-one knows who he is, but there no doubt is a definite man to whom this description is applicable.

In the first chapter of *The Problems of Philosophy*, Russell gave these theories practical muscle by pointing out that the painter "wants to know what things seem to be, the practical man and the philosopher want to know what they are; but the philosopher's wish to know this is stronger than the practical man's and is more troubled by knowledge as to the difficulties of answering the question." He then took as the illustrative "thing", the uniform table whose uniform top is "really" the same colour all over, whose appearance seems different under different lights, and whose apparent shape changes with perspective. From this table, which later occupied a position in his examples as common as moving trains and flashes of light in Einstein's Relativity, he led on to the existence of matter and the relationship between the physicist's and the philosopher's world.

While "the Shilling Shocker", Russell's first book on general philosophy, deals essentially with the relationship between human knowledge and the experience on which he stresses it must be based, it went beyond this elementary analysis to emphasize what Russell saw as the need for philosophy in the full life. Philosophy, he says towards the end of the book in a passage which has some of the broad sweep of "The Free Man's Worship", does not merely help "to keep alive that speculative interest in the universe which is apt to be killed by confining ourselves to definitely ascertainable knowledge". Its main good lies elsewhere. With the air of throwing down the gauntlet, he says that

> The life of the instinctive man is shut up within the circle of his private interests: family and friends may be included, but the outer world is not regarded except as it may help or hinder what comes within the circle of instinctive wishes. In such a life there is something feverish and confined, in comparison with which the philosophic life is calm and free. The private world of instinctive interests is a small one, set in the midst of a great and powerful world which must, sooner or later, lay our private world in ruins. Unless we can so enlarge our interests as to include the whole outer world, we remain like a garrison in a beleaguered fortress, knowing that the enemy prevents escape and that ultimate surrender is inevitable. In such a life there is no peace, but a constant strife between the insistence of desire and the powerlessness of will. In one way or another, if our life is to be great and free, we must escape this prison and this strife.

The Problems of Philosophy was particularly unusual in that its material was not only understandable by laymen but was also important enough to be presented to professionals. Not only was chapter five, on "Knowledge by Acquaintance and Knowledge by Description", basically the paper he had read to the Aristotelian Society, but the account of universals and particulars covered much the same ground, in much the same words, as his Presidential Address to the society in the autumn of 1911, "On the Relations of Universals and Particulars".

When the book appeared in 1912, it was mainly the Idealists who found points to carp about; in particular Bernard Bosanquet, with whom Russell had often crossed swords, and who now wrote a pained review in *Mind*, strongly criticizing the author's sharp distinction between universals and particulars. "It is a distinction which divorces the being & logic of his universe from its life and love," he said. "I cannot say how deeply I regret that such a doctrine, absolutely fallacious, as I hold, in logic, and in its general bearing a mere formulation of popular prejudices, should go out to the world with Mr. Russell's great authority." Russell was unabashed. "What *is* one to do with such a resolute confusion between what the world is & what one would like it to be?" he asked. "Bosanquet is typical among philosophers in having never felt the pure intellectual impulse, which merely wants to understand. This vice in philosophers is due to their determination to find religion. They are men of little faith."

Religion was in fact beginning to loom up in his preoccupations, pushed there by Ottoline and held in reserve by her as they read Spinoza or Hume in the woods, discussed the daily round at Cambridge or decided on their next surreptitious rendezvous. She had caught him – or, more accurately, had been caught by him – as he emerged from the dark tunnel of *Principia Mathematica*, and the deep sincerity of her religious convictions immediately began to influence him in a way that would have been impossible a decade earlier, or later.

Certainly his views were at times coloured by the ardent lover's accommodating compromise. Nevertheless, his innermost attitude to revealed religion was to lesser or greater degree affected by Ottoline's persuasion during the first five years of their friendship. Yet if the final reaction to her promptings was to be the bitter denunciation of Christianity which marked the Russell of the 1920s, some of her influence stuck fast. No less a figure than Father D'Arcy, the Catholic theologian, having read Russell's autobiography in 1967, wrote of "being very impressed by the intensity of [his] appreciation of the mystical element". Dean Matthews of St Paul's once wrote that Russell "could have been a saint and a mystic".

Ottoline's religious influence, from which Russell only slowly shook himself free, began to show within a few weeks of the March meeting in Bedford Square. "When we first found each other," he wrote the following year, "everything in me was quite buried and put away. I had all the cruelty of the ascetic. Then . . . the religious things came up & rather overpowered everything else."

At first he was uneasy about the change. "In very early days," he admitted, "I had a feeling of treachery to what I believe most deeply when I became sympathetic to your religious outlook, & that gave me a recurrent mental aloofness." But the most obdurate aloofness had difficulties in the face of Ottoline's charms. "It is funny about religion," he was soon writing. "I should have said beforehand that I shd. mind you believing in God & a future life – but now I only feel I *ought* to mind. I must some day try to tell you why I don't believe in them – but at present it seems dusty & I feel it doesn't matter."

The conflict between what he believed and what he was trying not to believe had to be analysed and resolved if he were ever to have peace. As early as May 1911 he had written,

> I want to get free from business, & away from purely technical jobs, & really try to write out something of what I live by in the way of faith. It will take time, because of jobs already undertaken; but it will come about gradually, more & more. And if you can have leisure & health you can make all the difference to me in that – because I should write everything for you in the first instance, & then prune it to do for others.

A groping for a different kind of faith from Ottoline's was the response to a religion which was a mixture of the conventional and the imaginative. She believed in the immortality common to many revealed religions, and in their accounting methods which balance good deeds against bad, and the minor purgatories of this world against the rewards to come. Yet her run-of-the-mill acceptance of what had been pumped into her as a child was set against a background of mystic wonder at natural beauty; at the inexplicables of the world; and at the things which she failed to understand, a category which included much natural science but less of human nature.

Under her influence, Russell began to adulterate the brave pessimism of "The Free Man's Worship". His position, that of a dyed-in-the-wool agnostic desperately in love with a religiously devout woman, was delicate. He was honest enough not to conceal his feelings yet sufficiently infatuated to fear that his views might cause trouble. From the first, therefore, he played down those dogmatic points on which he knew they would disagree, played up the underlying beliefs which he hoped they had in common. In particular he was always careful to pay tribute to Mother Julian of the Truro Sisterhood, a vital and sympathetic *religieuse* whom Ottoline had met some years earlier and whose combination of saintliness and modernity – "she read all Wells's novels as they came out"–influenced her life more than did Russell's scepticism. He told her,

> More than 20 years ago, with infinite slow pain, I put away God. Now you revive the old pain, & it is greater because of all the accumulated experience of sorrow which would be transformed by Him. Your bird that you gave to Mother Julian, your Mantegna, & your prayers–I can't tell you how profoundly I feel them–it is like the ghost of a dead friend speaking poignant words & then vanishing into the night.

But if there was a vestigial desire for the cosy comfort of belief, Russell still knew that it was not genuinely for him. He wrote to her,

> Your belief only survives because you do not believe in reason. That is the serious division, not God who is a mere symptom. When I say you don't believe in reason, I mean that passionate feeling seems to you a ground for belief, which exempts one from further minute examination. When I am with you I am not conscious of antagonism, I am only conscious of intense endeavour to find ways of meeting on fundamental things without being false to my creed. My view is that passionate feeling is often sufficient ground for judging things good or bad, but not for judging that they exist.

So they would argue things out sensibly, as rational human beings. At least, he hoped they would. But whatever he hoped, he knew that in argument he would be unable to restrain himself, that although his opponent was Ottoline, his bite would still be worse than his bark, and that unless he was careful he would do her emotional injury. He tried to reassure her:

> It is true that I shall sometimes publicly attack things which you believe, but it will be for the sake of other things that you will also believe. It is my business in life to do my best to discover the truth about such things, & to explain what I have come to think, & why. I do not think it matters so much what people believe, as how they believe it. People who are speculatively minded cannot believe honestly anything they have not tested by every possible test–& a belief which is not honest is poisonous. Among philosophers, belief seems to me generally purchased by some sacrifice to truthfulness, & so I find myself combating it. But it interests me far more to try to preserve what I value than to attack what I disagree with. Only, I think the absolutely fearless pursuit of truth is the first condition of right-thinking for me and for all who spend much time on abstract thought. And so attacking what seem to me comfortable fictions is bound up with my positive beliefs, & has to be done along

with the rest. But you will know the spirit in which I do it, & you will not mind, will you, Dearest?

She did not mind; at least, not very much – possibly because throughout the first eighteen months of their relationship her power over him steadily increased, its upward line taking only an occasional minor lurch downwards after he had made the rare mistake of confronting one of her beliefs head-on. He wrote to her somewhat bitterly, after one discussion,

> You with your God and your immortality escape the hardest things, the eternal partings, the waste, the sense of injuries which can never be repaired. How anyone can believe that a good God devised such a hell is astonishing to me. You & I are among the very most fortunate of mankind, but tho' we are happy now, we have both suffered much in the past, & one of us at least will in all likelihood suffer more in the future than in the past. Few people would inflict so much on their worst enemy – yet God inflicts much more on most people.

But it was not all iconoclasm. "To give religion to those who cannot believe in God & immortality has been for years my deepest hope," he wrote in August 1911, "but the fire left me, & I lost faith. Now I have a deeper, wider, calmer vision than ever before, & your faith makes mine easy."

By this time he had already tried to put down his beliefs in a form which would suggest that they were not wholly irreconcilable with hers. This was "Prisons", an intellectual discussion of the philosophy of religion in which he desperately tried to bridge the gulf between his own views and Ottoline's. "The world's a prison and Denmark one of the worst wards" was a line, he told her, that had once been constantly in his mind – "& now there is no prison for me. I reach out to the stars, & through the ages, & everywhere the radiance of your love lights the world for me."

In this exhilarated mood he had set to work – while still grappling with *Principia* proofs and *The Problems of Philosophy*. "I feel like Napoleon playing 6 games of chess and dictating to 7 secretaries all at the same time," he wrote. He began work on the book at Ipsden, having forecast that the atmosphere there would give him ideal conditions. "If they will let me have a key & spend half the night walking about, it will be best of all," he added. "If I can do something great it will set your conscience at rest. If it turns out as I hope, it might be to our time what 'Sartor Resartus' was to an earlier generation. I believe together we have the capacity for it." But he sensed his limitations. "I have no skill in that sort of thing," he wrote a few days later; "it is a pity: it would gain by some imaginative setting."

Lacking this, he decided to handle in more academic fashion what he later described as a statement of how easily human life becomes a prison and how religion should be the escape from it. The first chapter, he said, would deal with the nature and value of religion which

> provides worship, acquiescence, love. Some discussion of nature of worship. Contemplation to a great extent, provides all 3. Must learn to view things in regard to which we can act as we should view things in regard to which we cannot act. This requires a discipline, through contemplation, where action is impossible. This discipline in following chaps. *Chap. II* The world of universals. Will deal with math'cs. etc. showing their value. *Chap. III* The physical world. Deals with the empire of matter, the immensity of space, & the beauty of nature. *Chap. IV* The Past. Here objects contemplated are of same sort as those in regard to which we have to act, but being past we see them without distortion. Value of history. At this point, the preliminary discipline is supposed finished, & we apply contemplation to purify emotion & action. *Chap. V* Contemplation & the Emotions. *Chap. VI* Contemplation & Action. *Chap. VII* Union with the universe. These chaps. will merely expand what I wrote before; I think the last might actually be what I wrote before, which sews up the whole. I don't know what to call the book. "On Contemplative Freedom" or "The Religion of Contemplation"?

Even here, deeply moved and deeply committed, his passion rubs incongruously against practicalities. Thus after outlining the development of "Prisons" he continues, "The Vision is very strong in me tonight – the night is unbelievably beautiful & the wind is full of mystic wonder. I finished my last Chapter of the S[hilling] S[hocker] before tea, & sent it to be typed . . . I took some sentences on Contemplation out of the Prisons MS & the denunciation of those who make man the measure of all things." Even at this stage, before he had become the prolific polemical writer, he took care to get the maximum mileage out of all he wrote.

From the first, Russell was uncomfortable about "Prisons", a feeling reinforced when he showed it to the Whiteheads. "[Alfred] has not read it yet & tells me he doesn't expect to be able to get through it – anything ethical bores him," he reported to Ottoline.

> Mrs. W. criticised it very severely – not the ideas, which she agrees with, but the style. She says it is dull – the most severe criticism there is. She says it appears *voulu*, that the emotions spoken of are not spoken of so as to be felt; & that the intellectual & emotional parts don't belong together. The gist of the matter is that being written when I was happy it fails to appeal to those who are not so – not that she put it that way. I knew in my instincts she would not like it. She says the beauty of "The Free Man's Worship" is lacking.

1 Bertrand Russell as a boy

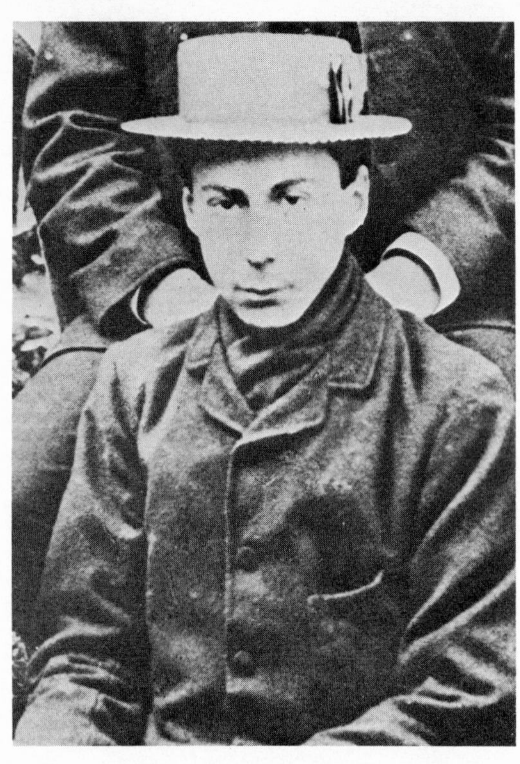

2 Russell as an undergraduate at Cambridge

3 The Pearsall Smith family at Friday's Hill, Fernhurst, about 1894: (*front, left to right*) Robert Pearsall Smith, Karin Costelloe, Hannah Pearsall Smith, Ray Costelloe, Mary Costelloe (later Mrs Bernard Berenson); (*back*) Alys, Logan

4 Russell and Alys, 1894

5 Friday's Hill: (*left to right*) Hannah Pearsall Smith, Robert Pearsall Smith, Alys, Logan, about 1894

6 Alys in her wedding-dress, 13 December 1894

7 Russell about 1896

8 Alys outside the door of Millhanger, Fernhurst, 1897

These reactions are significant pointers not only to the quality of "Prisons", a manuscript which has never come to light, but to the extent of Russell's feelings during the intellectual honeymoon. Alfred Whitehead, claiming that ethics bored him, was clearly skirting the unpleasant task of telling the truth; Mrs Whitehead, who certainly understood Russell, implies that he was writing largely for Ottoline's benefit. "Prisons", she later told him, "has the dullness that comes to middle-aged men when they marry."

He took the criticisms to heart, worried away at the manuscript for the next few weeks and as late as mid-December was asking Ottoline's advice. She had her opinions. Russell had his, and the manuscript was worked over intermittently during the early weeks of 1912. Then it quietly slid from view as a book, although Russell was to incorporate material from the last chapter in "The Essence of Religion" which was to appear in the October 1912 issue of the *Hibbert Journal*.

"Prisons" had been started as Russell grappled with *The Problems of Philosophy*. The prolonged inquest on it was held as he prepared for the Michaelmas Term and sought about for something on Bergson to add to the paper on Bergson's philosophy, written a few months later and published in the *Monist*. He had little regard for Bergson's battle against the influence of logic, or for his attempt to explain evolution by a creative urge. "One of his chapters", he noted to Ottoline, "ends with a wonderful peroration in which he compares human life to a cavalry charge – he describes the whole human race careering so madly that they pass all obstacles, 'perhaps even Death'. I think after a cavalry charge lasting 70 years one would be sorry to pass that obstacle successfully."

Quite fortuitously, he had the chance of listening to Bergson, whose beliefs he regarded as "merely traditional mysticism expressed in slightly novel language", and whose language itself he considered "that of the company-promoter rather than the philosopher", at the Aristotelian Society at the end of October. The evening meeting cut short his time with Ottoline so that he "felt like a gourmet who has been given the most wonderful soup & then told that is his whole dinner for tonight". However, it was almost worth it, sitting between Bergson himself and Francis Younghusband, the soldier, explorer and mystic of whom he approved at first sight. Back in Cambridge the following day, he described how some of the company had dealt with the great man.

> Shaw explained Bergson's philosophy lucidly, Bergson protesting that that was not what he had meant, & Shaw patronisingly silencing him. Shaw said we wanted to get rid of the oriental element in religion at which Zangwill fired up. They struck me as pert street-boys, laughing at the policeman because they know it is not worth his while to

notice them. They all professed such marvellous power over matter that they seemed to be Gods.

While research for the main Bergson paper continued the problem of the *pied-à-terre* in London had been solved by the discovery of a small flat in Russell Chambers, Bury Street, Bloomsbury. This was ideal; the nearby Morrell home at 44 Bedford Square gave Ottoline permanent justification for being seen in the area and the British Museum did the same for Russell. She supplied rugs, pictures and basket-chairs, while Alys sent up Lord John's desk, silver and linen, and the small table, made out of Doomsday-book oak, at which Russell had written the *Principia*. To mark the start of a new era he bought a Cambridge–London season ticket. This enabled him, he wrote with a touch of abandon, to go up and down as often as may be without extravagance.

It was now November. A few weeks later Ottoline moved to the Morrells' Black Hall in Oxford for Christmas, and Russell prepared to spend the holiday with the Whiteheads at their Wiltshire cottage. "While I am in the midst of the Whiteheads' family life I feel very much separated from you – what is going on is so insistent & makes so many different appeals that it is difficult not to feel as if you were a dream," he was soon writing. "I go back in feeling to the times when I have been with them & past years claim me. It has been a day full of jollity – Xmas dinner, charades, songs & so on. I like to be there – but inwardly I have a feeling of remoteness."

The feeling was to be relieved within forty-eight hours. Before leaving London they had arranged to escape from their respective house-parties for a day as soon as possible, and on the 27th they met in Russell's flat for 1.30 luncheon and early tea. And here, about religion, they had their first serious row. It escalated into an argument threatening to end the whole affair.

Ottoline stayed longer than intended and missed her fast train back to Oxford. He left later for Marlborough. Each wrote letters to the other as they travelled back, Russell posting his as he changed trains at Reading. She, fearful that she was going to lose him, sent a "bless you" telegram on arrival in Oxford. But the argument was ominous, with Russell reluctant to slacken the assault on her beliefs and Ottoline fearing that, beneath his protestations of love, he would regard her as dishonest.

He compromised as much as conscience allowed, and retrieved the situation in a spate of letters which claimed his beliefs were not really incompatible with hers. On December 29,

> What you call God is very much what I call infinity. I do feel something in common in all the great things – something which I should not think of quite as you do, tho' it is very mysterious & I really don't know what to think of it – but I feel it is the most important

thing in the world & really the one thing that matters profoundly. It is to me as yet a mystery – I don't understand it. I think it has many manifestations – love is the one that seems to me deepest & that I feel most when I am very deeply moved. But truth is the one I have mainly served, & truth is the only one I *always* feel the divinity of . . .

And the following day,

I think Christ was right to put love of God before love of my neighbour. Only I don't think God *exists* ready-made. I think he is an idea we can conceive & can do something to create, tho' he will never exist *fully*. That is why human actions are important – *because* God does not exist already. There is of course one *great* difference between your beliefs and mine. I do not think any spiritual force outside human beings actually helps us – there may be such a force, but if so it is only as incarnated in human beings that it helps us. Therefore I cannot pray or lean on God. What strength I need I must get from myself or those whom I advise. And this view does seem to me nobler, sterner, braver than the view which looks for help from without, besides seeming to me truer . . .

He felt strongly and planned to put his case to her in Oxford but at the last minute she cancelled the meeting. Mrs Morrell, she decided, would be suspicious if she were away for too long, and Philip had – reluctantly one gathers – advised that it would be unsafe for them to meet.

The austere guide-lines for moral self-sufficiency which he had put forward during what he later called "the Christmas crisis" covered only one side of the Russell coin. The other, put forward frequently during the next few years, revealed a totally different character, showman rather than philosopher, hungry for action as well as for thought. It was this second Russell who could explain to Ottoline not only his deepest religious impulses but also what he called his "*real* morality" apart from thoughts and principles. He had discovered it, as he had discovered the departure of his love for Alys, while bicycling.

I was much amused by it. It is, to behave as one might in grand opera or in epic poetry. That is why my violence does not offend me, whereas taking up with a woman for whom I have no passion does offend me. I could behave like Hamlet or Othello or even Macbeth without feeling degraded, but if I behaved like Richard Feverel I should not think myself fit to live. It came to me through thinking of Tristan & Isolde, & of how rapturous it would be to die together like the people in Rosmersholm. I am afraid it is a morality hardly suited to this age. This is only my morality of passion; besides that, I have an ascetic morality of religion, & my intellectual morality of thought. You will see from all this that I am out of the wood, & enjoying life again.

Ottoline had by no means won the day. She might have been vaguely surprised at Russell's comment to Gilbert Murray that he had been writing on religion, "only my own, but also devilish edifying". But she was nevertheless beginning to sap the high wall of agnosticism with which he had surrounded himself. That she got no further was the result not only of a limit to his powers of adaptation but of exterior circumstance which was to weaken their togetherness far sooner than either expected.

There was still the hankering to concentrate on philosophy, although philosophy of a more popular, less technical, nature. He had been side-tracked by Ottoline, but he was already coming back to the path he was really intent on pursuing. In the last weeks of 1911 he wrote that

> During this past year I have written 3 Paris lectures (of which 2 are published & the 3rd soon will be), my shilling shocker, the Aristn. paper, & Prisons. Considering how much time has been taken up in lectures & proofs & seeing pupils, I don't feel seriously dissatisfied. But I have an uneasiness about philosophy altogether; what remains for *me* to do in philosophy (I mean in *technical* philosophy) does not seem of first-rate importance. The shilling shocker really seems to me better worth doing. It is all puzzling and obscure. For so many years I have had absolutely no choice as to work, that I have got out of the way of wondering what is best to do. I think really the important thing is to make the ideas I already have intelligible. And I ought to try to get away from pedantry. My feelings have changed about all this; I did think the technical philosophy that remains for me to do very important indeed.
>
> I will try to write out what I think about philosophy; it will help to clear up my own ideas. All the historic problems of philosophy seem to me either insoluble or soluble by methods which are not philosophical, but mathematical or scientific. The last word of philosophy on all of them seems to me to be that *a priori* any of the alternatives is possible. Thus e.g. as to God: traditional philosophy proved him: I think some forms of God impossible, some possible, none necessary. As to immortality: philosophy can only say it may be true or it may be false; any more definite answer would have to come from psychical research. As to whether nothing exists except mind: philosophy, it seems to me, can only say that all the arguments adduced on either side are fallacious, & that there is absolutely no evidence either way. And I should say the same of optimism & pessimism. Except as a stimulus to the imagination, almost the only use of philosophy, I should say, is to combat errors induced by science & religion. Religion says all things work together for good: philo-

sophy says this belief is groundless. Science leads people to think there is no absolute good & bad, but only evolved beliefs about good & bad which are useful to gregarious animals in the struggle for existence; philosophy equally says *this* belief is groundless.

All this is rather dismal. But as a stimulus to the imagination I think philosophy *is* important. But this use is not so much for the technical philosopher, but rather for the man who wants to see his own special pursuit connected with the cosmos; therefore it is popular rather than technical philosophy that fulfils this need. This is fundamentally why I think it is more useful to write popular than technical philosophy.

Still seeking certainty, he was now anxious to explain the task in simple words.

7

Enter Wittgenstein

By the start of 1912, Russell should, on the face of things, have been sailing into calmer waters. His *affaire* with Ottoline had been successfully manœuvred round two dangerous corners, and if he was now forced to live a double life, that was an experience which the conspirator in him rather enjoyed. The emotional block had been removed and his pent-up sexual demands at least partly satisfied, a relief which meant more to him than to many men – "how right you are about chastity," he wrote to a woman friend years later. "I gave it a good try once, but never again." Intellectually, also, he now seemed to be on easier ground. He had recovered, abilities unimpaired, from the punishing mental demands of *Principia*, while *The Problems of Philosophy* was soon to be the first success in the semi-popular writing at which he was to become such a dab hand.

Yet neither emotionally nor intellectually was the immediate future to be as calm as it looked. Ottoline's connubial loyalty was to become increasingly irksome. He thought of breaking with her entirely, an escape-route contemplated at regular intervals. As always, he failed to take it.

Intellectually, also, he was soon being pulled in opposite directions. He saw the value of popular writing, both as a duty and as an exercise which cleared his own thoughts; but having grappled with the complexities of *Principia* he was satisfied with nothing less than working at full stretch. From the first months of 1912, therefore, he began to concentrate his efforts on the theory of knowledge and the problem of matter, two complex and interlinked subjects being made even more complex by the new atomic theories of Thomson, Rutherford and Bohr. The effect of these conflicting demands on his time, combined with the strain put on his emotions, gives his life during 1912 – and indeed until the whole pattern was changed by the outbreak of war in August 1914 – a kaleidoscopic, almost patchwork air, in which the only constant factor is the background of university terms.

The galaxy of talent at Cambridge included not only Moore, Keynes and Hardy, but also a miscellany of walk-on characters who in any other company would seem larger than life. The galaxy, moreover, was soon to be overshadowed by the figure of Ludwig Wittgenstein, enigmatic and slightly ominous, disruptive, unpredictable, striding at the most unearthly hours from his own room to Russell's, and with equal bull-headedness along the narrow path dividing genius from madness.

Russell wrote to Lucy Donnelly,

> I do not come in contact with very many people – not more than 20 in each year – but those few I see a great deal of. They drop into my rooms at odd times, & come to my Thursday evenings; I try to civilise them, accustom them to free talk, liberalism, religion, politics, whatever comes up. Sometimes we have a regular Platonic dialogue, beginning with the young man propounding a rash thesis, going on to the dogmatic fallacious refutation by another young man, whom I sit on; then I take up the matter in a Socratic way; after perhaps 3 hours the young man sees that the world is not so simple as he thought. That seems to me the sort of thing that education really consists of, and that is independent of the system.

These Thursday "squashes", limited to fifteen since that was the number of Russell's chairs and coffee-cups, had a stern earnestness which contrasted strongly with a strain of the facetious which might have shocked his pupils had they known of it. "In my lecture yesterday I changed my mind in the middle," he wrote in March 1912.

> I had gone to prove that there probably is an external world but the argument seemed to me fallacious when I began to give it, so I proved to my class that there was no reason to think anything existed except myself – at least no *good* reason – no such reason as would influence a man in investing money, for instance. That was very sad, but it doesn't seem to matter much. It made a better lecture than if it had been more pat.

The light-heartedness was real, the new effervescent Russell, never far below the surface, bubbling up through even the high seriousness of philosophy. However, there were constant problems in combining the life of a Cambridge don with that of the Bury Street romantic. At Cambridge he had the benefits of the lecturer's job, while writing and coaching added a taste of jam to the bread-and-butter. But that was all. A good deal of the money he had inherited at twenty-one had already been spent, and a letter to Ottoline helps explain his genuine shortage of cash.

> I have grown more and more careful about spending money as time went on. It is one of the things I have a vigorous conscience about. I save money on clothes & cabs & books, & I try to travel cheaply & only when it is important. I have given away large sums

of my capital, because definite things seemed so important that I couldn't keep it, & also because I am afraid of growing stingy as I grow older. But if I had spent money on myself, I should not have procured any admirable result. I have always been willing to spend any sum on keeping efficient. – I quite agree that politics is *the* important thing. But just when I am thinking of getting a new great coat, I get a letter from some young man, educated but penniless, who will be all right in a few years if he can just get enough food to keep alive till he gets work – & so on. I don't as a rule help weak people – I help strong people who will soon need no more help. And I have found that very successful – it produces successful useful self-reliant people, whereas weak people never grow independent of one's help if they have once grown used to it.

Never an extravagant liver, he rubbed along contentedly enough, if rather frugally. "I dined at an inn on my way from the station – cold lamb and stewed apricots – and got to my rooms at 9.30," he said on returning to Cambridge from London one evening,

found stacks of proofs as expected, wrote some letters, sorted & dated your letters & put them into their box & made a bonfire of the envelopes, & got to bed before 12. This mng. my 2 young men arrived as I was finishing breakfast (2 boiled eggs as always) & talked to them for 1½ hours about fractions, real numbers, positive & negative, & such topics. Then I read my paper, with much pleasure in Asquith's announcement [Mr Asquith's revelation that the government intended to ignore the Lords' amendments to the Parliament Bill, and had obtained the king's agreement to exercise the Royal Prerogative and overcome resistance to the bill]. Then I looked through some of the proofs & took a sheet to the Press; since then I have written a number of letters, lunched (bread & marmalade as always) & begun looking through the typed stuff about tables etc. (I hope you noticed that the table was not your table, but the big one I found here). I have to finish this, take the other chapters to be done, look through 2 sheets of proofs & lecture again Monday.

His life, not spartan after Pembroke Lodge but in striking contrast to the champagne-for-breakfast programme of Frank, was softened by the affection which he felt for Cambridge in general and for Trinity in particular. "Here I have the sort of love of every separate stone & tree & corner that only comes of long association," he wrote. "... There is an odd satisfaction about having a place in a machine – it makes one less dependent upon one's inner springs." He also enjoyed the academic life itself, the closed professional shop whose members had few links with the privateering world outside and saw little reason for forging any. He kept the interest in Women's Suffrage and Free Trade which had roused him a few years earlier; he followed international affairs with a keen if donnish eye, and frequently castigated the iniquities of politicians. But in all this he was still the objective observer, looking out from his privileged watch-tower and only slowly becoming aware of the savage cut-and-thrust through which Ottoline was trying to help Philip along his rocky road towards the top.

"First McTaggart came before the official time, to discuss the nature of aggregates, on which depends (so it seems) his 'proof' that the universe is good," he wrote of one typical evening in the Cambridge cocoon.

> Then came a number of Moral Science men, Geach, the ex-High Churchman who has become a materialist; Dorward, a solemn Scotchman, silent but rather able; Ogden, Secretary of the Heretics; Chrouschoff, a very lazy Russian (he has no sense of humour, and was a little vexed by some very harmless jokes I made at his expense); Larrington, a man who has been in a Bank but is now doing economics, a Conservative Free Trader, older than most undergraduates, & more real, very likeable; and Hardy came in for a time. We talked about Bergson, whether lectures serve any purpose (I hold they don't), the philosophy of religion, universals & particulars, & various other topics. I enjoy having the young men – being less hard-worked and less part of the machine than most of the dons, I can give them more freshness than most of the others can.

It was a good enough life, in spite of the penalties sometimes to be paid. "After dinner I got entangled among a lot of old people – Horace Darwin, Lord Farrar, Sir Henry Hardinge Cunynghame of the Home Office, & J. J. Thomson," he complained on one occasion to Ottoline. "They talked about sea-sickness, livers, rattle-snakes and such things – all the dull topics elderly gentlemen love. I escaped as soon as I could."

But the penalties were more than counter-balanced by his "young men", the bright mathematical undergraduates who were to continue the work he and Whitehead had started. The most remarkable was Wittgenstein, the cantankerous, inscrutable figure who had entered Russell's life the previous autumn and who did not leave it completely until he died nearly forty years later. He had been a disciple of Russell's for some time, but not until February 1912 did he become a member of Trinity, and not until the following June did the Degree Committee of the Special Board for Moral Science admit him to a course of research as an Advanced Student and formally ask Russell "to be kind enough to act as the Director and Supervisor of the Student".

Their first meeting had been in October 1911. Russell had returned to his rooms for tea, read Ottoline's latest letter, and begun discussion with C. K. Ogden, later for the *Cambridge Magazine*, and later still the originator of Basic English, when a tall, gangling visitor arrived, knowing very little English but refusing to speak German. Russell explained,

> He turned out to be a man who had learned engineering at Charlottenburg, but during his course had acquired, by himself, a passion for the philosophy of math's, & has now come to Cambridge on purpose to hear me. This took till 5.15: in the next few minutes I settled my business with Ogden, & then went off to my lecture, where I found my German duly established. I lectured very well, owing to excitement and insufficient preparation. I am much interested in my German, & shall hope to see a lot of him.

Wittgenstein was twenty-two, not German as Russell had at first thought, but Austrian, a son who had severely disappointed his father by so far deserting common sense as to study philosophy. In Russell's opinion he was "perhaps the most perfect example [he had] ever known of genius as traditionally conceived, passionate, profound, intense and dominating", and he now crashed into Russell's own field and began to cultivate it with a vigour and professionalism that Russell himself appreciated more quickly than most of his contemporaries.

From the first, he knew that he was up against something exceptional. "My German friend threatens to be an infliction," he wrote a few days after the first meeting; "he came back with me after my lecture & argued till dinner-time – obstinate & perverse, but I think not stupid." The visit outlined the future pattern, and throughout the next few weeks Russell was full of complaints. "My German engineer very argumentative & tiresome" – "My lecture went off all right – my German ex-engineer, as usual, maintained his thesis that there is nothing in the world except asserted propositions, but at last I told him it was too large a theme" – "My German engineer, I think is a fool. He thinks nothing empirical is knowable – I asked him to admit that there was not a rhinoceros in the room, but he wouldn't." Years later Russell recalled how he had "looked under all the desks without finding one, but [Wittgenstein] remained unconvinced".

Within the month Russell had almost had enough. "My ferocious German came & argued at me after my lecture," he wrote on 16 November. "He is armour-plated against all assaults of reasoning – it is really rather a waste of time talking with him." However, the turning-point was near. Wittgenstein, like the late Lord Cherwell whose Continental ancestry often poked through his bowler-hatted Englishness, could sink obstinacy in a sea of charm when he wanted to, and after Russell had called on his pupil for the first time, Ottoline noticed a change of tone. "I am getting to like him," she was told; "he is literary, very musical, pleasant-mannered (being an Austrian) & I *think* really intelligent." But now he faced Russell with a question more brutally direct than was expected from a student.

> My German is hesitating between philosophy & aviation; he asked me today whether I thought he was utterly hopeless at philosophy, & I told him I didn't know but I thought not. I asked him to bring me something written to help me judge. He has money, & is quite passionately interested in philosophy, but he feels he ought not to give his life to it unless he is some good. I feel the responsibility rather, as I really don't know what to think of his ability.

Doubt was removed by Wittgenstein's paper. "Very good, much better than my English pupils do," was Russell's verdict. "I shall certainly encourage him. Perhaps he will do great things." A month later it seemed that he might. Wittgenstein brought Russell "a very good original suggestion, which I think is right, on an important point in logic". More was to follow, and the Austrian was soon being accepted by Russell as part of the philosophical future. "Moore thinks enormously highly of [his] brains [and] says he always feels W. *must* be right when they disagree," Ottoline was told. "He says during his lectures W. always looks frightfully puzzled, but nobody else does. I am glad to be confirmed in my high opinion of W. – the young men don't think much of him, or if they do it is only because Moore & I praise him." The impression of "odd man out", of whom the most unexpected might be expected, was strengthened a few days later. "I like Wittgenstein more and more," Russell wrote.

> He has the theoretical passion *very* strongly – it is a very rare passion & one is glad to find it. He doesn't want to prove this or that, but to find out how things really are. He is very excitable & rather sad, but has excellent manners – tho' in argument he forgets about manners & simply says what he thinks. In spite of it all, tho', something about him makes him a bore. In his flat moments, he still talks, slowly, stammering, & saying dull things. But at his best he is splendid. There is very much more in him than in any of my other pupils.

To Lucy Donnelly he was equally enthusiastic. Wittgenstein "never believes what I say, & always has admirable reason for his dissent; it is not *barren* dissent, but that of a man who has absorbed what one has to teach & gone farther. *He* has *no* respect for authority, which is a great comfort to me."

Wittgenstein was excitable, full of a boiling passion which might, as Russell put it, drive him anywhere. "He has more passion about philosophy than I have," he ruefully admitted.

> His avalanches make mine seem mere snowballs. He has pure intellectual passion in the highest degree; it makes me love him. His

> disposition is that of an artist, intuitive & moody. He says every morning he begins his work with hope & every evening he ends in despair – he has just the sort of rage when he can't understand things that I have ...
>
> And later: "I have the most perfect intellectual sympathy with him – the same passion and vehemence, the same feeling that one must understand or die, the same sudden jokes breaking down the frightful tension of thought."

Even more auspicious was his performance in Nevile's Court during the sessions that went on into the small hours. "In discussion with him I put out *all* my force & only just equal him," Russell admitted. "With all my other pupils I shd. squash them flat if I did so."

It was not only philosophical matters on which they disagreed. Forty years later Russell said bluntly to a friend, "Wittgenstein was witty but was a homosexual." To Ottoline, at least in writing, he merely passed on innumerable veiled and disapproving hints. Though never believing that homosexuality should be illegal, he exhibited a personal distaste for the subject, shying away from it with the prudishness of a Victorian matron confronted with the word "legs".

In March 1912, Wittgenstein left Cambridge to spend the vacation in Austria, rather formally telling Russell that the happiest hours of his life had been spent in his rooms. "When he left I was strangely excited by him," he told Ottoline. "I love him & feel he will solve the problems that I am too old to solve – all kinds of vital problems that are raised by my work, but want a fresh mind and the vigour of youth," he went on a few days later.

> He is *the* young man one hopes for. But as is usual with such men, he is unstable, and may go to pieces. His vigour & life is such a comfort after the washed-out Cambridge type. His attitude justifies all I have hoped about my work ... he has even the same similes as I have – a wall, parting him from the truth, which he must pull down somehow. After our last discussion, he said: "Well, there's a bit of wall pulled down."

With term finished, Wittgenstein gone, and Ottoline in Paris for Easter, Russell decided on a brisk and solitary week's walking. Loneliness, the turbulent spring weather, and the realization that he had been in love with her for a year, created an uprush of emotion and an uninhibited outpouring which reveals a Russell of rising forty with a sharp eye for nature and a romantic depression with the universe.

On the evening of 19 March he dined with the Whiteheads, heard Karl Pearson lecture, then returned to his flat still uncertain where he would travel the following day. Chance brought him to the station in time to catch a West Country "slow", and he spent most of the day impatiently hoping he would reach Lulworth on the Dorset coast that evening. He was unlucky and spent the night at Wool, six miles inland. But he had written Ottoline two letters in the train, posting them at stations *en route*, and had caught a glimpse of the hills above Studland where they had said goodbye the previous April.

The following day he was off, with a pack that included a Keats she had sent him for the trip, a volume of Shakespeare, a pocket Blake and "the Oxford book", almost certainly the *Oxford Book of English Verse*.

"It was incredibly beautiful," he wrote from Lulworth that evening; "the road climbed slowly up & up till one could see everything, & then plunged madly down like the Gadarene swine. I never saw anything more beautiful than the western sea when I got here – there was a black downpour of rain, with a break on the horizon, so that the distant sea was as white as a mist."

From Lulworth he set out for the twelve-mile tramp over the cliffs to Weymouth,

> a splendid walk, up and down along the coast, very wild at first, like the chalk cliffs you & I went to one day at Studland. There were several bouts of violent rain & hail, & the whole way I had to fight against a hurricane. But the worst of the rain came while I was lunching, so I didn't get very wet. It was again a day when everything is beautiful. I enjoyed battling with the elements & it did me a lot of good . . . I love being alone these days – all this last year I have enjoyed solitude, but before that I hated it. All the spectres used to come out & gibber when I was alone. Now I think about you & about plans of work, & I have no spectres. But while I was walking today I hardly thought at all, the wind made it impossible.

Weymouth Harbour was full of battleships and the town awash with sailors on leave. The following day he sought sanctuary on Portland Bill, his batteries recharged by a letter from Ottoline, forwarded by his London charlady to whom he regularly telegraphed his latest address. "I have found a sheltered spot in the sun at the extreme end of [the] Bill, with nothing but rocks & a wild sea & strange melancholy sea birds of kinds unknown to me," he wrote. "The waves are magnificent & the place altogether makes me very happy. It is the kind of place I like best – tumultuous, cruel, unchanging & inhuman."

Warming to his subject, he went on,

> This place does speak to my soul. Nothing but rocks & sea & sky. The sea is metallic & glittering, not at all beautiful; the rocks are tumbled & unimpressive. I don't know what I like – the vastness & horizon, the movement & noise, the sea-birds & the solitude. But – there is something more – I think the movement gives me a sense of

> a life which is not the life of man or of anything sentient, & which must be strong because it is unfeeling. The endless battle within me makes me like what acts without inward battling: that is why I like necessity & the laws of motion & the doings of dead matter generally. I can't imagine God not full of conflict; my God, like the one in Genesis, would have repented & sent the flood. So I prefer no God. Life seems to me essentially passion, conflict, rage; moments of peace are brief & destroy themselves. A calm God must be like Spinoza's, merely the course of nature. All this is autobiography, not philosophy.

Soon after he had left the Bill where he had written this, he passed two men, one of whom he heard saying, "When the Deity wakes, the world wakes; when the Deity sleeps, the world sleeps. Who is the Deity on earth? No one knows. He is the Three in One, the One in Three, an unfathomable mystery. Not all the eastern sages . . ." Russell, looking back, out of earshot, thought him mad. "I *longed* to go & demand his gospel, but I hadn't quite the necessary aplomb."

After a good night and another letter from Ottoline, he set off for Wareham, twenty miles away.

> It was raining a great part of the time, but fine at the end – the spring is wonderfully forward – horse chestnuts in leaf, even elm-twigs green, blackthorn in blossom, & houses covered with pirus, it was lovely even while it was raining. But I was in a fit of madness & did not enjoy anything. About the 18th mile I began to laugh at myself & became sane, so it is lucky my walk was long. All emotions depend on circulation. Today I feel dry & hard, prepared to demonstrate the idiocy of everybody & everything, but otherwise sane.

But the thought of her return to England – and the knowledge that it would be return to Philip rather than to himself – had begun to rouse his devil. He tried to exorcise it by walking further & faster, and succeeded, even though arriving at Christchurch "terribly fresh still". But at Christchurch the devil was expelled by the beauty of the Priory. That evening, as he sat writing in the Ship Inn, it began to return:

> I do wish I could get inside your skin & know what it feels like to be you. Sometimes I think I know, & sometimes I think I don't. Also sometimes I think you know about me, & sometimes I think you don't. I doubt if ever you know how nearly I am a raving madman. Of all the characters I ever read about in fiction, none was so intimate to me as Rogojine. It is only intellect that keeps me sane; perhaps this makes me overvalue intellect against feeling. I remember when I wanted to commit murder, the beginning was a sudden picture (I hardly have pictures at ordinary times) of a certain way

of doing it, quite vivid, with the act visible before my eyes. It lived with me then for ever so long, always haunting me; I took to reading about murders & thinking about them & always with that picture before me. It was only hard thinking that kept me straight at that time – the impulse was not amenable to morals, but it was amenable to reasoning that this was madness.

Two days later, back in London, he collected a handful of letters from Ottoline and learned that she had undergone a painful operation to her nose. "When physical pain flares up beyond a point it is utterly *ghastly*," he wrote, "the most ghastly thing on earth. God made it for his pleasure, having full power to make a world without it. King Leopold, Caligula & the rest were all gentle lambs compared to their Creator. But hush. I must & will be good."

Soon afterwards they met at Bedford Square. There were one or two meetings, alone, at Bury Street. Then, after a week, he was off again, this time with Frank and his wife. The journey had its perils, since Frank was in a state of nerves and quickly lost his temper on the road.

He sits inside the car with his mouth glued to the speaking-tube, calling out "faster", "slower", "not more than 23 miles an hour", "go up to 38", "keep that other car in sight", "don't pass it", "keep out of its dust", "when you stop, don't stop in the middle of the road, leave that to horsedrivers". When carts don't get out of his way, he turns and swears at them with concentrated passionate fury.

Frank was not the only hazard. Russell had observed after his brother's second marriage that he had "wanted a wife and a cat – he got both in one", a verdict justified by her actions when she got Russell on his own. "[She] began at once on sex questions, assuring me that women are far more sexual than men, but are restrained from speaking the truth by convention & propriety," he explained. "Why does every woman think that all other women are like herself? She is very full of her writing; told me she had written a wildly passionate love-scene, & Frank had questioned her as to who the man was. All this in a fat even voice. I think variety & physical pleasures are her only real passions."

They all drove west from Salisbury, walked on Dartmoor, went over the prison – "but rather to my relief", Russell wrote, "we couldn't see the convicts at work, because of its being Saturday" – and continued into Cornwall where, passing through Truro, he tried to pick out the place where Ottoline had met Mother Julian. Then on to St Ives where he sat by the sea and pondered on all that had happened since he had stayed there with the Whiteheads three years previously. Finally, back to London and, after a note to Ottoline, a "moment of heaven" in Bury Street.

Then Cambridge and Wittgenstein. The Austrian started to unburden himself immediately on arrival, not stopping to explain where he had been or what he had been doing. "I have got a number of new technical ideas from him, which I think are quite sound & important," Russell wrote. "I shan't feel the subject neglected by my abandoning it, as long as he takes it up. I thought he would have smashed all the furniture in my room today, he got so excited."

Wittgenstein's potential was beginning to counter-balance Trinity's initial distaste for a prickly customer. "Everybody has just begun to discover [him]," Russell wrote.

> He was very good at tea. He is the only man I have ever met with a real taste for philosophical scepticism; he is glad when it is *proved* that something can't be known. I told Hardy this, & Hardy said he himself wd. be glad to *prove* anything: "If I could prove by logic that you wd. die in 5 minutes, I shd. be sorry you were going to die, but my sorrow wd. be very much mitigated by pleasure in the proof."

The illustration was after Russell's own heart. "On reflection," he told Ottoline, "I found that I agreed with him."

From the early summer of 1912 Wittgenstein's relationship with Russell, little more than six months old, began to change. On paper it might still be that of pupil and teacher, but the teacher was already eager for the pupil's opinion of his work; work which had been outlined to Ottoline a few months earlier in a long letter.

> There is one great question. Can human beings *know* anything, & if so what and how? This question is really the most essentially philosophical of all questions. But ultimately one has to come down to a sheer assertion that one does know this or that – e.g. one's own existence – & then one can ask why one knows it, & whether anything else fulfils the same conditions. But what is important in this inquiry can, I think, be done quite popularly; the technical refinements add very little except controversy & long words. I was reinforced in this view by finding how much I could say on the question in the shilling shocker ...

His hopes were not to be easily or quickly fulfilled. As he grappled with the question of what was ultimately knowable he found it inextricably tied up with the problem of matter. For a while his work on both subjects went forward on parallel lines: in an unpublished paper, "On Matter", and an unpublished synopsis, "Philosophy of Matter"; and in the series of evolving ideas presented in his Lowell Lectures published as *Our Knowledge of the External World*; in "The Relation of Sense-Data to Physics" and in "The Ultimate Constituents of Matter": a progress leading from the Cartesian dualism of *The Problems of Philosophy* in which matter and mind had no points of contact, to the neutral monism of *The Analysis of*

Mind in which they were merely different arrangements of the same raw material.

Some of his early ideas were incorporated in the paper, "On Matter", read to the Philosophical Society of the University College of Cardiff in May. He had been invited as a guest speaker, had proposed "Philosophical Implications of Symbolic Logic" as a subject, and on being asked for something of more general interest, had suggested "Matter". He expected it to be "a model of cold passionate analysis, setting forth the most painful conclusions with utter disregard of human feelings", as he warned Ottoline.

> I haven't had enough courage hitherto about matter, I haven't been sceptical enough. I want to write a paper which my enemies will call "the bankruptcy of realism". There is nothing to compare to passion for giving one cold insight. Most of my best work has been done in the inspiration of remorse, but any passion will do if it is strong. Philosophy is a reluctant mistress – one can only reach her heart with the cold steel in the hand of passion ...

A discussion with Wittgenstein confirmed his view that all was going well. "It will shock people, especially those who would like to agree with me," he told Ottoline. "It is altogether too sceptical. Wittgenstein (who has just been here) is delighted, but no-one else will be." When he had finished, he still thought the same.

> It is not as clear as it ought to be. I don't think anybody will understand it. But I don't see how to improve it. I think the thought is all right, it is only the arrangement that is faulty. However, it will have to do.

Cardiff appears to have been satisfied. So was Wittgenstein. "*He* thinks my paper on Matter the best thing I have done – but he has only read the beginning & end."

His preoccupation with Wittgenstein's future, with his other "young men", with preparations for a Mathematical Congress to be held in Cambridge in August, and above all with the surge of inspiration that was producing "On Matter", would have been enough to keep several minds occupied through the summer of 1912, quite apart from the constant need to keep the relationship with Ottoline in good repair.

In addition, however, he now embarked on a programme of imaginative writing. This was an entirely new operation and would previously have been uncongenial. However, Ottoline had worked a remarkable sea-change. "It is really amazing how the world of learning has grown unreal to me," he confided.

> Mathematics has quite faded out of my thoughts, except when proofs bring it back with a jerk. Philosophy doesn't often come into my

mind, and I have no *impulse* to work at it. My whole impulse, in mental things, is towards imaginative writing. I long to have leisure of mind for it, and to live the sort of life that would suit it. If I go on having any power of writing, I think I must give up teaching here at the end of my five years. By that time Wittgenstein can take my place ...

Some weeks earlier he had given Ottoline an autobiography revealing and analysing the torments of his upbringing, the agonies of his marriage to Alys and the intellectual battles he had fought before he had met her. He wrote in April,

> I think if I ever publish that autobiography, I might publish it anonymously, under the name of Simon Styles unless you can suggest a better name. I might invent an author of that name, & publish lots of things of his. No one would guess it was me. That's not at all the sort of person I am supposed to be. I *am* relieved that you liked the autobiography – I felt it had made no impression in scraps – I might any moment be inspired with a perfect torrent of writing now, if only I could hit on a central idea. But it must not be exposition. It must be more imaginative, more artistic.

The reason for this urge towards creative writing was explained the following day. "It worries me rather having discovered that I have so little belief in philosophy," he admitted.

> I did seriously mean to go back to it, but I found I really couldn't think it very valuable. This is partly due to Wittgenstein, who has made me more of a sceptic; partly it is the result of a process which has been going on ever since I found you. It may be temporary, and I rather hope so; but I doubt it. The other sort of writing, even if I can do it, ought hardly to fill all one's time, because inspiration is rare.

Rare maybe, but Ottoline soon stimulated it. Why not, she suggested, turn the autobiography into conversations between a young and an old man? Why not, he replied, "but I will put the bulk of it – all the passion & the experiences – into the mouth of the young one, leaving the old one merely occasional comments. The old one shall be 'I' & see the young one at intervals throughout a number of years. Do you think that a good plan?" The answer was "not entirely", and the project was eventually reshaped into *The Perplexities of John Forstice*, a novella in which Russell used an even more tortuous method of describing his intellectual pilgrimage.

Forty years later he stated that Mallock's *The New Republic* had been the model for *Forstice*. Published posthumously after he had kept it quiet throughout his life, the book does indeed use the same device of bringing together a group of morally diversified characters who sit down to straighten out the world and in doing so reveal their own beliefs. But the resemblance with Mallock's little masterpiece goes no further. *The New Republic* is a coherently articulated work of art in which personalities bat the shuttlecock of argument to and fro in a way both intellectually and artistically satisfying. *Forstice* is Russell's anguished attempt to expound the religious ideas and ideals which had occupied his mind during the first forty years of life, an exposition developed with the help of Ottoline, who personally wrote in a character of her own.

The Perplexities of John Forstice describes the predicament of an eminent physicist whose cool, splendidly isolated, scientific soul is without warning convulsed in a moral turmoil of doubts, bewilderment and uncertainties. At the same time his unsuspecting mind is subjected to a cataract of political and ethical problems. Perplexed he certainly becomes, and in his endeavours to introduce order and clarity into this mental chaos, he undertakes his own kind of Pilgrim's Progress which leads, by way of emotional upheavals, remorse and self-analysis, into a state of intellectual grace. After which he returns to his job of professing.

On this framework Russell pinned a good deal of thinly disguised autobiography. The nun, contributed by Ottoline, was based on Mother Julian. In some places no disguise was used, as Russell revealed a few years later when writing to Ottoline. "I copied out for 'Forstice' part of a letter I wrote you about 23rd March, 1912 – I enclose it – every word of it is true now, except about fierceness – that is gone – I am altogether less fierce than I was then."

The manuscript, written at the usual break-neck speed, was finished on 2 July. "It wants changes, but it really is good," he confided in the first flush of enthusiasm; "the best of it is your part, *really*; I am sure anybody would say so. I have much less doubt about it than I had about 'Prisons' even at the time; it really is worth something, I feel sure. And I think it is only the beginning of many things. It is all due to you, my Dearest. Don't forget that, if times of discouragement come later."

The optimism faded when he read the manuscript on its return from the Cambridge typist.

> It wants to be approached much more slowly – the mood must be more created, less taken for granted – the whole thing wants to be fuller, less bold, less clipped . . . I used to be unable to feel the importance of imaginary things when I wrote them myself, but I don't in this, & the reason is that I have a real affection for the man Forstice, as if I were a friend, & I feel it important to make people see what a lovable person he is.

The ever-ready Whiteheads were now conscripted as literary guinea-pigs. Alfred appears to have reacted as with "Prisons", and preferred to keep discreetly quiet. His son North did the same. However, it was liked by Whitehead's daughter Jessie. "I found myself alone with her for 2 or 3 minutes," Russell told Ottoline, "so I asked her, not knowing what else to say. She liked the poet best; next to him the philosopher. The Russian novelist, she said, talked the sort of stuff one might expect of a Russian novelist. She had the cool critical detachment of the very young. I had practically never talked to her before."

Touchstone of the operation was Evelyn Whitehead. She liked the manuscript, which Russell found a comfort, although she had criticisms, all of which he felt could be attended to without difficulty. She had, however, taken exception to the nun, a point which Russell made to Ottoline with some glee. "[She] thought the nun quite unreal – obviously an intellectual man's conception of a nun – she, who knew nuns, knew they were much less sentimental," he wrote. "So she hadn't guessed for a moment that it was not by me." A few days later Mrs Whitehead qualified her remarks. "About the nun," Ottoline was informed, "it really is *only* the inappropriateness of my long speech in the middle of your writing that she felt, & as to that I expect she is right – you will see that the two styles clash, & my remarks are more tentative than hers would be. Your part (wh. I didn't tell her was yours) she really likes. This is a comfort to me."

More comfort came from Lowes Dickinson, who had himself written dialogues in the Platonic manner. He went so far as to describe *Forstice* as a very great piece of writing, a verdict which suggests that even the originator of the phrase "League of Nations" had his critical off-days. "I do really think it has the quality of the best seventeenth-century prose, which is the highest praise one can give," he went on, before adding: "then you do the nun with extraordinary beauty and sympathy", a pat of praise which Ottoline was justifiably pleased to hear about.

However, the more Russell considered the manuscript, the less satisfied he became and the more his own inadequacies weighed him down. "I wish I knew more of the world," he lamented, in deciding that there should be more action; "it is a dreadful thing to have been a student up to the age of 40!" A few days later he added,

> What I should like to do would be to exhibit some kind of strife resulting from too finite an outlook in the people concerned. But I can't think how to do it. I am afraid of being too didactic. One ought to show Forstice like Dostoyevsky's idiot, or like the Fool in Lear, vaguely feeling something bigger than the matter of contention. But that wants so much Art.

Frustration continued to niggle away:

> I feel so hampered by want of art & lack of knowledge. I long to know all human life & all history & everything. Arnold Bennett gets his effects through his immense knowledge of industrial life. It is quite useless to get things up, as Flaubert did, in order to write about them. One must have some genuine interest in them or some real contact with them before they become sufficiently part of one to be written about. It is hard for a student to change his spots.

Nor was it only Bennett whom the "student" yearned to emulate. "I do *wish* I were more creative – it is such a miserable trickle," he complained. "A man like Mozart makes one feel such a worm".

Months later, he was still anxiously wondering how to make the story jell artistically, perceptive enough to realize that he was out of his depth in the kind of problems that fiction, even polemical fiction, inexorably poses.

> I was wrong in thinking Forstice ought to see wars & pestilences & so on – those are not the things I can do. He must see remarkable people of various sorts – as many as possible – men who believe in war are more useful for my purpose than war itself. There ought to be all kinds of theoretic sinners, all the people whose ideal contains strife in some form – imperialists, plutocrats, futurists, Bergson, etc. etc. Strindberg c'd. come in – hosts of people really. All these *before* the Amanti del Pensiero. I will try to do them all with love, not with contempt – make them seem blind & worthy of pity, not successful & strong tho' they think themselves so.

Bennett's *Milestones*, which he saw a few days later, triggered off a long analysis of how the novella could be improved. There should, he thought, be

> another dialogue for Forstice, in which believers in progress of different kinds assemble together & jubilate – with as much refinement as I can give them – & are met by an Ecclesiastes pessimist. That will make 3 pessimists – one for each of the 3 temptations in the wilderness – the first says life is bad, the second says it is trivial, the third says it is unjust. The new man will be quite different from the other two. He will be very literary, & will begin on the text "there is no new thing under the sun". For that purpose I will (if I can) invent quotations from Chinese, Persian & Indian sages saying just what the previous people in the dialogue have said; I will draw a parallel between Chicago & ancient Alexandria, & do anything else of that kind that I can think of. Then by insensible stages the speech will pass into a profound inexhaustible despair owing to

the transitoriness of all things & the ultimate extinction of life in the universe. The philosopher whom I have already done will be an answer to this man – not formally, but in fact. The previous speaker must be all the different species of futurists – all the men who wish to cast off the burden of the past, to pretend the world is young & the Golden Age about to dawn; the scene must be laid in America, perhaps at a celebration of the opening of the Panama Canal? (The Pharaohs made a Suez Canal. My pessimist might find a papyrus relating its inauguration). One would have a collection of men assembled to witness this landmark of human progress; the pessimist wd. have come to elucidate certain obscure passages in his papyrus by observing what men say on such occasions. No, this is all too farcical. I must have a simple setting. But one could make a wonderful Voltairean little story on that theme.

At this stage he put the manuscript aside, pulling it from the drawer again only towards the end of the year. After that, *Forstice* dropped into the background until Russell, making use of a new friendship with Joseph Conrad, asked his professional advice. Conrad was penetrating rather than encouraging. Russell told Ottoline,

His view is that I might leave the 1st. and 3rd. parts as they are, but that the middle part, in Florence, should be expanded into a long book, with conversations of the various characters singly. He says I must not attempt to embody the dialogue – I rebelled but he was inexorable. I can't bear to sacrifice the poet's speech! He seemed to think that by a great deal of work I could make something of it, but not to be sure whether it was worth my while to give so much time to it. He seemed to think very well of the garden party at the beginning . . . And I am happy to say he liked the nun.

Despite this qualified approval, *Forstice* once again sank out of sight. From time to time during the years ahead, the manuscript was dredged up, but most of the problems it symbolized had been submerged by the tidal wave of the war years. Not until half a century later did Russell agree to eventual publication, but only after his death. "Whilst I am satisfied with the first part of the work," he wrote in his last years, "the second part represented my opinions during only a very short period. My views in the second part were very sentimental, much too mild, and much too favourable to religion. In all this I was unduly influenced by Lady Ottoline Morrell."

Throughout the summer of 1912, as he poured out to Ottoline his thoughts and the gossip of Cambridge, he repeated his claim that nothing would ever equal his feelings for her. But he was still irked by her loyalty to Philip, and at times leaned on mathematics to bring the point home.

"Seeing that you, who have the whole of two men, would suffer greatly if you only had one & a half," he wrote, "you can perhaps imagine that it is hard to be content with a half, which is three times less than what would *not* content you." He had believed he could ride away to a new world in which a writer-philosopher, cut adrift from academic ties, would live a dream-existence with a magic Ottoline who had tossed aside a parliamentary husband, a young daughter and a bright social future. Instead, he was left with a letter-writing love-affair and discreetly arranged meetings, which may have satisfied Ottoline's grand plan but which became progressively and even more unsatisfactorily platonic.

He persevered. But he eventually put forward the tentative suggestion that he might, just conceivably, turn elsewhere occasionally. Here his ability to make little of things was strained beyond breaking-point, and he was obliged to send, post-haste, a back-tracking letter.

> The thing I was thinking of when I talked of another woman was not *so* shocking as you seem to have thought. I was thinking of a certain woman whom you don't know, who cares for me and for whom I have a very real affection. I believe it would be for her happiness & wd. do her good. I only say this because I think you thought of worse things & it is true they did cross my mind, but no more ... Sometimes I think we ought to give up everything sexual altogether. It may be we should get more of the best of each other that way. Only I doubt if I could stand it; I might find it necessary to break altogether.

He did his best. There were, after all, the deepest platonic feelings as well as the other sort, and following one more than usually tense altercation he sent an appealing letter of apology accompanied, as on other occasions, by some poor verse. "I must try to make my passion less; but it is hard;" he promised;

> today it was overwhelming – & it is dreadful when you cry. Dear heart, I was really *very* happy when I came, & was only talking of old things. Discipline will grow easier with time, & then it won't interfere so much. You won't know me in time: I will give you a nice pretty well-behaved tea-table poodle-dog kind of love, which will sit up & beg & be grateful when it is fed. Then you *will* like me!

He fought on; if not to the end, at least for a considerable time. And even in the throes of deep despair he was pleading his case for meeting her abroad again, for the psychological change of setting which would dissipate the aura of family and household distractions which in Britain surrounded the wife of Philip Morrell, M.P.

Earlier in the year she had visited Dr Combe of Lausanne, a specialist who, she hoped, would cure her migraine. Russell, learning that she planned a second visit, jumped at the chance of joining her abroad. She was cautious. Philip welcomed the idea, commenting that Russell would look after her. Nevertheless, care would have to be exercised and Russell felt it necessary to reassure her. "*Of course*, I shouldn't dream of letting anyone know I was going to Lausanne," he pleaded. "I shall say I am going abroad for a walking tour, & Mrs. McGowan will manage letters. It is very natural to be going abroad, & I couldn't well manage to conceal the fact of my being abroad." But he still had his doubts. "Would you not, as far as your own happiness is concerned, prefer that I should not come to Lausanne?" he asked. "For God's sake answer at once & truly. If you *would* like me to come I will arrive Wed., get a room, & then come to Hotel Richmont. There may be some sober happiness still in store for us; at any rate it is worth hoping for." He was nervously on edge and heard by bad luck, just as he was ready to go, that Helen Thomas, by this time married to Simon Flexner, was living outside Lausanne. "I ought not to come," was his first reaction, "but it is not in my power to stay away. I will go home again at once if you like, or always stay indoors till after dark."

The readiness of the distinguished philosopher to hide the contrast between public image and private reality does highlight Russell's inner fears as in the summer of 1912 he began to realize that relations with Ottoline had reached their limit, that she was determined to stick to her way of life and that he had only a well-defined, even if an exclusive, paddock outside her private stables. In a letter written as he decided to go to Lausanne whatever the chances of discovery or rebuff, he revealed how greatly he was being torn apart:

> You say you know what I feel, but at the very times when you say you love me, you prove by your actions that you don't. I know you are meaning to speak the truth, so I think you don't know what words mean. I will try to take what you give me; at Lausanne the outward circumstances may make it easy to put up with its being so little. And perhaps I shall forget for a time how little it is. Dearest, I haven't even the very tiniest resentment; it is Fate, no one can help it, you could not have foreseen it. And I am certain that by nature you are capable of great love; it is only physical exhaustion that prevents it. But meanwhile loving you is like loving a red-hot poker, which is a worse bedfellow than even Lytton's umbrella: every caress brings an agony.
>
> One can't transfer love to another person, as if it were a piece of luggage to be taken from one train to another. It takes me nine years to recover the freshness of feeling that is wanted for love. In nine years I shall be 49, & shall be too old for anyone I could care for; even if they could care for me, I should wither their life by the depth

of my pessimism & despair. Therefore nothing remains but frivolities. Of course I ought to be strong & live the "quiet bachelor life" my cousin thought so nice. But apart from anything else, I must escape from memories – I have too many & they are too painful. I rule out drink & morphia & such things, because they would spoil my intellect, & if that were spoilt it would be simpler to die.

He sincerely meant it all, suffering the same agonies of make-or-break decision that he was to suffer nine years on, with a new mistress expecting marriage and the first of three future wives expecting the same. Meanwhile, he travelled to Lausanne.

Russell stayed at what was then the Old Hotel, remembering how a century and a quarter earlier Gibbon had written in a summer-house there the last lines of the last page of the great history and laid down his pen. In the same garden he worked throughout the morning. After luncheon, he and Ottoline read Leopardi and explored the surrounding hills. "The afternoons we spent together, talking and reading and going expeditions until dinner," she wrote. "Leopardi's poems were a great inspiration to him then; we read them together. He grew, indeed, most gentle, more imaginative and less logically definite, more open to spiritual ideas." They walked by the lake, watched the last light fade from the Dents du Midi and lost themselves in a welter of romantic eighteenth-century regret that life was nothing more than it seemed. For the first time Ottoline fully unburdened herself, revealing the frustrations and unhappiness of her own childhood and later life, at last accepting his sympathy.

This mattered to him, perhaps more than anything else. Looking back on the visit two years later, he found every detail still photographically recorded on his mind. "I remember all the changing moods from day to day," he said, "– single conversations almost word for word; it was the most *wonderful* time of my life – not quite as happy as some earlier times, but more wonderful. I suppose nothing nearly so wonderful will ever come to us again." In particular he remembered her birthday when they had gone by lake to Geneva, then on to Ferney where they had peered through the gates at Voltaire's house:

> the extraordinary beauty of the evg. as we came back into Ferney after being in the fields – one of those moments of inward & outward peace, when time stands still for an instant. I have only had a very few, & they remain with one – generally some goad of desire prevents one from resting in the present. How happy we were in Geneva, getting your watch – somehow it all seems to have happened in a previous existence, long, long ago. It is like days of sunshine one remembers from early childhood – motionless & detached, without past or future.

He had been right. The intellectual climate of Lac Leman had eroded her psychological barriers, and a new understanding had begun to grow up between them. But he was not so bemused as to believe it could be more than temporary, that his relationship with Ottoline would ever give him the security that he looked for. He knew that he had to be satisfied with second-best. It was as well. Ottoline herself was in no doubt when she recalled the visit to Ferney in her diary some years later. "Fate and chance seem to draw one to certain spots as if they are the stages where one has to play one's little part," she wrote. "Only the partners are changed – the emotions are so varied. It was here that a year before I had sat with **** and it was here that I was to sit again, far more happily, with Philip."

Back in Britain, Russell nevertheless settled down again with confidence that the relationship could take the operational strain. Care had to be taken that no hint was dropped of his trip abroad and at one point he warned anxiously against the secret leaking out. Moreover in London, where the Bury Street flat had become a regular base, there was always the possibility of bumping into the past. This happened with disturbing results a few weeks after the return from Lausanne. A Cambridge friend, Arthur Dakyns, was also in London and the two men decided, apparently on the spur of the moment, to visit the Russian Ballet at Covent Garden. As they were moving into their seats Dakyns suddenly said, "There's Karin." Russell looked, and saw not only Karin Costelloe, Alys's niece, but, in the next seat, a radiantly smiling Alys looking beautiful and not unhappy. "I turned and fled," he wrote to Ottoline the same evening. "[Dakyns] hadn't seen her, thought I didn't know where the places were, and hung on to my arm all the way out trying to stop me."

In the street, Russell explained to Dakyns. For a few moments the two men wandered about, apparently not sure whether to go back. Then Russell looked up. Coming towards him was Alys. "I didn't see her till we were passing," he said; "she looked haggard and in torture – as she passed she gave me a look which was intended to pierce my heart, and did so . . . I was very much upset, especially by the 2nd meeting. I walked on a few steps, and then had to lean against the railings for some time – but she was out of sight by that time." They walked back to Russell's flat, where he recovered quickly by talking metaphysics. "At last," he wrote, "we went out to a cinematograph to see if it bore out Bergson's philosophy, which it did. Darling, I can't tell you how awful it was."

The incident, which, as he told Lucy Donnelly, "was inexpressibly painful to me, & so raked up old things that I was upset for some time", continued to rankle, perhaps because on second thoughts it was clear that Alys was able to survive without him. "On reflection, I think her look at me was not all tragedy, but also partly to see how I looked without my moustache," he confided to Ottoline.

Our eyes met before I knew she was there. She has a terrible hold on me still. Her power of making me suffer irritates me against her, but it persists all the same. There is something that never dies if one has cared deeply for a person . . . There is nothing for me but to forget her – only having lived with her so long, it is hard.

A footnote to the encounter soon came from Lucy Donnelly, to whom Alys had also described the incident. She had, it appears, been "softened" by the meeting, a fact which Russell confessed was a great comfort, and a little later returned to him a bundle of his letters.

Throughout the late summer and early autumn, before term began, his meetings with Ottoline continued on their "as and when possible" basis. "Let us go to Putney on Wed. as the time is not very long, & come to my flat for dinner," he wrote on one occasion. "(I agree with Mirabeau that you shd. say *chez toi* and not *chez vous*). Don't bring chicken – Mrs. McGowan can get it & cook it. I will have chicken too. But do as you like about thermoses to Putney."

If some meetings were prosaic others ended on a note that was almost comical. Thus there was the occasion, a few weeks after the Opera House incident, when Ottoline was staying at her brother's farm near Churn in the Vale of the White Horse. Russell spent the day with her on the downs. They parted only at dusk, but the time had seemed terribly short, he lamented: "I had just begun to feel really alive when the time came to an end." Then he set off in failing light for Cholsey, walking fast to catch the last train back to London. First the stars disappeared. Then he lost his way. Only by jog-trotting could he reach the village at 10.00. The station was deserted, all lights out, and only a sleeping railwayman in the signal-box. The 10.08 ran but twice a week, and not that night, a maddening discovery for one who carried large parts of "Bradshaw" in his head and could become incensed by the suggestion that he could conceivably miss a train. "I went into the village and had a most exciting time," he wrote.

Everybody was in bed, and when I knocked they thought I was a burglar. At first they pretended not to hear, and when they did answer they refused to open. I had already spent an hour trying about four inns, and several cottages where I saw lights, and was beginning to despair, when I met a villager coming home on his bicycle, and laid my sad case before him. He took me to an inn where he knew the people, and woke them out of a sound sleep.

Here he was let in, for a bed and breakfast that cost 1*s*. 9*d*. "It was thoroughly enjoyable," he wrote on arriving back at his flat the following afternoon. "Today I am all the better and have made a good start with my Aristotelian paper."

The following week he was down again, this time deeply sunk in depression and self-pity. Ottoline tried to help. She wrote in her diary:

> While we were sitting out on the downs he sobbed and sobbed, and this of course melted me, and I felt how cruel and unsympathetic I had been. He is so lonely, and tortured by his brain incessantly working, and he cannot be sympathetic in the things that so much affect me. His body and mind seem to have a huge gap between them. His hands are like the paws of a bear: no feeling in them, only force. His intellect is so immense but *en l'air*: not *en rapport* with the things of this sensual life. No visionary power or imagination in that direction, or what there is is very arctic and bare. No fancy. He is not narrow, only shorn.

One ray of light in the darkness was his enjoyment of the conspiratorial approach, and a few weeks later he was savouring preparations for another visit to her in Lausanne. He would join her, he wrote, as long as he could arrange his lectures suitably. "That means 3 days quite clear," he said. "I will put my lectures Monday & Wed. to start with, then I will remember that the Arist'n. meets on Mondays, & alter them to Wed. & Friday. By that means I am free from Thursday night to Wed. after'n. This is cunning." It was also successful, and the visit passed off without hitch. "Last Sunday," Russell wrote on his return, "the 'Heretics' here had a paper on 'The Religion of Mr. Bertrand Russell' – they little knew what practical form Mr. B.R's. religion was taking at the moment! Everybody here *wd.* be surprised!"

All the same, Mr Russell's absences were becoming increasingly difficult to conceal or to explain away. The reputation founded on the first volume of *Principia Mathematica* was already strengthened by the acclaim given to *The Problems of Philosophy*, which sold some 13,000 copies within a few months of publication. He was again president of the Aristotelian Society, a personality in university affairs. And he was an important figure in the Fifth International Congress of Mathematicians held that year in Cambridge, again meeting Peano who twelve years earlier had sparked alight his imagination. "He looks the ideal picture of a logician," he told Ottoline; "he has quite extraordinary nobility from singlemindedness – I have a very great reverence for him."

On Russell, already lured far out of his ivory tower by Ottoline, the meeting had a disturbing effect. "I have an odd sense of treachery when I meet these people, because learning does not absorb me as it does them," he admitted. Nevertheless, there was another side to this particular coin.

> I find it excites me and gets hold of me to think of seeing so many people interested in math'al philosophy – my interest revives & the

scent of battle stirs my blood. The love of power is terribly strong in me – I can't help reflecting that all these math'al. philosophers have different thoughts from what they wd. have had if I had not existed. But of course the real thing that makes an occasion of this kind feel important is the sense one has of scattered missionaries of truthful thought, each fighting a rather lonely battle, all coming together & finding encouragement in this common purpose. For the moment that feeling has swallowed up personal things altogether.

But not for long. "My Darling Darling Darling," he wrote the following day. "I slipped away from all the math'ns. one moment & found your letter – oh such a joy it was – I kissed it madly many times my Dearest Love." Then back to the Congress whose demands are described in his account of the following day:

From 9.30 to 1 I was in the chair, trying to get men not to exceed their 20 minutes (quite impossible, tho' I stood beside them till they stopped), occasionally getting into terrific arguments with Frenchmen, Germans, Italians, Russians, etc. Then I lunched with 3 Italians & gave them coffee afterwards – discussing the whole time. Then I had a breathing-space in which I walked with Whitehead – then the Dean of Bryn Mawr (a Miss Reilly, who is a math'al. Logician) came to tea; then a fierce young Italian named Padoa, with whom I had differences that seemed capable of adjustment: 2 hours of him, argument, exhortation, vituperation – I told him he was deliberately propagating error, he told me my work was so complicated that I needn't hope it would survive me – but we were really excellent friends, & parted on the best of terms. At dinner I was next to a man from Sofia who could only talk a little bad German; then more argument. Now at last they have all trooped off to a party which I have cut – I really enjoyed my day, tho' I am half dead. The constant changes of language make it much more tiring; but it is worth while, & exciting.

But not all entertaining could be cut, and the daily letters suffered in consequence. "In the evening there was a party at [St] John's where I had to talk to millions of foreigners," he reported a couple of days later. "It was dull. Now it is too late for tonight's post, so this will have to go in the morning."

While the mathematical congress no doubt stirred Russell's professional instincts, the later summer and autumn of 1912 was a period during which his recovery from the strain of *Principia Mathematica* was making itself felt. He was getting his second intellectual wind, thinking more deeply about the adventurous inquiry into matter and the basis of knowledge, which he had begun in the spring, yet still finding time for serious thoughts on a range of peripheral subjects. One was "The Essence of Religion", a paper for the *Hibbert Journal* taken or adapted from "Prisons" which bears the imprint of Ottoline's influence and which carried Russell a long step from "The Free Man's Worship" along the road to mysticism. The paper – discussed by the Heretics while Russell had been in Lausanne with Ottoline – started conventionally enough with the familiar distinction between the two natures of man, one "particular, finite, self-centred; the other universal, infinite and impartial". But he sheered away from the follow-ups offered by Christianity and the other religions of the East. "The infinite part of our life does not see the world from one point of view: it shines impartially, like the diffused light on a cloudy sea," he wrote.

> Distant ages and remote regions of space are as real to it as what is present and near. In thought, it rises above the life of the senses, seeking always what is general and open to all men. In desire and will, it aims simply at the good, without regarding the good as mine or yours. In feeling, it gives love to all, not only to those who further the purposes of self. Unlike the finite life, it is impartial; its impartiality leads to truth in thought, justice in action, and universal love in feeling.

The philosophy of a religion which presupposed the existence of a knowable good – a supposition which Russell was soon to cast overboard – was unlikely to cause offence except to those who protested that it was an attempt to plan a religion without a God. Whether Russell himself took it with quite that high seriousness may be questioned. Wittgenstein, who had been unhappy about the article, felt that Russell "had been a traitor to the gospel of exactness & wantonly used words vaguely; also that such things are too intimate for print". Russell disliked the verdict and explained the reason to Ottoline – "because I half agree with him".

One result of the *Hibbert* article was to bring Russell into touch once more with Francis Younghusband. He had been nearly killed in a motoring accident, had reflected on life during his recovery and published his findings in a book entitled *Within.* In Russell's view this was nothing but "atheism implanted by a motor-car ... It is a very amateurish book, but has a quality of simple sincerity which makes one like him. He goes on to build up a religion of atheism, interlaced with irrelevant things such as free divorce." Younghusband sent Russell a copy, and the following month appeared at a meeting of the Aristotelian Society to congratulate him on the *Hibbert* article.

Friendship quickly sprang up between the two basically dissimilar men. In describing how he took tea in Russell's rooms, Younghusband wrote,

> A more brilliant intellect I never met, but he was much more approachable than McTaggart had been at first; and he had a pecu-

> liar charm of his own. His writings were most pessimistic, but he himself always appeared in the best of spirits – a feature which I had also noticed in pessimists on frontier expeditions. Apparently the way really to enjoy oneself is to be full of dark forebodings and expect the worst; then if the worst actually happens it is only what one had expected, and if anything less than the worst occurs one can be in uproarious good-humour.

While the soldier approached the philosopher with an interested quasi-reverence, Russell was intrigued by the action-packed life of the soldier. "I love him, he is very full of universal love," he said, "and his stories of his life are thrilling." The words were typical of the man who could write a few months later: "What is important, I wonder? Scott and his companions dying in the blizzard seem impervious to doubt."

Younghusband was but one of the growing band of characters drawn into Russell's orbit and described in sharp detail in the two-a-day letters to Ottoline. Yet however much he might be intrigued by the idiosyncrasies of the human animal, however much he might revile the wickedness of politicians, cast doubts on the wisdom of Grey's policies or comment with neat iconoclasm on the foibles of dons and undergraduates, only two subjects really absorbed him throughout the autumn of 1912. The first was Wittgenstein whose demoniac ferocity in pursuit of the truth was transfixing Russell much as the stoat transfixes the rabbit; the second was the great inquiry which had started with "On Matter".

Russell's preoccupation with Wittgenstein, who returned to Cambridge in September, was like that of an enthusiastic racing trainer with a promising horse. "We talk about music, morals, and a host of things besides logic," he related to Ottoline. "He gives me such a delightful lazy feeling that I can leave a whole department of difficult thought to him, which used to depend on me alone. It makes it much easier for me to give up technical work. Only his health seems to me very precarious – he gives one the feeling of a person whose life is very insecure. And I think he is growing deaf."

Before term started, Wittgenstein was to be off on a quick visit to Iceland, but first he had to furnish a new set of rooms. "He is *very* fussy, and bought nothing at all yesterday," reported Russell.

> He gave me a lecture on how furniture should be made – he dislikes all ornamentation that is not part of the construction, and can never find anything simple enough. Then I gave him sage advice, not to put off writing till he had solved *all* the problems, because that time would never come. This produced a wild outburst – he has the artist's feeling that he will produce the perfect thing or nothing – I explained how he wouldn't get a degree or be able to teach unless he learnt to write imperfect things – this all made him more and more

furious – at last he solemnly begged me not to give him up even if he disappointed me. I love his intransigence; he makes me feel myself a puny compromiser. But I have such a strong protective feeling towards him that I find it hard to be as reckless for him as he is for himself, though I think he is quite right. This morning I made him read two pages on sense-data by a muddleheaded person named Dawes-Hicks, but the muddle made him quite ill. He declaimed for a long time and I thought he would murder me! The strength of his passion is really splendid. He is still here tonight but leaves tomorrow morning.

When Wittgenstein returned to Cambridge the following month he was in bad shape, deep in a trough of depression like those which periodically engulfed Russell, who now reported,

He is on the verge of a nervous breakdown, not far removed from suicide, feeling himself a miserable creature, full of sin. Whatever he says he apologises for having said. He has fits of dizziness & can't work – the Dr. says it is all nerves. He wanted to be treated normally, but I persisted in treating him physically – I told him to ride, to have biscuits by his bedside to eat when he lies awake, to have better meals & so on. I suppose genius always goes with excitable nerves – it is a very uncomfortable possession. He makes me terribly anxious, & I hate seeing his misery – it is so real, & I know it all so well, I can see it is almost beyond what any human being can be expected to bear. I don't know whether any outside misfortune has contributed to it or not. I had him to meet Keynes yesterday, but it was a failure. W. was too ill to argue properly.

Ottoline, ever helpful, replied with the homeliest of remedies. "Thank you very much for the cocoa, which duly arrived today," Russell answered. "I will remember the directions, & try to get W. to use it – but I'm sure he won't"

Cocoa notwithstanding, the mental turbulence remained. A few days later, after Russell had taken Wittgenstein to see North Whitehead rowing on the river, he was told that they might as well have spent the time at a bullfight, and that *all* competition was of the Devil. "I was cross because North had been beaten, so I explained the necessity of competition with patient lucidity," said Russell.

At last we got onto other topics, & I thought it was all right, but he suddenly stood still & explained that the way we had spent the afternoon was so vile that we ought not to live, or at least he ought not; that nothing is tolerable except producing great works or enjoying those of others, that he has accomplished nothing & never will, etc. – all this with a force that nearly knocked one down.

9 Mary Costelloe (later Mrs Bernard Berenson) and Bernard Berenson at Friday's Hill in 1903

10 (*far left*) Russell in 1910

11 (*left*) Lady Ottoline Morrell about 1910

13 (*right*) Lady Constance Malleson (Colette O'Niel)

12 (*below, left*) Lady Ottoline, Philip Morrell and their daughter Julian about 1913

14 (*below, right*) Russell outside Bow Street at the time of his trial in 1918

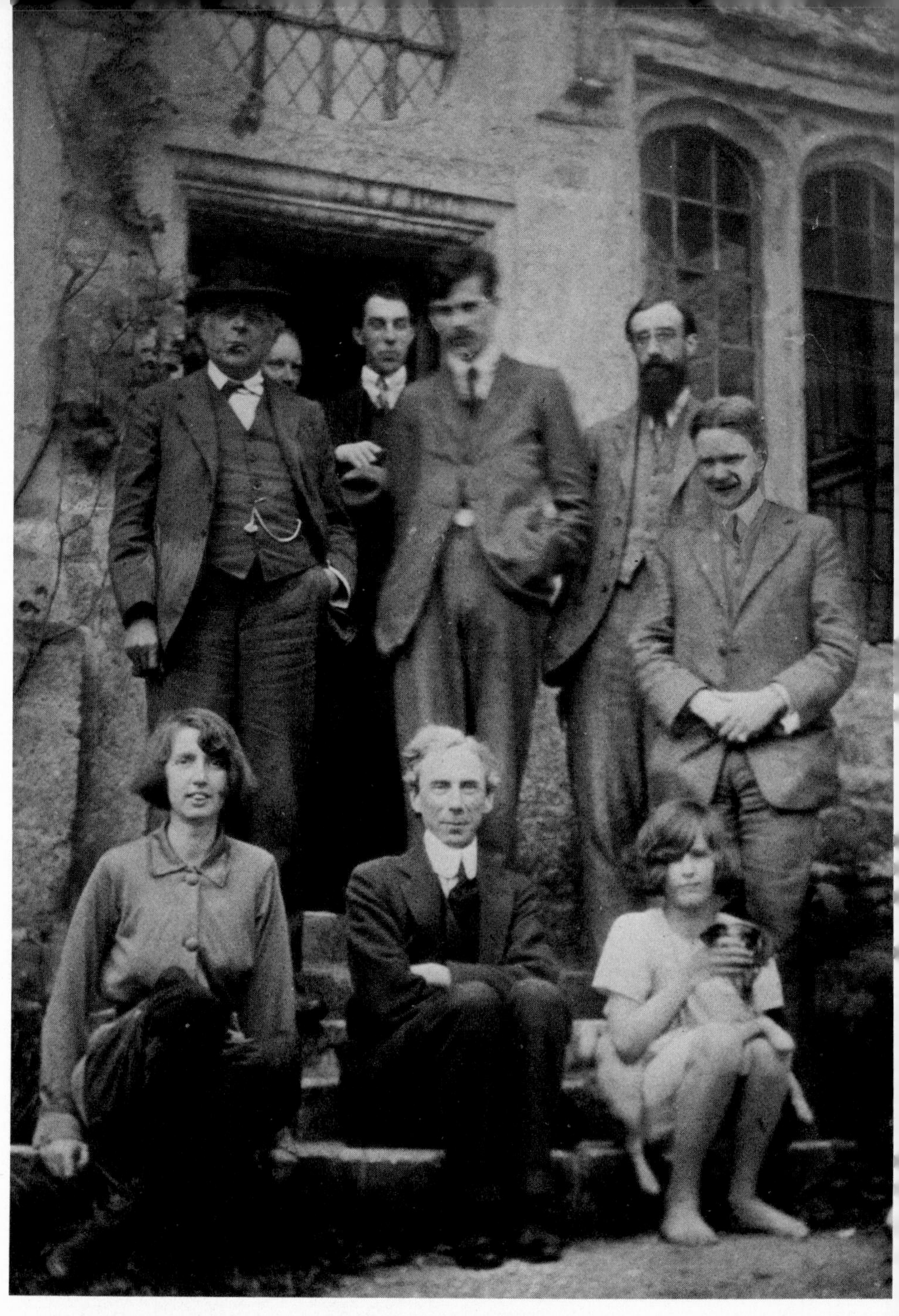

15 Russell at Garsington about 1916, with (*left to right, standing*) Augustine Birrell, unknown, Augustine Birrell's son, Aldous Huxley, Lytton Strachey, John Tresidder Sheppard; (*sitting*) Dorothy Brett, Russell, Julian Morrell and her dog, Socrates

This was the man who was shortly to be in and out of the Apostles, Russell's love of his younger days, within the week – in circumstances which Russell was later to fudge. Lytton Strachey's account of the affair reveals how it looked to Cambridge: "The poor man [Russell] is in a sad state," he said.

> He looks about 96 – with long snow-white hair and an infinitely haggard countenance. The election of Wittgenstein has been a great blow to him. He dearly hoped to keep him all to himself, and indeed succeeded wonderfully, until Keynes at last insisted on meeting him, and saw at once that he was a genius and that it was essential to elect him. The other people (after a slight wobble from Békássy) also became violently in favour. Their decision was suddenly announced to Bertie, who nearly swooned. Of course he could produce no reason against the election – except the remarkable one that the Society was so degraded that his Austrian would certainly refuse to belong to it. He worked himself up into such a frenzy over this that no doubt he got himself into a state of believing it – but it wasn't any good. Wittgenstein shows no signs of objecting to the Society, though he detests Bliss, who in return loathes him. I think on the whole the prospects are of the brightest. Békássy is such a pleasant fellow that, while he is in love with Bliss, he yet manages to love Wittgenstein. The three of them ought to manage very well, I think. Bertie is really a tragic figure, and I am very sorry for him; but he is most deluded too.

Half a century later Russell told Strachey's biographer, "I knew nothing at the time about Wittgenstein's relations with the Society, nor had I any strong views as to whether he should be elected or not."

But it was not quite like that, even though Strachey was exaggerating Russell's opposition to Wittgenstein's proposed election. On 9 November Russell in fact attended the Society "to warn them of dangers about Wittgenstein, but they elected him and a man called Bliss", as he wrote to Ottoline the following day. "They say W. and Bliss hate each other, but I know nothing of that. I *feel* it will lead to some disaster, but I cannot see any reason for feeling that."

Before the election could be confirmed Wittgenstein had to appear, and on the 11th Russell voiced his misgivings to Keynes.

> All the difficulties I anticipated have arisen with Wittgenstein. I persuaded him at last to come to the first meeting & see how he could stand it. Obviously from his point of view the society is a mere waste of time. But perhaps from a philosophical point of view he might be made to feel it worth going on with. I feel, on reflection, very doubtful whether I did well to persuade him to come next Saturday, as I feel sure he will retire in disgust. But I feel it is the business of

the active brethren to settle this, before next Saturday. If he is going to retire, it would be better it should be before election.

A few days later Ottoline learned the worst. "Wittgenstein has left the Society. I think he is quite right, tho' loyalty to the Society wd. not have led me to say so beforehand. I have had to cope with him a good deal. It is really a relief to think of not seeing him for some time, tho' I feel it is horrid of me to feel that . . ."

For this reason, if for no other, Russell was absent when a few days later Wittgenstein read a paper to the Moral Science Club in his own rooms on "What is Philosophy?" "The paper", says the club's minutes, "lasted only about four minutes, thus cutting the previous record established by Mr. Tye by nearly two minutes. Philosophy was defined as all those primitive propositions which are assumed as true without proof by the various sciences. This definition was discussed, but there was no general disposition to adopt it."

With Wittgenstein battling through incipient breakdown, Russell moved steadily back into the philosophical arena with a determination which over-shadowed his preoccupation with Ottoline and the different kind of intellectual excitements into which she had encouraged him. It would be an over-simplification to infer that he was either falling out of love with her and returning to his old intellectual pursuits as a consolation, or that his professionalism, no longer to be denied, forced lesser interests, including Ottoline, out into the cold. The simplest analysis of a complex situation is that he had now completely recovered from *Principia Mathematica* and that the recovery coincided with the opportunity for serious work once again.

He reviewed his position in a letter which is transparently sincere, obviously effective, and which yet staked his freedom to do what he wanted.

> It *is* true that at the moment *all* my feelings (not only about you) are at a low ebb – but that is because instinct is driving me back to technical thought. It is almost exactly two years now since I finished what I had to write of the big book – since then, except about a week at Ipsden, I have done no really hard thinking, & now the necessity is revived. While it lasts, it dims everything else for the moment – but it doesn't last, & it is only the preoccupation of a difficult task, not any real change in one's feelings. I *know* that when the fit leaves me, you will find me quite as full of love as I ever was. In early days, I used to tell you these fits wd. come – but it has been so long I had almost begun to hope they wouldn't.
>
> Dearest, do believe that my real deep love is not less. I know passion is less, but that can't be helped. You explained to me once how you have to keep me on an island of your life; for a long time I kept you in the centre of mine, but in the long run that was incompatible

with one's duties, & I had to put you on an island too. As you know from your own self, one can't feel quite the same strength of passion permanently when that is the case.

With the decks thus cleared, and lack of passion explained away, he turned to the subjects whose exploration was to absorb so much of his energies during the next decade. His remarks during three successive days early in November illustrate the ferment of his mind during this creative period.

"As regards Matter, I have got into deep water – it grows frightfully difficult, but I am more & more pleased with the problem," he wrote on the 7th. "It is like getting hold of the right end of a tangled skein – you see how it will all get unravelled, tho' at moments the intricacy is maddening. Just at this moment, I can't go on, but I shall soon." Twenty-four hours later he was writing,

It is a vast & very difficult subject – it may easily grow into years of work & a big book. The complexity is frightful – my head reels when I try to think it out. But I shall get it disentangled in time. The whole point of view is very new, & so will the details be – it wants a great effort of imagination to conceive things as I am trying to do. I am glad to have got hold of something really fresh, not a mere development of old ideas.

The next day he touched on a more important development. "At present it is appallingly difficult – it is finding the way, trying to imagine the world in an unfamiliar way, fitting together bits of a very complicated puzzle," he began.

I haven't the least idea yet what is the truth of the subject, but I am sure I have hit upon a real thing, which is very likely to occupy me for years to come. The problem requires a combination of physics, psychology, & mathematical logic – as soon as I see my way more clearly I shall have to refresh my knowledge of both physics & psychology, which is rather out-of-date. It is not really only matter that I am concerned with, but the basis & extent of our knowledge of things & people other than ourselves; matter is merely the technical form that the question takes. I perceive daily a whole new science to be created. At present, tho' it absorbs all my energies, I can't actually work at it more than about 2 hours a day, because it is difficult & thoughts come slowly. Later on, it will take more time.

What had happened was that the problems of matter had been swallowed up by the greater problems of the theory of knowledge.

Meanwhile, as a dummy run, he explained to the members of the Moral Science Club the position he had reached on the lesser subject. "No good argument for or against the existence of matter has yet been brought forward," says the club's minutes in describing his amended version of the "On Matter" paper read at Cardiff earlier in the year. "Can we, therefore, know an object satisfying the hypotheses of physics from our private sense-data?"

The relationship between the hypotheses of physics and the broader questions of philosophy were in fact to pre-occupy Russell increasingly from the autumn of 1912 onwards – with results which spread far beyond the purely academic. He had tended to shy away from much of science, looking on it as consisting largely of experimental work in the laboratory, an occupation at which he was all fingers and thumbs, a ham-handedness shared with Einstein and J. B. S. Haldane, as though great mathematical expertise goes with a facility for dropping things. However, he had quickly seen the significance of the new ideas that marked the last decade of the nineteenth century and had written in 1896 of Hannequin's "Essai critique sur l'Hypothèse des Atoms dans la Science Contemporaine" as being "a serious attempt at a unified and systematic Philosophy of Nature [which deserved] the attention of all who are interested in the philosophical bearings of the atomic theory". But as the great *bouleversement* of traditional physics became apparent with the acceptance of radio-activity the Quantum Theory and Relativity, Russell became so immersed in symbolic logic that little time was left for thought on other things. Only now early in the second decade of the twentieth century, did he appreciate how much physics was demanding not laboratory experiment but the mathematical expertise which he understood so well.

The outcome was important. From now onwards mathematics and philosophy took him more frequently on to ground common to himself and the physicists, the men who in less than half a century were not only to revolutionize society but to help substitute the research team for the cavalry as queen of the battlefield. During the inter-war years he was thus well placed to assess the links between philosophy and Einstein's General Theory, to understand wave mechanics, and to foresee the consequences which would follow the fission of the atomic nucleus. Apart from anything else, this gave him a head-start in 1945 over those who imagined that the atomic bomb was merely a more powerful explosive.

Russell's method of briefing himself in science was described a few days after he had realized how useful it would be to his philosophical researches into the basis of knowledge. "I am going on reading popular books on physics," he said. "When I have read enough of them to know my way about, I will start on things that are not popular. A new big piece of work like this produces the sort of tightening-up & sudden alertness that you see in a dog who startles a hare. It is a fine big canvas that may easily take me 10 years to fill in. The mere thought of it makes my blood tingle."

It was in this frame of mind, eager for work, that he was invited once again to the United States. His rejection of Professor Perry's invitation in 1911 had not been allowed to rest, and George Santayana, visiting England early in 1912, renewed the invitation on Harvard's behalf. Russell balanced separation from Ottoline and from Cambridge against the undoubted attractions of America. Not until November did he agree to a three-month visit to begin in March 1914. This would bring him what he called the princely sum of £600. He would give two courses, one on logic and one on a more general philosophical subject, and also the Lowell Lectures in Boston for which he would receive an additional fee. His letter of acceptance illustrates his ideas on education in general and on how his own beliefs in particular should be judged.

> From my experience both as a pupil and as a teacher, I should say that really advanced teaching of clever people is best done in personal talk. I should be glad if there were some way of meeting the cleverer men individually & informally not more than one or two at a time, when they felt so disposed; say by being known to be accessible at certain hours of certain days. Is this possible? In that way anything in my lectures which they disagreed with could be argued out.

His mind made up, he still felt it would "be quite dreadful when the time comes; but I know I ought to go, & the work-half of me wants to go". He expected to be invited to lecture in New York as well – as indeed he was – and before sailing he agreed to visit the University of Chicago, a journey whose repercussions were to be more personal than professional. "America contains a number of people who are ready to take up my sort of stuff," he explained to Ottoline; "& I think [the visit] would be very useful. I only wish the Americans had more brains and were less superficial." But he had no intention of leaving Britain for good. When Professor Royce asked if he would "go to Harvard permanently as their chief professor", he firmly refused.

By the end of 1912 the anomalies of existence were becoming more bearable. His frustrations with Ottoline continued and his philosophical difficulties at times looked insuperable. Nevertheless, as the problem of dovetailing her into his programme became part of routine logistics, as his philosophical work developed, the two halves of a double life began to look less incompatible. In London the cosy Bury Street flat, stocked with China tea for Russell and cigarettes and peppermints for Ottoline, was still the rendezvous where the frustrated lover was involved in the most anguished torments over his mental and physical relationship with his dearest darling. The Trinity rooms looking out on the Master's Garden were still the habitat of the erudite member of the Aristotelian Society. Yet from the letters which poured out daily from one or the other it is evident that the two worlds were merging. Russell, star risen and still rising, now found it possible to balance the humiliations of a mistress who refused to leave her husband against the plaudits of an academic world which fully recognized him. As the First World War approached, the figure waiting in the wings was neither the mathematical academic nor the romantic lover, but rather "Bertie", the highly idiosyncratic, one-off mixture of both.

8

Ottoline: Ebbing Tide

Russell's renewed philosophical ambitions, temporarily eclipsed by his attempts at imaginative writing, had begun to re-emerge towards the end of 1912. The next year they were riding high as he began to prepare the Lowell Lectures for America, imperturbably switching subjects when he found that his initial choice was unacceptable; wrote a major book on "Theory of Knowledge", only part of which was ever published; and weathered a storm of criticism from Wittgenstein.

However, the atmosphere within which his relationship with Ottoline flourished began to change. In March 1913, Philip Morrell bought Garsington Manor, an Elizabethan house outside Oxford which was eventually re-created as an exotic cultural conservatory. The building was in a state of decay when the Morrells bought it, with chickens running through the rooms, the garden a wilderness. Considerable time and money were needed, and not until May 1915 could they move in. While the house at Peppard had been a country retreat, Garsington was to be both a political centre and a stage on which Lady Ottoline could display her genius as mistress of a literary and artistic forcing-house. Here, for almost a decade, she was to attract with courageous confidence Prime Ministers actual and potential, poets such as Siegfried Sassoon, the Liberal protesters who went under in the wartime deluge, as well as a few of the men who opened the sluices. Ottoline made Garsington and Garsington made her. In the process, Russell was ground between the millstones.

He complained in one of the periodic re-assessments of their relationship,

> Ever since you went [there], the ways of seeing you that I found easy have almost entirely ceased – the long days together in the country – the times of freedom in my flat – all the things that eased the difficulty of the situation for me ... I see I must make up my mind to it, but I don't think you know how hard it is. It does involve a complete absence of any real happiness with you. And that led me to seek a second-rate happiness elsewhere. Anything else can never be more

> than a *pis-aller*. But when you went to Garsington there was a loss to me which was infinitely greater than you have ever realised.

All this despite the fact that Russell, like many others, almost made Garsington his second home. He had gone to the house-warming and birthday party at which the guests had helped complete the interior decorations, climbing up on to high steps to paint the beams of the red room. He lived, sometimes for weeks at a time, in one of the small houses on the estate, coming across to the manor to eat when he wished. In the summer, when Ottoline helped the estate-workers with the harvest, Russell too was conscripted, a task which she noted failed to relieve the tension of his pure intellect. "He only feels life through his brain, or through sex, and there is a gulf between these two separate departments," she added.

Before this there had appeared Santayana's *Winds of Doctrine*, giving Russell's ideas set-piece assessment and clinical criticism. After benevolently noting that *The Problems of Philosophy* might more accurately have been called "the problems which Moore and I have been agitating lately", Santayana outlined the doctrines which emerged from Russell's writing:

> that the mind or soul is an entity separate from its thoughts and pre-existent; that its substantial elements may be infinite in number, having position and quality, but no extension, so that each mind or soul might well be one of them; that both the existent and the ideal worlds may be infinite, while the ideal world contains an infinity of things not realised in the actual world; and that this ideal world is knowable by a separate mental consideration, a consideration which is, however, empirical in spirit, since the ideal world of ethics, logic, and mathematics has a special and surprising constitution, which we do not make but must attentively discover.

It was on to the ethical aspect of this doctrine that Santayana directed his criticism with an accuracy which caused Russell to change his views. Up to now, his ethical beliefs had been basically those set forth some years earlier in "The Elements of Ethics", an essay which leaned heavily on Moore's *Principia Ethica* and testified to Moore's influence on Russell in the philosophical soul-searchings of the later 1890s. Their essence was that the substance of ethics was as independent of human judgment as the substance of philosophy or mathematics. Right and wrong, good and evil, were entities as unalterable as the redness of fire or the softness of wool, and a statement involving them would be as true or as false as a statement involving any other fact of the universe. "Thus *good* and *bad* are qualities which belong to objects independently of our opinions, just as much as *round* and *square* do; and when two people differ as to whether a thing is good only one of them can be right, though it may be very hard to know which is right."

Now came Santayana with his argument that ethics involved the unknowable. At first, Russell's reaction was cautious. Soon, however, there came the admission that if it were not possible to obtain certain knowledge of ethical facts then ethics must be pushed from the philosophical field. "Driven from the particular sciences, the belief that the notions of good and evil must afford a way to the understanding of the world has sought a refuge in philosophy," he conceded in "Mysticism and Logic". "But even from this last refuge, if philosophy is not to remain a set of pleasing dreams, this belief must be driven forth." However, this limitation, allowing in theory the statement "I think this is bad" but not "this is bad", was airily ignored by Russell in practice. After expounding his views on one matter to Lowes Dickinson, he was heard to comment of a politician: "But he is a *scoundrel.*" Here he stuck for some thirty years, still believing even in 1943 that "where ethics is concerned, I hold that, so far as fundamentals are concerned, it is impossible to produce conclusive intellectual arguments ... In a fundamental question of ethics I do not think a theoretical argument is possible."

The public comments in *Winds of Doctrine* were nevertheless not so outspoken as Santayana's private views. Writing to B. A. G. Fuller, he gave what was in 1913 a widely held professional view of Russell:

> ... not a very trustworthy thinker; he has the fault common to the political radicals of being disproportionately annoyed at things only slightly wrong or weak in others, and of flaming up into quite temporary enthusiasms for one panacea after another. His theory of the natural world is Mill-ish and almost Humian; it is, in comparison with the reality of nature and even of experience, what the report of a battle might be in the mind of a telegraph wire through which a full description of it had been sent. There would be a perfectly adequate representation of everything in dots, dashes, and pauses, but no blood, no passions, no drama, no heroes, and no poor devils. On the other hand, Russell's lectures on logic (one or two of which he has shown me) are very clear and enlightening.

The view was underscored when Santayana, again writing to Fuller, added, "There is a strange mixture in him, as in his brother, of great ability and great disability; prodigious capacity, brilliance here – astonishing unconsciousness and want of perception there. They are like creatures of a species somewhat different from man."

Santayana's criticism may well have suggested the subject that Russell first proposed for the Lowell Lectures, the place of Good and Evil in the universe. However, during the spring of 1913 he was concentrating on the theory of knowledge and, before he could start work on the lectures, received a letter from President Lowell himself. Owing to a provision of the will of the founder of the institute, it said, the president preferred him to take some subject not so distinctly religious. Could he choose a subject of more scientific character? Russell took the problem in his stride. "I can give them the same stuff as 'the scope & limits of scientific method' – perhaps the need of some restraint will improve it," he blandly informed Ottoline.

Before this confident decision he had made an important change of emphasis in his work. Ever since his paper "On Matter", early the previous year, he had planned to expand it into a major book before doing the same with his views on the theory of knowledge. Now he reversed priorities, influenced partly at least by the fact that material on the theory of knowledge could be used in the Harvard lectures.

Once he had a logical reason for putting "Matter" into cold storage, he turned to the theory of knowledge with a ferocity which is reflected in his letters.

> The excitement of philosophical construction is coming over me – more than I have had it for a long time. When it comes, the whole great structure shoots up before one's vision with the swiftness of an Aurora Borealis, & rather like it – great shafts of sudden light piercing the darkness. I suppose people who are not philosophers don't mind so much when things are puzzling – to me it is intolerable until I understand. I am too excited to write about other things now.

A few days later he was preparing to start work. There were great masses of detail held ready in his mind but, he told Ottoline, it was all so simple that her young daughter Julian could understand it. It would be a 500-page book, but if he could get through ten pages a day, fifty days would see it finished.

Before starting, he allowed himself an evening out, going to a formal dinner at which he sat between Mrs Winston Churchill and the famous Venetia Stanley. To Ottoline, who had departed for Lausanne once more, he described the occasion.

> Winston monopolised Venetia, & Mrs. Winston wanted to hear him, so I was relieved from responsibility. When the ladies were gone, Winston asked me to explain the differential calculus in two words, which I did to his satisfaction ... Everybody was friendly. They are an extraordinarily prosperous healthy fighting breed – it gives one a sense of safety to be one of them. One feels that whoever is oppressed it won't be them. But they are not good people to marry, unless one can look after oneself, like Winston – they are too strong & thick & insensitive & combative.

This was 6 May. The next day he was off, working with his usual concentration and stimulated not only by the difficulty of the task but by the news that *Principia Mathematica* was selling in what he regarded as astonishing numbers – nearly five hundred copies of volume one by the end of 1912, nearly three hundred of volume two when it had been out only ten months. "I can't think who buys it – it must be the libraries," he admitted.

To discourage friends who would interrupt his work he invented non-existent engagements, and to Ottoline he reported on the progress of his ten-pages-a-day programme. "I feel so bursting with work that I hardly know how to wait for the days to roll themselves out," he confided. "I want to write faster than is physically possible. I haven't had such a fit for ages – it keeps me as happy as a king." By 22 May, he was past 160 pages and still going on at the same rate. It meant being very busy, he added, as the rest of life had to go on as usual. "Work is a desperate business & can't be done genteelly – there has to be something rough & primitive in the fight," he pointed out a few weeks later, of the battle into which friends were also conscripted. "[Causality] depends on induction which depends on probability, which is being treated by Keynes, who has just been put on a Royal Commission on Indian currency," he told Ottoline – "so the fluctuations of the rupee will delay my work indefinitely! The connections of things are queer."

On the summer evening of the 23rd, as he looked out from his rooms over the Master's Garden, he was still hitting his target of ten pages a day and wrote with bubbling confidence to Ottoline,

> The night is hot & delicious, with just a sound of summer breeze, – a night that seems made for love – ah me – we grow old & tiresome doing our duty & the moments when we might live slip away. I have written so much today that I can allow myself a few sinful thoughts – 20 pages today – to the end of "Acquaintance" – & tomorrow will have to be the Day of Judgment ... Day by day my writing grows more simple & naive – with comprehensive confessions of ignorance. I grow capable of greater sincerity as time goes on – what I am writing now is amazingly sincere – there is absolutely nothing "clever" anywhere, except possibly a few words on the very first page, which I shall alter some day. It is wonderful when one's thoughts grow together into a pattern, & one can write them out as one whole ...

Five days later all had changed. The transformation was brought about by Wittgenstein whose growing significance in Russell's life had been appreciated by Ottoline for some months. As far back as the previous summer he had noted, "Oddly enough [Wittgenstein] makes me less anxious to live, because I feel he will do the work I should do, & do it better.

He starts fresh at a point which I only reached when my intellectual spring was nearly exhausted."

But his confidence was continually being qualified by his fears that Wittgenstein would wander across the line dividing genius from insanity. "I had a terrific contest with [him] late last night, because I told him it wd. do him good to read French prose, & that he was in danger of being narrow and uncivilised," he wrote after one visit.

> He raged & stormed, & I irritated him more & more by merely smiling. We made it up in the end, but he remained quite unconvinced. The things I say to him are just the things you would say to me if you were not afraid of the avalanche they wd. produce – & his avalanche is just what mine wd. be! I feel his lack of civilisation & suffer from it – it is odd how little music does to civilize people – it is too apart, too passionate, & too remote from words. He has not a sufficiently wide curiosity or a sufficient wish for a broad survey of the world. It won't spoil his work on logic, but it will make him always a very narrow specialist, & rather too much the champion of a party – that is, when judged by the highest standards.

And three weeks later, enclosing to Ottoline an anguished note from Wittgenstein, he observes, "Poor wretch! I know his feelings so well. It is an awful curse to have the creative impulse unless you have a talent that can always be relied on, like Shakespeare's or Mozart's." Shortly afterwards Russell writes that Wittgenstein had just called on him announcing that logic was driving him into insanity. "I think there is a danger of it, so I urged him to let it alone for a bit & do other work – I think he will," he said. "He is in a shocking state – always gloomy, pacing up & down, waking out of a dream when one speaks to him."

This tempestuous figure had called on Russell soon after he had started on "Theory of Knowledge" and had voiced his disapproval. The result, Wittgenstein warned his tutor, would be exactly like the Shilling Shocker all over again. When Russell had some 225 pages of the manuscript finished, worse was to follow. Wittgenstein called again. Russell explained,

> We were both cross from the heat. I showed him a crucial part of what I have been writing. He said it was all wrong, not realizing the difficulties – that he had tried my view and knew it wouldn't work. I couldn't understand his objection – in fact he was very inarticulate – but I feel in my bones that he must be right, & that he has seen something I have missed. If I could see it too I shouldn't mind, but as it is, it is worrying, & has rather destroyed the pleasure in my writing – I can only go on with what I see, & yet I feel it is probably all wrong, & that Wittgenstein will think me a dishonest

scoundrel for going on with it. Well, well – it is the younger generation knocking at the door – I must make room for him when I can, or I shall become an incubus. But at the moment I was rather cross.

On reflection, three years later, he described the criticisms as "an event of first-rate importance in my life [which] affected everything I have done since. I saw he was right, and I saw that I could not hope ever again to do fundamental work in philosophy. My impulse was shattered, like a wave dashed to pieces against a breakwater. I became filled with utter despair."

In 1913 Russell had to decide two things without delay. Were Wittgenstein's criticisms as sound as he intuitively felt them to be? And if so was he to incorporate them or ignore them? "I think in all likelihood they are just," was his first reaction. "But even if they are, they won't destroy the value of the book. His criticisms have to do with the problems I want to leave to him – which makes a complication."

A few days later he got down to the nub of the difficulty. He still wanted to obey what he called "a sort of inner voice [which kept on] as persistently as the rumble of a train, saying 'Get on with your work – get on with your work', leaving no peace when I am doing anything else ... The feeling of writing that must be done is like being in the middle of a mountain & having to tunnel one's way through before one can reach light and air." But he admitted that he had got over Wittgenstein's attack only superficially, and by an act of will, which now made the work a task rather than a joy. "It is all tangled up with the difficulty of not stealing his ideas," he went on. "There is really more merit in raising a good problem than in solving it."

But he carried on, though more slowly, and in a mood of depression which increased when Wittgenstein arrived once more. "He came analysing all that goes wrong between him and me, and I told him I thought it was only nerves on both sides and everything was all right at bottom," he wrote to Ottoline.

> Then he said he never knew whether I was speaking the truth or being polite, so I got vexed and refused to say another word. He went on and on and on. I sat down at my table & took up my pen and began to look through a book, but still he went on. At last I said sharply "All you want is a little self-control". Then at last he went away with an air of high tragedy. He had asked me to a concert in the evening, but he didn't come, so I began to fear suicide. However, I found him in his room later (I left the concert, but didn't find him at first), told him I was sorry I had been cross, & then talked quietly about how he could improve!

Russell pressed on for another 125 pages after the blast – to the end of the analytical section. Then he ground to a halt, for reasons that are implied in Wittgenstein's reply to Russell's first reaction: "I am very sorry", he had written, "to hear that my objection to your theory of judgment paralyses you."

The nub of Wittgenstein's objection has not survived in the record. But Kenneth Blackwell, whose detective work in the late 1960s on the surviving part of the original manuscript has made its reconstruction possible, points out that Russell had by this time developed his theory of judgment to a much more sophisticated level than that outlined in *The Problems of Philosophy*. He had in fact analysed a judgment (or statement of belief) into several constituents and created a formula to represent the logical form of the archetypical judgment. "But Wittgenstein's objection", Blackwell has pointed out, "was a fundamental blow. He saw that Russell had omitted the binding factor, the element which would combine the disparate constituents into a significant whole, and make it impossible for a piece of nonsense – such as 'the table penholders the book' – to result from the formula."

What was to have been Russell's first full-scale effort since *Principia Mathematica* was in fact to have an even stranger history than that three-volume, ten-year work which had cost each of its authors £50. A good deal of the raw material was used in the Harvard lectures in 1914; the first six chapters, whose manuscript pages have disappeared, were published, possibly with minor amendments, in the *Monist* in 1914 and 1915; the remaining 208 pages lay among Russell's papers until they were discovered by Blackwell. The book, as reconstructed from these elements, becomes divided into analytic and constructive sections, the first of which contained parts called "Atomic Propositional Thought" and "Molecular Propositional Thought" – significant pointers to the way he was now thinking.

Wittgenstein's attack was part of a bad summer. Ottoline was in Lausanne and firmly decided that it would be indiscreet for Russell to join her there again. Hopes dashed, he waited impatiently for her return, then poured out his sorry story.

> It was very difficult to be honest about [Wittgenstein's attack], as it makes a large part of the book I meant to write impossible for years to come probably. I tried to believe it wasn't as bad as that – then I felt I hadn't made enough effort over my work & must concentrate more severely – some instinct associated this with a withdrawal from you. And the failure of honesty over my work – which was very slight and subtle, more an attitude than anything definite – spread poison in every direction. I am pure in heart again now, thanks to your divine gentleness & long-suffering. And so my love goes out

freely to you again. I must be much sunk – it is the first time in my life that I have failed in honesty over work.

During June 1913 this bitter internal conflict, added to emotional *bouleversements* by Ottoline, almost unbalanced him. As evidence there is the extraordinary letter he sent her on the 28th, the day after a fractious meeting in his flat. It is not certain what triggered off the scene, but with Russell's "instincts" in their normal state of excitement it is not difficult to guess. "It seems to me today that we ought to part for good, because continuing leads straight to the madhouse," he began.

> Besides, a scene of such degradation as yesterday's makes it impossible to stand spiritually upright in a person's presence again. Would you mind if I talked about it to Mrs. Whitehead? I want an understanding outside point of view. I wonder whether some day you wd. talk with her. I shd. like you to know that I am not *all* bad – that I *can* be unselfish, & understanding, & sympathetic, where my madness doesn't come in. I know you must be very unhappy. But it is cold abstract knowledge. I am not either happy or unhappy in the slightest degree. I suppose what is happening is tragic, but I don't feel it so. Yesterday you thought I shd. make a mistake in parting from you, & you thought I was only hurt when I said the opposite. I am not hurt today, but full of clear vision. It seems to me all but certain that to save my reason I must part from you. Don't imagine I say this in anger, or that I shall plunge into reckless immorality. I only want to live quietly & work. It is not anger, but dedication, that prompts me. I have *no* anger. I think always you have been divinely patient & gentle. And I really don't now underestimate your love. We love each other, but neither gives the sort of love the other wants. Some time back when I said I wd. win you, I decided to keep silence about my unhappiness, & to lie to you. I thought if in that way storms could be avoided I should in time become as happy as I said I was, & all wd. be well. But instinct is too strong for me. However I behave, nothing but insanity lies ahead of me if we go on. I haven't felt you the least cold lately – that is why I feel it is hopeless.
>
> I am afraid I can't make a letter reach you tomorrow. I will write tomorrow to Bedford Square. I come back here tomorrow. If you permit me talking with Mrs. W. I will try to see her Monday or Tuesday. Forgive this dreadful letter. Nothing lives in me today except the fear of madness.

The storm subsided. He saw sense, decided that he was over the moral hump with Wittgenstein, must make the best of things with Ottoline, and prepared to face the Long Vacation with unexpected equanimity. First he spent a fortnight in the Scillies. Like Shelley, he could have remained there forever, entranced by the islands' healing beauty, the quiet seas and skies, low hills and an Atlantic beauty which, more mystical than the Mediterranean, reminded him of the Hebrides. "I have never known any place so absolutely satisfy my soul," he wrote to Ottoline; "– I came to love it almost in the way I love you."

From the Scillies he returned to London and after a brief interval set off for Innsbruck with Charles Sanger for a month's trans-Alpine walking that was to bring them eventually to Punta San Vigilio on Lake Garda and to a party of mutual friends that included Lucy Silcox, headmistress of the Southwold school where Ottoline had settled Julian.

He left London on 1 August, after a long day with Ottoline, to whom he wrote a brief note from the train: brief because it was difficult to write much without being noticed, and he still felt his companion should not suspect what was going on. The prospect of nearly a month's separation was already inducing a mood of sentimental romance and Russell, keeping a careful eye on Sanger in the corner of the carriage, signed himself "Your Knight-at-Arms".

They left the train at Modane, near the northern end of the Mont Cénis, and the following day walked over the pass and down to Susa, bathing in streams on the way, descending from the heights through pine trees, then chestnuts, then vines, and marvelling at the transformation with the delight of all those who cross the Alps on foot from north to south. "It seems", wrote Russell, "a sin to live in fog & rain & darkness when there are such heavenly places in the world."

For the next three weeks they wandered: down to Turin where Russell had hoped to meet Peano but was disappointed, and where he left Sanger to deal with the luggage while he rushed off to the main Post Office to collect the awaited letter from Ottoline; to Bergamo and up to the mountains again; and finally to Brescia and Verona before arriving for their rendezvous on Lake Garda.

He practised his Italian on everyone available. He read the whole of Congreve and started on the *Purgatorio*. He found the absence of English papers maddening and arranged for the *Nation* to be sent out *poste restante*. He was moved by fine art as well as by fine scenery, as when he revisited the statue of "Victory" at Brescia. "It has that strange sense of peace that very great things have – something about the Titanic struggle that Northern genius suffers from," he wrote. "It belongs to a world I feel to be above anything I can ever hope to reach – I always have a sense of being left outside the gates of Paradise when I see such things."

Yet despite all these distractions there remained a growing sense of unease, unaffected by the letters from Bedford Square awaiting him at the bigger Italian towns, shown in the replies which he scribbled while Sanger had a daytime nap or after he had gone to bed.

In substance, Ottoline's letters were not so very different from those she had been writing for more than two years. But to Russell they were stern reminders that whatever happened she was determined to go her own way, living her own full life. By the time he reached Verona the strain was getting too much. And at Verona there was awaiting him a letter implying that it might be better if they parted. It had been written over three days and ran to sixteen pages, a long passionate reiteration of love which nevertheless came from a woman almost bowed under by the constant stream of criticism and grievance to which she was subjected. She did not want to break with him, but was it not by now the only thing? Russell had time to read it only once, and quickly, before dashing off a reply which began "My dearest dearest dearest", and continued at the same level. "I am utterly and absolutely miserable. I find I *cannot* face life without you – it seems so bleak & dark & terrible. I know I should not go on with it long." He brought up her refusal to let him join her at Lausanne, a refusal to let him share in her Italian lessons. "I feel like a tree in a pot in an attic – roots pressed against the side, top against the ceiling, no room to grow anywhere," he continued. And, separated from her by hundreds of miles, he now raised the complaint that had been festering in his mind for months – "which is that at the beginning you said you & P were only devoted friends which is not true. For the last year & a half this criticism has troubled me frightfully. I am afraid there is no hope of anything approaching happiness for me for the rest of life – I cannot face losing you, & I cannot be content with what you give without a greater moral effort than seems possible to me." There was much more in the same vein, and Ottoline was implored to help him "out of the tempest and the night" and, with no doubt a remembrance of her Christian background, to "have mercy on a struggling sinner".

That posted, he spent the day with Sanger and at night, after his companion had gone to bed, wrote once again, a long and more studied letter which, read in its entirety, gives a moving picture of the emotional cul-de-sac in which he now found himself.

> I feel even more hopeless than I did at first. If *you* decide that we must now part, I shall bear you no grudge, & only feel that you have done what you had to do. – Since your letter came, everything has seemed strange & unearthly. I went to San Zeno, where the beauty moved me infinitely. Sanger left me alone inside, & I found myself on my knees praying. I can't justify it, but it was a deep & sincere prayer – a prayer for strength to subdue my instincts. If we are to go on, I must give up wishing for companionship, or for any escape from loneliness, or for children – you do not know the depth & passionateness of my desire for children. As long as those desires exist in me, I cannot help instinctively resenting the fact that you would never satisfy them even if you were free & cd. If I can conquer these

desires (which unfortunately I let loose at the beginning of our relations) I should be then able to get great religious happiness from being with you. But I should have to become a saint to do that. Can I? I don't know. I have grown cynical about moral efforts & reformations. – We sat in the Piazza looking out on the Arena, & dined there – immense crowds of gay people listening to the band – many of them I loved from their faces, but they seemed separated from me by a vast gulf – I felt so utterly alone that I hardly could keep from calling to them that I too was a human being, & really one of them. This place has more moving beauty to me than any other except Venice – the river is quite wonderful – & many things.

You say you think at bottom I wish to part. No, not at bottom. Often the vision of a peaceful family life with a home & children comes before me & maddens me. But I know that is a dream. Even if we parted, I should always care for you too much to have a right to ask love of any woman I respected; for you hold the deepest depth of me, which no one else but one has ever touched, & from which no one will ever dislodge you. Then besides: if the rest of my life is to be of any use, it must be in teaching, & for that I must avoid scandal. What I wish at bottom is to become a saint, & be able to bear your not giving more; then, as a reward, I should get the good of what you do give. But I really think you still don't at all realize how hard the thing is that you demand of me. You speak as if it were rare to desire another person's whole devotion, whereas it is normal; you differ from the normal in desiring *two* people's whole devotion. But forgive me – this is not the road to saintship! I must learn not to consider you morally at all, but to take you like the weather – sometimes propitious, sometimes not, but never to be praised or blamed. It is the only way. – I am sorry about the Don in me; he only comes out because of checked impulses. Of course my constant criticism has chilled you; I quite see that it must cease if we are to go on. – Now, my dear dear Love, I am in your hands. If you think me capable of doing better, after all these many many failures, I will try to conquer those instincts & put them right away, & make the best of what you can give. I am *quite sure* that is the right course if I can do it, & that any other course means absolute irretrievable ruin. It is very late, & I am worn out & dead in feeling – but I am less miserable than a few days ago, because I do wish to be good, whereas then I wished nothing. I must not wish to win back your love – if that comes, it must be without my thinking of it as possible. I want to say God bless you – if I had the right. If we part, I shall always love you & wish all possible good to you. Your B.

Such a letter might suggest a writer who had passed the point of no return. But Russell had more than ordinary resilience. On the horizon, moreover, there was Punta San Vigilio, with its "curious sudden adventure" which he described to Ottoline only after his return to England.

"There was a solitary young German lady whom we all noticed & liked the looks of – at first she had an aunt with her, & then she was quite alone," he wrote.

> She seemed lonely, so Lucy Silcox invited her to join our expedition to Salo the day before yesterday to see the Martinengo-Cesaresco gardens. It turned out she had two children who were going to join her in a week. She may be a widow but seemed more as if she were separated from her husband. At the end of the evening I had an hour's tête-à-tête with her & liked her enormously. She is well-educated (has been at 3 universities!) very nice-looking, gentle but strong-willed ... In saying goodnight I kissed her hand, & she appeared on the veranda at 7.30 to wave goodbye yesterday morning. I don't suppose I shall ever see her again – the only importance of the incident is that I felt I could now give an affection worth having to someone else. I feel it shameful that it should be so, but so it is. It shows a great poverty of nature in me, & I wish it were otherwise.

Whatever the poverty of nature, his letter displayed considerable diplomacy. He was soon in correspondence with his German lady. The details of their subsequent meetings as transmitted to Ottoline were to exemplify the art of the ingenuously misleading. At first, the episode, which might have ended very differently had the First World War not broken out, appears to be nothing more than a straightforward sexual need. Yet the truth is more complex and helps to explain the tangle of relationships from which Russell was hardly ever free during the four decades following the summer of 1913. Each woman in a long line offered a selection of agreeable, and usually complementary, attractions. Sex was sometimes an important, and occasionally the overwhelming, factor, but it was never more than part of a relationship, and sometimes no more than a *bonne bouche* to something less transient. For Russell, moreover, the conventional one-to-one relationship, which had been sorely strained during his tentative premarital frolics with his sister-in-law, was quickly dissolved in the acid tests of logic and psychology. Thus with little more than a touch of split personality he was able to love two – or more – women with equal intensity, equal devotion, and with only a slight difference in the mix of emotions felt for each.

At first the encounter showed only minor therapeutic side-effects, and back in Cambridge he settled down for a term's work which was to be disrupted by even more than the usual number of emotional crises. Before term began, Ottoline introduced him to Joseph Conrad whose books Russell had long admired. Superficially the two men had little in common. However, Russell felt that they shared the same outlook on human life and human destiny, and he described Conrad's philosophy as considering "civilized and morally tolerable human life as a dangerous walk on a thin crust of barely cooled lava which at any moment might break and let the unwary sink into fiery depths".

On 11 September, he visited Conrad at his home in Ashford, Kent. His report to Ottoline is more revealing than his later reminiscences.

> It was *wonderful*. I *loved* him & I think he liked me. He talked a great deal about his work & life & aims, & about other writers. At first we were both shy & awkward – he praised Wells & Rothenstein & Zangwill & I began to despair. Then I asked him what he thought of Arnold Bennett, & found he despised him. Timidly I stood up for him, & he seemed interested ... Then we went a little walk, & somehow grew very intimate. I plucked up courage to tell him what I find in his work – the boring down into things to get to the very bottom below the apparent facts. He seemed to feel I had understood him; then he stopped & we just looked into each other's eyes for some time, & then he said he had grown to wish he could live on the surface & write differently, that he had grown frightened. His eyes at the moment expressed the inward pain & terror that one feels him always fighting. Then he said he was weary of writing & felt he had done enough, but had to go on & say it again. Then he talked a lot about Poland, & showed me an album of family photographs of the 60's – spoke about how dreamlike all that seems, & how he sometimes feels he ought not to have had children, because they have no roots or traditions or relations. He told me a great deal about his sea-faring time & about the Congo & Poland & all sorts of things. At first he was reserved even when he seemed frank but when we were out walking his reserve vanished & he spoke his inmost thoughts. It is impossible to say how much I loved him.

Years later, Russell was asked to account for the strange sympathy between himself and Conrad but admitted that he could not pin it down. He continued,

> I think I have always felt that there were two levels, one that of science and common sense, and another, terrifying, subterranean and periodic, which in some sense held more truth than the everyday view. You might describe this as a Satanic mysticism. I have never been convinced of its truth, but in moments of intense emotion it overwhelms me. It is capable of being defended on the most pure

intellectual grounds – for example, by Eddington's contention that the laws of physics only *seem* to be true because of the things that we choose to notice. I suppose that the feeling for Conrad depended upon his combination of passion and pessimism – but that perhaps is a simplification. You ask whether my feeling for Conrad was based upon a common sense of loneliness. I think this may have been the case, but the experience, while it lasted, was too intense for analysis.

Perhaps the truth is that both men were linked by an understanding of loneliness as the great fear, a fear that Conrad used as the mainspring of several novels and Russell knew as the mainspring of his own life.

It was natural that, after half a century, Russell should invoke physics in discussing his relationship with Conrad. For as the friendship developed in the autumn of 1913 he began to see, even more clearly than before, how the nuclear revolution begun in the last years of the nineteenth century was bringing physics on to a collision course with philosophy. The realization was speeded up by the annual meeting of the British Association, whose members now heard for the first time how Niels Bohr had successfully explained Rutherford's nuclear atom in terms of Planck's Quantum Theory.

"It seems one of the Danes has been reading a revolutionary paper on Physics at the British Ass., & poor J. J. Thomson, who had always been the very foremost in innovation, took the conservative line & was squashed (so they say) by an eminent German who agreed with the Dane," Russell reported to Ottoline. "The nature of matter has been changing about once a year for the last 15 years, but this change (from what Littlewood told me) is much more serious than any previous one. Physics is a most sensational science."

The most recent development did not attract Russell merely by its relevance to "Matter" and theory of knowledge. The scientific iconoclasm of the nuclear revolution, whose opening salvoes were echoing round the world, elated him by its intellectual daring: a few days later he said,

> I have been hearing more about the new physics – it is very exciting. The atmosphere of the Scientific world in this age is wonderfully exhilarating as compared to the world of culture – the people are tremendously alive, feeling that it is for them to do great things, not at all dominated by past achievements, tho' they know them thoroughly – all the best people have a tremendous sense of adventure, like the Renaissance mariners. They question everything that has been done, & are willing to pull down because they have enough energy & power to build up again. It is *the* thing in which our age excels – I am thankful to be able to have a part in it.

His reaction was immediate and typical; a few of the abler science and mathematical students would visit him once a week after dinner and discuss philosophical questions linked with science. The traffic was two-way, and while Russell would be rousing consciousness of philosophy in them, they in turn would be broadening his knowledge of the discoveries which so disconcertingly changed the nature of matter every year. The idea got off to a slow start, but before the end of October he was reporting success – eleven visitors whom he expected to settle down to seven or eight, with five or six seriously interested. "I am sure it is *far* the most useful thing I have yet found to do here," he wrote. "I enjoy it hugely, but it is frightfully tiring."

His renewed interest in physics further weakened his belief in the brute distinction between mind and matter which had characterized *The Problems of Philosophy*. A first step was taken in "On the Nature of Acquaintance", in which he pointed out that "the things commonly regarded as mental and the things commonly regarded as physical do not differ in respect of any intrinsic property possessed by the one set and not by the other, but differ only in respect of arrangement and context". The theory could be illustrated, he went on, "by comparison with a postal directory, in which the same names come twice over, once in alphabetical and once in geographical order; we may compare the alphabetical order to the mental, and the geographical order to the physical". One result of this move towards neutral monism was to nudge "mind" from its position as mental substance, radically different from matter. The view of *The Problems of Philosophy* that we are acquainted with ourselves was now replaced by a denial that we ever have more than self-consciousness; and that we can thus be acquainted only with the contents of our consciousness.

This change of stance was to be followed by a modification of his former view about matter itself. "If physics is to be verifiable," he wrote, "we are faced with the following problem: Physics exhibits sense-data as functions of physical objects, but verification is only possible if physical objects can be exhibited as functions of sense-data. We have therefore to solve the equations giving sense-data in terms of physical objects, so as to make them instead give physical objects in terms of sense-data." This apparently insoluble problem was solved in "The Relation of Sense-Data to Physics" by replacing matter with *sensibilia* as the ultimate physical entities, *sensibilia* being "... those objects which have the same metaphysical and physical status as sense-data, without necessarily being data to any mind". Russell, ever ready with the practical illustration, and putting his thoughts alternately into pigeon-holes marked philosophy and Ottoline, explained the evolution simply: "Thus the relation of a *sensibile* to a sense-datum is like that of a man to a husband: a man becomes a husband by entering into the relation of marriage, and similarly a *sensibile* becomes a sense-datum by entering into the relation of acquaintance."

Transmutation of the physical objects of *The Problems of Philosophy* was only a partial solution, but for the moment it gave Russell a world picture which could without problems contain both physics and perception. It also presented a later wit with material for a limerick:

> Said Lord Russell to Lady Cecilia,
> I certainly wish I could feel ya,
> Your data excite me,
> It would surely delight me
> To sense your unsensed sensibilia.

The process which blurred the sharp outlines separating Russell's physical and mental worlds continued later in "The Ultimate Constituents of Matter". It would have continued whatever happened. But it is clear that it was greatly influenced by the explosion of new ideas in the physical sciences which took place before the start of the First World War.

One of the young men attracted by Russell's efforts to integrate science and philosophy was Norbert Wiener, a youthful prodigy later to become famous as the creator of cybernetics. Just eighteen, Wiener had already received a Ph.D. from Harvard for his thesis on "A Comparison between the Treatment of the Algebra of Relatives by Schröder and that by Whitehead and Russell". A travelling fellowship now brought him to Europe in the train of a lengthy letter of introduction from his father, a distinguished professor at Harvard, whose glowing account of his son's abilities noted that "in philosophy he has pursued studies under Professors Royce, Perry, Palmer, Münsterberg, Schmidt, Holt, etc. at Harvard and Cornell Universities", a staking of claims to which Russell added the note: "Nevertheless, he turned out well."

The youth had been accompanied to Cambridge by the father, who launched his first meeting with Russell by giving a eulogistic account both of his son's virtues and of his own. Russell wrote of the encounter,

> While this information was being poured out, his son – after a period of dead silence – suddenly woke up & began an equal torrent, on the subject of his Doctor's thesis – pulling out books from my shelves & pointing out crucial passages, pointing out, kindly but firmly, where my work is one-sided & needs his broad view & deep erudition to correct it. Both went on at once, like children shouting "look at the castle I have built". "No, look at *mine*" – I believe the young man is quite nice & simple really, but his father & teachers have made him conceited. I asked him what he had read in philosophy – he at once reeled off the names of *all* the great philosophers, tho' he couldn't remember the titles of their books. Mathematics of course he professed to know pretty well, tho' he admits it would be as well to know more.

Russell's first impressions were reinforced before the end of the month. "Yes, the infant phenomenon is staying here till I go to America," he told Ottoline. "I have read his Dr's. thesis & think him more infant than phenomenon. Americans have no standards." To Lucy Donnelly he confided, "The youth has been flattered & thinks himself God almighty – there is a perpetual contest between him and me as to which is to do the teaching." And although he could not entirely support Wittgenstein's verdict, he was obviously glad to pass it on: "Wiener good at mathematics? Then mathematics must be no good."

For his part, Wiener has contributed one of the few accounts of Russell's impact on his students, a three-faceted picture of Russell at forty-one. There was first his position as the distinguished, aristocratic central figure of the Mad Hatter's Tea Party of Trinity. "McTaggart, a Hegelian and the Dr. Codger of Wells' *New Machiavelli* with his pudgy hands, his innocent, sleepy air, and his sidelong walk, could only be the Dormouse," relates Wiener.

> The third, Dr. G. E. Moore, was a perfect March Hare. His gown was always covered with chalk, his cap was in rags or missing, and his hair was a tangle which had never known the brush within man's memory. Its order and repose were not improved by an irascible habit of running his hand through it. He would go across town to his class, with no more formal footwear than his bedroom slippers, and the space between these and his trousers (which were several inches too short) was filled with wrinkled white socks.

Russell was different; his slight air of caricature was subconscious; McTaggart and Moore appeared to have cultivated theirs. "They had the flavour of a crusty old port – a flavour that does not reach its full perfection without the intervention of the cellarman."

In contrast to the air of inconsequential disorderliness which at times surrounded Russell, there was the clear logic of his teaching which could make the complexities of the *Principia* seem almost simple, the speed with which he had grasped the significance for philosophy of Einstein's Relativity and the new atomic theories.

Both the caricature Russell and the logical Russell could be expected. But it is faintly surprising that, according to one paragraph in Wiener's recollections, the green eyes of the satyr were already beginning to show.

> My New England puritanism clashed with his philosophical defence of libertinism. There is a great deal in common between the libertine who feels the philosophical compulsion to grin and be polite while another libertine is making away with the affections of his wife and the Spartan boy who concealed the stolen fox under his cloak

and had to keep a straight face when the fox was biting him. This does not endear the philosophical libertine to me. The old-fashioned rake had at least the fun of don't-care; the puritan is working within a code of known restrictions which tend to keep him out of trouble. The philosophical rake is as bound as the puritan, and has to steer a course in as narrow a channel; but it is a channel which is poorly lighted and poorly buoyed. I expressed myself very freely in this manner, and I am quite certain that Russell heard my comments to a friend one dark night when we met on the street as we were returning to his quarters. Though he never gave a sign of hearing me, this experience rendered me particularly apprehensive of his criticism.

While Russell was bearing with Wiener, Wittgenstein arrived with news that brought relief and distress at the same time. He was just back from Norway and was determined not only to return at once, but to live there in complete solitude until he had solved all the problems of logic. "I said it would be dark, & he said he hated daylight," Russell wrote to Lucy Donnelly.

> I said it would be lonely, & he said he prostituted his mind talking to intelligent people. I said he was mad & he said God preserve him from sanity. (God certainly will). Now Wittgenstein, during Aug. and Sep. has done work on logic, still rather in the rough, but as good, in my opinion, as any work that ever has been done in logic by anyone. But his artistic conscience prevents him from writing anything until he has got it perfect, & I am persuaded he will commit suicide in February.

Wittgenstein's work included a number of very difficult logical ideas which Russell, who was as keen to have them expounded as Wittgenstein was to do the expounding, "could only just understand by stretching [his] mind to the utmost". However, talks were hardly enough and Wittgenstein eventually promised to make a written statement before leaving for Norway. This presented problems. His artistic conscience intervened and when he felt he could not get down his ideas properly he backed out. Russell tried one method after another. First he persuaded him to dictate extracts from his notebook to a German shorthand writer. The latter was unimpressed and greeted Wittgenstein's "A is the same letter as A" with the comment, "Well, that is true, anyway." Russell, seeing the transcript, felt that much of the material was not properly explained and finally induced Wittgenstein to sit himself down and try to do better. "After much groaning he said he couldn't," he wrote to Ottoline.

> I abused him roundly and we had a fine row. Then he said he wd. talk, & write down any of his remarks that I thought worth it, so we did that, & it answered fairly well. But we both got utterly

> exhausted, & it was slow . . . All this suits me to perfection & prevents me from feeling impatience, or indeed anything except the wish to drag W's thoughts out of him with pincers, however he may scream with the pain.

At the last moment, when it looked as if Wittgenstein would disappear into the Norwegian snows without properly disclosing his discoveries to anyone, Russell took desperate measures. The secretary of Philip Jourdain, a young historian of mathematics with whom Russell had been in close correspondence while writing *Principia Mathematica*, arrived to borrow a book. Russell, acting on the spur of the moment, persuaded her to come back later in the day and take down in shorthand Wittgenstein's explanations and his own questioning interjections. They were to prove invaluable, and have been published as "Notes on Logic". "I have been translating & copying & classifying the notes of Wittgenstein's work," he wrote four months later as he completed preparations for his journey to the United States, "as I shall want them for lecturing on Logic at Harvard." However, these notes were to have even greater significance, since they suggested directions for further research from which Russell was to produce Logical Atomism five years later. They also served as Wittgenstein's programme for his *Tractatus Logico-Philosophicus*.

Reluctance to talk about his work to Russell did not spring entirely from Wittgenstein's inarticulateness. Commiserating with Moore that there was no one in Cambridge with whom Moore could discuss his work, Wittgenstein concluded, soon after his arrival in Norway, "Even Russell – who is of course most extraordinarily fresh for his age – is no more pliable enough for *this* purpose." A few months later Moore visited Wittgenstein in Norway and took down extensive notes about his work. These were passed to Russell, to whom Wittgenstein, picking up the threads again after the war, remarked, "I should never have believed that the stuff I dictated to Moore in Norway six years ago would have passed over you so completely without trace."

Eventually he was gone, and Russell could set about completing the Lowell Lectures. He had written provisional drafts during the first twenty-five days of September, finding the work easier than he expected, but well aware that they would need much going over. "They will all have to be re-written," he told Ottoline when roughly half-way through; "– they must be easier, longer, in better style, & with more jokes – I will get a book of jokes & put in one from each page. I am told one joke at least is *de rigueur* in an American lecture." The following month, while deep in the problem of extracting what he could from Wittgenstein, he decided to change the order of the lectures, bringing the easier ones to the earlier part of the course and re-grouping all of them round the central problem of the external world.

The re-writing, to which he now applied himself following Wittgenstein's departure, was more taxing. The last three lectures were troublesome, and on 2 November he wrote that he had "worked for 3 hours & finished lecture VI, the only erudite one of the lot. I am glad to have it done with." A day later he had finished No VII and announced with relief that there was now only one to go. "I shall be thankful when I have done with them," he added. On 5 November he reported that he hoped to finish the last lecture over the weekend. "Then," he went on, "I shall be free to go on preparing the other two courses I have to give in America – each about 36 lectures, wh. means a lot of work. It is hard not to get dusty when one has so much to do, but as long as I am fit I enjoy it." Finally, on Saturday 8 November, he wrote that he hoped to finish the job that day, "which will be a relief". A week later, the lectures at last completed, he admitted that he had been burdened by the thought of them ever since June. "Now I am free from that weight, & it makes me feel as if a cope of lead had been taken off. The work that remains to be done is straightforward & offers no difficulty."

In old age Russell claimed that the Lowell Lectures had been written in 1914 and gave at least two colourful accounts of the process. However, it is obvious – not least from his letters to Ottoline – that his recollection was in fact of another paper, "The Relation of Sense-Data to Physics", written for the New York Philosophical Society. In retrospect the mistake was easy enough to make, since a number of ideas in the paper were eventually incorporated in the published version of the lectures.

Shortly afterwards he was faced with a difficult decision. "Chicago University wants me to go there from June 15 to end of July & offers £200," he announced. "I am to cable my answer. In some ways it is desirable to go, but I shd. hate to be away longer than I had planned, & of course it wd. be a great fatigue, & mean losing the summer for my own work. I find I can't make myself think you wd. miss me, tho' I try to; if I could, I should let it weigh with me. We must settle about it tomorrow mg." Before the end of November he accepted; but only a briefer, and earlier, visit.

The end of term was approaching and he began to plan for the Christmas Vacation. Ottoline had earlier left for Lausanne, where she was to see her doctors again before visiting Leysin, high on its shelf above the eastern end of Lake Geneva, where her daughter Julian had been sent for her health. Here she would be joined by Philip, after which she would go on to Rome. Russell arranged to meet her there.

However, in Rome he would not be entirely dependent on Ottoline, to whom he had already inserted, in the middle of a long letter, the casual news that on returning from Italy he had written to his German lady about some books she had lent him. "She has just now answered, but

I find I have lost all interest in her," he went on. "She is in Rome, & I might see her at Xmas I suppose, but I have no wish to."

As far as it went, this was probably true, but Russell knew Russell and towards the end of November he thought it prudent, as well as honest, to make a confession to Ottoline that would have been significant even without its closing sentence. "There is a thing I have it on my conscience to say, & it is this," he began.

> At times when I am chilled by your aloofness, as I was last June, I am liable to seek affection elsewhere, tho' I shd. always have the sense to keep out of anything serious. I found it then very disagreeable to speak to you about it, & except as required by honesty it wd. have been better if I had quietly extracted myself. I think it is really better not to speak, as it is humiliating & causes quite useless pain & strain. Of course I wd. speak of anything at all serious. Your affection is intermittent, & one has to have ways of living through the times when it is in abeyance, without reproaching you, as that only prolongs the harm. This is all only by way of foresight in case of future bad times.

It was not at all clear whether Rome was to count as bad. He stayed in one hotel for a few days in the pre-Christmas week, Ottoline in another. Together they walked in the Campagna, visited the usual sights. At the Sistine Chapel Philip put in an unexpected appearance which, despite his acceptance of the situation, gravely disturbed Russell. Then Ottoline was off, first to Florence, then back to Leysin, from which she would descend to see him at Aigle, the little village below the health resort. She knew that he would soon be meeting his German lady again, and in the train she wrote asking him to let her know how things went. Her letter, and the longer and more detailed one she sent him from Florence the next day, are extraordinarily revealing. She did not want to lose him. But it is quite clear that she understood his loneliness, understood her inability to assuage more than a part of it, and was unselfishly willing to let him go if needs be.

In Rome, Russell spent an enjoyable Christmas with his German lady. He took her for a day in the Alban Hills, escorted her and her children through the Borghese Gardens, and dined and lunched with her. It was all, he assured Ottoline in Florence, very low-key. He admitted to liking his new acquaintance very much, but dispelled fears of anything more in a series of letters which included a variety of reassurances. "You need not be afraid of my plunging into things with my German lady. She does not excite me or make me lose my head, or much attract me physically" – "I know that whatever happens I shall never give to any one else the kind of feeling I give to you – the kind of feeling that has all the magic of the western islands & all the passion of Beethoven." This, and much more, was poured out in a few days, concluding with a long and reassuring account.

> The situation perplexes my instinct & makes everything go crooked. I lunched with [my German lady] today, & after her children had been sent to their nap there were a few moments' peace, during which she read poems by a man named Moericke whom Wittgenstein has always raved about – he even left a vol. of him in my rooms, hoping I should read him, but I never did. However, I liked the poems she read. All this is for the best as far as she is concerned. I like her, but she does not touch my imagination, because I feel I can see all round her. I am not in love with her, & shall not be, nor she with me. The people that really move one are those who are like mountains whose heads are hidden in the clouds – one does not know how high the summit may be. I am sorry to have given you so much needless pain – I ought to have waited till all was cleared up. I have a very strong affection for her, & shall try not *to lose sight of her; but things will never go further*. She dines with me tonight. I may see her again in the summer, but of course that is doubtful.

The war in fact ensured that. Russell never saw her again. It is difficult to know how seriously this affair might have developed had the First World War not broken out, or the repercussions it might have had on Russell's subsequent career. His "things will never go further" perhaps "made little" of events, and in old age he suggested that they did in fact go further; even so, it is hard to believe – particularly in the light of future events – that he would deliberately have misled Ottoline.

All tidily settled with his German lady, Russell left for Aigle. Here the brief meeting with Ottoline aroused all the old doubts and they again discussed the hardy perennial: would it be better to part? There were recriminations, he lost his temper, she decided that the answer was "Yes". Stunned by her decision he continued his homeward journey to England and his London flat.

Here there awaited him a letter from Conrad, who had just read "The Free Man's Worship". "You have reduced to order the inchoate thoughts of a life-time and given direction to those obscure *mouvements d'âme* which, unguided, bring only trouble to one's weary days on this earth," Conrad ended his letter of appreciation. "For the marvellous pages on the Worship of a free man the only return one can make is that of a deep admiring affection, which, if you were never to see me again and forget my existence tomorrow, will be unalterably yours *usque ad finem*."

To Russell, brooding on the future, the letter had an artificial significance. He sent it immediately to Ottoline, still in Leysin, telling her to read it before going on with his letter to her. "[It] has somehow brought me a flash of insight – the insight I have not had all these days," he went on.

> I have had the same insight before, but have lost it. Dearest, we must not break with each other. As I read, a sense of shame came to me. I felt No, the man who wrote that is not the man Conrad sees now – the affection he gives is not now deserved – the man who would face a hostile universe rather than lose his vision has become a man who will creep into the first hovel to escape the terror & splendour of the night. The feeling was so strong and swift that I felt for a moment as if I must never see him again. It would be spiritual suicide to give you up for the sake of peace. It would not matter to give up physical things, & it would not matter to have other relations if they were compatible with our spiritual union – but that must not be broken. Whatever the pain, love is a sacred thing. And anything else ought to be as serious & deep. I did think this before – I meant to say it yesterday – but I was only half alive – spiritually I was dead.
>
> Everything I said to [my German lady] was said on the basis of what I am saying now, & my relations with her are quite satisfactorily settled on that basis & need no altering. If I cared for her spiritually, it would be another matter – but it is affection, admiration, intellectual companionship, without a touch of flame. It is hard for you to bear my pain & not to urge me to seek relief. But the pain is not all you – it is partly in the essence of living seriously. It would be death to form a serious relation based on anything but the most serious side of life. Yesterday of course you thought my love was dead. Passion grows less, but you know that passion is not the same as love; & my love is utterly unalterable. I find, to my surprise, that if we part I shall not wish ever to see [my German lady] again.
>
> You will think this letter is written in a passing mood. Of course the opposite mood will come back, but this is based on insight. All this time I have been in perplexity, not knowing the right. Now I know it. But if you, for your sake, decide to break, I cannot wonder.
>
> This letter is the utter truth.

He had done all he could, at least for the moment, and now he travelled up to Cambridge, the only place he knew as home. Here, slotted into his natural academic habitat, his intellectual ambitions freshened once again.

> My rooms looked very friendly and nice when I got home – it is a comfort to creep into one's hole. It is very quiet here – very few people are up. What an odd detached thing the part of one's mind that does work is. I have done as much work today as I should usually

do in a week, & I find myself intensely interested & very fit, in spite of travelling, a cold, & a fit of constipation wh. pills have failed to cure – not to mention all our troubles. The work-machinery seems to follow its own laws, & to exist in the same body without really belonging to the same person. For the moment, the sheer delight of clear vision as to the problem of matter makes the whole world look bright. It is odd. To see clearly after being long puzzled is one of the god-like things in life. I suppose what makes people philosophers is finding it intolerably painful to be puzzled & correspondingly glorious to see clearly. It is like surveying from a hill-top a country strewn with battlefields where desperate victories have been won against what seemed irresistible odds. It is worth being mad & hateful & filling oneself & others with pain if that is the price one must pay – merely to write down what I have in germ in my mind about matter will probably take me the rest of my working life. I have a vast synthesis in my head, bringing together what had seemed discrepant facts from physics, physiology & psychology; & if I can fully succeed it will be in the end as definite as the multiplication table. It may turn out to be a better piece of work than any I have yet done. But it will want health & energy & a terrific driving force. My work really is creative in a very high sense, because it consists in bringing scientific method & demonstration into regions where hitherto there has been nothing but conjecture. Forgive all this boasting – it is really the things I see, not my part in them, that I find intoxicating. After an interval, they are so much clearer and more solid – like things appearing in the dawn, growing more visible while one turns away. These big things make one ashamed of personal troubles – happiness & unhappiness seem small things beside science.

Even so, he did not want to lose her. Before she received the Conrad letter, and his enclosed plea, she had written confirming her decision that they should part, and for the next few days he waited anxiously to see if she would change her mind. She did; by stages; in a series of letters saying she would reconsider her decision – there might have to be temporary partings – she would continue with the relationship until he left for America.

Once again he had saved himself at the edge of the precipice. And once again he had fallen back on Mrs Whitehead's good counsels. "Talking to her was very soothing," he confessed; "the talk was kept very *piano*, & she urged with all her strength that it would be madness to part permanently or even to put away passion. She thought temporary partings would do."

But following Ottoline's return to England they did more than patch things up. She agreed, reluctantly it seems, to visit her doctor and discover, once and for all, whether it would be possible for her to have a child. There was, she was told, virtually no chance. Russell reacted to the news with a letter and a note. "I am very sorry indeed that the doctor's decision is what it is," he wrote in the first, "it makes everything so useless." In the second he tried, he said, to make her understand what he had been feeling recently.

> I had no anger with you about the main thing – it hurt, but seemed right. Only I felt hopeless because of your not realising it would hurt. The longing for children has grown & grown in me, & the pain of not having a child by you has been terrible. And from the very beginning I have felt pain because you didn't understand the things of instinct. When you spoke the other day, the bitterness of all the pain & hunger I have suffered became too much & I couldn't bear it any more, & I lost all power to think of anything but anguish in connection with you. You have heart, but not understanding, & so over & over again without meaning it you hurt. I must break with you, or I shall be broken, & I must not be broken yet ...

But underneath the pain she wanted a complete break as little as he did. They met a few days later and he wrote to her afterwards recalling her "sudden outburst ... asking me not to give you up altogether". He repeated his sense of having to protect himself or be destroyed, but went on, "I perceived more & more that, whatever crises we have, we shall always come together again. That being so, I must try to put out of my head the three things I want & can't have – children, daily companionship, & imaginative writing."

With this temporary truce in hostilities, and a mutual agreement to go on seeing one another, Russell took up once more the serious work to be done before he set out for America in mid-March.

9

An American Adventure

During the first weeks of 1914, Russell had been deep in creative work. "Since I came back," he wrote early in January, "I have read and analysed innumerable articles, prepared a number ... on the theory of knowledge, made some important discoveries, written a long paper for a New Yk. Phil. Soc. – about 12,000 words – & compiled most of a lecture on the philosophy of evolution. This is five days' work ..." The paper for New York – "The Relation of Sense-Data to Physics", to be read before the New York Philosophical Society – had taken him only three days, he subsequently confided to Lucy Donnelly. "Don't tell them," he said, "or they will think it worthless, whereas it is one of the best things I ever did."

He was also preparing a new course of lectures for the coming Trinity term, and writing a preface to Poincaré's *Science and Method*. "It cost me a frightful lot of time & thought for such a short thing," he wrote of the Preface; "it was a delicate matter, as the book contains a fierce attack on me, which I thought ignorant and unfair, but which nearly destroyed my reputation in France. It doesn't prevent my finding delight in Poincaré & loving him; but I felt it would be affectation to ignore it, & yet difficult to mention it in the right way."

He was in no doubt about the quality of the sudden burst of production. "From the time I came here in 1910 until lately," he wrote in mid-January, "I did not get any important new work done, & it worried me. Last June I hoped I was doing well, & then Wittgenstein reduced me to despair again. But this time I am *sure* I have done well. Worry about work colours all one's thoughts & feelings about everything, & takes the joy out of life. I know Wittgenstein would like the work I have done lately."

As he dealt with philosophy, he was also writing what became one of his best-known papers, "Mysticism and Logic". Its genesis lay in the discussions on religion with Ottoline when, for a while, she had almost made him believe it was possible to reconcile himself with a God. Scepticism had eventually won that battle, but it had been an indecisive victory.

"I don't at all discard what belongs to mysticism, but I feel it is rather an inspiration & a refuge in great moments than a mood to live in while one has difficult work to do," he had once written to her. "It rises up, at the last moment, when I might go to the devil, & turns me the other way instead."

He now wanted a popular lecture to give in the United States and felt that this would be a good subject. "I know now what I really believe about it," he said. "I no longer oscillate with changing moods. If I could do it right it would be very good." He wrote most of the paper in twenty-four hours, thought it inadequate, and almost completely re-wrote it within the next few days, finally achieving what one writer has called "an intense exercise in religious philosophical autobiography". It did not, Russell said, "aim at eloquence, but only at careful exact statement". Not as good as he wished, was his final verdict: but sober, careful and balanced.

As he prepared for his journey to America, there came good wishes from Wittgenstein in Norway. "Perhaps [the visit] will give you at any rate a more favourable opportunity than usual to tell them your *thoughts* and not *just* cut and dried results," he added. "That is what would be of the greatest imaginable value for your audience – to get to know the value of *thought* and not that of a cut and dried result." The good wishes were not to remain unqualified. In two subsequent letters Wittgenstein spoke of a quarrel with Russell, a quarrel whose cause remains unidentified. "I dare say his mood will change after a while," Russell phlegmatically commented to Ottoline. "I find I don't care on his account, but only for the sake of Logic. And yet I believe I really do care too much to look at it. It is my fault – I have been too sharp with him." He was right, and in the second letter Wittgenstein modified his decision:

> Now I'll make a proposal to you. Let's write to each other about our work, our health, and the like, but let's avoid in our communications any kind of value-judgment, on any subject whatsoever, and let's recognise clearly that in such judgments neither of us could be *completely* honest without hurting the other (this is certainly true in *my* case at any rate). I don't need to assure you of my deep affection for you, *but that affection would be in great danger if we were to continue with a relationship based on hypocrisy and for that reason a source of shame to us both.* No, I think the honourable thing for both of us would be if we continued it on a more genuine basis. I beg you to think this over and to send me an answer *only when* you can do it without bitterness. Feel assured in any case of my love and loyalty. I only hope you may understand this letter as it is meant to be understood.

Russell did not reply immediately. There were pressing problems about his American trip, of which finance was one. He was, he told Ottoline, utterly desperate. "I haven't been living within my £20 a month – the rent of the flat ran away with the whole of it, except 6d., in one fell swoop," he had confessed to her a few weeks earlier. The jaunt to Rome had been costly, he was overdrawn at the bank, there was very little to come in for some time, and he would even have to borrow money to pay his fare to the U.S. "Will America be shocked if I come second class?" he asked Lucy Donnelly. He would be glad of the saving. "I have tried to get help from my brother, but he is hard up too," he told Ottoline. "My Aunt Agatha, I know, would sooner see me cut in little pieces & eaten by cannibals than lend me sixpence. She is very fond of me, but fonder still of money ..." The problem was eventually solved by Philip Jourdain. He had links with a firm of philosophical publishers who agreed to pay £100 in advance for the right to print the Lowell Lectures.

Even more agonizing than the threat of financial shipwreck was the prospect of three months' separation from Ottoline. They had often been parted for weeks at a time, but never by the Atlantic, a more formidable barrier then than now. Would her letters arrive regularly? Would they arrive at all? And would she continue to receive his running commentary on day-to-day life? Throughout the first months of 1914 these desperate questions distressed him with all the torments of a youth firmly in the grip of first love. As the parting came nearer, he resolved on one thing. "It is awful to have to leave you now," he wrote on the last day of February. "I hope when I come back you will be still in town. If you are I will settle in my flat." Rooms in Trinity would of course have to be kept on, but just as there are absentee landlords so there could be absentee lecturers.

Russell's reluctance to put an ocean between himself and Ottoline was compounded when he arrived in the United States. The contrast between her way of life and what seemed to him the comparative barbarism of America was too much. The effect was to be fundamental and lasting. The bitter and at times unbalanced criticism of most things American which he unleashed in his letters to Ottoline was certainly put in proportion by time. Yet an undertow of feeling remained. He had more than another half-century to live, and for much of it he was to feel great respect for individual American achievements and for individual Americans. After the Second World War he wished – however surprising it looks in the light of his later statements – that the United States would assume the hegemony of the world. Yet beneath all this he never forgot the three months based on Cambridge, Mass., in 1914 which had separated him from Ottoline for such an intolerable time.

Almost to the last he remained on hand. On 8 March Ottoline again left London for Leysin. He sailed for America only on 7 March, a date which brought him to Harvard behind time, with the result that his opening lectures on logic had to be given by Harry Costello, then a young Harvard instructor.

The voyage was made agreeable by the company of Younghusband, who was once again impressed. "[Russell] is a socialist, and I know from his conversations has a very deep and genuine sympathy with the labouring classes," he later wrote.

> But a greater natural individualist I have never come across. He was *born* to stand by himself. Working with others in a body, as we have to in a regiment or in a Government Department, is wholly unnatural to him. Everybody would love him for his charm. But he would make a rank bad Prime Minister of a Socialist State ... He was great at argument in philosophical or political debate; but he did not carry his argumentative habit on to an Atlantic steamer. On board ship he was a simple-minded and delightful companion. We had a small table to ourselves at meals; and we paced the decks together all day long; and there was no end to the subjects which interested him.

In New York, Russell was met by Lucy Donnelly and Helen Flexner who shepherded him on to the train for Cambridge, his base of operations for the next three months. Here, his arrival created a stir, and not only because he was co-author of *Principia Mathematica*. Being the heir to an earldom was an advantage but the main reason for his lionization was that New Realism – the American opposition to Idealism which had been started by William Montague and Ralph Perry in the first years of the century – was now the 'in' movement in American philosophy. Not only was *The Principles of Mathematics* one of its holy books, but two of its six leading exponents, the authors of *The Progress and First Platform of Six Realists*, were Ralph Barton Perry, Chairman of Harvard's Philosophy Department, and Edwin Bissell Holt of the Psychology Department.

Russell's own opinion of the movement – and of its disciples – had been given two years earlier after he had read the account by its six founding-fathers in their joint book, *The New Realism*.

> It is a comfort reading some philosophy that seems at last right in method; they wd. make a good atmosphere for an able man, but none of them are really able, & all fail in the final edge of accuracy on which beauty depends in thinking, ... These American Realists have evidently studied all the sort of stuff I think important, yet every now & then they lapse into gross blunders that make one feel they haven't *really* understood a single word. But they come much nearer to clearness than other phil'ers. do.

Russell thus found himself the centre of an enthusiastic circle of devotees as for four weeks he delivered his lectures at the Lowell Institute on Monday and Thursday nights, lectured in Harvard twice a day three days a week, and for social entertainment took his pick from a thick stack of invitations.

At first he stayed at the Colonial Club, humble, shabby and cheap as he described it, a temporary home from which he sent Ottoline his first impressions. "This is a regular American place," he said "very dirty, disgusting food, windows *never* opened, spittoons distributed tastefully about the floor, hard efficient un-meditative men coming and going, talking in horrible American voices." The servants were all coloured, he wrote a few days later; "the one I have most to do with is jet-black – was a printer in the West Indies, so he is used to English ways. I find the coloured people friendly & nice – they seem to have something of a dog's liking for the white man – the same kind of trust and ungrudging sense of inferiority. I don't feel any recoil from them." But he was unhappy in the club and was glad to be taken in hand by a former colleague, H. A. Hollond, who had been granted a year's leave of absence from Trinity and was now studying at the Harvard Law School. Hollond had a small flat off Harvard Square and before the end of March Russell moved in with him, the two men "doing" for themselves for breakfast and lunch so that, as Russell wrote to Ottoline, "it only leaves dinner in the stuffiness among the spittoons".

Hollond took his visitor to supper with Roscoe Pound, soon to become head of Harvard's Faculty of Law. Russell was delighted at the contrast between the simplicity of the great scholar and the pretentiousness of many people who had entertained him in Boston. "As we walked back along what I think were deserted tramlines you chanted 'Pound', 'Pound', 'Pound'," Hollond recalled. Russell was outraged by what he considered the banality of Alfred Noyes's poems, read by Noyes himself at an evening recital; but apparently happy at a dinner-party foursome in the house of the formidable Amy Lowell. The guests were Elizabeth Perkins, Russell and Hollond. After a luxurious dinner she sat in a huge armchair smoking a long cigar and Russell, one-third her weight, upright on a hard chair smoking another, each capping the other's stories.

Russell's Harvard visit got off to a bad start, although his own version of events may have been influenced by the fog of depression that descended whenever he counted the days which would elapse before his letters arrived in Bedford Square. "My first Lowell lecture was a failure," he told Ottoline. "There were 500 people, I was seized with shyness, I felt they wouldn't like what I had to say & that it was foolish of them to come; so I didn't speak loud enough, and half couldn't hear. No doubt there will be much fewer tonight."

He was right, and a fortnight later his audience had settled down to about two hundred and fifty. "It seems to me futile, but as they pay me I don't scan the matter too closely," he reported. "I am expected to dress, tho' none of my audience do. The people who run the place are fussy and old-maidish – fearfully particular about punctuality in starting and stopping, & everything else except the excellence or the reverse of the lectures."

He attempted, he later said, "to show, by means of examples, the nature, capacity, and limitations of the logical analytic method in philosophy". The method had, he went on, insistently forced itself upon him "as something perfectly definite, capable of embodiment in maxims, and adequate, in all branches of philosophy, to yield whatever objective scientific knowledge it is possible to obtain", and in the lectures he illustrated how it could operate by considering "the problems of the relation between the crude data of sense and the space, time, and matter of mathematical physics". The result, he claimed, was "a merely popular outline", a fair description only if the course were compared with the higher flights of *Principia Mathematica*.

Russell may well have sensed that he was giving his audience more than they were prepared for. Certainly the criticisms which he sent back to England tended to condemn Americans in general and the Harvard Establishment in particular, and exonerated only the students, for whom he had considerable respect. Even on the train to Boston, he had noted "the American tendency to slow platitude". Arrived there, he remarked that "America produces a type of bore more virulent, I think, than the bore of any other country – they all give one exactly the same information, slowly, inexorably, undeterred by one's efforts to stop them". The criticism was not only for Ottoline. To Margaret Llewelyn Davies he reported, "Boston prides itself on virtue and ancient lineage – it doesn't impress me in either direction. It is musty, like the Faubourg St. Germain. I often want to ask them what constitutes the amazing virtue they are so conscious of – they are against Wilson, against Labour, rich, over-eating, selfish, feeble pigs." As to Harvard itself, his verdict was damning: "Nobody here broods or is absent-minded, or has time to hear whispers from another world – except poor old Royce, whom I like, tho' he is a garrulous old bore. Everybody is kind, many are intelligent along the narrow lines of their work, & most are virtuous – but *none* have any quality. Yes, they 'make much' of me, but it gives me less pleasure than I thought it would."

The dirge, which continues almost unbroken through scores of letters, may have been due to an inherent belief in the superiority of Cambridge, England, over Cambridge, Mass.; it may have been due to the long line of Russells which stretched so far back into Britain's history – of one dinner-party he commented, "they were the kind of people who are frightfully proud of their ancient lineage because they go back to 1776". More certainly, his complaints were the result of an irrational irritation which troubled him whenever he reflected that these men, with their kind invitations, were keeping him away from Ottoline for a monstrous thirteen weeks. But he intended that it should be no longer. Invited to lecture in San Francisco, he agreed that he wanted to see the Pacific – "its mere name is romantic to me"; but the trip would have kept him out of England for at least another three weeks, and he turned it down.

Impressions of his pupils were the bright side to the coin, partly because they sparked alive his sympathy with the young and the sceptical, partly because they at least could not be saddled with inveigling him across the Atlantic. And he liked their iconoclastic questions, particularly those which came from the more senior men who had studied under Royce. "When we who were trained in such a school went riding into the visiting professor that spring," says Harry Costello, "Professor Demos tells me that we horrified the younger students, that Bertrand Arthur William Russell should be treated just like an ordinary man. But Royce and Russell were big enough to take it and like it."

The class in logic was small and for specialists, that in theory of knowledge of more general interest and attended by Professor Perry as well as by students. In addition, Russell held open house for tea and discussion in Hollond's flat once a week. He also read theses, set examination-papers for the first time in his life, and entered into the academic lives of the students in a way they found unusual and stimulating. One reason for their enthusiasm is suggested by Russell's account to Ottoline: "In teaching able men it seems to me one's relation to them should be like that of Columbus to his crew – tempting them by courage & passion to accompany one in an adventure of which one does not know the outcome."

The most famous of these pupils was T. S. Eliot, who sailed into Russell's life on 27 March.

> This morning two of my pupils came together to ask me a question about work. One, named Eliot, is very well-dressed & polished, with manners of the finest Etonian type, the other is an unshaven Greek, appropriately named Demos, who earns the money for his fees by being a waiter in a restaurant. The two were obviously friends, and had on neither side the slightest consciousness of social difference. I found they were not nearly so well grounded as I had thought; they were absolutely candid, & quite intelligent, but obviously had not been taught with the minute thoroughness that we practise in England. Window-dressing seems irresistible to Americans.

To Lucy Donnelly he wrote that Eliot was "proficient in Plato, intimate with French literature from Villon to Vildrach, very capable of a certain exquisiteness of appreciation, but lacking in the crude insistent passion that one must have in order to achieve anything. However, he is the only pupil of that sort I have; all the others are vigorous intelligent barbarians..." Eliot himself later said that Russell's account of symbolic logic seemed to have nothing to do with reality. "But", he conceded, "it gave me a sense of pleasure and power manipulating these curious little figures."

At Harvard Russell also met John Dewey, the philosopher with whom he frequently disagreed and whose path was to cross his own in China nearly a decade later. "To my surprise I liked him very much," he wrote. "He has a large slow-moving mind, very empirical and candid, with something of the impassivity and impartiality of a natural force. He & Perry & I had a long argument about 'I' – Dewey saw a point I was making but Perry didn't – he is a good man but not a very clever one, as the country gentleman said of Dizzy."

Russell's first break from Harvard came early in April when he visited the Flexners in New York for the weekend. He enjoyed it. He enjoyed being driven round the city by Helen and taken up the tallest skyscraper from whose summit he had "a view which is really marvellous; the whole town, the sea & islands, the inland country ending in hills as blue as Italy". And, in one of his confessional notes to Ottoline, there is an ominous touch of the emerging Russell, triggered off by any pretty woman within chatting-up distance. He had been horribly starved and rasped and, he went on, "I am afraid it made me more affectionate to Helen Flexner than I should have been in Europe. However, she was glad to find me so, & no harm was done." Eliot, seeing his tutor as Mr Apollinax, and thinking "of Fragilion, that shy figure among the birch-trees, And of Priapus in the shrubbery Gaping at the lady in the swing", was not slow to perceive the new and more sensual Russell now emerging.

Back in Harvard, which he had left while desperately waiting to hear from Ottoline, he now received three letters in close succession, an event which transformed even his view of the university. "Your very dear letter of this morning has just come," he wrote on 15 April, " – it is such a joy to me – it is so wonderful the happiness in each other now – I feel so full of affection for all the people here – love seems to brim over – I have seen all the world, lectured, dined, shopped, written letters, & walked out to the only wood, where I gathered a bunch of bluebells, the first I had seen this year."

He had a good deal of hard work to round off before leaving for a week's peripatetic lecturing. It was not all academic, as he made clear when he wrote after five days during which the thaumaturgic effect of Ottoline's letters had begun to wear off.

> On Friday, I spoke on suffrage to a crowd of fashionable ladies in a Boston drawing-room – a futile proceeding. Mrs. Jack is the only woman I have met who is not genteel – they all seem as if they ought to be governesses. Friday I dined with the Münsterbergs – *awful* people – & all their guests *horrors*. The ugliness of the faces along the table made me almost unable to eat – fat, stupid, complacent, with-

out any redeeming trait of any sort or kind. I find myself *thirsting* for beauty to rest the eye – any kind of visible beauty. I did not know how much I should miss it. It makes me parched and dry. As I think of Cambridge, Mass., I find I have an intimate horror of every corner of the place – it all screams at one, like living always with the screech of a railway engine. Thank Heaven half of it is over ...

He was by this time in Bryn Mawr, by courtesy of Lucy Donnelly and in spite of the bitter opposition of Dr Carey Thomas, who eighteen years earlier had invited him to lecture there. Lucy had wanted him to visit her and had asked the president if he could formally address the students. "I do not like to have Bryn Mawr students miss what students in other colleges are getting and prizing, and I think that we have had here this year unusually few speakers of real intellectual eminence," she added. The appeal had no effect on the president, who still had uncomfortable memories of Russell's previous visit during which Alys had discussed free love with her students. The fact that with Russell's abandonment of Alys this attitude now appeared to have brought its own reward was hardly to the point. Alys and Dr Carey Thomas were after all related members of the tightly knit Quaker community and Dr Thomas, now batting as stoutly for the family in its adversity as when Alys and Russell had made their joint visit to Bryn Mawr, firmly forbade all official contact between Mr Apollinax and her young girls.

What the president could not forbid was an informal meeting in Lucy Donnelly's rooms. The occasion was Sunday tea. "Miss Thomas might just as well have let you speak to the whole body of students, for the praise and inspiration of your lecture has spread like wild fire, and the people you moved intellectually are moving others in some sort at least," Lucy wrote to Russell shortly afterwards. "My happiness is in no degree malicious, believe me. There is nothing I have cared for so much as to have you get hold of the place, as I have never known anyone else to get hold of people, intellectually as well as personally."

The pleasant job done, Russell moved on, first to Johns Hopkins in Baltimore, then to Princeton – "full of new Gothic, & ... as like Oxford as monkeys can make it" – and thence to the Flexners' again in New York. This was merely a staging-post on the way to Smith College at Northampton where he read "Mysticism and Logic", – "suitable for an audience of whom some have not gone very far in philosophy", as he described it – before returning completely exhausted to Hollond's Cambridge flat. He still had a few weeks at Harvard. He finished his courses, set examination-papers, tied up loose ends, dined out most evenings and found time to write a dozen long letters to Ottoline in which he metaphorically struck off the days until he could be with her again. "You can't think the happiness it is to be near the end of this long exile & to feel that we shall be together again before long," he wrote when about to leave Cambridge. "I long to kiss you and hold you in my arms my Dearest Dearest Dearest."

He left on 26 May; but not for England. First there was Chicago. "I stay with some people named Dudley, whose daughter I used to know at Oxford," he wrote to Ottoline. "He turns out to be a very eminent surgeon – I know nothing about them beyond having met the daughter when I accepted the invitation. I am told she writes – when I knew her she tried to, but with quite amazing lack of success." The statement was, at the least, somewhat disingenuous. It was the daughter who had invited him to stay at her parents' home while Russell had wanted to know her better ever since he had first met her. His omission of these hardly irrelevant details from his normally frank and open letters was unconscious but significant.

From the moods revealed in his letters, changing from brightest optimism to darkest pessimism with switchback variation, it seems that in spite of the almost mystic understanding that only rarely deserted his relationship with Ottoline, mysticism was often not enough. The reason was simple. Her early refusal to renounce her life and be carried off into the setting sun by a piratical philosopher was not only due to love of Philip and her daughter, or even of her social position and political ambitions. There was also, with Russell at least, a background of sexual reserve. Russell did his best to understand this, however little he was willing to accept it. The situation might have been satisfactory for some men: not for Russell, of whom it could be said that even in his sixties his "terrific sexual urges ... caused him to assume the repulsive expression of a lustful satyr".

During the first few years of their relationship he was usually able to keep this trait in check. Only with the advent of his German lady did it begin to present serious problems. Russell the logician had a simple solution. "I half think if women were free", he wrote to Ottoline on hearing that one of her friends had reluctantly cut down a blossoming love-affair, "their sex-feelings would be much more like men's – there would be serious relations, which would bring tenderness, & light relations, which would merely assuage instinct."

Ottoline, with antennae well developed for sensing changes in human relationships, may well have had a tremor of premonition on reading Russell's account of the Miss Dudley he had known in England. If so, she was quickly to be justified. "My Darling", he began on his way home, having finished his travels by lecturing at the University of Michigan, "This is the last letter before I sail – thank heaven. I am *longing* to be with you again my Dearest." After this he came to a more serious matter.

> When I started I assured you I should not have any adventures here, but I have had one. The more I saw of Helen Dudley & the

more I read of her work, the more remarkable she seemed. Yesterday, she & I spent a long day in the woods together & I found that I care for her a great deal – not with the same intensity or passion as I feel for you, but still very serious. I told her I cared for some one else with whom I would not break, but she did not mind that. It ended by our spending the night together – & she will come to England as soon as she can – probably in Sept. or late August. I do not want you to think that this will make the very *smallest* difference in my feeling towards you, beyond removing the irritation of unsatisfied instinct. I suppose it must give you some pain, but I hope not very much if I can make you believe it is all right & that she is not the usual type of American. The whole family are extraordinarily nice people. The parents have the morals of their generation, & will suffer greatly if it became necessary for them to know – but her sisters all sympathised ...

Russell then went on to describe her, explained that he had found her withering, like a flower in drought, for want of love and understanding, and concluded with a reassurance:

I am sure my judgment of her is right, & not merely because I have been away from those I care for. The only really doubtful question in my mind is whether to keep the matter secret or not. For the moment of course it must be secret. My Darling, please do not think that this means *any* lessening of my love for you, & I do not see why it should affect our relations. I do mind most intensely giving you pain, I do indeed. I long to be with you & to make you *feel* that my love is absolutely undiminished. The impulse that came over me was like the impulse to rescue a drowning person, & I am *sure* I was right to follow it. And now Darling goodbye until we meet & do not let this prevent the happiness of meeting if you can help it. My deepest most intense devotion is with you always.

None of this was much beyond the guide-lines that Russell had laid down for himself. Nevertheless the self-portrait as life-saver was plausible only with some stretch of imagination, and it says much for Russell's powers of persuasion that he was, without too much difficulty, able to make Ottoline accept the situation with no more than a controversial exchange of letters. However, in one respect Ottoline had been put on the higher ground from which she could deal with the situation as it developed during the next few months: while she had been told of his relationship with Helen Dudley, Helen Dudley had been carefully prevented from knowing that the person he "cared for" was in fact his mistress, and had been so for some time.

With the confessional safely in the post, he turned towards England, home and Bedford Square.

10

Against the Stream

Russell sailed back across the Atlantic in the comfort of the *Megantic*, idly observing how the sea "was beautiful beyond belief, with the rare gentleness of fierce things"; enjoying the relaxation excited by his first sight of an iceberg, "sticking up in a conical shape, just as they do in pictures", and joyfully adding as a P.S., "I have now seen four icebergs." It was still only June 1914, and England to the east was still the untroubled country he had known since boyhood, the England he later described in reviewing Santayana's *Soliloquies* as centred on "the well-to-do unintellectual graduate, and [including] the country-house from which he comes, the sports which are his most serious pursuits, even – with some reserves – the dons by whom he is taught, provided they are sufficiently mellow and remote from modern research. This is the England which was fashioned in the time of Queen Anne – a land of leisure and beauty, of aristocratic culture, of tolerance and good humour." Cambridge was still the Cambridge of his dreams, while as for the surrounding countryside – "Ah God! to see the branches stir / Across the moon at Grantchester!"

After the liner docked at Liverpool he made for his London flat. He was by now a good deal more able to deal with delicate situations than the ingenuous young man who had returned from his first visit to the United States eighteen years earlier. Three years as Ottoline's lover had taught him more about the ways of the world than the previous thirty-nine; the accomplished man of parts, casually telling Lucy Donnelly that he had "stayed with Helen Dudley's people in Chicago – they are a nice family, & I found, rather to my surprise, that she has a good deal of literary talent", had grown quite experienced in making little of things. Expertise was called for; and more besides, since he was soon to be faced not only with the awkward problem of Helen Dudley but also with the crisis of conscience caused by the war, an event which drew him out of the academic world into the hard light of public scrutiny and transformed both his political views and his personal life.

By the end of June he was settled once more into his Cambridge rooms and his Bury Street flat. And now, to an extent which was quite new, he found himself dominated by the need to escape from the personal cul-de-sac into which he had run. The susceptibility to women which he had kept buttoned up for so long had got the better of him in America, as it had in Punta San Vigilio. This time, however, things were working out differently: Helen Dudley, he discovered, would soon be embarking for Britain, a possibility which he had gaily thrown off to Ottoline but had not contemplated seriously until the awful event was imminent. If this were not enough, Ottoline had, apparently to his surprise, been hurt by the matter-of-fact tone of his references to Miss Dudley and now needed careful handling if their special relationship was to be maintained. Thus Russell's concern with Britain's progress down the slope to war trotted in tandem with a campaign aimed at reassuring Ottoline of his affections and disengaging himself from the adoring Miss Dudley.

The trouble with Ottoline was solved first, and with a combination of logic and persuasive charm. During his absence in America she had begun to think that their relations should be merely platonic: and she wondered, on his return, whether he would still wish to see her. Russell dealt with the situation simply and quickly. He implored her forgiveness, pleaded that he could not live without her. They met briefly within twenty-four hours of his return. Within forty-eight she was visiting his flat once more, converted as much by the challenge of Helen Dudley as by anything else. They arranged to meet once a week and for a while went to Burnham Beeches every Tuesday. Russell's problem for the next few weeks was how to keep it that way.

Helen Dudley posed greater problems. At first it was her eagerness to bring the *affaire* into the open that caused him most concern, presenting him with "practical problems – when & how to leave Trinity – the necessity of telling the Whiteheads, which I dread doing more than I can say". In fact the more he thought of Helen, the more attractive Trinity became. "Cambridge holds a great part of my affections," he wrote. "I should be homesick for it if I were shut out from it. So much has happened to me here, & the place is so bound up with whatever continuity there has been in my life, that it has a hold on all my habits." As for the Whiteheads, Evelyn had helped cope with Ottoline three years earlier, and he must have feared her almost inevitable "Not again!"

By 23 June, six weeks before the outbreak of war, five days before Sarajevo, Russell had seriously begun to face the facts of the situation. "It happens that tonight I am unusually clearsighted, so I will put down the simple truth, as I may lose it again tomorrow," he wrote.

> I am less fond of H.D. than I have tried to persuade myself that I was; her affection for me has made me do my utmost to respond. This has brought with it an overestimate of her writing. The truth is that I think well, but not very well, [of] her capacity for writing,

> and that I care enough for her to desire a relation which would not deprive me of you or of Cambridge, but that I shrink from anything open.

After this literary red herring, and the more honest footnote the following morning that "the lonely nights grow unbearable & ... I haven't enough self-discipline to overcome the desire to share the night with a woman", he sat down to write yet another letter to Ottoline, poignantly revealing his particular human needs.

Although he had spent the day meeting people – his brother, Karin Costelloe, Margaret Davies, Oscar Veblen the mathematician – his mind had been on other things.

> The chief thing I have been thinking about is how to make you understand what is your importance to me – but I suppose it is useless to try to make you understand that at this date. However, I will try.
>
> The root of the whole thing is loneliness. I have a kind of physical loneliness, which almost anybody can more or less relieve, but which would only be fully relieved by a wife & children. Beyond that, I have a very intense & terrible spiritual loneliness. You & the woman I cared for many years ago are the only two human beings who have touched that in any way. I have dreamed of a combination of spiritual & physical companionship, and if I had had the good fortune to find it, I could have become something better than I ever shall be. But both in your case & in the other, physical instinct was left unsatisfied, & its insistence interfered with the real spiritual companionship, until it had been got under. I wish I could explain to you what I feel about spiritual companionship. Most people, even when I am very fond of them, remain external to me. Alys, even when I was most in love with her, remained outside my inner life. H.D. would never touch it. What I get from most of the people I like to be with is escape from the inner life, which is too painful to be endured continuously. But what I get from you is an intensification of it, with a transmutation of the pain into beauty and wonder. But owing to the weakness of your physical instinct I fail to get this as long as I am starved physically. If you could believe it, I could really have a much better relation with you (if your nature permits it) if I were not dependent wholly on you for what it is hard for you to give. If H.D. finds my keeping up with you intolerable, I shall part from her. I am sure this is right, & that anything else would lead to an unspeakable tragedy.
>
> Physical instinct, at least in me, is not satisfied by the physical act alone, but cries out for constant companionship, especially in the night.

> With most people, the basis of my relationship is sympathy – by living in their world, I escape for a time from mine. But with you it is different – that is why I am not sympathetic with you. Except where sex comes in, I do really live a very unselfish life – much more so than you know. But I do find sex too strong for me.

With these honest, if somewhat tardy, statements, the decks were cleared for an equally honest admission of his feelings for Helen which plummeted like a stone once he had got the truth off his chest. He felt great tenderness, and wished to develop her best. "But I feel no passion, & if she came to care for someone else that seemed capable of helping her, I should be glad – not only reasonably, but with all my instincts."

He was soon feeling reassured: "I don't think H.D. will do any harm between you and me, and I think her existence is in a way a safeguard for the future." But there was an undertow of resentment that the newcomer would disrupt their weekly visit to Burnham Beeches. "I am really most regretful", he went on, "that H.D. will interfere with our day the week after next."

For Miss Dudley and her father were leaving for England on 3 August, she hopeful for the future and he innocent of what was going on. As the meeting grew nearer Russell's feelings hardened. "I feel now an absolute blank indifference to her except as one little atom of humanity," he wrote the day before she sailed. "I simply *cannot* act as I had intended. I feel I shall break her heart – but the whole affair is trivial on my side, and just now I cannot play at things. If I had even the faintest hope that she could understand, I might come to care for her seriously; but I know she will think it monstrous to forget her because of public things. This day week I must face her." Five days later he wrote that she was to arrive on Sunday or Monday. "Unless", he added, "captured by Germans."

The Germans did not oblige. What is more they had now, with the invasion of Belgium, turned a Balkan war into a European one, thus effectively blocking what might have been a convenient escape-route. "I have had a postcard from my German lady saying she is with her children by the sea near Rimini & inviting me to visit her," he had informed Ottoline during the second half of July. "I think I might go late in August. Since Xmas I have had three letters from her – quite friendly, but obviously showing that she could not *think* of anything more. So there seems no reason why I should not visit her." The war was to end that possibility.

Miss Dudley and her father arrived in England on 8 August. As Russell admitted in a lengthy pen-portrait, her mouth and her nose were ugly. But her brown eyes were Chinese-shaped and interesting, and she had a good figure. Her face showed character and her movements, thought and talk all suggested a sincere and passionate temperament. She planned to stay in England indefinitely, ostensibly to carry on with her literary work, while Dr Dudley was to return home after a round of professional visits.

During his short stay he and his daughter were introduced to the Morrells. The outcome was to be convenient for Russell, since it was soon arranged that Miss Dudley should stay temporarily at Bedford Square. "When I saw with what hopes and preparations for a honeymoon she had come," commented Ottoline, "I could not help feeling extremely sorry for her."

Russell took the situation in his stride. "I don't think she realises *quite* what you and I are to each other," he assured Ottoline, "and now there is no reason why she should. It would be very unfortunate if she thought you had anything to do with my change towards her; she certainly doesn't now, and has (so far as I can see) *no* feeling of hostility or suspicion towards you."

Far from hostility, Miss Dudley felt relief that in Ottoline she had someone in whom to confide her troubles in general and her emotional ones in particular. Thus the Morrells' hospitality strengthened Russell's hand. Just as Mrs Whitehead had three years earlier obligingly passed on the confidences received from Alys, so now Ottoline was able to give Russell her own assessment of Helen's feelings. At times this produced its own troubles. "I am very very sorry that H.D. goes on telling things that bother you," he wrote on one occasion; "*do* try to stop her – there is no use in her telling them & you really know all about it now." From Ottoline this brought a pained response, to which he replied: "I couldn't understand your saying my letters to her were more passionate than any I ever wrote to you. I think you must have forgotten." This was not the objection. What irked Ottoline was that the letters, confidently shown to her by Miss Dudley, were not so very dissimilar from those she herself had been getting a few months earlier.

The situation required delicate handling. Russell and Helen were to be invited to Garsington for the same dates and guests remember how Helen would be heard knocking on his bedroom door when refused admission. His evasive actions had quickly brought a protest. He wrote to Ottoline from Bury Street,

> Yesterday morning, I had a letter from Helen ... You can't say I have deceived her since she came. I saw her here yesterday (she proposed herself) – at first I was aloof – She begged me not to be – I said we must talk things out first. She said she couldn't talk now, but had made up her mind for more friendship after the next few days, but wanted to wait a few days before coming to that. Then I yielded and became affectionate. She made me promise to give her one night – this morning I have written retracting the promise. I *can't* do it – it would drive me mad.

She might be encouraged to return to America, but this was ruled out by Russell's fear that she would commit suicide on the voyage. He therefore battled to keep her at arm's-length. But she was still around, a fact which in view of his relations with Ottoline was a temptation to providence.

Providence did its best on 25 August, bringing Helen to the Bury Street flat where she failed to get an answer. Later in the day she confided the fact to her hostess. Ottoline, properly shocked at the young girl's forwardness, was not unduly surprised. Almost at the moment when Helen was describing her abortive visit, Russell was writing to Ottoline. "It was *wonderfully* happy today," he said, " – tho' it was painful when Helen rang at the door – it seemed so intolerably brutal. – But it could not spoil the great joy of feeling at one with you again."

The situation had all the elements of disaster. "Nothing on earth would induce me ever again to go an inch beyond friendship with her," he now wrote. A fortnight later he was telling Ottoline: "I was sorry not to see you tonight, but I didn't want to see H.D. She came and knocked ever so long, soon after you were gone. Poor girl, I wish I had not been so headstrong in giving her hopes – but the whole thing is utterly dead – I haven't even a remnant of affection now." He realized he was cutting the safety-margin a bit thin, and impressed on Miss Dudley that for the moment he was willing to meet her only out of doors, an effective side-step she was forced to accept with good grace.

That done, he left London for a few days' walking in Somerset. Ottoline kept him posted on Helen Dudley, who had now left Bedford Square for lodgings nearby. After being told that Ottoline had found her a useful job he wrote that he was "amused & pleased to hear you have provided H.D. with work. Never mind if she is hurt."

Back in London, Russell continued his disengaging manœuvre. At this point they agreed not to meet again but some weeks later she could no longer resist the temptation to visit his flat. "I wouldn't let her in," he told Ottoline, "& though she asked me for a glass of water I kept her waiting on the stairs while I fetched it. I made her go home & walked as far as the door of her lodgings with her." Eventually he extricated himself; before the end of the year Helen had moved from London and when she returned, months later, it was with her sister Katherine.

However, Helen's retreat into the background did not mean that Russell was now free of emotional entanglements: from this time onwards he rarely was. Nevertheless, it is surprising that he had barely subsided with relief at Miss Dudley's retirement before he was writing to Ottoline about the "queer talk we had about Miss C.W." He went on,

> At present, I have not the *slightest* impulse towards anything of the sort – but it may grow in time, I suppose. But if so it would not be

> for passion but for the sake of companionship. However, I suppose I may be wrong about that. I have made so many mistakes that I incline to rely on your opinion, which seems to be very definite & emphatic on this occasion. I don't know how much unselfishness there is in your view – I feel it would be a relief to you not to feel responsible for my happiness.

This time it was Irene Cooper Willis, unusual and talented, for long the companion and research assistant to Vernon Lee, the enigmatic *littératеuse*. "She was beautiful, severe and Spanish-looking," says her friend Enid Bagnold.

> She had dark hair which curled over her ears, held in with a pair of dark green combs. She dressed in a way which fascinated me, and which for a time I copied. Her white collar and cascading linen frill gave her a Portia-like air. She was, in fact, a barrister. She looked always as though to answer a Shylock – with beautiful indignant gravity, shy, but rigid for the right. This air, later on, had the same effect on Bertrand Russell as it had had on Desmond MacCarthy. Her gravity (and beauty) drove certain intellectual men in and out of love with her. I don't think she was ever in love with any man. She loved and liked women; she had tender warmth for women. But if it led to passion she was unaware of it. The two women she venerated were Ellen Terry and Vernon Lee.

She had been introduced to Russell by Ottoline early in December 1914, when he needed a research helper for a political pamphlet, *The Policy of the Entente*, and it was at Ottoline's London house that Enid Bagnold saw them together.

> He was, as Margot Oxford said, looking like a knife – you can never see him edge on. He has to be turned flat. He was buzzing round her like a wasp – trying to get her to talk, turning away in exasperation, turning to me with half a question – hoping for light but getting none. Most women would have been flattered. But not Irene. If she had looked shy he could have borne it. But she looked full of talk and silent.

Ottoline's first questionings were quickly justified. "I think I may easily come to have a *very* great affection for Irene," Russell was soon writing early in January, " – not a very passionate feeling, but one which might give happiness & be free from the pain of passion. And I feel pretty sure she would respond, tho' she would be shy & would need to be led gently. And I think she would interfere as little as anyone could between you and me."

The news that he was now seriously interested in the woman she had introduced to him just four weeks previously came as a shock, even to the nearly unshockable Ottoline for whom both the German lady and Helen Dudley had been competitors within less than a year. Nevertheless, she reacted generously, appreciating that Russell needed more companionship than she could give. His response was bitter and Ottoline was forced to deny that she was trying to pass him on to Miss Cooper Willis.

He was now thinking of leaving Cambridge, apparently as prelude to a hoped-for divorce, but Ottoline urged that before taking drastic action he should consult the usual adviser and referee, Mrs Whitehead. However, this was unnecessary since Miss Cooper Willis turned up for a long talk with Ottoline at Bedford Square, asking for advice, and pleading the need to look after her sister. She had no intention of being cited in a divorce case; and she found it difficult either to control her feelings and be a platonic friend or, as Ottoline suggested, go away with Russell from time to time and live with him.

However, Russell was already having second thoughts. If she feared scandal, he disliked caution. "I have written to her saying I don't see much hope for the future," he told Ottoline, "that I don't think she would be happy in the sort of position I could give her. I feel sure, almost, that the whole thing will come to nothing. I profoundly regret her help over work, & I wish to goodness I had not made love to her, so that I could have kept that. I don't want the rest." Nevertheless, Miss Cooper Willis continued to work for him for a few more months, fading only slowly from his life before he delivered – to Ottoline – his final verdict: "I have a real and great affection for her, but I do like people to be willing to shoot Niagara."

Russell's anguished outpourings about his problems with Helen Dudley and Miss Cooper Willis suggest that emotional entanglements dominated his life during the early months of the war. This was not so. His personal feelings were extravagant and intense enough to fill out the pigeon-hole reserved for them. But when Helen Dudley had been dealt with for the day, or the current feeling about Miss Cooper Willis analysed and recorded, that was that: all thought and energy could then be switched to the main topic on the agenda, which was of course the war. It is true that in the autumn of 1914 he wrote the Herbert Spencer Lecture on "Scientific Method in Philosophy", using much material from the Lowell Lectures and complaining to Ottoline during its preparation, "It worries me because I can't get interested or feel that it matters whether I do well or ill. It will bring me £20, but it will be a miserable pot-boiler." It was not quite that, but the remark underlines how he already felt that time spent even on philosophical writing was time taken off from more important things.

Russell's attitude to the war is frequently misconstrued, both by those who believe that he did not care about Britain and by those who claim, with as little truth, that he was an all-out pacifist. As far as the Germans are concerned, he agreed that there was much to be admired in them; nevertheless, his comment to Lucy Donnelly after visiting Niagara with one was fairly typical: "Insufferable race." As for pacifism, Russell declared from the first that he did not think all wars unjustified; only that most of them were, and that in this particular case Britain would have best served her own interests, and those of Europe, by remaining neutral.

In 1914 this attitude had more support than is usually appreciated today. In Russell's case, its roots stretched back to the Co-efficients and his ineradicable belief that Grey's policy at the Foreign Office had been a recipe for war. Later, in 1911, he had been blistering in his opinions on the outcome of the Anglo-Persian Treaty. "We help in the perpetration of a crime against liberty, justice & civilisation," he wrote: "*Motive*: fear of Germany – which nearly caused war last summer, & is the ground for our vast naval expenditure. *Cure*: Friendship with Germany. *Means*: Assassination of Grey."

Dislike of the Russian autocracy was certainly a factor in his attitude to the events of 1914, as it was in that of his friend Charles Sanger. "As you know," Sanger wrote to Russell three days after the outbreak of war, "I have always regarded Grey as one of the most wicked and dangerous criminals that has ever disgraced civilisation, but it is awful that a Liberal Cabinet should have been parties to engineering a war to destroy Teutonic civilisation in favour of Serbians and the Russian autocracy." Russell heartily agreed. "If we succeed," he wrote to Lucy Donnelly, "the only power that will ultimately profit is Russia – the land of the knout."

Sanger's phrase, "engineering a war", also reflected Russell's feelings. With his habit of following a step logically through to its consequences, he could not believe that the Foreign Office record was anything less than a Machiavellian progress. That men could reach Cabinet rank and still do no more than muddle through without foreseeing the consequences was literally unbelievable; the alternative was intent, the conspiracy view of history from which he rarely deviated and which made it almost inevitable that half a century later he should regard Macmillan and Kennedy as "much more wicked than Hitler", and the assassination of President Kennedy as a skilfully devised plot.

This was the background to his feelings as, throughout July, the repercussions of assassination at Sarajevo began to spread across Europe. At the beginning of the month, at one of Ottoline's Bedford Square dinner-parties he was introduced to the Prime Minister, Herbert Asquith, who had asked to meet him. Whether they talked much is not on record but he at least had a short talk with Miss Asquith – "I don't know how sincere she was, but she seemed *quite* sincere," he later confided – and there is one entry in his diary which suggests that the meeting led to something more. It is for 27 July and reads, "10 Downing Street, 5 p.m."

Britain was by this date already sliding towards war, although many still wished to hold her back. Thus on 31 July Lord Edmond Fitzmaurice, who would have been Foreign Secretary had Grey refused the appointment in 1906, wrote of the war-threat to J. A. Spender, "I can see no mortal reason why we should be dragged into this affair unless Grey has given pledges of which the House of Commons knows nothing."

Nevertheless, the feeling for neutrality remained strong throughout the country. "I have not found a *single* person, of whatever party or class, who is in favour of war, or thinks anybody else would be," Russell wrote from Cambridge; "*all* think it folly and very unpopular, Tories as well as Liberals; and they hardly realise that we are being drawn in. At first I found people incredulous when I said Grey would join in if France was attacked; now, regretfully they see he will." His rationally argued case for British neutrality ended in the same letter with a plea for German *Lebensraum* and an appeal for the Germans that was to be repeated within Germany twenty-five years later – "when they try to protect their homes and their wives and daughters against vast hordes of Russian savages, we do our best to prevent their efforts from being successful, and to threaten them with starvation if war breaks out".

Russell's views were held by many members of the university. J. J. Thomson, soon to be both President of the Royal Society and Master of Trinity, was among the eminent men who issued a plea for neutrality saying,

> War upon [Germany] in the interests of Serbia and Russia will be a sin against civilisation. If by reason of honourable obligations we be unhappily involved in war, patriotism might still our mouths, but at this juncture we consider ourselves justified in protesting against being drawn into the struggle with a nation so near akin to our own and with whom we have so much in common.

Russell himself signed with many others a statement published two days later which expressed "the supreme conviction of the supreme importance of preserving England's neutrality in the existing situation", of those who considered "that at the present juncture no vital interest of this country is endangered such as would justify our participation in a war". His feelings were no doubt reinforced when, dining months later with Lord Courtney, the standard-bearer of conciliation, he heard Lord Morley's indiscreet admission "to the effect that if Germany had delayed her violation of Belgian territory 48 hours the Cabinet would have broken up and there would have been a *coalition Government*".

At the start of what was to be the last weekend of peace he was still in Cambridge. Keynes had just lent the proofs of his *Treatise on Probability* to Russell for the latter's critical comments and the two of them, together with C. D. Broad, had been going over them night after night in Russell's rooms. On Sunday 2 August there came a telegram from Ottoline urging him to come down to London without delay. He left early the following morning and lunched at Bedford Square in a state of mind revealed by two letters written within the previous seventy-two hours: "I seem to feel all the weight of Europe's passion, as if I were the focus of a burning glass – all the shouting, angry crowds, Emperors at balconies appealing to God, solemn words of duty & sacrifice to cover red murder & rage. It seems as if one must go mad or join the madmen." Then, as common sense struggled back, "I am fixing some things in my mind which I forgot during the Boer War: not to hate anyone, not to apportion praise & blame, not to let instinct dominate. The force that in the long run makes for peace & all other good things is Reason, the power of thinking against instinct."

In Bedford Square Ottoline agreed that Philip should make a pacifist speech in the House that evening. According to Russell, she "told Philip he was to make a pacifist speech in the House, and he feared her more than the British Government and nation". The speech was, in fact, a simple plea that Britain should stand aside. Failing to gain admittance to the Public Gallery, Russell walked home via Trafalgar Square without hearing it, dejectedly marvelling at what he took to be the average person's delight at the prospect of the coming war.

He spent the night at his flat, met Ottoline the following morning, and for half an hour walked with her along the streets around the British Museum, speculating on what the future held. Almost two decades later, when the area was being transformed for the extension of London University, he told Ottoline that he could "never pass the empty region behind your house without remembering how we walked there the day war began". He went on to the weekly staff-lunch of the *Nation*, and handed in a letter pleading for British neutrality, which the editor, H. W. Massingham, promised to publish. The following day, according to Russell, the situation had changed. Massingham wrote saying "Today is not yesterday" and published the letter only after vehement protest by Russell, who later said, "After about three years of war, he forgot that he had ever been in favour of the war. I did not remind him."

Massingham was not the only one who decided to support the government when it came to the crunch. That evening Russell quarrelled with his old friend George Trevelyan on the issue of British intervention, and attended the last meeting of the British Neutrality Committee which, with Charles Buxton, the former Liberal M.P., J. A. Hobson the economist and Lowes Dickinson, he had helped found under the chairmanship of Graham Wallas, the Fabian friend of his Friday's Hill days.

When he left London on Wednesday Britain was at war, but there still seemed a faint hope that neutralist feeling, strengthened by Grey's admission of secret military talks with the French which had been concealed from the House of Commons, might bring about an early armistice. Back in Cambridge he was quickly disillusioned.

"We are terribly alone in this terrible world," he wrote to Ottoline in the evening; "I have been home 10 minutes and have had a letter from Mrs. Whitehead in favour of war, and a talk with Professor Hobson, who got most of the signatures to our manifesto, but has gone over completely because of Belgium. One can only suffer and wait." The following day he reported, "The prize bore of the College reproached me tonight with not taking the war more seriously, and said perhaps in time I should find out what a grave matter it is." He met Keeling, "the Socialist firebrand, and he told me he was enlisting and could not imagine a greater joy than to see a German fall to his rifle".

In London the following day, things were little better. Here he met his old friend Eddie Marsh, "immaculate in evening dress, blooming and happy, enjoying his importance" as Churchill's Private Secretary at the Admiralty. This was the beginning of the end of a friendship. A few weeks later they met again and to Russell's protests about Britain's attitude Marsh replied, "Oh well, we couldn't have the Germans over here." Russell, according to Marsh, said that he didn't see why not. Four years later, when their respective opposition to and support for the war had both intensified, Marsh had become, according to Russell's invective to Ottoline, "the kind of obscene philosophic insect that ventures out from its crevice in the darkness provided by the war, crawling over defenceless corpses and polluting them with its slime".

To Lucy Donnelly he said on 22 August that

> Wells writes that he is "enthusiastic" for this war. Shaw favours it; secretaries of peacetime societies welcome it; vegetarians and anti-vivisectionists support it to a man. Hardly anyone seems to remember common humanity – that war is a mad horror & that deliberately to cause the deaths of thousands of men like ourselves is so ghastly that hardly anything can justify it.

A few weeks later he reiterated his sentiments; "... Clearly the Germans are the worst – but Maeterlinck & Gilbert Murray & Robert Bridges are almost as bad."

However, despite his initial and firmly held belief that Britain could and should have remained neutral, despite his contempt for the men over Service age who declaimed the glories of war, Russell throughout the next few weeks was far more reserved, and far more in line with majority opinion, than he later became. "I do see the point of those who believe in the war, and it is a comfort, because it makes it easy not to hate them," he wrote to Ottoline. "And I think at the very last it couldn't be helped;

but until the very last it could have been." And to Lucy Donnelly: "We are all patriots in one sense, that we ardently desire the victory of the Allies; but we don't want a *brutal* victory, and many of us think that a wiser policy in the past might have prevented war altogether, tho' now that war exists there is nothing for it but to prosecute it, tho' it will probably involve the death of about half of the men in the country between 20 and 30." He also wrote strongly to Ottoline of the line Philip should take in the House.

> I take it for granted that P. on Saturday will make it clear that he will not oppose Government while the war lasts, and that he recognises the need of prosecuting it with all vigour now we are in. It is important to dissociate *political* opposition, which must begin when the military danger is past, from opposition of the sort that might conceivably be thought damaging to our success in the war.

His early acceptance of the political situation gradually changed; so did the climate in which even such qualified dissent could be expressed. As the casualty-lists lengthened and passion took control, the wall dividing opposition to the war from the policy of fighting to the bitter end became higher and thicker. Nevertheless, many links of family and friendship held firm. Alys, who continued to follow his fortunes closely, had temporary doubts, writing in September 1914, "I agreed with thee at the beginning of the war, but am not sure that I do now." But when Russell came under heavy attack two years later, she offered to sell investments to raise cash for him. Gilbert Murray, whose public defence of Grey brought a bitter response from Russell, refused to break an old friendship although he might have acted differently had he known that Russell felt "ashamed of ever having liked him" and considered him "as squashy as a slug". Even Aunt Agatha, always happy to make the scathing pronouncement on Russell's personal life, mentioned the word "war" only in the penultimate paragraph when congratulating him on his work, and added, "My very good Bertie, let this dark shadow between us be removed by the love on both sides which can dispel all misunderstandings and misconceptions."

Most remarkable, as well as most poignant, was the situation which developed between Russell and the Whiteheads, quietly patriotic and quietly shocked, as unable to doubt the sincerity of their old friend's attitude as they were to understand it. Russell's surprise at Evelyn Whitehead's first letter supporting the war was increased by a second that arrived in Cambridge a few days later. "When I got here," he wrote on returning from London, "I found a *very* war-like letter from Mrs. Whitehead saying North wants to enlist & she thinks he is right. I can't tell you how much I mind – I feel as if my relations with the whole family could never again be quite the same. Next to you they are much the most important people in my life." A fortnight later he told Ottoline he had replied in an effort to narrow the breach. "I hope it will answer," he went on. "But I shall never get over the sense of estrangement from them. I could do with other people, but the Whiteheads touch me too nearly."

Alfred Whitehead did his best in a long letter written after he had seen off his elder son for France. "I am miserable at differing from you on so great a question," he wrote. "I cannot see what other course was open to us than the one which we actually took . . . it seems to me that it would have been national suicide for us to stand out."

Early in September Russell visited the Whiteheads at Lockeridge, hoping for the best, expecting the worst, especially as Evelyn had been "meeting Belgian refugees at Charing X and getting their horrors first-hand", as he described it. His anticipations were justified. "It is perfectly awful here, worse even than I expected," he wrote to Ottoline.

> I hold my tongue – there is nothing else to do. Every tale against Germany is believed – there is no hint or trace of justice or mercy. I am only now realising how very remote we are from the general feeling of humane people. Everything they say confirms me in anti-war feeling – but I find myself utterly remote from them, in a different world altogether. I suffer most from the absence of any attempt at justice, at imagining how matters look from the German side. It goes against all that I feel most deeply, & it hurts terribly coming from them. I fear sooner or later they will attack me, & I don't know what I shall do then. I want to escape. I don't know if I shall be able to hold out till Saturday. They have read about Louvain, & it has steeled their hearts against mercy – there is an orgy of hate, running through all their humanity to Belgian refugees & other sufferers. The world has far to travel yet before compassion & understanding take the place of anger. It is really dreadful to feel so cut off from old friends. I should not dare to say anything to Mrs. Whitehead – to Whitehead alone, when he spoke of Louvain, I suggested that perhaps we did not quite know the exact facts, & he immediately changed the subject . . .

He continued to visit them, but the visits grew less frequent. By April 1915 he was admitting, "I dread the Whiteheads. I would as soon walk over red-hot plough-shares." Mrs Whitehead had become "more or less sane, but he is utterly wild and mad in his determination to crush Germany & [in] his belief in the quite special wickedness of Germany". The easy way out would have been to dissent in silence, but this was not Russell's way: "something that if I had been religious I should have called the Voice of God, compelled me to persist".

Throughout the next four years Whitehead stood his ground as Russell stood his; but there existed between them a gulf that Whitehead at least believed to be unbridgeable. As the war went on, the gulf deepened. "I had meant to avoid discussion with you – where feeling is acute, and divergence deep, discussion among intimates is often a mistake," Whitehead wrote in April 1916. But a letter from Russell compelled him to re-state his belief – that "on the whole, men who refuse military service are avoiding a plain, though painful moral duty – often no doubt with the excuse of a mistaken conscience".

If Whitehead's wartime correspondence with Russell reveals a logical admission that rational men must sometimes agree to differ, a more emotional overtone suffuses the letters from Evelyn Whitehead, the very woman whose agony in the spring of 1901 had aroused Russell's frustrated sympathy and forced him to the belief that the horrors of war were only rarely justified. In August 1914 she maintained that where she differed from him was in believing that "the bully must be stopped"; and, almost as a *non sequitur* half-way through her letter, writes "goodbye Bertie". There is a gap of eighteen months, then she writes almost from out of the blue, that she "hated challenging" him – apparently at one of his public lectures where she intervened – and admitting with despair "well, it is no good and yet I know that perhaps someday we will talk again like old friends". All except one man in her elder son's last unit was a volunteer, she said, and Eric, the younger son, would soon be old enough to serve.

> All of them will go, many for that ideal of freedom which Germany opposes, it is their precious young lives that buy it and they are glad to give them for the sake of all that makes life worth living and I felt bitter through the blinding pain, and I wanted you to see that they care with their lives and to give them a parting bow as they go, do you see, Bertie? . . . There is no need for forgiveness dear Bertie, I expect we both pay full measure for those convictions which are dearer than life.

In reply, Russell demanded a thought for the German mothers too, a demand which Mrs Whitehead appeared to evade – "if I have not made myself clear it is hopeless to try".

Yet the friendship still held. Later in the war, when the threat of prison hung over him, Russell received a letter from Evelyn that epitomized both his wartime relations with the Whiteheads, and his position in their world.

> Dear Bertie,
>
> Try and think out a place of work, do, your mind is so fine & your work is so valuable – After all, what you care for most in the world is your work – It is your early love and you are always faithful to it, you never over-estimate it.

Your métier is to write, to write philosophy, ultimate truth is worth slaving for, your mind is always at its best when you are living for this. If at any time we can do anything to mitigate, or to make the present more endurable, let us know it at once – However passionately we may disagree with your present views to us, you are you, the friend we value, whose affection we count on, the friend whom our boys love, & in many ways still our Infant Prodigy – If we don't write later on it is only because you will prefer to hear from, & to see others, not because the pain and the bitterness of this very vital divergence has altered the strength of our long & tried friendship – Do come soon ring me up – Affectionately,

EVELYN WHITEHEAD

It was not only friendship with the Whiteheads that struggled for survival during the war. Across the lines there was Wittgenstein. "It seems strange that of all the people in the war the one I care for much the most should be [one] who is an 'enemy'," he wrote. "I feel an absolute conviction that he will not survive – he is reckless and blind and ill. I can know nothing until the war is over. If he does survive, I think the war will have done him good." A few months later, when he heard that Keynes had somehow received a letter from Wittgenstein, he revealed his feelings to Ottoline. "I never knew till the war came, how large a place he has in my life – next to you, I think, because he holds my imagination so completely. He never fails one in that respect – he is wonderfully pure."

Before long Russell himself received a letter. Wittgenstein told him,

If I should perish in this war, my MS which I showed Moore will be sent to you, with another which I have written now during the war. If I remain alive, I should like to come to England after the war, & explain my work to you by word of mouth, if you are willing. Even in the former case, I am persuaded that it will be understood by someone sooner or later. May heaven soon again vouchsafe me good ideas!!!

Thy LUDWIG WITTGENSTEIN

Please greet Johnson kindly from me.

At the mention of Wittgenstein, Russell still responded with the crackle of excitement that comes from touching genius. But the excitement was personal rather than professional; philosophy had now been pushed almost entirely from his mind to make space for political work. Before the end of August 1914 he had became a founder-member of the Union of Democratic Control, born during meetings held in the Morrells' Bedford Square house. The initial idea had come from Charles Trevelyan, who had resigned from his Private Secretaryship at the Board of Education on the outbreak of war, and E. D. Morel, a man of high conscience and crusading fervour. Trevelyan and Morel were joined by Ramsay MacDonald, Norman Angell, Lord Ponsonby and Joseph Rowntree. Together they founded an organization which was to continue, with varying fortunes, not only throughout the First World War but until after the Second.

In the early days Russell was greatly unimpressed by the U.D.C. "The evening was dreadful," he wrote of one meeting, "– P[hilip] admirable, Angell full of good ideas but silent, the rest a set of selfish fools – except MacDonald, who has much virtue, and some sense, but not much. If many Quakers are like Rowntree, I understand why they instituted silent meeting. They talked of starting a new party – it seemed like 8 fleas talking of building a pyramid." However, he strongly supported the Union's three main aims. These were to secure real parliamentary control over foreign policy, and to prevent it being again shaped in secret and forced upon the country as an accomplished fact; to open direct and deliberate negotiations with democratic parties and influences on the Continent when the war ended; and to secure such peace terms as would not "either through the humiliation of the defeated nation or an artificial re-arrangement of frontiers merely become the starting point for new national antagonisms and future wars".

Even in 1914 the aims were respectable enough. So were the supporters, many of them present or future Members of Parliament from the left wings of the Labour or Liberal Parties. The U.D.C.'s statement stressed that serious campaigning was to start only when "the country is secure from danger" and Russell, writing in October to Charles Trevelyan, puts an interesting gloss on the charges of pro-Germanism so constantly made against him. "It would be unwise in the extreme to publish anything at present containing explicit criticism of Grey or of the immediate causes of the war," he said.

> I see no harm in denouncing "secret diplomacy", which may be taken as Grey's *alias*; but I feel *very strongly* that until the Germans have been expelled from France & Belgium it is better to confine ourselves to terms of peace and other *future* matters, leaving the past to be dealt with when the country is out of danger. Otherwise you will alienate many who are with you in opinion, & incur so much odium as to render yourselves useless.

But material dealing with recent policy and suggesting lines of action for the future was urgently required. Here Russell's ability to tailor together almost any sort of article or paper came into play, and from now onwards he was to devote an increasing amount of time to such political propaganda, first for the U.D.C., later for the No-Conscription Fellowship.

An early pamphlet was *War: The Offspring of Fear*, written for the

U.D.C. at the suggestion of Trevelyan, who read the draft and suggested additions. It contained, like much else that Russell wrote during the war – and afterwards, his critics may add – a curious mixture of sound common sense and fantasy. Dealing with the violation of Belgium he observed that "every student of strategy has known for many years past that this must be an inevitable part of the next Franco-German war, and ... Sir E. Grey expressly stated that if it did not occur he would still not promise neutrality", an admission by Grey, published in a White Paper, which threw a new light on pity for poor little Belgium. But as well as this pemmican of common sense, the pamphlet contains some phrases which might have come from Germany a generation later. Thus the war was, essentially, "like the barbarian invasion of the Roman Empire, or the medieval wars of Christian and Musselman ... a great race-conflict, a conflict of Teuton and Slav, in which certain other nations, England, France and Belgium, have been led into co-operation with the Slav ..."

Russell, and others of like mind, pinned their hopes on the quick expulsion of the German armies from France and Belgium followed by a peace imposed by powerful neutrals on combatants before the fabric of European civilization had been torn apart. If these hopes were to be fulfilled it would be necessary to counter the stream of official propaganda directed at the neutrals from Britain and France, and as early as September 1914, he had tentatively considered making a lecture-tour in America, the most powerful of the neutrals, and the possibility of interviewing President Wilson. The scheme, less grandiose than it sounds, had been encouraged by his meetings in London with Elizabeth Perkins, the Boston writer he had encountered at Harvard six months previously. Back in America Mrs Perkins sounded out the authorities but received a discouraging reply. No foreigner could be presented to the president unless introduced by his own ambassador or minister, a service that Britain's representative was in the circumstances unlikely to provide. "The present is not the time to discuss peace," William Phillips, Assistant Secretary of State, tactfully noted on 2 November; "and I fear that Russell will find a very small audience in this country at the present moment, but the time will come, undoubtedly, when everything he has to say will be listened to with intense interest."

However, if a Russell peace-tour in America was a non-starter, Mrs Perkins's efforts brought results of a different kind; it was she who now put him in touch with American editors, notably Ellery Sedgwick of the *Atlantic Monthly*, thus paving the way for the long stream of articles which were to cause such gnashing of teeth in Whitehall. On the face of it these articles – among them "Is a Permanent Peace Possible?", "The Future of Anglo-German Rivalry", "War and Non-Resistance", and "Individual Liberty and Public Control" – were harmless enough. Some of his statements had a surprisingly respectable cast, as when he wrote of the post-war peace, "No solution will be possible until it grows clear to the

Germans that they cannot reasonably hope to become superior to us at sea." As for pacifism, he held that, "broadly speaking . . . the use of force is justifiable when it is ordered in accordance with law by a neutral authority, in the general interest and not primarily in the interest of one of the parties to the quarrel".

The articles were finely tuned for one particular market, and Russell showed considerable skill in judging what would affect the Americans in any particular circumstance. Thus he rightly sensed the reaction to the sinking of the *Lusitania* by the Germans in May 1915. His article on "How America Can Help to Bring Peace" was already in type when the *Lusitania* was torpedoed with the loss of nearly twelve hundred passengers, including about a hundred Americans. Without delay, Russell cabled to stop publication.

The occasions when his views in the *Atlantic Monthly* chimed in with the gospel as handed down from Whitehall were more than counterbalanced by the intellectual context in which they appeared, and by the persistence with which he would take a question, weigh up the pros and cons, and state his opinion without regard for person, country or prejudice. Two specific ideas which he favoured were officially considered especially harmful, or impractical, or both. One was for an international organization, "able and willing to secure obedience by force", which seemed equally objectionable to the government and to out-and-out pacifists but which Russell saw as the best hope of peace. The other was his advocacy of passive resistance. "If it were adopted deliberately by the will of the whole nation, with the same measure of courage and discipline which is now displayed in war," he wrote, it "might achieve far more perfect protection for what is good in national life than armies and navies can ever achieve, without demanding the carnage and waste and welter of brutality involved in modern war."

However, it was not only Russell's opposition to this particular war which made him disliked in Whitehall. What also stuck in the official gullet was the non-religious, non-national approach, as well as the effectiveness of his prose. These traits were well illustrated by the paragraph ending his "War as an Institution".

> Men have learned gradually to free their God from the savagery with which the primitive Israelites endowed him; few now believe that it is his pleasure to torture most of the human race in an eternity of hell-fire. But they have not learned to free their national ideals from the ancient taint. Devotion to the nation is perhaps the deepest and most widespread religion of the present age. Like the ancient religions, it demands its persecutions, its holocausts, its lurid, heroic, cruelties; like them, it is noble, primitive, brutal and mad. Now, as in the past, religion, lagging behind private consciences through the

> weight of tradition, steels the hearts of men against mercy and their minds against truth. If the world is to be saved, men must learn to be noble without being cruel, to be filled with faith yet open to truth, to be inspired by great purposes without hating those who try to thwart them. But before this can happen, men must first face the terrible realisation that the gods before whom they have bowed down were false gods, and the sacrifices they have made were vain.

Here spoke the essential Russell, opinions unqualified by expediency, undeterred by the fact that in linking religion with national ideals he was handing his enemies an invaluable weapon.

He had not been slow to realize how the cold steel of his logic could deal with political problems as easily as with those of philosophy, and his letters are full of plans for projected books, pamphlets and articles. In describing a work on the Foreign Office which he had in mind, he wrote,

> I can make a terrific piece of invective in the book I want to write. One might head each chapter with a quotation from Asquith's speeches since the war – "We are fighting in defence of small nationalities" – Boer War; "for democracy" – how we paid the Tsar to suppress the Duma & send its members to Siberia; "in defence of the sacredness of treaties" – Algeçiras & Persia; & so on through the whole chapter of our crimes. I cannot discover an infamy in the whole wide world which the F.O. has not done its best to support – it is beyond belief.

It was a plausible thesis – until he laid his flank open to attack with an over-statement typical of the kind with which he often ruined a good case. "I think", he concluded, "every word the Germans say against us is justified."

The diatribe against the Foreign Office was never written, although what did appear was *The Policy of the Entente* in which Russell shot his arrows into the body of Gilbert Murray. There also appeared in 1915 "The Ethics of War", prepared for the *International Journal of Ethics*, then edited by Russell's old friend Philip Jourdain. In this Russell distinguished four kinds of war: of colonization, of principle, of self-defence and of prestige. "Of these four kinds," he says, "I should say that the first and second are fairly often justified; the third seldom, except as against an adversary of inferior civilisation; and the fourth, which is the sort to which the present war belongs, never." If this is surprising, more is to follow. For although wars of colonization "are totally devoid of *technical* justification, and are apt to be more ruthless than any other war," there is, Russell avers, another side to the coin, since

> if we are to judge by results, we cannot regret that such wars have taken place. They have the merit, often quite fallaciously claimed

> for all wars, of leading in the main to the survival of the fittest, and it is chiefly through such wars that the civilised portion of the world has been extended from the neighbourhood of the Mediterranean to the greater part of the earth's surface.

The paper contrasted strongly with the views of the radical, loosely joined groups which strove for an early end of the war, even if this came before the decisive defeat of the Central Powers. Nevertheless, Russell remained one of their most impartial spokesmen. In 1915, moreover, he severed his links with the Liberals, relinquished academic work for full-time propaganda, and swung himself away from the Union of Democratic Control into the vastly more activist ranks of the No-Conscription Fellowship, all moves which reflected his hardening opposition to this particular war.

The first move came in April. "One of my chief reasons for supporting [it]", he wrote when notifying the secretary of the Cambridge Liberal Association that he did not wish to renew his membership, "was that I thought [the Liberals] less likely than the Unionists to engage in a European war. It turns out that ever since they have been in office they have been engaged in deceiving their supporters, and in secretly pursuing a policy of which the outcome is abhorrent to me. Under these circumstances I can do nothing directly or indirectly to support the present Government."

Even so, he could not yet quite bring himself to support the Socialists. "I have been for some time in two minds as to joining the ILP," he told Herbert Bryan, the Labour leader.

> I agree most warmly with the attitude which the ILP has taken up about the war, & that makes me anxious to support the ILP in every possible way. But I am not a socialist, though I think I might call myself a syndicalist. I hardly know how much I commit myself to in joining; it is always difficult to sign a declaration of faith without reservations. Perhaps my hesitation is unduly scrupulous; perhaps it will cease; but for the moment I do not quite feel as if I could join you.

Without party, he was by no means without cause, and by early 1915 his political journalism was already hardening into a major job. As early as the previous November he had thought of throwing in the sponge at Trinity. "What I can do further in philosophy does not interest me, & seems trivial compared to what might be done elsewhere," he had then written.

> ... I don't want to be in Parliament; it seems to me one is freer outside, & can achieve more. I should want to write, to travel, to speak

in foreign countries, to be unfettered in saying what I believed. If I went into ordinary politics, I should become an object of jealousy to labour men, which would be a hindrance. I can't bear the sheltered calm of university life – I want battle and stress, & the feeling of doing something. I might get a year's leave of absence from here as a time of experiment, so as not to burn my boats. What do you think?

Ottoline agreed in principle, as he became more and more impatient to leave a Cambridge so radically different from the place he had looked on as home. Nevile's Court had been turned into a hospital. A primitive blackout was in operation and members of the Officers' Training Corps guarded the local reservoirs. The recruiting campaign had all but emptied the colleges of students, since no system of keeping essential men from the forces was yet in operation, and by December his class consisted of two Americans, an Italian, a Japanese and a woman. "All the white men are gone or drilling," he protested in disgust. Many of the younger dons had already joined up, and control of university and college affairs was gradually falling to the elderly and more conservative Fellows. "These fussy bloodthirsty old men are so unutterably contemptible," he complained. "My soul is full of black horror and impotent hate." By contrast, the opposition groups were, compared with those in the Second World War, more numerous, more vocal and more aggressive. Apart from the unqualified pacifists who opposed killing in any circumstances, there were many such as Russell who objected, on grounds as much political as anything else, to this particular war at this particular time. Unlike most fully fledged pacifists, they tended to be vehement and many of them – notably Russell himself – developed to a fine art the technique of quietly exasperating their opponents to screaming point. Thus they acted as lightning conductors, attracting not only pacifists and political activists but all those who were constitutionally "against".

During the first months of 1915 one of Russell's pamphlets – probably *War: the Offspring of Fear* – achieved local fame in Cambridge. "One of the divinity professors discussed it with a gathering of his friends who were all highly-educated and very intelligent men – school inspectors, clergymen, etc.," Russell was told, "and after a very careful discussion it was gravely burned with the consent of the whole company; and one of their number expressed the opinion that it ought to have been burned by the common hangman."

As the nation became more warlike, Russell grew more depressed with the Cambridge scene.

All that one has cared for is dead, at least for the present; & it is hard to believe that it will ever revive. No one thinks about learning or feels it of any importance. And from the outer deadness my thoughts travel to the deadness in myself – I look round my shelves at the books of mathematics and philosophy that used to seem full of hope & interest, & now leave me utterly cold. The work I have done seems so little – so irrelevant to this world in which we find we are living. And in everything except work I have failed so utterly.

The gloom remained even when he moved among sympathizers. Meeting with a score of men determined not to join the armed forces, he experienced "the same impression as the letters of Apollinaris Sidonius in the break-up of the Roman Empire, when the barbarians were invading Gaul".

However, while Russell was preparing to leave this dispiriting atmosphere, the Council of Trinity was preparing to hold on to him. Whatever views might be held about his political opinions, there was no doubt about his growing reputation, and for such a man to be living and working in college, but to hold a post only as Lecturer, seemed faintly ridiculous. On 12 February, 1915, the Council decided to elect him to a Research Fellowship as soon as his Lectureship ended.

"If I accept it, it decides my settling permanently into a don," he told Ottoline. "I suppose it is the right thing to do, but I should have liked not to have to make my mind up at present." Then, before an offer was formally made, he applied for leave of absence during the coming Michaelmas and Lent Terms. What followed next was a courteous but cool exchange. The Council pointed out that the Fellowship would presuppose his being engaged in the systematic study of philosophy and mathematics. He would have to stick to the job although the Council members "would consider favourably an application for leave of non-residence if he informs them that the purpose of the application is the better prosecution of those studies". This, as the members of the Council probably knew, was not at all what Russell had in mind. His reply was that his philosophical work was "improved by occasional excursions into other fields, from which one returns with renewed freshness of mind", an ingenious statement but one unlikely to pass any Council member with eyes open. A gentlemanly compromise was proposed and accepted. On 28 May the Council agreed that Russell should not be offered a Fellowship; that when his Lectureship ran out in October it should be renewed for another five years; and that he should be granted leave of absence for the coming Michaelmas and Lent Terms.

The decision, Russell later maintained, had been taken purely on "party" lines, with only the two U.D.C. members of the Council supporting him. "The College has been rent into violent factions," was his description to Ottoline. " ... They all suppose I must mind dreadfully not being a Fellow, but I don't care two pins ... Both friends & opponents in the dispute about me have rather disgusted me. I have never before known much about College politics. I *am* thankful I shall be away for a time.

Dons are stifling." Later he gave his reasons. "I lose £140 but gain in freedom ... I am only just realising how Camb. oppressed me," he wrote from his London flat. "I feel far more alive here & far better able to face whatever horrors the time may bring. Camb. has ceased to be a home & a refuge to me since the war began. I find it unspeakably painful being thought a traitor. Every casual meeting in the Court makes me quiver with sensitive apprehension. One ought to be hardened ..."

So far, his political writings had been mainly confined to U.D.C. publications, small in circulation: the pages of the *Atlantic Monthly*, influential among a limited readership in the United States but little known in Britain; and the *Labour Leader*. Now he was to embark on a more ambitious project: a series of political lectures subsequently published as *Principles of Social Reconstruction*, the first of his popular political books and possibly the best of all his political writings. The genesis of the lectures, like much else in Russell's story, can be traced back to Ottoline, in this case to the meeting which she engineered with D. H. Lawrence. The relationship which developed not only helped thrust Russell into the public arena but after an initial period of friendship eventually aroused in both men a mutual hatred, mutually enjoyed.

Ottoline had been attracted by Lawrence's writing, in particular by the descriptions in *Sons and Lovers* and *The White Peacock* of the Nottinghamshire countryside she had known as a girl. After their first meeting, she gave Russell her impressions in a letter which also casually warned him that Helen Dudley had reappeared in London.

"Fancy Helen being back!" he replied as though whistling to keep up his spirits. "What a bore. I thought she had gone for good ... I am glad you like Lawrence. One feels from his writing that he must be wonderful – a man with a real fire of imagination. I should like to know him."

Ottoline responded by taking Russell to Greatham, where the Lawrences were living in a cottage under the lee of the South Downs, lent them by Viola Meynell. "From the first," she recorded in her journal,

> these two passionate men took to each other and Bertie Russell, as we drove away, exclaimed "He is amazing; he sees through and through one." "Yes. But do you think he really sees correctly?" I asked. "Absolutely. He is infallible," was Bertie's reply. "He is like Ezekiel or some other Old Testament prophet, prophesying. Of course, the blood of his non-conformist preaching ancestors is strong in him, but he sees everything and is always right."

The two men were thus drawn together as potential friends. Yet the Lawrence of the coal-field community, with a sackful of chips on his shoulder in the days when this was no assurance of success, faced the confident product of the Stanley and Russell families who was only now emerging from the Cambridge cocoon. The impractical revolutionary, aching to lean against the pillars of society and quite certain they would crack if he did, faced the grandson of Lord John who had sucked in with his mother's milk an understanding of the political machine. The believer in *Blutbrüderschaft*, whose prognathous ideas could not be entirely argued away by his supporters, faced at the other end of the lists the calm logician armed at all intellectual points.

Thus it was almost inevitable that within a few months the two men would mount their hobby-horses and charge each other full tilt, without benefit of button on the lance. After the encounter each veered off. But Russell, less damaged than Lawrence, eventually came to harbour the more bitter dislike, which burst out in a broadcast almost half a century later. Lawrence contented himself with fictional lampoons of Russell and a remark recorded by William Gerhardi, after Russell's mind had been praised. "Have you seen him in a bathing dress," Lawrence asked. "Poor Bertie Russell! He is all Disembodied Mind!" Even so, for Lawrence it must have been maddening that Russell's scrawny five foot seven was such an irresistible attraction for women; jealousy within the *Blutbrüderschaft* was no prime mover in the dispute between them, but its overtones were there.

None of this was in view when Russell wrote to cement the friendship after their first meeting. "Your letter was very kind to me, and somehow made me feel as if I were impertinent – a bit," Lawrence replied. "You have worked so hard in the abstract beyond me, I feel as if I should never be where you have been for so long and are now – it is not my destiny." He was right. Cambridge, to which Russell now invited him, was not his destiny. It would be, he warned Russell in advance, a quite momentous occasion for him. "I don't want to be horribly impressed and intimidated," he wrote, "but am afraid I may be. I only care about the revolution we shall have. But immediately I only want us to be friends. But you are so shy and then I feel so clumsy, so clownish. Don't make me see too many people at once or I lose my wits."

He arrived on Saturday 6 March. Russell did his best to make him feel at home, but without obvious success. In hall that night Lawrence sat with Russell on one hand and on the other G. E. Moore, with whom he was instinctively at cross-purposes. There were friendly exchanges with Hardy and apparently less friendly ones with Keynes. Recollections of the evening are few and inconclusive, but Lawrence seems to have thrown up a psychological palisade to protect himself from the influences of such an assured and confident company.

The following morning Keynes was among those invited to a breakfast in Russell's rooms which Lawrence later described as one of the crises of his life. According to Keynes, he "was morose from the outset and said very little, apart from indefinite expressions of irritable dissent". Russell tried to draw his guest into the conversation but, Keynes has said, most of the talk "was *at* Lawrence and with the intention, largely unsuccessful, of getting him to participate ... I came away feeling that the party had been a failure and that we had failed to establish contact".

Few reactions could have made Russell more anxious to consolidate the new friendship, particularly in view of his personal feelings about Keynes's intellect which frightened him, and Keynes's homosexuality which distressed him.

> Lawrence had rather liked him before, but seeing him this morning at 11, in pyjamas, just awake, he felt him corrupt and unclean. Lawrence has quick sensitive impressions which I don't understand, tho' they would seem quite natural to you. They are marvellous. I love him more & more. I wouldn't dream of discouraging his socialist revolution. He has real faith in it, & it absorbs his vital force – he must go through with it. He talks so well about it that he almost makes me believe in it ...

Keynes came to dinner that evening and Russell's account to Ottoline suggests that the battle-lines between his two guests stiffened.

> Keynes was hard, intellectual, insincere, using his intellect to hide the torment in his soul. We pressed him hard about his purpose in life – he spoke as tho' he only wanted a succession of agreeable moments, which of course is not really true. Lawrence liked him but can't get on with him. I get on with him, but dislike him. Lawrence has the same feeling against sodomy as I have; you had nearly made me believe there is no great harm in it, but I have reverted; & all examples I know confirm me in thinking it sterilising.

For his part, Lawrence failed to be impressed, either by Keynes or by the visit. "It is true Cambridge made me very black and down," he wrote to Russell on his return to Greatham. "I cannot bear its smell of rottenness, marsh-stagnancy. I get a melancholic malaria. How can so sick people rise up? They must die first." All the same, Lawrence still had for Russell the attraction of the outsider for the insider.

The next step was a second meeting at Greatham. From it there emerged the first rough ground-plan for *Principles of Social Reconstruction*. "We talked of a plan for lecturing in the autumn on his religion, politics in the light of religion, & so on," Russell told Ottoline. "I believe something might be made of it. I could make a splendid course on political ideas; morality, the State, property, marriage, war, taking them to their roots in human nature, & showing how each is a prison for the infinite in us. And leading on to the hope of a happier world."

Lawrence's account was complementary.

> Bertie Russell is here. I feel rather glad at the bottom, because we are rallying to a point. I do want him to work in the knowledge

of the Absolute, in the knowledge of eternity. He *will* – apart from philosophical mathematics – be so temporal, so immediate. He won't let go, he won't act in the eternal things, when it comes to men and life. He is coming to have a real, actual, logical belief in Eternity, and upon this he can work: a belief in the absolute, an existence in the Infinite. It is very good and I am very glad.

We think to have a lecture hall in London in the Autumn and give lectures; he on Ethics, I on Immortality; also to have meetings, to establish a little society or body around *a religious belief, which leads to action.* We must centre in the knowledge of the Infinite, of God.

The "we" was still there, although Lawrence was already qualifying his views. To Ottoline he wrote that Russell was "vitally, emotionally, much too inexperienced in personal contact and conflict, for a man of his age and calibre. It isn't that life has been too much for him, but too little. Tell him he is not to write lachrymose letters to me of disillusion and disappointment and age; that sounds like 19, almost like David Garnett. Tell him he is to get up and clench his fist in the face of the world."

What Russell did was to work at his customary speed and, within a few weeks, send Lawrence a draft outline of what he thought the lectures should contain. It was speedily returned, spattered with underlinings, single, double, treble and quadruple, and with one "must" underlined no less than fifteen times; with marginal notes and with the occasional "No, no" scrawled across whole paragraphs. In addition, written on the title-page of the 22-page draft, was the following:

Don't be angry that I have scribbled all over your work. But *this* which you say is *all social criticism*; it isn't social reconstruction. You must take a plunge into another element if it is to be social reconstruction. Primarily you must allow and acknowledge & be prepared to proceed from the fundamental impulse in all of us towards The Truth, the fundamental passion also, the *most fundamental* passion in man, for Wholeness of Movement, Unanimity of Purpose, Oneness in Construction. *This is the principle of Construction.* The rest is all criticism, destruction. *Do, do* get these essays ready, for the love of God. But make them more profound, more philosophical. Make them not popular, oh, not popular. The best is to attack the spirit, then proceed to the form. You call the spirit Subjectivism. Do go to the root of this; kill it at the root. Show how everything works upon this great falsity of subjectivism, now. I like it where you take them one by one. The State, Marriage, etc. But you *must* put in the *positive idea.* Every living community is a living state. You must go very deep into the State, & its relation to the individual.

We shall be at 32 Well Walk, Hampstead, Mrs. Radford – this weekend. I must see you.

> Above all don't be angry with my scribbling. But above all, *do* do these lectures.
>
> I must lecture – or preach – on religion – give myself away. But you must dare *very* much more than you have done here – you must dare be positive, not only critical.

Russell reacted calmly enough, although his next note to Ottoline foreshadowed the approaching rift.

> Lawrence, as was to be foreseen, is disgusted with my lecture-syllabus; it is not mystical and Blake-ish enough for him. He says one ought to live from the "impulse towards the truth" which he says is fundamental in all of us. It seems to me, in him, merely an impulse to mistake his imaginations for the truth. He talks of a desire for oneness with others which he believes to be the same as the "impulse to truth". I don't believe these things exist in most people. But I find those who have a strong imagination generally read their own natures into other people, instead of getting at other people by impartial observation. Lawrence is just as furious a critic as Wittgenstein, but I thought W. right and L. wrong. He is coming to see me Sat. I dread it. I don't know whether I shall still be able to feel any faith in my own ideas after arguing with him, although my own reason is all against him. He is lacking in humour; he takes my irony seriously and protests against it ...

Much as he wished to, he was unable to shake off the influence. "I am depressed, partly by Lawrence's criticisms," he wrote. "I feel a worm, a useless creature. Sometimes I enumerate my capacities, & wonder why I am not more use in the world. I suppose scepticism is my real trouble. It is always only by an act of will that I keep it under, & it weakens me."

However, disagreement was not the root of the trouble. Disagreement was the stuff of his life. What he had begun to object to in Lawrence was the hectoring schoolmasterly manner which assumed God-given omnipotence. This would have been bad enough had not the crime been compounded by Lawrence's impracticality, a weakness which Russell always found it difficult to condone. "There must be a revolution in the state," Lawrence had written to him in his first letter.

> It shall begin by the nationalising of all industries and means of communication, and of the land – in one fell blow. Then a man shall have his wages whether he is sick or well or old – if anything prevents his working, he shall have his wages just the same. So we shall not live in fear of the wolf – no man amongst us, and no woman, shall have any fear of the wolf at the door, for all wolves are dead.
>
> Which practically solves the whole economic question for the

present. All dispossessed owners shall receive a proportionate income – no capital recompense – for the space of, say, fifty years.

Fine ideas but, as Russell knew even without the help of Keynes, totally irrelevant in terms of solving "the whole economic question".

However, the friendship lumbered on, and later in the month Russell persevered by sending Lawrence an essay for his magazine, the *Signature*. Entitled "The Danger to Civilisation", it emphasized the perils of a long war but ignored the factors in society which had helped bring it about. Lawrence reacted with a long semi-hysterical letter which ended, "The enemy of all mankind, you are, full of the lust of enmity. It is *not* the hatred of falsehood which inspires you. It is the hatred of people, of flesh and blood. It is a perverted, mental blood-lust. Why don't you own it.

"Let us become strangers again, I think it is better."

At first Russell was unable to shrug off Lawrence's denunciations. "I was inclined to believe that he had some insight denied to me," he wrote nearly forty years later, "and when he said that my pacifism was rooted in blood-lust I supposed he must be right. For twenty-four hours I thought that I was not fit to live and contemplated suicide. But at the end of that time, a healthier reaction set in, and I decided to have done with such morbidness." However, it had not been quite as bad as that. "The idea of suicide has never been long out of my thoughts since I was a boy," he wrote at the time to Ottoline, "but it won't come to anything till I have no more work in me – it is really a possibility I play with in imagination to help one through the days. It is not a thing to be taken seriously."

Russell's comparatively innocuous essay hardly warranted Lawrence's outburst, but a clue to the reason for it is given in a letter from Lawrence to Lady Cynthia Asquith: "I've got a real bitterness in my soul, just now, as if Russell and Lady Ottoline were traitors – they are traitors," he complained. "They betray the real truth. They come to me, and they make me talk, and they enjoy it, it gives them a profoundly gratifying sensation. And that is all. As if what I say were meant only to give them gratification, because of the flavour of personality, as if I were a cake or a wine or a pudding." Bitter as he was, uncomfortably aware that to Cambridge he was an outsider and to Garsington possibly no more than an interesting specimen, Lawrence had a point. When Ottoline invited Russell to meet the Lawrences at Garsington, he replied that discussing Lawrence's philosophy with him would be rather difficult. "It is rather uneducated stuff," he went on; "I feel as you would if I wrote about pictures."

In spite of his reluctance to take seriously either Lawrence's philosophy or his political plans, Russell continued to feel a grudging respect for the man's vitality and an envy of his imagination, which mirrored his envy of Conrad's power and style. But his feelings were more than counter-balanced by his judgment of Lawrence's ideas as distinct from his creative literary genius. Concepts of blood-consciousness and blood-being were, he felt, "frankly rubbish"; in addition Lawrence "never let himself bump into reality". This was too much for Russell, who was content to let the friendship slide apart.

It slid quickly enough, and into a bitter enmity whose course should be traced before Lawrence's impact on *Principles of Reconstruction* is assessed. In 1917 Russell, handed a copy of Lawrence's *Look! We Have Come Through* over the Garsington breakfast-table, drily remarked, "They may have come through, but why should I look?" Fourteen years on, when he wrote the first draft of his autobiography, he completely ignored Lawrence, although this was perhaps not to be wondered at. Lawrence had died a year earlier, and the flood of posthumous praise was reaching high tide. Russell, by contrast, was in one of his deep periodic troughs, at low ebb both personally and professionally. His real feelings surfaced four years later in one of his last letters to Ottoline. "Lawrence", he wrote, "is one of a long line of people, beginning with Heraclitus & ending with Hitler, whose ruling motive is hatred derived from megalomania, & I am sorry to see that I was once so far out in estimating him." Two decades later he wrote a long and bitter condemnation for the B.B.C., "the harshest words [he] ever hurled at an opponent in a lifetime of abuse," as they have been called. To a correspondent he gave a more urbane explanation:

> As to the effect of Lawrence on me, many people had told me, and I had supposed it possibly true, that the habit of analytic and rational thinking had rendered me incapable of the kind of intuitive understanding that Lawrence claimed to possess. Knowing that the forces that move people are often unconscious, I was prepared to think that he might be right about me. I only thought this for a few hours. After that, the instinct of self-preservation took care of me and I decided that he had been talking nonsense.

Lawrence struck while his opponent was still alive. In "The Blind Man", Bertie Reid is "a little dark man, with a very big forehead, thin, wispy hair, and sad, large eyes", a man "whose mind was so much quicker than his emotions, which were not so very fine"; and in *Women in Love*, Sir Joshua Malleson, whose Hermione Roddice is a thinly disguised Ottoline, is – with "a mental fibre so tough as to be insentient" – "an elderly sociologist . . . a learned dry Baronet of fifty who was always making witticisms and laughing at them heartily in a harsh horse-laugh", a description which probably rankled as much as Lawrence's bravado in giving the baronet the name of Russell's current mistress.

In the summer of 1915, as he veered sharply away from Lawrence, he began to immerse himself in the preparation of his lecture-plans. Philip

Morrell arranged for him to have a flat in the farm-bailiff's house, Ottoline decorated it, and Russell settled down to work. When visitors he wished to meet came to Garsington he took meals in the manor house. Usually he worked in the mornings, in the afternoon he often walked with Ottoline, becoming more gloomy, more tied up in his work. Slowly but steadily, relations between them grew more cantankerous. "He gets dreadfully on my nerves," she wrote in her diary in mid-July; "he is so stiff, so self-absorbed, so harsh and unbending in mind or body, that I can hardly look at him, but have to control myself and look away."

To his face she was more diplomatic. But he sensed her reaction. "The result", he wrote months later, "was that the impulse stopped dead." He put the lectures aside for a while, and turned instead to denunciation of a political pamphlet written by his old friend Gilbert Murray. In old age, he said of the dispute merely that Murray had gone "out of his way to write about the wickedness of the Germans, and the super-human virtue of Sir Edward Grey". In fact, the argument was a good deal more personal, reflecting Russell's current view of Murray, whom he described in a letter to Lucy Donnelly as "a snivelling sentimental ass".

Murray had already won his reputation for an impartiality that could be neither bought nor curried. It was therefore something of a feather in the government's cap that his pamphlet, *The Foreign Policy of Sir E. Grey, 1906–15*, of a size and make-up convenient for propaganda purposes, not only exculpated Sir Edward but attacked the "pro-Germans" in Britain in knockabout terms. Conveniently for the Cabinet, two of those lambasted as "often very clever" but "not at present in a state of mind which enables them to see or even to seek the truth" were Brailsford and Russell. They were among the small minority, Murray went on, who

> become naturally so wrapped up in their own immediate controversy that, as far as their combative feelings are concerned, the central enemy of the human race is Sir Edward Grey; next to him come the British Cabinet and the most popular Generals. The Kaiser is to them a prisoner in the dock, a romantic unfortunate, to be defended against overwhelming odds.

This, Russell felt, was some way below the objectivity expected of Murray. Shortly afterwards, waiting on a station platform on his way back from Garsington, he heard a voice from the incoming train calling, "Bertie." It was Mary Murray, who tackled him at once about her husband's pamphlet. "We had a very painful conversation," Russell wrote to a friend, "and at one moment I thought we were going to become enemies for life. I have a very strong affection for her, and I should have minded dreadfully. But we smoothed it over and parted friends."

Whether this encounter alone would have tipped him into action is not clear. But a few weeks later he was informed by Delisle Burns that copies of Murray's pamphlet were being distributed free to all lecturers of the University Extension Delegacy (an unofficial term to cover the body of extra-mural lecturers working for the Board). "If you are writing anything you might notice this," Burns added. Russell duly did so. The result was *The Policy of the Entente, 1904–1914, A Reply to Professor Gilbert Murray*, a pamphlet which in the climate of the times was likely to be read only by the converted.

Russell buttressed his case by the use of official British documents – as had Murray. Both men were selective. But whereas Murray's selection patted on the back both British honour and British circumspection, Russell's raised awkward questions. He was certainly in complete agreement "with the whole of what Professor Murray says as to the wickedness of Germany's invasion of Belgium". He pointed out that an earlier pamphlet of his own, condemned by Murray as pro-German, had been prohibited in Austria "on the ground of the vehemence of its pro-British bias". And when it came to the claim that the invasion of Belgium had in fact been the cause of the war, Russell made damaging use of the statements in the British government's White Paper No 123. "The German Ambassador asked Sir Edward Grey whether he could promise neutrality if not only the integrity and independence of France (including colonies) but also the neutrality of Belgium, were respected," he said. "Sir E. Grey replied that he could give no such promise." To Murray's claim that such bargaining would have been illusory, dishonourable and dangerous, he went on,

> That is to say, honour or interest, or both, so bound us to France that we could not, even to save Belgium from invasion, stand aside while France was attacked. So far from Belgium being the cause of our intervention, we were precluded from making any effective diplomatic attempt to protect Belgium by the fact that we could not promise neutrality even if Belgium were respected.

The controversy with Murray would represent only a shot in the dogged battle between Russell and the rest, were it not for a curious sidelight cast on the affair by Clifford Allen, later Lord Allen of Hurtwood, a founder-member of the No-Conscription Fellowship with which Russell was to have such a close connection. After the war he and Russell visited Brailsford in his Hertfordshire home. Allen later wrote,

> On the way back, Bertrand Russell told me what he knew of [Mrs Brailsford's] history. She had been a brilliant student of Gilbert Murray's, had fallen in love with him though he was married, and at last wrote that she would go to the devil unless he had an affair with her. He consulted Bertrand Russell who said that the only way to

deal with the situation was to do one thing or the other. Either he must have nothing to do with her or must agree to her wish. Murray instead merely philandered, and she ultimately married Brailsford on the understanding that there should be no sexual intercourse because of her love for Murray. This was her stipulation. Bertrand Russell did not know the result although it appeared that Lady Mary Murray forced the false relationship to an end so far as her husband was concerned. When the war broke out, Murray seems to have revenged himself on Bertrand Russell and Brailsford by his vicious attacks on them in connection with the pacifist cause.

The story seems strangely at variance with Murray's character, while Allen was by no means an objective witness after all he had suffered. Nevertheless, it is difficult to believe that there was no fire behind the smoke, even though it was a curious tale for Russell to relate about an old friend. After Russell's pamphlet had appeared, Murray wrote a friendly note to Russell who replied that he was sorry if he had been offensive and added, "I feel our friendship still lives in the eternal world, whatever may happen to it here and now. And I too can say 'God bless you.'" Maybe. But the blessings went, in Russell's more private opinions, to the man who he had described to Ottoline as being "as squashy as a slug".

With Murray's pamphlet disposed of, Russell turned again to *Principles of Social Reconstruction*. But it was only late in the autumn that the lectures were finished and he was ready to hire the Caxton Hall, Westminster, for eight evenings in the coming January, February and March.

The programme was announced in the *Cambridge Magazine*, now reaching its high tide of anti-Establishment criticism under C. K. Ogden, but the announcement aroused little enthusiasm. "I wonder if you or Bessie or either of you will come to any of my lectures?" Russell wrote to Bob Trevelyan. "I gather very few people are coming & I am in despair about it." However, old friends rallied round and even the critical Whiteheads came. "They must have hated it," Russell admitted. After a poor start, attendance perked up, helped by the enthusiasm of Ottoline and the support of Russell's Cambridge friends. Lytton Strachey wrote,

> Bertie's lectures help one. They are a wonderful solace and refreshment. One hangs upon his words, and looks forward to them from week to week, and I can't bear the idea of missing one – I dragged myself to that ghastly Caxton Hall yesterday, though I was rather nearer the grave than usual, and it was well worth it. It is splendid the way he sticks at nothing – Governments, religions, laws, property, even Good Form itself – down they go like ninepins – it is a charming sight! And then his constructive ideas are very grand; one feels one had always thought something like that – but vaguely and inconclu-

sively; and he puts it all together, and builds it up, and plants it down solid and shining before one's mind. I don't believe there's anyone quite so formidable to be found just now upon this earth.

Subjective as it was, Strachey's account gives an idea of the impact made by the lectures on the small, receptive group which alone could be expected to attend them. Together with "The Free Man's Worship", Kingsley Martin later wrote, the lectures were "the nearest things I had in my day at Cambridge to a textbook of political aspiration and a basis for philosophical thinking". Outside the Establishment, one of the few critics was Lawrence, still angrily astonished that Russell did not expect to transform the world in an hour or two. "His lectures are all right in themselves, but their *effect* is negligible," he wrote to Ottoline. "They are a financial success. But all the people who matter are too busy doing other things to come to listen. He lives only for fussy trivialities, and for nothing else." To Russell himself he was more blunt.

I don't believe your lectures *are* good. They are nearly over, aren't they.

What's the good of sticking in the damned ship and haranguing the merchant-pilgrims in their own language. Why don't you drop overboard? Why don't you clear out of the whole show ... ?

"My love to you," he concluded. "Stop working and being an ego, and have the courage to be a creature."

Far from being too mealy-mouthed, as Lawrence objected, Russell's lectures were in 1916 considered the apotheosis of revolution, and caused consternation among the directors when they arrived in the office of Stanley Unwin, who had offered to publish them. His colleagues were only won over after he remembered that his co-directors had the greatest respect for Professor J. H. Muirhead, editor of the firm's Library of Philosophy, to whom he proposed that Russell's typescript should be sent. He later wrote,

They unhesitatingly agreed, but to their chagrin his verdict was as follows: "I have read most of Russell's 'Principles of Social Reconstruction' with the greatest possible interest. It is a brilliant book and I congratulate you on having the publication of it. Parts of it, especially the part on marriage, will give rise to a great deal of discussion, possibly even opprobrium, but people ought to be sufficiently familiar with the point of view and it is one that has to be faced and reckoned with. The central problem that is raised – the place of institutions, family, state, church – is a vital one, and it is of quite extraordinary interest to find William Godwin's polemic against them revived in so brilliant and up-to-date a fashion ... "

To have one's second political book compared to Godwin was no bad start. Its basic aim, Russell wrote in a preface, was

> to suggest a philosophy of politics based upon the belief that impulse has more effect than conscious purpose in moulding men's lives. Most impulses may be divided into two groups, the possessive and the creative, according as they aim at acquiring or retaining something that cannot be shared, or at bringing into the world some valuable thing, such as knowledge or art or goodwill, in which there is no private property. I consider the best life that which is most built on creative impulses, and the worst that which is most inspired by love of possession. Political institutions have a very great influence upon the dispositions of men and women, and should be such as to promote creativeness at the expense of possessiveness. The State, war, and property are the chief political embodiments of the possessive impulses; education, marriage, and religion ought to embody the creative impulses, though at present they do so very inadequately. Liberation of creativeness ought to be the principle of reform both in politics and in economics.

This was Russell's first statement of the political ideas he was to maintain with few changes for the rest of his life. His method of work was revealed a couple of years later when a Rugby master wrote explaining that he had taken a passage from the chapter on education, discussed it with his class, and then rewritten it. Now he wanted to know what Russell thought of his effort. "The logical meaning is, of course, unchanged," he was told,

> but what is lost is the movement and rhythm. In a passage of this kind one instinctively develops a theme in the kind of way in which Beethoven does. One works it gradually free from antagonistic feelings, until at the end it emerges triumphant. This of course affects the whole rhythm of the sentences and the changes in cadence. I do not mean that all this is deliberate or conscious: indeed it is only through comparing it with your reconstruction that I became aware of a certain crescendo in the original, which I feel to be lacking in your reconstruction. You begin with the triumph and end with the terror, which would suggest thought as a tyrannic master rather than an inspiring leader into freedom.

The argument for the new philosophy of politics was worked out in chapters dealing with the principle of growth, the State, war as an institution, property, education, marriage and the population question, religion and the Churches, and a final account of "What We Can Do". Russell attacked both the State and private property; concluded that both for Britain and Germany, "at every moment during the war the wisest course would have been to conclude peace at once, on the best terms that could have been obtained"; stressed the need for what would be, in effect, an armed League of Nations; claimed that "neither the right to dispose of property by will nor the right of children to inherit from parents has any basis outside the instincts of possession and family pride"; and on marriage, education and the Church, put forward views then considered as offensive as they are today considered reasonable. Lawrence, true to earlier form, was shocked by their mildness. "I have not read Bertrand Russell's book," he wrote, "but I can assure you it is no good."

Every chapter did in fact contain a few sentences which were certain to shock or infuriate a majority of British readers in 1916. In contrast to the sober praise of the left-of-centre journals there was much echoing of the *Athenaeum*'s denigration of what it called "the monastic detachment of which Mr. Russell is at once so distinguished and so despairing a representative". Lord Cromer, reviewing in the *Spectator*, described it as a "thoroughly mischievous book" and a delighted Mr Unwin printed the verdict on the jacket of the next edition.

11

Into Battle

Nine months had passed between the delivery of the lectures on *Principles of Social Reconstruction* early in 1916 and their publication in the autumn. The controversy which they then aroused was not entirely due to their advanced thinking or because they were directed to a nation which now realized it was in for a long war. Equally important was the fact that Russell had in the interval become one of the most hated men in Britain, the result of a translation from mathematical academic into militant propagandist which sprang from his support for the No-Conscription Fellowship and the *cause célèbre* in which this support involved him in the summer of 1916.

The new Russell had been stirred alive first by the coming of war and then by lecturing on social and political affairs. The outcome was revealed in a letter to Lucy Donnelly written in the immediate aftermath of the Caxton Hall lectures. "... Power over people's minds is the main personal desire of my life; & this sort of power is not acquired by saying popular things," Russell wrote.

> In philosophy, when I was young, my views were as unpopular and strange as they could be; yet I have had a very great measure of success. Now I have started on a new career, & if I live and keep my faculties, I shall probably be equally successful. Harvard has invited me to give a course of lectures 12 months hence on the sort of things I am now lecturing on, and I have agreed to go. As soon as the war is over people will want just that sort of thing. When you once understand what my ambitions are you will see that I go the right way about to realize them. In any large undertaking, there are rough times to go through, & of course success may not come till after one is dead – but those things don't matter if one is in earnest. I have something important to say on the philosophy of life and politics, something appropriate to the times. People's general outlook here has changed with extraordinary rapidity during the last 10 years; their beliefs are disintegrated, & they want a new doctrine.

But those who will mould the future won't *listen* to anything that retains old superstitions & conventions. There is a sharp cleavage between old & young; after a gradual development, I have come down on the side of the young. And because I am on their side, I can contribute something of experience which they are willing to respect when it is not merely criticism ...

The first of his contributions was made to the No-Conscription Fellowship, founded in November 1914 by Fenner (now Lord) Brockway, editor of the *Labour Leader*. Although its appeal was mainly political, it aimed at bringing into one group all men of military age who opposed compulsory service but were outside bodies such as the Society of Friends which held pacifism as an intrinsic belief, or the Independent Labour Party which opposed the war on political grounds. At first there had seemed little for the Fellowship to do; the belief that the war would soon be over lingered on throughout 1915, and there was as yet no conscription, the government still hoping that the necessary forces could be raised by rousing appeals to patriotism or by carefully induced shame. Only when the appeals failed was it admitted that those who did not come must be dragged; in November 1915 the Derby Recruiting Campaign showed plainly what the future held, and conscription was introduced two months later.

Russell himself was over-age, but many of his friends were not and many sought his advice. "Bertie was most sympathetic," Lytton Strachey wrote to Ottoline soon after conscription was seen to be inevitable. "I went to see him this morning and we had lunch with Maynard [Keynes] in an extraordinary underground tunnel, with city gents sitting on high stools like parrots on perches, somewhere near Trafalgar Square." Significantly enough, Keynes, soon to be made a Companion of the Bath for his services at the Treasury, supported the National Council Against Conscription with a cheque for £50 soon after the Conscription Bill was passed.

It is still difficult to separate facts about the N.-C.F. from fiction; legend and propaganda from brutal truths; or to assess what the organization actually achieved. But at the least it brought a wriggle of embarrassment from the more thoughtful of the powers-that-be; prepared the way for the evolution of ideas during the inter-war years; and helped ensure that during and after the Second World War, those who stuck to their pacifist guns were treated in a less uncivilized way than their fathers. In all this, Russell played a part that should not be obscured by the image sedulously built up by the authorities: that of the dilettante professor, stepping into a strange arena and usually making a fool of himself. The reverse was the case. From the thick Home Office files bearing his name it is obvious that the government knew that in Russell they had a formidable opponent.

As early as March 1915, he reported to Ottoline that a friend had found the N.-C.F. far more inspiring than the U.D.C. Further, according to a young Cambridge mathematician who had refused an Admiralty demand to work on the mathematics of aircraft, supporters were "joining at the rate of thousands a day". Russell felt moved to speak for it. "The U.D.C. will be all right *after* the war," he continued,

> but for the moment they are tumbling over each other in their eagerness to disclaim any lack of patriotism or of determination that the victory must be ours. This puts such a restraint upon what one can say that it half paralyses one. And I grow less & less interested in the politics of the war, & more & more to feel the important thing is to denounce *all* war. If one could have made any defence of Germany, I dare say I should not have felt as I do. But Germany seems to me very nearly as bad as the most rabid people say, & yet I feel it is wrong to fight Germany. And I don't like getting involved in irrelevant controversies on questions of fact, which don't really matter one way or the other.

His move from the predominantly political climate of the U.D.C. into the more emotionally charged Fellowship took time. He certainly wished to help the No-Conscription people. "But I have a good deal to do for my lectures," he wrote while still preparing *Principles of Social Reconstruction*, "& I don't want to get over-worked again." Thus it was not until the first months of 1916 that his strong personal feelings combined with disgust at the "idleness" of U.D.C. supporters to drive him into the welcoming arms of the N.-C.F.

"The non-resistance people I know (in the Cambridge U.D.C.)", he had told Ottoline, "are so Sunday-schooly – one feels they don't know the volcanic side of human nature – they have little humour, no intensity of will, nothing of what makes men effective. They would never have denounced the Pharisees or turned out the money-lenders." Very different was Clifford Allen, just twenty-six, secretary and general manager of the Labour *Daily Citizen*, and chairman of the N.-C.F. since its formation. Early in 1916, Russell heard him address a No-Conscription meeting a few weeks after conscription had been brought in. "Very able as an organiser & leader," he wrote; " – not attractive personally, but capable of becoming a power, & sure to be always on the right side. He has decision & energy & a capacity for making people follow him." The last assertion was certainly true. Shortly after making it, Russell walked into the N.-C.F. headquarters and offered his services. His decision was to have repercussions on the pacifist movement; on the caricature-portrait of Russell presented to the British public for much of the next half-century; and, through a strange quirk of fortune, on Russell's deepest emotional life.

Apart from one fine and one six-month sentence, he suffered none of the hardships and few of the inconveniences which wrecked the professional lives, and often the health, of many conscientious objectors. Even so, he was one of the most effective single opponents to conscription, a fact recognized by the government in the lavish amount of time and energy devoted to him. His influence was partly due to ability as a propagandist; partly to the dedicated skill which he gleefully exercised in outwitting the authorities, and which rapidly earned him the nickname of "Mephisto"; partly to the position which this political outsider who was yet a house-party acquaintance of Asquith, and the heir to an earldom, occupied on the social inside. At first he was merely a helper, willing to turn his hand to the most pressing task, whatever it was. With Clifford Allen's second imprisonment in 1916, he became Acting Chairman and as such was able to deploy his considerable powers at a higher level. The work itself, concerned very largely with policy decisions, was always demanding, frequently monotonous, and totally lacking the excitement of the N.-C.F.'s activities in the field which brought it to the verge of conflict with the law. Nevertheless it was essential and it runs like a necessary backbone through Russell's effect on the Fellowship.

His early work coincided with publication of *Justice in War-time*, a collection of political essays written since the autumn of 1914. Its appearance was received along party lines, with denunciation from the Right and praise from the Left, although even *The Times Literary Supplement*, which headed its review "A Superior View of the War", had to confess, "We freely admit that the volume contains not a few smart sayings and well-turned epigrams and that there are individual sentences and paragraphs which express wholesome truths."

The decision openly to support the N.-C.F. caused some bristling among his friends. "I hold that the State has the right to compulsion both in taxes and in personal services," wrote Whitehead. "Here I agree with all the great Liberal statesmen e.g. Cromwell, the French Revolutionary Statesmen, Lincoln, J. S. Mill, etc., – You used to admire these men: I never suspected your fundamental divergence." Beatrice Webb, harking back to an occasion when Russell had spoken eloquently of the need to resist, thought all the speeches "might have been delivered at any gathering of persons dissenting from the verdict of the bulk of their fellow-citizens because they felt themselves possessed of a higher standard of morality".

From some, the criticism might have been expected, as when Lawrence wrote,

> You are satisfying in an indirect, false way your lust to jab and strike. Either satisfy it in a direct and honourable way, saying "I hate you all, liars and swine, and am out to set upon you", or stick to mathematics, where you can be true – But to come as the angel of peace – no, I prefer Tirpitz a thousand times in that role.

> You are simply *full* of repressed desires, which have become savage and anti-social. And they come out in this sheep's clothing of peace propaganda. As a woman said to me, who had been to one of your meetings: "It seems so strange, with his face looking so evil, to be talking about peace and love. He can't have *meant* what he said."

It was not only Lawrence. Lytton Strachey reported to Vanessa Bell that Russell was "working day and night with the N.-C.F. and is at last perfectly happy – gloating over all the horrors and moral lessons of the situation". Like Russell, Strachey often made his point by exaggeration.

Russell's move into what was to all intents and most purposes full-time voluntary work for the N.-C.F. made economy essential. He therefore left his Bury Street flat, let it to the first of a succession of tenants, and moved into semi-permanent quarters with Frank, taking a top-floor room in his brother's house in Gordon Square, conveniently situated almost midway between Bury Street and Bedford Square. Here he hung above his desk framed portraits of Leibniz and Frege, introducing them to visitors with the words, "I have these two Huns to keep me company."

Frank had in the meantime, during the progress of his matrimonial adventures, obtained a divorce from his first wife, and also from the second whom he had married bigamously. Then in 1916 he had married Elizabeth von Arnim, formerly Elizabeth Beauchamp, a widow who had already achieved considerable fame as a novelist and as author of *Elizabeth and Her German Garden*. She had known her new brother-in-law for some years and welcomed him into the household: "My two men ... afford much excitement and variety in the ménage," she was later writing. "Bertie is the most charming creature – elf-like ... imp-like, a Christ and a devil ... The weirdest of human beings."

From his new quarters he walked most days to the nearby N.-C.F. offices and here put himself under the control of the formidable Catherine Marshall, a martinet if ever there was one and an old acquaintance from the Suffragist Movement who had left it on the outbreak of war to devote herself to the pacifist cause. A hard driver, she made no exception for eminent philosophers, and under her instructions Russell answered letters, spoke at public meetings, briefed Members of Parliament and acted until the end of 1917 as intellectual vanguard of the movement. For the first and probably last time, he was regularly presented with a long agenda, some items marked with a brief "B.R. to do." Obediently, he did.

Two sides to Russell's involvement, an infectious enthusiasm and a gross over-estimate of what the movement was likely to accomplish, were illustrated in his report to Ottoline of the Fellowship's April conference, "the most inspiring and happy thing that I have known since the war began", as he described it.

They got through immense masses of business, all of it important, with extraordinary speed; one saw how business was done in the French Rev'n. Allen wields the sort of power over them that leaders had then. He is a man of genius – not at all simple, with a curious combination of gifts. At the opening of the Conference, when he first rose, they wanted to cheer him till they were hoarse, but he rang his bell & held out his hand for quiet: they stopped at once, & he began "Will you turn to p. 1 of the Agenda" – it is something like the way Parnell treated the Irish Members. I have never seen anyone comparable to him as a Chairman. All the intervals were filled with Com'ee. meetings, so we were all kept pretty busy. I said a few words of sympathy, & they gave me a great cheer. I really believe they will defeat the Government & wreck conscription, when it is found they won't yield.

I can't describe to you how happy I am having these men to work with & for – it is *real* happiness all day long – I feel they can't be defeated, whatever may be done to them.

The thought of battle invigorated him and Ottoline soon noted in her diary that he was a changed man, using up all his energies, with none left over to go bad. "I hope it will last, for it makes him so happy," she added. "I think if he can keep up his present enthusiasm he may really lead a movement."

Shortly afterwards Russell, together with Clifford Allen and Miss Marshall, met Lloyd George. The ostensible reason was to interview him about the conscientious objectors who were being kept in prison, although as Lloyd George was still Minister of Munitions it seems more likely that the main reason was to discuss the non-Service work which conscientious objectors might be willing to do. "He was very unsatisfactory," Russell reported to Ottoline, "& I think only wanted to exercise his skill in trying to start a process of bargaining. Still, it was worth something that he should see Allen & know the actual man. It will make him more reluctant to have him shot." Whether Russell's intervention on this occasion was a good thing may be open to doubt – "At the end, as we were leaving, I made him a speech of denunciation in an almost Biblical style, telling him his name would go down in history with infamy" – but he was ideal for the day-to-day output of letters implementing the strategic decisions of the Associates' Political Committee. Produced with Russell's deft touch, they not only explained the Fellowship's point of view but stood at least some chance of publication in the generally hostile press.

He was a propagandist who could make people listen in spite of themselves and a letter in the *Labour Leader*, over the signature "F.R.S.", has all the stigmata of this particular Fellow of the Royal Society. Under the heading "Practical War Economy", it proposed that since Britain had now adopted Continental conscription there existed a more economical method of conducting the war. "Let all the Great Powers of Europe agree that boys, when they reach the age of 18, shall be divided by lot into three classes, one containing the half of them, the other two each containing a quarter," it proposed.

> The class containing one half shall be painlessly executed in a lethal chamber. Of the other two classes, the members of the one shall be deprived of an arm, a leg or an eye, at the discretion of the surgeon; the members of the other shall be exposed day and night to defening noises, until they acquire some nervous affliction – madness, speechlessness, mental blindness, or deafness – after which they shall be liberated to form the future manhood of the country.

In the cut-and-thrust of such N.-C.F. work, in writing an editorial nearly every week from the summer of 1916 onwards for the Fellowship's *Tribunal*, and in a snowdrift of pamphleteering, Russell found good scope for the intellectual dynamiting that was both an enjoyable exercise of his skill and a weapon in the good fight. Even so, it is doubtful whether the moral magnetism of the work would alone have kept him in the Fellowship for two long years. But there happened to be an extra something. If Russell lacked appetite for physical struggle, he more than balanced it with a delight in making rings round authority. This helped to sustain him, to keep him in the cause when service under Miss Marshall, and the sheer weight of uninteresting drudgery, might otherwise have pushed him back into a more intellectual shell.

For their part, the authorities handled him a good deal more gingerly than their published records admit. "He writes and speaks with a good deal of misguided cleverness," allowed Edward Troup, Permanent Under-Secretary in the Home Office, in advising against prosecution on one of the numerous occasions when this was considered. Herbert Samuel, the Home Secretary, agreed that the whole course of Russell's action "made him dangerous", while a special five-page report to the Prime Minister in the autumn of 1916 was needed to explain and interpret the convolutions, distortions and deliberate lies into which Russell's careful actions had forced the authorities. Russell himself loved it all. "For my part," he exulted to Ottoline, "I get so much fun out of it that I have difficulty in looking the part of a martyr."

He not only loved it. His efforts helped tremendously to keep the ship of protest afloat, and if there is one lesson to be learned from the papers of Clifford Allen and of Catherine Marshall, as well as from the reminiscences of the crew who remain, it is that Russell's influence in the N.-C.F. was greater than is generally appreciated. He, far better than anyone else, could discard the emotion when it no longer served, and use instead the cool intellect beneath; an example of private practice serving public purpose.

Miles Malleson, the actor who was to become deeply and intimately involved with Russell before the war was over, was one of Russell's converts. He had enlisted early and been wounded in France. "In 1915 I was wandering about London very unhappy because I didn't feel quite the same as when I joined up," he has said.

> My friends at Cambridge, the best of them, were being killed off one by one. Every day there was another name. And in this state of almost despair as to what I felt about it, I sneaked into the back of a very big meeting, of a very full hall, and there was Russell on the platform making a speech. And I heard a passionate and reasoned argument that this slaughter of my generation should be brought to an end as soon as possible. And somehow my doubts and uncertainties were cleared away and I think that that afternoon probably was a turning point in my own attitudes and thoughts about the world.

Russell's strong points included the honesty of his beliefs and his equally whole-hearted concern for ordinary men and women. "There is a man in Wandsworth called Gardner who is pining for a message from you to generally 'buck' him and the others up," he was told on one occasion in a message from Fellowship headquarters. "Do you think you could spare five minutes to write one? I hate to trouble you, but it won't be the same for them if anyone else does it." The wife of a conscientious objector wrote that she and her husband had once tramped eighteen miles to hear him speak. And even Clifford Allen, contained in his own shell more than most leaders, could write to Russell from prison, "I don't think I shall ever forget Sunday with you. How exhausted you must sometimes get, giving strength to other people."

Not only exhausted but often bitter. "I am living all against impulse," he wrote.

> – my impulse is to write biting things about the pleasure men derive from having their sons killed, or about what fun it is to be a journalist of military age on the Morning Post – or about the Bishop of London at the last Judgment, full of surprise to find himself not appreciated. It drives me wild that peace can so *obviously* be got & hardly anybody wants it; except the soldiers, who don't count, because there is so little affection in the world.

At times in his pacifist work, as elsewhere, he put a foot wrong. His claim to Gilbert Murray that the risk conscientious objectors ran of being shot by the military authorities in France was as great as the risk the ordinary soldier ran of being shot by the Germans was a damagingly misleading statement. His joke that since the king was giving up alcohol for the duration of the war he would start drinking, since teetotalism must have something to do with killing Germans, was trite. And his scepticism of early German atrocities was an error of judgment which he admitted in private, and which drove one of his potential supporters to ask, "You can't be meaning to suggest that there is evidence of the same kind to convict our troops and their commanders, e.g. of systematic rape and arson. We have burned no Louvain and sunk no *Lusitania*."

Nevertheless, his ability to bait the authorities and encourage them to make fools of themselves was a useful weapon in a struggle sometimes fought in disconcertingly mixed company. "This has been a most glorious and beautiful week-end, and also a very interesting one," wrote Keynes to his mother in describing a May 1916 visit to Garsington. "Into a nest of rebels, Philip Snowden, Massingham, Bertie Russell, Lytton Strachey, the Morrells, two young ladies from the Slade and me, who are the house party, enter this afternoon the Prime Minister, Sir Matthew Nathan, Lady Robert Cecil and Lady Meux – a queer mix-up."

Garsington, to which the Morrells finally moved in the early summer of 1915, had become a main focus of the pacifist movement in Britain, and while Russell's emotional links with Ottoline had been loosening, his political links with both her and Philip had been strengthened by the war. Russell in this new and more militant habitat is well described in a letter from Naomi Bentwich, a young Newnham girl and an ardent N.-C.F. supporter who wrote of Garsington with its "brilliant colours everywhere ... huge log fires and bowls of spice all over the place. Not ostentatious but every comfort." Into this scene there came the man himself. "The lady was very excited about his coming, although he seems a pretty regular visitor," Miss Bentwich went on;

> she made herself look young and beautiful, and her spirits were high. He was in the drawing-room when I came down to dinner, and when I was introduced he said "We have corresponded have we not?" At dinner he didn't stop talking about the N.-C.F.; he described the Conference almost exactly as I had described it in a letter I wrote to Cambridge people who were not there – just the same things struck him, and in the same way. He talks exactly as he writes, perfectly expressed in very simple language; he is extremely sociable, speaking in just the same open kind of way to Maria or Mlle as he did to Lady Ottoline. When we adjourned to the drawing-room and all the ladies took up their embroidery (I had some too, but I didn't do much) he was still very much the centre of the party; by the way I have not told you that Lytton Strachey (the French literature person, something like Michael Lange, and an out-and-out conscientious objector) was there, and an American poet called Eliot, a friend of Russell's.
>
> Russell began business after dinner; he brought out a number of letters he had received from imprisoned C.O's., and one particularly

> pathetic one from a young poet called Chapellow, and he got Morrell to promise to read it in the House. (Philip Morrell is an M.P., a typical Liberal, very pleased with life, very fond of his wife, tall, handsome, jolly, not stupid). Then he got Lady Ottoline to send an invitation to the Bishop of Oxford to tea next day, and discussed a manifesto to be sent to Asquith with Morrell. He kept turning to me to corroborate what he said about Clifford Allen and the Conference, and once we had a real argument about the wisdom of refusing exemption on condition of pursuing the employment in which you were engaged at the time; he thought the men ought to accept that, and I thought not; with Strachey on my side and Morrell on his, we concluded that Strachey and I were the more consistent, he and Morrell perhaps wiser.
>
> He went for a walk in the moonlight with Lady Ottoline and Eliot and then they came back alone and he did not come in for about half-an-hour. He and Lady Ottoline seem to be on rather brother-and-sisterly terms; she goes into his bedroom and he into hers, and they read one another's letters, and altogether he seems extremely at-home there. Maria gives a false impression of them both.

Next morning Miss Bentwich found Russell alone at breakfast. He at once began talking about Cambridge, making the revealing remark that if he had not renewed his Lectureship the previous year he would have thrown himself entirely into N.-C.F. work as he really wished to do.

> He asked me if I had suffered any persecution yet from Newnham authorities; it was so sweetly sympathetic the way he asked, Marge; humane, that's what he is, in every respect, even when he's talking about the military authorities and Cambridge dons and Lloyd George; there's no trace of pettiness in him, nothing but large-hearted human understanding and clear moral vision. I asked him if he didn't grudge the time taken away from philosophical speculation to spend on social reform like this, and he said that ever since the beginning of the war he could think of nothing else; he *had* to be up and doing; so I asked him if he thought it was a matter of temperament and pointed at Moore as an example of the other attitude, and he supposed it was.

A few days later Miss Bentwich wrote again to her friend. "His main weakness", she concluded of Russell, "is that he is open to flattery I think; and also I doubt whether he is very sensitive and refined about *les affaires du cœur*; one or two remarks of his about divorce and his wife suggested this. But he impressed me deeply; he's a very great man indeed I'm sure."

Miss Bentwich's judgment of "brother-and-sisterly terms" was probably correct. Years later Russell looked back on the Garsington epoch as marking a basic change in Ottoline's attitude to him. After the move, he wrote, "she gave me less and less while at the same time she gave more and more to others. For instance, I was never allowed to enter her bedroom but Aldous Huxley was habitually present while she undressed. (I do not think that she ever had physical relations with him). In the end I rebelled and decided that the pain and frustration were more than I could endure."

At Garsington he was the centre of an admiring throng of the already converted. Outside the circle, he was still known only to the academic world. All this was to be changed by the events which began in the spring of 1916 when Ernest Everett, a young St Helens schoolmaster, was called up for service, contested it on conscientious grounds, and was granted exemption from combatant service. He ignored the military notice for non-combatant duties, was arrested as an absentee on 31 March, handed over to the military, and after refusing to obey orders was sentenced to two years' hard labour. Today the sentence has a medieval ring. Even in 1916 it was tailor-made for protest and on 15 April Russell drew up in his brother's house the draft of what became known as the Everett Leaflet, a document that in this initial form did little more than recount the facts of the case. The following day, in the N.-C.F. offices, a further paragraph was added, not all of it by Russell himself. The additional words, after pointing out that Everett had been sentenced solely for abiding by his conscience, said that he was "fighting the old fight for liberty, and against religious persecution, in the spirit in which martyrs suffered in the past". Then it asked, "Will you join the persecutors? Or will you stand for those who are defending conscience at the cost of obloquy for conscience sake in the same way as Mr. Everett? Can you remain silent while this goes on?"

Even with this addition, the leaflet was not specially inflammatory, and Russell later maintained that the Archbishop of Canterbury had said as much in the House of Lords. It was printed in bulk by the N.-C.F. and shortly afterwards two members of the Fellowship's Liverpool branch were charged with distributing it. The defendants insisted that they had been told by Allen that the Press Censor had passed it, but this was not so and each was sentenced to a month's imprisonment. Other distributors were arrested and sentenced. "Why do they leave me alone?" Russell demanded of Ottoline with all the frustration of the overlooked martyr. Then he realized that the arrests offered just the opportunity he had been waiting for; he seized it with both hands.

On 17 May *The Times* printed a brief letter from him, pointing out that six men had been imprisoned for distributing the Everett Leaflet, and concluding, "I wish to make it known that I am the author of this leaflet, and that, if anyone is to be prosecuted, I am the person primarily responsible."

There is no doubt that Russell's letter seriously embarrassed the authorities; it was meant to. "Prosecutions are helpful to us, & would be especially so if they ended in imprisonment without the option of a fine," he had stressed to Allen. "I don't think we ought to do anything to diminish the odium which the Govt. must incur in silencing us." A fortnight later, when the government had at last been forced to risk the odium, Russell again underlined his position. "This prosecution is the very thing I wanted," he wrote to Ottoline.

> I have a very good case morally – as good as possible. I think myself that the legal case is good tho' no doubt they will convict, and I rather hope they will . . . I saw Miss Marshall and Allen and a number of the others – they were all delighted and hoping that I should get a savage sentence. It is all great fun, as well as a magnificent opportunity. The sort of opportunity I have longed for – and I have come by it legitimately, without going out of my way.

For the authorities had, after ten days' dickering, finally decided that they had to prosecute regardless of the dangers and on 30 May two detectives arrived at Russell's rooms in Trinity armed with the Everett Leaflet and *The Times*. They politely asked if he acknowledged authorship, and on his admission served a summons for impeding recruiting and discipline.

In London the following day he conferred with the N.-C.F. solicitors and decided to plead his own case, although in Frank's opinion writing the leaflet was not as culpable as publishing it. "Don't you make any admission as to publication," he added. "Send me a copy of the leaflet to read – I hope your people will have a good counsel." Whitehead rallied round. "Let me know if and how I can help or show any office of friendship," he wrote as soon as he heard of the prosecution. "You know well enough that the mere fact that I think your views of state policy and of private duty in relation to it are mistaken, does not diminish affection."

To Ottoline, as he prepared his own case, Russell wrote with his usual frankness, "I am not anxious to secure an acquittal. It is delightful to have brought it on in just this way – a way which no one can regard as wanton or groundlessly provocative, because there were the poor men to champion. I fully expect them to inflict only a fine. I wonder if they will call Lord Derby. I should enjoy cross-examining him." As for defending himself, the reason was forcefully stated in a letter written to Allen when the case was over and when it appeared that the N.-C.F. had had no shorthand writer in court. "If not, it was a serious omission," Russell wrote, "*absolutely the only point* of making a speech and defending myself was to have it reported, & to have someone to report it was the only thing that mattered – because a report can be printed."

The government in its wisdom did not call Lord Derby, the Director of Recruiting, bluff, hearty and always smiling, possessed of "what Englishmen admire: geniality, generosity, public spirit, great wealth, and successful race-horses", a decision much to be regretted by all with a sense of drama or of the ridiculous. Nevertheless, the case heard at the Mansion House on 5 June was sufficiently colourful in its own right. Russell, cheated of cross-examining Derby, a man "at times hesitant when faced with a dilemma", defended himself in a Court bedazzled by the flamboyant figure of Ottoline and her companion Lytton Strachey, angularly seated beside her in the Public Gallery like a giraffe-sized Toulouse-Lautrec. Philip, she had told him a few days earlier, would stand bail. Presiding was Sir Charles Wakefield the oil king, Lord Mayor of the City of London, a fifty-seven-year-old who "took a very energetic part in the recruiting movement". Prosecution lay in the hands of Mr A. H. Bodkin, later Director of Prosecutions, who now exhibited a genius for making the worst of a bad case. As G. H. Hardy remarked in his account of Trinity's reaction to the case, "a verbatim report is cruel to an indifferent speaker; but Mr. Bodkin's oratory was worse than his law."

From the start, the prosecution concentrated on the claim, difficult to support, that the Everett Leaflet would hamper recruiting: it was left to Russell himself to suggest it might less implausibly be claimed that the leaflet prejudiced discipline. The nub of Bodkin's case was not only that the leaflet tended to prevent recruiting. "One thing which is perfectly certain about it is that there is not a syllable in it from beginning to end which is likely to assist recruiting," he added. This of course was true, if not surprising; but neither was it actionable.

Russell's defence is a delight to read, and even after half a century it is easy to sense the embarrassment of all but the most insensitive government supporters as they listened.

He began by employing the statements only recently made in the House of Commons by the Home Secretary. "I agree with Mr. Herbert Samuel in holding that a man who, in these circumstances, decides to break the law, is a man who can be respected," he said. "If Mr. Samuel and I have committed an illegality in declaring this opinion, I hope he will issue new regulations before he finds himself in the position in which I am today." After this irritating preliminary, guaranteed to produce the greatest offence with the smallest effort, he came to the crux of his defence.

> I do not think that there is any evidence possible to adduce, and no evidence has been adduced, in favour of the view that this leaflet prejudiced recruiting. At the time when it was issued, single men were already subject to conscription, and therefore any supposed effect would have been only in regard to married men. Now, the

> married man who contemplates voluntarily enlisting is *ex hypothesi* not a conscientious objector. The leaflet informs him that if he chooses to pose as a conscientious objector he is liable to two years' hard labour. I do not consider that knowledge of that fact is likely to induce such a man to pretend that he is a conscientious objector when he is not.

A logical argument indeed. But it was an argument, as Hardy says, "put in a way more likely to appeal to Fellows of Trinity than to Lord Mayors with inelastic minds". It was, moreover, an argument which if followed to its end might lead to a dangerous verdict of not guilty.

"I would say, my Lord, that whether I personally am acquitted or convicted, matters little," Russell continued.

> But it is not only I who am in the dock, it is the whole tradition of liberty which our ancestors built up through centuries of struggle and sacrifice. Other nations may surpass us in other respects; but the tradition of liberty has been the supreme good that we in this country have preserved more than anything else, and for that liberty of the individual I stand. Under the stress of fear the Authorities have somewhat forgotten that English tradition. To me the fear seems unworthy, and I think the effect will be disastrous if it does not cease.

Russell spoke for about an hour, "quite well – but simply a propaganda speech", Lytton later wrote. "The Lord Mayor looked like a stuck pig. Counsel for the prosecution was an incredible Daumier caricature of a creature – and positively turned out to be Mr. Bodkin. I felt rather nervous in that Brigand's cave."

Eventually the Lord Mayor's impatience got the better of him. "I have allowed you a great deal of latitude because you are inexpert," he interrupted, "but I think I must tell you that you are now making what is a political speech." Brushing aside Russell's protest, he said that he had been unconvinced and would therefore find the defendant guilty. The fine would be £100 or sixty-one days' imprisonment, with eight days allowed to pay.

The Everett case gave Russell his first taste of publicity and personal drama since the Wimbledon by-election, nearly a decade previously. He liked it. "I have learned how to speak now – I am glad," he wrote two days later. "Some reserve or shyness has been broken down in me by all this time, and I can bring out all that is in me in a way I couldn't before." And there was more to it than that. He was not a man who sought the limelight for its own sake, but when it shone he enjoyed the experience as much as the benefit it brought his cause. "What I want permanently," he once wrote to Ottoline, "not consciously, but deep down, is stimulus, the sort of thing that keeps my brain active & exuberant. I suppose that is what makes me a vampire. I get a stimulus most from the instinctive feeling of success. Failure makes me collapse." Appearance at the Mansion House was success.

There was still the appeal to face, but that would not be until the end of the month, and he now left London for a ten-day walking holiday to Ludlow, Newtown, the Devil's Bridge and Aberystwyth, a break before the storm which found him in a mood of almost delirious happiness with the open air:

> This country goes on being perfectly heavenly. I have got over my fatigue now and into the way of walking. It makes one feel placid about everything. I am amazed that people don't know this part of the world. It was Peacock's Maid Marion that made me want to come here. I have lovely weather. The country is extraordinarily deserted ... I am very well, very happy, and entirely without thought – existing in a delicious animal fashion, enjoying fields and woods and birds and rivers in a slow quiet way.

He needed the rest, for his appeal against the Everett case verdict was to lead on to a tumultuous few months.

It was heard, and rejected, on 29 June before the City Quarter Sessions at the Guildhall. Russell refused to pay the fine, but there was no question of his going to prison: the value of his personal belongings in Trinity was rather more than £100 and a Distress for non-payment was therefore levied under the Defence Regulations. The local auctioneers arrived at the college and removed to the Corn Exchange his carpets and furniture, some fifteen hundred books, "upwards of 100 ozs. of PLATE, Plated Articles, Gentleman's Gold Watch and Chain" and the Butler Gold Medal which he had been awarded by Columbia University the previous year for his contributions to logical theory.

However, although keen bidding was expected there was no danger of his belongings being dispersed. As the *Cambridge Daily News* put it, "Some disappointment was accordingly caused when at the commencement of the sale the auctioneer announced that he had an offer of £125 for all the plate, and plated articles, medal and library of over 1,500 books, which was a sufficient sum to pay all expenses."

What had happened was described to Russell in a letter from H. T. J. Norton, one of his former mathematical students: "The £125 was subscribed, as I suppose you know, by a number of people, and as it was sufficient to pay the fine and the expenses, the forced part of the sale came to an end, and the books, the silver, the watch and chain, medal, your tea-table, and some small things were withdrawn. The remainder – that is to say, carpets, bookshelves, settee, writing table – were then put up for sale and actually sold."

The rejection of his appeal and the forced sale of his belongings was only one move in what appears to have been a deliberate government campaign to clip Russell's wings. The next was to follow swiftly. When, early in 1915, it had become known that Russell was obtaining two terms' leave of absence from Trinity, Harvard had immediately invited him for another visit. At first he thought it might be possible to revive the idea of seeing President Wilson and for a period he contemplated joining forces with Jane Addams, International President of the Women's International League. He dropped the scheme on finding that Miss Addams was "regarded in Washington as the Pankhursts were in Downing Street, & is about as welcome there as the Black Plague". In addition, he wrote to Ottoline, "it doesn't seem now as if America wd. be so important in the [peace] settlement; & if I went, I shouldn't want to be there so long as to have to talk philosophy. I have nothing new to say in philosophy, & I don't want to have to think about it just now ..."

Then, in January 1916, Professor Woods of the Harvard Philosophy Department offered him a lectureship. Further, he had offered to include in the appointment a course based on his political views of the war. Russell's reactions were mixed. "*Against*, there is, first, that going to America is horrid," he argued to Ottoline.

> Then, that it would rather interfere with anything I might want to do here in the way of peace-work. Also, that it would be tiring, & make me less likely to get good ideas for writing. *For*, the chief argument is financial. They would pay me £400, & I could cover expenses by odd jobs, so that the £400 would be clear profit. That would make it possible for me to have a nice cottage in the Chilterns, near Prince's Risborough, & pay for you to come all the way in a motor if you would visit me there. Another argument for, is that it enables me with decency to postpone the decision whether to leave Trinity for another year. A third argument is that America is important internationally, & that I have vastly more influence there than here. The course on Logic would want no preparation, & I could give it in my sleep. The other would be worth working on, & probably worth giving. I should be able to go about a good deal, & get to know important men. The F.O. would let me go for lecturing at Harvard, but would probably refuse unless I had some good reason of that sort; & I do think America is worth going to now ...

Before the end of the month he had accepted; at the same time he posted a copy of the lectures he was giving in London on "Principles of Social Reconstruction". The impact in America of these "mischievous" lectures – eventually published there as *Why Men Fight: A Method of Abolishing the International Duel* – is indicated by a letter which he received in March from

Woods, who had discussed Russell's proposed political course with the president of Harvard. Woods wrote,

> He quite agrees with me that there can be nothing but good in the course, and, in fact, I know he would be delighted to have the benefit of your fresh treatment of these problems on which we need so much light in America. Royce, in spite of an entirely different ethical point of view, says the course will be heartily welcomed and so do all the others. I wish to say myself that I think you have an extraordinary opportunity in America due to the fact that our thinking on the political presuppositions has been so hopelessly optimistic and infantile. Just now we are aware that all that has been in the main stream in the tradition must be recast. Accordingly, instead of thinking that we should approve your course, it would be more fitting if you counted it as creating and satisfying a need of which we were only dimly aware ...

However, as the effects of the London lectures spread, and as Russell's bogy-man image began to harden up, he himself began to have doubts about the official British attitude. "I think I ought to warn you", he wrote to Professor Woods in April, "that it is just possible the Foreign Office here may refuse me permission to leave the country. If the move came from Harvard, permission would almost certainly be given." He had good reason for doubt. Woods had managed to arrange lecture-engagements at half a dozen other universities or colleges; but Michigan, he stressed pointedly, wanted Russell only on philosophy, "owing to the strong local feeling for the Allies".

The invitation had in fact handed the British government a ticklish problem, since Russell's reputation in the United States was still growing, as shown by the award of the Butler Gold Medal. On that occasion he had written to Ottoline, "It is to be given by the American Embassy. As my Atlantic Monthly article is certainly treasonable, I hope it may be brought to me in prison." His reputation for stirring the pot had not diminished during the months that followed, and the fact that he planned to lecture in America not only on logic but also on politics was bound to cause misgivings in Whitehall.

Eleven days after his letter admitting authorship of the Everett Leaflet had appeared in *The Times*, the Foreign Office received a cipher from Sir Cecil Spring Rice, the British Ambassador in Washington: "President of Harvard University", this went, "says University wants services of Bertrand Russell as lecturer. Latter thinks he may be refused permission to leave. He might be warned that Germans will circulate any anti-British utterances he may make here."

The Ambassador's message was discussed. One official minuted that "[Russell] ought by all means to be prevented from going". Another:

"I think his effect would be disastrous in the United States just now with so much peace talk about. On the other hand he is crying out to be made a martyr." However, it was the Private Secretary, Treaty Department, who first suggested a way out. Ignore the martyrdom for the time being, he proposed. "First let us ask the Home Office confidentially if any steps are contemplated against him. If so, it will pave the way for refusing to issue a passport – which is the only real means I know of by which we can stop him leaving the country." This was on the 29th. On the following day Russell was served with the summons – apparently without the knowledge of another official who added his belief that Russell was "one of the most mischievous cranks in the country". He continued, "I submit that it would be folly to let him go to America. He has invited prosecution, and I cannot think why the Public Prosecutor leaves him alone, more especially since he has prosecuted the people who distributed the seditious literature in question."

To less simple souls the reason for the delay was plain enough. The illegality of the Everett Leaflet was highly debatable: but while it might be possible to ride roughshod over the protests of five humble distributors, Russell would be a more formidable defendant. However, the need to prevent him from speaking in America appears to have weighed down the scales. The summons was issued and the Home Office was informed that Grey had decided not to allow Russell a passport. Since the case was not to be heard for another four days, an interesting light is cast on the Foreign Office note to Washington two days after the case but three weeks before the appeal had been heard. "Mr. Russell has been convicted under the Defence of the Realm Act for writing an undesirable pamphlet and no passport will be issued to him to proceed to the United States. Please inform the President of Harvard." Not even the Foreign Office could screw up the effrontery to call the Everett Leaflet either seditious or treasonable; but in the circumstances "undesirable" was enough.

Russell had mixed feelings. "Personally I am relieved except as regards money," he wrote on hearing the news. "I *loathed* the thought of the exile. But you cannot imagine how it *infuriates* me as a piece of tyranny. I want a fuss made about it. I want it pointed out that I was going to teach logic & that the Government thinks logic wd. put America against us."

The last claim, completely ignoring the contentious political course, was typical of two weaknesses which made him, in later years, a less formidable opponent than he might have been. He could blinker himself to unwelcome facts; worse still, he could at times ignore their existence in a way that laid him open to the charge of deliberately twisting evidence.

Refusal of a passport was the first of two steps which followed the Everett case – if "followed" is the right word to describe the government's actions – and on July 11 the Council of Trinity unanimously dismissed him from the Lectureship renewed for five years the previous October. The grounds were that he had "been convicted under the Defence of the Realm Act, and his conviction has been confirmed on appeal". The Council had at least waited for the appeal, which is a better showing than Grey's at the Foreign Office. Nevertheless, the Foreign Office had a point, if a weak one, in preventing a man of Russell's standing from spreading what even Michigan obviously considered to be anti-British propaganda. The case of Trinity was very different.

A memorial protesting against the dismissal was signed by twenty-two Fellows, but it was mild in tone, merely placing on record the fact that the signatories were "not satisfied with the action of the College in depriving Mr. Russell of his lectureship". Many hung fire. Among them was A. E. Housman who had once remarked "If I were The Prince of Peace, I would choose a less provocative Ambassador." Russell had countered, "I don't know how one *can* advocate an unpopular cause unless one is either irritating or ineffective."

The dismissal immediately became the centre of a storm which raged far beyond academic circles. The Council had been legally within its rights, having the power to expel any who were "convicted by a court of competent jurisdiction of a crime of whatever nature or description". But the real issue was another matter: in general, the propriety of taking such action for a purely political offence, and in particular the judgment of taking it in this case. G. H. Hardy, discussing the question later from the viewpoint of the college, suggested that "the important question is not whether the Council could put up a sound technical defence of their action, but whether it was sensible, and likely to promote the real interests of the College". Judging by the full story, as well as by the immediate reaction, even these necessarily narrow interests hardly seem to have been served. "My first impression on hearing of the course the Council had taken was to treat the story as incredible," wrote Gilbert Murray. D. S. Robertson, a Trinity Fellow on active service in France, took the view that while Russell's action had been illegal the College Council had been free to judge whether it was dishonourable. "Their refusal to draw such a distinction", he added, "seems to me an inexpressible disaster to tolerance and liberty." A former Senior Scholar from Trinity, A. E. Heath, wrote to the *Manchester Guardian*: "Mr. Russell suffers penalties for his opinion; those who have left Trinity to fight or to work in factories pay the penalty of the opposite opinion. The residue disgrace England in the eyes of the scientific world." Moore suggested that chapel services should be banned in Trinity, since the precept "Love your enemies" was obviously subversive, and a decade later D. H. Lawrence, although allergic to Russell, observed that "something seemed to go out of Cambridge when Bertie Russell had to leave". Whitehead, asking Russell two months later, "Have you seen my pamphlet on you, to the Fellows of

Trinity? I sent it round in July," apparently joined the protest, although no copy of the pamphlet seems to have survived.

Jane Harrison spoke for many when moving a vote of thanks to Mr Milukow, a distinguished Russian who had lost his Chair of History for his political opinions and had addressed a meeting at Newnham. "The words were on my lips, a hackneyed cliché enough – 'such a thing in England would be impossible' – when I remembered suddenly that not only was it not impossible, it had actually happened in our midst," she later said. "I gave utterance to my shame as an Englishwoman." Hilton Young, later Lord Kennet, who had been up at Trinity in 1900, wrote from H.M.S. *Centaur* asking, "What brings me here?" and answered, "The desire that England should remain, and that Europe should become, a place in which the Russells whom fate grants us from time to time should be free to stimulate and annoy us unpersecuted ... That Trinity should gratuitously number itself among the persecutors, this is more discouraging than a German victory."

The comparison with Germany was also made outside the purely academic arena. It was pointed out that Professor Förster of the University of Munich had for long been preaching pacifism and criticizing the German government on the grounds that they were partly to blame for the war; but although the German government had done its best to secure Förster's removal, the University of Munich had refused to budge. Neither was the comparison with the Russell case lost on neutrals. "The opinion of the academic world may be thought little of in this country," the *Manchester Guardian* pointed out, "but in America, and generally in lands where people believe in education, it is a serious factor in the formation of public opinion, and in this world the dismissal of a leader of thought like Mr. Russell has the same sort of effect as the degradation of a bishop would have in the church."

Through all this the Council remained silent. But their position was defended privately, some months later, in a letter to Hilton Young from McTaggart, who had voted for the sacking.

> About Russell, I should like to tell you the way I look at it. I should not have been prepared to remove him for the expression of opinions, whatever those opinions, while the expression of them was legal. But it is quite different – or so it seems to me – when he had done something the law pronounced to be a crime. The conviction was for making statements "likely to prejudice the recruiting and discipline of His Majesty's forces". The removal of Fellows from the College (and the same principle would apply to Lecturers) for conviction of crime is contemplated in Statutes, if the conviction is grave enough. We had to consider whether, in time of such a war as this, a conviction on such a charge was so slight a thing that we could pass it over.

> There was doubtless much on the other side. (1) Most crimes are committed for vicious motives, and no-one doubts that Russell acted as he did because he believed it to be his duty. This makes, of course, a very important distinction between the cases. (2) Academic freedom is very precious and fragile. (3) Russell's eminence at his work makes his removal an exceptionally serious loss to the College.
>
> I did not form my opinion lightly – I need not tell you that. And, while I recognise the force of the arguments I have mentioned, I have never wavered in my conviction that I voted rightly.
>
> The loss to me is greater, perhaps, than to any other Trinity man, if one takes account both of old friendship, and of our common work. I miss his criticism very deeply, but it is not what I miss most.
>
> Well, he acted as he thought right, and so did I. That is something left . . .

Russell himself was less worried than his supporters: "Yes," he wrote to Ottoline, "I am delighted at the way the question of Cambridge has been solved. I hope the Council will be made to feel that they have acted unworthily – I feel quite impersonal about it, as I am glad to have my own course decided for me. Every bit of persecution is useful – it makes people see that no good comes out of war."

This was more than making a virtue out of necessity, and probably owed at least something to Lawrence, who even before the prosecution had an intuitive feeling of what Russell's letter to *The Times* might mean. "If they hound you out of Trinity, so much the better," he had written. "I am glad. Entire separation, that is what must happen to one: not even the nominal shelter left, not even the mere fact of inclusion in the house. One must be entirely cast forth." Russell took the hint. Deprived of his Lectureship, he had his name formally removed from the Trinity roll.

A reaction, immediate if unexpected, came from St Andrews. Would Russell be prepared to stand for Lord Rectorship of the university, asked C. D. Broad. "Some of the most prominent students who are left and those who would be mainly concerned in running your election, are very anxious to get you, both because of your eminence in philosophy and because you are a prominent Pacifist," he said. "Your election would make all the fire-eating old gentlemen on the Court and the Senators simply foam at the mouth; but from the constitution of a Scottish University they could do nothing to prevent it, save by getting some other student or students to propose someone else and beat you in a contested election." No record of Russell's reply has survived although his first response was to describe the proposal to Ottoline as "great fun". Having a full hand already, he presumably said "no".

The damaging impression created in neutral countries of a government unable to fill the ranks without the most rigorous imposition of the law was but one counter-productive result of the Everett case. There was also the spur which it gave to a Russell whose principles had now been honed a shade sharper by persecution that was no less persecution because it was sought. From now on he threw himself into the fight with renewed vigour and increased ingenuity. "The war, it seemed to me, was folly, and every bit of energy that could be diverted from the business of killing was so much to the good," he wrote in a sidelight on the situation.

> This was a reason, not only for oneself refusing to kill but also for providing as much innocent work as possible. Policemen who might otherwise have been drafted into the Army, were kept busy making inaccurate reports of pacifist speeches for the benefit of Scotland Yard; prison officials were kept from the front by the need of guarding conscientious objectors; lawyers and lawyers' clerks were occupied with their misdeeds. In one way or another, quite a number of people were prevented from engaging in the official business of killing each other.

During the next eighteen months secret meetings, code messages, all the paraphernalia of what at times looked like schoolboy antics, were invoked to ensure the continued publication of the *Tribunal*, and to keep the organization one step ahead of the authorities, determined as they were to cripple the N.-C.F.'s activities without incurring the odium of suppressing it. Russell enthusiastically took part in it all; staff-managing operations with a keen eye for publicity and an uncanny sense, perhaps learned at Granny's knee, of what would embarrass the government most; drawing in helpers both by his reputation and his caustic assessment of what they could do.

Francis Meynell remembers what he considered an early accolade: "I like you, Meynell," Russell told him, "because in spite of your spats there is much of the guttersnipe in you." Fenner Brockway remembers that Russell, "although an heir to an earldom ... was very hard up during this period and arrived late for committees more than once because he hadn't any copper to pay for a bus – but perhaps this was due to his forgetfulness of mundane things, or, more likely, because he had emptied his pockets for some down-and-out. He was full of a spirit of fun, like some irrepressible but clever Puck." One night, when arrests seemed imminent and there were six detectives in the street, the committee crowded into three taxi-cabs and directed the drivers to 57 Gordon Square, "Bertrand gleefully wondering what his absent brother would say if we were arrested on his premises." There was also the occasion on which Brockway left important documents in a cab, whose driver was expected to hand them over to Scotland Yard. "Well," said Russell, "I move that we adjourn to Scotland Yard – we may as well save the police the trouble of arresting us." Instead, a cutting-out operation was mounted by Catherine

Marshall, who had a brother at the Yard. She phoned him with the distressed plea that a young country friend had left a bag in a cab but was returning to Derbyshire. Could it be collected? It was: unopened.

The records leave no doubt that Russell played a lion's part in helping to keep the N.-C.F. afloat in its most depressed moments. He was resourceful, irrepressible, and enlivened all situations by a *panache* that combined the spirit of a believer and the confidence of a Russell.

Even before the Everett case and its repercussions turned him into a notorious national figure, his work for the N.-C.F. had drawn him across his own personal Rubicon into direct contact with ordinary men and women. Especially was this so through the letters from families of conscientious objectors who needed help or advice. However, it was a propaganda tour in South Wales which set the seal on his relations with those outside his own academic and social worlds. Compared with this, the Wimbledon election was a tame affair of middle-class tea-parties.

He was of course experienced in lecturing to undergraduates and to fellow-guests in country houses. His talks on "Principles of Social Reconstruction" had been given to less specialized yet still restricted audiences. But the tour through grey mining villages where opposition to the war had been bubbling for nearly two years was another thing. Politically, the audiences would be receptive. But they were naturally critical, even of those who knew their language, their ways, and the fine print of their traditional prejudices, and to any Daniel with Russell's background their world of bleak valleys leading up to uncomfortable moorlands could be a lions' den.

His first meeting was at Merthyr Tydfil in June 1916. Here he spoke in a hall packed with more than two thousand, mostly miners. Even the Chief Constable was friendly, possibly because the official shorthand-writer had been lifted from the Chief Constable's control and ordered to report direct to London. In Merthyr, then in Cardiff, he was listened to with the silence of rapt attention, the crowd-consciousness sensing his "liberation of pent-up passion", as he described it to Ottoline, his feeling that it was "glorious to be speaking out at last, saying what one thinks, facing what may come of it". In one village the authorities cancelled their letting of the local hall and he spoke in the open air. In Swansea, a meeting was held almost impromptu on the outskirts of the city and he found himself on a common, shouting at the top of his voice to a steadily growing crowd. After half an hour hoarseness brought him to a stop. "But I had said all that mattered. Every single person agreed, though it was an entirely accidental crowd."

At Port Talbot, the largest steel-town in South Wales, he again spoke out-of-doors, to a meeting organized by one of the steel-workers on a common between two chapels. Just as he was about to begin, the congregations emerged, most of them "starred" men who were reserved, earning good wages and personally unaffected by the war. Some four hundred, in their Sunday best, stopped to listen until he had finished. That evening he went on to Briton Ferry – "a really *wonderful* meeting – the hall was packed, they were all at the highest point of enthusiasm – they inspired me, and I spoke as I have never spoken before. We put a resolution in favour of immediate peace negotiations, which was carried unanimously." But, he added, the two plain-clothes men taking notes presumably abstained. Finally he spoke at Ystradgynlais, to a smaller number of miners, intelligent, thoughtful, but with minds still not made up. That did not worry him, since this "sort of meeting is really more useful than an enthusiastic one".

The meeting in Cardiff was in some ways the most important of the tour since here Russell knowingly risked a sedition charge. "The police took down every word I said & I have no doubt whatever that they will get me on what I am saying," he wrote. "I shall be in till the end of the war. I am wondering whether I shall come out with my mind undamaged. I should be sorry if it were injured – it is at its very best just now & there are so many things I want to do with it."

There was to be no sedition charge – although for a while it was a close thing. Even had there been, his letters to Ottoline suggest that he would have taken it in his stride, so aroused had he been by the reception in South Wales. Here, possibly for the first time in his life, Russell found that emotionally he was giving as well as taking. His intellect had always been at the disposal of all who asked for it; but until now he had invariably been the emotional debtor, demanding more than he could ever repay. Now, packed with an emotion that not only flowed out to the crowd as though from a bottomless well, but also evoked a deep response, he felt a tinge of the demagogue's delight at finding he could make the public heart beat faster.

There was also the exultation of the struggle. "I personally shall go down in this fight I expect, but it is worth it," he also wrote.

> I enjoy it all . . . Quite lately I have somehow found myself – I have poise and sanity – I no longer have the feeling of powers unrealised within me, which used to be a perpetual torture. I don't care what the authorities do to me, they can't stop me long. Before, I have felt either wicked or passively resigned – now I feel fully active and contented with my activity – I have no inward discords any more – and nothing ever really troubles me.

In Wales he had been impressed by the number of working-men who knew *The Problems of Philosophy*, and their enthusiasm led him to think of teaching "all the working-men who are hungry for intellectual food . . . I foresee a great and splendid life in that sort of thing, dealing with political ideas, but keeping out of actual politics", building up an educational system that would be not only financially free but free from State control.

> I see my career after the war quite clearly now. I will be at the head of a movement of freer education for politically-minded working men and for the really progressive intellectuals. It is tremendously needed. It will differ from things like the W[orkers] E[ducational] A[ssociation] by having a definitely political object – it will try to teach men what they should know in order to be politically effective, and to give them a philosophy that will make their politics stable ... It would be ideal work for me. One would preach the abolition of the whole wages system – no more work for wages, no more slavery to capitalists or government officials. Freedom, growth unimpeded, free play for people's best energies. It is the essential preliminary to any successful movement of fundamental reform.

Life had at last found a meaning. During the philosophical work ahead, "seeing all sorts of people and getting to know all sorts of human facts", he might at times be "overwhelmed by the passion for the things that are eternal and perfect, like mathematics". But in this field there would always be ample work to be done. With interests requiting his emotional and intellectual needs, he was sure that Ottoline would satisfy the rest. If not, there might be desultory philandering. But it need be no more than that. It looked as though he could steer comfortably ahead, on course at last. Yet within a few weeks he was to be deeply involved in a traumatic and romantic *affaire* which was to hold part of him until he died; politically, he was to be drawn into a series of skirmishes with the government which, in spite of their important ethical overtones, have in places an air of almost knockabout farce.

Up to this stage, to Russell's South Wales tour in the summer of 1916, the authorities had been comparatively cautious in their dealings with the N.-C.F. movement in general and with Russell in particular; an awareness of what might be politically counter-productive had limited the employment of the wilder official expedients. Thus there was reluctance to use a specially written article attacking Russell under the heading of "Mugwumpery" and beginning: "The Ass in the Lion's Skin and the Wolf in Sheep's Clothing represent familiar human types, but we have no image for the traitor who pretends to be a Mugwump." Minutes on the official idea of distributing the article surreptitiously included the view that it seemed to be an advertisement for Russell, and the comment that "however much one dislikes B. Russell, one can't dismiss a man of his eminence and genius with this kind of vulgar heavy-handed fun". Finally, it was proposed that the article be sent to Petrograd, Tokyo and Rome, who "need not use it if they don't like it." The official file suggests that however much the men in Whitehall detested Russell personally, they had until now kept their heads.

In the wake of the South Wales tour, they ran to panic stations in actions which revealed startling inefficiency, crossed departmental lines, and consummate lying. The Cardiff speech started the trouble – or, to be more accurate, pressure from the *Daily Express*, following the speech. The meeting had been attended by a Chief Inspector W. H. Harries, and a detective and detective-sergeant who that evening reported to the Head Constable in the city and who then, on request, obtained the shorthand notes of the speech taken by the *Western Mail* reporter. According to government statements in the House of Commons, the editor had been unwilling to publish the speech but had patriotically made the reporter's text available to the police triumvirate, who had apparently been unable to muster a sufficiently expert shorthand-writer of their own. Little happened until a Captain Jones who had intervened with questions at the Cardiff meeting wrote to the local paper and to the *Daily Express*. The effect, in the words of Sir Charles Mathews, the Public Prosecutor, "was to throw a blaze of limelight upon B.R. and to give a fictitious importance to his pro-German utterances".

At this point the Home Office felt obliged to step in, and Edward Troup wrote to Mathews saying that Herbert Samuel, the Home Secretary, had taken a serious view of the speech as reported in the *Daily Express*. Revealingly, the most offensive passage was not apparently Russell's assertion that there was no longer any need to continue the war, but his remarks about Russia. "We cannot dismiss [his] remarks as insignificant," Troup continued.

> He writes and speaks with a good deal of misguided cleverness, he is anxious to go on an Anti-British mission to the U.S.A. and a letter stopped by the Censor (Boyd, my private Secretary, could find it, I think) shows how deliberately hostile he is.
>
> Still, it is a difficult question whether we should do more harm than good by prosecuting. He would make a clever defence and would publish it as a pamphlet.

The letter stopped by the Censor had been written to Professor Woods. It referred to the Everett case, and went on, "Since then the same offence has been punished by the death sentence, commuted to 10 years' penal servitude. Anyone who thinks that I can be made to hold my tongue when such things are being done is grossly mistaken." The Censor had passed the letter to M.I.5, whose General Cockerill asked the Home Office whether it should be stopped. "Lord Robert Cecil said in the House of Commons 10.8.16, 'The Foreign Office do not think it desirable that Mr. Russell should leave this country at present and that they are unlikely to alter their decision," Cockerill went on, almost inviting the comment pencilled on the letter: "Is he to be allowed to convey [by letter] that which he cannot say by word of mouth?" The answer was "no", and the letter was thus retained in the Home Office "with the papers relating to Mr. Russell and his activities in case it may be useful if further proceedings should have to be taken against him hereafter".

Proceedings now seemed inevitable. They were prevented only with some difficulty by Mathews, who informed Sir Ernley Blackwell at the Home Office that the House of Commons had decided to allow debate of peace terms. In addition, he went on, considerable strain would be placed on his department by the effort of bringing all but an infinitesimal part of Russell's speech within the range of prosecution. However, Mathews was unwilling to give Russell a free hand. He continued,

> The action I would respectfully recommend is (a) The issue of an instruction to the Official Press Bureau that under no circumstances is any meeting attended by BR ever to be mentioned in the Press, nor is any correspondence which relates to any such meeting to be allowed to become public; (b) The issue of an instruction to the Police to seize whatever BR may print, either in pamphlet or in leaflet form, and to justify such an instruction, were it to be challenged in the House of Commons, by the production to the challenger of the Cardiff speech.

Sir Ernley, obsessed though he was with the danger that Russell seemed to threaten, doubted whether it was practical to carry out Mathews's proposals. However, he was as reluctant as Sir Charles to let the quarry get clean away and an opportunity to prevent this now came fortuitously to hand. For the police surveillance which was providing detailed information of N.-C.F. operations reported that on 1 September Russell was to visit Haverhill in Suffolk where fifty conscientious objectors were making roads. According to the Home Secretary, who was subsequently asked by the Prime Minister to explain the action which now made the government look ridiculous, Russell planned "to harangue them, obviously with a view to induce them to refuse to work, and thus break down the whole scheme for the employment of conscientious objectors". The inaccuracy of this assessment can be judged from a note about the Haverhill group which Miss Marshall had sent to Russell three days earlier. "I am quite sure that it is important to see the men there individually, or at any rate in small groups, as well as *en masse*, so as to find out the individual points of view, which vary considerably." The Home Secretary, Herbert Samuel, was out of London at the end of August, but Sir Ernley, acting off his own bat, now persuaded the military to issue an order banning Russell from Haverhill. The initial idea was that he should be barred from visiting either the village itself–just within one of the prohibited areas declared at the start of the war – or an area ten miles around it. However, the War Office discreetly explained that the idea of creating banned areas had been to ban spies or potential spies from coastal regions and that it doubted whether the regulations could be stretched to cover what the Home Office wanted. The answer seemed to be simple: the War Office reluctantly agreed to make an order excluding Russell from all prohibited areas, an act which was to cause the Home Secretary much embarrassment but Russell very little.

The following morning, 1 September, two Scotland Yard officers arrived at Gordon Square with an order forbidding entry to prohibited areas without special permission. Yet as they were serving it, the Home Secretary himself, now back in London, was writing on Sir Ernley's minute to the War Office, "I think it would be difficult to defend an order excluding [Russell] from all prohibited areas as they cover about a third of the country. There is no question, of course, that he is an enemy agent."

Samuel had seen that in his absence the authorities had made a highly damaging error of tactics. Russell had seen this too. He was to be mildly inconvenienced by the ban; but he was aware, as soon as Samuel, that the authorities would be in danger of making themselves look silly, vindictive or both, in the all-important eyes of the neutrals. "I have no notion why they served the notice on me, or whether there is any hope of getting it rescinded," he wrote a few hours after the Scotland Yard men had called. "I am much more angry than ever over anything yet. It is a power conferred on them for dealing with spies, & they choose to suppose that I want to give military information to the Germans. It makes my blood boil."

The slur on his character more than counter-balanced his pleasure at the sight of the authorities making fools of themselves, and he at once invoked the aid of Younghusband, who promised to do what he could, called on the War Office to make the right noises, and reported back that there was little hope of help from that quarter. At first Russell thought of ignoring the ban; then he decided that acquiescence was the better tactical move. "The whole thing cheers me up," he wrote to Ottoline. "It is such a comfort to have something immediate and small to fuss about. Younghusband will probably discover why they have done it. I hear today that they have searched my flat from top to bottom, or more accurately from end to end. There is lots of sport to be got out of this matter. I am enjoying it."

A few days later he was still warming to the subject: "I begin to feel any day wasted in which there is nothing about me in the Stop Press! If they don't withdraw the order, I have great schemes for a dramatic challenge."

As news of the War Office ban spread and liberal opinion reacted, his initial feeling was reinforced. "There is no reason to be miserable for me," he wrote.

> I am thoroughly enjoying it, & I think I shall get the best of them in the end. Everyone is indignant. For my part, I get so much fun out of it that I have difficulty in looking the part of a martyr. The time will come for seeing Ll[oyd] G[eorge] or the PM but not yet ... I am flattered by their making such a dead set at me – it is the first thing that has persuaded me I was doing any good. I could not have affected anything if they had let me alone. They *are* fools.

The Home Office might well have agreed since what had been intended as a move to stop a leading member of the N.-C.F. from speaking to conscientious objectors, a debatable yet nevertheless defendable action, now took an unexpected turn.

Earlier in the year the N.-C.F., impressed by the impact of Russell's lectures on "Principles of Social Reconstruction", had conceived the idea of exploiting his unsuspected flair for popular political speaking. "Allen", he wrote to Ottoline, "has a scheme for me to give a course of lectures in the autumn, like the one I gave at Caxton Hall in the spring, but more popular – to be given in 6 large towns simultaneously, free, but at the expense of the local Quakers – each town to pay me £100. I like the plan from every point of view & I expect it will come off ..."

It was now about to do so, with Russell lecturing on "Philosophical Principles of Politics". But three of the six cities in which he was to speak were in areas from which he was now banned. Furthermore, one of the six was Glasgow, already a centre of anti-war feeling and, as the political base of "Red Clydeside", a constant worry to the authorities. The government was therefore faced with a disagreeable choice: that of banning Russell from giving a course of popular political lectures or of lifting the restriction with the obvious implication that someone had blundered.

Sir Ernley's hurried order had firmly put the authorities on a hook from which Russell would do nothing to remove them. It had also given the opposition, and the opposition press, an effective stick with which to beat the government. In the view of the *Daily News*, the authorities had "preferred to treat an Englishman of distinction as though he were an alien of suspicious antecedents, presuming apparently on the unpopularity of his views to protect conduct from inconvenient criticism". The *Manchester Guardian* wished that "Providence would favour the War Office in dealing with such matters with a touch of humour, or if it cannot spare it, a modicum of common sense."

During the next few days the War Office achieved the difficult feat of remaining in the trap where the Home Office had placed it. On 8 September, Russell asked for permission to "proceed to Glasgow to deliver a lecture on 'Political Ideals', being the first of a course of six arranged before the Order was issued forbidding me to enter prohibited areas". The letter was addressed to the correct officer, who by chance happened to be Lt.-Col. the Hon. A. V. F. Russell, a distant cousin. Russell the War Office replied to Russell the philosopher asking if he would be good enough to forward the lecture for censorship. The philosopher countered by pointing out that since the lectures would be spoken and not written this would be impossible; but he enclosed a syllabus, which showed that the original N.-C.F. idea had evolved into "The World As It Can Be Made". Its six lectures dealt with Political Ideals, Evils of Capitalism and the Wages System, Pitfalls in Socialism, Individual Freedom and State Control, National Independence and Internationalism, and Education and Prejudice. From the brief descriptions under each heading it was plain enough that each subject was to be handled in a serious, not to say sober, manner. The harshest claim that authority could genuinely make was that they might make people think. Even the War Office felt it necessary to explain itself, and on the 11th a General Brade wrote to Russell saying it had been suggested that their action implied that he was "held to be a person likely to communicate military information to the enemy". But the Order, he went on in the kindest way possible, had been made under No 14 of the regulations and this enabled the government to keep out not only suspected spies but those suspected "of acting, or of having acted, or of being about to act, in any manner prejudicial to the public safety of the Defence of the Realm". Furthermore, he went on, the Army Council would be willing to withdraw the order if Russell "would give an undertaking not to continue a propaganda which, if successful, would, in their opinion, militate to some extent against the effective prosecution of the war".

Here the authorities revealed a weakness in their hand, as did General Cockerill who wrote to Russell two days later, metaphorically begging him to toe the line so that the order could be withdrawn. "The subjects on which you wish to speak could, I think, with little difficulty or loss of interest, be treated without any direct or obvious reference of the day," he said. "On the other hand they might not." Would it not be possible, he added, for Russell to give an honourable undertaking not to use the lectures for propaganda?

But Russell was in no mood to help them out of the morass into which they had stumbled. Such an undertaking, he pointed out in a "Personal Statement", would be completely unworkable. "May I say that I consider homicide usually regrettable," he asked.

> If so, since the majority of homicides occur in war, I have uttered a pacifist sentiment. May I say that I have a respect for the ethical teaching of Christ? If I do, the War Office may tell me that I am praising conscientious objectors. May I say that I do not hold

> Latimer and Ridley guilty of grave moral turpitude because they broke the law? Or would such a statement be prejudicial to discipline in His Majesty's Forces?

Furthermore, he pointed out, his lectures would undoubtedly be followed by questions. Would he really have to reply to some with the statement, "I am under an honourable undertaking not to answer that question"?

A long sparring-match went on almost until the end of September, Russell operating from the higher ground since the War Office was anxious to repair the damage which the prohibition had caused. "I think it quite likely that the Order against me will be rescinded but I cannot pretend that I am particularly anxious that it should be, except for the honour of the country," he wrote to Elizabeth Trevelyan, the wife of his old friend. "Personally I find the whole matter very amusing and I should find the papers dull if they contained nothing about myself." The government had made itself look ridiculous to the neutrals, and as a result many of those who detested Russell's opinions came to his defence, both in the House and outside. Even Alys, whose devoted loyalty was usually concealed, now wrote, "Dearest Bertie, I have felt most indignant at Trinity's treatment of thee, and now I am very sorry that the Government is persecuting thee so unjustly and unwisely. I had been saving up £100 to invest in Exchequer Bonds, but I would rather give it to thee, if I may, as I am afraid all this persecution interferes very seriously with thy income."

The situation had become one from which all except the most leather-skinned government supporters would have been happy to retire. Even the most adamantine of War Office staff were now vaguely uncomfortable at preventing the country's leading philosopher from speaking on philosophy in any major city which happened to be near the coast. They were to feel more awkward still, the following month.

Russell's first lecture was due to be given in Manchester in mid-October. The following night he had planned to speak in Glasgow. On cancellation of the Glasgow meeting due to the War Office ban, a substitute had been organized by what had been the National Council against Conscription but had recently become the National Council for Civil Liberties. Under the chairmanship of Sir Daniel Stevenson, the city's Liberal leader who two years previously had been Lord Provost, more than one thousand people met in the Central Hall. After normal formalities the proceedings were opened by the miners' leader, Robert Smillie, "a man of transparent integrity, in whom pity and indignation were passions wholly selfless". Smillie began with an explanation. It was most unusual for him to read his speeches, but a watch was being kept on people like himself. He might be prosecuted and he was therefore taking the precaution of reading from a text.

"On dark days," he began, "men need a clear faith and a well-grounded hope and, as the outcome of these, the calm courage which takes no account of hardships by the way." The press took it down. As he continued, some of those who had often reported him began to look at one another with surprise. "When I finished the lecture," Smillie later wrote, "I informed the audience that that was the beautiful message that Mr. Bertrand Russell had been prevented from delivering to the people of Glasgow."

Once Smillie had thus given with impunity in Glasgow the lecture Russell himself had been prevented from giving, although he had already delivered it in Manchester, the government's position slipped from untenable to farcical. Lloyd George, obliged to defend in the House the action taken on behalf of the Home Office, but apparently still uninformed of the Haverhill incident, did his best to brazen it out, claiming that the government "had information from a very reliable source that Mr. Bertrand Russell was about to engage in the delivery of a series of lectures which would interfere very seriously with the manning of the Army". It was difficult to see how quasi-academic talks on such subjects as "The Sphere of Compulsion in Good Government" would be likely to have this effect, particularly since conscription was now in force, and doubly difficult since the effect was apparently expected to operate in Glasgow but not in Manchester. As the *Daily News* summed it up, if Russell's activities were a peril to the State, it was "ridiculous to pretend that, while perilous in maritime towns, they will be harmless further inland – a danger in Brighton but not in Birmingham, in Hull but not in Halifax".

There was, in fact, a far more plausible argument, which had been put forward on 3 September, with a proposal far more drastic than banning Russell from certain areas. Lloyd George, however, was either unaware of it or felt it inexpedient to produce this particular rabbit from the hat at this particular time: "A man who goes about preaching such doctrines as this at the present moment," said an officer in M.I.5 after describing Russell's claim that there was no good reason for continuing the war, "is a danger to the State, and as such is not a suitable person to be allowed into prohibited areas, where he would have special opportunities of airing his vicious tenets amongst dockers, miners and the transport workers. If Mr. Russell should still persist in making speeches similar to his Cardiff one in unprohibited areas, then the next step will be to confine his movements to a particular area." What the authorities obviously feared, and with some reason, was not a rise in the number of conscientious objectors but an increase in the industrial unrest which simmered just below the surface. In fact Russell, writing a brief foreword to the lectures when they were published for the first time in England in 1963, stated, "[The War Office] charged me with inciting industrial disaffection in order to stop the war." The "charge" presumably refers to some remark by General Cockerill since no such accusation was ever formally made.

Even his personal confinement might have done more harm than good. "If you have not already arranged for someone else to do it," wrote one of his correspondents,

> could you let me have a copy of your first lecture given in Manchester, and by Smillie in Glasgow, so that I could have the honour of reading it in Liverpool, which is a prohibited area? A good crowd would turn up – the meeting would be organised by the Women's International League or by the N.-C.F. & ILP Joint Committee – and so your message would get to the people in spite of Government idiocy.

On 19 October the cudgels were taken up in the House of Commons by Philip Morrell, whose assertion that Russell had "been persecuted and pursued with a malignity recalling the methods of the Middle Ages" would have been given an added piquancy had his listeners known that he was defending his wife's former lover. The Home Secretary himself came galloping to Lloyd George's rescue, but with a defence made up in almost equal parts of cautious tergiversations and incautious lies. Samuel maintained that Russell's Cardiff speech "could undoubtedly have been made the subject of a prosecution", although the Public Prosecutor himself had specifically stated, "I do not advocate the prosecution." When challenged by Charles Trevelyan to repeat phrases to which objection was taken, he sought cover by means as sly as they were successful. "I should be sorry to repeat them", he said, "because it would give additional publicity to them." He also contended that Russell had been prevented from going to America because the government feared he "would be carrying on propaganda similar to that in which he was engaged in Cardiff". This was arguable enough in view of the plans for political lectures, but Samuel then went on to state that Russell had been "asked whether he would give an undertaking, if he were given a permit to go to America to give lectures at Harvard, not to engage in anti-British propaganda", a remark which recalls Hitler's dictum that the bigger the lie the better the chance of getting away with it.

In the House, Samuel continued to state that the order banning Russell from all prohibited areas had been made at the time of the Haverhill camp episode "because in those areas almost all the camps are situated", whereas a different story is revealed by the files. More sinned against by his staff than personally sinning, Samuel later beat a tactical retreat from this exposed position, admitting that he was in error on some points but still maintaining that Russell could go to the United States if he would give a guarantee of what the government considered to be good behaviour.

Russell did not ask for the ban to be raised. The government let it remain, a gift to German propaganda which Whitehall presumably felt was counter-balanced by the limitation of Russell's personal appearances.

12

Colette

During the summer of 1916 Russell emerged into the full light of public scrutiny. He was now a man about whom questions were asked in the House, a tilter against windmills, acceptable material for the cartoonist. Evolution into this new role, ever afterwards to compete with the professional logician and philosopher, was soon to be followed by a parallel emotional development which was to affect the rest of his life. Thus for Russell in mid-span – past it for the average man, approaching it for the nonagenarian-to-be – 1916 was a climactic year both publicly and personally.

On the evening of 31 July, Clifford Allen arrived at the police station in Lavender Hill, a drab and indeterminate area of South London on the fringe of the railway-yards at Clapham Junction, gave himself up and was shortly afterwards sentenced to three months' imprisonment for desertion under the Military Service Act. With him to the station went Lady Constance Malleson, a young actress using the stage-name of Colette O'Niel, and working at the N.-C.F.'s offices in her spare time. Russell arrived soon afterwards: to give Allen moral support and to get the story for the *Tribunal*.

At the far end of the wooden bench in the waiting room, Colette saw "a small man, with a fine brow, aristocratic features, silver-grey hair, and a passionate expression. He was conventionally dressed in dark clothes and he wore a high stiff collar. He seemed detached in mind and body – but all the furies of hell raged in his eyes."

From his end of the bench Russell regarded a beautiful, slight, auburn-haired girl still a few months from her twenty-first birthday. The younger daughter of the 5th Earl Annesley and his wife, Priscilla Cecilia Armytage Moore, she had been sent from Ireland to Darwin's Downe House in Kent, then a boarding school which she re-christened Damned Hell. After a few unhappy terms she persuaded her mother to remove her and was sent first to Dresden, then to Paris, a city she left only reluctantly for the ritual London season that demanded presentation at Court.

However, she conformed only on one condition: that she should train at London's Academy of Dramatic Art.

She soon became a confirmed agnostic, a move which dismayed her family as much as her espousal first of the Independent Labour Party, then of the No-Conscription Fellowship. It was in character that in 1915, still in her teens, she should marry Miles Malleson, actor-grandson of the man who had been honorary secretary of John Stuart Mill's election committee, and that the marriage should have been unorthodox even by today's standards. "I never cease being glad and grateful that M and I set our faces against conventional matrimony from the very start and that we've stuck to that," she was to write to Russell. "We're free to go or stay. That was our undertaking and promise. As you know, the legal ceremony had to be because it was the only way in which we could be together while I wasn't yet of age." By the summer of 1916 Colette, with the winds of youth ruffling her hair, was irresistible to all but the most hardened, and Russell was not a natural resister.

He and Colette were briefly introduced on the evening of 31 July. They did not meet again until 13 September. This time it was in an upper room of Gustave's Restaurant in Soho, where a changing group of Left-wingers – Ramsay MacDonald, the Robert Smillie who was to deliver Russell's lecture at Glasgow, Henry Nevinson the war correspondent, Francis Meynell and Gilbert Cannan the writer – met every Wednesday evening. Here, as Colette later wrote, "we found ourselves placed side by side," a table-seating that may conceivably have been coincidence but is more likely to have been the result of Russell's dropping the right word into the right ear.

After dinner Colette, Russell and Gilbert Cannan walked back to the small flat in Bernard Street that she still shared with her husband and which she called the Attic. "Cannan was stopping the night with us ... and as we walked back, I found myself hoping Russell would not come in," she wrote. "Cannan had a way of preventing any real talk – and one didn't want any but very real talk with Russell ... It was only a short walk back from Gustave's through the quiet Bloomsbury squares – but I had an odd feeling that it was perhaps the most important thing that had ever happened to me – or would ever happen to me: this meeting with Russell." Russell did not go in, but returned to his brother's house in Gordon Square less than half a mile away.

Ten days later the annual N.-C.F. Convention was held in Portman Square. Russell, still wearing the martyr's crown of dismissal from Trinity, was given an immense ovation as one of the main speakers. When the meeting was over he left with Colette. They dined at Canuto's, across the road in Baker Street, before walking back to the Attic. This time she was alone, and this time he stayed. Before morning they were lovers; and before morning both had become trapped in a lifetime's complex relationship from which neither was able entirely to escape.

In his autobiography, Russell gives the impression that this was an *affaire* which ended when he abandoned Colette after five years; when, as she herself put it, she "woke up one fine morning in 1921 to find life finished". At its best, this is an urbane example of his ability to make the best of his own story. The truth is very different. In the late 1920s, he renewed the relationship in a number of idyllic meetings in Somerset and Cornwall. More than a decade on, and after an ecstatic holiday together in Sweden, Russell had again become convinced, as he told her, that they "should never have parted". Yet the story was still the same, and the two persistent lovers parted for the third time, Russell perhaps fearing that marriage would ruin it all. But nearly twenty years later, in his nineties, he was still to be filled with love and affection at the regular arrival of Colette's red roses every birthday. And on the eve of Christmas 1968, she could still write to him, "Nothing on this earth could have given me greater delight than getting your dear letter of the 16th this very day. My thoughts are constantly with you. I send you all the most devoted love always and for ever."

All this, and much more, is chronicled in the hundreds of letters which passed between them during the half-century that followed their meeting. Russell's correspondence with Alys two decades earlier had glittered with the surprised excitement of first love. His letters to Ottoline had been on a totally different level, deeply passionate and often of a quality which makes them among the most moving love-letters of the twentieth century. Those to Colette, like hers to him, are yet again of another quality, bubbling with a sexuality they both relished, avidly discussing their personal relationships and, between intermittent bursts of disillusion and despair, reiterating avowals of eternal love.

Russell wrote first: two letters from Gordon Square to which he had returned in the early hours. "I woke to the dim fog and hoarse shouting of the newsboy in the street below," said Colette in acknowledging them. "Instantly my thoughts flew to you. Yes, contrasts in these days are strange; here in my room the fulfilment of being with you: but outside the flames of a Zepp crashing to earth. At most times nowadays one is half numb from the horror of the war."

They met again on the evening of the 27th. And walking back through the Bloomsbury squares the following morning he met a street flower-seller and sent him to the Attic with a bunch of red roses, a symbol that neither was to forget.

At the beginning of October they spent a day together in the country, and on the hills above Goring in Oxfordshire Russell told her of his relationship with Ottoline. Colette, who had stayed at Garsington the previous year, took the news equably – "I remember her splendid bearing and her real kindness," she wrote to him the following day. But he had learned to temper frankness with caution; he made no mention of Helen Dudley or of another entanglement from which he was to have difficulty in extricating himself. Colette was equally cautious; thus far, her husband Miles was told nothing of the *affaire*.

For the next few weeks she was the stimulating background to Russell's daily life. It was easy for her to drop in notes to him at Gordon Square on her journeys between the Attic and the N.-C.F. offices. "Having daily work more or less in common makes it almost seem we're together in all the working hours," she wrote to him early in October. "So you mustn't think or feel that you've to write to me or see me. Our love doesn't depend on those things for its life. All the same I've jotted down your engagements and find that I do have Friday evening free. So it would be perfect if we can have it together."

They exchanged photographs. "I've sent you the Hoppé . . . you asked for," she said in a note to him. "*When* shall I have one of *you*? I'd like one taken when your heathery hair hasn't been all shorn off by the damned barber, I'd like it looking robustious and revolutionary. Or do I mean rebellious?"

Soon afterwards Colette, whose relationship with Miles was now only platonic, told her husband of her *affaire* with Russell. "He was so gentle and tucked me up so tenderly," she wrote the following day.

> I felt a bit exhausted, but before I went to sleep I saw the sun spreading wings across the sky, and the smell of early morning was fresh and good. And now, all this day, and all the time until I see you again, you'll be in my heart. I feel utterly one with you now, not only as lovers but in an almost deeper way. I feel outward bound into the storm.

Russell himself also began to clear the emotional decks. Responding with his usual intuition, he had sensed her suspicion that his revelation about Ottoline had not been quite the whole story. There were in fact two addenda, quite apart from Helen Dudley, about whom he continued to remain silent. One concerned Katherine Mansfield, cousin of Elizabeth von Arnim, Frank's third wife, whom he had met at Garsington earlier in the year. She had needed a reference for a flat and had turned to him after St John Hutchinson had refused on the ground that she was living in sin with Middleton Murry. Half-way through 1916, she exchanged manuscripts with Russell and in sending hers stressed, "I cannot tell you how much I value your friendship". The friendship continued throughout the early euphoria of Russell's relationship with Colette; and when, during the last weeks of 1916, that relationship seemed in danger of ending, the bond with Katherine Mansfield strengthened. "I have just re-read your letter and now my head aches with a kind of sweet excitement," she then wrote.

> Do you know what I mean? It is what a little girl feels when she has been put to bed at the end of a long sunny day and still sees upon her closed eyelids the image of dancing boughs and flowering bushes.
>
> To work – to work! It is such infinite delight to know that we still have the best things to do and that we shall be comrades in the doing of them. But on Tuesday night I am going to ask you a great many questions. I want to know more about your life – ever so many things. There is time enough, perhaps, but I feel definitely impatient at this moment.
>
> You have already, in this little time, given me so much – more than I have given you, and that does not satisfy me. But at present my work simply springs from the wonderful fact that you *do* stand for life. And until Tuesday I shall not read your letter again – It troubles me too greatly, but thank you – Thank you for it.

A few weeks later she wrote again, enclosing her letter in an envelope on which she had written the circled words "I am 25 1917".

> You wrote me such a lovely letter, mon cher ami. Yes, let us dine together on Friday evening. I shall be well enough if you will please come for me here. Then *we shall talk*. I feel there is so much to be said that I am quite quite silent until then; that it is an age since we have seen each other; and yet while I haven't seen you my "friendship" for you has gone on and grown ever so much deeper and profounder.
>
> Let us be very happy on Friday night. I give you my two hands.
>
> KATHERINE.

More than thirty years later, Russell was surprised when he unearthed the letters in his files. "They read", he wrote, "as if we were having an affair, or about to have one, but it was not so. She withdrew, possibly on account of Colette, though I never knew. My feelings for her were ambivalent; I admired her passionately, but was repelled by her dark hatreds."

The relationship with Katherine Mansfield, which ebbed and flowed through the war years, had its roots in a mutually intellectual approach to the world, however seriously he may have regarded her as a reserve player in the sexual game. Not so simple was that with Vivien Eliot, the young wife of his former student at Harvard.

Early in 1915 Russell, hurrying out from his Bury Street flat to buy tea, had literally bumped into T. S. Eliot, who had arrived in England unknown to him and was now at Merton College, Oxford. Shortly afterwards he had invited him up to Cambridge where Eliot spoke to the Moral Science Club in Russell's rooms on "The Relativity of the Moral Judgment". Their friendship gathered pace and was soon careering along the path that friendship with Russell often followed. A few years previously it was Wittgenstein who had been the disciple and Russell who described how he loved him. He continued to do so until, a decade later, the disciple struck out on his own and they agreed to differ. Relationship with Lawrence had followed a similar course. "I love him more and more and I wouldn't dream of discouraging his socialist revolution", he had declared before falling out with him on the means of social reconstruction. Now came Eliot and Ottoline once again was reading, "I loved him like a son."

In 1915 Eliot was about to be married. Russell was soon introduced to the new Mrs Eliot and passed on to Ottoline his intuitive view that she might develop into saint or criminal; her apparently post-war, but undated, letter to Russell stating that she had stolen jewellery from him and lacked the courage to return it, suggests that the judgment was not much out. There seems little doubt that Mrs Eliot was addicted to drugs, and that the burden she became had a traumatic effect on the development of Eliot's poetry. She was also extremely pretty, "slim and rather small, but by no means insignificant", as Brigit Patmore has described her. "Light brown hair and shining grey eyes. The shape of her face was narrowed to a pointed oval chin and her mouth was good – it did not split up her face when she smiled, but was small and sweet enough to kiss, added to this, she did not quiver, as so sensitive a person might, but shimmered with intelligence."

Russell's version to Ottoline was rather different. "I expected her to be terrible, from his mysteriousness," he confided after he had dined with the young couple, "but she was not so bad. She is light, a little vulgar, adventurous, full of life – an artist I think he said, but I should have thought her an actress. He is exquisite and listless; she says she married him to stimulate him, but she finds she can't do it. Obviously he married in order to be stimulated. I think she will soon be tired of him."

She had swum into Russell's orbit at a moment when Ottoline's influence had become paralysing and, as he admitted to her later, when he felt he had to regain his independence. She had just forced him to lay aside the "Social Reconstruction" lectures and he wanted to prise loose her hold for a while. Vivien Eliot, he made clear in subsequent letters, had happened to turn up at a convenient moment, and he had "used her for the purpose", an explanation which in fact does less than justice to Russell. For from his intimate letters to both Ottoline and Colette there can be no doubt that he gave the Eliots considerable and unqualified financial help with motives at least far removed from the obvious ones; and that he and Mrs Eliot did not, in the expected progress of night following day, become lovers. To Ottoline, to whom he never lied however much he might prevaricate, he could say, "I never contemplated risking my reputation with her, & I never risked it so far as I can judge."

From the first, Russell was interested in the effect which marriage would have on the young man whom he still regarded as a potential recruit to philosophy. And from the first he was the willing confidant of Mrs Eliot, who like so many women was happy to pour her troubles into the ear of the understanding and sympathetic Bertrand Russell. She had many troubles. "I am worried about those Eliots," he confided to Ottoline.

> It seems their sort of pseudo-honeymoon at Eastbourne is being a ghastly failure. She is quite tired of him, & when I got here I found a desperate letter from her, in the lowest depths of despair & not far removed from suicide. I have written her various letters full of good advice, & she seems to have come to rely on me more or less. I have so much taken them both in hand that I dare not let them be. I think she will fall more or less in love with me, but that can't be helped. I am interested by the attempt to pull her straight. She is half Irish, & wholly Irish in character – with a great deal of mental passion & *no* physical passion, a universal vanity, that makes her desire every man's devotion, & a fastidiousness that makes any expression of their devotion disgusting to her. She has suffered humiliation in two successive love-affairs, & that has made her vanity morbid. She has boundless ambition (far beyond her powers), but it is diffuse & useless. What she needs is some kind of religion, or at the least some discipline, of which she seems never to have had any. At present she is punishing my poor friend for having tricked her imagination – like the heroine of the "Playboy". I want to give her some other outlet than destroying him. I shan't fall in love with her, nor give her any more show of affection than seems necessary to rehabilitate her. But she really has *some* value in herself, all twisted and battered by life, lack of discipline, lack of purpose, & lack of religion.

The chance to be helpful was not long in coming. Accommodation in London was difficult and dear, and he offered the young couple the use of his flat in Bury Street. On 11 September 1915, Eliot wrote to Russell, "As to your coming to stay the night at the flat when I am not there, it would never have occurred to me to accept it under any other conditions. Such a concession to convention never entered my head; it seems to me not only totally unnecessary, but also would destroy for me all the pleasure we take in the informality of the arrangement."

Ottoline, knowing Russell, had her premonitions. "There is no occasion for your fears," he assured her. "He is not that sort of man & I will be much more careful than you seem to expect. And I feel sure that I can make things come right. We can talk about it when I come. I would not for the world have any scandal, & as for the Eliots, it is the purest philanthropy – I am sorry you feel worried – there is *really* no need."

As it happened, this was true. Nevertheless, Ottoline's subconscious worry about Russell's feelings was not without reason. "I am getting very fond of Mrs. Eliot," Russell had written before offering the couple the flat, "not in an 'improper' manner – she does not attract me much physically – but I find her a real friend, with a really deep humane feeling about the war, & no longer at all unkind to her husband. I feel her a permanent acquisition, not merely an object of kindness, as I thought at first." Within a few months he admitted to having "a very great affection" for her: a feeling, he told Ottoline, "utterly different from the feeling I have for you. What makes me care for her is that she affords an opportunity for *giving* a kind of affection that hitherto I have only been able to give in a slight, fragmentary way to pupils – I don't mean that is the whole of it, but it is what is important." By November he could say, "I shall be seeing a great deal of her – the affection I have for her is what one might have for a daughter, but it is very strong, & my judgment goes with it."

Towards the end of 1915 he arranged to take Mrs Eliot to Devon and they spent five days together at Torquay. Ottoline received a detailed analysis of the episode. She would not, he said, be able to see at all what it was that attracted him to Mrs Eliot. "I have found out what it is mainly, but I am rather ashamed of the discovery," he went on.

> It is that she is trustful & thinks me wise & good – at least as regards her – & as regards her I have been. Partly this satisfies my love of despotism, partly it makes me feel not such a wretch as I have always felt for a long time in relation to you. I have had moments when I have thought I might like a closer relation with her, but that is not the truth – the whole satisfaction I have depends on being useful both to her & to Eliot, & would vanish if I began wanting anything inconsistent with that. I dare say if I settle in the country after Camb. Term is over I shall have visits sometimes from both, sometimes from her alone, but I shall never have a physical relation with her, which in any case she would not at all want ... The problem for as regards Mrs. E is this: All the faults you suspect exist but they are gradually improving. I have made her trust me & look to me & care for me to a considerable extent. In spite of her faults I have an affection for her, because I feel they spring from a root of despair & that she might become quite different. And apart from affection, I have incurred responsibility. The affection is not constant, but the sense of responsibility is. I don't want to quarrel – I think with time I can

avoid giving her the feeling that I have played her false, without getting into any permanent entanglement. But it will want time.

However, all was not well, a turning-point in the relationship was near, and a few months later he was writing that his thoughts and his feelings were in confusion at the prospect of a coming meeting. "I don't know what I want or what I ought to want," he went on. "I feel sure the result will be a violent quarrel, whatever I may intend – if not this time then next."

Ottoline for her part had been equally disconcerted. "I had a long talk with Bertie about Mrs. Eliot," runs an entry in her diary. "I don't really understand her influence over him. It seems odd that such a frivolous, silly little woman should affect him so much, but I think he likes to feel that she depends on him, and she looks up to him as a rich god, for he lavishes presents on her of silk underclothes and all sorts of silly things and pays for her dancing lessons." However, a move towards disengagement was near, the result of Ottoline's cautions and the realization by Russell of what Robert Sencourt has called Mrs Eliot's "fragile grasp on sanity" and what he has described as "her taking of drugs and the consequent hallucinations". He kept up friendly relations with the Eliots for a number of years. He helped them financially. But from the summer of 1916 there is little doubt that the picture is the unusual one of Russell as much pursued as pursuer.

It was soon afterwards that he became the target for a stream of unqualified affection from Colette, a beautiful and passionate woman with a formidable ability to express her feelings, to demonstrate that she felt no allegiance elsewhere, and to convince a man old enough to be her father. Russell, not unnaturally, was bowled over. Only after some three months did he begin to regain his balance.

Early in November he travelled to Manchester, a city from which the War Office could not exclude him, to make another speech in the series inaugurated by Smillie in Glasgow. Then he went, by train and on foot, to the Cat and Fiddle, high up on the Derbyshire moors and one of the most lonely inns in England. Here Colette was waiting for him and here they spent an ecstatic week, walking in all weathers during the days, sitting by the open fire in the evenings.

At the end of the holiday she moved to Manchester, for a week in theatrical lodgings. He travelled to Birmingham, the city where he was to give his next popular lecture, before returning to his brother's house in Gordon Square.

Troubles now followed in quick succession, the least being the temporary flight to America of Frank's latest wife, unable to put up with his savage treatment any longer. Fenner Brockway, one of the N.-C.F.'s founders, had been arrested and was soon to be serving a sentence of twenty-eight months, six of them in solitary confinement. Clifford Allen had been released from prison after his three-month sentence but was about to be re-arrested, and it was only with difficulty that Russell obtained a special permit to attend the court martial, held at Newhaven, Sussex, one of the restricted areas. He was accompanied by a military escort for the day, and the final paragraph of the permit reminded him that "The Pass will not enable you to stay the night in Newhaven, or to go anywhere else in the Town except to the Court Martial room and return to the Station". Hitting even more closely was the news that Jean Nicod, one of Russell's pre-war Trinity pupils, and a French citizen, now feared that he might be shot for refusing military service.

Nicod was one of three "regulars" who came to Russell in Gordon Square for private coaching. A second was one of his Harvard students, Victor Lenzen, while the third was Dorothy Wrinch, a young woman who had written to him in 1914 with a question about "Mysticism and Logic". Some months later she had called on him. "She wants to learn logic but Girton doesn't want her to, & threatens to deprive her of her scholarship if she does," Russell had told Ottoline.

> She has just finished her mathematical tripos, & is just the sort of person who ought to do it – she is very keen, but has not a penny beyond her scholarship, and is at the mercy of Miss Jex-Blake, a Churchy old fool. It makes me mad. If she could get £80 a year, she would ignore the College. But she doesn't see how to. If I had it, I would take her on as my Secretary, but I don't see how I can manage it.

In London, in 1916, he could at least give her tuition, and Miss Wrinch had joined the small group in his rooms who discussed symbolic logic, the prospects for the pacifist cause and the outcome of the war, beneath the stern gaze of Leibniz and Frege. All were of similar outlook and all were on one occasion weekend guests at Garsington.

Tuition was efficiently spatch-cocked in with Russell's N.-C.F. activities. But it all took time and early in December Colette received a note saying that his work and his other engagements would prevent him from seeing her for "some very considerable time". The words were a warning, although she was not yet to know this, often used when Russell was starting a disengaging operation.

His feelings had certainly been affected by the renewal of his acquaintance with Katherine Mansfield. "I want to get to know [her] really well," he had recently written to Ottoline. "She interests me mentally very much indeed – I think she has a very good mind, & I like her boundless curiosity." Yet the warning that work might keep him from seeing Colette was at least partly justified since he was about to carry off a considerable propaganda-coup.

He had long respected President Wilson and had the previous year written of one presidential speech, "It was amazingly fine. One felt a lonely man, fighting bravely to keep his country from blind rage, reminding men of ideals in direct simple words – something of Lincoln's quality was in it." In November 1916, Wilson had been overwhelmingly re-elected on the slogan, "He kept us out of war", and he shortly afterwards addressed a peace appeal to the Central Powers and the Allies. Both rejected it with equal distaste. However, Russell sincerely believed that Wilson could now muster sufficient power among the neutrals not merely to recommend but to impose peace and in advocacy of this he now wrote a 1,200-word open letter to the president.

The document – in whose drafting, Russell confided to Ottoline, Philip had been most helpful – was to draw down even more wrath than his work for the No-Conscription Fellowship. He began with an eloquent appeal – "You have an opportunity of performing a signal service to mankind, surpassing even the service of Abraham Lincoln, great as that was." And he ended with words that reflected an undertow of feeling in Britain.

> Like the rest of my countrymen I have desired ardently the victory of the Allies; like them, I have suffered when victory has been delayed. But I remember always that Europe has common tasks to fulfil; that a war among European nations is in essence a civil war; that the ill which we think of our enemies they equally think of us; and that it is difficult in time of war for a belligerent to see facts truly. Above all, I see that none of the issues in the war are as important as peace; the harm done by a peace which does not concede all that we desire is as nothing in comparison to the harm done by the continuance of fighting.

It was not only Wilson who at his best could subconsciously echo Gettysburg.

The letter completed, one problem remained: how to get it to the United States through a censorship which Russell rightly guessed was giving his mail special scrutiny? A solution presented itself with the help of Helen Dudley and her younger sister Katherine.

Since September the two girls had been living in Russell's flat, which they had taken over from the Eliots, but Katherine was about to return home for Christmas. And to Katherine was now entrusted Russell's small four-page letter which she concealed before passing through the Customs at Southampton.

Katherine arrived in New York on 20 December, uncertain of how to deliver the letter. She soon found that the American Neutral Conference Committee would be holding a private luncheon two days later in the Hotel Astor, and to the committee she presented herself, unannounced, unnamed, but as a confidential agent of Bertrand Russell. Henry Holt, president of the conference, introduced her to the meeting before reading Russell's letter. Then it was decided that a delegation of three should leave for Washington that evening and, if possible, ensure that Wilson got the letter. First, however, it was copied and made available to the press, an action ensuring that whatever the president's response, neither he nor the rest of the world would remain in ignorance of the appeal. The first part of the operation was certainly successful, and the *New York Times* printed the letter in full under the front-page banner headline: "Mysterious Girl Brings Russell's Peace Plea Here; Famous English Philosopher and Mathematician Asks Wilson to Stop War Ere Europe Perishes."

In Washington, the committee's delegation was equally successful, and the letter was put before the president by Walter Lippman, Wilson's unofficial press attaché.

The impact on the British authorities of this audacious cutting-out operation was immediate, and on 26 December Spring Rice, the British Ambassador in Washington, sent a special report to the British Foreign Secretary, A. J. Balfour. "It has been brought to the President's knowledge, together with other communications of a similar character from allied sources, and is supposed to have received the President's earnest consideration," it said.

There is no evidence that the letter had the slightest effect on American policy, but in England it added fuel to the bonfire already burning round Russell's feet. "Mr. Russell cannot have it both ways," the *Morning Post* declared. "Either he was worthy of the attention of the President of the United States, in which case his smuggled letter was a treachery to his own country; or he was unworthy of attention in which case the intrusion upon President Wilson was a piece of sheer gratuitous and, we will add, mischievous impertinence."

Whether treachery or impertinence, the authorities were worried that the document had slipped under their guard, and an Inspector Edmund Buckley was given the task of discovering how this had happened. "Having pursued quiet enquiries re same," he recorded, he had identified the Dudley sisters as the occupants of Russell's flat, found that Katherine had sailed to New York in the second half of December and drawn his own, correct conclusions. But Helen was still in Britain, and Inspector Buckley ended his report with the warning that "if the elder Miss Dudley tries to embark she should be carefully searched".

The letter, and the intensification of his activities which it foreshadowed, seriously endangered Russell's relationship with Whitehead. They remained friends until Whitehead's death in 1947, as Russell was always careful to stress. But on 8 January 1917, Whitehead sent Russell two separate letters. In the first he announced that he would no longer continue sending him his notes for the fourth volume of *Principia* which it had been decided he would write on his own. "I don't want my ideas propagated *at present* either under my name or anybody else's – that is to say, as far as they are at present on paper," he said.

The result will be an incomplete misleading exposition which will inevitably queer the pitch for the final exposition when I want to put it out.

My ideas and methods grow in a different way to yours and the period of incubation is long and the result attains its intelligible form in the final stage, – I do not want you to have my notes which in chapters are lucid, to precipitate them into what I should consider as a series of half truths. I have worked at these ideas off and on for all my life, and should be left quite bare on one side of my speculative existence if I handed them over to some one else to elaborate. Now that I begin to see daylight, I do not feel justified or necessitated by any view of scientific advantage in so doing.

I am sorry that you do not feel able to get to work except by the help of these notes, but I am sure that you must be mistaken in this, and that there must be the whole of the remaining field of thought for you to get to work on – though naturally it would be easier for you to get into harness with some formed notes to go on. But my reasons are conclusive.

To Russell the letter was an extension of Whitehead's disgruntlement at not being sufficiently acknowledged, as he believed, in *Our Knowledge of the External World*. Certainly he did not send any further notes. Yet it is difficult not to believe that his reaction was, at least in part, a reflection of his dislike of Russell's political beliefs. This is borne out by the second note, more brusque, sent on 8 January. With it he enclosed a cutting from *The Times* reporting Maeterlinck's protest against the German deportation of French and Belgians. "As the result of damping down amongst neutrals – America in particular – of the first protests against earlier atrocities, this is now happening. What are *you* going to do to help these people?" he demanded. A single line about his younger son was added below his initials: "Eric leaves us in April – Flying Corps."

Russell's concern with the specific issue of conscientious objectors was now being broadened by the Russian Revolution. His initial enthusiasm for the explosion was natural, since he supposed that the abdication of the Tsar and the formation of the Provisional Government would automatically mean the withdrawal of the Russians from the war. However, some Russians believed the country could wage a war and manage a revolution at the same time. Kerensky himself, first War Minister and then Prime Minister, urged the vigorous prosecution of the war and vainly tried to mount a major offensive during the summer of 1917. But these events tended to be overlooked in Britain except among those who pinned their faith on the Council of Soviet Workmen and Soldiers' Representatives who they hoped would soon overthrow the new Russian Government.

Russell, and men like him, saw the fall of the Tsar as a panacea for almost every political trouble, especially in the climate of the meeting held on 31 March 1917 to welcome the Revolution. The Albert Hall was packed, he told Ottoline, adding that 20,000 people had to be refused tickets. "Every person there was wanting a real absolute change in everything, not the sort of piecemeal niggling reforms that one is used to, but the sort of thing the Russians have done," he went on.

> There was *no* opposition. The C.O's. came in for their due share of applause – that one had expected. But besides that, people cheered for a republic, for freedom for India, for all the things one never hears mentioned. Jos Wedgwood, who represented moderation, suggested that it was possible to believe that some good objects could not be obtained without war, but he could only get a hearing after an urgent appeal from the Chairman. The whole atmosphere was electric. I longed to shout to them at the end to come with me & pull down Wormwood Scrubs. They would have done it. The Reporters applauded, but did not take notes. A meeting of the kind would have been utterly impossible a month ago. Smillie & Williams were admirable as regards Labour. The regular pacifist gang were not speaking, & the general public did not know what sort of meeting it was going to be. "To cheer the Russian Revolution" sounded quite respectable. But the speakers one and all urged that we should do likewise. The audience was largely Russian Jews. I saw my little friend Tchitcherin (the Sec. of one of their organisations) afterwards, beaming like a cherub. There was a lot said about Ireland – the Sinn Fein martyrs were enthusiastically cheered. The Russians have really put a new spirit into the world, & it is going to be worth while to be alive.

Russell's unqualified and uninformed optimism was general, and early in June, as Kerensky was marshalling his forces for the offensive, the United Socialist Council convened a conference in Leeds to work out ways of co-ordinating their efforts with the Russians. Russell travelled to Leeds with Colette, her husband Miles and Ramsay MacDonald, "who spent the time telling long stories of pawky Scotch humour so dull that it was almost impossible to be aware when the point had been reached". On arrival in the city they were identified as going to the meeting and were hissed through the streets, while small boys threw stones.

The occasion itself was slightly disappointing. "Snowden & MacDonald & Anderson are not the right men," Russell complained. "The right man would be Williams (of the Transport Workers), but he is not yet sufficiently prominent. Smillie is perfect except that he is old. The enthusiasm & all-but unanimity were wonderful – out of 2,500, there were only about 3 dissentients. Nothing was lacking except leaders." Russell, in the audience, rose to speak, but there were shouts for his presence on the platform and when he got there he was cheered enthusiastically. He spoke in support of a resolution which called on the British government to establish immediately "complete political rights for all men and women, unrestricted freedom of the Press, freedom of speech, a general amnesty for all political and religious prisoners, full rights of industrial and political association, and the release of labour from all forms of compulsion and restraint". He concentrated on the conscientious objectors in prison, stressing that "it is by their refusal to serve that they have shown the world that it is possible for the individual to stand in this matter of military service against the whole power of the organised State".

They applauded everything that had to do with conscientious objectors, he told Ottoline. "It was a good beginning, but a very great deal remains to be done – MacDonald, whom I travelled down with, was persuaded we should be broken up by soldiers – he has lost his nerve – he does the things, but expects disaster."

By a quirk of coincidence, this ecstatic account from a man who was later to lambast the new Russia was matched mirror-fashion by a critical report from Beatrice Webb, later to become a eulogistic Communist admirer. "The thousand or more delegates to the Leeds Conference were – so one of them declared – mentally drunk – and quite incapable of coherent thinking," she confided to her diary. "They were swayed by emotions towards peace and an emotion towards workers' control. It is an odd irony that the concrete example of the 'workers' control' arising out of the Leeds Conference was the seamen's refusal to permit MacDonald and Roberts to proceed to Petrograd to forward the propaganda for a negotiated peace."

At the Leeds meeting it was decided to follow the Russian example and set up organizations in England and Scotland aimed at the formation of workers' and soldiers' councils, and Russell was quick to bring the N.-C.F. into the movement. In a letter to Branch Secretaries asking them to send delegates to Divisional Conferences, he said that these would

> be at least as much concerned with economic reconstruction as they will with the question of peace. But probably a large majority of members of the N.-C.F. would agree that a great change in our economic system is implied in the principles which under-lie our basis. We should therefore be not going seriously outside our province by joining in the advocacy of some such changes, though as pacifists we should wish to do all in our power to secure that the changes should occur without the use of force and not in a spirit of violence or hate.

> The new movement will aim, as the Russian Government does, at bringing the war to an end by a general peace, but it will not be an out and out pacifist movement, and if it were it is not likely that it would succeed in securing peace ...

Russell's role as the focus for thoughtful opposition to the war was underlined soon after the Leeds Conference with the arrival in England of Siegfried Sassoon, a young officer in the Royal Welch Fusiliers. A bundle of contradictions, he had joined up the day before war broke out and had won the Military Cross before being wounded and recommended for the Victoria Cross. But Sassoon was acutely sensitive to the wastage of the war and growing steadily critical of the way it was being run; a poet already drawn into Ottoline's Garsington circle, a military hero among pacifists.

Russell had sent him a copy of *Principles of Social Reconstruction*, and once back in England Sassoon acknowledged the book. So far, he said, he had only read the foreword, which he liked. But, he was only a soldier-poet of thirty-one, and it is clear that he was cautious of expressing any very definite views about the quasi-revolutionary ideas of a man as eminent as Russell. He went on to say that he expected his wound to keep him in England for about a couple of months. After that, one could infer from the tone of his letter, he would soon be back in France. Yet in England the need to do something else slowly but steadily became more apparent.

Shortly afterwards Sassoon wrote to H. W. Massingham of the *Nation* proposing that he "publish something outspoken so as to let people at home know what the War was really like". A few days later he called. "You said the other day that you couldn't print anything really outspoken," he said, "but I don't see why I shouldn't make some sort of statement – about how we ought to publish our War Aims, and all that, and the troops not knowing what they're fighting about." Massingham felt this might backfire. He advised caution. And he passed his visitor on to Bertrand Russell.

Some account of Russell's share in what follows was given, thinly disguised, in Sassoon's *Memoirs of an Infantry Officer*; but Russell's own papers, and his letters to Ottoline, reveal the full importance of his part in what was to be, for Sassoon, a traumatic experience deeply affecting his future career. Massingham, the Markington of Sassoon's *Memoirs*, advised him to call on Russell – the Thornton Tyrrell of the book – who telegraphed to say that he could see Sassoon that evening. Sassoon wrote,

> My first impression was that he looked exactly like a philosopher. He was small, clean-shaven, with longish grey hair brushed neatly above a fine forehead. He had a long upper lip, a powerful ironic

6 Russell with Dora Black (later Russell's second wife) at the National University, Peking, in 1921

17 (*far left*) Russell on the Great Wall of China, 1920

18 (*left*) Russell in Japan with Mr Kegawa, a Japanese Labour leader, 1921

19 (*below, left*) Russell outside Peking University, 1921

20 (*right*) Russell with his son John, aged two, during the Chelsea election, 1923

21 (*below, right*) Russell with Dora (*seated*) during the Chelsea election

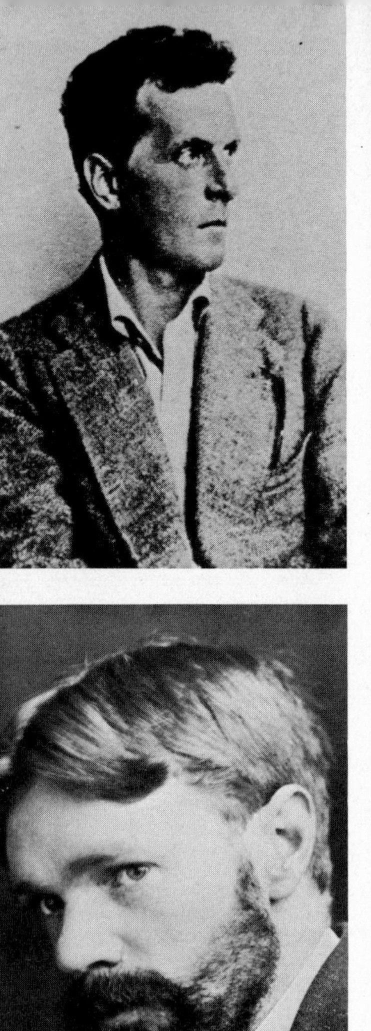

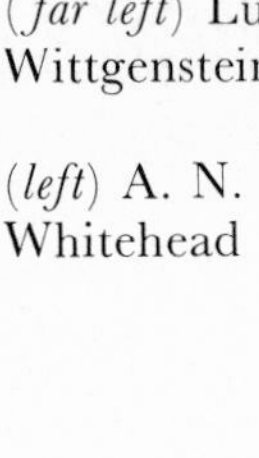

22 (*far left*) Ludwig Wittgenstein

23 (*left*) A. N. Whitehead

24 (*far left* D. H. Lawrence

25 (*left*) Lytton Strachey

26 (*far left*) George Santayana

27 (*left*) Stanley Unwin

mouth, and large earnest eyes. I observed that the book which he put aside was called *The Conquest of Bread* by Kropotkin, and I wondered what on earth it could be about. He put me at my ease by lighting a large pipe, saying as he did so, "Well, I gather from Markington's letter that you've been experiencing a change of heart about the War."

Sassoon agreed. "Tyrrell poured me out a second cup of tea and suggested that I should write out a short personal statement based on my conviction that the War was being unnecessarily prolonged by the refusal of the Allies to publish their war aims. When I had done this we could discuss the next step to be taken."

Russell recommended a maximum of two hundred words. He asked Sassoon to bring him the finished manuscript and promised to see that as many copies as possible were printed and circulated. "I had", said Sassoon, "taken a strong liking for Tyrrell, who probably smiled rather grimly while he was reading a few more pages of Kropotkin's *Conquest of Bread* before going upstairs to his philosophic slumbers."

For his part, Russell had been equally impressed. "He is altogether splendid, physically, mentally and spiritually," he wrote to Mrs Swanwick, a leading N.-C.F. supporter. "He has shown amazing courage in battle, and is now showing still greater courage by his defiance. There is nothing in the faintest degree hysterical or unbalanced in his attitude which is the inevitable development of the thoughts and feelings expressed in his poems. The sheer impulse of humanity is the basis of his action."

A week later Sassoon was back with his statement:

> I am making [it] as an act of wilful defiance of military authority, because I believe that the War is being deliberately prolonged by those who have the power to end it. I am a soldier, convinced that I am acting on behalf of soldiers. I believe that this War, upon which I entered as a war of defence and liberation, has now become a war of aggression and conquest. I believe that the purposes for which I and my fellow soldiers entered upon this War should have been so clearly stated as to have made it impossible to change them, and that, had this been done, the objects which actuated us would now be attained by negotiation. I have seen and endured the sufferings of the troops, and I can no longer be a party to prolonging those sufferings for ends which I believe to be evil and unjust. I am not protesting against the conduct of the War, but against the political errors and insincerities for which the fighting men are being sacrificed. On behalf of those who are suffering now, I make this protest against the deception which has been practised upon them; also I believe that it may help to destroy the callous complacence with which the

majority of those at home regard the continuance of agonies which they do not share, and which they have not sufficient imagination to realise.

After the second meeting, Russell gave his impressions of Sassoon to Ottoline. "You are quite wrong in thinking I don't like him. I thought I saw some faults, but not of a kind I mind; & his courage is really wonderful." While Sassoon was obviously intent on having his statement published, whatever the repercussions on his own fortunes, Russell was still uncertain how the situation could best be turned to the advantage of the No-Conscription movement, even though H. B. Lees-Smith, one of the few pacifist M.P.s, was apparently ready to air the matter in the House of Commons. "I talked to Massingham about [Sassoon], took him to see first Francis Meynell & then Lees-Smith, & arranged the programme as far as possible – but the legal obstacles can only be overcome through questions or speeches in the House of Commons," Russell wrote. "Lees-Smith was very kind and helpful. I suppose P. will also be willing to help in the House? I wrote to Ponsonby but he was away so I have not yet heard from him. S.S. had *quite* decided, & has now taken the irrevocable step – at least he was just going to when I left him yesterday. So now the matter should be spoken of everywhere – the more the better. I think he is happier now than he was."

The irrevocable step was the posting of the statement to Meynell at the Pelican Press. Meynell printed it as a leaflet and circulated it until, after some weeks, the remaining copies were seized by the police.

Meanwhile Sassoon came to the end of his leave and failed to report to the Fusiliers depot at Litherland on the outskirts of Liverpool. Some days later he received a telegram: "Report how situated." "There was nothing for it but to obey the terse instructions, so I composed a letter (brief, courteous, and regretful) to the Colonel, enclosing a type-written copy of my statement, apologising for the trouble I was causing him, and promising to return as soon as I heard from him," Sassoon has written. The response was, "Report immediately."

Before leaving London he visited Russell again, "hating the prospect of painful interviews with people he is fond of, but quite resolute, & much happier inwardly than before he took the plunge". He was, Russell went on, "wonderfully brave. I admire his courage more than I can say ... I don't want to appear in the matter myself, as S.S. is not an out & out pacifist, & it would be a pity if he became identified with those who are."

At the Litherland depot they were baffled. There was at first no response except tolerant kindness and amiability, and extreme unwillingness to take action. The military had consulted "higher authority", and when Sassoon told them that the thing had gone beyond their control, they showed little understanding of the serious situation that was developing.

Up to this point the pacifists held all the aces. An officer whose courage and intellect were equally beyond dispute was risking court martial and disgrace in order to attack the continuation of the war. Nothing could be better propaganda. However, within the next few days the situation was drastically reversed.

To Robert Graves, a brother-officer in the regiment, Sassoon had sent a newspaper-cutting of his statement. But while Graves had a similar disillusioned view of the war he saw little point in this particular form of protest.

> I knew, too, that as a gesture it was inadequate. Nobody would follow his example either in England or in Germany. The war would obviously go on, and go on until one side or the other cracked.
>
> I decided to intervene ...

Graves's action was quick and to the point. To a potentially sympathetic major at the Fusiliers depot he wrote urging that Sassoon be brought before a medical board and given indefinite leave. Shortly afterwards he himself arrived at the depot.

His first efforts to talk Sassoon out of his protest were unsuccessful, since Sassoon was determined not to appear before the medical board. Graves then played his untrumpable card. "He said," Sassoon wrote, "that the Colonel at Litherland had told him to tell me that if I continued to refuse to be 'medically-boarded' they would shut me up in a lunatic asylum for the rest of the War. Nothing would induce them to court-martial me. It had all been arranged with some big bug at the War Office in the last day or two." Sassoon capitulated.

"So far so good," Graves later observed. "The next thing was to rig the medical board." This he successfully did with a good deal of skill. In the words of the War Office, Sassoon was reported "as not being responsible for his actions, suffering from a nervous breakdown", and was sent to a Scottish hospital for shell-shocked officers.

Graves then invoked the aid of an old friend, Evan Morgan, private secretary to W. C. Bridgman, Minister of Labour. "I expect you can help me," he wrote.

> You have I expect heard about the poet Siegfried Sassoon being exploited by the pacifists Bertrand Russell & Lees-Smith when in a state of (now certified & official) nervous breakdown after being wounded in some marvellously brave fighting in France. He wrote a letter of wilful defiance to his Colonel refusing to do any more service. After enormous struggles I've smoothed things down & got him certified suffering from nerves, etc. by a Medical Board & told the pacifists that they've been thwarted, & that their protégé is now

in a convalescent home in Scotland. Well, you belong to the Trades Union of poets & so you must see what you can do in connexion counter-propaganda bureau to stop his "defiance letter", copies of which he has sent to B. Russell & to Henderson's "Bomb Shop" [a shop in the Charing Cross Road which sold a lot of peace propaganda], going any farther. Everything is being hushed up now. James Hope the M.P. (Treasurer of the Household) has been working on behalf of a quiet solution to the business. I have told him about what I've done – Any scandal would spoil all our efforts.

However, if the police had successfully infiltrated the No-Conscription Fellowship and other pacifist movements, they in turn had their own lines well laid. Two days after Graves had written to Morgan, a copy of the letter was in Russell's hands. "It is just what was to be expected on the part of the authorities, but I had thought better of Graves," he told Ottoline. "Could you make him see that he is not acting the part of *real* friendship, tho' he thinks he is? I have told Lees-Smith, who heard from S.S. this morning. S.S. remains absolutely unshaken. *We* have to see that there *is* 'scandal' & no 'Hushing-up'. Lees-Smith is raising the matter in the House."

Lees-Smith received a somewhat dusty answer from the Under-Secretary of State for War, who announced that Sassoon had been guilty of a breach of military discipline but that the authorities instead of court-martialling him had discovered that he was suffering from shell-shock. "I do not think even my hon. Friends opposite", he added, "would go so far as to say that a medical board, knowing the man to be guilty of a breach of discipline, in order not to assist the political attitude of my hon. Friend and his colleagues, would say that this man was suffering from shell-shock. I have a great respect for medical boards, but I do not believe for a single moment that they would solemnly send a man to an institution of this sort under those circumstances, and I hope my hon. Friends opposite will not press me to accept that view."

As far as Russell was concerned, the episode was brought to an abrupt end by a letter from Graves.

Dear Bertrand Russell, Sassoon has been forced to accept a medical board & is being sent to a place in the country as suffering from nerves: which is certainly the case as anyone can easily see. The evidence supplied by various friends for the medical board is most conclusive. His opinions are still unchanged but there is nothing further for you to do (with him for your cause). I blame you most strongly for your indiscretion in having allowed him to do what he has done, knowing in what state of health he was (after his damnable time at Arras). Now you can leave things alone until he's well enough again to think calmly about the War & how to end it.

Sassoon's statement, and its results, were indicative of the gulf which, as the war approached the end of its third year, widened between those who believed in a fight to a finish and those who saw Europe's best chance for the future in a negotiated peace. By 1917 the polite disagreements between the Union of Democratic Control and the rest had gone for good. On the one side the authorities had reached the dangerous stage where criticism was equated with treason and where any suggestion of leniency towards the critics was quickly dispelled by a look over the shoulder at what was happening in Russia; "Reds under the bed" first became commonplace in the summer of 1917. On the other side, too, tempers frayed, emotion kicked reason out of the window and the niceties of constitutional action went by the board. In the civilian world, "Revolt on the Clyde" became more than a headline, while in the Services there could be heard, by those willing to listen, the first faint cracks which were not the stirrings of disobedience but a falling away of faith, so beautifully analysed in C. E. Montague's *Disenchantment*. The British army escaped the mutinies which riddled the French after the Nivelle offensive, and even in 1919 the post-war revolts on demobilization presented no serious problem. Even so, victory came only just in time.

Russell experienced the new ferocity soon after the close of the Sassoon incident. On 28 July, he attended a meeting held in the Brotherhood Church, Southgate, North London, to welcome the Russian Revolution. "I got shaken out of the mood of doubt and depression I was in by the events at our meeting this afternoon which was broken up," he began in an account to Ottoline.

> A vast crowd of roughs & criminals (paid) led, or rather guided from behind, by a few merely foolish soldiers (Colonials) broke in – it was only due to great self-restraint on the part of the delegates that there was no bloodshed. It was really very horrible. There were two utterly bestial women with knotted clubs, who set to work to thwack all the women of our lot that they could get at – the roughs had horrible degraded faces. The crowd outside as we were leaving was very fierce – several women had almost all their clothes torn off their backs. But absolutely no one showed the faintest trace of fear. Most women would have been terrified, but ours were not even flustered.
>
> I realized vividly how ghastly the spirit of violence is, & how utterly I repudiate it, on whatever side it may be. The mob is a terrible thing when it wants blood.
>
> The young soldiers were pathetic, thinking we were their enemies. They all believed we were in the pay of the Kaiser.
>
> At one moment they all made a rush at me, & I was in considerable danger – but a woman (I don't know who) hurled herself between

me & them – they hesitated to attack her – & then the police appeared. She showed wonderful courage.

I found the whole thing bracing. I realized that there are things I believe in & that it is worth living for – love, gentleness, & understanding.

The mob got in by smashing the doors, before our proceedings had begun.

It is strange how the world loves its enemies rather than its friends.

Russell in fact needed the battery and barricade of the Southgate meet ing. He had been going through a bad phase, alternately seeing the mil lennium as just round the corner and then convinced that things wer going from bad to worse. At times the thought of peace and of a lif devoted to philosophy made things bearable – "when the war is over shall vanish from the world & devote my time to solitary contemplation" he told Lucy Donnelly. "There are still mathematics, & the stars, & th wind at night." Then the drudgery of work at the N.-C.F., and the visio of an England intent on fighting to extinction, once again submerged hi hopes. The need for action, the threat of physical attack, worked wonders So did the thought of a long-awaited holiday with Colette, which wa to start the day after the Southgate affair, for he needed to be pulled ou of the trough emotionally, as well as politically.

After the warning to Colette six months earlier that he would be unabl to see her for some considerable time, Russell had withdrawn into himsel almost completely. It was not only the prospect of Katherine Mansfiel that had diverted him. He had become acting chairman of the N.-C.F. he was determined to maintain his coaching; there was Ottoline, and th temptation of Garsington, an ever-handy refuge. There was also Mr Eliot, not so easily shuffled off as was Helen Dudley. Even Russell ha his hands full.

By the spring, however, he was imploring her to give up acting for politics, a switch which would mean an end to her periodic departure for the provinces. She refused. Nevertheless, they continued as before meeting as and when they could, promising themselves an escape as soon as opportunity offered. When it eventually came, Russell still had tw worries on his mind.

For one thing his *affaires* with Ottoline and Colette were becoming th subject of rumours and tittle-tattle picked up by the family. From Aun Agatha there came a note marked "Private – Burn":

For a long time, I have been burdened with the pain of hearing of your misconduct with women – and married women. At first I refused to believe and longed for denial – but so hate the subject, or asking you, that I refrained. Names mentioned were Lady Ottoline

> Morel [sic] & Lady Constance – ? for the moment I forget – You will I know tell me the truth – for this has been spoken of as positive fact – *if I can truthfully deny* will thankfully do so, for your sake. If not, will of course leave it all in silence – & hope & pray that the future will be nobler and higher. You have I know always inferred that I have only narrow views as to marriage. Promiscuous connections I hate. On the deeper question of marriage I cannot write, but reserve all interchange of thought till we meet.

There is no evidence of any interchange. But Russell did not "burn".

More important than the question of how much or how little to tell Aunt Agatha was the question of how much to tell Ottoline. Here Russell had teetered perilously along the borders of deception. The previous autumn he had thrown off the news that "In a gay boyish mood I got intimate with Constance Malleson, but she doesn't suit serious moods". A few months later he had warned Ottoline against believing that he saw Colette often – "only now and then, when I happen to have nothing to do".

By the early summer of 1917, however, this sleight of statement was becoming less credible. Russell was again at Garsington, and one afternoon he and Ottoline took a walk to their favourite wood. "I asked him about Lady Constance Malleson," she remembered years later, "and he told me that she had been for some long time his mistress. It was a shock to find that it had been going on for nearly a year and that he had not mentioned it to me. It only showed how far apart we had drifted, and how little of our old intimacy remained." But she was charitable. "I always laugh at Bertie's parting thrust," she added; "as we were climbing the stile on the way home, he said, 'What a pity your hair is going grey.' "

The admission having been forced out of him, Russell tried to explain. "I wanted to tell you more about Constance Malleson," he wrote in an undated letter across which Ottoline has written "June 1917".

> – I began to know her well in the autumn, & meant to tell you, but your attack both made me afraid of you & set me to thinking I wanted to break with her. I set to work to withdraw, & almost completed the process. It was at that time that I hated everybody – I found it set me against you too. At last I came to the conclusion that I really didn't want to withdraw – it was practically the first time I had deliberately disagreed with your judgment of anyone – I did have a rather superstitious respect of your judgment of people. When I gave up withdrawing, I no longer hated every one & no longer felt an instinctive grudge against you. I think there *may* be more seriousness in it than I implied when we talked.
>
> It could never make a *shadow* of a difference to what I feel for you.

Nearly a year & a half ago now I realized once for all that I *must* detach my *instinct* from you, because otherwise life was too painful to be borne. That left me with a feeling of grudge, unless I could let my instinct go to some one else. Now, I do not feel on my side anything to interfere with what is possible. I give you always a *deep* love, & a profound sense of spiritual comradeship. And that is quite indestructible. Goodbye my Darling.

Yours B.

Shortly afterwards he spelt out the position more clearly. "You speak of being shut out from so much of my life," he wrote. "It is *only* C.M. I don't want to discuss with you. If you remember how in old days you hated discussing your relations with P. with me, & how the subject practically had to be avoided between us, it will help you to understand."

There were many similar despondent letters. His belief in philosophy had been undermined by Wittgenstein and by the war. His plans for social reconstruction were useless in the face of human nature, about which he had been much too optimistic. His love for her had turned to despair and he longed for death as much as he longed for the end of the war. There was much more in the same vein. Across one of them Ottoline later wrote in her long sloping hand, that Russell was living with Constance Malleson at the time and she thought he was very happy. And across another, even more pessimistic, she wrote the same conclusion once more. In fact, it is doubtful if Russell was very happy for any long period during the war; quite apart from emotional chaos, his intense feeling about the slaughter made happiness impossible except for the rare intervals when thoughts of the real world could be pushed to the back of his mind.

It was just such a break that he and Colette had been promising themselves. "You'll read to me out in the woods, and we'll have the peace and joy of being together day after day and night after night," she had written. "We'll walk and talk and be happy and free and feel like gods."

Now the time had come. With the sound of the mob only a few hours away, they left Paddington for the remoteness of Knighton in Radnorshire. There they stayed at the Norton Arms for one night, moving on the following day to the Feathers in Ludlow. Accounts of the Southgate meeting had already spread, and Russell probably feared being recognized. Their stay in Ludlow was almost as brief. Two days later they moved on to a lonely farmhouse near Ashford Carbonell, south of the Clee Hills, and here they lived idyllically for a fortnight.

Colette remembered years afterwards,

We walked enormously, read Voltaire, bathed in the Teme, and shamelessly enjoyed the good farmhouse cooking. When we lay reading in blazing sunshine out in the orchard, Russell's heathery hair

> seemed almost to give off sparks like a heath fire. He wore it extremely short. Gun-metal dark above the ears, it was jet black where it ended in a widow's peak at the nape of the neck. And when he threw back his head and roared with laughter, the roar of his laughter echoed almost to the distant Clee Hills.

They walked in good weather and in bad, talking most of the time, Russell on one occasion reeling off the whole of Shelley's *Ode to the West Wind*; expanding on the delights of philosophy; and becoming so immersed one day in "egocentric particulars" that he added eight miles to the journey home.

For him it was one of the best fortnights of his life. But belief that he could really isolate himself in the Welsh Border country, or opt out of the battle for even a fortnight, was pure illusion. He had to remain in touch with Ottoline, and dropped her a brief note after they had left Ludlow, assuring her that while there were times when he was completely in tune with her, these "would not be quite genuine unless they were interspersed with moods of a different kind". After this recipe for having one's cake and eating it, he continued, "I have left 'The Feathers' and moved into a farm about 3 miles from Ludlow – it is delicious country. I have been sleeping 10 hours every night, and have grown full of vigour. I am coming home Friday, and next week I hope I shall be able to come to Garsington if you can have me." And he ended with the first hint of a major change in his feelings and commitments: "I wish I could get out of the N.-C.F. but I don't see how I can."

13

From War to Peace

Back in London, Russell found his enthusiasm for the No-Conscription Fellowship ebbing fast. When he had been made acting chairman following Clifford Allen's second imprisonment, he had written to Ottoline complaining that the appointment was a nuisance. "I did not want to do that sort of work any more," he said, "– but I owe an obligation to the N.-C.F. because of having already worked with them so much, so I must stick here & go down to their office every day." Now, months later, the obligations were becoming increasingly difficult to fulfil.

One reason was an undercurrent of dissatisfaction he had sensed as early as the summer of 1915. "This morning I read a paper to a Pacifist Conference," he had then written to Ottoline. "They were an awful crew. Pacifists are really no good. What is wrong with mere opposition to war is that it is negative. One must find other outlets for people's wildness, and not try to produce people who have no wildness."

Closer acquaintance had brought disgruntlement of a different sort when he came under the thumb of Miss Marshall, that born sergeant-major, "very difficult – bullying everyone, dilatory, untruthful, hating to part with power" as he described her. His dislike was not diminished by Miss Marshall's brisk ability to put him in his place, as when he had sent her a long letter voicing his dissatisfaction with the human race.

> The thing to remember in reading history is that the mad extravagant things people did are exactly what people do now. The book about Napoleon in this list tells you how Ll.G. became P.M., the book about Russia will enable you to understand the position of Rasputin. Contemporaries know nothing. Nero was thought a saint: caricaturists alluded to his time as "a sweeter simpler reign" ... I do not think Ll.G. worse than the rest of mankind ... on the contrary I think he belongs to the best 10 per cent – it is the human race that is vile. It is a disgrace to belong to it. Being busy is like taking opium, it enables one to live in a land of golden dreams. I must get busy again. The truth is not the sort of thing one can live with.

Miss Marshall made short work of this. "For goodness sake," she replied, "get busy again quickly, & get rid of the distorted visions of Truth to which idleness – or plum pudding? – seems to have given rise. Remember *you* are a 'Contemporary' of the European war and Ll.G. and this generation of the human race, & are therefore wrong in your views about them!"

At times their exchanges grew fiercer as when she accused him of wriggling out of Fellowship duties. "I am sorry that I have to write you such a wholly nasty letter," she added. "I wish I could think of just one nice thing to say, but there is not one I have in my mind at present, and I have no time to hunt." He in turn warned her against writing such letters and added, "If I did not realise that you are so tired as to be hardly responsible, I should be seriously annoyed."

Friction apart, most N.-C.F. workers, not least Miss Marshall, realized Russell's value to the cause. As a propagandist he combined in a rare way the virtues of enthusiasm and professionalism. As a visitor in high places he could talk with Lloyd George or Asquith or Haldane on terms of equality that most of the others could only envy. And as a man who could speak his mind with terrifying honesty, he was one of the few who had a chance of bridging the gulf which at times divided policy down the middle. Significantly enough, it was Russell whom the Fellowship sent in May 1917 to visit the Home Office camp at Princetown on Dartmoor for men who had accepted non-combatant duties. Without much trouble he convinced them they were not being neglected by the Fellowship.

Soon he was also to be campaigning for the Absolutists, those men who refused service of any kind. In the early summer of 1917 Russell was approached by Margaret Hobhouse, the first wife of Henry Hobhouse, the politician and local-government reformer. Their eldest son was in prison as an Absolutist and Margaret Hobhouse, although supporting the war, co-opted Russell to help produce *I Appeal Unto Caesar*, a plea for the Absolutists which in four months went through four printings of 18,000 copies. Although Russell's connection with the book was kept strictly secret, it is now clear that he ghosted the major part of it. The propaganda was at least partly successful: Absolutists dangerously ill in prison, including Clifford Allen, were released before the end of the year.

By this time, Russell had in fact diverted his activities from the No-Conscription Fellowship. Early in 1917 his disgruntlement had been accentuated by a belief that replacements for N.-C.F. officials imprisoned by the authorities were not of sufficiently high calibre. "Full of petty quarrels & sordidness" was the opinion of a man never to feel happy in a second eleven.

As early as May 1917, he had rationalized his feelings and set them down in a Private and Confidential letter to the members of the National Committee. He felt uncomfortable as acting chairman, he said, and for more reasons than one. First, he was a poor administrator – a failing that in practice was more than counter-balanced by his energy and ingenuity. Secondly, the work which the N.-C.F. could now do effectively was not as important as other things to which he could devote himself. Then came two linked and more substantial points. "It seems to me clear that so long as the war lasts, any work that hastens the coming of peace is more important than anything else, particularly if peace comes in the spirit advocated by the Russian Revolutionaries," he went on. "The N.-C.F. is not a suitable body for action in general politics, because thousands desire an end to the present war for every one who accepts the extreme pacifist position. I think we ought as individuals to do what we can to help those who aim at ending the war, even if they do not accept the view that war is always wrong."

His attitude to the unadulterated pacifist creed was what really mattered, and the time had now come for an unequivocal statement. In "The Ethics of War" he had bluntly written, "I cannot believe that war is under all circumstances a crime." This was unpalatable to many N.-C.F. members, but Russell was too useful an asset to be questioned on theological points. Most members, reasonably enough, were content to use his opposition to this particular war. The Tottenham branch had, it is true, withdrawn his nomination as vice-chairman in view of "the divergence of view as expressed in your lectures, regarding the necessity of armed force, and the basic principles of the N.-C.F." There was also the occasion on which, as he wrote to Miss Marshall, he had had a "fearful rumpus" at one particular meeting about the use of force. But these were isolated instances – and remained so if only because the issue had been largely academic.

But the situation had been transformed, in Russell's eyes, by the Russian Revolution. "I am a conscientious objector to the present war," he wrote,

> and to almost any imaginable war between civilised states. But I have always held, and publicly stated, that the use of force in revolutions is not necessarily condemned. Until lately, this was mere academic reservation, without relevance to the actual situation. Now, however, it has become a pressing practical consideration. A certain amount of bloodshed occurred during the Russian Revolution, probably unnecessarily. If it was unnecessary, I can of course condemn it; but if the revolution could not be accomplished without it I cannot condemn it. And I should hold the same opinion as regards this country, if the circumstances were similar. If the "sacredness of human life" means that force must *never* be used to upset bad systems of government, to put an end to wars and despotisms, and to bring liberty to the oppressed, then I cannot honestly subscribe to it.

He stuck to his beliefs. Months later he was writing to Clifford Allen, "The world grows more full of hope every day. The Bolsheviks delight me; I easily pardon their sacking the Constituent Assembly, if it at all resembled our House of Commons."

Nevertheless, he may still have had qualifications. It is not certain that the letter, intended for the National Committee, was ever posted. Certainly the Committee took no immediate action. For six months Russell struggled with the problem of his beliefs. On one side there was the need to support the morale of such a man as Allen – "it was very largely for his sake that I kept on with [the N.-C.F. work] so long", he wrote to Ottoline. On the other hand there was the uncomfortable feeling of sailing under false colours and a growing disillusion with the practical business of keeping the movement afloat, an operation almost indistinguishable to Russell from the wheeler-dealing of politics which he detested.

On 3 September, 1917, his sister-in-law Elizabeth, now returned, recorded in her diary, "He is getting tired of the lot he has been associating with and says by Christmas he hopes to have withdrawn. He thirsts after philosophy once more." He confirmed her judgment two days later when he wrote to Philip Jourdain,

> My interest in philosophy is reviving, and I expect before long I shall come back to it altogether. I want to write (1) an Introduction to modern logic, (2) a new edition of "The Principles of Mathematics", and I want to do a lot of work, applying mathematical logic to the principles of physics along the lines of my book on the "External World". If I had done all this, I could die happy.

The decisive step was finally taken in the autumn when he resigned from the N.-C.F., handing over with relief to Dr Alfred Salter. "I long to be back at philosophy," he added to Ottoline. "My head is full of things to work at . . . I feel as if I should like never again to feel any strong emotion of any sort or kind. I want a quiet methodical existence, like the end of Candide – emotions are always dreadful in the end. But I don't suppose I shall be able to stick to such a humdrum programme."

He agreed to carry on writing for the *Tribunal* until the end of 1917, and most weeks subjected the government to an attack which mixed facts, logical argument and a gadfly presentation that repeatedly stung authority on its most sensitive parts. Nevertheless, he was effectively bowing out from pacifist involvement. And he wasted no time in getting to work on *Roads to Freedom: Socialism, Anarchism and Syndicalism*, undertaken for an American publisher "solely for the sake of filthy lucre".

Like most of Russell's rush-jobs, it was competent, a plea for Guild Socialism which revealed him, according to one reviewer, as an anarchist whose anarchism was "of a kind with which, as regards one of its tenets, a good many people who are not anarchists will sympathise".

When he had finished *Roads to Freedom*, he told Ottoline, he wanted to write a bigger book on the lines of *Principles of Social Reconstruction*. "Pacifist work, except by those who were *not* pacifists from the start, seems to me now quite useless, & the sense of futility drives me mad," he went on. "But since I decided to give it up, I have grown sane again, but rather sober & drab".

There remained the War Office order banning him from large chunks of Britain. Here Frank Russell offered to intercede. On 14 December, 1917, he visited General Cockerill of M.I.5, who was courteous but cautious, and stressed that both the Home Office and the Foreign Office would have to be consulted. There was, in any case, one minor problem. Russell was prepared to state that he was giving up pacifist work; but he was unwilling to guarantee that he might not return to it at some future date. To a man of his precise turn of mind this was no more than common sense; to a man of General Cockerill's professional suspicion it looked like hedging. Nevertheless, polite interchanges continued between the 2nd Earl and the War Office. It looked as though Russell, tacking back into philosophy again, might be heading for calmer waters.

The same was true of his private life. During the months following his return to London from the Clee Hills he had weathered a succession of storms with Colette which would have left most ardent lovers unfit for further battle. Russell, even more emotionally battered than during his bouts with Ottoline, managed to survive, but before the end of September he had decided to finish the *affaire*. However, this was not easy. Colette's tour was ending, and within forty-eight hours she was back in London where there took place first a reconciliation, then another break. This time it was enough to spur him into writing a 600-word analysis of her character charging her with lack of religion, lack of self-control, lack of public spirit, love of cheap success and notoriety, acquisitiveness, envy, commercialism, competitiveness, crudeness, hypocrisy, sexual vanity, shoddy work, selfishness and shirking.

Colette survived it, ignoring the charges and keeping her head until Russell about-turned, took it all back and sought forgiveness. Repentance lasted only a few days. Then he wrote a curt letter of about a dozen lines breaking with her for ever, and delivered it by hand. But later that evening he visited her as usual. As he was to remark later, philosophers and mathematicians in love "are exactly like everybody else, except, perhaps, that the holiday from reason makes them passionate to excess".

By November they were back to normal. So much so that Russell, his Bury Street flat still being let to Helen Dudley, sought about for an alternative to his rooms with Frank. "Tomorrow morning at eleven sharp", wrote Colette on 7 November, "I'll be waiting on the doorstep for you, and we'll walk out together to find a home." They found it in a studio on the ground floor of a rather dilapidated house in Fitzroy Street.

There they settled, Russell's more contented mood being reflected in a letter to Ottoline describing his writing of *Roads to Freedom*. "I enjoy immensely doing work that doesn't seem wholly futile," he said. "I shall be happier still to get back to philosophy in the spring. Today I went to the Westminster Cathedral & sat there some time – I always think it very beautiful – & listening to the chanting one's mind gets gradually to permanent things, away from exasperation and despair. Mankind are terribly tragic, but there is a splendour through all their blindness."

He spent Christmas Day with Colette, her husband and her mother Lady Annesley, then travelled on to Garsington for the rest of the holiday. And here, taking time off from the jollifications, he put the finishing touches to a series of lectures which were to reveal his philosophical progress of the previous two decades.

Russell often stressed the value of the subconscious in solving technical or literary problems. He would, he said, push them to the back of his mind and work at something else; then they would present themselves fully solved. While he drummed up support for the No-Conscription Fellowship, castigated Lloyd George and raised blood pressures with his articles in the *Tribunal*, the thoughts of the last twenty years had kept bubbling away in his subconscious like a soup-stock on the simmer. There was his jettisoning of Idealism, and the road to the logicizing of mathematics that this made possible; there was his Theory of Descriptions, his Theory of Types and his urge to apply to the broader questions of philosophy the logical methods so successful in revealing the foundations of mathematics; and there was the growing influence of the new physics which had begun to cast fresh, if disturbing, light on the relationship between mind and matter. No less compelling, there was the dynamite of Wittgenstein which had forced him to reconsider his beliefs as surely as Thomson and Rutherford had forced physicists to reconsider the idea of the billiard-ball atom.

Now, as he abandoned hope of giving further help to the pacifists, the implications of the past presented themselves in good order, a coherent company of ideas lined up as the philosophy of logical atomism. Russell outlined this in eight London lectures early in 1918, and when they were printed shortly afterwards he added in a characteristic prefatory note that they were

> very largely concerned with explaining certain ideas which I learnt from my friend and former pupil Ludwig Wittgenstein. I have had no opportunity of knowing his views since August 1914, and I do not even know whether he is alive or dead. He has therefore no

> responsibility for what is said in these lectures beyond that of having originally supplied many of the ideas contained in them.

He later stated that he had "adopted the philosophy of logical atomism" in 1899–1900. In 1905 he had written to a friend that he believed "all things are discrete and atomic. But that is a large question ... " In 1914 he used the phrase logical atomism in his Harvard Lectures, while *Our Knowledge of the External World* contained a chapter on "Logic as the Essence of Philosophy" which stressed the value of logical analysis if philosophy was to progress.

Now he showed how this policy could be followed. Logical atomism had, he said, been forced upon him "in the course of thinking about the philosophy of mathematics", and what he now proposed was that the practice successfully used there should be applied to the basic problems of non-specialist philosophy. The structure of mathematics had been broken down into individual bricks, each of which could be inspected separately. This process, which had been carried out with symbols, must now be carried out with words, a process only possible, of course, for those who did not see the world as a quivering jelly, each part affected by each other part. Here, however, Russell had no difficulty. "When I say that my logic is atomistic," he said at the start of his first lecture, "I mean that I share the common-sense belief that there are many separate things; I do not regard the apparent multiplicity of the world as consisting merely in phases and unreal divisions of a single indivisible Reality." The emphasis on "logical" was just as simply explained.

> The reason I call my doctrine *logical* atomism is because the atoms that I wish to arrive at as the sort of last residue in analysis are logical atoms and not physical atoms. Some of them will be what I call "particulars"–such things as little patches of colour or sounds, momentary things– and some of them will be predicates or relations and so on. The point is that the atom I wish to arrive at is the atom of logical analysis, not the atom of physical analysis.

The working tool for this particular job was not the austere symbolic language of *Principia Mathematica*, which had syntax but no vocabulary, but everyday language. It was an imperfect tool, but by analysing into constituent parts the statements which could be made in it, Russell found it possible to approach the belief that all philosophical perplexities were the outcome of slovenly use of language, a belief later held more firmly by the logical positivists and the exponents of linguistic analysis, both of whom made use of the ideas he now put forward. The results of such critical analysis were the data of personally experienced colours, shapes and smells which mirrored common-sense propositions about everyday objects like chairs and tables. On the truth or falsehood of these simple propositions rested the truth or falsehood of all the more complex propositions, embracing even the sophisticated statements about the new physics, since they could be induced from the most simple propositions. Logical atomism thus combined the picture theory of language with the verification theory of meaning, and as a result was able to describe the universe without the aid of metaphysics.

The lectures were published in the *Monist*, and finally brought to an end the friendship between Russell and Philip Jourdain. In spite of the similarity of their views about the war, their relations had been deteriorating gradually, the main reason being Jourdain's obsessional belief that the "axiom of choice", introduced as a newcomer to the foundations of mathematics in 1904, was provable from traditional principles. Russell, together with most other mathematicians and logicians, reluctantly accepted that the axiom must be accepted *as* an axiom. Disagreement, which loomed larger in Jourdain's mind as disease – Friedrich's ataxia, a palsy which made writing difficult – took firmer hold, was further aggravated by the fact that Jourdain had paid out of his own pocket the £100 which Russell had received for publication in the United States of *Our Knowledge of the External World*, and had apparently never recovered the money from the American publishers.

It was against this background that, midway through publication of the lectures, the chief editor of the *Monist* died. He was succeeded by Jourdain. One of the new editor's first acts was to write to Stanley Unwin asking whether there was any likelihood of his firm starting proceedings against the *Monist* for copyright because some parts of the articles were very like passages in Russell's latest book. Russell pointed out that the lectures were given from notes, but that the book was written quite separately. This did not rule out the possibility that he had committed the author's crime of self-plagiarization, and he generously offered to stop publication of further articles in the *Monist* if Unwin wished. Unwin did not wish and the storm in the teacup subsided. However, the new situation between Russell and Jourdain can be judged by two letters which show how each was determinedly thinking the worst of the other. Russell, writing to Unwin before he knew who had complained, said, "I hope it was not Jourdain, who was annoyed with me, along with all other competent people, for not admitting the validity of a mathematical discovery which he believes himself to have made." And Jourdain, believing that Russell's demand for payments for the logical atomism articles was linked with possible support for this discovery, wrote, "It is practically asking me to bother [the former editor's widow] especially for you in order that I may get some approval from you of what I have written."

Long before this breach, in fact while Russell was still giving the lectures at the start of 1918, he had again run foul of the authorities. Christmasing at Garsington in 1917 and discussing with Ottoline's sophisticated company the American entry into the war and the build-up of American troops in Europe, he threw out one of his typically mischievous exaggerations. Even if the Americans were not efficient against the Germans, surely they might be used to intimidate strikers in Britain? No one appears to have taken the idea seriously, and it is doubtful if Russell intended them to.

However, Christmas was barely over when the editor of the *Tribunal* invoked his aid. Russell was giving up his regular weekly article. But there was now an unexpected gap for the first issue of 1918, and would he please fill it? He responded immediately, producing in a rush a column and a half on "The German Peace Offer" in which he pleaded for early negotiations, and painted a grim picture of the situation in the coming year if they were not successfully concluded. The argument was plausible. But Russell was unable to let well alone. The Garsington conversation returned to his mind and entranced him with its opportunity for tweaking authority's tail: "The American garrison which will by that time be occupying England and France," he wrote, "whether or not they will prove efficient against the Germans, will no doubt be capable of intimidating strikers, an occupation to which the American Army is accustomed at home." He had done his homework thoroughly and was later able to quote a U.S. Senate Report which dealt with the use for strike-breaking purposes of American troops in America.

That single sentence in the *Tribunal* was a godsend to the authorities. It was, as pointed out by G. H. Hardy, one of Russell's stoutest defenders, "a foolish and reckless sentence, the kind of sentence which an able man could write only after a long course of exasperation". Russell himself later admitted as much, telling Gilbert Murray " . . . Of course if I had known the blaze of publicity that was going to be directed upon that one sentence of the 'Tribunal', I should have phrased it very much more carefully, in such a way as to prevent misunderstanding by a public not used to the tone of exasperated and pugnacious pacifists." Its wording was, in fact, less rather than more provocative than one he had written a few months earlier, commenting that "we may hope to have an American garrison in the country, ready to shoot down strikers".

However, the timing of the later article was unfortunate. Frank Russell's pleading for his brother had at last won over the authorities and on the day that the *Tribunal* article appeared a War Office memo was prepared lifting the ban on Russell visiting the restricted areas. The *Tribunal* article changed all that, and the following day General Cockerill wrote to Frank Russell pointing out that, while he had been doing his best, there was now this latest article to consider.

Nothing happened for a fortnight. Then action was taken. "Two detectives visited me yesterday morning when I was in my bath, & asked me if I had written an article (about a month ago) called 'The German Peace

Offer' & in particular a certain sentence about the American garrison being useful for intimidating strikers," Russell wrote to Clifford Allen on 2 February. "So I said I had. They then asked me if I edited the Tribunal; so I said I didn't. I thought they would ask who did, but they didn't; they went away, after saying it was about the Tribunal they were inquiring."

Three days later a summons arrived. "It is very annoying," he wrote to Ottoline, "particularly as the remarks were rather foolish & not good for propaganda. I won't pay the fine, & I don't want friends to pay it for me. I am so little good for work just now that I would just as soon be in prison; it is the only way to be useful when one is so slack. And a time of *recueillement* might be good for me."

The case was heard five days later at Bow Street. Shortly before, a review in *The Times Literary Supplement* of *Mysticism and Logic*, a new edition of Russell's *Philosophical Essays*, had reflected the puzzlement of many academics. What was Russell really up to? Publication, the reviewer said, would help to prevent the spread of a false idea about Russell. "It would be a pitiable thing if this philosopher and mathematician of European fame were to be thought of only, or even principally, as a politician whose ideas have offended the mass of his countrymen," he went on. "Those who know Mr. Russell, whether as his pupils at Cambridge or in unofficial intercourse at Oxford, have always shrunk from the very idea of his being associated with raids, police courts, and snapshots in the daily papers; it seemed the desecration of a classical temple."

At Bow Street the temple was charged with "having in a printed publication made certain statements likely to prejudice His Majesty's relations with the United States of America". There is no doubt that he was technically guilty; nevertheless, according to Gilbert Murray, the American military attaché in London, having been asked by the British government to give evidence on their behalf, had not only refused but had been supported in his refusal by the Ambassador, Walter Page.

Although there was no evidence that Russell had, in fact, prejudiced His Majesty's relations with America, it was arguable that his statement was "likely to", and he was summarily found guilty and sentenced to six months' imprisonment in the Second Division. That the sentence aroused regret even in the mind of Sir John Dickinson, the magistrate who handed it down, is shown by his letter to T. J. Cobden-Sanderson, Russell's godfather, two days later, in which he stated that he had done what he believed, and still believed, to have been his duty. However, it is obvious from the tone of his letter that it was only with sincere regret that he had punished a man who had such a high place in science, but the higher the position the graver the responsibility. "I can only hope that the admonition will be understood by all."

Russell was convinced that the authorities had seized on the article as their last chance of prosecuting him. "I had completely withdrawn from pacifist agitation, & the authorities knew it," he wrote to E. S. P. Haynes. "That, I imagine, is why they have prosecuted me now, because they knew I should commit no more crimes, & therefore if they did not act at once I should escape them." His attitude gives too much weight to the conspiracy view of history, and completely ignores the chronology of events: Frank's plea that his brother was giving up pacifist work to return to philosophy, the War Office decision to raise the ban, and the appearance of the *Tribunal* article. Even the most liberal-minded bureaucrat might be pardoned for seeing a breach of good faith that warranted a lesson.

At first, Russell was not much perturbed by the sentence. "It is the fortune of war, & one mustn't take it too seriously," he told Ottoline. "I never felt anything equal to the concentrated venom of the magistrate in sentencing me: it was a blast of hatred, quite astonishing. The appeal comes on April 12. There is very little chance of any change in the sentence, but at any rate it gives one time, & means that I shan't be in while it is cold, which is a mercy."

Another consolation was the sympathy shown by friends, even those who strongly disagreed with him. Thus Whitehead's elder son North sent from his Army posting an extremely affectionate letter, reminding Russell of the holidays he had spent with North and his brother Eric, and hoping that they would all meet when the nightmare of the war was over. "I am writing to tell you how sorry I am that you are in trouble," he wrote, "and to tell you what a warm feeling of friendship I feel for you."

Another letter was from Cobden-Sanderson, now nearing eighty, enclosing a letter written to Kate Amberley on Russell's birth in which he had forecast "a life fitted to the wonderful scene about you". "Ah, that your mother, 'm'amie', had lived to know you now!" Cobden-Sanderson went on.

> How you would have loved one another! When it was proper to do so, indeed a little earlier! I hurried down to Ravenscroft to see her, and you, my godchild, for it had been long arranged that, boy or girl, I was to be godfather. And now with old and constant affection I send you my love on the eve of your own [appeal] and pray that whatever outward destiny may decree for you, you will, within yourself, as heretofore and always, "plant yourself firm in Nature's midst, conscious of all its untold mysteries, erect, listening, prayerful"!

The Establishment viewed the crime as enormous, although there was a touch of the ludicrous in sentencing Russell for a few unwary phrases after he had stumped the country with impunity while preaching the pacifist cause.

Russell himself was chiefly concerned with the jobs to be finished before he began his sentence, notably *Roads to Freedom – Proposed Roads to Freedom*, as it was called in the United States. This, with its subtitle of *Socialism, Anarchism and Syndicalism*, was to be the only one of his books in which he seriously considered anarchism as a social and political philosophy. He was against it; but he was against it with certain qualifications, and even the anarchists themselves agreed that he understood the principles he criticized. His answer was Guild Socialism, "which concedes what is valid, both in the claims of the State Socialists and in the syndicalist fear of the State". When the book was re-published thirty years later he saw no reason to change his views, although he was, he said, much less sympathetic to anarchism. *Roads to Freedom* went through three editions in fourteen months, being published in the highly relevant period immediately following the 1918 Armistice. It was lucky that Russell completed the manuscript before his sentence began, thus leaving his time in prison free for philosophic work.

Writing would be impossible in the Second Division, and before the end of February he was discussing with his friends ways in which it might be possible to have the sentence altered. "I think there is practically no chance of getting the sentence changed into a fine, or even reduced in length," he wrote to Gilbert Murray. "But I do think that, after the Appeal, it will be possible to bring pressure to bear on the Home Secretary in effective ways."

At first, he planned to plead his own cause on appeal. "I would certainly employ counsel if there was any chance of getting off," he told E. S. P. Haynes, "but if you had followed prosecutions under DORA [Defence of the Realm Act] as closely as I have had to do, you would know that the greatest advocate that ever lived could not obtain any mitigation of the sentence. That being so, the only thing remaining is to make as good an impression as may be upon the general public; & for that purpose I am sure it is best to appear in my own defence."

The longer he thought about it, the less worried he became. "I have become gradually more satisfied with my case," he told Ottoline; "– it no longer seems to me a bad one for propaganda ... I gather that in 2nd Division one has a certain number of books, but not writing materials. And I don't have hard labour, which is a relief. I don't really much mind the prospect – absence of responsibility will be so delicious."

At this point, with Russell half-reconciled to six months in prison, another threat arose. He wrote to Murray,

> It seems decided that the military age is to be raised, and that being so, I feel it is necessary for me to be prepared before I go to prison. As you know, I have been a supporter of the Absolutists, and I could not conscientiously accept alternative service. But if the Tribunal chose to recognise my work in philosophy as of national

importance (!) I could simply go on doing it, and avoid prison without compromise. I don't the least mind a definite 6 months' sentence, but I do mind being in indefinitely for perhaps a number of years, as I believe I should be no good for work after that. And there is a lot I want to do still, in directions to which the Government would have no objection ... There will be need of a good deal of preparation for presenting my case to the Tribunal. I propose to enter into a contract to do a book on modern logic, so as to show that my intentions are definite. I think testimonials from eminent men, *philosophers and others*, to the effect that I ought to be allowed to do philosophy, would be necessary. I think some also should be got from America; e.g. from Professor Dewey of Columbia, and Professor R. B. Perry of Harvard. Probably Carr might be willing to do this. Any person in this country whose name would be known to the Tribunal would be useful. If any such person would come and give evidence, it would be a very great help.

The easiest way from the point of view of the Government might be if the National Service Representative were instructed not to object to exemption in my case. Then there would be no need of a fuss. And the Government would be perfectly free to withdraw my exemption at any moment if they found me again obnoxious. This is a question of pulling strings. I don't know whether you would see any way of doing it. I am sorry to bother you with all this, but when I am once in prison I shall have no means of attending to the matter, and it is really important for my whole future.

However, Russell was not forced into the corkscrew position of standing firm with the Absolutists who refused all work of national importance, while at the same time claiming exemption himself on the grounds of his nationally important philosophy.

Even so, as the date of appeal approached, the prospect of the Second Division looked increasingly disagreeable. "It seems to me very improbable that my sentence will be reduced on appeal," he wrote to Carr,

but it is possible that the Home Secretary might grant First-Division treatment if strongly urged by persons of influence. I am venturing to ask whether, if the sentence is confirmed, you would see your way to approaching eminent philosophers for this purpose. I believe Gilbert Murray is willing to do something of the kind, so you would have to avoid overlapping, but there are many whom you know and he doesn't. I should not make such a request, but for the fact that I find six months in the Second division is a more serious matter than one naturally supposed. The food allowance has been reduced lately below the point consistent with health, so that released prisoners are practically always ill for a considerable time after their liberation.

> While in prison, one only has three-quarters of an hour a day for reading: the rest of the time is occupied with work and prison tasks. There is much work in philosophy that I had intended to do; but I doubt whether my brain will be good enough for it after such a sentence, and as I am no longer young I feel time presses.

Murray and Carr rallied round and organized a joint petition pleading for his sentence to be served in the First rather than the Second Division. The aid of Lord Haldane, out of office but still influential, was invoked by Alys, who wrote of her husband, "I do not share his present views, but I know that he is haunted by the fear of his father's malady & I very much fear that what is to anyone a very severe punishment might be fatal to his intellect." When the appeal was heard on 2 May by Mr Lawrie, Deputy Chairman of the County of London Session, the sentence was amended to imprisonment in the First Division. Russell was, according to the magistrate's summing-up, "a man of very great distinction, and it would be a very great loss to the country if he were confined in such a form that his great abilities would not have scope..." It seems possible that this happy outcome was at least partly due to careful lobbying. A note on the Home Office file dealing with the decision says that "the precedent is unfortunate", although it was thought that Mr Lawrie would "be more circumspect in future". Russell himself has stated that it was by the intervention of Arthur Balfour, then Foreign Secretary, that he was placed in the First Division; and that the credit was also shared with the Home Secretary, Herbert Samuel. "My brother knew everybody concerned," he has said, "and when the Home Secretary wasn't being very obliging, my brother went to see him: 'Oh, you know, he was my fag at Winchester. He'll do it.' He did." The story is less unlikely than it sounds. Frank Russell, Colette's "huge blustering pink-cheeked schoolboy inextricably entangled in motor cars and electrical gadgets", could turn on not only a bullying ferocity but also a devastating charm.

Whether or not the 2nd Earl had a hand in the affair, his brother was to serve his sentence as an aristocrat of the prison world. "The rules affecting them", it has been said of First Division offenders, "have a class flavour about them, and are evidently intended to apply to persons of some means who are in the habit of keeping servants." Thus Russell was not only allowed a special cell but, for 6*d.* a day, the services of another prisoner – who received a third of the pay – to relieve him "from the performance of unaccustomed tasks or offices". He was allowed his own food and any books or newspapers "not of an objectionable kind". And the fortnightly visits by three friends or relations and the one letter a fortnight could be augmented by the Visiting Committee "to such reasonable extent as they deem advisable". Doing time in the First Division was thus more like internment than imprisonment: the object of the exercise, in the words of the Labour Report of the Prison System Enquiry Committee, being "either to deter such offenders, and others also, from repetition of their offences, or else to isolate them temporarily from society, inasmuch as their liberty of action is regarded by the Government as being dangerous to itself and to the community". Russell was, in fact, to be basically a political prisoner. It allowed him to get on with his work, but it lacked the glamour of martyrdom.

Once a change of Division seemed likely, he began to plan for four hours of philosophical writing each day, four hours of philosophical reading and four hours of general reading. He was worried by the ban on smoking, but agreed to settle for chocolate as a compensation. "I am sure I shan't mind the time in prison. I am really glad to be going," he admitted to Ottoline. "But I don't feel as if it were in my power to do much for the country – I wish it were. But I am not near enough in outlook to the average man to be able to have much immediate influence. One has to aim at being, like Shelley, an influence upon the comparatively few in the rising generation, not a power in the present."

While Russell was struggling with the problem of arranging his prison life to suit his working plans, he heard that Whitehead's younger son Eric had been killed in the Royal Flying Corps. The news, ironically enough, came as he was appealing to the Whiteheads to visit him. His immediate letter to Evelyn no longer exists. Her reply is affectionate and understanding. "Don't think your reason going, dear," she wrote,

> you can keep your will and you must try your hardest – Hearts don't break so here we are; indeed, I will try to make life sweet still for North and Jessie, but I am not clever at facing it without my Eric ... I cannot tell you about Alfred, he looks much older. North has a return of shell-shock. J. is wonderful and I must not think of myself so much. Dear Bertie, which ever one of us you prefer to see will go; just choose the one who will best fit your mood – You will hold out – old friendships strain but do *not* break. Later on we will talk of all this time of divergence and of my beloved Eric – With dear love from us all, Yours affectionately ...

Early in May he arrived at Brixton Prison in a taxi, regretting that the authorities had not arranged for a Black Maria. With a schedule of work carefully planned, the prospects of Prisoner No 2917 were somewhat less intimidating than they had looked at first. However, he was still a prisoner and he was to suffer from the dark psychological overtones of that state. He might write to his brother soon after passing through the prison gates, "All goes well with me – everybody treats me kindly, from the governor downwards." He might add a few days later that "Days here succeed each other monotonously but not very disagreeably. I believe I missed my vocation by not being a monk in a contemplative order." Nevertheless, the respite from responsibilities, the relief of no longer having to make up his own mind, were soon overwhelmed by the fact that "one lives here in constant irritation from lack of liberty ..."

Irritation was emphasized when he found that personal application to the Governor was necessary for leave to see his solicitors who wished to amend a book-contract; for permission to send the review of a philosophical book to the *Nation*, or philosophical manuscripts to Wildon Carr. Neither was this all. He was required to make special requests for his own clothes, for a private room, and for books, papers, and money for food – all allowed in the First Division. He would have been further irked had he known that while the Governor, Captain Haynes, was agreeable to all these ameliorations, the Chairman of the Prison Visiting Committee, Sir Vansittart Bowater, a former Lord Mayor of London whose reactions conjure up a rather Neanderthal image, took a very different view. "Personally I think this prisoner should have little or no consideration," he pronounced on hearing of the requests. "This prisoner", he added a few days later, "appears to think that he can live in the same comfort and with the same facilities as he would if he were in his own house, with the exception of his being kept within four walls." However, Sir Vansittart was told that the law had to be followed. Russell got his books and his papers.

He was also allowed three visitors per week instead of per fortnight. They had to come together, and while preparing for Brixton he compiled lists of "compatibles". Thus Clifford Allen could arrive with Lady Russell, and a third congenial companion; and the philosophers would come together. More than compatibility was involved. Ottoline and Colette were not on the same week's visiting-list. There was some uncertainty about who should be available when, and a list of extra people for visits, in order of preference, was headed by Gilbert Murray followed by Charles Sanger, Littlewood the mathematician, Desmond MacCarthy, Margaret Davies, Neville the mathematician, Mrs Hamilton, T. S. Eliot, Miss Burdett, Francis Meynell and his old friend Arthur Dakyns.

To his brother Russell gave an early account of his reactions to Brixton. "The only real hardship of life here is not seeing one's friends," he wrote on 6 May.

> It was a great delight seeing you the other day. Next time you come, I hope you will bring two others ... I am anxious to see as much of my friends as possible. You seemed to think I should grow indifferent on that point but I am certain you were wrong. Seeing the people I am fond of is not a thing I should grow indifferent to, though thinking of them is a great satisfaction. I find it comforting to go over in my mind all sorts of occasions when things have been to my liking. Impatience and lack of tobacco do not as yet trouble me as

> much as I expected but no doubt they will later. The holiday from responsibility is really delightful, so delightful that it almost outweighs everything else. Here I have not a care in the world: the rest to nerves and will is heavenly. One is free from the torturing question: What more might I be doing? Is there any effective action that I haven't thought of? Have I a right to let the whole thing go and return to philosophy? Here, I have to let the whole thing go, which is far more restful than choosing to let it go and doubting if one's choice is justified. Prison has some of the advantages of the Catholic Church.

The ordering of visits was largely the work of Frank, who had two qualifications for the job. In the England of 1918, a title helped to oil the machinery even more than it does today; and he himself, having served his sentence for bigamy in Brixton, was on Christian-name terms with some of the warders.

The question of letters came next. It was not in Russell's nature to be content with the single weekly outward letter permitted by the regulations. His method of jumping this particular fence was simple. He was at work on research of a kind which meant little to the authorities; it was unlikely that writings in French would be closely scanned, or indeed scanned at all, by those supposed to censor them. Thus the ostensible letter from the French Girodin Buzot to Madame Roland was in fact a letter to Colette. "Boismaison", referred to in another letter as the "place where one at least of the agents in that drama derived much of the strength and vigour required", was the farm run by Mrs Woodhouse where Colette and Russell had stayed. And a regular stream of apparently historical information, presumably the result of his reading, was actually the gist of correspondence which Frank, or other recipients in the know, sent on to those concerned.

In addition there was a flow of intimate undated letters to Colette, written on rough, lined paper, often on both sides of a torn sheet. These were smuggled out as and when possible.

Her messages to him went via *The Times* which he read daily. The first was on 7 May when the Personal Column contained the entry, "G. J. Back from country. All, all love, Lonely but busy." It was followed at intervals of a few days, sometimes of a week, with other entries to "G.J." which reported "Happy beyond Words", "only living until Boismaison. Longing and longing for that", and "So lonely. You have all my love." In wartime this could not last, and an alert Scotland Yard, given at least the hint of a clue by a birthday message on 18 May, called on Colette in mid-July to question her. No offence had been committed; but the messages stopped.

With channels of personal communication properly organized, Russell began to make the best of Brixton. The speed with which he knuckled down to serious work is shown by the first item in a long-term programme which he outlined to Frank on 27 May. "I have nearly finished an 'Introduction to Mathematical Philosophy', 70,000 words," he began. When this was finished – a logical counter-part to other prison-literature such as Bunyan's *Pilgrim's Progress* and Cervantes' *Don Quixote* – he would start on *The Analysis of Mind* before going on with logic.

> (a) I want to tackle first the analysis of belief and shall be grateful if [Carr] will send me any book I ought to read bearing on this. For purposes of logic, I *must* know whether there are atomic facts containing no verbs, such as beliefs *appear* to be. (b) I want to be clear as to the relation of symbolism to psychology, and generally the status, in relation to the real world, of what logic calls the 'proposition'. (c) I want a precise theory of the nature of vagueness. These three problems I want to solve for the sake of *logic*: there are others which I wrote to Carr about before, which are rather *metaphysical*, i.e. concern the question "are there specifically mental entities?" I expect to take several years over this work, as there is a lot of reading to be done before I can begin writing. (NB I don't know *what* reading). Then I shall be free to turn to: III. Elements of Logic. This will set forth the logical basis of what I call "logical atomism" and place logic in relation to Psychology, Mathematics, etc. IV. Then I must do a metaphysic: as it were an *Encyklopädia* – summing up results, in criticism of Physics, Psychology, Mathematics, etc. V. When too old for serious work, I should like to write a book like Santayana's "Life of Reason", on how to behave reasonably in this preposterous world. I hope by then I shall know. As always hitherto, I shall occasionally abandon philosophy for a short spell of other work or mere holiday: I have found that in that way one's thoughts remain fresher. I become more and more fixed in the determination, which I came to last autumn, to do no more pacifist work. It seems to me that since Brest-Litovsk there has been nothing for pacifists to do: on the other hand my philosophical interests are very keen.

He kept them that way, judging by the occasional note that Frank passed on to his brother's philosopher-friends. "Lord Russell", said one of the notes, "is desired by Mr. Bertrand Russell to convey the following message to Mr. Broad: 'I have read him in this month's *Mind* with much pleasure and approval, but I don't altogether like shrieks upside-down. ["Shrieks": the notational device Whitehead and Russell adopted in *Principia* to symbolize such propositions as "The *x* satisfying '*x* wrote Waverley' exists."] Tell him he should get into communication with Whitehead as to notation."

He was soon at work on a 10,000-word appraisal of Dewey's *Experimental*

Logic for the *Journal of Philosophy*, and began to tackle for *Mind* a review of Husserl's *Logische Untersuchungen*, "very like trying to swallow a whale", as Colette described it. Unfortunately, it was never completed.

Although prison-life was bearable in the First Division the burdens, both psychological and practical, steadily became more trying. By the summer, Russell was beginning to realize that prison was not the place for serious work, and he was soon including in a letter to his brother a message to Ottoline:

> I have lived on charity since September 16 [1917], and although I am immensely grateful, I can't plan my whole future on that basis. It is very easy for me to earn money by writing on social questions, but impossible to earn by philosophy. When I come out from prison I must set to work to earn at least £200 a year somehow. I should not have worried over this, but for the fact that I should *like* to give myself to philosophy, whereas if I am earning I can only do philosophy in odd moments. Is there any possibility that those who wish me to do philosophy could establish a research fellowship for me? This would also have the advantage of being something definite to put before Geddes. If this is impossible, could you enquire as to ways of earning £200 a year which would leave some leisure for philosophy?

In August he was imploring his brother to pull all possible strings for his release.

> My principal reason is that I have ideas for what I believe to be a really important piece of philosophical research, with which I am exceedingly anxious to make progress, but in spite of my utmost efforts I find it very hard to accomplish much while I remain here. During my first two months of imprisonment I did a great deal of work, as appeared from the MSS I sent out. But at the end of that time I had a series of bad headaches, which obliged me to be careful; & ever since I have found that I cannot work much without a return of the headaches, & that the work I can do is not very fruitful. Philosophical research is not like the work of a clerk or a housemaid: diligence alone is not enough to ensure success in it. One needs also that condition of mind & body in which new ideas come; & for that, diligence, though necessary, is not sufficient.

Frank was unable to help on the question of release, but he induced the authorities to relent on a number of minor matters. Russell was allowed to keep his light on "after hours" and thus continue with his philosophical reading and writing as long as he wished. His friends were allowed to bring in flowers, and it is difficult not to believe that the ease with which letters were smuggled in and out owed something to Frank's persuasive hints that a Nelsonian blind eye should be used in certain directions.

Despite these minor ameliorations, Russell grew increasingly depressed. "My instinctive belief is that the war will go on until Germany is as utterly defeated as France was in 1814, and that that will take about another 10 years," he wrote to Miss Rinder of the N.-C.F. in June.

> I do not believe either that we or the Americans will stop sooner. Probably Russia will rise against Germany some six years hence, and that will correspond to 1812 – all pure guessing. I think of Godwin who roughly corresponded in that war to me in this. In his later years he gave it up and wrote novels. His only effects on the next generation were two: (1) Shelley from love of him ran away with his daughter. (2) Malthus from hatred of him invented the theory of population. The more useful of these two effects was the one inspired by hatred, but neither was enough to justify a life. Fortunately as I have no daughter that part of the analogy must fail. But perhaps I shall have an effect on G.D.H.C[ole]. comparable to that of Godwin on Malthus. Speriamus. Joking apart, feeling impotent is very horrible.

By midsummer he was so low in spirits that he seriously contemplated going on hunger-strike with the aim of forcing the authorities to release him. He was eventually dissuaded, but only after strong arguments from Colette, at this date probably the only person who could induce him to do anything against his own judgment.

> Were you in for several years, or even for 12 months, it might be worth thinking about. But for 6 months it really isn't. Not that I think it'll make you ill; it is something more psychological than that. There are a number of good reasons against it, but I'll mention only 2. First, the psychological one. I'll not go into it but only *beg* you to promise to consult Pethick-Lawrence before you think any more about it, because *he* knows exactly how badly the whole thing might turn out.
>
> Second, Frank. He's been doing everything possible to get things made better for you, and *has* got them made better. And now you propose to start a hunger-strike behind his back. From *no* point of view is it a good idea, Beloved. Please don't brush this aside as rubbish. Please think it over very soberly. Please.

He was persuaded. Even so, his restlessness grew. He had gone into prison with high expectations that he would be able to write in peace. But as the mood worked itself out the problems took over. After a few months, moreover, he began to realize that it was not only in his professional life that a change was taking place; in his private affairs as well, the disadvantages of incarceration began to outweigh the benefits of isolation.

Something of the deep spiritual passion of his relationship with Ottoline still remained, but since his meeting with Colette there had been less passion and more spirit. Nevertheless, he had found it difficult to believe that the strong physical longing for her had entirely disappeared. Now, measuring his feelings for the temporarily unattainable Ottoline with those for the temporarily unattainable Colette, he knew. Ottoline dotted the i's and crossed the t's of the situation in a number of letters which he received in prison, and these he passed on to Colette. "I'm so glad you are glad that things between you & her have sorted themselves out ..." she wrote after reading them.

Prison also braced him for a final break-away from Mrs Eliot. He had never wanted to give her more than affection, but though the spirit was unwilling a man of Russell's strong personal predilections found this difficult. Now, in prison, common sense strengthened his resolution, and early in July he asked his brother to tell Eliot that he would probably have to give up all financial interest in the Eliots' house. In practice it meant little; symbolically it meant a lot.

These were entries on the credit side of imprisonment, but they were entries that concerned lesser emotional traumas. What mattered to Russell above all was Colette; and with Colette, as the separation lengthened, as he thought of her travelling on tour, jealousy once again began to bite. When she was in London she visited him almost every week, going to bed early the preceding night "anointed with Madame Helena Rubinstein's face cream, so's to look presentable for you tomorrow; if not the Lord's Anointed, anyway the Hon. Bertrand's". There was a bitter-sweet touch to the visits. "It is terrible when I come to see you & cannot tell you anything of the love in my heart, cannot throw my arms around you, cannot take yr dear face in my hands," she wrote. "It is unbearable to see yr hands so close to mine on the table & yet not be able to fill them with kisses. I cld cheerfully wring the warder's neck, if it'd be any use. A good pacifist sentiment, anyway."

Her letters were equalled by his, inspired by the prospect of the future and bringing out the contrast between the austere logic-chopper of popular sentiment and the deeply passionate man that Russell was.

And to Colette he now confided the deeper longings which had driven him all his grown life, the ambitions which a few years earlier he had described so well to Ottoline. "I must, I *must*, before I die, find *some* way to say the essential thing that is in me, that I have never said yet," he wrote after describing his plans for the future;

> a thing that is not love or hate or pity or scorn, but the very breath of life, fierce and coming from far away, bringing into human life

> the fearful passionless force of non-human things ... I want to stand for life and thought – thought as adventure, clear thought because of the intrinsic delight of it, along with the other delights of life. Against worldliness, which consists in doing everything for the sake of something else, like marrying for money instead of for love. The essence of life is doing things for their own sakes ... I want to stand at the rim of the world, and peer into the darkness beyond, and see a little more than others have seen of the strange shapes of mystery that inhabit that unknown night ... I want to bring back into the world of men some little bit of new wisdom. There is a little wisdom in the world; Heraclitus, Spinoza, and a saying here and there. I want to add to it, even if only ever so little ...

Colette's tender, passionate replies to the lonely man in his prison-cell were a touching testimony to love and devotion. But among the gossip in her letters, the stories of people met and of old acquaintanceships renewed, there came the news that she had once again seen the film-producer whose advent had been the cause of her earlier break with Russell. There was also an American colonel "with a most touching physiognomy: a heavily built creature like a St. Bernard mastiff with sad, honest, brown eyes". The colonel was not only anxious to help T. S. Eliot, with whom he too was friendly, but was unburdening his personal affairs to a sympathetic Colette. To Russell's over-imaginative mind, this became an army of men eager to supplant him in Colette's affections. Before the end of July she was having to reassure him.

Then, as worry about her affections turned to fear, a diversion was provided by Helen Dudley who was still the tenant of Russell's Bury Street flat. With thoughts of leaving the Fitzroy Street studio when he came out of prison, Russell wrote ending her tenancy and with naive optimism apparently thought this would not affect his now-platonic relations with her. However, a difficult situation arose – made no less difficult by the fact that Colette was still totally unaware that Miss Dudley had been Russell's mistress.

The predicament might have been embarrassing. Russell, however, kept his head and waited for something to turn up. It did. Helen decided to go back to the United States. On 15 August, a few days before she was due to sail, she visited him in prison. He arranged that there would be no other visitors that day and she stayed for the permitted thirty minutes.

After she left, Russell was filled, temporarily at least, with pain and relief, remorse and satisfaction. After the parting he had to write once more. Colette was the least unsuitable channel of communication; and Colette knew some of the circumstances, though still ignorant of the most important. His farewell letter to Helen was thus enclosed in a letter to

Colette, its privacy ensured by the psychological gambit of telling Colette she could read it if she wished.

"If you possibly can," he went on in the covering letter,

> write me longer letters, and more *definite* news. Don't leave answering until the last minute. Remember what it is like being shut away here, thinking, imagining, seeing how much you don't tell, noticing the faintest sign of coldness, fearing that by the time I come out all your passion will be going elsewhere, as it did once before. If I were not in prison I could get rid of profitless thought of this kind, but in prison it is fearfully difficult. And the result is a mood in which one sees nothing happy in the future either ...

At the end, he added, "Please do your utmost to get my letter to Helen Dudley before she sails on Tuesday." Colette dutifully obliged, delivering it by hand to Helen at her London club shortly before she left for Southampton.

Helen replied that night in a singularly moving letter. Russell, relieved that his parting note had been delivered, wrote to Colette the day after Helen had sailed, telling her that he had completely recovered his sanity and briefly summarizing the whole of the Helen Dudley affair. It was to be thirty years before he again mentioned her to Colette.

It was appalling, of course. Yet outrage gets little support from Helen Dudley herself. Three years later, hearing that he was going to China, she wished him every happiness: "It does sound as though you had really reached harbour." Another two years on she gaily describes a friend talking about Russell. "Then he asked me if I could explain what your attraction was for women!" she continued. "Couldn't understand it himself, but knew three women in this country on whom you'd made a lasting impression – when you were spoken of, their expressions changed. Mine didn't change and he was left guessing about a possible fourth woman." In love, as in war, what Russell roused was the fury of the non-combatant.

When Helen Dudley left for the United States, he expected to be out of Brixton in about six weeks – apparently not knowing he might get remission for good conduct – and from now onwards his correspondence with Colette centred on the celebration of his release: where they would breakfast, where they would lunch, where they would find complete isolation for the following few days. "I keep thinking of the moment I'll open the door & you'll be standing there, come home at last," she wrote on 7 September, "and we'll be together alone at last; & I'll put my arms round yr dear straight shoulders, & stroke yr heathery hair, & kiss you like a starving man & love every bit of you."

A few days later she was getting the Bury Street flat ready, collecting his pipes, laying in supplies of his favourite tobacco, detailing in letters

28 Russell and companions picnicking on the Cornish coast

29 Russell on the south coast of Cornwall, near Carn Voel, in the later 1920s

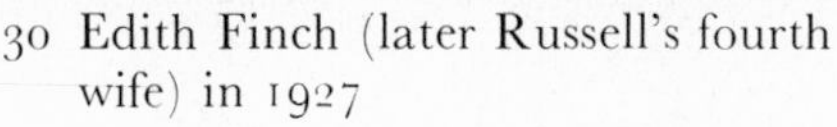

30 Edith Finch (later Russell's fourth wife) in 1927

31 Lucy Donnelly in 1927

32 Russell and Dora outside Telegraph House

33 Russell in the grounds of Beacon Hill School, with his own children and other pupils; (*second from left*) John Russell; (*on Russell's left*) Kate Russell

34 Dora at Beacon Hill School

35 Russell on the steps of Beacon Hill School (Kate is sitting on his knee, and John is standing, fifth from left)

36 Russell with Gerald Brenan and Peter Spence (later Russell's third wife) at East Lulworth, 1934

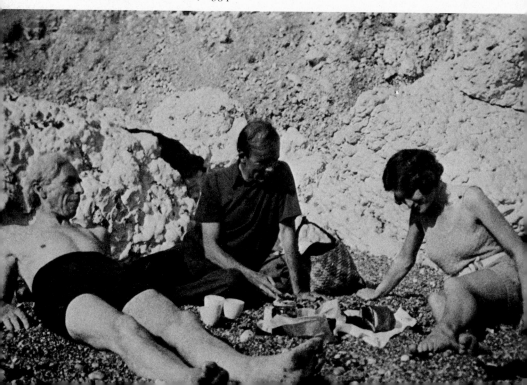

how she was preparing the flat in which they would set up home together. "I walk fr. room to room," she wrote, "loving it all & no longer needing to remind myself of Granny Annesley's advice: 'My child, count yr blessings'. Because I do: each day, hour, moment that brings you nearer home. In my heart you live always & for ever, for better or worse."

Now at last, it seemed, Russell was coming emotionally to port. Nothing was to be further from the truth.

On 11 September he wrote that less than three weeks of his sentence remained to be served. But remission was more than he expected and he was out in seven days. He emerged therefore while preparations for welcoming him were still incomplete and, in his unsettled semi-neurotic state, this chance circumstance seemed almost a personal affront. Colette was waiting for him as planned. She welcomed him as planned. But before the day was out a jealous scene, based on his assumption that she was in love with the American colonel, had blown them apart. The idyllic week in the country was abandoned and that evening he left the Bury Street flat for Gordon Square. Here there was soon to arrive a note from the ever-faithful Alys. "I am thankful that thee is free again, and do trust thy health is none the worse," it went. "I thought of thee every day with greatest regret, and dreamt of thee almost every night."

Sexually frustrated and bitterly disappointed by the scene at Bury Street, Russell now escaped to Telegraph House, his brother's country-home on the Sussex downs, but not before he had visited Clifford Allen, who noted in his diary, "BR arrives. He is very child-like in his engrossment with his own emotions, virtues, vices, and the effect he has upon other people. The oddest mixture of candour and mystery, cruelty and affection, fearless concern for constructive philosophy and enormous personal interest in attitude to himself of other philosophers."

For his part, Russell believed that the visit had done him untold good. "Now," he went on to Ottoline, "I enjoy getting back to work and having secure privacy – no telephone, no post, no visitors – it is as good as prison, with the advantage that I can walk out whenever I like."

Unsure of where he stood with Colette, as desperate as ever for Ottoline's comforting mental reassurances, disillusioned with much of the pacifist movement and already fearful that a hard peace imposed on Germany would make another war inevitable, Russell found consolation in his work, sheet-anchor for his sanity in times of trouble. The uncertainty, insecurity and doubt do much to explain his almost aimless movements and fluctuating emotions during the next few weeks. He had already written to Ottoline, inviting himself to Garsington and urging her to spend a week with him in October at Lulworth on the Dorset coast. They had often promised themselves an escapist holiday together, she free from household worries, he free from work; in prison, where the idea of visiting Lulworth had arisen, the prospect had special attractions. "It will be a *great* disappointment if you give it up," he wrote to her. "Oh, I do *long* for talk and freedom – think of the wind off the sea blowing through one's hair, and the smell of the sea and the sound of the sea and the great sky, and to shout and embrace the glory of the world – no walls, no gates and locks, no wardens ..." Now, outside at last, he stressed his need for her with an underlined "please".

Before receiving a reply he returned from Sussex to Gordon Square. Ottoline herself was frequently visiting London and before the end of September she and Russell had spent an ecstatic day in Richmond Park – "the way it developed *utterly* unexpected to me, but it is a great joy to find things so imperishable", he wrote. Nevertheless, the ties of Philip and family were as strong as ever. Lulworth was impossible. Usually ready with a reserve, Russell decided to field Colette, with whom his relations had been following a shuttlecock course between ecstasy and despair. He had continued his guerrilla warfare on the subject of the American colonel, been relieved when she agreed to see no more of him, then confessed that he had no right to put her in a cage. "I see CM at her place, hardly ever here, & then only for a moment," he wrote to Ottoline.

But this could not last. Colette was drawn to him as irresistibly as he to her and they were soon at Lulworth together. Here they spent a few idyllic days that in Russell's words were as great and splendid as any they had ever had. She, for her part, admitted to being happier than she thought possible. He countered with the affirmation that he would not desert her.

He had barely set foot again in London before he was off once more, this time for Abinger where Clifford Allen had begun two months' complete rest on doctor's orders. "Talked much with BR about peace prospects," Allen noted in his diary.

> He is entirely opposed to any thought that even now a properly ordered map is the essential thing. He would have preferred an indecisive military ending, believing that this would produce a better after-war spirit, and that this would be better than a good map with a decisive military victory. I didn't agree. I still think that we should never have got anything decisive for the world's future out of an indecisive ending to the war. A good map will give a chance to the right spirit, especially with a League of Nations.

Allen's ambivalent feelings about Russell were illustrated by a further entry, made after a second visit a fortnight later. "B.R. sat by the fire for nearly an hour and recited from memory Shakespeare's sonnets and Blake. He was like a happy child, and he made me realise from his tenderness and brilliant mind why, with all his waywardness, I love him so devotedly."

On the face of it, Russell was going to be very hard up, and under

Gilbert Murray's leadership his friends rallied round. "Mr. Bertrand Russell has now been released from prison and is desirous of devoting himself to philosophical work," read a printed memorandum circulated by Murray.

> It is to be feared, however, that he may find this impossible, since in the present state of public feeling no ordinary university institution is likely to be willing to employ him as a teacher after his expulsion from Trinity College, Cambridge. Consequently some admirers of his work, unwilling that his rare talents should be wasted, have formed the project of collecting privately a fund sufficient to provide £150 or £200 a year for three years to be paid to Dr. Russell as a special Lectureship in order to enable him to devote himself to philosophical work, in the form of teaching or research or both. The undersigned venture to ask if you would be inclined to make a subscription to this fund & allow your name to be mentioned as having done so. Sums from £1 upwards will be received, & the amounts contributed by each subscriber will be treated as confidential.
>
> By the present regulations of the Ministry of National Service exemption is granted to "teachers above the age of 45"; Mr. Russell is over 45, & by profession a teacher; & although, of course, if he remains unemployed, it is not clear he will have any claim to exemption, the regulations will presumably apply to him when once he resumes his regular work as a teacher and lecturer. [Signed by S. Alexander, Bernard Bosanquet, H. Wildon Carr, G. Dawes Hicks, T. Percy Nunn, A. E. Taylor, James Ward, A. N. Whitehead.]

Russell saw no need for charity. "I hope Murray's lectureship scheme will fall through, now that it is not necessary for escaping prison," was his response. "I want to have time for my original work." Nevertheless, it was the money now raised by Murray which, early in 1919, financed the lectures he gave at the London School of Economics on "The Analysis of Mind".

For the moment, bread-and-butter income was provided by articles for popular journals. By contrast there was a renewal of his philosophical papers. The first was "On Propositions: What They Are and How They Mean", a paper which reflected both the behaviourist books he had read in Brixton and a fresh assessment of the nature of propositions which showed the persistent influence of Wittgenstein. It indicated, moreover, the future trend, the increased attention to psychology and linguistics which was to reveal itself in *The Analysis of Mind*. It was probably this paper that Colette glanced at when she visited him at Bury Street before telling him: "It was grand seeing all those pages immaculately covered in words with never an alteration. Heavenly to know you are properly started on real work again, beloved."

"Real work" was coming along, though hope for the future seemed precarious in the political climate that was to generate the Coupon Election. Yet whatever stood on the credit side was more than counterbalanced by personal devils, and the ability to make a mess of his personal life that dogged him until he reached his eighties. The war, as he later wrote, had certainly shaken him out of himself and given him an interest in the world beyond philosophy. But his personal problems had merely been compounded between 1914 and 1918.

"It is very difficult to adjust oneself to the new world," he wrote to Ottoline the day before the Armistice. "I find it hard to resist the feeling that I have lived long enough: the energy wanted for new beginnings, which I felt in prison, I no longer feel. Nothing in my personal future seems interesting or vivid or worth the pain of existence. But that is a mood, & would pass if I could get to Italy. It is due to unspeakable weariness of spirit."

Ten days later he wrote a longer letter revealing the fraught state in which he faced the peace:

> This letter is a cry of distress & an appeal for help. I find it is utterly impossible for me to do any work or endure life if I live in London, & I know I can't live alone – I must find some way of enduring life, or else give it up.
>
> Could I for the present come to Garsington say 4 days a week? In lodgings if there are any of them where one can get a fire. Perhaps with Clive demobilising it will be possible. I should be really happier if I could get a man to live with me by the sea. And of course what I *really* want is a wife – but the world contains no one available in either capacity. The truth is I am worn out. I need looking after, & some one to see after the mechanism of life & leave my thoughts free for work. Since I quarrelled with Alys I have never found any one who would or could take me away for holidays when I am tired or take care of me & now I find without something of the kind I am no good.
>
> I put myself in your hands – except that I have a duty to C which may interfere. What would answer best with her would be if I saw her 2 days a week & lived elsewhere the rest of the time – I don't want emotions but I want quiet companionship & good air & exercise.
>
> C has behaved angelically but the shock was so severe that I cannot get any rest except away from her – and the feeling that my work is suffering makes me horrid to her, & that makes us both miserable.
>
> When do you return from Welbeck? I *may* go away with C next week for a short time but I doubt it – If I do, other arrangements would only come into force when I return.

Forgive the brutal frankness of this letter. It is my only chance of escape.

The situation was not entirely concealed from Colette; but to her he merely threw off the brief remark that he might regularly spend a couple of days a week at Garsington. Thus for Russell the war ended on a note very different from that of August 1914. Now he was trying to deal not with Helen Dudley but with himself.

On Armistice Night he was in London. "The crowd rejoiced and I also rejoiced," he said. "But I remained as solitary as before."

14

Turning-Point

The end of the war left Russell high and dry. His political views had been transformed and he had discovered an unsuspected prowess as a popular speaker, but he was too much of an individualist to fit comfortably into any party. There seemed much to support his current pessimism. "I profoundly hate the social upheavals that I foresee," he wrote to Gilbert Murray, "but there seems no hope of Capital voluntarily permitting a better world to grow up – or at least very little. I am conscious that revolution would make me violently pacifist & lead to my head being amongst the first to fall; nevertheless, I think the probable alternatives are even worse."

The war had thrust him out into the world of ordinary people and what he saw there raised a number of perplexing problems:

> When I examine my own conception of human excellence, I find that, doubtless owing to early environment, it contains many elements which have hitherto been associated with aristocracy, such as fearlessness, independence of judgment, emancipation from the herd, and leisurely culture. Is it possible to preserve these qualities, and even make them widespread, in an industrial community? And is it possible to dissociate them from the typical aristocratic vices: limitation of sympathy, haughtiness, and cruelty to those outside a charmed circle?

These were questions which Russell, who had lived entirely within the circle until his mid-forties, had never previously asked himself. From now onwards they were to loom ever larger in his mind, standing beside the sublime questions of philosophy and just as persistently demanding an answer.

In his own subject he still clung to the hope of getting through the maze and discovering philosophic certainty, but he now had to march on alone, without the academic comradeship which had meant so much to him at Cambridge. Even were he invited back to Trinity there might be difficulties in accepting, since his personal affairs were still in a constitutional state of disarray. He was nearing fifty, passionately in love with a woman half his age, still emotionally dependent on Ottoline and still married to a woman he had left almost a decade before.

These circumstances brought no comfort, and for some time he wavered, concentrating his intellect first on the development of logical atomism, on the problems which he tried to solve in *The Analysis of Mind*; later, on the implications of the new philosophical system which Wittgenstein had been perfecting in the enemy trenches. He filled the gaps in his working life with whatever minor *ad hoc* jobs were offered and personally allowed himself to be blown by chance. A little more resolution, a little more willingness to risk the hazards of command, and he might have steered himself. As it was, almost two years passed before he at last took the tiller and turned towards a new life. His hopes were high. Nevertheless he sailed into years of disappointment and near-despair, when once again even suicide had its attractions.

During the last weeks of 1918, aching for quiet and a rest from emotional manœuvres, he found peace at Garsington. Here, Ottoline was now attracting not only the writers, artists and pacifists of the war years but those who hoped to take a political hand in making the future. A little more baroque, she was now more resplendent and bohemian than ever, and still able to twist Russell round her little finger. The Ottoline of this period has been vividly evoked by Vivian de Sola Pinto, taken to Garsington by Sassoon, with whom he had served in the Welch Fusiliers.

> She was dressed in a bright scarlet frock in a style suggestive of the Elizabethan period and a sort of hoop or small crinoline. Her voice was as remarkable as her appearance. I can only describe it as a richly musical grotesque but the impression made on me by Lady Ottoline was far from grotesque. She had an aura of radiant charm, vitality and intellectual power, and I felt that I was in the presence of the modern equivalent of Fox's Duchess of Devonshire or Byron's Lady Oxford.

The Duchess was beginning to have her reservations about Russell. Russell was again at Garsington, she wrote to Mark Gertler. He was very nice, she went on, but there was one thing of which she complained: that he kept too rigidly to intellectual matters while she, as she put it, wanted at times to sing and dance.

At Christmas she had her chance. Russell left Garsington for a break at Lynton, on the north coast of Devon, with Colette and Allen. They stayed at the Cottage Hotel where the three of them walked in the wooded grounds, sat on the stone-paved veranda five hundred feet above the sea, and amiably discussed the fate of the world and their own personal futures. They remained until mid-January. The day before they left, as Russell impatiently got ready for a walk, Colette wrote to him, "You are sitting puffing at your pipe almost close enough for me to reach out my hand to stroke your heathery head, and you haven't the least idea that I'm writing to you, but I want you to have a word to welcome you at Garsington." Everything had been perfect. For all three it had been a rest before problems ahead.

From Lynton, Russell returned to Garsington, living again on the estate where Santayana found him "in a spacious upper chamber, with plank walls and many books about", but eating in the manor-house. At Lynton he had agreed to take up quarters in Allen's Battersea flat and at the end of January he moved to London. A few days later Allen became seriously ill, the flat was invaded by female N.-C.F. colleagues and Russell, lamenting that the place was full of psychology and that he did not care to compete with furious women, moved back to the ever-welcoming haven of Garsington.

Basking for part of each day under Ottoline's stimulating influence, writing in the quiet of French's Farm, he finished off a great deal of work. There were a few ephemeral articles for American journals, written to keep the financial stock-pot boiling, and the more important "Democracy and Direct Action" which foreshadowed the Russell of forty years on. "Direct Action has its dangers," he concluded in the paper, written for the *English Review*, printed also in the *Dial* and reprinted as a pamphlet by both journals, "but so has every vigorous form of activity. And in our recent realisation of the importance of the law we must not forget that the greatest of all dangers to a civilisation is to become stereotyped and stagnant. From this danger, at least, industrial unrest is likely to save us."

Making both ends meet was a necessity; of still greater consequence was his struggle with *The Analysis of Mind*, started in prison and finally to see the light of day in the series of lectures paid for by his friends. While he was grappling with this task he was distressed by an unexpected turn in his relations with Mrs Eliot. A few weeks earlier they had dined together, and she had been firmly told he would be unable to see her for some considerable time, the Russellian euphemism for the chop. To the brush-off, Mrs Eliot had replied that she disliked fading intimacies and was therefore ending the friendship. Ignoring this unexpected gift from the gods, Russell continued to write. Now, early in February, he received a letter from her husband. On the face of it, the trouble was minor and purely financial; there were difficulties about the Eliots' house, which Russell had helped furnish, and it was proposed that he might like to take it over.

At first, Russell was in favour of Eliot's proposal and persuasively put before Colette the advantages of having their own country house to which they could escape. She, trying to keep his feet on *terra firma*, pointed out that he had only just finished paying rent for accommodation at French's Farm, was not yet free of the Fitzroy Street studio, was still responsible for a half-share in Allen's flat in Battersea and would, if she died suddenly, have the Bury Street flat on his hands. "I think", she added, with an unconscious touch of ambiguity, "you are really trying for two birds with one stone."

Eventually he patched up the business and disengaged himself finally from Mrs Eliot. That done, he got down to the work that mattered.

The heart of his problem was the relationship between mind and matter. Until almost the start of the century, the Cartesian doctrine of an absolute division between the two still retained not only respectability but immutability. Old Lady Russell's oft reiterated jingle, "What is mind? no matter; what is matter? never mind," was simply the lay dismissal of a question that had continued to puzzle even the most brilliant of natural scientists and philosophers. Kipling's East and West might be separated for ever, but no more certainly than mind and matter, forever staring at each other across the unbridgeable gulf.

Yet as the nineteenth century passed into the twentieth, this comfortable doctrine had been assaulted from two directions. From one there came the psychologists of the behaviourist school, denying the existence of mental processes, objectively studying the overt responses of humans and other animals, paving the way for an analysis of mind that reduced it to a series of chemical or electrical responses. From the other came the larger and in many ways more formidable battalions of the physicists, finding that the electron, an invisible riddle wrapped in a negative electric charge, formed part of the world's solid stuff. Thus they put forward the apparently preposterous idea that even the solid tables which formed the substance of Russell's philosophical explanations consisted mainly of empty space in which minute and almost unimaginable particles circled for ever round even more unimaginable nuclei – themselves soon to be revealed as no more than further collections of electric charges. Matter, thus dethroned, was to receive yet a further shock with the exposition of Einstein's Relativity, which regarded mass itself as depending, so to speak, on the eye of the beholder, a variable rather than an absolute in a world consisting of "events" from which "matter" was derived by logical construction. As Russell now pointed out, "Whoever reads, for example, Professor Eddington's 'Space, Time and Gravitation' will see that an old-fashioned materialism can receive no support from modern physics."

These developments, which were steadily leading one group of men to consider mind very largely in terms of matter, and yet another to dismiss matter as little more than a convenient shorthand expression of more complex things, profoundly disturbed Russell's sense of rightness, and before the war he had tentatively begun to deal with them in "Knowledge by Acquaintance and Knowledge by Description". Now, as Einstein was driven on to produce the General Theory of Relativity which covered more than his earlier Special Theory, Russell felt it necessary to deal more thoroughly with the problem of mind and matter and the nature of consciousness. In *Our Knowledge of the External World* he had treated matter as a logical construction based on sense-data. Now he was to treat mind as a logical construction based on sensations – and to consider sensations as just another form of sense-data. He tended to see the subject in practical terms. "If you have a nightmare," he once wrote, "the one school will say that it is because you ate too much lobster salad, and the other that it is because you are unconsciously in love with your mother." When a publisher suggested illustrating his paper on "Mind and Matter", Russell asked, "Would you have a picture of a living skeleton talking to G. K. Chesterton?"

The best starting-point seemed to be William James and the New Realists he had met in Harvard five years previously and for whom the "stuff" of the world was neither mental nor material, but a neutral substance out of which both were constructed. With this premiss he had started on the subject in Brixton, but by the time of his release he was still plagued with difficulties. They persisted for another four months and it was only at the end of January that he saw his way through them. So excited was he that he telegraphed Colette from Garsington, telling her that he had made an important discovery. As a result, he wrote in a follow-up letter, he was not merely happy; he felt just as he had when he had come back from meeting Peano in Paris about two decades earlier.

Seriously getting down to work, he now began to construct a non-dualistic account of the world which agreed with the accepted facts of both psychology and physics, a task of unification in which he tried to analyse mind and matter in terms of neutral elements. He was not entirely successful. None the less, he did succeed in clearing away a great deal of undergrowth – especially the idea of consciousness as essential to life or mind – and establishing a base from which others could advance.

His conclusions were delivered first in the series of London lectures, later in *The Analysis of Mind*, a book which he half-jokingly suggested the Americans might call "Do Men Think", or even "I Don't Think" – they had, after all, published *Principles of Social Reconstruction* under the title *Why Men Fight*. Basically, his thesis revolved around the first of six points with which he concluded the book. "Physics and psychology", he wrote, "are not distinguished by their material. Mind and matter alike are logical constructions; the particulars out of which they are constructed, or from which they are inferred, have various relations, some of which are studied by physics, others by psychology. Broadly speaking, physics group particulars by their active places, psychology by their passive places."

The Analysis of Mind broke new ground and a lot of it was understandable by that hypothetical reader, the educated layman. It was, moreover, of a singular clarity, a quality which had always distinguished Russell's technical writing and which now came through, as it had in *The Problems of Philosophy*, when he addressed himself to those who knew little of the subject. Joseph Conrad was typical of the non-technical readers to whom Russell brought light out of darkness. He praised the book as

> an habitation of great charm and most fascinatingly furnished; not to speak of the wonderful quality of light that reigns in there. Also all the windows (I am trying to write in images) are, one feels, standing wide open. Nothing less stuffy – of the Mansions of the mind – could be conceived! I am sorry for the philosophers who (like the rest of us) cannot have their cake and eat it. There's no exactitude in the vision or in the words. I have a notion that we are condemned in all things to the *à-peu-près*, which no scientific passion for weighing and measuring will ever do away with.

Once *The Analysis of Mind* was out of the way, Russell reverted to his minor work: writing for the *Dial*, reviewing for *Mind*, and turning out an assortment of miscellaneous journalism which had little to do with philosophy. In fact by the summer, back with Allen in Battersea, he could write happily to Ottoline, "I am glad to be no longer worried about money – 'The Athenaeum' & the 'Dial' suffice, with my lectures, so that I am by no means poor any longer."

But he was badly needing a break. First he wrote to his Cambridge mathematical colleague, J. E. Littlewood, proposing that they should share rooms or a farmhouse for a couple of months. Then he wrote to Colette: could she help find somewhere suitable? The choice eventually fell on Newlands Farm, Lulworth, a five-bedroomed building close to the beach with good bathing, a vista of sea and hills, and a pine-wood behind it.

Although he could have rented it for £50 a year plus the cost of a caretaker, Russell decided to take it for three months from 24 June. The countryside captivated him, giving back to him what he called "the big simple eternal things – the sound of the sea on the shingle, the cry of gulls, moonlight on the waves, the setting sun on cliffs". It reminded him of Ottoline, never far from his thoughts, whatever diversions might exist. "All the large and simple beauty of this place brings you into my thoughts continually," he wrote to her; "it is the beauty of free sweeping lines, hills, cliffs, sea and sky, nothing to stop the eye. If I take on the place, as I probably shall, you must come down here next year as soon as the weather gets good ..."

A few days before departing he dined with Colette and told her of his plans for the summer, how Littlewood and he hoped to be joined by a succession of friends. She had already been told that he might "in time get a daily companionship from someone else" and on 25 June she received a curiously contradictory letter. He hoped for no new joy except from her; but although he had not stopped loving her – and doubted if he ever could – things would have to be different. Would she give him his freedom?

He received her reply the following day, as he was about to leave for Dorset. The letter was no more final than others that had marked their relationship during the past three years; yet thinking it over on the journey, he did feel that this time it really was the end. The belief lasted a few hours. Shortly after he arrived at Lulworth, the post-boy delivered a telegram: "Will be with you ten o'clock tonight with Allen. Colette."

She arrived on time, having come in a hired car. They embraced in the dusk. The reconciliation seemed as complete as it was sudden, and appeared to be confirmed by the long letter Russell wrote after her return to London less than forty-eight hours later. Apart from her, his only deep feelings were those of despair; all the worries of the past few months had been wiped out by the few hours at Lulworth; he had been filled with wonderful happiness once more, and they must now begin a new life.

His account to Ottoline was the same but different. "The parting with Colette did not come off – she wanted to try again, so I agreed. So I shall be seeing her again some time soon. I don't know what will come of it."

During the next few weeks Newlands Farm saw a steady flow of visitors. They included Jean Nicod and Dorothy Wrinch, who with Russell and Littlewood applied themselves to Eddington's recent and revealing report on Einstein's General Theory of Relativity. Its impact on Newlands Farm induced the party to wire Eddington for advance news of the eclipse expedition which was testing the theory. Only preliminary news of the expedition's observations was available, but Russell was so overwhelmed by Eddington's argument, that he one day exclaimed in exasperation "… to think I've spent my life on *muck*".

While the implications of Einstein were being debated, there arrived at Lulworth what was to become one of the most famous philosophical manuscripts of the twentieth century: Wittgenstein's *Tractatus Logico-Philosophicus*, at this date bearing the title "Logisch-philosophische Abhandlung". Five months earlier, in February 1919, Russell had received the first post-war news of his pupil. Wittgenstein, fighting with the Austrian forces, had been captured on the Italian front only a few days before the Armistice. He was in a prisoner-of-war camp at Cassino and allowed to send only two small postcards a week. Then he succeeded in smuggling out, via a medical orderly, a letter in which he announced the completion of a book incorporating all his work of the previous six years – that is, roughly since he had parted from Russell in Cambridge. "I believe I've solved our problems finally," he wrote.

> This may sound arrogant but I can't help believing it … I've got the manuscript here with me. I wish I could copy it out for you;

> but it's pretty long and I would have no safe way of sending it to you. In fact you would not understand it without a previous explanation as it's written in quite short remarks. (This of course means that *nobody* will understand it; although I believe it's all as clear as crystal. But it upsets all our theory of truth, of classes, of numbers and all the rest.) I will publish it as soon as I get home.

Russell was at once anxious to see the manuscript even without the explanation which Wittgenstein regarded as essential. He found an ally in Keynes, now principal representative of the Treasury at the Paris Peace Conference, to whom he forwarded Wittgenstein's letter. Keynes was in fact being tackled direct by Wittgenstein, who had told him, "I wish I could see [Russell] somehow or other for I am sure he won't be able to understand my book without a very thorough explanation, which cannot be written. Have you done any more work on probability? My MS contains a few lines about it which, I believe, solve the essential questions."

Keynes, no doubt as anxious as Russell to see the manuscript which would solve the essential questions, had promised to help. The Italians would let Wittgenstein send out letters or manuscripts and might agree to release him out of turn, he told Russell, before adding, "Heaven give me escape from this Paris nightmare as soon as possible."

Now came the manuscript itself. Russell discussed it with Miss Wrinch and Nicod, and the result was a long list of questions dispatched to Wittgenstein. Before they arrived in Italy Wittgenstein had received the *Introduction to Mathematical Philosophy*, sent by Russell as soon as he had Wittgenstein's address. The effect of the book was unexpected. "I should never have believed that what I dictated to Moore in Norway six years ago would pass over you so completely without trace," Wittgenstein now wrote.

> In short, I am afraid it might be very difficult for me to reach an understanding with you. And my small remaining hope that my manuscript would convey something to you has now quite vanished. Writing a commentary on my book is out of the question for me, as you can imagine. I could only give you an oral one. If you attach any importance whatsoever to understanding the thing, and if you can arrange a meeting with me, please do so. If that is impossible, then be so good as to send the manuscript back to Vienna by a safe route as soon as you have read it. It is the only corrected copy I possess and it is my life's work!

While the Lulworth party was still mulling over the profundities of Wittgenstein's manuscript, an urgent plea arrived from Philip Jourdain. While Russell was in prison, Jourdain had prepared for the press *The Philosophy of Mr. B*rtr*nd R*ss*ll*, which claimed to be a manuscript of the late Mr Russell, saved with his interleaved *Prayer-Book of Free Man's Worship* when "a body of eager champions of the Sacredness of Personal Property" burned down his house. The book consisted of forty-three very short chapters each of which developed a philosophical joke. One, a parody of Russell's Theory of Types, explained how an Oxford don reduced all jokes to thirty-seven primitive proto-Aryan types, and went on to discuss second-order, third-order and even fourth-order jokes and those "jokes of transfinite order [which] presumably only excite the inaudible laughter of the gods". There were also twenty appendices containing quotations from Lewis Carroll, and relevant cross-references linking such matters as Russell's treatment of nonexistent entities and the White Knight who, when told "I see nobody on the road," replies, "I only wish *I* had such eyes." Even without the coincidence of Tenniel's Mad Hatter, in appearance surprisingly like the Russell of Edwardian Cambridge, the congruities between Carroll and Russell were numerous: in the world which Carroll invented and the world which Russell perceived, things were rarely what they seemed.

Jourdain had sent the manuscript to Russell, who gave it his blessing. There was much mutual goodwill and some of it had survived the wrangle over the *Monist* articles with Unwin. Now Jourdain was dying, still obsessed with his final proof of the axiom which had so long set him at loggerheads with most of the mathematical world. Would Russell, Littlewood or Miss Wrinch, but by preference Russell, visit him and listen to his proof? Littlewood and Russell discussed what should be done. As mathematicians, neither of them expected to agree with Jourdain's "proof"; but would it perhaps be justifiable to tell a dying man, for his own comfort, that his proof was viable? Neither felt that it would be.

Finally, Littlewood and Miss Wrinch travelled to Jourdain's home in Fleet and listened to his proof. "I said that a new point was involved, and I would have to consider it closely and at length," Littlewood has written. "Then he burst out: 'My dear fellow, you know perfectly well that you can see whether a proof is right or wrong in 5 minutes.'" Russell, hearing their story when they got back to Lulworth, appears to have been moved by their account and telegraphed an offer to visit the dying man. "Your telegram came just too late to arrange for Philip to see you," Mrs Jourdain replied. "He is now quite unable to talk or see anyone, but just lies in a semi-conscious state. Why didn't you make an effort to come a little sooner? You have made him so unhappy by your inability to see his well-ordering [i.e. his new proof]. You are the only person he wanted to see and talk with months ago." Jourdain died five days later.

During this long summer on the Dorset coast Russell was not involved only in philosophical business. He was also taking the first steps in an emotional progress that was to change his life. With Dorothy Wrinch there had come to Lulworth her friend Dora Black. Russell had first met Miss

Black, a Fellow of Girton, a few years earlier on a weekend's walk in Surrey with Miss Wrinch and Jean Nicod. They had stayed at the White Horse in Shere, then walked up to lunch at Bob Trevelyan's home on the nearby slopes of Leith Hill. The meeting lodged in Dora Black's mind, and fifteen years later she recollected how the day when she had first met Russell still had wonderful associations for her.

Miss Black was not only physically attractive; she also exhibited a questioning intelligence of a high degree and an iconoclastic approach to the accepted order of things. She had, moreover, a hunger for intellectual experience and for children which Russell found pleasing. Her appearance in Dorset was casually reported to Ottoline in a brief sentence: "We have here Nicod and his wife, who seems rather nice and Miss Wrinch and her friend Miss Black." Colette was told only that Miss Black was "nice", and that he doubted whether he would "take up" with her. However, as they swam in the sea together and walked on the neighbouring hills, his doubts quickly evaporated. "Dora and I became lovers ..." as he later wrote.

After the Newlands Farm party had broken up, Dora crossed the Channel to study in Paris. Russell returned to Allen's flat in Battersea where the two men very soon began to grate on each other's nerves. "More intellectual 'ticking off' from BR at dinner because I used the word 'sentence' when I should have said 'phrase'," Allen wrote in his diary. "I'm dead sick of it." And, ten days later: "A dull, provocative spirit is rising between Bertie and myself. I am becoming more and more frozen and inarticulate. This academic atmosphere with its flashes of unreality and contemptuousness stifles me."

Russell was in one of his deepest troughs, but with little apparent reason. Only a few weeks after the latest drama with Colette he was writing in the old glowing terms, protesting that he clung to the thought of her and continued to love her with all his heart and soul. Colette, remembering Lulworth, gave him a small gold coin for his watch-chain, with around it the engraved words she had often written to him, "Car, chaque jour je t'aime d'avantage, aujourd'hui plus que hier, et bien moins que demain." He in turn gave her a small diamond arrow. Ever afterwards they called it "Conrad" – the name of his friend whose *The Arrow of Gold* had just been published, and a name he was later to give to both his sons.

Meanwhile, discussion with Wittgenstein had moved on apace. Earlier, he now said, he had sent the manuscript to Frege. "He wrote to me a week ago and I gather that he doesn't understand a word of it at all," he added. "So my only hope is to see *you* soon and explain all to you, for it is VERY hard not to be understood by a single soul." It was next agreed that the two men should meet in The Hague as soon as Wittgenstein was released. Then another problem arose. Wittgenstein, having decided that money was no use to a philosopher, had given away the considerable fortune recently inherited from his father, and was now penniless. However, he suggested that a way out might be found by selling his furniture from Trinity. Russell offered £80 to the firm still storing it. They accepted and the problem of Wittgenstein's fare was solved.

While Russell was involved in this transaction there came an echo from 1916. Then his dismissal from Trinity had brought a proposal that he should stand for the Rectorship of St Andrews. Now his wartime record brought him a similar offer from Glasgow. The newly formed University Socialist Club had first taken the daring decision to select Karl Liebknecht, but their letter of invitation arrived in Germany as the Socialist leader was murdered. Their next choice, Rosa Luxemburg, had barely time to reply before she too was murdered.

"I can remember our committee meeting to decide who next (we had made no announcement about Liebknecht) and the most exciting and controversial figure we could think of was Russell," says Dr Stark Murray, one of the club's founders. "He accepted at once and we made our announcement in time. Being first in the field, we had the right to call our propaganda magazine 'The Lord Rector' which was considered a triumph." The Conservatives and Liberals had previously agreed not to contest an election but, after an unsuccessful attempt to persuade the Socialists to withdraw, were forced to find their own candidates. The Conservatives chose Bonar Law; the Liberals, Gilbert Murray.

In the campaign that followed, a number who might have been expected to support Russell decided on discretion. "Alas, No time," wrote H. G. Wells in answer to a request for help. Shaw replied that while he supported Russell politically, he was a friend of both Russell and Murray and would therefore stand aside and watch the fight. The showpiece stunt of the Socialist campaign, in the days when undergraduates specialized in this kind of demonstration, was the production of a large red flag on to which the black letters "BR" were sewn. On the eve of voting day, this was run up the flagpole in front of the university, where it could be seen for miles, and the ropes to it nailed so high that only the fire brigade could haul it down.

The result was what might have been expected in the climate of the times. Bonar Law came first, Russell a bad third with a meagre eighty votes in a poll of many hundreds.

Soon afterwards he was on his way to meet Wittgenstein in The Hague, happy to be at the heart of philosophical adventures again. At Trinity, also, things were going his way once more. Back in the spring, thirty of the thirty-four Scholars of the college then in residence had formally petitioned the Master and Fellows "to consider the desirability, now that the war has ended, of inviting the Hon. Bertrand Russell to resume his work in the College". They stressed that they were not concerned with the rights and wrongs either of Russell's political attitudes during the war or with the Council's decision. "The motive that has led us to appeal to you in this way", said a covering letter to the Master, "is simply the belief that Mr. Russell is capable of rendering invaluable service both as a teacher of philosophy and as an influence in the general life of the college."

The memorial was duly noted, and although no action was taken immediately, it cleared the air for the next move. This was made by Professor Hollond, now back in Trinity from Harvard, where Russell had stayed with him in 1914. "I cannot remember how it came about that I took the lead in the matter," he has written. "What happened was that in the Michaelmas Term of 1919 I assumed the task of writing a letter to the Master and obtaining signatures to it." The number of Fellows was then limited to sixty, and of these twenty-eight signed Hollond's memorial expressing the "hope that Mr. Russell may be appointed to a lectureship". An indication of real feelings was that they included every Fellow who had served in the armed forces. Eddington, Rutherford, G. H. Hardy and G. I. Taylor as well as E. D. (now Lord) Adrian, signed. So did Whitehead. "He [had] found himself ... in a terribly difficult position," wrote Hardy, "and the letters in which he explains his difficulties are really moving ..." Five others preferred not to sign for an assortment of personal reasons, but told the Master they approved reinstatement. The pro-Russell faction thus commanded an absolute majority, and while the Council did not legally have to accede to their wishes, a refusal would have started damaging guerrilla warfare. The Council acted accordingly. On 28 November it ordered the letter to be circulated; and on 12 December,

> It was agreed that a lectureship in Logic and the Principles of Mathematics tenable for five years from 1 July, 1920 be offered to Mr. Russell; that he be required to reside in Cambridge during full term and to deliver one course of lectures a term on the subjects of his lectureship; and that he receive a stipend of 250 guineas a year payable from the general corporate revenue, together with rooms in College to be held under the conditions applying to Fellows in Class B, and dinner in Hall.

Russell had by this time left England for The Hague. But he had been kept informed by Littlewood of the preparations to get him back and realized that he might soon be put in a quandary. The Cambridge of 1919 was not quite the Cambridge of 1911, which would have ostracized him had his liaison with Ottoline been known. But it still operated a sexual code which might have demanded resignation from a new appointment had he begun to live openly with either Colette or Miss Black.

His future actions were not foreseeable, even by himself. It is true that on the train to The Hague he wrote to Colette in what appear to have been unequivocal terms. She had been dear and loving to him ever since Lulworth, and he felt that nothing could now ever come between them. However, he omitted one detail; that Miss Black, who had been spending the autumn in Paris on her Fellowship work, was also travelling to The Hague, ostensibly to read manuscripts in the library; actually, as he wrote to Ottoline, in order to be with him. Important, of course, but it could all be shuttled to the back of his mind to make way for Wittgenstein and philosophy.

They had been at The Hague a week when Wittgenstein arrived – accompanied by Arvid Sjögren, apparently his close companion. He stayed for seven days and throughout each of them discussed his manuscript with Russell. "I came to think even better of it than I had done," Russell wrote to Ottoline before leaving Holland. "I feel sure it is a really great book, though I do not feel sure it is right. I told him I could not refute it, & that I was sure it was either all right or all wrong, which I consider the mark of a good book; but it would take me years to decide which. This of course didn't satisfy him, but I couldn't say more."

The fundamental idea of the *Tractatus*, which Russell mulled over with Wittgenstein in the lounge of the Hotel des Deux Villes, was that philosophical problems sprang basically from a misunderstanding of the logic of language, since everyday language failed to reveal its logical structure completely. In Gilbert Ryle's words, Wittgenstein had generalized the departmental conclusion provided by Russell's Theory of Descriptions: "All logic and all philosophy are enquiries into what makes it significant or nonsensical to say certain things. The sciences aim at saying what is true about the world; philosophy aims at disclosing only the logic of what can be truly or even falsely said about the world." However, with the use of symbolic logic, it was possible to conceive of a language whose logic would be completely known; and if this language were used, then the problems of traditional philosophy would be seen to be nonexistent. But it did not end there. Wittgenstein's reduction of the problems of philosophy to semantics also meant the reduction of mathematics to tautologies, since every mathematical proof was merely a tautological transformation of what was contained in its premisses. Or, as Russell put it thirty years later, "All mathematical proof consists merely in saying in other words part or the whole of what is said in the premisses."

Neither of these two conclusions was agreeable to Russell. "I found Wittgenstein's 'Tractatus' very earnest and this implied a genuine philosophical outlook in its author," he was to write. "I did not appreciate that his work implied a linguistic philosophy. When I did we parted company ... I felt a violent repulsion to the suggestion that 'all mathematics is tautology'. I came to believe this but I did not like it. I thought that mathematics was a splendid edifice, but this shows that it was built on sand."

Wittgenstein left The Hague a few days before Christmas with his manuscript, Russell's encouragement and an offer to write an introduction. When he received it, he objected vehemently and told his friend Engelman, "My book will probably not be printed, as I could not bring myself to have it published with Russell's introduction, which looks even more impossible in translation than it does in the original ... " To Russell himself he protested, "All the refinement of your English style was, obviously, lost in the translation and what remained was superficiality and misunderstanding."

By June, five German publishers had turned down the book. Then, apparently in desperation, Wittgenstein told Russell that if he could arrange publication in England he could have the manuscript. It arrived as Russell was about to leave England once again, and he passed it over to Dorothy Wrinch, who was asked to do her best to find a publisher. The Cambridge University Press rejected it, but Wilhelm Ostwald, the ageing Russo-German physical chemist, then editor of *Annalen der Naturphilosophie*, agreed to publish, and the *Tractatus* finally appeared in German in the issue of autumn 1921.

Before Wittgenstein left The Hague, Russell heard that Trinity had invited him back. "There is eagerness for your lectures on the part of an overwhelming majority of the education staff," Hollond told him in a gloss on the official news from the Master, "and I feel sure that those who do not share this feeling will stand loyally by the decision which has been arrived at."

For Russell it raised problems, since it was not only truth-functions which he had been discussing in The Hague. He had been planning his future, this time with Miss Black. "The present intention is, as soon as possible to begin a common life, with the hope of children," he wrote to Ottoline on 20 December.

> This is not a sudden idea. We discussed it at Lulworth and decided to think it over while she was in Paris. There are outward difficulties – her people, Girton, Trinity (which has asked me back). These are serious, but I am satisfied that there are no difficulties as far as she and I are concerned – I believe (tho' it is rash to prophesy) that you would like her very much. There is a complete absence of the usual academic faults – there is courage, adventurousness, love of colour, unbounded generosity and gentleness. And at the same time very good brains and the most delicious wit. After this, you will at least believe that I care for her.

Whether the "common life" was to include marriage is not mentioned, although Russell later wrote, "We both thought that marriage should be compatible with minor affairs ... and at the end of 1919 we made a compact in writing to the effect that we would mutually tolerate them. But

I stipulated that if she should have a child that was not mine there should be a divorce."

He ended his explanatory letter with the information that he was leaving The Hague that night and that his address for the next fortnight would be the Cottage Hotel, Lynton, where he would be staying with Allen. In London he found a letter from Colette. "Beloved, I'm wanting to stroke your heathery head," it said. "But there's not long to wait now. A thousand welcomes back – from your Colette." Indeed there was not long to wait. Russell had omitted to tell Ottoline that while Allen would be with him at Lynton, Colette would also be there.

The three of them arrived on 22 December, and stayed for nearly three weeks. Throughout the Christmas, walking on the cliffs, and in the snug parlour of the Cottage Hotel, Russell discussed at length with Colette his possible future with Miss Black; the future of a man desperately uncertain of himself, torn between his simple passions but also anxious to cause as little unhappiness as possible. For Colette, the discussion was bearable only because it was plain that Russell's own mind was not yet irrevocably made up. Moreover, the situation favoured her. In all struggles for control, absence is a handicap, and while Colette was present in Lynton, Miss Black was absent in Paris. The effect on Russell, a subtle change in his attitude, was conveyed by two letters to Ottoline, who had already given the new liaison with Miss Black her affectionate blessing. "As for divorce," Russell told her on 27 December, "I think it will come to that – we have discussed it endlessly – I should like to be free to marry but she dislikes legal matrimony, which seems to me very rational – so things are still in some doubt." They continued that way and shortly afterwards he wrote, "I don't think I can avoid going to Cambridge for at least a year, and that of course entails respectability." Eventually he accepted the offer from Trinity while still uncertain of his long-term plans.

"My dearest O.," he wrote, "I forgot to say in so many words that of *course* anything that happens with regard to Dora Black will not interfere with our friendship in any way whatsoever." His relations with Colette, he went on, continued "tho' in the nature of things they will grow less intimate with time". But, he added, "all plans are quite uncertain as yet – so many different things have to be considered."

Within the year anything might happen, and to Colette it at first appeared to be happening very quickly. For, on returning to London, Russell found a letter from Paris whose contents he relayed to Colette: Miss Black now thought that a career would be preferable to rearing a family – in which case he would break off relations with her. But by the following evening the situation had been restored. A cable from Miss Black told him to ignore her letters. She was, after all, willing to raise a family.

The start of 1920 thus found Russell still emotionally bedevilled: in love with Colette yet desperately aware of the more practical advantages of life with Dora; only partly helped by the worldly advice of Ottoline, talking to him over their dinner tête-à-têtes like understanding aunt to disturbed nephew. "His mind is rather wearing him out, beating itself against its bars – his hunger for companionship – and his mind works like a steel rasping machine – and shakes him too much without diversion," she confided to Mark Gertler. "I am now to write to him once a fortnight and have just written him four pages in tiny hand-writing and my hand aches so from having done it and my *mind* aches too."

Early in the year Colette was on tour again and for a few weeks she and Russell batted their passions to and fro through the post in an exhausting volley. To her he poured out his troubles about Dora, the would-be Empress of all the Russells as Colette described her. To him, from the cheap hotels of the small touring company, she sent an unquenchable flow of love-letters, reminiscent, passionate and deeply moving. She was rewarded by the news that Russell and Dora had made up their differences.

For him, work was the great healer and he enjoyed a political lecture-tour in Scotland, addressing enthusiastic audiences in Edinburgh, Clydebank, Paisley and Glasgow. He spent five days in Paris, meeting Romain Rolland and signing his appeal for European peace. Then he thankfully accepted an invitation to lecture at the Catalan University in Barcelona, and decided to give them his lectures on "The Analysis of Mind". Before leaving England he wrote Colette a letter which brought the reply that it had frozen her: "I'm alone, existence is painful, and it takes considerable effort not to go under," she wrote. "If I hadn't work I certainly shouldn't manage not to. Beyond struggling to keep my head above water, I'm paralysed. Forgive these clichés." But she sent ahead a cable to welcome him to Barcelona. He arrived with Dora and, lectures completed, travelled on with her to Majorca. But, he wrote back to England, it was of Colette that he dreamed each night.

Russell returned to London in the early spring of 1920 to find that a three-year-old ambition might at last be fulfilled. Ever since the Russian Revolution he had been anxious to discover what was really happening beyond the battles of the interventionist forces and the struggles of the White Armies to put the clock back. So far, there had been scant chance of this. But now plans were being made for a Labour delegation to visit the Soviet Union and Russell found it possible to go with it. His enthusiasm for the great new experiment was at white heat and as he made preparations for the visit he wrote a long article for the New York *Liberator* supporting the new Bolshevik government. It contained qualifications but could nevertheless be reprinted under the headline "Bertrand Russell Goes Bolshevik". When he returned from Russia weeks later, almost completely disillusioned, his statements were "still floating like a flag almost from the masthead of all the pro-Bolshevik publications throughout the western world". He had a difficult task hauling it down.

The day before he left England, Colette met him at Lewes for one of their long, carefree walks. On the Downs he asked her, "I suppose you wouldn't come to Russia?" He knew what her answer would be; he would have been as embarrassed as elated by a "Yes". In the train to the coast the following morning he wrote one of his impromptu passionate letters declaring that the memory of their last day and night together would serve him during the long Russian journey. He wrote again from Bergen, and again from Oslo. In Stockholm he received her cables of love and affection.

And from Stockholm, last port of call before entering Russia, he wrote to Ottoline, "I feel sure I shall have an extraordinarily interesting time, & see everybody I want to see. Probably it will have a great effect upon me – but what effect I don't know. The only thing I feel sure of is that Trinity High Table will feel very funny after Russia. I don't believe I shall like even my best friends among dons." On 10 May he crossed the frontier.

Russell's visit to the Soviet Union was to affect his political beliefs and his public image as radically as the break with Alys had affected his private life. He entered Russia in a mood of almost unqualified optimism; he left it with a detestation of Communism that isolated him from many of his Socialist friends and was to last the remainder of his life. Two things should be said about the transformation which prepared the way for his attitude towards preventive war in the later 1940s. The first is that it did not spring exclusively from his philosophical reluctance to accept, with Plato, that the State should be master over man, or from the impression of bureaucratic inefficiency which affronted his tidy mind. A more fundamental reason, and one which points to the heart of his character, was distress at the spiritual vacuum he saw as the price of Communism. "I am infinitely unhappy in this atmosphere," he wrote from Petrograd, " – stifled by its utilitarianism, its indifference to love and beauty and the life of impulse. I cannot give that importance to man's merely animal needs that is given here by those in power." In different circumstances he might have weighed the arguments differently. But strung up as he was with his own emotional problems, it was more than he could do to assess objectively the way things looked to a population exchanging one tyranny for another. Thus it seems almost certain that the personal view of conditions which set hard in his mind not only was that of the outsider but was considerably more critical – if more percipient of the future – than that of most Russians. They saw the upheaval of history in 1920 as the least objectionable alternative in a world that offered only a choice between evils; Russell saw it as a lurch towards dictatorship by the Commissars which would be quite as bad as dictatorship by the Tsars.

Even so, his dedicated anti-Communism, expressed immediately on his return to England, and retained almost unqualified through the years, is more critical than the day-to-day journal made during his journey in Russia. Writing later of the disease and famine which, with the other two Horsemen, were riding roughshod through the country during those awful months, he makes little allowance for the aftermath of the First World War, for the battles of the civil war still raging in the Caucasus, the Baltic and Siberia, or for the fact, acknowledged in his resignation from the No-Conscription Fellowship, that there are times when battery and barricade are justified. In his journal, which has a quality of immediacy he never quite recaptured, the balance is held more finely. The cruel dogmas of the State are not condoned but are at least partly attributed to the brute necessity of the times.

The British delegation included Mrs Snowden, Clifford Allen, Robert Williams (Secretary of the National Transport Workers Federation) and Tom Shaw (soon to be Minister of Labour in the first Socialist Government), with Haden Guest as medical adviser. From the start, the party responded in conflicting ways to the banquets and ballets, the tours and the concerts. Emma Goldman, the American anarchist and journalist then in Russia, wrote,

> Most members of the mission fell for the show and became the more pliable the longer they stayed ... There were certain members of the British Mission, however, not entirely inclined to look in open-mouthed wonder at the things about them, with their mental eyes shut. These were not of the labouring element. One of them was Mr. Bertrand Russell. Very polite but decisively he ... from the very first refused to be officially chaperoned. He preferred to go about himself. He also showed no elation over the honour of being quartered in a palace and fed on special morsels. Suspicious person, that Russell, the Bolsheviki whispered. But then, what can you expect of a *bourgeois*?

A similar impression was registered by Marguerite Harrison, another member of the delegation. "In spite of his profession of Socialism," she says, "Russell was essentially an aristocrat. His thin, hawk-like profile, his slender hands and feet, and the indescribable air of breeding about him proclaimed the fact. He could not mix with the proletarians and there was an air of aloofness about him."

They arrived in Petrograd on 12 May. "View over Neva to Peter-&-Paul from windows of palace extraordinarily beautiful," Russell wrote.

> After late breakfast taken to see trade union central offices, a former aristocratic girls' school. Then drive in motors round the town and

> through suburbs to the sea. The town seemed a city of the dead, nearly all shops closed, big houses empty, roads full of great holes, no traffic except trams & a few army waggons. Completely opposite impression in the evenings: vast dinner & reception for us & a Swedish deputation of metal workers, given by trade unions; followed by singing, dancing and music, extraordinarily beautiful, full of vigour & life. The same impression in their painting, which we saw in a museum during the afternoon, & sp. "The Dead Communist". There is no doubt that their art is wonderful, & that, at the slightest opportunity, they are full of joy of life & a certain strange creative energy, unlike anything I have seen before.

The following day he met the President of the Petrograd Philosophical Society and three of its members. In his autobiography, Russell describes their pathetic appearance; in rags, unshaven and unkempt. But his account written after the meeting is more revealing.

> None like the Communists. Yet all agreed that there is no hope except in peace, & that the rigid orthodoxy & control which they dislike is due to the national peril. All said that the present atmosphere is good for research, & that admirable work is being done. Bloch stated that art has to be taught from a Marxian point of view; nevertheless he is now lecturing on rhythmics at the popular university, & he never got a chance of lecturing on the subject under the old regime. His proletarian pupils insist upon his teaching the subject *au fond*, not popularly, & he finds them admirable. One of them stated that lectures in metaphysics are not allowed in the university, on the ground that there is no such subject, & science is the only thing. Much to be said for this view.

Yet one of the mathematicians, he later wrote, told him that there was a university Soviet which gave each charwoman an equal voice with the professor in determining the mathematical curriculum. "I am a democrat, but ..." he protested.

The delegation spent five days in Petrograd, interviewing trade union officials, visiting factories, trying to understand in a few days what had eluded permanent observers for years. Some contrasted the poverty of the streets with the gargantuan banquets arranged in their honour; others carefully ignored the contrast.

According to Marguerite Harrison, Russell was theoretically interested in the Russian experiment. "Actually, he was revolted by the popular demonstrations, the crude propaganda and the misery and squalor of life in Soviet Russia," she says. "We wandered about together in the villages collecting information from the peasants. Russell took notes industriously, but he did not have the journalist's capacity for minute observation. He soon grew weary of collecting material and we frequently strolled off for long walks into the country while the other members were interviewing Communist officials or inspecting Children's Homes." But he nevertheless had an alert eye for some detail and indelibly registered the sight of a Commissar smuggling milk for his children in his official car; an illustration, he said years later, of how the instinct to provide for one's own family would bring down Communism's promises of equality and brotherhood.

He visited Maxim Gorky, consumptive and speaking with pain between fits of coughing: "He said he was more international than any Englishman could understand. I thought his opinions seemed exactly the same as mine." Summing up a few hours before the party moved on to Moscow, he wrote, "I feel that all they [the Soviet Government] have done is right for Russia, but none of it would succeed in the West. Admiration, not imitation."

In Moscow, between the acts of *Prince Igor*, he met Trotsky. "Very Napoleonic impression," he wrote in his journal.

> Bright eyes, military bearing, lightning intelligence, magnetic personality. Exceedingly good-looking, which surprised me. Would be irresistible to women, & an agreeable lover while his passion lasted. I felt a vein of gay good-humour so long as he was not crossed in any way. Ruthless, not cruel. Admirable wavy hair. Vanity even greater than love of power: the vanity of an artist or actor. He came back with us into our box. When the audience saw him, they gave a great ovation – quite spontaneous, we all thought. He stood in Napoleonic attitude while they cheered; then spoke a few words, short & sharp, full of transitional energy, & called for three cheers for the brave fellows at the front. 1914 over again; but without the hope engendered by communism, I think it would be impossible to revive this mood in a war-weary nation. Conversation banal.

Russell attended a meeting of the Praesidium, heard ordinary people in the Moscow streets complaining of the cost of living, and noted, "just as in England". He visited a group of Tolstoy adherents, mainly to discuss the position of conscientious objectors. "Almost exactly as in England," he wrote. "Good law, bad tribunals. Differences: some absolute exemptions have been granted; the Society of Tolstoyans is invited by Govt. to examine objectors & give certificate of genuineness, which it does, tho' some think it shouldn't & some won't come before it or any other tribunal; about 15 Tolstoyans have been shot" – a final comment that even Russell, however hard his thoughts of Derby and Lloyd George, must have found hard to square with "Almost exactly as in England".

On the evening of 19 May he was granted an hour's interview with Lenin. He wrote in his journal,

> His room is very bare – a big desk, some maps on the walls, 2 bookcases, one easy chair, for visitors. Throughout the time I was there, a sculptor was working on a bust of him. Conversation in English, very fairly good. He is friendly & apparently simple – entirely without a trace of *hauteur*, a great contrast to Trotsky. Nothing in his manner or bearing suggests the man who has power. He looks at his visitor very close, & screws up one eye. He laughs a great deal; at first, his laugh seems merely friendly & jolly, but gradually one finds it grim. He is dictatorial, calm, incapable of fear, devoid of self-seeking, an embodied theory. The materialist conception of history is his lifeblood. He resembles a professor in his desire to have the theory understood & in his fury with those who misunderstand or disagree; also in his love of expounding. I put three questions to him. (1) I asked whether & how far he recognized the peculiarity of English conditions. The answer was unsatisfactory to me. He admits that there is little chance of revolution now, & that the working man is not yet disgusted with Parliamentary government. He hopes this result may be brought about by a Labour Ministry, particularly if Henderson is premier. But when I suggested that whatever is possible in England may occur without bloodshed, he waved aside the suggestion as fantastic. I got little impression of knowledge or psychological imagination. (2) I asked him whether he thought it possible to establish communism firmly & fully in a country containing such a large majority of peasants. He admitted it was difficult. He laughed over the exchange the peasant is compelled to make, of food for paper – the worthlessness of Russian paper struck him as comic. But he said things would right themselves when there are goods to offer to the peasant. For this he looks partly to electrification in industry, which he says is a technical necessity in Russia & will take 10 years; but chiefly he looks to the raising of the blockade. He said that as late as July 1917 the Bolsheviks were not only persecuted, but even assaulted by the Moscow mob. He said that very few understand the theory of the gov't., but that many support it out of instinct. I got the impression that he despises the populace & is an intellectual aristocrat.
>
> He described the division between rich & poor peasants, & the government propaganda among the latter against the former – leading often (as he suggested with a great laugh) to the rich peasant being hanged on the nearest tree, or meeting some such fate. He seemed to think that the dictatorship over the peasant would have to continue a long time, because of the peasant's desire for free trade.

He spoke with glee of the advantages the government had gained from the harshness of Kolchak & Denikin. He said he knew from statistics that the peasants have had more to eat these last two years than they had before, "& yet", he said, "they are against us" – but in this he was only speaking of the rich peasants, I imagine. I asked him what to reply to critics who say that in the country he has merely created peasant proprietorship, not communism; he said that was not quite the truth, but he did not say what the truth is. (3) I asked him whether resumption of trade with capitalist countries would not create centres of capitalist influence, & make the preservation of communism more difficult. He admitted that it would create difficulties, but said they would be less than those of the war. He said that 2 years ago neither he nor his colleagues thought they could survive against the hostility of the world. He attributes their survival to the jealousies & divergent interests of the different capitalist nations; also to the power of Bolshevik propaganda. He said the Germans had laughed when the Bolsheviks proposed to combat guns with leaflets, but that the event had proved the leaflets quite as powerful. I don't think he recognizes that the Labour & Socialist parties have had any part in the matter. He likes Northcliffe's attacks on him, & wants to send N. a medal for Bolshevik propaganda. Accusations of spoliation, he says, may shock the bourgeois, but have an opposite effect on the proletarian. – I think if I had met him without knowing who he was I should not have guessed that he was a great man, but should have thought him an opinionated professor. His strength comes, I imagine, from his honesty, courage, & unwavering faith – religious faith in Marxian orthodoxy, which takes the place of the Xtian martyrs' hopes of Paradise, except that it is less egotistical. He has as little love of liberty as the men who suffered under Diocletian & retaliated (on heretical Xtians) when they acquired power. Says "Herald" completely misunderstands dictatorship of proletariat. Laughs at Cole for believing in Soviets without dictatorship.

Later Russell was singled out by Kamenev, President of the Moscow Soviet, and taken for the night to his country house. Here the two men discussed Russia's next step, and in his journal Russell gives a long objective account of their conversation. Only at one point do his feelings show through. Kamenev explained how the Soviets were dealing with the Mohammedans of Turkestan. "It seemed to me possible that a complete solution of the problem had been found, & that a socialist England might deal with India on similar lines," Russell recounted. "But of course India is more populous than Turkestan, & has a stronger indigenous culture. I felt a certain unconscious imperialist tone in his talk on this subject."

Then the party left Moscow for a long steamer-trip down the Volga.

During the voyage Clifford Allen fell ill with pneumonia; most of the delegation left the boat at Saratov, but Russell, Mrs Snowden and Haden Guest remained on board to nurse the invalid. At Astrakhan on the Caspian Sea – "more like hell than anything I had ever imagined" – Allen was given two days to live. Finally, a fortnight later, he was convoyed out of Russia to Reval, barely alive.

Another week and Russell was back in Stockholm. He immediately wrote to Ottoline. "Partly owing to [Allen's] illness but more because I loathed the Bolsheviks, the time in Russia was infinitely painful to me, in spite of being one of the most interesting things I have ever done," he said.

> Bolshevism is a close tyrannical bureaucracy, with a spy system more elaborate and terrible than the Tsar's, and an aristocracy as insolent and unfeeling, composed of Americanised Jews. No vestige of liberty remains, in thought or speech or action. I was stifled and oppressed by the weight of the machine as by a cope of lead. Yet I think it the right Government for Russia at this moment. If you ask yourself how Dostoevsky's characters should be governed, you will understand. Yet it is terrible. They are a nation of artists, down to the simplest peasant; the aim of the Bolsheviks is to make them industrial and as Yankee as possible. Imagine yourself governed in every detail by a mixture of Sidney Webb and Rufus Isaacs, and you will have a picture of modern Russia. I went hoping to find the promised land.

In these sentences, Leonard Woolf remarked, Russell obtained "the best of all his worlds – dislike and hatred of Americans, Jews, and even his personal friends".

The accusation is less unfair than it sounds. In no sense an anti-Semite – as his writings make abundantly clear – Russell nevertheless sometimes exhibited a personal allergy to Jews which is betrayed in his private correspondence from time to time, lasted until the 1930s, and should not be brushed under the carpet. It dissolved quickly as Hitler rose to power, and before the end of the Second World War Russell saw the creation of a Jewish state as essential to post-war peace.

In 1920 his disillusion with Bolshevik Russia welled up in the tranquil security of neutral Sweden where the contrast between Russia and Democracy hit him between the eyes. It was soon reinforced by the annoyances, if no more, of the situation he now found awaiting him.

He had telegraphed Dora Black from the port of Reval on the Gulf of Bothnia but had received no reply. Now, in Stockholm, he heard from friends that she was in the same city. Then came more definite news. "Miss Black, against my wishes, set out in pursuit of me, missed me, & is now travelling round by Murmansk," he wrote to Allen. "I only discovered this yesterday evening ... Heaven help her! I am too sorry for her to be angry." But he realized that she might be put in prison, a possibility which worried him. However, "there was nothing one could do about it, so I came back to England, where I endeavoured to recover some kind of sanity, the shock of Russia having been almost more than I could bear", he wrote. The action had its implications. Russell lacked neither physical nor moral courage and the return to England suggests that his feeling for Miss Black was something less than that of the ardent suitor.

He arrived back in London at the end of June. Colette was waiting for him on the platform and they drove to his Battersea flat, festively decked out with fresh bunches of the same lilies she had sent him in prison two years previously.

He was ready to take a deep breath, politically and emotionally. Russia had been brutally disillusioning, the revolution of his ideals no more than a squalid nightmare. Almost as bad, there was the example of Clifford Allen, the paladin of the No-Conscription movement on whose behalf Russell had struggled and spoken and written for so many weary months when he had other things to do. Outside the Soviet Union, Allen would, he feared, quickly forget the critical opinions of Allen inside. The fears were justified. Within three days of his return, Allen was writing that he and Russell were "for the first time in [their] lives ... like two cats, fighting bitterly over Russia".

If Russell was now even more deeply concerned about the post-war world, his personal life still presented its own intractable problems. Always prone to ups and downs, he could be kept from damaging vacillations only by such sedatives as a long, planned programme of work; a background of chronic unhappiness to which he could resign himself; or, when luck went his way, a years-long, if tempestuous relationship such as that with Ottoline.

No such sedatives were now available; indeed, all ahead looked particularly feverish. After the years of miscellaneous experience with Ottoline, Helen Dudley, Colette and Dora, he was no longer willing to retire into the celibate agony which had helped to give birth to the *Principia*. Ottoline would never become a phantom for him – "I shall come back from the other side of the world, perhaps happier, but not changed towards you," he was soon to write – but she would never be the reliable mistress for all seasons. As for his future with Colette or with Dora, it presented an uncomfortable choice between ecstatic happiness tinged with a poetry he never found elsewhere, and a family affair more likely to give him the children he longed for, the heir he felt it his duty to provide.

None of these unsettling circumstances helped in the weeks ahead. They explain his irresolution, the distraught contradictory actions which at first glance have all the signs of a man playing a double game with two women. The truth is otherwise but no less uncomfortable. Russell, the steel-cold philosopher forced into deciding his future, now displayed the human failings of the over-passionate man, more buffeted by emotion than others and responding with more haphazard indecision.

In his flat, he and Colette opened the post which had accumulated during his absence in Russia. There was much political material, letters from Cambridge friends, a long letter from Ottoline. There was an offer from a London publisher to take anything he wrote at a starting royalty of twenty per cent, a pointer to the way his literary stock had risen but an offer that Stanley Unwin quickly castigated as an effort by "competitors who would probably not have considered your work during the war ... to tempt you away from us".

There was also a letter from the Chinese Lecture Association which invited one foreigner to China each year. Would Russell visit Peking University and give a year's course of lectures, it asked? Russell's instinct was to wait before committing himself. He wanted first to think out the horror of Russia. He wanted rest, and he wanted to be alone with Colette, who would be free until her next tour in July. But he decided, in principle, that he had to go.

With Dr Haden Guest he now prepared for the *Lancet* an account of the difficulties experienced with the Russian authorities following Clifford Allen's illness. Then he wrote to Ottoline saying how heavenly it was "to be back among people who are sane and kindly. Russia seemed like an asylum of homicidal lunatics, where the warders are the worst lunatics. It is very hard to keep one's sanity."

He now left London with Colette for a week in the isolation of Rye. They stayed at the Mermaid Inn and walked each day on the marshes between Appledore and Winchelsea, pushing the future and the coming year of separation into the back of their minds. "Every moment together was perfect from first to last," Colette wrote on their return. "And I've added that straight white road, past Stone-on-Oxney, to my imperishable store. I feel you still beside me, I see your hair glinting against the Winchelsea sky. You have my whole and undivided heart, now and forever."

Back in London Russell found Allen, better in health than he had expected and, as he had feared, still praising Russia. "He has half forgotten what he felt about the Bolshies while he was there, and will soon be quite in favour of them, I expect," he wrote to Ottoline. He also heard from Dora, who had succeeeded in getting to Russia under her own steam; learned to his disgust that she "loved the Bolshies" as fervently as Allen; and wrote to Colette with the news that he might break for good with Dora. Two days later he formally accepted the invitation to Peking, having already asked Trinity for a year's leave of absence from the Lectureship due to start in October.

Allen increased Russell's restlessness with London, to him as dreadful a place now as it had seemed after Lulworth; its effect intensified the deep-down misgivings which filled him now that he had decided on the voyage out. Only at Garsington did he find a haven where he could sit and think, take stock, and dare to face the future. From that refuge he wrote to Colette on 24 July, half in hope, half in despair, a long spontaneous letter filling page after page of Ottoline's elegant, narrow writing-paper with his impressions of Russia, "a world of dying beauty and harsh life". Did not the hunger and want that powered the revolutionary forces in themselves narrow the horizon, lessen the chances of successful reform? "But an uneasy doubt remains, and I am torn in two ..." But one doubt was dispelled. On the last page Russell comes to his feelings for Colette, the woman whose love will be beside him till the crack of doom, through all sorrow and all disaster. Here at last was certainty, an area swept more clean of doubt than any he had found even in the heroic world of mathematics. Thus set, he prepared for China.

At the Attic, to which Colette was soon to return, he left a suitcase packed with the letters she had written to him since their first meeting almost exactly four years previously. With it was a note reminding her to bring it to the West End hotel, where he had asked her to provide Alys's lawyers with the evidence for divorce proceedings. For now, after a quarter-century, he had briefed his lawyer, Charles Sanger, and Sanger had written to Alys. "A divorce will be a relief," Russell confided to Gilbert Murray. "Hitherto it would always have interfered greatly with my work; now it won't. The law is certainly very ridiculous ..." Alys no doubt agreed. "I have always felt it would be better for both of us to be divorced," she replied, "though I very much dislike the hypocrisy involved."

Colette arrived back in London early in August and came as arranged to the London hotel. The following morning, she was off to Portsmouth. Within hours, Russell was grasping at the chance of another meeting, pleading that she should take the midnight train from Portsmouth or, if necessary, have herself driven up to London through the night. There was an urgent criss-cross of telegrams, proposing and rejecting dates, as he struggled with preparations for China and she moved on tour from town to town. He wondered in his letters to her why he had ever decided to accept Peking, so awful was it to live apart from the person one loved. On 4 August, he wrote again, assuaging any fear that his love for her would ever dim or that anything could keep him from her if she wanted him.

On 4 August he also wrote to Ottoline, arranging for her to meet Dora, now due in four days' time. "I haven't seen her for so long, and so much has happened to us both, that we shall meet almost as strangers," he said. "I rather dread it. Perhaps after five minutes we shall no longer be on speaking terms." But he made no bones about the fact that if all went well she would be coming with him to China. Marriage was another matter. "I don't feel much disposed to [it]," he wrote. "In any case it would be impossible till after my return from Peking, which is just as well."

Dora arrived in London on the 8th. From the first, she and Russell sank their differences. "I am very happy," he told Ottoline; "my feeling for Dora has become a more profound one since her return – before that we were always in difficulties about Colette and I never got the best out of her – also Russia has brought out the best." It was now decided that Dora would come with him to China and before leaving they provided his lawyers with evidence for a divorce. Nevertheless he continued to write to Colette, stressing how difficult the long parting would be, how much he loved her.

Meanwhile he learned that the boat for China would be leaving Marseilles a fortnight late. He refused to stay in London, ostensibly because he could not work easily there, more probably because he mistrusted his emotions if he delayed departure. Instead he would spend the time in Paris and, as he wrote to Stanley Unwin, try to write a short book on Bolshevism. He confirmed that he would be happy with the usual terms, although adding, "I should be grateful if you could let me have £25 on account of royalties now instead of on publication. My reason for suggesting this is that I find expenses connected with going to Peking unexpectedly heavy, whereas when I get there I shall be well off." Unwin obliged by return.

The book was *The Practice and Theory of Bolshevism*, an uncompromising account of his Russian experiences. Early on, he had given Unwin a percipient warning: "I expect universal abuse," he said, "but that won't do the book any harm in the long run." He was right on both counts. To his sister-in-law Russell later wrote that the book had "involved being quarrelled with by most of my friends, & praised by people I hate – e.g. Winston & Lloyd George". But it was certainly a success, and twenty years later Unwin wrote that it could be reprinted without change. Russell himself had mixed views, and as early as 1923 advised, with a touch of lordly grandeur, that it should not be kept in print. "The book deals with a situation which ended with the adoption of N.E.P. [New Economic Policy], in advocating which Lenin adopted all my criticisms of Bolshevik policy," he said. "Even the theoretical part of the book seems like flogging a dead horse since the Bolsheviks have ceased to advocate world-revolution."

With only hours to go in London, he achieved a minor triumph. Dora's people, he informed Ottoline, "are coming to the station to see us off and give the family blessing! They accepted me as if I were a son-in-law, though they are in no way advanced." On the same day Colette, who now knew that he would not be alone, wrote to him from the provinces. "My heart is gone to you: it is the Brixton feeling, of danger, of some kind of death. But I'm still glad for your sake that you're going. It will all be so strange, the ancient beauty of China, and the Chinese gaiety of spirit which you'll love. And I'm glad that you won't feel lonely, but you will have someone to warm your heart." She bought a large map of the world on which to follow his journey. She posted a batch of messages addressed to him at various points *en route* to the East. "There will be a letter for you at every port of call," said a farewell telegram. "So always ask. Good luck. I can't bear to say goodbye."

He had met her first only four years previously. He was to see her only once again in the next eight. But as Sir Frederick and Lady Black watched him and their daughter depart from Waterloo, he might this time have quoted Arnold back to Colette – "I go, Fate drives me, but I leave half of my life with you."

Arrived in Paris, Russell and Dora Black had a fortnight to wait before catching the boat at Marseilles, and once again he began to make emotional ends meet. His semi-frantic and often contradictory letters to Ottoline during the previous few weeks indicate that he had been in two minds about taking Dora to China, that he had resolved to let circumstances decide and had then, following her return to London, accepted the situation and persuaded himself that there could be corners in his life for both Dora and Colette – as well, of course, as a special enclave for Ottoline. But at the back of his mind there had still remained doubts; they dissolved in the atmosphere of Paris. "I am quite extraordinarily happy," he wrote to Ottoline; "no qualms about the future. Everything has worked out right as if by a miracle."

His only qualms were about the book on Soviet Russia. He had finished it in a hurry but only now decided to go ahead with publication. The upshot was a book whose tone and judgments were epitomized in two sentences. "One who believes, as I do, that the free intellect is the chief engine of human progress, cannot but be fundamentally opposed to Bolshevism as much as to the Church of Rome. The hopes which inspire communism are, in the main, as admirable as those instilled by the Sermon on the Mount, but they are held as fanatically and are as likely to do as much harm." However, circumstances alter cases. On the voyage out he was asked by passengers to speak on Russia. "In view of the sort of people that they were," he has written, "I said only favourable things about the Soviet Government."

The voyage from Marseilles lasted nearly six weeks and in the heat of the Red Sea Russell momentarily began to have second thoughts about Dora. "I was sensitive because of the contempt that [she] had poured on my head for not liking Russia," he later wrote. "I suggested to her that we had made a mistake in coming away together, and that the best way out would be to jump into the sea. This mood, however, which was largely induced by the heat, soon passed."

They called at Singapore, Saigon and Hong Kong, and as they approached China Russell began to write back home. To Colette he protested that she was constantly in his thoughts, that he longed for her arms and her lips. To Ottoline he sent a travelogue giving his first impressions of the Far East:

> [Saigon] is a nightmare place – up a river, absolutely flat, surrounded by swamps in which they grow rice, even hotter by night than by day, full of mosquitoes, bats and large lizards. The Europeans are all enormously rich & very ill – the women drive about in motor cars, gorgeously dressed, rouged, but with hollow cheeks & all suggesting Death. The tropics strike me as cruel & nightmarish – the impression is like "The Heart of Darkness".

In Hong Kong, where Dora's father had once had connections, she was invited to a ball given by the Commodore's wife. "No one seems to mind our relations," Russell observed. A Chinese acquaintance gave them a ceremonial meal near Saigon where they were introduced as "Professor Russell and the very intellectual Miss Black", and Russell noted that this was apparently to be their official style. He had expected that their relationship might cause difficulties and the fact that it failed to do so surprised and almost disappointed him. "It is not literally true that I introduced my present wife as 'Miss Black, my mistress'," he wrote some years later. "I introduced her simply as Miss Black, leaving the rest to be inferred; & she always referred to me simply as Mr. Russell. Some missionaries and such were so anxious (out of curiosity) to see us that they persuaded themselves our relations were 'innocent' even after we had shown them over our house and they knew we had only one bed." Even British officials dealt diplomatically with the situation, smiling outwardly if fuming inwardly. "The Legation people are tumbling over each other to ask us to dinner together," Russell wrote. "What has become of morality? I am quite shocked – I hoped we should avoid conventional people."

His first stops in China created problems for the British Representative in Peking, who on 22 October informed the Foreign Office that Russell had arrived in Shanghai accompanied by a Miss Black. "He is stated to have expressed pro-Bolshevik and anti-British sentiments during the voyage," he added before asking whether he should take action.

Whitehall's response was unequivocal. Russell, it was minuted on the cable from Peking, "though discredited in this country, would certainly prove subversive and dangerous to British interests at a Chinese educational institution where his pronouncements would be decidedly 'ex Cathedra'". To deal with this peril it was at first recommended that the War Powers Order-in-Council might be invoked, since that appeared to give the authorities power to detain and deport him from Shanghai. However, the Foreign Office's Legal Adviser warned that such action would raise a storm of criticism, and pointed out that the Order would soon be superseded anyway. Frank Ashton-Gwatkin, then Second Secretary, brought a final touch of sanity to the situation. "But Bertrand Russell returned from Russia thoroughly disillusioned as to the benefits of Bolshevism," he minuted. "He is a crank and would no doubt antagonise his fellow-passengers and provide ample material for gossip on board ship. But he is a man of great intellectual attainments and of honest purpose." However, the Foreign Office was not beaten yet. "Would it not be possible," Peking was finally asked, "in the event of [Russell] indulging in subversive utterances to arrange for Chinese Government to call your attention to his activities and their deleterious effect upon the public safety?"

The Chinese refused to oblige. But Russell was not forgotten. In a list of murderers, spies and other disreputable characters listed under "Suspected Persons" in a Secret Abstract to the Director of Military Intelligence a few weeks later, Bertrand Russell was No 6. The report made his crime clear. "Stayed at Changsha and lectured to the Chinese on Socialism. He stayed in a Chinese Hotel with a lady who was not his wife. The American Mission entertained them both before this was known."

However, these irregularities lay in the future as they landed at Shanghai. They were met by their interpreter, Yuen Ren Chao, a twenty-eight-year-old Chinese who had recently returned from ten years in the United States to teach mathematics and physics at Tsing Hua College in Peking. "Very nice and good, but quite Americanised, quite Y.M.C.A.," was Russell's description of Chao, who despite his Americanization seems to have viewed Russell as equably as did the rest of his countrymen – "very much what I had expected from photographs and descriptions, except that he looked stronger, taller, and more gracious-mannered than I had thought. He looked like a scholar."

After three hard days in Shanghai during which Russell packed in numberless interviews with Chinese academics, was interviewed by the press, and gave impromptu lectures, he and Dora were taken up-country to Hangchow. "This place is wonderfully beautiful on a lake where poets and Emperors lived for 2,000 years, each adding some element of loveliness," he wrote to Ottoline. "The country is even more humanized & ancient than Italy – the landscape exactly like Chinese pictures – the people all gay and delightful, more full of laughter than any people I have ever known, & as witty as 18th century French people. They accept Dora quite readily."

From Hangchow, where they enjoyed a day's tour of the lake in sedan-chairs, they travelled to Nanking and then up the Yangtze to Hangkow before taking in an educational conference at Changsha on their way to Peking.

In Changsha, they met John Dewey and his wife. Dr Dewey had been invited to China the previous year by the same organization which had invited Russell, and even without the bond that linked two leading philosophers they might have been expected to become friends. Russell in fact reported to Ottoline that the Deweys were kind and helpful; and months later, when Russell was desperately ill in Peking, Dewey did all that he could to help. Nevertheless, references to Dewey in Russell's long letters from China are as conspicuous by their absence as the barking of Holmes's dog in the night. A letter to Ottoline reveals why. "The Americans sprawl all over this place, all convinced of their own righteousness ... The Deweys, who are here, & who got into trouble in America during the war for their liberalism, are as bad as anybody – American imperialists, hating England as Maxse used to hate Germany, & unwilling to face any unpleasant facts. In 1914 I liked Dewey better than any other academic American; now I can't stand him." The dislike was mutual. "Dewey's feelings about Russell", the philosopher Sidney Hook later wrote, "began in China ... What concerned Dewey was Russell's insensitiveness to other people's feelings. He believed that there was a streak of cruelty in Russell and an aristocratic disdain for the sensibilities of other human beings outside his class." The fact that Hook apparently agreed does not invalidate the judgment. But Dewey's attitude may also have been influenced by another factor: Russell's frequent claim that pragmatism, a word that could be used to cover Dewey's own philosophy, was a justification of industrialism and collective enterprise.

Before reaching Peking, where his real work was to begin, Russell sent Ottoline a long diary-record of his travels, asking her to have it typed and sent on to Massingham of the *Nation*. "He can print extracts if he wants to. But if not I can send him something more interesting later, which I should prefer," he said. This insistent eagerness to turn the odd journalistic penny was combined with expediency. Would Ottoline please type a number of copies? "I should like [Clifford] Allen, Elizabeth [Russell] & Colette to have the diary because I haven't time to write," he added.

In Peking, Chao found for them a single-storey house built round a courtyard in the eastern part of the city, and here they settled down with their interpreter. "We have 3 rickshaw boys, one each, a cook, & a boy who acts as parlour-maid & housemaid," Russell reported.

> We have old wiggly Chinese bookshelves, heavy black Chinese chairs, a big divan of the sort they used to use for smoking opium, lovely square tables, all black – we get bright colours for curtains & rugs – the sun shines in & makes it hot, although it is by way of being cold now here. We have stoves, which are the only thing not beautiful. We found lovely things in stacks of lumber, not appreciated. Our Chinese friends are amazed at our not wanting European rubbish! Rugs & silks are lovely here – as is heavy old furniture.

Writing this in the first enthusiasm for new surroundings and new friends, he prepared for a winter of work. But before he got down to it he wrote one important letter. It was to J. J. Thomson, the Master of Trinity: in it Russell burnt his boats with Cambridge, resigning from the Lectureship which he had accepted a year earlier and from which he had already been granted a year's leave of absence. "I resigned," he subsequently explained, "because I was living in open sin."

Among the Peking University staff responsible for Russell's visit was Chang Sung-nien, a professor of mathematical logic. However, Chang was also an ardent Guild Socialist. Russell's *Principles of Social Reconstruction* and his *Roads to Freedom*, as well as *The Problems of Philosophy*, had been published in China, and his selection as guest rested as much on his political views as his professional qualifications. The visit had, indeed, been sponsored by leaders of the Chinputang party, of which it has been written, "The party members' political views were various and included guild socialism, democratic socialism, capitalism, and republican or monarchial constitutionalism. To a certain degree, its leaders' sponsorship of Russell's lectures was conducted in the hope of strengthening their ideological position." But because of his pro-Socialist views – and in spite of his reaction to Russia which was not yet widely appreciated – Russell was also welcomed by the more extreme Left.

In Peking he gave five "official" lectures: on Mathematical Logic, The Analysis of Matter, The Analysis of Mind, The Problems of Philosophy, and On the Structure of Society. The first was delivered to an audience of about fifteen hundred in the university and later lectures were given alternately in the university and the teachers' college. It is reputed that both Mao Tse-tung and Chou En-lai attended. In addition to this regular programme there were also talks on Idealism, causality, relativity and gravitation. Even this was not all, and a place was found for informal talks to small study-groups and seminars. In fact interest was so great that a Society for the Study of Russell was organized and a *Russell Monthly* published.

"We have settled down to a regular life here, very hard working, & most of the work very futile," he told Ottoline shortly before Christmas.

> A great deal of lecturing (by both of us) to students who are eager & enthusiastic, but ignorant & untrained & lazy, expecting knowledge to be pumped into them without effort on their part. A good deal of writing articles in Chinese & Japanese papers. Less social life than at first, but still too much – the Europeans here are mostly old-fashioned & boring, polite to us because they are afraid of what I may say to the Chinese (the Bolsheviks are in touch with them, not *very* far from Peking), but of course really hating us & furious at having to condone our flouting of conventions & decencies. The Chinese

> are infinitely polite & flattering, but one always feels they have secrets, & that they say things to each other of which we get no hint. However, on the whole we live a quiet life.

Dora usually lectured on subjects of a more social or political nature. Chao filled in as translator, and although chosen by the authorities mainly because of his specialist knowledge of mathematics and philosophy, coped adequately in other directions. At times he stumbled, and later recalled that when Dora had been speaking to a large audience at the Women's Normal School, she had mentioned unmarried men and unmarried women. "There being different words in Chinese for 'marry' for men and for women," Chao says, "I happened to use the wrong verbs and it came out something like 'men who have no husbands and women who have no wives' at which the audience roared with laughter."

All seemed to be going well. Certainly things had worked themselves out well with Dora, and Russia was now a subject for debate rather than argument. As for the Chinese, they were already giving Russell a sense of perspective which was to endure. "China did one thing for me that the East is apt to do for Europeans who study it with sensitive sympathy," he wrote in 1944; "it taught me to think in long stretches of time, and not to be reduced to despair by the badness of the present. Throughout the increasing gloom of the past twenty years, this habit has helped to make the world less unendurable than it would otherwise have been."

Nevertheless, a hint of homesickness crept into many of his letters. He loved England with a youthful, romantic love which mocked reason and would have been barely credited by those who vilified him in the First World War and in the 1950s. He was never very happy when long out of the country and his home thoughts from abroad had more than a dash of the Browning whom he despised as a sickly sentimentalist. But it was not Oh, to be in England, merely for the spring, although he enjoyed the scents and sounds of the English countryside as much as anyone. The Russells had long had a hand on the tiller of state. It was unendurable to be out of touch with affairs, and his appeals to Ottoline for news of what was going on at home reflect a feeling that China, whatever its advantages, was really on the edge of the world.

Although it was a good life, by the first weeks of 1921 the advantages were beginning to wear a trifle thin. Russell was a man of moods, giving in China a hint of the weathercock judgment that in later years was sometimes to cause confusion. News of the Irish troubles caused him to long for even deeper retreat from the world. "People seem good while they are oppressed, but they only wish to become oppressors in their turn," he said; "life is nothing but a competition to be the criminal rather than the victim. The world is rushing down into barbarism, & there seems nothing to do but keep alive civilisation in one's corner, as the Irish did in the 7th and 8th centuries. So I study Einstein & dream of retiring to a Buddhist monastery in the hills."

A few weeks later Russell is another man. He told Ottoline,

> We are both very happy here, but one couldn't stay here for ever unless one were prepared to retire from the world. It is not here that important things begin. And one can't get books or information about them, so that one would stagnate mentally. We read the papers carefully & manage to keep more or less up-to-date in politics, but in literature & science it is quite impossible. And it would be unendurable never to see one's friends again.

On 14 March he was driven a hundred miles south of Peking to speak on education at the Yu Te Middle School in Paoting. "It was still wintry and windy and he lectured as usual without an overcoat while I shivered beside him even with my overcoat on," says Chao. Shortly afterwards, taking tea before the drive back to Peking, Russell began to feel cold. The decision to return at once was followed by a series of mishaps. First they had a puncture. Then the car refused to start. When they reached Peking the gates were shut and an hour's telephoning was needed before they were opened.

Russell, now running a high temperature, was taken first to the Legation to be cared for by Dr Dipper of the German Hospital and later to the hospital itself. Here double pneumonia was diagnosed. His condition quickly deteriorated and by the 26th he was being given oxygen. A diary entry made by his interpreter Chao that evening shows his condition. "Prof. Dewey made out form for Mr. Rus. to sign," it runs. "He could mutter 'power of attorney?' (to Dora Black that is), then tried to sign. The doctor was afraid 'er kenn nicht'. But he did scribble out B. Russell. He could recognise me and called me in, whispered 'Mr. Ch'. He called Dewey by name and said 'I hope all my friends will stick by me'."

The next day he was worse, and Dr Dipper abandoned hope. He would have died then had not a young but undaunted doctor refused to be beaten, taken over treatment, and slowly began to pull him back from the precipice. Dora, who was caring for him by day while the only English professional nurse in Peking took over at night, was constantly pestered by Japanese journalists since they had planned to return *via* Japan where Russell was to lecture. "At last," he later said, "she became a little curt with them." He was then reported dead in a Japanese paper. The news was immediately cabled to America, then to London, where a surprised but imperturbable Frank Russell was asked by an Associated Press reporter whether his brother had died – not in Peking but in Japan. "I told them I thought it was very improbable," he later explained to his brother; "first because you wouldn't do such a thing, secondly because you weren't in Japan, thirdly because you hadn't told me and fourthly because if the news came from America there was a *prima facie* assumption that it was untrue."

The report was like Mencken's lie going round the world while truth was putting on her boots. It was widely, if temporarily, believed, and one missionary paper published a one-line obituary: "Missionaries may be pardoned for heaving a sigh of relief at the news of Mr. Bertrand Russell's death."

Colette heard the news in Paris where she had gone with Sybil Thorndike and Miles who were playing Lady Macbeth and the Porter. "That news broke me," she wrote.

> A neat job: short, sharp and permanent. Death admits no argument, anguish, or wild regret. Only the brain in its extreme agony (provided it remains intact) photographs what passes in front of it: a tall Frenchman walked down the street; he had a black beard, a black coat, a black portfolio under his arm; on his head he wore a sailor hat. A dish of red cherries stood in a café at the Rond Point, a white china dish with pale blue rings; the cherries were dark red and bright red. Those things alone were real: more real than anything that had happened before or has happened since: the sum total of life, the remains of life, photographed on your brain, burnt into it in a moment of agony that lasts till the end of your days.

Only days later did she learn that Russell had not died. He had remained delirious and for three weeks it was touch and go, and it seems likely he was saved only by a serum from the city's Rockefeller Institute and the efforts of the English nurse. "[She] says my recovery is literally a miracle, only explicable by the direct interposition of Providence. I suggested to her, in Gibbonian phrase, that Providence works through natural causes, but she rejected this view, rightly feeling that it savours of atheism," he wrote at the time. "She was a deeply religious woman," he added later, "and told me when I began to get better that she had seriously considered whether it was not her duty to let me die. Fortunately, professional training was too strong for her moral sense."

On 28 April he came to. "I have missed much by not dying here," he wrote, "as the Chinese were going to have given me a terrific funeral in Central Park, & then bury me on an island in the Western Lake, where the greatest poets & emperors lived, died, & were buried. Probably I should have become a God. What an opportunity missed."

On emerging from his delirium his first action was to write to Ottoline.

> Dearest O,
>
> I am just able to write again so I want to tell you how profoundly you have been in my thoughts all this strange time. I am told I tried

to write to you during my delirium but of course I could only produce a meaningless scrawl. In the early days of my illness, my mind was more filled with beauty than ever before or since. I am sending you a dream I had which may interest you. I also had music – unreal & mystic – always in my head. In all this I kept thinking of you. I am nearly well now, very grateful for your letters, which are an *immense* joy to me. I have had the one about Colette & C.A.

Before getting ill I had begun to dislike N. China. It is parched and the people are cruel. We shall come home as quickly as possible. Too tired for more.

My most true love, B.

As a footnote he asked her to send to Colette, or to anyone else she wished, a copy of the enclosed description of his dream. "The following was dictated on March 20, 1921, the third day of my illness, at a time when I was already partly delirious, just before delirium obtained complete possession of me," it began.

The dream which it relates was dreamed on the same day. I took the utmost pains to make my account verbally identical with the dream, and the dream was so vivid that I think it likely I approximately succeeded.

I dreamt that my bedroom was transformed into a vast cavern on a vast precipitous hillside. In the middle of the cavern I lay sleeping on my bed, while all round, tier above tier, innumerable hermits likewise slept. The next room was transformed into a similar cavern on the same hillside, connecting with mine, filled also with hermits but not asleep. They were hostile to us & might come to destroy us in our sleep. But I in my sleep spoke to my hermits in their sleep, & said: "Brother hermits, I speak to you in the language of slumber, & the language which only sleepers can utter & only sleepers can hear or understand. In the land of sleep there are rich visions, gorgeous music, beauties for sense & thought such as dare not exist under the harsh light of the cruel sun. Do not awaken from your sleep, do not resist the other hermits by their own means, for though you win you will become as they, lost to beauty, lost to the delicate vision, lost to all that ruthless fact destroys in the waking world. Sleep therefore; by my slumber language I can instil into you what is better than success & war & harsh struggle, & the worthless grating goods which wakers value. And by our magic, as one by one the other hermits fall asleep, we shall instil into them the bright vision, we shall teach them to love this world of gentle loveliness more than the world of death & rivalry & effort. And gradually from us will radiate to all the world a new beauty, a new fulfilment. Men's dreams will lead them through the livelong day along grassy lawns by sparkling brooks

& through the dream night to the majesty of the stars, made gentle & warm & lovely by the rustling twigs through which they shine; to edifices of emblazoned glory, inaccessible mountain tops whose whiteness makes the blue of the sky more visible; & the mysterious sea, majestic in storm & gentle as a playful child in the sparkling calm.

"In these visions mankind shall forget their strife, happiness shall come to all, pain shall fade out of the cruel world, & mankind shall come to know the beauty which it is their mission to behold."

With its overtones of Blake and high moral purpose, the dream reaches back to the Russell of a decade earlier, the man who under Ottoline's influence had toyed with religion without the help of double pneumonia. It also suggests that beneath the philosopher of logical atomism there still lay the mystic, held in only by the normal constraints of consciousness.

He recovered slowly, hampered by a succession of complications that included inflammation of a vein in one leg which completely immobilized him for three weeks. However, he was still alive – and overjoyed at the fact. "I am astonished to find how much I love life," he wrote in May. "When I see the sun I think I might never have seen him again, & I feel 'Ugh! it *is* good to be alive'. Out of my window I see great acacia trees in blossom, & think how dreadful it would have been to have never seen the spring again. Oddly enough, these things come into my mind more instinctively than human things."

He was still weak and even by the end of June, after seven abscesses on his leg had been cut, still had to hobble with a stick. And now, only half-way along the road to recovery, he learned that Dora was pregnant. "I mildly regret that the divorce has not gone through in time for the child to be legitimate," he wrote – prematurely – to Clifford Allen, "but Dora does not care a damn. It is a pity she did not know while I was at death's door, as it would have comforted her – but it only became clear later . . ."

Since the early years of the century, if not from the first years of his marriage to Alys, he had desperately wanted children. The feeling had affected his relations with Ottoline and with Colette, and he was now deeply moved. "We are both overjoyed," he wrote, "though it is a little awkward that we should both be feeble just when we have to pack up and travel." He himself faced many months of convalescence and would be more in need of care than able to give it. All at once he saw their position: that of two white people alone in a sea of Chinese millions with not a glimpse of shore around the full circle of the horizon. "We both long for home," he confessed. "This place seems cruel to Europeans. When one is robust it is full of charm, but in bad health it is terrifying." Later, returned to England, his viewpoint steadied back between the poles of admiration and distaste. "I would do anything in the world to help the Chinese, but it is difficult," he wrote. "They are like a nation of artists, with all their good and bad points. Imagine [Mark] Gertler & [Augustus] John & Lytton [Strachey] sent to govern the Empire & you will have some idea how China has been governed for 2000 years."

Early in the summer he & Dora were rescued by a Girton don who providentially turned up and offered to shepherd them across the Pacific and home via Montreal and the Atlantic. Even the voyage had its problems. An attempt to book a double cabin brought a rebuke from the shipping line in Shanghai: "Regret to advise that it is entirely out of the question for a lady and a gentleman to be berthed in the same cabin on our steamers unless they hold passport, marriage certificate, or some other document as evidence that they are legally husband and wife," it said. However, either Russell or Miss Black might secure the exclusive use of one cabin while the other took an ordinary berth. "In this way they would not be shown on the books officially as in the same cabin."

By early July all was ready, and plans completed for the short stay in Japan before leaving for North America, *en route* to England. Russell and Dora gave their final lectures, Russell offering a parting word of advice to his listeners: "You will have to pass through a stage analogous to that of the dictatorship of the communist party in Russia," he is reported to have said, "because it is only by some such means that the necessary education of the people can be carried through, and the non-capitalistic development of industry effected."

This English version, reaching the Foreign Office via the *Peking Leader*, confirmed Whitehall's worst fears. But there is some doubt about the accuracy of more than one statement made by Russell in English, translated into Chinese, quoted in Chinese papers and then translated back into English. The author of *The May Fourth Movement* quotes another of Russell's statements about Communism as, "I hope furthermore that every civilised country in the world should experiment with this excellent new doctrine." But, the author adds, some of the final translations into English must be incorrect. "Hence," he says, "while their essentials are true, the translations should not be taken too literally as representing Russell's own views."

In Peking the Chinese decided to make a presentation to Russell before he left on 7 July. They had heard that the English liked cups and Russell was therefore presented with a fine silver two-handled specimen with his name in Chinese on one side and an inscription on the other. Its twins are to be seen on a thousand English sideboards and it was, he later said, the only athletic cup he ever won.

Arrived in Tokyo, still weak from pneumonia and pregnancy respectively, they were once again hard-pressed by journalists. Dora eventually shook them off by pointing out that as Russell was dead according to their own reports he obviously could not be interviewed. Then they crossed the Pacific to North America, and after an exhausting trans-continental journey embarked for England.

They reached home on 27 August 1921. Alys had been granted a decree *nisi* the previous May, but Dora was expecting to give birth in mid-November. Six months had normally to elapse before a decree absolute made remarriage possible, a hiatus which would in this case make legitimacy a close-run thing. To Russell, whose child could one day be heir to the earldom, the point was of some importance, and he had already instructed his solicitors to apply for a reduction of the waiting period.

There was also Colette, by now half torn apart by contradictory hints and letters from Peking, and writing, "I memorise the Chinese saying: 'You cannot prevent the birds of sorrow from winging overhead, but you can prevent them from nesting in your hair.'" Six months earlier there had come to her ears the tittle-tattle of Logan Pearsall Smith, who had described Russell's affairs in some detail at a dinner-party, then added, "Miss Black is going to marry him directly my sister's divorce is through." The gossip may not have worried Colette too much. Certainly she had reassurance a few weeks later when Russell, strengthening his hold on life in Peking, wrote to her in faint unsteady pencil-hand. The message was clear. Colette was his beloved and when he returned they could be together as before. He wanted her love and her comradeship in the deep things he could share with no one else. Her reply left equally little doubt. "My Beloved, I don't know how to wait until you're safe home again and I can take you in my arms, look into your dear eyes, and be one with you again: be whole." Before he received the reply he sent one more letter. It had a single promise: he loved her and would not lose her.

Then, in mid-June, the situation was dramatically changed. Dora, he wrote back to England, was pregnant.

Russell went first, with Dora, to the Battersea flat which he had been sharing with Clifford Allen. As soon as the two men were alone Russell anxiously questioned Allen about Colette. Allen handed him a stack of letters, written but not posted when she had learned he was to start for home. Russell read them and wrote her a brief note.

There had been a time when he had hoped for a child by Colette, but misunderstanding had ruled that out. Half a century later he claimed that she had never been agreeable to the idea. Her story was different. Now, however, any freedom of manœuvre he had hoped to retain had been removed by Dora and the embryonic presence of a possible 4th Earl. "On my return from China, when my son John was about to be born," he later wrote, "[Colette] told me that she had now changed her mind and would be willing to have children by me. But by this time it was too late."

This time he had driven himself into a cul-de-sac from which there was no honourable retreat. As he now wrote to Colette, he was so distraught that he knew neither how to think nor to feel nor to speak. But he was doing the only thing possible. As he explained in terms as kind as he could make them, but as unambiguous as they had to be, he had committed himself to marrying Miss Black and setting up house with her, immediately and permanently. "In the autumn of 1921," Colette wrote a decade later, "there was an epidemic of marriage. B.R. was the first to go down."

She wrote a brief note which Russell tucked away at the end of a thick bunch. "There's no new pain left for me to learn," it ended. "I shall never deny my love for you. In the past I wasn't grown enough to give everything I could now give. I'm not too proud to admit my pitiful striving. I shall not write again, you are not to write to me, I am your Colette." It was to be four years before Russell did write. Meanwhile, he turned to other business.

First, there was the decree absolute. He had to wait a fortnight before his lawyer announced that the application had come before the judge. "The King's Proctor mildly objected to the procedure," he said. But the ever-accommodating Alys had supported the petition and it had gone through successfully.

The papers came through on 21 September, and Russell and Dora were married at Chelsea Registry Office on the 27th, thus bringing her safely home to matrimonial port with more than six weeks to spare. Russell's lawyer trusted that Mrs Russell was free from anxiety. That was far from the case. Nobody was more disappointed over the marriage than she had been, she wrote to a friend some months later. She would have been quite happy if the divorce had come too late, and wrote later of the shameful action and disgrace of marrying.

At the small reception following the ceremony Frank appeared in his normal form. In his speech he paid little attention to the bride but concentrated on his own matrimonial problems and referred to Elizabeth, now deserted though not divorced, as "that wife who libels me".

Russell, a man who recognized the pattern of events, trusted that his second marriage would prove more successful than his brother's third.

A Long March Downhill

15

Start of an Experiment

When Russell returned from China, more than twenty years had passed since the comfortable routine of life at Fernhurst had been shattered by the realization that he no longer loved Alys. The context in which he now made a second attempt at family life was very different from the first. Then he had been no more than a young philosopher of promise, who might or might not set the tinder ablaze; now his reputation, in the United States as well as in Britain, had behind it not only *Principia Mathematica* but a lengthening row of books, papers and honours. By contrast, he now not only lacked any academic appointment to measure against his Trinity Fellowship of the early 1900s, but had cut his Cambridge links with his recent resignation. Furthermore, the money which had offered a safety-net during the early years of his first marriage no longer existed, and Dora Black's family could not offer a second net as reassuring as the Pearsall Smiths' had been.

His path was also made more difficult by the fact that he was now not merely famous but notorious. The heir to the earldom who has also done time in Brixton Prison is not a familiar figure, even among English eccentrics; neither is the potential earl whose wife-to-be arrives eight months pregnant for the marriage ceremony. These black marks, double-scored by his Socialism and his agnosticism or atheism – agnosticism when talking to laymen, atheism for Churchmen, he used to boast with a determination to be wicked – won him enemies enough on the political Right. Thus he was fair game for supporters of things as they were, a man who could expect his public statements to be misinterpreted as a matter of duty, and his public life attacked from all sides. Yet his excoriation of the new Russia had the same effect on many from the Left. His reputation as intellectual rogue-elephant continued to grow.

Russell and many old friends thus became disillusioned with each other. "He is now so busy with politics and money-making that I doubt if he ever thinks about probability," he wrote of Keynes. "He has become enormously rich, and has acquired 'The Nation'. He is Liberal, not Labour . . . " As for the Webbs, he disliked and distrusted their adulation of Soviet Russia and rarely resisted a chance of disagreeing with them. Thus when the argument at one country-house meeting turned to Japan and China he was quick to jump in. "You, Beatrice," he said, "only like the Japanese because they are efficient and sanitary, and read the Webbs' books; you dislike the Chinese just because they are dirty and have no urinals at their railway stations."

The constitutional love of stirring the intellectual pot often brought in return a subjective verdict. An unpublished entry in Beatrice Webb's diary is typical. "Physically aged, with an impaired vitality: but more brilliantly intellectual than he has ever been," was her opinion after she had reluctantly decided to acknowledge his second marriage.

> He is cynical and witty. His paradoxes are more impatiently perverse than those of G.B.S. He never seems serious; and his economic and political views follow on his temperamental likes and dislikes. His last book–*An Analysis of Mind*–is amazingly well written; intensely sceptical. He throws about his hypotheses and comes down lightly on one or the other, as provisional conclusions; but as conclusions which he will toss on the scrap heap of *rejected opinions* whenever he finds something more to his taste. This is markedly so with his political and economic views. He thinks he believes, with an almost fervent faith, in libertarian pacifism. But I doubt it. If, for instance, there arose a creed war he would be on the side of a secularist rebellion. Religious faith with puritan morality is to him "L'infame". He has no interest in the scientific method: he would even object to applying science to society, seeing that it might mean constraint on the will of some who desired to do anything they pleased without considering like liberty in others. He is too indolent or impatient to work out the problem of maximising freedom by deliberate social action.
>
> I should be sorry to bet on the permanence of the present marital tie. She is a singularly unattractive little person to me ... I think she adores him, and she may have a pleasant temper. Possibly the boy may keep them together for Bertie seems inclined to dote on this son and heir. His bad health may also be a restraining factor preserving his domesticity. But there is a strangely excited look in his eye (does he take opium?) and he is not at peace either with himself or the world. His present role of a fallen angel with Mephistophelian wit, and his brilliantly analytic and scoffing intellect, makes him stimulating company. All the same, I look back on this vision of an old friend with sadness: he may be successful as a *littérateur*; I doubt whether he will be of value as a thinker, and I am pretty well certain he will not attain happiness of love given and taken and the peacefulness of constructive work. When one remembers the Bertrand Russell

of twenty years ago, with his intense concentration on abstract thought, his virile body and chivalrous ways, his comradeship and pleasant kindly humour, the perfect personal dignity with a touch of puritanism, it is melancholy to look on this rather frowsy, unhealthy and cynical personage, prematurely old, linked to a ... girl of light character and materialist philosophy whom he does not and cannot reverence. However, the boy may save him and the marriage.

Amidst the spite of an old friendship there was a good deal of truth in what Beatrice Webb wrote. Certainly the Russell of Friday's Hill was now overlain with a more complex character. As in those distant days, he still sincerely wanted children, his peace, and the time to push on with philosophical work. He had been through the fire. Yet if this tended to settle him down, to lure him into the comfy armchair of the normal family-man, two other factors had a diametrically opposite effect. A decade earlier Ottoline had released both his pent-up romanticism and the latent sexuality which had been kept under hatches for the first forty years of his life, and there was not the slightest chance of pushing either of them back below decks. While this added a dimension to his personal life unthinkable at the turn of the century, his intellectual interests outside logic, mathematics and philosophy had been strengthened. The war had transformed his social conscience from an item among the baggage into a weapon for the fight.

The emotional and intellectual developments which had turned the prim pre-war figure of Blakeney-Russell into the Pimpernel-Russell of 1914–18 were first publicly noticed by an astute observer in the *London Mercury*, who devoted an essay to "Three Philosopher-Prophets", Dr Inge, Bertrand Russell and George Santayana. He wrote of Russell,

> Side by side with an austerely logical and scientific philosophy, he has entered on a fresh outlook in which impulse and feeling play the most important part. So much so that he might seem to be a logician doubled, as the French say, by an emotionalist; and though this may be too simple a way of putting the matter, it suggests that there are two sides to Mr. Russell. There is no reason why the same person should not combine logic and emotion; was not Coleridge "logician, metaphysician, bard"? And Mr. Russell, as we have seen, believes that philosophers have a mystical and logical strain in them. But this thought is not metaphysical, nor much like Coleridge's, and it makes a contrast which almost passes into a cleavage.

As soon as this new Russell, *un homme fatal* if ever there were one, tried to settle down in London he discovered the full handicap of his new image. His first efforts to lease a house in London were frustrated. To many, harbouring Russell was like harbouring the powers of darkness, and, as he wrote to Unwin, he was "objected to by landlords on the ground that, unlike them, I preach what I practise". Eventually he bought the house in Sydney Street that was to be his home for the next few years. That done, he had, as a first priority, to set about keeping his family financially afloat.

The heir which he had so long yearned for, John Conrad, had been born on 16 November 1921. A fortnight earlier Eliot, harking back to the Russell of "Mr Appollinax", had sent a message via his wife – "Tom says he is quite sure the baby *will* have pointed ears, so you need not be anxious," Vivien had written. But Russell was anxious. "The night seemed just like Tristram Shandy – the Dr. and I sat up together all night, gossiping & talking of carefully irrelevant topics," Russell told Ottoline a few hours after the birth. "I am so relieved – I made sure the child would have 3 arms & no eyes, or something queer, but he seems no worse than other people's babies." The confinement revealed at least one unbroken link with the past. From Evelyn Whitehead's son North, there came an invitation on behalf of his parents: if things were difficult while Dora was in hospital, Russell was to come round when he wanted, to eat with the Whiteheads whenever he wished, to make use of them whenever he felt inclined.

Two years later a daughter, Katharine Jane, was born, and at the age of fifty-one Russell was faced with bringing up a young family. What energies and time remained over from the business of earning a living would be devoted to propagating his political views. And as background, and never very far from his thoughts, there were his grand schemes of philosophical investigation, powered by a head of steam that in the general dispersion of activities became temporarily less effective throughout the 1920s.

The bread and butter, and as time went on a good deal of the jam, came from his freelance writing. He was willing and able to contribute a popular article on going to the cinema as efficiently as he would review *Life in the Middle Ages*, write an introduction to Lange's *History of Materialism*, or discuss Durant Drake's *The New Morality*. Whatever the problem, he would come up with a solution, whether the subject was politics, sociology or the morality which science and scientists should adopt. At times the omniscience looked a little over-done. "Does the world have some little problems of peace or injustice? He leaves both fools and angels dawdling at the post to provide us with a four-point programme which can be enacted next Tuesday, and that will be that," wrote James L. Jarrett. "He is sanguine in his notions of what a little more logic or intelligence, a little less muddle, would do."

Yet in his own field his position was unchallenged and Moore, asking if Russell would review C. D. Broad's new book, *The Mind and its Place in Nature*, could say, "Broad himself is very anxious that you should do it, though he says that you will dislike it extremely."

He lectured, and the honoraria certainly came in useful. But the bulk of his income, which rose in the later 1920s to the then respectable figure of more than £3,000 a year, did not come from lectures, or from the royalties on philosophical works, but from the hard grind of routine journalism. He worked under pressure, noting despondently in mid-March 1925 that he "must write 50,000 words before May 1st" – probably his book *On Education*.

His writing, whether for the popular Hearst papers, in the pages of *Our Knowledge of the External World*, or when generally discussing the ever-enjoyable war between the sexes, has the twin virtues of appeal and clarity. One reads on, even in the face of mounting disagreement; furthermore, one understands, and from an exposition which has more in it of Eddington than of Jeans, and takes the reader to the heart of the most complicated subject with a minimum of confusion or doubt. Russell's ability to make his point, whether in a technical review or a Sunday newspaper article, was the product of a long course of self-instruction, as he described to an American correspondent in the summer of 1925.

> Gradually, as a result of a complex development, I have come to prefer the 18th century to the 17th; but it is still the early 18th-century that I like best – Swift, & (in his way) Defoe. From the age of about 16 onwards, I formed the habit, in thought, of turning a sentence over & over in my mind, until I had a combination of beauty, clarity, & rhythm. I would do this with every idea that came into my head. Brevity, especially, I always greatly desired. I wrote very carefully, with many corrections, until I had passed the age of 30; i.e. down to & including the year 1902. After that, I felt that my style was formed, for good or evil. I now hardly ever make any corrections in a MS, beyond altering a word where there is an unintentional repetition. I think over a book before beginning to write, & when I begin the real work is finished. Of course I always compose each sentence fully in my head before beginning to write it out.
>
> As to what I think best in my own writing, "The Free Man's Worship" is the best in one style, but it is a style which I have deliberately abandoned as too rhetorical. "Why Men Fight" (as it is called, without my consent, in America) is, I suppose, the best example of my newer style, though it still has echoes of the old manner, for instance the passage about Thought near the end of the chapter on Education. I still think this passage rather good. I wrote it after being stuck for an hour, & sitting all that time before a blank page. I think also that there is a rather good bit of writing at the beginning of my book

"The Problem of China". It is the end of the first chapter, beginning "It was on the Volga in 1920", or something like that.

No one can doubt the importance of style who has ever had to explain difficult ideas or make propaganda for unpopular opinions. In France, this is generally recognized, with the result that French mathematical books, for instance, are vastly more intelligible than books of equal profundity written by Englishmen or Germans. Style consists, fundamentally, not in ornament, but in following the reader's natural development – his breathing, as regards rhythm; his thoughts, as regards ideas. To ignore style is to make of life a succession of jolts & jars, a football scrimmage instead of a dance.

As for reading, prose style can only be formed by reading good prose, but for modern use it should not be too ornate. Jeremy Taylor may still be read, but hardly Milton's prose or Sir T. Browne. Swift is admirable; Lamb is good, but a trifle affected, owing to his passion for the 17th-century. The Book of Common Prayer is perfect in its way – better even than the Authorised Version. Shakespeare's prose – for instance "what a piece of work is Man, etc." – is perfect. I think some really good things should be learnt by heart. My experience was, when I was younger, that one unconsciously reproduced the rhythms of what one was reading.

Much of this practical working knowledge, acquired over almost half a century, was distilled into three short rules which he put down in various ways over the years. A writer, he maintained, should first state his main idea in a single sentence without any qualification at all. Next he should insert whatever qualifications were needed to prevent his idea being misunderstood. And once again, a separate sentence should be used for each qualification, thus preventing the main idea from getting lost. The second rule was that a writer should never use long, unusual or technical words when short, well-known or non-technical words would do the job just as well. This would mean that the reader could keep his attention on the idea rather than having it led aside by a flurry of exciting but unnecessary words. The third rule was that a writer should never revise. If he went back and tried to improve, he would usually do the reverse.

Usually he did the job in long-hand. Like most master-craftsmen, he took it as part of the job to deliver on time. In addition, he had that other mark of the professional, the ability to squeeze the last drop of literary juice from the orange. The "rather good bit of writing", which he had tailored into *The Problem of China* so efficiently that the seams did not show, was in fact the text of the letter written to Colette from Garsington. Personal reminiscences would be worked into discussions on philosophy as well as into autobiographical notes, jottings and articles, while almost any journey or experience could become the substance of articles long and short, popular and learned.

Practice, which over the years had become habit, brought its reward after his return from China when the need for money became urgent. China itself was of course a rich seam to work, and soon after his return he wrote to Unwin proposing a book. "I will try to get it finished during the Xmas holidays," he added. His alternative titles of "The Chinese Puzzle" and "The White Peril" were rejected and it ultimately appeared as *The Problem of China*. Here he surveyed Chinese history, linked her future with that of Japan, and dealt with the Washington Conference which had recently replaced the Anglo-Japanese Alliance with a four-power pact between America, Britain, France and Japan. Following chapters contrasted Chinese and Western civilizations, and discussed the prospects for education and industrialization. After half a century, *The Problem of China* still stands up well. It also expresses Russell's emerging distrust of industrial civilization, which he feared would endanger the worthwhile things in life. For years this view had been implicit. Now he put it down explicitly:

> The main things which seem to me important on their own account, and not merely as means to other things, are: knowledge, art, instinctive happiness, and relations of friendship or affection. When I speak of knowledge, I do not mean all knowledge; there is much in the way of dry lists of facts that is merely useful, and still more that has no appreciable value of any kind. But the understanding of Nature, incomplete as it is, which is to be derived from science, I hold to be a thing which is good and delightful on its own account. The same may be said, I think, of some biographies and parts of history. To enlarge on this topic would, however, take me too far from my theme. When I speak of art as one of the things that have value on their own account, I do not mean only the deliberate productions of trained artists, though of course these, at their best, deserve the highest place. I mean also the almost unconscious effort after beauty which one finds among Russian peasants and Chinese coolies, the sort of impulse that creates folk-songs, that existed among ourselves before the time of the Puritans, and survives in cottage gardens. Instinctive happiness, or joy of life, is one of the most important widespread popular goods that we have lost through industrialism and the high pressure at which most of us live; its commonness in China is a strong reason for thinking well of Chinese civilisation.

A year later the theme was elaborated in *The Prospects of Industrial Civilisation*, which he wrote with Dora. The idea of the book had come to him on the ship to China, and he had been half through it when struck down in Peking. Like the majority of Russell's books from this time onwards, it sold well in the United States, a country whose publishers both pleased and maddened him. As he told Unwin some years later, the American public read him very much more than the British; but he was irritated by the way that sober titles had to be popularized out of recognition. Negotiating a few years later over *Freedom and Organisation*, he offered to call it "One, Two, Three – Bang", remarking that this "would be a fairly accurate title. You could add, as a sub-title, 'An Historico-Economic Investigation of the Socio-Political causes of the War 1914–1918'."

Russell's eight months in China did more than yield material for two books. He had become attached to the Chinese way of life and as firmly attached to the idea that the country was considered by the West solely as a field for capitalist exploitation. Therefore, throughout the 1920s, he wrote regularly for both British and American journals on the evolving situation there, an operation which aroused periodic bouts of apoplexy and despair in the Foreign Office. In 1924 an article on "British Imperialism in China" in the *New Leader*, circulated in Whitehall for comment, brought a regretful reaction from Sidney Waterlow, an old Trinity friend and a nephew of Elizabeth Russell. He minuted on the offending article,

> I have known Mr. Russell for many years, at certain periods intimately, & I greatly admire his genius. But he has always been a psychological puzzle to me. How is it possible that a man with his scientifically-trained mind should permit himself to write assertively & dogmatically on questions of fact of which he has only the most superficial knowledge? This peculiarity too often leads to mistakes and mis-statements, which must in the long run injure his reputation. The present article is an example of this. It hardly seems worth detailed comment, & it would be troublesome to disentangle its interwoven strands of fact & fiction.

However, Sir Charles Addis, the banker, did his best. His lengthy rebuttal was refused by the *New Leader* and *The Times*, but finally accepted by the *Morning Post*, which backed up his letter with a leader excoriating Russell. For Russell this was but a start. Before long he was writing on "British Folly in China" and earning a rebuke in the Foreign Office files for writing "a monstrous article".

However, the most telling interaction between Russell and the China lobby arose out of the Boxer Indemnity Committee. In his autobiography Russell says merely that he and Lowes Dickinson were appointed in 1924 to the Committee, set up by Ramsay MacDonald's short-lived Labour government to decide how the British portion of the Boxer Indemnity should be used for the mutual benefit of Britain and China, and were sacked six months later when the Conservatives were returned to power. The files reveal a more interesting story.

Russell and Dickinson were invited to serve as representatives of education, and from the first there was no doubt that the Labour government favourably viewed the idea that the bulk of the money should be used for this purpose. A hitch occurred immediately. MacDonald had, for reasons unknown, asked Lord Phillimore to preside over the Committee. A judge and international jurist, Phillimore was better known for his ecclesiastical exactitude, being much sought after as a counsel to argue on such questions as "the use of lighted candles on the Communion Table, the wearing of certain ecclesiastical vestments, the eastward position during the prayer of Consecration, the singing of the 'Agnus Dei', and the legality of a reredos with sculptural representations of the Transfiguration and Ascension". Phillimore and Russell would have made curious committee-fellows.

However, Phillimore's action on receiving MacDonald's invitation was to hurry to the Foreign Office for an appointment with Sir Eyre Crowe, the Permanent Under-Secretary. He was, he protested, embarrassed. Sir Eyre minuted,

> Lord Phillimore's embarrassment arose from his opinion concerning Bertrand Russell. His objection to the latter [was] as a highly immoral character and as a man holding views on education subversive of accepted theories of conduct (ethics) and training (education) with which he [Lord Phillimore] so strongly disagreed that he could not possibly preside over a Committee, or attend one, of which Mr. Russell was a member. He begged me to explain confidentially to the Prime Minister. If Mr. Russell's membership were still an open question Lord Phillimore thought the Prime Minister might agree to consult him (as the chairman-designate of the Committee) as to its constitution in which he could put forward his objections to Mr. Russell. If however things had gone too far for this, Lord Phillimore would, to his sincere regret, see himself constrained to decline the honour offered him. I could only promise to lay the matter before the Prime Minister. It is of course well known that Lord Phillimore is a very earnest and rather puritanical high churchman (if such a combination is possible). I believe his objection to Mr. Russell would be unsurmountable even if only the latter's rather unsavoury matrimonial adventures were in question, but he is in addition severely critical of Mr. Russell's avowed atheistic teaching & his known opposition to church & missionary schools, the latter of which must of course be an important factor in any scheme of education on European lines in China.

MacDonald refused to be browbeaten. "I am not disposed to yield if Mr. Russell has accepted," he wrote to Phillimore. "It is of the greatest importance that on this committee should be at least one of a school more modern than that which has hitherto dominated Western Education in China which with its good results nevertheless has shown great defects. Apart from anything else Mr. Russell's qualifications for this work are undoubted & special, & a boycott such as Lord Phillimore proposes cannot be countenanced."

However, before the Committee could begin work, a November election had replaced the MacDonald administration with Baldwin's. Industry, which had for months been demanding that the Indemnity be spent on trade rather than education, at once seized its opportunity. On 2 December Sir Eric Geddes, writing to the Foreign Office on behalf of the Federation of British Industry, protested that the existing Committee was not sufficiently representative. "Moreover there exists, in the opinion of the Federation," he went on, "a serious danger that a Committee including two representatives of education without the presence of representatives of other important interests would tend to prejudice the important questions of principle involved in the allocation of the funds." The following day Waterlow minuted from the Foreign Office, "Beyond circulating the [Boxer Indemnity] Bill to the Cabinet I suspended the action authorised by the Secretary of State . . . because on reflection an improvement occurred to me. The problem is to get two better members of the Committee than Mr. Bertrand Russell and Mr. Lowes Dickinson . . ." Both were now informed that their services were no longer required.

Russell replied with "British Labour's Lesson" in the *New Republic* and an interview with the London editor of the *New York World*, declaring that the previous government had definitely decided to spend the money on education, which they had not, and that the new government would devote it to trade and missionaries, which was roughly correct. "Like Tweedledee," the Foreign Office noted, "Mr. Russell when he is angry seems to hit at everything whether he can see it or not. He is now proving how unfit he was to serve on the Indemnity Committee; & his statements – and mis-statements – may be of use to us if the matter is raised in Parliament."

During this unhappy period of the 1920s, there were a few things that Russell would not turn his hand to – "I am sorry but I do not wish to do a book on Confucius. He bores me" – but only a few. He was apprehensive not so much of science as of how it might be controlled, and *Icarus or the Future of Science*, his contribution to the famous "Today and Tomorrow" series launched by Frederic Warburg in the 1920s, prophetically spelled out the warning. "I am compelled to fear that science will be used to promote the power of dominant groups rather than to make men happy," he wrote. "Icarus, having been taught to fly by his father Daedalus, was destroyed by his rashness. I fear that the same fate may overtake the populations whom modern men of science have taught to fly."

Icarus was an intellectual *jeu d'esprit*, but it was not only at this level that Russell was now finding himself journalistically fluent. He tried his hand at scientific popularization, first with *The ABC of Atoms* – in which he forecast that work on the structure of the atom would "ultimately be used for making more deadly explosives and projectiles than any yet invented" – then with *The ABC of Relativity*. Both were short books that did their job perfectly until, years later, they were out-dated by events. One reason for their success was the attitude reflected by Russell's assertion that "most men of science, when they attempt popular writing, display contempt for the reader and talk to him as elderly gentlemen talk to adventurous little boys".

Other more important if less remunerative tasks also occupied him during the first years of his second marriage. One was the preparation of a new edition of *Principia Mathematica*. Early in 1920 the Cambridge University Press had inquired about the projected fourth volume. This was to have been written entirely by Whitehead, but was never completed. However, in 1923 a reprint of the existing three volumes was discussed. The work was in constant demand by students, but the economics of printing further copies were not eyed with much favour by the Syndics of the Cambridge University Press. The type was still standing, which was just as well since the prospect of re-setting the huge book, with its scores of pages littered with the complex symbols of mathematical logic, would have stopped in their tracks more adventurous publishers than the Cambridge University Press. Moreover, mathematics had moved on since the early years of the century and it was essential that new ideas should be dealt with.

Russell, after consulting Whitehead, suggested that a very brief addition should be made to the existing Introduction. "I think this chapter could be made to fill exactly one sheet, if desired," he added helpfully; "certainly that would be about the length of it." This was in March 1923. A few months later he wrote to the Press asking for more time. Whitehead was within a few months of accepting a chair of philosophy at Harvard and was preparing to leave Britain for ever. The friendship had not been restored to its pre-war strength and it appears that Russell now decided to go it alone. Certainly the 127-page manuscript which he sent to the Press in September 1924 was influenced by Wittgenstein's ideas as expounded by Russell in his lectures on "The Philosophy of Logical Atomism" in 1918. Whitehead had little sympathy either with logical atomism or with Wittgenstein, and it appears that he let Russell get on with the task, without comment but without collaboration.

Whitehead's biographer, Professor Victor Lowe, believes that there was probably an understanding between the two men that Russell should state plainly that Whitehead had no hand in the revision. Years later Russell himself said that he had sent the material to Whitehead in the United States, received no reply – quite customary with Whitehead – and eventually posted the manuscript to Cambridge. Whatever the details, the edition of 1925 contained no mention of the fact that Russell alone was responsible for the new material, footnotes to the new introduction in fact stating that "the authors" – in the plural – were "under great obligations" to F. P. Ramsey and that *they* were indebted to many readers for pointing out misprints and minor errors. Whitehead responded with a grumpy note to *Mind*, and a few years later dissented, in a lengthy paper, from most of the new ideas, which had in effect been slipped in below his name. Among mathematical logicians the dissent was hardly needed. "To some extent," Whitehead's biographer has remarked, "its author's standing with them had been affected by his publication of metaphysical books, almost as being divorced affects a man's standing in some communities."

The reissue of *Principia* underlined the fact that Russell had become an essential part of the philosophical establishment. Meanwhile, however, the establishment had been changing and his Tarner Lectures, published in 1927 as *The Analysis of Matter*, were in some ways the end-product of the ideas which he had been changing and re-formulating since he had first rushed them off in letters to Ottoline fifteen years earlier. The lectures harked back to his pre-war interest in the physics of Rutherford and Bohr, and aimed at demonstrating the logical structure of the world when viewed in the light of relativity and quantum physics. They asked how the laws of physics were connected with the data of sense-perception, which provided the ultimate evidence for such laws, and they then speculated on the most plausible view of nature which this connection suggested. Reading the lectures might, C. D. Broad commented, "be compared to attending a Rugby football match under the guidance of Mr. W. W. Wakefield".

By contrast there was Russell's *An Outline of Philosophy*, a popular guide tapped out at speed for the American market. He was not particularly happy either about the book or its consequences. For one thing, he grumbled to Ottoline after its publication, "every few days Americans descend on me. I hoped they would not come so far, but they do – I think of buying an aeroplane & having a house in the Azores; I don't see what else to do about Americans, & Hindoos, who are even worse."

During the 1920s Russell was also much in demand as a left-wing speaker, although his unpredictability meant that no organizer could be quite certain what he was in for. He spoke on politics, on the wider social questions, on education, and also on religion. Here he had drawn sharply back from the mysticism towards which he had been encouraged by Ottoline before the war and uncompromisingly opposed the Church, often in bitter terms.

His new and harder line was exemplified in what became one of his most famous lectures – "Why I Am Not a Christian", given for the National Secular Society in Battersea Town Hall. A straightforward recapitulation of the Rationalist argument, neither very deep nor very searching, it was enlivened by Russell's ability to write on the subject as competently as he could write "On Wife-Beating", "The Back to Nature Movement" and "Furniture and the Ego". It was bitterly anti-religious in a way quite unlike the reluctant despair of "The Free Man's Worship", the thoughtful *Hibbert Journal* essay on "The Essence of Religion" or the equally well-argued "Mysticism and Logic". Reaction against what he now saw to have been Ottoline's ameliorating influence was one reason for this new virulence that creeps into his polemics against religion in the 1920s, and does not begin to disappear until three decades later. Another clue is given in a letter telling her that his dearly loved son John has been dangerously ill after a double mastoid operation. "On Tuesday, the critical day, I had to come to London to debate the Xtian religion against Bishop Gore," he says. "I was told that suffering is sent as a purification from sin. Poor little John never sinned in his life. I wanted to spit in their faces – they were so cold & abstract, with a sadistic pleasure in the tortures their God inflicts."

His bitterness – evoked by the same Bishop Gore whose *Lux Mundi* had driven Julian Huxley by "the sheer intellectual perversity of its attitude" along the road to scientific humanism – came clearly through in "Why I Am Not a Christian". The reaction was strong, and epitomized by his old friend T. S. Eliot. Their friendship had withered away, and after publication of *The Waste Land* in which Eliot had used Russell's wartime vision of a disintegrated London, Russell was told "Vivien wanted me to send you the MS to read, because she was sure that you were one of the very few persons who might possibly see anything in it. But we felt that you might prefer to have nothing to do with us . . ."

A recent convert to the High Anglican Church, Eliot reviewed the published version of the lecture as a "curious and pathetic document", adding that Russell's views rested on emotional grounds and that anything else "would have been too profound for the comprehension of an audience at the Battersea Town Hall".

This was perhaps a little harsh, on Battersea as well as on Russell. Yet it is certainly true that between the two world wars his disdain of Christianity carried bitter overtones that had been lacking from almost all his previous discussions of the subject. One possible reason is obvious: personal external influence, such as it was, now came from Dora rather than from Ottoline. Thirty years later, when "Why I Am Not a Christian" was reprinted, *The Times* reviewer remained just as loftily critical: "the things which had worried Russell about Christianity in the 20th century were merely those which had worried Bishop Colenso in the 19th".

The dedicated anti-Christianity which Russell wore like a prized decoration made him something of a political liability in the 1920s. Nevertheless, in 1922 and 1923 he stood as Socialist candidate for Chelsea, a Conservative stronghold whose sitting member was Sir Samuel Hoare, Secretary of State for Air. A few months earlier it had been suggested that he should be chosen to represent London University, a far more promising constituency for a Socialist. H. G. Wells had first been proposed. "Whereupon", Mrs Webb noted in her diary, "R. H. Tawney resigns from the chairmanship of the N.L.P. but before doing so proposes as the alternative Bertrand Russell. He declares that BR is a gentleman and HG a cad, which is hardly relevant if it is sexual morality which is to be the test." At least in university circles, Wells's personal imbroglios, which he tended to advertise in his own novels, counted for more than Russell's race to the registry office with a pregnant bride-to-be. The idea came to nothing and it seems very likely that Russell turned down the offer for fear that he might be elected. As he later made plain to both Gilbert Murray and Ottoline, he had no intention of standing for a seat he was likely to win: "I never wanted to get in but only to do propaganda."

There was certainly no chance of success in Chelsea, especially as he opened his campaign in the Town Hall by unequivocally supporting a programme for full-blooded Socialism that included a capital levy and nationalization of the coal-mines and railways. As for Russia, he soft-pedalled the tyranny he had described in such detail two years previously, criticized intervention, and advocated recognition of the Soviet government. Even the voters who were prepared to support such a programme received little of the usual political buttering-up from their candidate: after one Labour canvasser had suffered a mishap Russell brusquely refused, for what he considered sufficient reason, to visit him either with or without the expected accompaniment of fruit and photographer. "I don't like him and I won't go to see him." The recipe for failure produced 4,513 votes for Russell and 13,437 for his opponent, a result only slightly improved the following year when his supporters increased to 5,047 and his opponent's dropped to 10,461.

In the General Election of 1924 Russell stood down, but Dora took over. Still less compromising than her husband, she had an even smaller chance of success, the prevailing mood being demonstrated by an incident on polling-day when their son John walked unprompted up to the Mayor of Chelsea and said, "Vote for my mummy." "Vote for a Red," replied the Mayor. "Never."

Russell's double failure was undoubtedly a relief for him and an escape for the Labour Party. Completely alien to the wheeler-dealing tactics of parliamentary in-fighting, he had also the occasional wildness in judgment and the facility for the unfortunate phrase that are the elephant-traps of politics. Thus at the time of the General Strike he could write, "I think if [the Government] wins it will put all the leaders in prison, make trade unionism illegal, & perhaps disenfranchise all who struck, on the ground that they are criminals as that foul beast Simon explained ..."

Although Russell would have been of little use to Socialists in the House of Commons, he was nevertheless a propagandist of growing power and influence, and in 1923 he decided to test both in the United States. A lecture-tour should fill the pocket as well as spread the gospel, and he engaged William B. Feakins, "transcontinental tour agent for lectures by Men of Fame". Feakins arranged an elaborate programme, and on 1 April 1924, Russell arrived in the United States for the third time. He was braced for nine weeks of engagements during which he spoke on Socialism, peace, world government, education, the problems of Western civilization and any other subject which he felt would arouse controversy, make people think, and fill a hall. All these subjects would have been potential sources of controversy even had Russell not dealt with them from a Socialist standpoint; but he sought to arouse opposition and he succeeded. On international affairs he criticized the League of Nations as pusillanimous and France as aggressive, a reaction to the occupation of the Ruhr of two years earlier very similar to that of Einstein who resigned from the League's Intellectual Co-operation Committee as a result of it.

It was for his attacks on American affairs, however, that Russell was criticized most savagely, notably after one long-remembered lecture to the League for Industrial Democracy on "What Is Wrong with Western Civilisation?" World government, Russell forecast, would come – if it ever came – not by voluntary federation but by imperialism.

> In this process, America will play the chief role. In spite of the immense amount of ignorant good-will in America, American policy since 1914 can be explained in terms of interest. Practically everything that has been done has furthered the oil interests and the house of Morgan ... I foresee at no distant date an extension of the American financial empire over the whole American continent, the whole of Western Europe and also the Near East ... The empire of American finance will be in the highest degree illiberal and cruel. It will crush trade unionism, control education, encourage competition among workers while avoiding it among the capitalists. It will make life everywhere ugly, uniform, laborious and monotonous. Men of ability in all countries will be purchased by high salaries. The world will enjoy peace, broken only by the dropping of bombs from

airplanes on strikers, but it will look back to the old days of war as a happy memory almost too bright to be true.

This was some distance from the hopes of only eight years previously when he had optimistically implored Wilson to save the world. But it was not the pessimism which stuck in the American gullet – although the *New York Times* reported the speech with the headline: "Bertrand Russell Sees Dark Future." What stuck was "oil interests and the House of Morgan", a phrase remembered long after much else had been forgotten.

It was not only fire from the Right that Russell drew down on his head. His views about Communist Russia had not changed since his visit four years earlier, and at a public debate organized by the League for Public Discussion, he argued with Scott Nearing, the well-known American Socialist leader, that the Soviet form of government was not applicable to Western civilization. In the debate, later published as *Bolshevism and the West*, Russell argued that the road to Socialism lay through education rather than revolution, an attitude that confirmed the view of many previous supporters that they had backed the wrong horse.

While he detested Scott Nearing's ideas, Russell was vehemently opposed to any attempt to censor them, and when interviewed by the *Crimson*, a Harvard student-newspaper, strongly criticized what he loosely called "the authorities" for having banned Nearing and two other radicals from speaking at the Harvard Student Union. He had done his homework badly, or been unduly vague, for in the ensuing argument with Harvard's President Lowell, conducted in the columns of the *New York Times* and the *New Student*, a national university weekly, Russell was forced to retreat and admit that it was not the university but the Student Union authorities who had done the banning.

Believing as he did, and expressing his beliefs in a society where, as he put it on his return to Britain, it was the "general feeling that socialism is something 'foreign' advocated chiefly by alien Jews", it was not surprising that Russell the political propagandist should get treatment different from that given to Russell the distinguished professor. Not everyone thought that it was inevitable, and *Unity*, a Chicago journal, bitterly alleged that Russell's contretemps with Harvard was the only fact about his tour that got proper coverage. "But this is not the worst," it went on.

> Turn from the newspapers to the colleges and the universities! ... How many colleges in America officially invited him to their halls? How many gave him degrees of honour? So far as we know, Smith College was the only institution which officially received him as a lecturer, though we understand that he appeared also at the Harvard Union. Practically speaking, Professor Russell was ignored. A better measure of the ignorance, cowardice and Pharisaism of American academic life we have never seen.

Maybe this was a little harsh. Russell had done what he set out to do, projected his political ideas and made a handsome profit into the bargain. Like most of his operations it had been carried out at full tilt, with astonishing energy, largely the result of Feakins's go-getting ways and the vigour with which he had fixed up engagements. At times Feakins's energy misfired – at least according to the story, possibly apocryphal, of Whitehead's invitation to dine at Harvard. The invitation was treated as business correspondence and Whitehead was told that Russell would be glad to dine with him: for a hundred dollars.

Every spare hour was filled with events that Feakins hoped would turn out profitably. Never before, Russell wrote to Lucy Donnelly, had he been so busy. "I preached leisure," he added, "but had no chance to practise it." What he did have time for, was a meeting with Helen Dudley. She had written to him more than once after the birth of John. Now she had been struck down by multiple sclerosis but had attended one of his lectures, and met him afterwards.

"[She] is entirely rational, but very easily tired and rather lame," he reported to Ottoline. "She is rather admirable because she keeps up her courage & her interest in literature & human beings in spite of everything." During their conversation, he later wrote, he could feel dark, insane thoughts lurking in the background. Her own response was less dramatic: writing to him shortly afterwards, she says that his lecture had reminded her of old times and somehow bridged the gap.

True to form, his most outspoken comments were reserved for Ottoline to whom, on his return, he gave a lively account of the visit:

> Most of my time, was spent travelling from town to town, leaping out of the train to lecture, & leaping in again as soon as my lecture was over. The train was the most restful part of the business. On arrival in a town, I was first surrounded by journalists all morning (after being turned out of the train at 6 a.m.), then had an enormous lunch with business men who unrolled slow platitudes that reminded one of the mills of the gods, then had tea (if I was lucky) with a crowd of sentimental ladies, then a heavy dinner with another crowd of business men, then a lecture, & then the train for the night. I can't imagine how I survived. In New York I stayed with a philosopher, Kallen, a Jew, whose friends are all Jews. All were kind, but I began to long for the uncircumcised. New York is mainly Jewish. My impression was that all well-to-do people in New York, both men and women, get drunk every night; they drink incredibly potent stuff. There is incredible sexual licence, especially among young girls, most of whom, however, observe the degree of caution which was proved inadequate in the Russell baby case [which despite its name had nothing to do with him].

He was glad to be back, he assured her, not least with his son and heir. "He was delicious when I arrived," he wrote. "He was waiting by the gate & received me with the greatest delight. Then he took me indoors & showed me a photograph of myself & said 'that is Dada' & set to work to compare it with the original. I thought he would have half forgotten me but he remembered everything we used to do together & insisted on doing it all again."

Russell's pleasure in his son, and later in his daughter, helped to keep him on course during the difficult 1920s when he was working overtime on routine journalism, trying to fit in the political propaganda towards which conscience prodded him, and usually despairing of getting back to what mattered: the philosophical thinking and writing which for the time being was shunted into a siding.

The fact that his second marriage appeared to be successful was also a point in his favour. "I've seen Bertie several times & his round little wife, & their little snug & happy house in Chelsea, full of tiny jackets & pilchers & powder-puffs and cradles, with Bertie looking *perfectly* blissful," his sister-in-law Elizabeth wrote to Katherine Mansfield. "She seems a nice little creature & they certainly are devoted to each other." Later, after Russell and his wife had visited her abroad, Elizabeth's views were strengthened. "I like [Dora] very much," she wrote, "& the more the more I know her, & Bertie has been great fun, & so happy that after all one feels a little warmed by it. Also, they both love being here & don't want to go away, & that always quite gets round me. I am persuaded Dora is the very wife for him, & if one succeeds in heading her (& him) off politics or indeed views of any sort she's a jolly, affectionate little dear." And, later in the year: "He is so happy now, & sparkles more than ever. She is the very wife for him – healthy, placid, sweet-tempered, & has such bright eyes that I am sure he is right when he says she is very intelligent. Also she has a dimple."

Russell relaxed into this family background as one sinking into a feather-bed. By 1924 it seemed likely that at least a part of his dream was coming real, and with his two children in mind he bought Carn Voel, a house at Porthcurno on the south coast of Cornwall a few miles from Land's End. Here, throughout the 1920s, the Russells spent the summer months of the year, and here he was happy as he had rarely been happy before. He wrote to Ottoline,

> It is so lovely here – the birds sing all day – there are larks & thrushes & blackbirds & cuckoos & curlews & sea-gulls all round the house & ships sail by, & at night one hears the sea in the distance booming on the rocks, & there is blackthorn & whitethorn, & bluebells & buttercups, & green fields & gorse moors, all without stirring from the house. The boy thrives amazingly – he is quite a different

creature from what he was when we came. He is full of fun & very roguish, with bright eyes which notice everything. He is altogether lovely, & I love him beyond measure.

At Carn Voel, he was telling her two months later, John had the advantages of "playing on the sands, then boating, then climbing on the rocks, & all the splendour of the sea, which is a good thing to have in one's memories of childhood – I want him to be an outdoor boy, not too precocious intellectually – he is so eager that he might easily overwork".

Ottoline – now moved from Garsington to Gower Street, a few hundred yards from her pre-war house in Bedford Square – received full details of Russell's delighted preoccupation with his son. "When I have any time to spare, I spend it playing with John, whom I love beyond all reason & measure," he told her. "He is very full of life – he has not been even slightly unwell for over a year (unberufen!) – he is full of gallant energy, marches against the wind till it throws him over. He has an amazing passion for flowers – the sight of a garden full of them sends him into an ecstasy. I keep thinking they will kill him in the next war, & have thoughts of becoming a Norwegian to prevent it." His son loved his school, but "he has not quite grasped that it is not his province to teach – on arriving one morning he gave the head-mistress a lecture on Saturn's rings. Another day he suddenly piped up: 'Have you been round the world?' & when she said no, he said 'my daddy has'."

There was another side to his character which he revealed to Lucy Silcox. "In spite of my efforts," he wrote, "John has considerable religious faith; he informed me that in the mornings he informs Apollo & Neptune what he wants them to do that day. But both children prefer magic to religion; they like the witches' cauldron in Macbeth Act IV, & know the passage nearly by heart."

One of Russell's favourite sayings was "men of wisdom love the sea; men of virtue love the mountains", and appreciation of Cornwall reflected his feeling for the non-competitive activities of swimming and mountain-walking. The Penwith moors which form the backbone of the Land's End peninsula can never claim mountain status, but they have a landscape ruggedness which satisfied at least some of his needs.

On the moors, on the little cliffs which drop down to the then deserted beaches, and in the sea beyond, Russell lived an almost idyllic life with his wife and two children. The ease with which he could sometimes scrub the memory of departed affections from his mind makes comparisons unreal, but the summer months of Cornish swimming and scrambling, of using sand and sea to explain to two bright children the riddles of nature, were a satisfying highlight in a long life.

Now in his fifties, Russell still retained the physical energy and mental agility of earlier years and shared the pleasures and excitements of his son and daughter with the understanding of a much younger man. When the children filled his empty tobacco tins with stagnant water and garden rubbish labelled "Poison for the Government", he pointed out that the government might hesitate to use it under this label and the more enticing one was substituted: "Nectar for the Gods". Neither child had much idea what the government was; but if father said it was wicked, then wicked it must be.

Parental fears were kept in hand. Controlling his dislike of heights – not as unusual in a mountain-lover as many might suspect – he would watch Kate or John scrambling on the cliffs and steep grass-slopes between Gwennap Head and Merthen Point, come up and convoy them down when they got stuck, hold back the "be careful", give them confidence and steadily train them into what Colette was to call "the children of one's dreams".

Russell could be as practical in physical activities as in the things of the mind. "If there's a current, always begin by trying to swim against it, to make sure you can" was one of his maxims. When one of the children got out of depth he prevented a panic by the confident shout, "Turn towards me: now swim."

There were many guests – on one occasion Miles Malleson and the wife he had married after divorce from Colette. Each afternoon they would all go down to the coast. "Bertie would say – it was about a mile's walk to the nearest beach – he would always say: 'Now, on this mile let us have a disquisition'. Those were always the words. 'What would you like to talk about?' And I would say, 'God, or anything you like'. 'Very well, I will tell you what I think'. It was the most stimulating two months I have ever had."

Another visitor was Arthur Cook, the miners' leader, brought to see Russell while on a tour of the West Country. "It had been raining all day, and Cook was wet and exhausted and so hoarse that he was almost unable to speak after having addressed small open-air meetings in spite of suffering from a bad cold," says one of his party. "While the rest of us chattered excitedly downstairs, Bertie, infuriated by the indifference shown to the Mine Union's leader's physical condition by his secretary, who was a hard-boiled left-winger, himself escorted Cook upstairs, carrying a can of hot water, and insisting that his guest change his sodden clothing, put on dry socks and take some rest."

At Carn Voel, as the family grew up, Russell's interest in education became more than academic. In *Principles of Social Reconstruction* and in *Roads to Freedom*, his theme was that education should encourage children to think for themselves, to question rather than conform. Now, with John and Kate developing fast, he began to study educational theory with a new interest. Most of it confirmed his views: that creativity should be stimulated, conformity discouraged; that while some discipline was necessary, the emphasis should be on self-discipline and that, in general, children should be given much more freedom than they had in a normal school. His teaching, largely assimilated into practice today, was dealt with in *On Education: Especially in Early Childhood*, the first of Russell's two major books on the subject and one which, he later remarked, seemed "somewhat unduly optimistic in its psychology". To John Dewey, who had reviewed the book, he was even more self-critical. "It is an amateurish and in some ways ignorant book, & I am relieved that it should not be despised by a man of your eminence as an educationalist," he said. "The book is addressed to parents as ignorant as I was when I first became a parent, & is only intended to give common sense. What you say about the effect of my children on me is quite just. I am as pessimistic as ever about politics, but I have now something else to think about. I seriously think of emigrating, however, as I expect disaster in England before my children are grown up."

Meanwhile, however, he had to educate them, not an easy task for one like Russell who disapproved of the conventional Public School education not only on social but also on practical grounds. The idea of handing John and Kate over to a State school was equally unattractive. His élitism favoured competitive examination for the universities at the age of twelve and special schools for exceptionally gifted children. "A great deal of needless pain and friction would be saved to clever children if they were not compelled to associate intimately with stupid contemporaries," he once wrote. "There is an idea that rubbing up against all and sundry in youth is a good preparation for life. This appears to me to be rubbish. No-one, in later life, associates with all and sundry. Bookmakers are not obliged to live among clergymen, nor clergymen among bookmakers." There remained the progressive schools, but most of those relegated the hard slog of learning to a position which horrified Russell. Dartington Hall had not yet been started, while for A. S. Neill's Summerhill Russell had only qualified sympathy. "It seemed to me, and still seems," he wrote, "that in a technically complex civilisation such as ours a man cannot play an important part unless in youth he has had a very considerable dose of sheer instruction."

With nothing satisfactorily filling the bill, Russell and Dora began "to consider whether human development might not be served by an attempt at providing a really modern education which, instead of training young children to maintain every prejudice of traditional society, or teaching them new dogmas, should try to help them to think and work for themselves, and so fit them for meeting the problems of the changing world they will have to face when they grow up. This was what we set out to do in our school."

The school was Beacon Hill, an institution whose reputation was a great deal better than that implied by the popular press. Even so, many of the stories printed about Beacon Hill were, though fiction, less remarkable than the truth. While the school was to be run jointly for its first few years by Russell and his wife, there was a difference of emphasis in their approaches. "It seemed as though not enough thought was being given to the type of people we hoped to have to build the future of socialism," Dora wrote years later. "Also it struck both Russell and myself that Labour had no real policy for education, only 'more education' not 'what sort', and concentration on equipment and buildings ... And certainly both then and now, not the least real notion of how to educate for democracy." Dora was thus primarily concerned with education for Socialism. Russell put the idea of the individual before the idea of the State, even the Socialist State. Education, as he had said years earlier, might be defined as the formation, by means of instruction, of certain mental habits and a certain outlook on life and the world.

The venture once decided upon, the Russells' first task was to find suitable accommodation; this was finally resolved by leasing Telegraph House, Frank Russell's home on the South Downs. Frank did not wish to sell his beloved Telegraph House to which he was as deeply attached as a sheikh to his harem. However, in 1927 he was deep in a bout of bankruptcy and was eventually persuaded to rent the estate to Russell. Negotiations were complicated, and Russell also leased Battine House, a building next to the rectory in the village of East Marden, two miles away.

Telegraph House was isolated for the south of England, even after Frank Russell had built a mile of road to connect it with North Marden. The nearest big village was South Harting, five miles away by road, and the house, surrounded by a wilderness leading up to the viewpoint of Beacon Hill, had to be largely self-supporting. Cook, housekeeper, matron and three maids were hired to service the community from their quarters below-stairs. Two chauffeurs, who sometimes warned new teachers of the perils to come, were employed to ferry children, parents or staff from Petersfield station and, in the summer, to take children on weekly excursions to the coast, a dozen miles away.

Eventually all was ready; unfortunately, just as Russell was about to start on another lecture-tour. He wrote to Ottoline towards the end of August 1927,

> Our school opens on September 22, and I go to America on Sept. 21, so Dora will have to manage without me for the first term. We have as permanent teachers our Mademoiselle (who is excellent) & a Miss Tudor-Hart, who has specialised on young children's schools in Vienna & America after being at Newnham; we have visiting people for music, etc. We start with 12 boarders & five day pupils, but contemplate going up to 24 or 30 later. We have terrible

> rows with my brother, who behaves like a common swindler. It is a difficult venture financially, & involves Dora giving up all her political work; but I am sure it is the best thing for the children. I *loathe* going to America.

Russell and Dora taught history, science, mathematics and geography. Methods, according to a brochure issued by the Russells, were to be "on the lines of Margaret McMillan, Dr. Montessori, some Froebel, and individual work". History followed Wells's *Outline of History*, published in 1920, which began with the planet Earth in space and time, outlined the geological story, dealt with the evolution of man and his early civilizations, and only then began to deal with the successive nation states and empires. Commonplace enough today, but almost the mark of the heretic forty years ago. Miss Tudor-Hart took the kindergarten class. Mademoiselle, a gorgeous Swiss girl with golden hair down to her waist, taught French. A succession of auxiliary teachers, part-time or permanent, served over the next few years to deal with the highly individual pupils, some in their early teens, some as young as three. Pay was only about a third of the going rate, but staff conditions were good, and everyone had their own well-furnished bed-sitter, either in a cottage near the main building or in Battine House, from which they were ferried to Telegraph House for breakfast. The attractions of working with Russell were considerable. "Whatever good it did to the children," says Boris Uvarov, who was science master for a while, "the life there was certainly good for the staff." During the first few years the auxiliaries included a number of striking young women and the school thus became a target for the R.A.F. pilots at nearby Tangmere, who would frequently do stunts over the house as a preliminary to dating them up.

Russell's ideas of running a school were those he outlined many years later. "I am afraid that education is conceived more in terms of indoctrination by most school officials than in terms of enlightenment," he said.

> My own belief is that education must be subversive if it is to be meaningful. By this I mean that it must challenge all the things we take for granted, examine all accepted assumptions, tamper with every sacred cow, and instil a desire to question and doubt. Without this, the mere instruction to memorise data is empty. The attempt to enforce conventional mediocrity on the young is criminal.

In a letter to one prospective parent, he described some of the practical ways in which his ideas were to be implemented. "With regard to religion there is no religious teaching of any sort or kind," he said.

> The children learn about the various religions of the world as historical facts but no one religion is treated differently from any other. A good deal of trouble is taken to make the education such as will

not inspire patriotism, more particularly in the teaching of history and geography which I do personally. As for teaching the brotherhood of man I have the same objection that I have to explicit moral instruction in that it tends to produce either hypocrisy or rebellion. Morality must grow, it cannot be implanted by precept.

Children below the age of five were given their own playroom where they could do what they liked with a wide range of materials, instruments and tools. "Even small children of 3 begin to use saws and hammers, and scissors to cut coloured paper designs," wrote Dora. "In our experience the child who has begun to live and work in this way, with a group of his own age, from 2 years upwards, is far more developed and independent at the age of 4 than the child who has had the old-fashioned life, surrounded by adult help, in his nursery." From five onwards the children were encouraged, but not forced, to start reading, writing and arithmetic. Elementary French and German were infiltrated into their studies. An interest in history was fostered first with the Roman pottery found in the grounds and afterwards from books. In the laboratory, where simple experiments were carried out before children could spell the names of materials they were using, crystals were grown, rocks and fossils were collected and discussed, and interest encouraged by observation of plants, animals, foods and chemicals. There were no prizes and no competitions except for an occasional test or class-game.

The basic programme, revolutionary half a century ago, was supported by a discipline midway between that of conventional enforcement and the unlimited freedom of Neill's Summerhill. There was no corporal punishment, and pupils were persuaded, rather than made, to work. Fighting and other jungle behaviour were kept at least partially in check by resolutions of the School Council, which included all the staff from Russell to the gardener, and every child aged five or more. When the best way of checking fighting was discussed it was at first proposed that "sloshing" should be forbidden. However, few children can live up to such a complete prohibition, so it was resolved that "this Council disapproves of sloshing as a method of settling disputes". Thereafter, Dora has said, when two children started to fight, others would run up chanting the Council resolution. Within this fairly loose framework a good deal of instruction was successfully given. Russell's own reliance on concentrated hard work kept the enterprise down-to-earth, and on one occasion his determined "I'll teach you mathematics if I have to break every bone in your body", said with a twinkle rather than a glint in the eye, was nevertheless effective.

In terms of results, the school was not startlingly different from many others. What caused misgivings in the popular mind was Russell's reputation, the encouragement of free thought on religion and sex, and the number of "new-fangled" ideas – even the virtue of daily orange juice for growing children was then little appreciated – with which it experimented. Out-of-the-rut practices not only gave Beacon Hill notoriety but caused the curious to look about for possible pegs on which to hang criticism. Thus it was tempting for the press to give Beacon Hill a rough time. True, one boy did set the scrub-covered downland alight but, as Russell wrote after the incident, "All goes well here. We find that the naughtiest children are the most artistic & imaginative. I don't mind mild naughtiness, but I rather object to attempts to burn the house down for the sake of a bonfire." One group did try to sacrifice a rabbit in imitation of Abraham's sacrifice of a ram. One child certainly was injured following a realistic game of Cowboys and Indians, and a primitive strike was organized by pupils against an excess of Brussels sprouts. But what would have passed as high spirits or animal vigour in a Public School was claimed to be anarchy at a "progressive" school run by an anti-war Socialist agnostic and his advanced wife. He was, moreover, something even worse in the eyes of many neighbours, since one of his first acts on taking over was to deny the local hunt access to the 240 acres surrounding the house. "Those who know English country society will realise", he later wrote, "that in so doing I have committed a worse offence than the advocacy of atheism, pacifism or free love. Yet I could not give the children at school a right outlook if I deliberately permitted the torture of animals for human amusement."

The sexual freedom of the school was a subject of constant prurient amazement. The children were, in Dora's words, "allowed to remove all their clothes in the summer if they wished to, especially for outdoor dancing and exercise". Special sex instruction was never required, since its fundamentals were incorporated in biology lessons, and the details of intercourse and birth taken for granted. Yet the Russells had surprising success in making naturalistic behaviour locally accepted when it could easily have raised conservative hackles. There circulated the apocryphal story of the local vicar arriving at Telegraph House where the door was opened by a small girl with no clothes on. "Oh, my God," exclaimed the vicar. "There is no God," replied the girl, firmly slamming the door. The truth was more interesting. Battine House, retained as an annex after Telegraph House was taken over, lay next to East Marden Rectory. The Rector and his wife were both characters of Victorian strictness, but did more than nip in the bud a local attempt to close the emerging school. "The children", remembers their son, the Rev. P. H. Francis, "wandered quite freely about the Rectory grounds naked in hot weather, and would ring the bell to talk with my parents. Then they would come indoors and sit on the kitchen table while my mother told them stories from the Bible."

Russell not only charmed away opposition but, according to the Rev.

Francis, was even able to "put the lie on the popular idea that he was somewhat fast and in favour of sexual looseness" – no inconsiderable feat. Press accounts certainly exaggerated isolated incidents, but the unvarnished truth would have been more titillating and, at the time, far more damaging. Writing to A. S. Neill, the founder of Summerhill, with whom he disagreed on the need for discipline, Russell noted that he did not in fact "absolutely insist upon strict sexual virtue on the part of the staff".

This was so. While some were traditionally conservative in sexual matters and actively distressed at the attitudes of their colleagues, great freedom was always allowed and sometimes taken. One matron remembers her time at Telegraph House by the endless sexual confidences on which she was asked to give advice. "I wish I had only nuns for staff," Russell exclaimed after one awkward dilemma; "then they'd only be concerned with the children." But the high-key emotional atmosphere did not concern staff alone. From 1927 onwards both Russell and his wife were themselves becoming entangled in the practical application of their beliefs in free love.

Poor Russell. "We both thought that marriage should be compatible with minor affairs," he later wrote of his second marriage, and during the later 1920s he practised his beliefs. "The first test came when I was in America on a lecture tour. While there I had a brief and unimportant affaire of which I told her on my return." This was in fact a case of "making little of it" since by 1927 Russell had reached the conclusion – voiced to more than one member of the Beacon Hill staff – that it was impossible to know any woman until he had slept with her, a belief supported by what had by this time become "his inability to restrain his abnormally strong sexual urges". He had no hesitation putting his beliefs to the test, and during the turbulent years of the Beacon Hill experiment he made determined efforts to find the combination of physical and mental happiness that was always one step ahead of him. There was the young woman with whom he disappeared on regular weekend sorties to his London flat, explaining this blandly to the staff with, "As we both have to go to London it saves a chauffeur if we both go at the same time."

There were others, and in February 1935, when Dora was finally granted a divorce, the judge noted that Russell "had been guilty of numerous acts of adultery in circumstances which are usually held to aggravate the offence ... infidelity ... with persons in the household or engaged in the business in which they were mutually employed".

However, the Russell who so ardently pressed a brand-new teacher – on her second night at the school, not her first – to sleep with him because he admired her, and who took her rebuff with amiable disappointment, was only one factor in the school's failure to make much impact on the educational scene and for the whole episode to deteriorate, in his own words, into "one of the most personally unhappy and unfortunate of my life". There were other reasons which in the best of circumstances would have been grave handicaps. One was lack of money. Started on the minimum of capital, the school was never self-supporting; it hardly could have been, even had all the fees been paid, and many were not.

Russell admitted the position in a report to one parent in November 1928. "We find that in the first twelve months of the school, in addition to a capital expenditure of £1,445.12.3., there was a nett loss of £1,847.10.1.," he said.

> We could of course make the school into a paying proposition by having a very much larger number of children, but that we do not wish to do, as it would alter the character and make it necessarily more institutional. At present we each of us know each child intimately, and can judge his or her psychological needs in a way that would be impossible if the school were large.
>
> We fixed the fee at a low figure, because we did not wish to have *only* children of the very rich; but in view of the magnitude of our loss (which has had to be made good out of my private earnings) I am writing to such of the parents as I do not know to be poor to ask whether they would be willing to pay somewhat increased fees. I do not mean that there would be any obligation to do so if parents felt a difficulty, but only that I should feel very grateful if those who could afford it would help somewhat to lessen my financial burden, which they could do by paying fees more nearly proportional to the cost.

There was also the background of the pupils. In the nature of things, progressive schools attract the children of non-conforming parents; even so, Beacon Hill accumulated an undue percentage of children from broken homes, illegitimates, and children with one or more American parents, sometimes separated. Thus the cross-section on whom Russell and his wife tried out their educational ideas was more caricature than fair sample. In addition, there were Russell's own personal limitations. He himself has written that "a school is an administrative enterprise and I found myself deficient in skill as an administrator". But it was not only in administration that he was sometimes unable to put the right foot forward. In strong contrast to his philosopher-friend Wittgenstein, engineer, architect and dab-hand at most jobs, Russell could be stretched by having to make a cup of tea. He had, moreover, a certain disinclination for the menial task; in theory the most democratic of men, Russell could not shake off the legacy of Pembroke Lodge; and the instinctive Russell outlook which divided life into below-stairs and above-stairs occasionally gave Beacon Hill the air of a comic film.

However, there was a more damaging factor which hampered its growth and the extension of its practices, most of which can be seen today as more enlightened than revolutionary, and suffering from nothing more than being half a century in advance of their time. This was Russell's delight in trailing his coat, a habit which dismayed some of those who believed that educational progress could only be achieved by gradualism. More than one parent, wavering about the merits of Beacon Hill, may have decided against it on reading Russell's statement in the *Daily Telegraph*. "I regard with horror all those whose business it is to keep the human spirit and the human intellect in fetters. I include among these all ministers of religion, a large proportion of school teachers, 90 per cent of magistrates and judges, and a large proportion of those who have earned the respect of the community by their insistence on what is called a rigid moral standard." With such an organizer, Beacon Hill needed no critical press to ensure that when Dora Russell took single-handed control it would have some difficulty in surviving. Miraculously, it held on until the mid-1940s when, transferred to the wartime West Country, its quarters were commandeered by the authorities.

In spite of Russell's sincere enthusiasm for progressive education, despite his personal anxiety to give John and Kate the education he felt was best, Beacon Hill could never be given the unremitting concentration it demanded. His diary jottings are themselves evidence of the time spent on his journalistic work – earnings of £3,000 for 1927; £3,500 for 1930; £4,000 for 1931 – and "Anyone with an idea for today's article?" was an appeal frequently heard at the Beacon Hill lunch-table. It all took time. In the evenings he would retire from the turmoil into the seclusion of his study in the hideously ugly tower, a sanctuary to which none was allowed without invitation. Here his thoughts on "The Twilight of Science", the popular articles for the *Daily Express*, *Harper's*, the *Atlantic Monthly*, the *Jewish Daily Forward* or the Hearst Press, were written out in a steady, regular hand, page after page with rarely a change of word or of comma. All necessary work if he were to keep Beacon Hill in funds, but little of it work he regarded as his particular mission in life. In such circumstances he might well have grown disenchanted, disgruntled, weighed down by a sense of failure.

In fact he had few such feelings. By a lucky chance there still exist his answers to a searching questionnaire sent out to him early in 1929 by the *Little Review* of Chicago. Russell answered its ten questions after warning the magazine that his replies were truthful rather than interesting. He would like best of all to do physics, to know physics and to be a physicist. He would gladly change places with about a dozen people – but first of all with Einstein. What he most looked forward to was watching the development of his children and what he feared most from the future was that he might become the sort of person people would find it tiresome to be with. Possibly tweaking the interviewer's attitude, he claimed that the unhappiest moment of his life had been his birth and the happiest would probably be his death, but he went on living because he enjoyed life. His weakest characteristic was his respect for bigwigs – a reply it is difficult to take seriously – while his strongest was an impersonal intellect. "I like most about myself the fact that many people like me; I dislike most the fact that I hate myself," he went on. He regarded himself as a moderately reasonable being in a totally unreasonable scheme. He had no views about art; but he liked the sea, logic, theology and heraldry. "The first two because they are inhuman, the last two because they are ridiculous," he added. "I dislike fools, tyrants, and women who speak of children as 'little darlings'."

That self-portrait was part of a continuing campaign to raise money in the United States, and his American lecture-tour in 1924 was followed by others in 1927, 1929 and 1931. On each, he made a useful profit, and during each he attracted a number of American pupils. Nevertheless, the debit entry was that Dora had far too often to cope single-handed with the multifarious, unforeseeable problems of running a controversial school. America, moreover, tended to arouse in him even greater interest in the problems of politics and world affairs which had for a while competed with the problems of education. As early as November 1927, he was describing the school as a nuisance which curtailed his freedom and entailed a lot of hard work. Two years later he was complaining that it made John and Kate ill and no longer served its primary purpose.

His three American tours were thus carried out while his own enthusiasm for Beacon Hill was evaporating. They were financially successful; but at the same time they laid a foundation from which the scurrilous if victorious attacks of a decade later could be mounted with comparative ease. Perhaps this was inevitable. A man who felt as strongly as Russell about the central issues of the times was bound to act as intellectual lightning-conductor – particularly when he readily debated in public such issues as "Is Democracy a Failure?" and "The Future of Education and of Modern Marriage". He sparkled, and those who disagreed with him were among the first to admit that his combination of logic and wit was persuasive. But in 1927, as in 1916, his enemies were warned.

At times, and in the rush of tours packed with every item that the indefatigable Mr Feakins could squeeze in, he let down his guard, admitting an attitude to his audiences that not everyone appreciated. Thus Max Eastman, who debated with him the course to be taken along "The Road to Freedom", has recorded how they walked away together after their discussion of progress through the class struggle. "Anyone who takes these debates and lectures of ours seriously", Russell declared, "must be an idiot." The remark, probably half-facetious, was typical of the mistakes that he could make. "I recoiled inwardly from this remark," Eastman says.

> As he was then making an enviable income out of these debates and lectures, gratifying the eagerness of a half-baked American intelligentsia to gaze upon, and gather pearls of wisdom from a great British philosopher, this roused my democratic indignation. I thought he ought to give the best he had for the money and adulation he was getting. I also thought – at that time – that his political opinions were as trivial and superficial as his philosophic speculations were profound.

His political opinions, nevertheless, did not arouse the anger of the previous visit. Furthermore, his lectures on education were in general accepted as the serious contributions they indeed were. The trouble arrived with his teaching on sex, expounded to Americans in a lecture on "Companionate Marriage", given to the American Public Forum on 3 December 1927. His sexual precepts were not new, and as far back as the pre-war Edwardian days he had qualified his belief that a happy marriage could be built on mutual respect by continuing, "... but if I had the devising of our institutions, I should make provision for those women who want children more than they want a man; it could be done if prejudice were less rigid". In the United States, trial-marriages for young people not yet ready to take on the responsibilities of parenthood had already been advocated by Judge Ben B. Lindsay of Denver among others. But Lindsay had been ousted from office and the subject was guaranteed to arouse fierce protest. Russell, discussing it even within a carefully thought-out and socially responsible context, was asking for trouble. "I hope and believe", he concluded, "that the greater sexual freedom now prevailing among the young is bringing into existence a generation less cruel than that which is now old, and that a rational ethic of sex matters will, therefore, during the next twenty years, more and more prevail over the doctrines of taboo and human sacrifice which pass traditionally as 'virtue'."

The first reaction threw a faint shadow across the future. When a student body at the College of the City of New York wanted Russell to address them, the president, Frederick Robinson, refused. "As you know," he later wrote to Bishop Manning, the Protestant Episcopal Bishop of New York, whose resolute convictions tended to make the more intelligent Christian wonder if he was batting on the right side, "I believe in the fullest discussion of educational, political and social questions in a truly liberal spirit." But when a man was known to advocate practices which were both illegal and offensive to the community, he went on, there was no need to expose young students to him in order to be liberal.

Dora Russell's *The Right To Be Happy*, which preached the same gospel of sexual permissiveness as her husband's lecture on companionate marriage, had just been published in America, and within the next few weeks both came under heavy attack from the churches. The Rev. Dr Milo Gates of New York devoted a scathing sermon to *The Right To Be Happy* and shortly afterwards Dr Horace Bridges, speaking in New York at the headquarters of the Society for Ethical Culture, delivered an unqualified blast against Russell: "He often delivers extraordinarily superficial judgments about human nature with an assured air, as though they were certainties," he said. "Bertrand Russell says they are true, therefore they must be true. This is frequently his attitude; he assumes what he ought to prove. His fundamental position is dogmatic atheism, based practically on materialism. Why not object as strongly to the dogmatism of the anti-theologian as to that of the theologian."

A few weeks later, and in ignorance of the big stick he had laid in pickle for the future, Russell sailed for England, more than 10,000 dollars to the good and justifiably pleased with what had been a successful operation. Before he left he saw Helen Dudley's three sisters, the people he liked best in America. "Helen herself I did not see," he told Ottoline; "apparently now she never has sane intervals."

When he returned to the United States in 1929, an elaboration of his thinking on companionate marriage put forward to the American Public Forum two years earlier had been thrown into the arena as a book, an offering presented with all the illusory mildness which was one of his specialities. *Marriage and Morals*, in many ways a routine piece of writing-to-order, was carried out with Russell's normal ability to keep the pot boiling. On receiving the manuscript, Allen & Unwin had sent it to Sir James Marchant, a well-known social worker whom Scotland Yard employed as their expert on obscenity. He passed it as unobjectionable. Some of it bore the mark of hurried research or judgment, and when it was about to be reprinted yet again Russell wrote to Stanley Unwin noting, "It has been drawn to my attention that on page 209 of 'Marriage and Morals' I say 'It seems on the whole fair to regard negroes as on the average inferior to white men'. I wish in any future reprint to substitute for the words: 'It seems on the whole fair', the words 'There is no sound reason'."

The changing relationships between the sexes down the years were described in the book, considerable emphasis being given to the coming of Christianity, to romantic love, to the taboo on sex knowledge, to divorce, population and eugenics. All unexceptional. Even more so was the conclusion on what was important in sexual morality. "The first thing to be secured", Russell stressed, "is that there should be as much as possible of that deep, serious love between man and woman which embraces the whole personality of both and leads to a fusion by which each is enriched and enhanced. The second thing of importance is that there should be adequate care of children, physical and psychological." Russell in fact came down heavily in favour of marriage. His main qualifications were that trial-marriages were in some cases desirable and that a lapse into sexual unfaithfulness by either married partner should not, necessarily, be a ground for divorce. It is a measure of his ability as a prophet that the first proposal has become widely accepted in the Western world and that the second has in fact been written into the English divorce-law. However, Russell suffered the usual penalty of the man out front, and was widely abused by those who criticized what were then revolutionary proposals but who ignored his accolade for the state of marriage. He expected as much and was not put out. When his sister-in-law Elizabeth told him that the book made a friend's hair stand on end he replied, "It should serve instead of vibro-massage."

In the United States, criticism was strong, particularly among those who had not read the book. It would have been strong even without the efforts of Bishop Manning. An expatriate Englishman who was later to lead the assault on Russell's appointment to the College of the City of New York, Manning was sincere, unbending and well versed in all tricks of the political as well as the clerical trades, a tough opponent whose abilities only a person innocent of the world would have been rash enough to underrate.

As soon as news reached him of the lecture-tour Russell was to make in 1929, Manning wrote to Dr Butler, president of Columbia University. President Robinson of the College of the City of New York, he said, had refused to allow Russell to lecture there because of his openly immoral teaching, and he did not believe that Butler would allow Columbia University to give its countenance or its moral support to such teaching as Bertrand Russell's. "He is an aggressive propagandist against both Christian faith and Christian morality. Adultery is just as much a sin as lying or stealing, and I do not see how the University can give its support to a man who advocates the one any more than to a man who advocates the others," he went on. Butler, who a decade earlier had awarded the Butler Gold Medal to Russell for his outstanding contribution to philosophy, obediently toed the line. Despite whatever arrangements had already been made, Russell would not lecture at Columbia.

In Britain, reaction to *Marriage and Morals* was more sophisticated, although Roy Campbell subsequently portrayed Russell as one of the masters at the summer school for love which is described in *The Georgiad*.

> Hither flock all the crowd whom love has wrecked
> Of intellectuals without intellect
> And sexless folk whose sexes intersect:

All who in Russell's burly frame admire
The "lineaments of gratified desire",
And of despair have baulked the yawning precipice
By swotting up his melancholy recipes
For "happiness" – of which he is the cook
And knows the weight, the flavour, and the look,
Just how much self-control you have to spice it with,
And the right kind of knife you ought to slice it with:
How to "rechauffe" the stock-pot of desire
Although the devil pisses on the fire:
How much long-suffering and how much bonhomie
You must stir up, with patience and economy,
To get it right: then of this messy stew
Take the square root, and multiply by two,
And serve lukewarm, before the scum congeals,
An appetiser for your hearth-side meals.
All who have learned this grim felicity
And swotted bliss up, like the Rule of Three,
As if life were a class-examination
And there were penance in cohabitation:
All who of "Happiness" have learned the ropes
From Bertrand Russell or from Marie Stopes,
To put their knowledge into practice, some
With fierce determination dour and glum,
But all with earnest faces, hither come;
And hither, too, the poets of the land
Even though in "Happiness" they take no hand.

The shadow of *Marriage and Morals* fell long across much of Russell's 1929 tour, but the notoriety paid dividends and enabled Feakins to draw a full house to his debate with John Cowper Powys on "Is Modern Marriage a Failure?" On this visit his reputation carried him to the West Coast by way of Salt Lake City. "The Mormons tried to convert me," he recalled, "but when I found they forbade tea and tobacco I thought it was no religion for me." In the West he spoke in San Francisco, Los Angeles and San Diego, a lecturer's battle-course that he described to Ottoline as he sank back into the comparative calm of Beacon Hill's persistent problems. "I have been North, South, East & West – down the Pacific coast from Vancouver to Mexico, across the Continent with visits to Mormons, Judge Lindsay, & other wild men en route." he wrote.

Queer country. At one place they asked me to speak to *men only* on Marriage & Morals, & when I got there I found they were broadcasting my speech! It didn't matter ladies hearing it if they were not *seen* hearing it. On the other hand, Texas, which on the movies is nothing but cowboys, contains the only known human beings who have read all three volumes of 'Principia Mathematica'. The South is the queerest place. Every man you meet assures you he is a gentleman, even if he is. But they lynch negroes with horrible cruelty, & a Rabbi told me his congregation ordered him to say nothing against a lynching that occurred in his neighbourhood. In strikes, the police fire volleys on the strikers, killing many; the survivors are hanged for having had the effrontery to remain alive. One woman, whose husband (not a striker) was shot in cold blood by the police, was informed that she had no redress, as she was an atheist & was therefore legally debarred from giving evidence. But they pay me vast sums to say what they kill their compatriots for saying.

Russellization of unpleasant truths ran parallel with a cool determination that American money was better in his pocket than theirs; just as Major Barbara enjoyed getting the hard cash from Undershaft, so did Russell chalk up a minor victory when commissioned to supply a weekly article for the Hearst Press. The contract came largely as a result of his American tours and produced a splendid series of articles which covered "Who May Use Lipstick", "On the Fierceness of Vegetarians", "Love and Money" and "Should Socialists Smoke Good Cigars". Then the contributor's fee was halved; then the series was stopped – according to Russell because he refused to visit Hearst's Californian castle, possibly because the original Citizen Kane had at last tumbled to the propaganda concealed in the articles.

Late in 1931 Russell returned to Britain from the third and last of his Beacon Hill fund-raising tours during which he lectured from coast to coast in the commanding guise of "The English socialist writer and peer of the realm" – his brother having died a few months earlier. They had taken him to the United States for only about six months in all, but they had transformed his position there. Even after his notoriety during the war, he had remained in America a figure better known within academic and left-wing circles than outside them. The whistle-stop tours had changed that, helping to make him in America the controversial, newsworthy, figure he had already become in Britain. Financially, the tours had been a success, but success had to be balanced against a darkening scene. The early 1930s marked a turning-point in the history of Europe and in much the same way they marked a change in Russell's. His relations with Dora began to go from worse to worst, Beacon Hill remained badly in the red and he saw no prospect of escaping from the journalistic treadmill into the calm of philosophy.

Only an almost perverse optimism kept him going. "Dearest O," he wrote, "you and I are shipwrecked mariners climbing the mast of a sinking ship – we must be engulfed in the end, but meantime we can enjoy the beauty of the angry sea."

16

End of an Experiment

In 1931, that watershed between the two world wars when Britain went off the gold standard and Hitler won the support of German industry, Russell succeeded to the earldom on the death of his brother in Marseilles.

Unconventional to the last, Frank Russell had told friends a few hours earlier that he was about to die, but so light-heartedly that they did not believe him. "It was very horrible as he had been dead rather a long time," Russell wrote to Ottoline after he had gone to France to identify the body. "He looked more than life-size and terribly cruel, like some dark heathen deity to whom human sacrifices are offered. I wish that had not been my last impression of him."

Succession to the earldom raised problems. Russell at once announced that he had no intention of taking over his brother's City interests. Frank's directorships, he wrote to Stanley Unwin, "lost him every penny that he possessed, but I find other forms of expenditure more agreeable". There was also the question of what he should be called, particularly worrying to some of his American colleagues and acquaintances, one of whom asked Whitehead what the answer was. "Well, it's difficult to say," replied Whitehead: "I always call him 'Bertie'." As for the title itself, Russell did not intend to capitalize on it. "A title is a great nuisance to me," he confided to his American publisher, "& I am at a loss what to do, but at any rate I do not wish it employed in connection with any of my literary work. There is, so far as I know, only one method of getting rid of it, which is [to be] attainted of high treason & this would involve my head being cut off on Tower Hill. This method seems to me perhaps somewhat extreme ..." Dora agreed, and together they issued the statement that neither would use the title except when strictly necessary for formal occasions.

Russell's first wife might have reacted differently. Alys, travelling in the Mediterranean with Lucy Donnelly, remarked on hearing of Frank's death, "And now I won't be a Countess, although I might have been."

More important than the question of title was whether Russell should take his seat in the House of Lords. He had a healthy irreverence for the institution, first shown two decades earlier when he might have been raised to the peerage had the Lords continued to block reforms. He would, he had threatened, choose the title of Lord Snooks.

Now, in 1931, he replied cautiously to Lord Marley, Chief Government Whip in the Lords, "I hope to take my seat before very long and I shall be a supporter of the Labour Party, unless possibly on some quite exceptional issue. I have been for many years a member of the I.L.P., and have every intention of remaining so. I do not, however, expect to attend regularly or to give a very great deal of time to politics ..."

Four days later he wondered whether he should have been more specific. "It seems that Marley is a very vigorous Whip," he complained to Fenner Brockway.

> He has been inundating me with letters practically saying that if I go out for the afternoon I must telegraph to him to say where I am going. I do not, however, intend to take much part in the affairs of the House of Lords. I shall take my seat, and probably once in a way speak on issues that are inconvenient for people with constituencies, such as divorce and obscene literature. But I do not intend to be turned aside by an accident from writing, which is clearly my proper job, nor do I think that it matters much whether the Labour case is stated well or badly in the House of Lords. If we had on our side any vigorous strategist, such as Lloyd George used to be, we should adopt the scheme which he adopted in 1909, of tempting the Lords to folly by not letting them know the strength of the forces they were antagonising.

A different view was taken by many of his friends. "You have more courage than I," wrote Gilbert Murray, "as well as more power of intellect, and I believe that the sort of thing you have to say to the world ought to be said – and said repeatedly – in some places like the H of L, where you have a quiet and intelligent though sleepy and reactionary audience, and where you can get a pulpit to address the country, instead of merely inspiring intellectual socialists and the like." In reply Russell explained frankly why he was refusing to enter the political arena, as he had refused to enter it more than thirty years earlier when on the verge of a career. "I shrink from the thought of addressing so hostile an audience as the Peers," he wrote, "and I cannot in any case do so as [Frank] did on behalf of the Government, even if the Government desired my support. I am too dissatisfied with them in many respects to be able to become a loyal Party man. I like their conduct of foreign affairs and their concordat with Gandhi, but not their complete inaction at home."

Russell's political stance, his aristocratic determination to go his own way regardless, was paralleled by his position in philosophy. He had held no permanent academic post for more than a decade and his views created enemies. But his known independence counted for a lot, and it was to Russell that Trinity turned when it needed advice on how to handle Wittgenstein. A few years earlier, during the printing of the *Tractatus*, Russell had met Wittgenstein at Innsbruck where they had discussed Russell's introduction to the book. Wittgenstein disliked both the introduction and Russell's plans for a new edition of *Principia Mathematica*, which he thought so wrong as to make a new edition futile.

But Russell was now quite unexpectedly asked to examine him for a Ph.D. based on the *Tractatus*. "I think ... that unless Wittgenstein has changed his opinions of me, he will not much like to have me as an Examiner," he told Moore, now Professor of Philosophy. "The last time we met he was so much pained by the fact of my not being a Christian that he has avoided me ever since; I do not know whether pain on this account has grown less, but he must still dislike me, as he has never communicated with me since. I do not want him to run out of the room in the middle of the Viva, which I feel is the sort of thing he might do."

He need not have worried. Moore and Russell first chatted informally to Wittgenstein as old friends rather than as examiners and examinee. Then Russell turned to Moore. "Go on," he said, "you've got to ask him some questions – *you're* the Professor." There was a short discussion. Russell made a brief attempt to argue that Wittgenstein was inconsistent in stating that little could be said about philosophy and that it was possible to reach unassailable truth. Then the Viva ended unexpectedly with Wittgenstein clapping each of his examiners on the shoulder and exclaiming, "Don't worry, I know you'll *never* understand it."

He got his Ph.D., and a grant from Trinity to carry on research. Nine months later a further grant was in the offing and the college once again turned to Russell for a report on the work his former pupil had done. He could hardly refuse. "At the same time," he went on, "since it involves arguing with him, you are right that it will require a great deal of work. I do not know anything more fatiguing than disagreeing with him in an argument."

It turned out that Wittgenstein had so far written nothing; but he would like to discuss his ideas with Russell. They did so during a mutually exhausting weekend at Telegraph House. "Of course we couldn't get very far in two days," Wittgenstein reported to Moore, "but he seemed to understand a *little* bit of it."

He reappeared some weeks later with the *Philosophische Bemerkungen*, a massive typescript made up almost entirely of rough notes which he tried to explain to Russell during a day and a half's visit. For his part, Russell wrote a brief note to Moore, hoping that that would be enough. "I have at the moment", he said, "so much to do that the effort involved in reading Wittgenstein's stuff thoroughly is almost more than I can face." However, he was finally coaxed by Moore into writing a formal report. "The theories contained in this new work of Wittgenstein's are novel, very original, and indubitably important," ran his final paragraph. "Whether they are true I do not know. As a logician who likes simplicity, I should wish to think that they are not, but from what I have read of them I am quite sure that he ought to have an opportunity to work them out, since when completed they may easily prove to constitute a whole new philosophy."

Russell's plea of having "so much to do" was very justified. He still had Beacon Hill on his hands. He was desperately short of money and he was writing round the clock to pay the bills. Moreover, as the 1920s turned into the 1930s, his private life, with what seemed to be its unavoidable agonies and accidents, once again began to demand more of his physical time and his emotional energy. His succession to the earldom, his renewed relationship with Wittgenstein and the growth of financial problems at Beacon Hill were all taking place against the background of increasingly personal complications. Throughout his previous adventures, Russell had kept firm control of the way things went. Now he was to be batted back and forth by events, so that for some years most of his energies were diverted to coping with *ad hoc* personal problems. Philosophy languished in a backwater, and in his tower at night he even wrote of *Principia Mathematica* that "the whole of this effort, in spite of three big volumes, ended inwardly in doubt and bewilderment". As for his belief that the sensible world was real, the crux of his abandonment of Idealism more than thirty years earlier, "this delight [had] faded, and I have been driven to a position not unlike that of Berkeley, without his God and his Anglican complacency". Depression descended and at least two sympathetic observers among the Beacon Hill staff feared he was going off his head. The master-touch had failed.

The main cause of the trouble was simple. During the first years of their marriage Russell and Dora had honestly believed that it would survive the strains inherent in their willingness to tolerate each other's *affaires*. The first test came when he was in the United States. Russell has said,

> While there I had a brief and unimportant affaire of which I told her on my return. She did not tell me until two years later that she meantime had had an affaire ... In view of the fact that we had been apart at the time, neither of us had much difficulty in tolerating what the other had done, but in later years things increasingly went wrong. She informed me that she was about to have an affaire with a certain young man and I who had been much attracted in another quarter thereupon followed her example.

These passing interludes might not, of themselves, have brought their chosen variety of marriage to an end. However, as he was to write of his break-up with Alys, he did not think it was within his nature "to remain physically fond of any woman for more than seven or eight years". By 1930 he had been married for nine.

This was bad enough; but it was not all. He was now past his mid-fifties, a distinguished figure and a man of the world who should have been difficult to capsize in even the most delicate of sophisticated situations. He was constantly endangered, however, by two characteristics: a genuine wish to introduce young people to the exciting world of books and science that he had inhabited all his life, and an insatiable appetite for personable and intelligent young women. In these circumstances he was obliged to skate over ice so thin that he was saved from public scandal more by good luck than good management.

There was, for instance, the case of Joan Follwell, a twenty-one-year-old girl whom he met after addressing a political meeting in Salisbury and whose story reveals the quintessential Russell of the period. "My family gave him hospitality as they did to visiting speakers," she later recalled, "and I remember that I walked home with him. When we had supper he asked my parents if he could talk to me alone. He asked me to read [an essay she had written] and I then realised that he was more interested in me than my writing."

The upshot was a series of letters to "My dear Joan (may I call you so?)" progressing to "My darling Joan", and thence to an invitation. When he returned to Telegraph House from Cornwall he would spend a night in his London flat, he said. "I should awfully like to know whether you will be willing to come to me for the night there," he went on. "My only fear is lest you may find me inadequate sexually, as I am no longer young, and not so satisfactory as a young man; but I think there are ways in which I can make up for it. And I do want you dreadfully, & I am sure I can help you in ways you will like – to know people, to come across books, to think out your problems and so on."

At this point a slight difficulty arose. Miss Follwell, it appeared, already had a young man. However, this was not necessarily an impediment. "I do not in the least mind anything you say about the man you love," Russell reassured her. "I don't want to possess you exclusively; how could I in fairness? I am sure that, with your temperament, you will not long continue to refuse all other men than your one occasional lover; if his attitude is such that you have to deceive him, that is a pity, but the fault is his, not yours." If she moved permanently to London he was willing to subsidize her rent with 10*s.* a week. That would make meetings easier. The alternative was for her to stay with him at a hotel. "This is not so nice & costs just as much as helping with the rent," he argued.

"The advantages of [a hotel]," he later pointed out, "are that you can have breakfast in bed; if you come to me we can only have what we can prepare ourselves, or else we could go out to breakfast. Also we must, in my flat, pay some slight deference to the landlady's scruples, by going out separately (if at all) in the early morning. (She is quite friendly, & only wants not to *have* to know.)"

However, he booked a room at a hotel. Then Providence willed otherwise. An argument had broken out among the Telegraph House staff and he was forced to cancel the arrangement with a hasty telegram.

Next, one of the journeys to the United States intervened. On his return he sent Miss Follwell a reminder: "Remember that I am very fond of you & very anxious to help you, & very anxious for a chance to be your lover." However, she still dithered. A year later, however, she was making firm inquiries about what their relationship was to be.

"It is true that I am by no means completely free," he replied.

> My lack of freedom has its source in my affection for my children, which has become the most important thing in my life. For their sakes, I must avoid causing their mother too much unhappiness. Neither she nor I make any pretence of conjugal fidelity, but she is still fond of me, & so certain decencies have to be preserved. If I failed in this, difficulties would arise between us, & the children would suffer. It is also for the sake of the children that I think it necessary to earn a good deal of money, which, of course, takes up much of my time, & involves occasionally going to America. All this lack of freedom is self-imposed, & is not quite absolute. But it means that I have to plan some way ahead to get free time.

Eventually, meetings were organized. "The second time", says Miss Follwell, "I had dinner with him and the third time I slept. He was very tenacious; this lasted over three years. But the sleeping wasn't a success so I gave him up."

Subsequently Russell sent her a parting letter. "My dearest Joan," this went. "Only a moment remains before the post goes – I have been rushed every moment since we parted – but I do want to tell you how happy I am in the memory of the hours during which you were with me – it was even more lovely than I had expected; and you were so kind & dear! Write me a word to say how you are & how the time composes itself in your memory. *Must* stop. Goodbye my love."

More than forty years later, Joan Follwell sold Russell's letters and, in a long tape-recording, regretted that she had not become a permanent feature of his life. "I think myself", she added, "that Russell is largely responsible for this so-called permissive society but that he wouldn't have liked it if he had seen it now ... He wanted to attain the ends he had in mind but he wanted to avoid hurting people."

The dual motives with which a man who was among the greatest philosophers of the century assiduously stuck to the seduction of the young girl over several years, nearly as anxious for her enlightenment as for her conquest, illustrates more than most episodes in Russell's life not so much the contrasting as the complementary aspects of his character. The supporter of the No-Conscription Fellowship in the First World War had a respect for action that could bring a genuine "I do so wish I'd done something like that" to a colleague describing the St Nazaire Raid of 1942. Years later a woman friend was to say that if he thought he was the nearest a man could get to being God he was also very close to being Satan as well. The parts made the whole man, an example in human terms of Niels Bohr's complementarity principle in physics: whether light consists of waves or moving particles depends entirely on their properties being investigated, since the subject under study has dual characteristics. So had Russell.

While Miss Follwell was reluctant to become too closely involved with a man thirty years her senior, he on his side was giving part of his attentions elsewhere. He had never been able to shut out from his mind the thought of Colette, still adoring and still undeterred by the worst he could do to her.

They had renewed contact a few years earlier when she found a letter from him pinned to the green baize board of the Hull theatre where she was playing. He had asked if he could bring John Conrad to see her, a plea barely concealing his inability to let the dead past bury its dead. Colette agreed and John was brought to the home of her mother, Lady Annesley, for an afternoon visit. A week later Russell and Colette dined and spent the evening alone there.

Slowly, like the tide coming in, their relationship crept on towards its earlier importance. Their correspondence ebbed and flowed, intermittently and unsatisfactorily as though each half-hoped, half-feared, that the other would make the next step forward. Then she was booked for a year's tour in South Africa. On hearing the news he begged her to spend her last day with him before sailing. He would be quite alone at Telegraph House except for the school staff.

The memory of that long day with her on the Sussex Downs never faded, a deep draught of the life he had known only ten years before but which now belonged to another world. He knew once again all he still felt for her, as he admitted in a brief anguished letter. During the following months she wrote weekly from South Africa to Lady Annesley, who shared the letters with Russell. Then she wrote to him direct. He replied immediately, hoping only that they would often be together again when she returned. He wanted to visit her Somerset home where she had been living between tours; the house on the top of the Mendips, from which she could see, "tramping home on winter evenings, the Clevedon lights swarm and cluster over the Channel – towards Lynton".

When Colette returned to England Russell was lecturing in America. When he came back, she was on tour again and it was some while before he finally arrived at Blagdon-in-Mendip. As they took long tramps over the hills, remembering Shropshire and Lulworth and Lynton, he asked if there was any reason why they should not be lovers as before. "On my side of course there isn't," she replied. Before leaving, he invited her to Cornwall where he would be quite alone with the children.

It was, as it turned out, to be an eventful summer. On 8 July 1930, Dora gave birth in London to a daughter. The father was a young American journalist, Griffin Barry, who had been living intermittently at Beacon Hill. Many years later Russell claimed that at the end of 1919 he and Dora had agreed that, while they would mutually tolerate each other's *affaires*, he had "stipulated that if she should have a child that was not [his] there should be a divorce". However, his first reaction to the coming birth was along different lines. He had, Dora has said, seemed "unable" to give her a third child and, hearing during his 1929 tour of the United States that one was apparently on the way from another source, had written, "Since I cannot do my part, it is better someone else should, as you ought to have more children."

Later he began to fear for the psychological repercussions on Kate and John, but believed that he would be able to reduce these to a minimum. "So I tried to endure the new child & behave towards her as if she were my own," he later wrote. At times the effort failed and a visitor to Beacon Hill, finding Russell cooing over a baby in a pram and asking if it was his, was told, "No, it's my wife's." The effort to treat the girl as his own was beyond his strength, he has admitted. "I did not at all dislike her & I felt strongly that it would be unjust & bad for her if, so long as we were nominally all one family, I allowed any preference for my own children to appear. But the resulting strain of daily and hourly insincerity was intolerable, & made family life a torture."

The child, Harriet Ruth Barry, was registered in Russell's name; not until five years later, when he found the child listed as his in Debrett, did he begin a campaign for removal of the name that was to last thirty years. But although he continually struck her name from the proofs sent to him, her birth-certificate showed her as his daughter, and no action was taken. Only on 11 July 1963 did his solicitors state that her birth-certificate would be altered. But although the name was thereafter omitted from Debrett, no alteration in the birth-certificate was made. Instead, the young woman had changed her name by deed poll.

The arrival of Harriet marked the beginning of the end of Russell's second marriage. He did in fact do his best to soldier on with it and only when Dora provided Griffin Barry with a son, two years later, did he begin to hanker for a divorce. Gentlemen did not divorce their wives in those days, but that presented no problem. Dora had ample grounds if she could be persuaded to take action.

In July 1930, with the girl safely delivered, Russell drove John and Kate to Cornwall, picking up *en route* a young woman whom Dora had engaged as governess for the summer. Marjorie Spence was a competent and beautiful Oxford undergraduate, usually known as "Peter", after she had changed her name to Patricia. John and Kate liked Miss Spence and remarked how unfortunate it was that none of the teachers at Beacon Hill were as nice. "She and I were left *tête-à-tête* every evening after the children were in bed," Russell has said, "and in the course of conversation we soon came to know a good deal about each other."

Their evening exchanges were interrupted by the arrival of Colette, who told her mother, "There's a nursery-governess to see to [the children] and pack them off to bed. She packs herself off as well, so he and I have the evenings alone together, which is blessed beyond words." During the mornings Russell worked at a small table in the front-room of Carn Voel while Colette worked on a book of reminiscences at the back. After lunch, there was a car drive and a picnic with the children; a walk on the cliffs or a ramble on the Penwith moors which rose inland. They sailed to the Scillies, stayed on St Mary's, and back in Cornwall had a glorious day with John and Kate visiting the *Cutty Sark* in Falmouth. "The children were the children of one's dreams," Colette wrote, "happy, fearless, free."

But beneath the idyllic exterior something was wrong. Russell, "his wiry leanness ... gone," as Colette wrote, was worried and beginning to show his age. Drawing on instinct and experience, Colette may have thought more than casually about Peter Spence. "B has told [her] that I'm an 'old friend'," she wrote. "Whether she believes it or not, I don't know. Though young, she strikes me as not inexperienced. The house is cramped, her room close to mine." Some cool ripple from the past blew across the happy surface of events, and one morning Russell asked somewhat querulously, "What keeps you going?" "I replied 'Work'," Colette later wrote, "(Precisely what keeps him going, naturally). There was a slight flavour of resentment in his question. Having left me to sink or swim during Peking, he seemed to resent that I didn't – utterly – sink. (Heaven forgive me if I do him an injustice.)"

Colette's departure coincided with the arrival at Carn Voel of Dora, Barry, the young daughter, and a male companion of Barry's whom Russell greatly disliked and whom he instantly, and no doubt irrationally, dubbed as a "spy". In the mornings and early afternoons he and Peter took John and Kate to bathe and climb the rocks or build sandcastles. They returned at tea-time after which Dora washed the baby, Barry looked on, and the maids remarked that "anyone would think he was the child's father". The situation was still further confused by the arrival of Freda Utley, an American friend of Russell whom he had known for many years. On seeing Barry's friend she shrank back and whispered to Russell that she had been warned against him. Remarkably, everyone survived.

When the summer of 1930 ended Russell and his wife returned to Beacon Hill school "to work out a *modus vivendi*", as he described it. Dora engaged Peter to come to Telegraph House for the Christmas holidays and it was then, according to Russell's story, that Peter and he became attracted to each other.

"There were various reasons for avoiding, if possible, a formal breach between Dora and me," he wrote years later. "Not only would it inevitably be bad for John and Kate, but it would make it impossible to carry on the school as a joint enterprise." There was as yet no ill-will between them, as Russell showed in his accounts of the situation to Ottoline. As for Dora, she told Ottoline that her husband had been as dear as he always was.

After Christmas Peter returned to Oxford to continue her studies, but the following summer a *ménage à quatre* was set up at Hendaye, where the Pyrenees meet the Atlantic coast. To the villa which Russell rented there came Dora and Griffin Barry, Peter and himself, John Kate and Dora's younger daughter. The weeks passed without serious incident, which says a good deal for everyone's tolerance. "Dora and I remain the best of friends all through our respective vagaries," Russell wrote to Ottoline after their return. "Apart from financial anxiety I am very happy about the whole thing."

In the late autumn, Russell left England for his 1931 lecture-tour of the United States. "I returned from America", he later wrote, "resolved to break off relations with [Peter], but she was determined to prevent this. I had a feeling of guilt towards her ... Also, I was still in love with her. There seemed no issue from this situation except divorce from Dora and marriage to Peter ..."

The transformation was to take three years and its progress should be briefly recounted before dealing with the work that Russell carried on with his right hand throughout the period while his left was dealing with the lawyers. At the start of 1932 he was still uncertain of what was to happen, an uncertainty made clear in numerous letters to Ottoline, some written by him, some by Peter. In March, Dora gave birth to a son by Griffin Barry. No special problems arose, since he was simply registered as Mr Barry's, while in Russell's eyes the event made a divorce from Dora more likely.

Dora carried on with the school and Russell carried on with Peter. Then, towards the end of the year, it was agreed that a Deed of Separation should be signed. It recited the existence of their matrimonial differences; it recorded the birth of Dora's two elder children; and it recorded the birth and parentage of her two other children, a statement which her counsel subsequently referred to as an admission of adultery. However, under a comparatively unusual clause in the Deed, both parties agreed that they would not invoke, in any future proceedings, any matrimonial offence which had taken place before the date of the Deed, 31 December 1932.

Russell's two children were made Wards in Chancery before Dora's petition for divorce was heard on 21 July 1934. An impediment now arose. While her counsel admitted her adultery before the Deed of Separation, he claimed that the special clause in it prevented her from going into details. The President of the Court declined to accept this until given further authority for the situation: and, when the case was resumed five days later, once again declined despite the fact that Dora produced her discretion statement. This time he invited "the assistance of the King's Proctor for the purpose of considering the whole matter".

That evidence was given four months later. "It suffices to say", commented the President of the Court, Sir Boyd Merriman, in eventually granting Dora her divorce,

> that her statement shows that both instances of her adultery of which she has spoken were preceded by at least two cases of infidelity on the part of her husband, and that he had been guilty of numerous acts of adultery in circumstances which are usually held to aggravate the offence. I am referring to the fact that she spoke of the infidelity of the respondent with persons in the household or engaged in the business in which they were mutually occupied. Finally, there had been, for at least two years before the Deed of Separation, association with the woman with regard to whom evidence of adultery after the execution of the Deed was given.

Early in 1935 Dora was granted her decree. Before it was made absolute there was bitter argument as to how Russell's two children were to be provided for through two Trusts he had earlier set up in their favour. A number of his close friends were drawn into the controversy. Some supported Dora, among them Francis Meynell, Russell's old friend from the Brotherhood Church battle of 1917. Meynell became trustee of a fund established for John and Kate, and to him Dora wrote in 1935, "I have never neglected or abandoned any of my children, and have done more for them than either of their fathers ever did." Great characters can have odd relapses into pettiness, Meynell later wrote.

> It was so with Bertrand Russell, always a hero of mine as well as a friend. When he and Dora were divorced I became involved in a dispute between them as to who should pay for their children's clothes. I did my best to make a reasonable accord between the parents. Dora was an equal friend, but I now saw more of her than of Bertie, and favoured her stance in this and other pathetically trivial developments of their quarrel. In May 1935 Bertie wrote grudgingly to me that he had accepted my decision about the payments for the

children's outfits. But his conclusion was definitely against me: "During the divorce proceedings, at a time when I had all the cards in my hand, you intervened and *forced* me to negotiate with Dora ... As you compelled me to enter into the concordat, it is clearly up to you to see that it is carried out". Dora was not, in my view, the trouble-maker, and I had clearly lost my influence over Bertie. So no accord was established. Yes, a great man can have his littlenesses.

Like many of Russell's friends, he may well have believed that whatever the individual rights or wrongs of the tangled situation, both parties were reaping, in almost Biblical fashion, what they had sown.

A sidelight on Russell's attitude, and on his handling of facts outside his professional orbit, is thrown by Elias Bredsdorff, then a young Danish Socialist student who invited him to Denmark later in 1935. To Bredsdorff, Russell said that he had been anxious to prevent Peter's name from being brought into the divorce-court and had gone through the customary motions of discovering a suitable co-respondent. Bredsdorff relates,

At the appointed hour the lady arrived, and both she and Russell were rather embarrassed about the whole situation. After having allowed themselves to be seen by as many people as possible in the hotel they went up to the bedroom, and Russell then told his co-respondent that unless she insisted on their going to bed together he would prefer them to sit up all night and talk. Russell was very pleased to learn that the lady was fond of playing chess. So they sat down at a table in the bedroom and played chess and talked in a much more light-hearted atmosphere than when they first met. But suddenly, just before mid-night, Bertrand Russell jumped up: "We forgot the shoes", he said, and they then hurriedly took off their shoes, and he put both pairs outside the door, neatly next to one another. Then they went on playing chess and talking.

What Russell omitted to state was that the petition for divorce in March 1934 had of course claimed "adultery with a Miss Marjorie Spence since the beginning of 1933".

Throughout the disintegration of his second marriage, spread as it was across an agonizingly long period, Russell continued to write books and articles with his usual prodigality. Many of them reflected the change in his interests which had taken place during the war, his heightened concern with social affairs, with politics and with the effect of science on society. They reflected, also, an attitude to human affairs which was less common then than it is today, an attitude which demanded that the organization of society should serve the individual, regardless of political or religious dogma. This feeling for the individual as the important unit infused a great deal that Russell wrote between the wars, and accounts for the immense popularity of his works, particularly among the young. This was very different from, and in many ways much more important than, the respect he had already earned in philosophical circles, and it was to come to his aid two decades later when the problem of dealing with nuclear weapons became the last great attachment of his life.

The Conquest of Happiness came in 1930, a book whose recipe was much in demand by Russell himself. With qualifications, the recipe worked. The Russell in whom, as Peter wrote to Ottoline, there was still "a great deal of the motherless small boy", was usually supported, even on his darkest days, by the intellectual lifebuoy he had built to make life bearable.

Two years later came *Education and the Social Order*. The book incorporated the lessons learned at Beacon Hill and qualified the over-idealistic recipes of *On Education: Especially in Early Childhood*. When it came to writing he was still in the familiar cleft stick, caught between the wish to say what he wanted and the need to make money, the latter gravely increased by the American slump which was causing a catastrophic drop in his U.S. sales. "I am anxious", he wrote in an illuminating note to Stanley Unwin, "to write a book which will sell well and not involve too much research. 'Marriage and Morals' and 'The Conquest of Happiness' both fulfilled these two conditions. The latter I am not very proud of, but as a propagandist I am not at all sorry to have written the former. Nevertheless I should prefer to write something more analogous to 'The Scientific Outlook'."

This easy option was not yet forthcoming. Instead there followed three books which were in no sense pot-boilers, in whose production Peter played a considerable part, and which in their own various ways were solid achievements. The first was *Freedom and Organization, 1814–1914* which traced the causes of political change during the century and balanced the effect of individuals against the economic techniques which they used.

"I do not want to write an ordinary history; what I want to do is to bring out the part played by beliefs in causing political events, the part which, I think, Marxists unduly minimise," Russell wrote in outlining the book to Unwin.

> I do not want to write something merely schematic and dry, and I hesitated for a long time as to the best method of dealing with such a mass of material. At the moment I incline to the view that the best plan is to take important individuals, portraying the world as they saw it. I want to bring out the extraordinary subjectivity of each man's cosmos. Consider, say, Marx and Disraeli, almost exact contemporaries, both Jews, and living in London within a stone's throw of each other. I suppose that Disraeli never heard of Marx, unless possibly in Scotland Yard dossiers. The interests, the knowledge, the

37 Russell with Sherwood Anderson before their debate on "Shall the State Rear Our Children?" in 1931

38 Russell meets pacifists in New York: (*front, left to right*) Rosika Schwimmer, Russell, Zola Lief; (*back, left to right*) Alfred Lief, Pierre Loving, W. W. Norton (one of Russell's American publishers), William Floyd

39 Russell at Harvard in 1940

40, 41 Bertrand and Peter (Patricia) Russell with their son Conrad in Los Angeles, 1940

42 Russell and Peter watching Conrad and his model train, Los Angeles, 1940

> whole universe of either was alien to that of the other. Every house in London that has at any period been inhabited by a distinguished man has a plaque, stating the fact, placed there by the public authorities, but they have refused any such mark of distinction to Karl Marx's house.
>
> My impulse is to give accounts of a number of eminent men – eminent some of them through real merit, others merely through their position. I see the period as framed between two emperors, Alexander I and William II, both completely silly, but both possessed of more influence upon the events of their own period than fell to the lot of many able men, with the exception of Bismarck. I should like to include Jefferson, although he is a little early, because I do not see how else to state the launching of the democratic idea. The whole middle period is dominated by Bismarck. Other men whom I should like to include are: Bentham, Malthus, Cobden, Robert Owen, Marx, Mazzini, Napoleon III, Disraeli, Darwin, Pasteur, perhaps Stevenson, Carnegie, Rockefeller, and as the grand finale of so much intellect, the Emperor William II ... The theme fascinates me, and if I could afford it, I should be glad to spend ten years over it.

Peter did "half the research, a large part of the planning, and small portions of the actual writing, besides making innumerable suggestions" according to a prefatory acknowledgment in the book to which an erratum slip added the word "valuable" before "suggestions". Russell liked the work – "I enjoy writing history so much that I feel prepared to continue doing it for the rest of my natural life," he told his American publisher – and before finishing it he had great plans for a successor. "I have in mind another big book such as I am doing now, on 'The Cult of Feeling' from Rousseau to Hitler," he wrote to Unwin.

> The break-up of 18th century rationalism, Wesley, Romantic Movement, medievalism (Scott, Coleridge, Tractarians, Dizzy); irrationalism in philosophy (Carlyle, Nietzsche, James, Bergson) & its connection with violence in politics. There should be an intellectual development accompanied throughout by appropriate events, from Marie Antoinette's Fêtes Champêtres to Hitler's pogroms, all of which spring from the cult of the heart as opposed to the head. There is a lot of material which I am having to leave out of my present book but which belongs to 19th century development. I want to do only substantial books for you & Norton henceforth.

The Cult of Feeling was never written, but for some while Russell continued to develop the idea and accumulate notes for what evolved into "The Revolt Against Reason", the title of an essay written for the *Political Quarterly* in 1935. Much of the material was incorporated into two later books, *Power: A New Social Analysis* and *A History of Western Philosophy*.

The first of these, which followed *Freedom and Organization* and *The Amberley Papers*, the latter a double-decker in which he and Peter reconstructed from family documents the life of Russell's parents, grew out of a series of lectures which he gave at the London School of Economics in the autumn of 1937 on "The Science of Power". "I am very keen on it myself," he wrote to Stanley Unwin. "I think of it as founding a new science, like Adam Smith's 'Wealth of Nations'." If *Power* did not quite achieve this, it was yet a remarkable document, dissecting the forms which authority takes down the years and outlining the means of directing them to the common good.

Such a spate of serious books, although lacking the high challenge of his professional philosophy, nevertheless put him in the running for many others. Some were turned down, as when he declined Gilbert Murray's proposal for a book on how to think, on the grounds that he had too much work in hand. He went on,

> Secondly, – and this is more important – because I haven't the vaguest idea either how I think or how one ought to think. The process, so far as I know it, is as instinctive and unconscious as digestion. I fill my mind with whatever relevant knowledge I can find, and just wait. With luck, there comes a moment when the work is done, but in the meantime my conscious mind has been occupied with other things. This sort of thing won't do for a book ...

Nevertheless, he pigeon-holed the idea away for future use and a few years later, when very hard up in the United States, wrote a forty-page pamphlet called *How to Become a Philosopher* (*The Art of Rational Conjecture*): *How to Become a Logician* (*The Art of Drawing Inferences*): *How to Become a Mathematician* (*The Art of Reckoning*). The publisher was E. Haldeman-Julius, one of the few Americans who helped him through a bad period. The pamphlet, later republished in the United States as *The Art of Philosophizing*, has a hint of Murray's proposal.

However, if it would not do in the 1930s, what would do was his autobiography, first proposed by Stanley Unwin. "I fully intend to write it before long," he replied,

> but I do not see how any publisher can make a very attractive proposal, seeing that it cannot be published until after I am dead – indeed, probably not until I have been dead some twenty or thirty years. I could perhaps have a Bowdlerised version published immediately on my death, and of course I could undertake to commit suicide on the day of publication, but I am afraid that if I did, you

would be liable to be hanged. For this part of the bargain, therefore, you would have to rely upon the honour of a gentleman. I have a certain hesitation in starting my biography too soon for fear of something important having not yet happened. Suppose I should end my days as President of Mexico; the biography would seem incomplete if it did not mention this fact.

Nevertheless, he decided to make a start and, sitting in the lonely tower of Telegraph House, dictated a short account of the first part of his life. He stopped, aptly enough, with his return from China with Dora. Quite aware of the manuscript's potential value, he estimated it might earn between £3,000 and £4,000, a small fraction of the sum it eventually made, but a sizeable expectation then. He sent a copy to his lawyer with a note instructing that publication be deferred until after his death and warning that parts of the manuscript might be considered obscene. He asked that persons referred to should be shown the references to themselves, and added that while there might have to be cuts, an unexpurgated copy could be kept for publication at a still later date and a limited edition perhaps issued right away.

At the same time he sent a copy to Ottoline. She liked parts of it. But the parts which dealt with her own life were another story and she begged him to leave them out. Even if they were published a hundred years on, she said, she could not bear it.

In response, Russell took evasive action.

> What you said about my autobiography worried me a good deal. Apart from the parts about you, I see on looking it over that the last chapter is not good, but I can't see what is wrong with the others. I think it will be better for me to go over the whole book, which in any case wants re-writing, before discussing details which may disappear. I have been wondering whether I am really a much nastier person than you thought I was, & this depresses me. Can we let it be till I have got my feelings in order about it all? I am still very unhappy that things I said gave you pain, & that I didn't know they would.

Soon, however, Ottoline was preparing her own version of their relationship, to be told through Russell's letters to her, although publication was to wait until both of them were dead. When Peter was told of the enterprise she asked that publication should come only after her death as well. The letters would, she feared, arouse a great deal of interest. Americans with whom he had had the slightest of relations would write books about him, she pleaded. Russell himself believed that that was not the real reason. "It worries her to think how much happened to me before she knew me," he told Ottoline.

In the face of this further complication, little more serious thought was given to the autobiography for the time being. A few cuts were made, and a few additions; Stanley Unwin was told that the manuscript existed, but it was now put away and no longer considered as a job in hand.

The complicated proceedings that preceded the divorce, the constant fear that he might be forced to see less of his son and daughter, and the ever-present difficulty in making both financial ends meet, all had their effect on Russell's health. Late in 1934 he planned an extensive European lecture-tour for the first months of 1935, but had to cancel it at the last moment. He was, his doctor considered, in a state of acute nervous exhaustion, necessitating complete rest, and was ordered to give up all work for three months. "At present," he wrote to Ottoline, "I cannot imagine any point in going on living. Nothing under the sun interests me ... At the moment I worry because I can't work & am therefore rapidly going bankrupt."

His health was saved by two months in the Canary Islands, but recovery was slow, and on his return to England at the end of March he declared himself "though sane, quite devoid of creative impulse, and at a loss to know what work to do. For about two months, purely to afford myself distraction, I worked on the problem of the twenty-seven straight lines on a cubic surface." By September he was fit enough to attend the Congress of Scientific Philosophy in Paris and, the following month, to carry out a lecture-tour in Denmark and to visit Sweden.

Only after his return did he finally decide to marry again – "the pro's and con's are fairly balanced, & sometimes one seems to preponderate, sometimes the other," he had written to Ottoline in November. Colette heard the news from a friend who sent her a clipping reporting the marriage of Russell and Peter Spence in mid-January 1936 in the registry office at Midhurst, Sussex. "Do you think he will perhaps come back to me," she wrote to Frank's widow, Elizabeth Russell, "– to die?" Years later she reflected, "In one sense my ship had gone down; on the rocks of B.R.; on the rocks of myself."

Shortly after their marriage, Russell and his third wife spent a brief holiday in Spain with their friends Gerald Brenan the writer, whom he had met from time to time in London, and his wife Gamel. Then they returned to Telegraph House, vacated by Dora after the divorce when she had moved Beacon Hill School to Brentford in Essex. Here he tried to settle down to work once again as his remaining capital steadily seeped away on the maintenance of a wholly uneconomic home. Eventually, in 1937, shortly after the birth of his son, Conrad Sebastian Robert, he was able to sell the estate. The sale hurt. Next to Cambridge, Telegraph House had been the nearest approach to a home he had known for years. He had watched the place develop under Frank's loving care for nearly forty years, and if he hated the ugliness of the house itself he loved the beauty of the surrounding countryside. Now he had cut free from that emotional anchor, an item to be balanced against the prospect of happiness with a new wife. On past form, this would last seven or eight years.

By the late 1930s Russell's earlier reputation had been reinforced by *The Analysis of Mind*, by *The Analysis of Matter* and by the occasional paper or essay in the serious philosophical journals. He had diversified his interests into education and foreign policy, written a weekly diary for the *New Statesman* for a while, trailed his coat on sex and marriage, polemically as well as practically, and frequently given the impression that he was, with Huxley and Haldane, among the last of the polymaths, able to talk eruditely but engagingly on any subject drawn from the hat.

His wide spread of activities as a professional writer made him sensitive to plagiarism and he had more than one brush with C. E. M. Joad, listed by the Sunday newspaper for which he wrote as "Britain's leading philosopher". For Joad, Russell mustered as much dislike as he could muster for anyone, once refusing to write a preface for one of his books with the words, "Modesty forbids." His dislike was partly due to Joad's inability to pass from one woman to the next without leaving a residue of bitterness or ill-will; partly to the boasting with which he conducted his private affairs. However, Russell's comment after Joad had been sentenced for defrauding the railway and had turned to religion – that "he lost his railway ticket and found his God" – was not entirely due to contempt for the way he ran his personal life. His real feelings were revealed when Joad had the temerity to ask for Russell's commendation of his *Guide to Philosophy*. Russell drafted a reply saying that for one reason he could not give it. He explained, in a letter which may never have been posted:

> I have observed in former books of yours a habit of quoting without inverted commas or other indication that the words are not your own; & in this book you carry the same practice to lengths which I cannot feel to be excusable. I cannot tell how far you have treated other authors in this way, but naturally I am not inclined to suppose myself the only person to whom you have shown this mark of respect.
>
> My chief criticism is concerned with pp. 474–483 and p. 387. No one would guess from what you say that
>
> (a) All the quotations from Marx & Engels given in those passages are in my book, & where I translated them you have used my translation;
>
> (b) the use of the theses on Feuerbach to interpret the dialectical element in Marx's materialism, & the reference to Dewey as similar, are not your own.
>
> There are, later, two quotations from Marx which are not from

me; I do not know where you found them. But you have given no evidence of what of course, I do not doubt, that you have ever seen any work of Marx & Engels.

It was not an isolated instance. "Joad had no influence upon me whatsoever, and in fact I thought him a charlatan," he later wrote. "His books consisted largely of plagiarisms from me without quotes or acknowledgements."

Russell's sensitivity to plagiarism, real or imagined, is underlined by the disgruntled note which he sent to Stanley Unwin on the appearance of Aldous Huxley's *Brave New World.* He had always remembered with dislike Huxley's picture of him as Mr Scogan in *Crome Yellow*, "like one of those extinct bird-lizards of the Tertiary", and years later would claim that the *Encyclopaedia Britannica* was the only book which had ever influenced Aldous: "You could always tell by his conversation which volume he'd been reading. One day it would be Alps, Andes and Apennines, and the next it would be the Himalayas and the Hippocratic Oath." Now he asked whether Unwin had noticed that Huxley's latest novel was "merely an expansion of the two penultimate chapters of 'The Scientific Outlook' ". "The only thing he has added is the Bokanovsky twins," he went on; "otherwise the parallelism applies in great detail, e.g., the prohibition of Shakespeare and the intoxicant producing no headache."

His touchiness about both Joad and Aldous may in large part have been due to his own failure to re-start work successfully in his own chosen field of philosophy. He had visited Copenhagen as a guest of the university and had addressed the Cambridge Moral Science Club on "The Limits of Empiricism", but he still despaired of making ends meet on what philosophy could bring in. To Moore he wrote that he wanted to develop the ideas on empiricism and to investigate the relation of language to fact. "But I am in the unfortunate position of being legally bound to pay between £800 and £900 a year to other people, & having only £300 a year of unearned income," he went on. "I cannot therefore work at philosophy unless I can get some academic job. I suppose there is no possibility at Cambridge. I should be very glad if there were, as my desire to get back to philosophy is very strong."

There was more behind this than the professional's desire to return to work at which he excelled. During the traumatic years which followed his break with Alys he had been kept sane by the problems of *Principia Mathematica.* As he had tardily realized that Ottoline would never abandon her family, the painful recognition was tempered by the excitement of great philosophical plans under way. Even in the agony of indecision which found him torn between Colette and Dora, the purely personal could be set against *The Analysis of Mind* and all that would follow it. But when life with Dora had slipped down into altercation and ill-will he had nothing better as refuge than humdrum journalism. He had no intention of being left so vulnerable again.

However, nothing came of the approach to Moore and his thoughts turned once again to America. "I gather", he wrote to Warder Norton, his American publisher, "that there is a university somewhere in America which has given Einstein and many others purely research jobs. Do you know which it is? If I had any chance of such a job I should apply for it. I should like to live in America if it were financially feasible." Norton obliged without delay and shortly afterwards Russell was writing to Abraham Flexner, Director of the Institute for Advanced Study in Princeton, set up three years previously as a "haven where scholars and scientists may regard the world and its phenomena as their laboratory without being carried off in the maelstrom of the immediate". On the face of it, this was an ideal harbour for Russell, while the Institute's endowment was so large that appointment to its staff would solve all financial worries.

At first, the prospects looked good. "I have been pulling wires and otherwise wangling for that Princeton post," Norton replied.

> All I can tell you at this time is that in the first place Veblen is the power on that faculty now that Dr. Einstein is out of the current picture owing to the illness and recent death of his wife. Veblen likes you very much and is rather put out that you had not written to him. I got this smoothed over on the grounds of your being so ignorant about the whole set-up of the Institute that you did not even know its name. Next, I can report that Dr. Flexner, when he was told by Mrs. Weyl that you would be interested, expressed definite interest. Mrs. Weyl told me "his face lighted up" at the prospect. But there are many difficulties. The question is practically what work you could be assigned. At the moment the two principal divisions of the work are mathematics, and politics and economy. But, confidentially, the political and economic people are pretty conservative and they are a little afraid of you! The question seems to be whether you would want to do further research and teach graduate students advanced mathematics, or whether they might create for you a kind of special chair of philosophy.

Einstein thoroughly approved of Russell joining the Institute. So did Veblen. So did Herman Weyl, who with the other two completed the triumvirate advising Flexner in mathematics and philosophy. But the triumvirate was over-ruled. Russell was informed by Flexner that his application had been rejected; no reason seems to have been given, and only later did he learn that Flexner himself had personally vetoed his appointment. But Abraham Flexner's close confidant and colleague was his brother Simon, head of the Rockefeller Medical Center in New York, and husband of Helen Thomas – cousin of Alys and a devoted member of that Quaker community which had been profoundly shocked by Russell's abandonment of his first wife.

With Princeton ruled out, he turned to Harvard, writing to Whitehead and reminding him that Harvard had six years earlier asked him to lecture, an invitation he had been forced to refuse. Was there, he asked, any chance of the offer being renewed? To Norton he was more outspoken. "I should *very much* like to succeed Whitehead at Harvard," he wrote, relaying an idea that had been proposed by Veblen when the Princeton post had fallen through. "... I have naturally thought of Whitehead's post but I have no reason to suppose that he contemplates retirement. Have you? I do not want to seem eager to step into his shoes, nor to have him hear at second hand about any move of mine in connection with Harvard." Nothing came of this and he next considered Chicago or California. But before these efforts met with success, he was to be helped out of the financial trough by his old friend George Santayana whose novel, *The Last Puritan*, had earned 35,000 dollars in the United States within a year of publication. Santayana, like most of Russell's friends, knew that he was hard up. Unlike most, he saw a way of delicately discovering the reaction to an offer of help. Ottoline, conscripted to sound out what it would be, found there was one possible snag. Negotiations for Dora's alimony were continuing. "Do you think Santayana would mind arrangements intended to prevent the money going to Dora," Russell asked. "There would be two ways. (1) an annual present, to which I should have no legal claim; (2) giving the money to Peter. But if *I* am given capital, or a claim to an annual sum, Dora will get her share." The first scheme was preferred and quickly produced results. "I got a letter this morning from Santayana's nephew, George Sturges, enclosing a cheque for £500 & saying I might expect a similar sum, for some years to come, every six months," Russell told Ottoline. "The source is anonymous, but the anonymity is very thin. It *is* good of Santayana." The generosity was not needed for long. Russell was soon at the University of Chicago. One of his first acts after appointment was to let it be known that he no longer needed the £1,000 a year.

Before this, however, there had been a change of fortune, as he explained to Ottoline in a letter telling her that Peter and he would soon be moving to Kidlington, a few miles north of Oxford. "I have gone back to philosophy," he said, "& I want people to talk to about it. I am lecturing (at Oxford) & shall get to know all the people in my line, of whom, among the younger dons, there are now quite a number. In Cambridge I am an ossified orthodoxy; in Oxford, still a revolutionary novelty."

The invitation had come late in 1937, for a series of lectures on "Words and Facts", "a first sketch of a serious philosophical work on Language & Fact intended to be important", as he told Stanley Unwin. The lectures came at a time when Russell was revising his view of the importance of linguistics to logic and philosophy. He had recently written a new introduction to the second edition of *The Principles of Mathematics* in which, while reiterating his fundamental thesis that mathematics and logic were identical, he had admitted that logic was "much more linguistic" than he had believed at the beginning of the century. But he was by now feeling that linguistics was demanding more from philosophy than its due, while some of its adherents "seemed inclined to treat the realm of language as if it were self-subsistent, and not in need of any relation to non-linguistic occurrences". Russell sought to rectify this imbalance in the Oxford lectures.

While working on them he renewed his efforts to find a permanent post in the United States. Like Aldous Huxley, he believed that Europe was no longer a place for a pacifist. As late as March 1939 he could write, "The best hope for the world, if Europe plunges into the madness of another great war, is that America will remain neutral, but will, when the fighting is over, use economic power to further sanity and liberalism, and to restore to the parent continent as much as possible of the civilisation that the war will have temporarily destroyed." However, unlike Huxley and others, Russell had more to urge him westwards than a despairing belief that sane and honest men should abandon the Continental ship and re-fit as best they could in the haven of the New World. "My feelings are three-fold," he wrote to Norton in explaining why he wanted to work in the United States. "(a) I have a lot of ideas in my mind that I long to work at and believe to be important. (b) I am faced with the likelihood of such poverty that I may be unable to give a proper education to the child that is coming, (c) that Europe is no place for children, with the imminent risk of war – particularly England, which is likely to suffer most in the next war."

But there was one formidable disadvantage to a move: it would put the Atlantic between him and the son and daughter for whom he had gone through so much and for whom he had an undiminished affection. After the divorce from Dora, John and Kate had continued to spend term-time with their mother or at school but shared the holidays between mother and father, and there seemed every prospect that this would work well if he remained in Britain. What would happen if he left the country – and the jurisdiction of the British courts – was another matter, and it was with mixed feelings that he continued to sound out the Americans.

Persistence was eventually rewarded. In March 1938, the Humanities Division of the University of Chicago invited him as Visiting Professor of Philosophy for the academic year of 1938–9. "We should expect you to dispose of your time in such fashion as to permit you a great portion of leisure for research or for outside lecturing if you wish," he was told; "apart from meeting with a group of students for a seminar in some subject to be selected by you, and apart from occasional special lectures, your time would be your own." Salary was to be 5,000 dollars, and while the invitation was for a year, Russell felt in his bones that absence would be longer, that when he left England in September all the future would be uncertain. For one reason, if for no other, his links with England had been weakened.

Throughout the 1930s he had kept up his correspondence with Ottoline, still confiding to her his most personal problems, asking whether he should bring Peter to live at Telegraph House while Dora was there, sending speeches and papers for her opinion, and still discussing politics and poetry as he had done for a quarter of a century. On 10 April 1938 he sent a letter full of fears.

> I have very little hope that a great war will be avoided. We took John & Kate to a cinema, & the news was all propaganda, including the rescue of gallant Russian explorers on an ice-floe, a black-out in Prag, a review of the French air force, etc., followed by a sentimental pro-Italian film. Our Government thinks it can detach Musso from Hitler; Hitler thinks we can't. We know America will be on our side; Hitler thinks it will be neutral. Therefore war is practically certain.
>
> Chamberlain is only talking peace till our re-armament is complete. No doubt he would like to preserve peace, but I don't believe he thinks it possible.
>
> I haven't read the book about Potemkin – I am sure it would interest me. I will get it. I read a book about Henry VIII – it was just like present-day Russia, even to the confessions.
>
> John & Kate are both convinced pacifists, though most of his friends are communists.
>
> I have to finish a book before June 30; after that, I shall not be very busy. But I may have to go to Chicago for the winter; it is still uncertain.
>
> Much Love.

Addressed to Gower Street, the letter, his 1,775th since the meeting in Bedford Square in 1911, was re-addressed to the Sherwood Park Clinic in Tunbridge Wells where Ottoline died ten days later. "My dear Philip," wrote Russell, "The news is a terrible blow and I feel stunned. I can imagine how dreadful it must be for you. A great part of my life, stretching back into childhood, is gone dead with her. I do not know anything consoling to say. I find that her gay courage, perhaps more than anything else, remains in my mind. Please believe in my very deep sympathy."

Russell was not mentioned in her will. But Philip sent him two of Lady Amberley's fans which Russell had given to Ottoline years earlier, and a picture from her bedroom which she particularly wanted him to have.

Now, in the summer, regret and masochism drove him to write once more to Colette. The initiative was possibly unexpected, since Colette had by now published a novel containing a highly detailed and barely camouflaged portrait of Russell. Before this, Lawrence, Sassoon and Aldous Huxley had each created their own Russells as individual characters in broad, set-piece contemporary panoramas.

Colette, in *The Coming Back*, told with the help of the astro-physicist Gregory Orellano, the story of her involvement with Russell between the day she had met him in Lavender Hill police-station and his return to England in the autumn of 1921. Many incidents were invented, contrived or disguised. Gregory's visit was to the United States rather than to China, and it is on board ship rather than at a dinner-party that she hears that Russell/Gregory is to marry Miss Black/West. Ottoline appears as Magdalena de Santa Segunda, while T. S. Eliot, Clifford Allen, Dr Joad and others among Russell's friends and acquaintances are there for the searching. So are the visits to the Clee Hills, to Lulworth and to Lynton. Few are spared the truth – Russell least of all.

Yet now, before she sailed east to Finland where she planned to settle, and he sailed west to the States, they had to meet once more. Would she come to Oxford? He knew what her answer would be.

He met her on the platform, white hair untidily leonine. Peter was waiting outside and drove them home. Here she met John and Kate, both silent, both perceptive. They lunched in a cool room, sheltered from the heat outside. After lunch they went out into the wall-enclosed garden of Amberley House, John and Kate lying full-length on the grass and Russell's young son Conrad lying naked in the sun . . . "The living image of my Grandmother Stanley," Russell insisted.

Colette remembered a decade later, how the day ebbed perceptibly. There was the same faintly aromatic blend of China tea which Russell had drunk most of his life – and which Harrods Stores persisted in addressing to Miss Bertrand Russell. On the mantelpiece there was the same bust of Voltaire. And there was the same exquisite Persian bowl Russell had wanted to give her.

She admired Peter with her aureole of Titian hair and her lithe figure. But, knowing Russell, she sensed the rocks ahead and found herself "wondering about the marriage rather as Santayana wondered about Elizabeth's to Frank".

Peter drove them back to the station in the late afternoon. Only when the train was about to start were they alone. "He stood at the open window of my carriage, looking up with an expression as if no years had passed since 1916," Colette remembered. "I expect that if we met in heaven (or Hell) it would be the same." As the train was about to move out he called up to her, "It's been too long, this separation; don't let it be so long next time."

A few weeks later he was crossing the Atlantic with Peter and Conrad, and with an agreement that if conditions worsened John and Kate would be allowed to join him in the States the following year. The parting with them had been made worse by the looming international crisis, and on 15 September he wrote to Gamel Brenan, "Yesterday I was in despair at the thought of leaving John & Kate behind to face the horror without me;" and he would, he stressed a few weeks later, have brought them with him had it been legally possible.

His own long-term future was by no means assured. The President of Chicago was Robert Hutchins who, in Russell's words, was occupied with the Hundred Best Books. More to the point, he was an ardent devotee of Aquinas, whom Russell didn't rate very high as a philosopher. Despite this acute difference, which induced a personal coolness between the two men and was influential in the non-renewal of his contract, Russell enjoyed Chicago, writing to Gilbert Murray after he had been there a number of months, "The University, so far as philosophy is concerned, is about the best I have ever come across. There are two sharply opposed schools in the Faculty, one Aristotelian, historical and traditional, the other ultra-modern. The effect on the students seems to be just right."

The family had sailed from England as the Munich crisis was rising to its climax, and when they arrived in New York Russell was closely questioned by reporters on his views of Chamberlain's decision to meet Hitler. The answer would have been obvious to any reporters who had read *Which Way to Peace?*, a short book which Russell had rushed off in 1936. In it he had done more than reiterate the point he had made twenty years earlier: that while some wars were justifiable, the vast majority were not. He had gone on to deal with the current situation in Europe and had concluded that the Germans under Hitler should not be resisted. The argument, which spelt out in detail how invading troops should be welcomed rather than fought, was that the horrors of bombing and of gas warfare, both of which were expected to be launched on the civilian population, were greater than those of German occupation. Plausible enough when advanced by an unqualified pacifist, the argument, when presented by a man who believed some wars to be justifiable, revealed an elephantine ignorance of Hitler's ambitions and of conditions in Germany. Yet in one part of a book showing extraordinary naivety Russell was strikingly percipient. There might, he suggested, be a new partition of Poland between Germany and Russia. "Everything possible is being done by Stalin to show that no question of principle divides him from Hitler," he said, "and I cannot doubt that he would be glad if the differences between the two countries would be composed at the expense of the traditional victim." However, Germany really wanted to be left alone to attack Russia; and if she did so, Russell proposed, Britain should remain neutral.

Which Way to Peace? was a book which Russell never wished to be re-issued. He had reservations about the policies he had advocated and he may also have had doubts about the lengths to which his logical approach had carried him. Gerald Brenan raised both issues in a long letter which reveals a great deal about both Brenan and Russell.

He admired Russell's analysis of the situation but disagreed on a number of points, notably the political interpretation of recent events. There was, however, one thing more personal:

> Your advice to individual pacifists to refuse to work in hospitals, to assist the wounded in the trenches or in air raids, to refuse to provide food, etc. is in my mind pedantic and hateful. The argument that by helping the wounded you are making room for someone else to fight may be logical, but it is inhuman and such pacifists will naturally and reasonably, in my opinion, draw on themselves the odium of their neighbours in time of war. That of course is what you want: the blood of the martyrs must flow. Yet I think you take it much too much for granted that the pacifist requires more courage than does, say, the happily married soldier who volunteers for the danger zone. And how can such pacifists hope to influence the peace settlement when the war is over? They will be the last people to be listened to.

Then, after returning to the practical political issues, he summed up in two paragraphs.

> I admire in you the combination of a strong intellect and the love of reason and justice that accompany it with a volcano of a very different sort under the surface. The tension produced makes you a great imaginative writer of the nature of Swift & Voltaire. That is why I regret you shd have such a desire to counsel & improve mankind: you use only half your powers when you write homilies. In my opinion you should always (except when you are writing philosophy), choose a subject which gives your secret fires (which show themselves in the form of wit, intolerance and unfairness) full play.
>
> Your book on peace is magnificently thought and written: as literature I have great respect for it: my objection to it is merely practical – that it does not help the cause we all care about. I believe we ought all to leave these things to our political Nursemaids and continue in peace at those things we are most fitted to work at. Sauve qui peut is now my policy. Pure cowardice. With Gamel to consider,

I am not ashamed of my wish to keep out, though it would be a *pleasure* to me, if war were to come, through Fascist aggression, not merely to tend the wounded but to meet their bombers in the air–just as it would be a pleasure to you, as a pacifist martyr, to face a firing squad. But your life is of such value to civilisation, that I hope you will go to America next year and not be self-indulgent.

A year after the publication of *Which Way to Peace?*, and as German threats against Czechoslovakia began to harden, Russell wrote to Gilbert Murray explaining his position further. "Spain has turned away from pacifism," he said.

I myself have found it very difficult, the more so as I know Spain, most of the places where the fighting has been, & the Spanish people, & I have the strongest possible feeling on the Spanish issue. I should certainly not find Czecho-Slovakia more difficult. And having remained a pacifist while the Germans were invading France & Belgium in 1914, I do not see why I should cease to be one if they do it again. The result of our having adopted the policy of war at that time is not so delectable as to make me wish to see it adopted again.

You feel "they ought to be stopped". I feel that, if we set to work to stop them, we shall, in the process, become exactly like them, & the world will have gained nothing. Also, if we beat them, we shall produce in time someone as much worse than Hitler as he is worse than the Kaiser. In all this I see no hope for mankind.

Russell, who a decade later was to be calling for the re-armament of Germany as a barrier against the Russians, put his faith in the Christian policy of turning the other cheek and supported Chamberlain's policy of appeasement. Like other men with less excuse for bad judgment, he did so not on the grounds that it bought time, even if dishonourably, but that it offered the prospect of peace. He had never held a high opinion of Chamberlain, he confessed on his arrival in New York, but after the decision to make the dramatic flight to Munich he began to think that his own judgment might be faulty. "I am afraid war would do an extraordinary amount of harm to the world," he said in a statement of mixed banality and percipience. "Even if we win, after the war I am afraid we would be just as mad as Hitler is. You go into such a thing believing that you are going to accomplish something but you get so angry that all proportion is lost."

But he was soon having reservations. "I was glad of the settlement, bad as it was," he was writing to Gamel Brenan in November. "But it does not look as if war could be avoided long."

In Chicago, he had three main tasks: to give an undergraduate course on "The Problems of Philosophy"; to run a graduate seminar on semantics; and to deliver a series of lectures based on *Power*. However, his first public appearance was to lecture on the international situation to the Chicago Council on Foreign Relations to whom he was introduced by Adlai Stevenson as one who for the better part of a generation had on and off "been swimming upstream against the current". He still backed Chamberlain for being among those "foremost on the side of peace" and maintained, "If the Labour Party were in power we should have had war by now." He saw little hope of America remaining neutral in the conflict which now seemed inevitable, and an acute observer might have seen a hint of attitudes to come: "Last time there was little to choose between the two sides," he maintained. "This time Hitler is definitely worse than anything found in England or France."

He was soon well settled in, hating the city but enthusiastic about the university. "I have some remarkably able pupils," he wrote to Lucy Donnelly. "The intellectual level is very markedly higher than at Oxford so I enjoy my work." He was lecturing, as in Oxford, on "Words and Facts", but had been told that such a title would be unacceptably simple and had changed it to "something like the Correlation between Oral and Somatic Motor Habits". "It was an extraordinarily delightful Seminar. Carnap and Charles Morris used to come to it, and I had three pupils of quite outstanding ability – Dalkey, Kaplan, and Copilowish [later Copi]. We used to have close arguments back and forth, and succeeded in genuinely clarifying points to our mutual satisfaction, which is rare in philosophical argument."

His contract with the university had been for a year, with an implied option for renewal which he hoped would be taken up. But there was no renewal and he might well have returned to England a few months before Hitler invaded Poland, and even become the gadfly of the House of Lords in the controversial debates of the Second World War.

The intriguing possibility was ruled out. First there came the offer of a three-year engagement with the University of California which he gratefully accepted, moving from Chicago to Santa Barbara in the spring of 1939. His duties did not begin until September and he filled in the first part of the waiting time with a lecture-tour which took him round the usual frenzied circuit, a combined marathon and obstacle race which, with its appointments, impromptu interviews and tight schedules, was a tough course for any man of sixty-six. That he could not always be certain of V.I.P. treatment is revealed in the account of one interview in Boston. "We had tea at the Ritz ... and then we had dinner there too – just the two of us," a college reporter later wrote.

> I still can't quite believe it. He was sixty-six and famous, obviously with an empty evening to fill, and I was a freshman and I didn't

know *anything*. I don't remember what we talked about, but he kept the conversation going and saw to it that I got a good story for the paper. And he paid for the dinner too. Looking back on it afterwards, I realised, of course, that *he* had interviewed *me*. And then, years later, I began to understand that he had been willing to spend that time with me simply because he was far more interested in my mind than I was.

By the time he arrived back in California, he was expecting John and Kate, and although they were technically only coming for the school holidays he frankly told W. B. Curry, the head of Dartington, that he would prefer them to finish their education in the United States.

> Even if there is no war, the atmosphere of England is now bad for young people. Nothing is so depressing as despairing preparations for a war which inspires no-one with enthusiasm. England's great days are over & the young therefore tend to be listless and cynical. Here, on the other hand, they are full of energy and hope. I am quite sure that Chicago University is better than either Oxford or Cambridge.

Work shed the only glimmer of light in a darkening scene, and in his depression he wrote a long letter to Colette, declaring that he already hated exile from England, that the public lectures had tired him and that he sometimes felt almost too weary to go on; but Dora, Peter and his three children were all dependent on his earnings and he must go on working until his dying day – a prospect that in brighter times would not have worried him unduly. As so often, the memory of his early days with Colette came to the rescue in a bad moment. He told her of his current work. He asked whether she remembered "egocentric particulars", bound up as they were in his mind with a stone bridge over a rushing stream – an image from a winter's day when they had stayed at the Cat and Fiddle. There were, he concluded, still things to live for.

A few weeks later John and Kate arrived from England for a visit that the coming war, and the danger of returning to Britain across the Atlantic, transformed into a years-long migration. Without delay, Russell took them for a brief trip to the High Sierra Camps, 9,000 ft up in Yosemite National Park, relishing their company after a year's absence. Then it was back to Santa Barbara – and the news that the Second World War had started.

17

The American Ordeal

In September 1939, when Germany invaded Poland, Russell was presented head-on with a dilemma he could no longer side-step. Was he or was he not still a pacifist? Or, to put the question more specifically, did he or did he not believe that Hitler should be opposed by force of arms? In 1914 he had proclaimed that he was not a pacifist in the usual, fully-fledged meaning of the word. There were circumstances, he admitted, when the evils of capitulation outweighed the evils of war. The Kaiser's Germany had in his opinion not furnished sufficient evils. Neither, it had seemed throughout the long ignominious retreat of the 1930s, had Hitler, although as early as 1933 Einstein, the epitome of pacifism, had made a smart U-turn in his ideas and announced that were he a Belgian he would cheerfully accept military service. Not so Russell.

He hung on even past Munich. "I supported the policy of conciliation," he subsequently wrote. "In this I was in agreement with the majority of my countrymen. I went further than the majority in believing that war should, at this moment in history, be avoided, however great the provocation." The policy was of little comfort to the Czechs, soon to be herded to the concentration camps, but it did allow the completion of Britain's vital radar chain and it bought time to encourage American aid. But Russell knew nothing of this and could thus be numbered among those who did good not by stealth but by ignorance. Even six months later, after the Nazis had marched into Prague and destroyed any remaining illusion that they were concerned only with German-speaking peoples, he still believed that Hitler's ambitions could be kept in check and was profoundly impressed by Roosevelt's attempt at mediation. "My dear Mr. President," he wrote on 15 April, "At the risk of being held guilty of unpardonable impertinence, I cannot resist expressing to you my profound gratitude and admiration for your peace plea to Hitler & Mussolini."

The change of heart came gradually and there are two indications of what brought it about. In a handwritten note attached to a letter to Stanley Unwin, Russell stated, "I remained in favour of peace until shortly before the outbreak of the Second World War when I became convinced that peace with Hitler was impossible." And to Gilbert Murray in September 1940 he pinned the matter even more definitely. The issue had become clear when "Stalin's Russia turned against us. I have no doubt that the Soviet Government is even worse than Hitler's, and it will be a misfortune if it survives." That the Russo-German pact of August 1939 helped to give respectability to this particular war was in line with Russell's uncompromising opposition to Communism and with the support he gave to the Finns in their struggle against the Russian invasion of November 1939. Since Thermopylae and Salamis, he wrote to Colette, there had been nothing so amazing and magnificent as the Finnish resistance. And to Lucy Silcox he wrote, "The Bolsheviks have at last shown themselves to all the world the monsters that I felt them to be in 1920."

With Stalin and Hitler leading each other down the same garden-path, Russell thus agreed privately that the war had to be fought, and it is ironic that the first realization was strengthened by the temporary *volte-face* of those who were to become Britain's glorious Russian allies. But he was under no illusion as to what it would all mean. "I share your gloom," he wrote to Norton early in September. "The war will be decided by starvation, & I should not be surprised if we starved first. I think we have very little chance of victory if America remains neutral. But I think the Germans would crack up as they did last time if they had any ill success. I cannot see the English giving in short of annihilation – they are as slow to stop as to begin. I wish I could have died before this time ..." His anxiety was felt by his graduate students, one of whom remembers how "we and Russell spent more time listening to radio broadcasts about the war in Europe than we did to discussing Hume, Russell and Carnap".

But although all now seemed clear if grim, Russell's instinctive distrust of a situation that mocked his earlier beliefs did not evaporate quickly. He still kept his views from the public arena. "I have so far abstained from all public expressions of opinion on the present war," he wrote to Stanley Unwin in January 1940, "because I find it difficult to be a complete pacifist about it, but reluctant to express a different view, which I might easily come to think mistaken." Not until the summer, as the Germans reached the Channel coast and held the French shore undisputed, a mere twenty-five miles from Dover, did emotion finally destroy his vestigial doubts.

One of Russell's least-appreciated characteristics was his love of Britain, a patriotism which so naturally coloured his thoughts and actions that it was as much part of him as the tang is part of the oyster. "To me," he had written to Gamel Brenan a few months after arriving in the United States, "love of England (not the political entity but the place) is almost as strong as love of my children, and very similar. I should find perpetual exile hardly endurable." During the First World War he had genuinely believed that Britain's fortunes would best be served by neutrality; as for physical invasion, that was as far from most people's thoughts as from those of the German General Staff. In 1940, Dunkirk altered all that. "Ever since the war began, I have felt that I could no longer go on being pacifist, but I have hesitated to say so, because of the responsibility involved," he now wrote to Kingsley Martin. "If I were young enough to fight myself, I should do so, but it is more difficult to urge others. Now, however, I feel that I ought to announce that I have changed my mind, and I would be glad if you could find an opportunity to mention in the 'New Statesman' that you have heard from me to this effect." In a personal letter to Elizabeth Trevelyan the following month he explained further. "I am still a pacifist in the sense that I think peace the most important thing in the world," he said. "But I do not think there can be any peace in the world while Hitler prospers, so I am compelled to feel that his defeat, if at all possible, is a necessary prelude to anything good; I should have felt as I do if I had lived in the time of Genghis Khan." The dominant belief that this particular war against the Germans, who were now supported by the Soviets, had to be fought to an end was reinforced by the emotions of the homesick patriot. "I am not a pacifist this time. I wonder what you and Bob feel about it. Being away from home makes one more patriotic," he wrote to Elizabeth Trevelyan a few months later. And to her husband he said that he saw a British victory as bound up with the future of civilization. "I don't think anything so important has happened since the fifth century, the previous occasion on which the Germans reduced the world to barbarism."

After the *New Statesman* "mention" had been reported in the *New York Times*, a brief statement by Russell was printed in the paper on 11 June 1940, and in February 1941 he put his views fully on public record. The occasion followed a speech in which President Hutchins of Chicago University expressed the belief that "the United States can better serve suffering humanity everywhere by staying out", an attitude, as Russell described it in a 2,000-word letter to the *New York Times*, "similar to that which I formerly took in regard to Great Britain". He pleaded that he had erred in good company, since Chamberlain, as well as Lord Lothian and Lord Halifax – the former and current British Ambassadors to the United States – had also been advocates of peace. The letter stressed that before 1939 Russell's "objections to the war that was coming were not of principle but of expedience ... There came a moment – some will say one moment, some another – when it became evident that Germany would destroy the independence of the democracies one by one if they did not combine in armed defence. From that moment the only hope for democracy was war." This was rather different from the claims of *Which Way to Peace?* But Russell was never a man to conceal a change of tack. "On the whole," he wrote to Emily Balch, the American Quaker,

> I no longer believe that non-resistance would have preserved any of the values that Nazidom aims at destroying. The Nazis are so efficient, thorough, and technically intelligent, that any country they subdue is likely to be subdued mentally as well as physically. So there seems nothing to be done except to meet violence with violence. It is a dreadful conclusion, and something deep in me rebels against it; nevertheless, I am forced to accept it.

The feeling grew, and W. J. Brown, the British M.P. and trade union leader, was reporting in 1941, after meeting Russell in New York, "[His] old pacifism is completely gone. He would like to see America in the war, preferably via Japan, and is quite reconciled to the view that any world order must be imposed by force and rest on force as its final sanction."

Thus repugnance at what had to be done was added to Russell's deep-seated fear for England, a combination that from the summer of 1940 onwards made his years in America among the unhappiest of his life. For the first few months, however, things were not too bad. Dora agreed that John and Kate should stay in America for the duration, and both were enrolled at the University of California. His pleasure at having them for an indefinite period was qualified only by wartime restrictions which stopped him getting money from Britain and the bewilderment and home-sickness that followed their transplant across the Atlantic. The first was a problem that remained for the rest of his stay in the United States. The second was unexpectedly ameliorated by a stroke of good luck when he discovered that two American children who lived nearby in Beverly Hills had spent a year at Dartington. He wasted no time in proposing twice-weekly meetings and weekend expeditions.

"When Tis and Ben went over to the Russells after school, Bertie always joined them for tea, and entered into their games and their conversation in a completely spontaneous way," says their mother, Mrs Kiskadden.

> He never talked down to them, even when discussion turned to matters about which he obviously knew far more than they. Instead, he asked questions and drew them out and encouraged them to express themselves. I nearly said that Bertie used the Socratic method with them, but it wasn't really that. He never minded leaving a discussion open, without conclusion, counting on maturity and experience to correct youthful assumptions. I admired this so much, because in this way he encouraged the children to think, and he never let them feel uncomfortably aware that the man with whom they were arguing was the greatest philosopher alive.
>
> I remember being convulsed with laughter one night just before

dinner when Tis returned from a visit to the Russells. She ran up the stairs calling to me "Mummy, what do you think! Bertie doesn't believe in Karma!" There was something so hilarious about Bertie gravely discussing Hindoo beliefs with a fifteen-year-old girl, and leaving her feeling quite free to follow her own thinking while making it clear to her that he didn't agree. Clearly it didn't occur to Tis that she had been engaged in anything but a discussion between friends whose opinions differed. She was certainly not squelched; she had had a glorious time trying to convince Bertie that she was right.

The same spontaneous delight in children as equals was shown when the Kiskaddens invited the Russells to an Easter-morning egg-hunt in their garden. John, Kate and Conrad arrived with their father. Then the hunt started. "I shall never forget watching that white mane of hair skipping about the paths on the hillside, holding his little basket of eggs," says Mrs Kiskadden. "He crowed with delight exactly as Conrad did, at each fresh trophy. No wonder the children adored him. Who could help it?"

To Russell, his family was the unit that mattered and it was not lightly to be split up. But when they all visited the Huntington Library and Art Gallery at Pasadena, an official informed him that children under six were not admitted. Russell offered to carry Conrad. The rule was inflexible, but he refused to allow a companion to look after the child while he joined the rest of the party inside. "He couldn't bring himself to enter a place where Conrad was denied," the friend said later. "Nor could he permit himself to ask for dispensation in consideration of his position."

Life in California had many advantages, not least the ease with which it was possible to get away from the cities into the solitudes of the Sierras. However, the country and the climate, though more agreeable than in Chicago, were counter-balanced by what Russell considered the almost totalitarian atmosphere of the university under its president, Robert Sproul.

Relations between Russell and Sproul were less than amiable, and when Russell, early in February 1940, and at the peak of disgruntlement, received the offer of a professorship at the College of the City of New York he resigned his current post and accepted the new one. Only then did he discover that the New York offer was not yet official. He at once tried to withdraw his resignation. However, this was too good an opportunity for President Sproul to miss and Russell was informed that there was no going back on his decision. Thus the way was opened for what turned out to be a *cause célèbre* which, in the words of the *New York Times*, "strick at the security and intellectual independence of every faculty member in every public college and university in the United States".

When accepting the New York post Russell had completely under-estimated both the opposition which his *Marriage and Morals* had raised a decade earlier and the tenacity with which the religious pack can pursue its quarry. Bishop Manning, who had so vigorously campaigned against Russell during earlier visits to the United States, now seized the proffered opportunity with both episcopal hands. First he addressed a circular letter to the leading New York papers denouncing the appointment on the ground that Russell was a "recognised propagandist against religion and morality who specifically defends adultery". John Dewey, Whitehead and many other academics came to Russell's defence, but Manning replied with a second salvo of letters deploring this "sinister but unhappily not ... surprising" support.

At this stage the size and danger of the rising storm was not quite apparent. Russell was accused of supporting unconventional views on sexual morality, which in itself was little more than the truth. But H. L. Mencken summed him up smartly:

> In one of his books he speaks very favourably of adultery, but he does so in the scientific way in which one might say a word for the method of least squares, the hookworm, or a respectable volcano. Multitudes of other men, both lay and clerical, have thought along the same lines, and if they have kept their ideas diligently to themselves, then the crypto-Earl's frank-blabbing is only the more to his credit.

The religious lobby took a different view, even though Russell would be employed by the college merely to teach logic, certain problems in the foundations of mathematics and the relation of the pure to the applied sciences – hardly erotic subjects. Teaching all-male classes on logic or mathematics, he was hardly likely to send rapacious urges coursing through the minds of his listeners. The New York Board of Education was in any case legally entitled to appoint anyone it wished and it therefore looked as though the bishop's protest, despite support from other religious bodies, would splutter out as little more than an exclamation of disgust.

Such might have been the case had the centre of controversy been anyone else. Russell's arguments, however, only too often had an assured air of superiority which goaded opponents into rash actions. As a waver of red rags before bulls, he was in a class of his own.

His ability to provoke opposition now goaded the anti-Russell lobby into a campaign that has many signs of genuine hysteria. In the United States *Tablet*, he was described as "the philosophical anarchist and moral nihilist of Great Britain ... whose defence of adultery became so obnoxious that one of his 'friends' is reported to have thrashed him". To the Jesuit *America*, he was the "desiccated, divorced, and decadent advocate of sexual promiscuity ... who is now indoctrinating the students at the University of California . . . in his libertarian rules for loose living in matters of sex and promiscuous love and vagrant marriage". An equally moved but less precise writer believed that "Quicksands threaten! The snake is in the grass! The worm is busy in the mind! Were Bertrand Russell honest even with himself, he would declare, as did Rousseau, 'I cannot look at any of my books without shuddering; instead of instructing, I corrupt; instead of nourishing, I poison. But passion blinds me, and, with all my fine discourses, I am nothing but a scoundrel.'" The writer, sending the letter as a telegram to Fiorello La Guardia, Mayor of New York, continued, "I beg Your Honour to protect our youth from the baneful influence of him of the poisoned pen – an ape of genius, the devil's minister of men."

These pleasantries were perhaps only to be expected in the rough-and-tumble of controversy. Certainly they seemed unlikely to decide the issue, and when the New York Board of Higher Education met on 18 March to debate a motion to rescind Russell's appointment, the motion was defeated. However, the voting was eleven to seven, and the leader of the anti-Russell faction warned, "The issue now passes from the Board of Higher Education to the public. Particularly in view of the close vote, public opinion will control in the end."

The opposition was not, in fact, to be satisfed with a simple democratic vote. The following day a Mrs Jean Kay sought in the State Supreme Court an order directing the Board to rescind Russell's appointment. The reasons given were that he was an alien; had not passed a competitive examination for the post; and was an advocate of sexual immorality. To support her case Mrs Kay claimed fear of what would happen to her young daughter were she taught by Russell.

There were loop-holes in her case; indeed, gaping chasms, not the least being that Russell would be teaching only male members of the college. This small point did nothing to deter Joseph Goldstein, who argued Mrs Kay's case in court. Ignoring such irrelevancies as the facts, Goldstein concentrated elsewhere, dredging what he could find from Russell's works and miraculously transforming it. Thus his brief contained the claim that Russell was "lecherous, libidinous, lustful, venerous, erotomaniac, aphrodisiac, irreverent, narrow-minded, untruthful, and bereft of moral fibre", a large claim for Russell's potential, even at the height of his powers. "Aphrodisiac" pleased him. "I cannot think of any predecessors except Apuleius and Othello," he remarked to Gilbert Murray.

But there was more to come. "Russell conducted a nudist colony in England," Goldstein continued in court. "He and his wife have paraded nude in public. This man who is now about seventy has gone in for salacious poetry. Russell winks at homosexuality. I'd go further and say he approves of it."

However, even Goldstein was forced to remember that Russell had been appointed to teach the theory of logic rather than the practice of love-play. He therefore delivered himself of the following judgment:

> He is not a philosopher in the accepted meaning of the word; not a lover of wisdom; not a searcher after wisdom; not an explorer of that universal science which aims at the explanation of all phenomena of the universe by ultimate causes; that in the opinion of your deponent and multitudes of other persons he is a sophist; practises sophism; that by cunning contrivances, tricks and devices and by mere quibbling, he puts forth fallacious arguments and arguments that are not supported by sound reasoning; and he draws inferences which are not justly deduced from a sound premise; that all his alleged doctrines which he calls philosophy are just cheap, tawdry, worn-out, patched-up fetishes and propositions, devised for the purpose of misleading the people.

Since Russell was not a party to the case, which had been brought against the Board of Higher Education, he could not himself be represented in court. But although he felt no need to answer the philosophical judgment, which revealed more about Goldstein than about Russell, he made a formal declaration denying the lies in the earlier part of Goldstein's statement.

Following the diatribe, there came the Board's counsel, who dealt merely with the point of law involved: the right of the Board to appoint an alien to a post in the City College. Justice McGeehan apparently considered it of little importance. A Roman Catholic who had earlier distinguished himself by trying to have a portrait of Martin Luther removed from a court-house mural illustrating legal history, he would have had difficulty in delivering an impartial judgment even with the best will in the world, and there is every indication that the best will was absent. His judgment in the City College case contained distortions, libels and *non sequiturs* galore. It revoked Russell's appointment, which was described not only as an insult to the people of New York but as, in a phrase which later became famous, "in effect establishing a chair of indecency".

In revoking the appointment, McGeehan stood firm on Russell's alien status and the fact that he had not passed a competitive examination – ignoring the escape-clauses in the regulations without which a sizeable proportion of New York's teaching staff would have to be sacked. Then he expatiated on the subject of Russell's character, and with a remarkable absence of chapter or verse made it clear that even had Russell been a true-born, competitively examined American, he would still have been totally unacceptable.

The judgment produced a flurry of articles in legal journals typified by Walter H. Hamilton's "Trial by Ordeal, New Style", in the *Yale Law Journal*, and it brought dismay and jubilation to the contending parties.

Russell's supporters, believing that attempts would be made to prevent the Board from appealing against the judgment, summoned up a formidable team to urge it on. The American Association of University Professors was one among the bodies which now, if rather late in the day, woke up to what was happening and set about trying to turn the tables.

On this occasion the academics came limping behind the rest of the field. Before the question of an appeal could be put to the test, Mayor La Guardia had moved with an audacity and a quickness worthy of a better cause. Russell's appointment had been cancelled. Therefore the Mayor could, and did, quietly withdraw from the Board's budget the appropriation that would have paid his salary. When this became known Ely Culbertson, the bridge-player who had made a fortune from the game, wrote to Russell promising that if he got the post without the salary, Culbertson would pay the salary out of his own pocket. But for practical purposes La Guardia's action had confirmed the abolition of the post.

The majority on the Board still attempted, unsuccessfully, to lodge an appeal, and Russell himself tried with equal lack of success to be made a party to the proceedings. "As Americans," said John Dewey when the case was lost, "we can only blush with shame for this scar on our repute for fair play."

Manning and his supporters had won the day, but it was a victory that may have done them more harm than good. To all except the most biased – and possibly to a few even of those – the sight of grown men in public office playing such antics was hardly edifying. In addition, Russell had been able to stake a claim for the future. After the judgment he had been upbraided by the *New York Times* – which had given a scrupulously fair account of the proceedings – for not retiring from the battle as soon as the fire became fierce. Taking up the charge, he replied in a letter that

> however wise such action might have been from a personal point of view, it would also, in my judgment, have been cowardly and selfish. A great many people who realised that their own interests and principles of toleration and free speech were at stake were anxious from the first to continue the controversy. If I had retired I should have robbed them of their *casus belli* and tacitly assented to the proposition that substantial groups shall be allowed to drive out of public office individuals whose opinions, race or nationality they find repugnant. This would appear to me immoral.

The situation was familiar. Russell had once again become the lightning-conductor, attracting forces from the darker areas of society and focusing attention on the need for eternal vigilance.

That was the public picture. The private one was less comforting. "You must forgive me if I am a little prickly just now," he wrote to Warder Norton on 11 May.

> To be suddenly reduced to the situation where I cannot support my children & shall very likely have to risk their death by sending them back to England, is painful. As things stand, it seems unlikely that my income for the next 12 months will reach 1,000 dollars. Everyone fusses about the public issue; my personal ruin passes unnoticed. So I am apt to feel cross, & as I mustn't let it out on my enemies, I snap at my friends.

Russell now had his back to the wall. He was out of a job: his resignation from the University of California came into effect with the spring, and the only future engagement was at Harvard where he was to give the William James lectures in September. Apart from personal troubles there arose, within the next weeks and months, the awful prospect that England might be invaded. It was therefore in a state of some mental chaos that he retired into the mountains to get his Harvard lectures into shape.

"In these days I am almost afraid to write to England, for fear of what may have happened before my letter arrives," he wrote to Lucy Silcox from Fallen Leaf Lodge, Lake Tahoe.

> Peter and I, for our own part, wish we were there, but for Conrad's sake one must think otherwise. John is not a pacifist & is prepared to go & fight whenever the British Government wants him; so far, there has been no call for Englishmen in America. Apart from the war we all flourish. John & Kate are both at the University of California; John is very studious & does very well in all his work. In his spare time he reads Lucretius – he longs to learn Greek also, but so far has not had time. Conrad is a delight, & in every way all that could be wished.
>
> I wish we could transport you here; you would find a place where the works of God still hold their own against those of man. We are spending the summer on the shores of a small lake (Fallen Leaf Lake) near a big one, Lake Tahoe, which you can find on the map. We are 6,000 feet up, with steep mountains all round – giant pines on the lower slopes, bare rock & snow higher up. The scenery is like the Tyrol; upland meadows with wild flowers kept luxuriant by the moisture of the melting snow, endless little lakes tucked away in folds in the mountains, streams and waterfalls & an endless variety of walks.
>
> With this, a heavenly climate – sun every day, cold clear nights, hot days. And water in plenty in spite of absence of rains, as on the southern slopes of the Alps. The whole region is a "national forest", taken over by the Government and preserved from ugliness. Though

the lake is surrounded by little houses like ours, they are hidden in the trees, & can't be seen. In the winter the snow is above the roofs, so the houses have to be shut up. When we first came, a month ago, there was still a lot of snow higher up. With the thermometer at 80°, one could dive off deep snow into water as warm as the Cornish sea in August. We go long walks of incredible beauty, & sometimes for a little while we actually forget the war – which is good, as we can do nothing about it.

On the shores of Lake Tahoe, sometimes sitting naked in the hard sunlight, Russell completed the William James lectures. They were in part a continuation of the quest for a definition of truth which he had followed in the early years of the century, returned to in his lecture to the Moral Science Club on the limits of empiricism, and discussed at Oxford in 1938, as well as at Chicago and California. Starting with the meaning of words and then going on to the significance of sentences, he now constructed a new correspondence theory of truth; asserting that "when a sentence or belief is 'true', it is so in virtue of some relation to one or more facts; but the relation is not always simple, and varies both according to the structure of the sentence concerned and according to the relation of what is asserted to experience".

At a different level the lectures, published as *An Inquiry into Meaning and Truth*, constituted Russell's attempt to deal with the philosophical conclusions of the Logical Positivists who had sprung from the Vienna Circle of the 1920s. They counted Russell among their philosophical ancestors, regarded themselves as applying his logical tools to perennial problems, and were anxious for his unqualified blessing. What he gave was qualified, although *Inquiry* shows their influence on his thinking – exercised largely through those, forced to flee from Europe, who were among his audiences at Chicago and Harvard. Men accustomed to controversy, they had argued Russell into changing his position on a number of points, and as a result *Inquiry* is more linguistically orientated than most of his books. But the problems with which it deals are essentially Russell's, centring on the role of evidence in our knowledge of the world.

Publication of the William James lectures enabled Russell to prepare a unique title-page. Below his name it carried a seventeen-line list of his honours, starting with the Nicholas Murray Butler Medal of Columbia University in 1915. There followed one final item: "Judicially pronounced unworthy to be Professor of Philosophy at the College of the City of New York (1940)". However, it appeared only in the English edition. His American publisher would have none of it.

The lectures gave yet further proof of the success with which Russell had returned to philosophy. His reception at Harvard, whose governing body had made their personal support for him unequivocally plain, helped him back out of the trough. The invasion of Britain soon looked less likely, although the start of night-bombing brought its own terrors of the imagination. "A hen, terrified by a motor-car, will rush across the road in imminent danger of death, in order to feel the safety of home," he wrote later. "In like manner, during the blitz, I longed to be in England."

In Harvard, there had arrived a letter from Colette in Finland. "It is impossible to say how overjoyed I was to get [it]," he replied.

> I had been wondering in a worried way what had become of you. In these days one never knows whether people are alive or dead ... I should like to see England again before I die, but God knows whether I shall, or whether it will be at all like the England I loved. I should like to see you again, and I know you will still be the Colette I loved. You have an unconquerable spirit – which one values more and more in these days when almost everything is shattered. Work remains. I plan a big book, a sort of history of philosophy, irreverent, showing up Plato, dealing with the problem of reconciling individuality with cohesion. One writes nowadays for a distant future, say 1,000 years hence, when the new shackles will have worn thin and the human spirit will again face the world unafraid. I feel it is worth while, and would rather not be dead.

There was soon another reason for optimism. By the time Russell reached Harvard he had a job once more; one which had been offered, moreover, as a direct result of the debacle of the City College affair. His defenders had been numerous, and if they were not powerful enough to affect the issue, they did include some of the most important names in contemporary American philosophy, John Dewey, Sidney Hook and Horace Kallen among them. Dewey and Kallen, both members of a Committee for Cultural Freedom formed to publicize the basic principles in danger, became editors of *The Bertrand Russell Case*, a series of essays on various aspects of the affair. It is rarely easy to raise money for a lost cause, and this was no exception. The Committee for Cultural Freedom was therefore happy to accept an offer to cover the 2,000-dollar costs of publishing the book, from Dr Albert Barnes, the highly individualistic founder, director and determined dictator of the Barnes Foundation at Merion, outside Philadelphia.

Barnes, who in the words of the Academic Freedom Committee's secretary had "been greatly excited by the attack on Mr. Russell, and has expressed himself publicly in very vigorous and unprintable terms", had built up a fortune from the manufacture of argyrol. This he had used to acquire a fine gallery of modern French paintings, and with his collection as examples, had taught the principles of aesthetics in a personal but not entirely unsuccessful way. Now it occurred to him that he could broaden his course to cover the philosophical and social background to art. Who better to do this than Bertrand Russell? The idea appears to have captured Barnes for a number of reasons. He would certainly be extending his curriculum; he would certainly be retrieving Russell from a particularly sticky financial situation. If any further inducement were required, it was that Russell at Merion would give the Barnes Foundation a câchet it would not otherwise acquire, however many Monets and Manets he was able to lay his hands on.

The doctor first sounded out John Dewey, who supported the proposal. Barnes sent Russell details of the Foundation and tentatively asked if he would accept a lectureship. Russell jumped at the proposal. "I cannot tell you what an immense boon your offer is to me," he wrote. "One is almost ashamed, at such a moment, to think of personal things, but when one has young children it is unavoidable." In a following letter he began to discuss the subject of his lectures – in embryo, the *History of Western Philosophy*. "I do not know whether you want me to lecture on philosophy or on social questions," he wrote.

> I should be very reluctant to lecture on sexual ethics, which have quite wrongly been supposed to be my special field. Actually the subject interests me much less than many others and I should be sorry to be diverted from philosophy and history to sociology. I could, if it suited you, lecture on different philosophies of the past, and their influence on culture and social questions: for example, Platonism and its influence, or the Romantic movement of the nineteenth century . . .

With Russell's agreement in principle firmly secured, Barnes flew out to him in California. He was generous not only with finance but with offers of help in finding a home for the star turn of the Foundation. Russell's letters, written just before and just after Barnes drew up a five-year contract, make no bones of his state of mind, and of his plans for the immediate future. Both he and his wife were grateful for the offer to find a house. "It is, I think, rather essential that we should be not less than fifty miles from Philadelphia and quite in the country," he stressed.

> Social life takes up time which we can ill afford to spare; I want to be able to concentrate on serious work. What is even more important, my wife's health needs care; she must live as quiet a life as possible, and ought, if at all possible, to be at some altitude above sea level. She intends to devote the first part of my time at Harvard to the question of a house. We shall need six or seven bedrooms and two other rooms; one living-and-dining room, and one not very small study . . .

But Dr Barnes did not fully understand the financial position and at first proposed that Russell should occupy what was almost a country estate. Russell explained,

> In the first place, it is *impossible* for us to buy; I cannot get money from England, and have here only what I have saved during the last twenty months. In the second place, I shall, out of 6,000 dollars a year, have to keep my two older children; I must therefore have a house which not only has a low rental, but is cheap to run and requires little service. I should not know what to do with 60 or 70 acres of farmland. It is much more important to my happiness to live within my means than to live in a beautiful house; and it is essential both to my wife and to myself to reduce the machinery of life to a minimum.
>
> Choosing a house is a very personal matter, like choosing a wife. I know that in China the latter is done by proxy, but although people make mistakes, we are apt to prefer our own folly to the wisdom of others. We should neither of us wish to decide on a house until we have seen a considerable selection. I am deeply touched at your even contemplating spending $35,000 on the matter, but I am sure we can be happy at very much lower cost, and we could not possibly pay a rent corresponding to such a price, so that, in effect, you would be paying me a bigger salary than was agreed upon.

However, before Russell took up the appointment Barnes did increase his salary. Russell had complained that he did not like having to give popular lectures elsewhere to boost his income. Barnes thereupon re-wrote the contract so that Russell should receive not 6,000 but 8,000 dollars a year, taking it for granted that Russell was thereby honourably bound not to give popular lectures; Russell took a different view, protesting later that it had been clearly understood he was under no *obligation* to discontinue his other work.

While he did not like having to depend on casual lecturing he seems to have enjoyed it, as when he was drawn into a long and controversial debate with Arnold Lunn. He had been invited to Washington to read a paper on "Education for Democracy" to the Open Forum, and Lunn was one of those invited to sit on the platform and ask a question or two at the end of the address. A formidable opponent who enjoyed as much as Russell an argument for its own sake, Lunn had asked for fifteen minutes during which he could pull his opponent's leg.

"The programme of the meeting informed us that the chief speaker was Earl Russell, but that he preferred to be known quite simply as Mr. Bertrand Russell," he later wrote. "I began by pointing out that if I were to wander round America describing myself as Lord Lunn, Mr. Russell would be very much surprised, and that I resented this aristocrat masquerading as a mister and stealing my democratic thunder."

Lunn laid into Russell, Russell replied with tolerance and a quick thrust of the rapier, and a good time was had by both. The next day Lunn called on the Russells and found that, while his host insisted on being called Mr, Mrs Russell was equally insistent on being addressed as Lady Russell. She had been asked if she did not feel guilty about this in the current democratic climate. "I said 'No'," she replied, "'but I should feel guilty if I was wearing your expensive mink coat.'"

Before Russell took up the appointment at the Barnes Foundation, it had been agreed that his course would consist not of a one-year series to be repeated annually, but of a single course spread over five years and covering the whole of Western philosophy. The result would be published as a book, and Barnes offered to provide a shorthand-writer who would present Russell with a verbatim transcript of each lecture.

Towards the end of the year Russell moved to Philadelphia – where on the application-form for a new passport he gave his profession as "Peer" – then on to Malvern where he took Little Datchet Farm, a 200-year-old house thirty miles from the city in pleasant rolling country that reminded him of Dorset.

Here he prepared to settle down, as happy as could be expected in the circumstances. Professionally, he was being well paid for work he enjoyed, and if he did not yet foresee that his lectures would become an unsuspected gold-mine, he was "learning things [he had] always wanted to know", as he described the process to Lucy Silcox. The horror of the war, and the looming problem of the Russian menace when it was over, threw their shadows across all he thought and did, even though the invasion of Britain, that most awful of possibilities which had chilled him in the summer of 1940, could now be ruled out. "Sometimes the longing for home is almost unbearable," he wrote to Elizabeth Trevelyan, asking later, "Are all the trees on Leith Hill cut down? I am haunted by the thought of disappearing beauty."

Homesickness was soon compounded by other worries, since guerrilla warfare now broke out between Russell and Dr Barnes, a warfare made almost inevitable by the juxtaposition of two such strong-minded men, the first determined to uphold his individual human rights, the other equally determined that his organization should be dominated by his own eccentricities. The battle ranked high as public entertainment and the *Philadelphia Record* at one stage proposed that Dr Barnes should "subsidise Russell so that a controversy enjoyed by all might be continued without undue hardship upon one of the principals". It is not entirely true that the initial cause of the trouble was Lady Russell's occasional practice of knitting during her husband's lectures; but there is enough in it to indicate the level at which the attack was made, and the knockabout air of the proceedings.

The first brush came in the spring of 1941, when Lady Russell tried to make contact with her husband while he was being interviewed by a journalist at the Foundation. Her action was, said a letter of complaint the following day, an infraction of the Foundation's regulations concerning decorum in the gallery – in the light of conflicting reports a hint that an anti-Russell faction was already in existence.

Peace prevailed for six months, although it is worth remarking that during this period Russell wrote to the British Ambassador in Washington, Lord Halifax, asking for advice about returning to Britain. "Many [English people in the United States] desire very strongly to be in England," he said, "but are in doubt as to whether they are wanted, and as to whether an extra mouth to feed would outweigh their possible usefulness. They would be very grateful for a simple statement as to whether or not their return would be likely to be advantageous to their country or the reverse." Simple statements, however, were not Halifax's strong point. He replied that it all depended.

Resigned to the situation, Russell carried on. Then, in the autumn, a letter to Lady Russell from the Secretary of the Foundation resurrected the earlier incident which had been considered by the Foundation's Board of Trustees. Peter replied that she had always helped to prepare her husband's lectures and sometimes found it necessary to attend. As to knitting, her husband had remarked that she had disturbed no one by knitting at far more difficult and technical lectures at the universities of Oxford, Chicago, California and Harvard. Russell himself wrote to the Trustees a short but blistering reply, pointing out that their complaint could have been made "orally, without formality and completely unnecessary rudeness".

If there was any doubt about the mood of the Foundation it was resolved a few days later when Miss Mullen, the Secretary, replied to Lady Russell in tones of high sarcasm. At this point a Mr Angelo Pinto wrote to Dr Barnes requesting permission to take colour-photographs during the lectures. This was given, subject to agreement by individual lectures. Lady Russell replied to Mr Pinto on her husband's behalf. He personally had no objection, she said, but he had "been officially informed that the class was disturbed by the less obvious distraction of knitting". Nevertheless he would put the matter to his class.

The reaction brought a confrontation less suited to the academic platform than to the theatrical. At the end of the lecture on 4 December 1941, Dr Barnes announced that he wished to discuss a problem. He put the case for Mr Pinto, saying that there was a great difference between his request and "one hour of knitting endured by at least a dozen people". Russell replied that complaints about knitting showed hypersensitiveness.

43 Russell interviewed by journalists at Harvard, 1940

44 Russell and Peter reading about the "Bertrand Russell case" which followed the proposal to appoint him to the City College of New York in 1940

45 Russell at Princeton in 1950, after hearing that he had been awarded the Nobel Prize for Literature

46 Russell, aged seventy-eight, after being rescued from the sea following the flying-boat accident at Trondheim, 1950

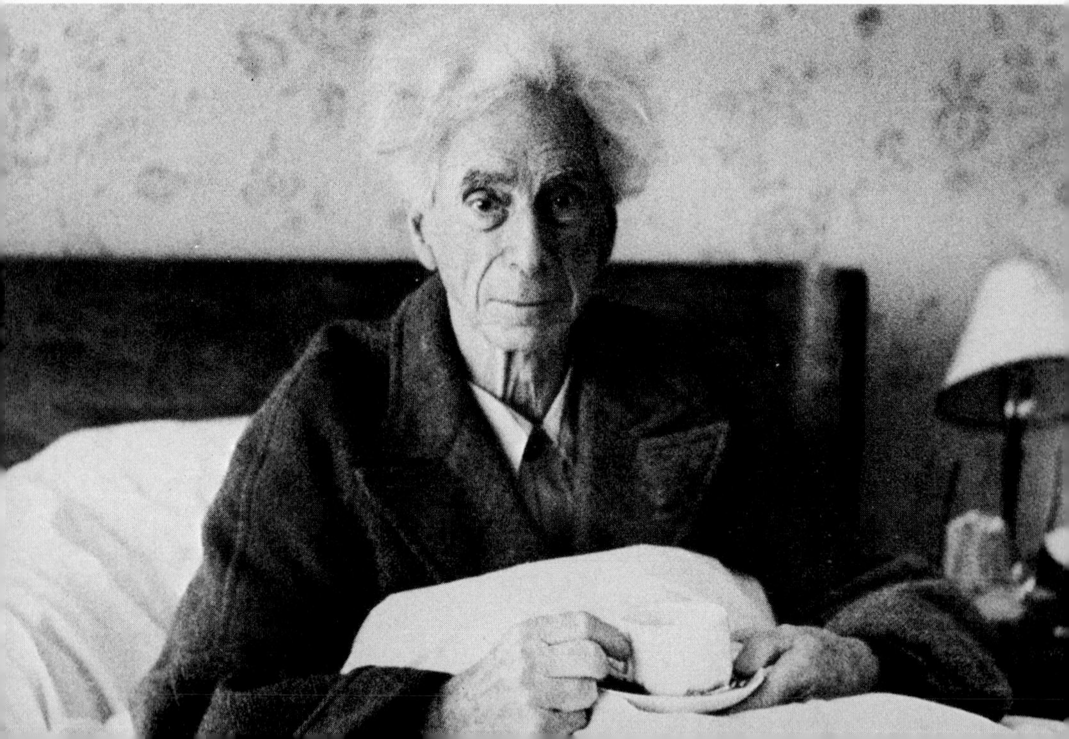

47 Russell with Sir David Maxwell Fyfe, Lady Violet Bonham Carter, Eleanor Roosevelt and Lord Boyd Orr, before taking part in a broadcast discussion in 1951 on human rights

48 Viscount Samuel, Hugh Trevor-Roper, Russell and Norman Fisher, in a "Brains Trust" programme, 1957

49 Russell sitting for Jacob Epstein, 1953

50 The Third Pugwash Conference in Vienna, 1958; Russell with Mr and Mrs Cyrus Eaton

Dr Barnes retorted that as Russell had said most of the class were not disturbed by the knitting, would those who agreed now put up their hands. At this Russell walked out, fearing that his supporters might have to pay for it. The result was a more than usually insulting letter from Barnes stating in plain terms that the Trustees "did not obligate [themselves] to endure forever the trouble-making propensities of your wife". Surprisingly, this particular storm was weathered, although Lady Russell was now in practice banned from the Foundation. Notwithstanding her retirement from the scene, Russell received a curt note on 28 December 1942 ending his engagement three days later for "breach of contract". There was an offer to renew it on a monthly basis, although its sincerity can be assessed by a sentence in the press statement which Dr Barnes issued a fortnight later. "Judging from the letters and verbal communications I have received," he announced, "Mr. Russell's departure from the scene has been a welcome relief not only to the best of his students but to all members of our official and teaching staff."

The dismissal had come entirely out of the blue. Behind the scenes, however, there had been some weeks of preparation on the part of Dr Barnes, who had learned that Russell was to give a series of popular weekly lectures at the Rand School in New York on "The Problems of Democracy". "With this gross breach of contract," he later said, "we began to consider the question of his dismissal from the staff, but delayed action for several months while we submitted the entire evidence to a group of distinguished authorities in ethics and law. The legal experts' opinion was that he had broken his contract by popular lecturing and by his upholding of Mrs. Russell's disorderly conduct."

The authority of Barnes's experts was eventually found to be nonexistent. Meanwhile Russell, although lodging a claim against the Foundation, was out of work once more, having, as he wrote to Stanley Unwin, lost his "whole income (illegally) at three days' notice".

In these depressing circumstances he struggled on, tidying his lectures into what was to become *A History of Western Philosophy*, producing for Haldeman-Julius the series of *How to ...* booklets, writing articles on the future of pacifism and on citizenship, and serious essays for Professor Schilpp's "Library of Living Philosophers". And for *Glamour* he advised readers on what to do "If You Fall in Love with a Married Man", a revealing example of his understanding of other people's human problems, if not of his own. Judged by title alone it was little more than a frivolous pot-boiler of the "do mothers make good wives" *genre*. In fact, it took a cool look at the assorted possibilities, analysed them, and then proposed common-sense solutions more to be expected from a marriage-guidance clinic than a popular magazine.

In spite of the income from *ad hoc* journalism, Russell's immediate poverty was worse than was implied by his casual comment, "financial stringency [was] not so much as I had feared". As a start, he and Peter moved from Little Datchet Farm to a primitive three-roomed cottage. Built for servants, it had three stoves, each of which had to be stoked every hour or so. "One was to warm the place, one was for cooking, and one was for hot water. When they went out it was several hours' work to get them lighted again," Russell has written. "Conrad could hear every word that Peter and I said to each other, and we had many worrying things to discuss which it was not good for him to be troubled with."

He was no luxury-lover; at times he had been poor, although for a Russell in his native habitat this was not too desperate a state. But here, isolated in America, the lack of hard cash was really worrying. John was now at Harvard, Kate at Radcliffe, and the fact that Frank's second ex-wife Mollie had recently died, thus ending a £400-a-year drain on Russell's resources, did not help in view of the wartime currency regulations.

The start of 1943 was thus a very bleak period and only a 3,000-dollar advance from Simon & Schuster for *A History of Western Philosophy* enabled him to keep John and Kate at university. When a publisher required a publicity photograph Peter told him that they could not afford to have one taken; they had only just enough money to pay for their food. On one occasion, travelling to New York to deliver a lecture, Russell had only the cash for a single ticket: the return-half was bought with a part of the lecture fee. After Dr Schilpp published the volume on Whitehead he received a note from Russell. Could he have a free copy, as he could not possibly afford to buy one? Already, family tradition asserts, there had been the awful day when Conrad's money-box had to be opened to pay the household bills.

The troubles were not only financial. Russell and Peter had now been married for seven years. While still at Little Datchet Farm they were visited by Freda Utley, the friend of pre-war days. She later wrote of Peter,

> I realised by now that [Russell] had a stormy petrel on his hands. She was a young and beautiful woman and needed to be courted and entertained as well as loved. While never, I feel sure, unfaithful to Bertie, whom she adored, she needed the society of younger men as escorts to parties and admirers and for youthful companionship. She was totally unsuited to live in a remote house in Pennsylvania often without servants (because few couples stayed long) while expected by herself as well as Bertie to maintain the kind of household which English people of the upper classes take for granted.

This was before the move to the cottage. Soon after they had settled in to their new and confined quarters, Alys Russell's niece Karin, who had married Adrian Stephen during the First World War, came to stay.

She may not have been entirely impartial in her reactions. But her friends back in England were left in little doubt that Russell's third marriage was heading for the precipice. A few months later he was telling Beatrice Webb that if he returned to England he would leave Peter and Conrad in the United States, and not long after that, when plans for his return were maturing, he wrote to Colette, hoping they would meet when he arrived and sending much love.

His enthusiasm for Peter, as evidenced in his published letters and unpublished remarks, had become rather muted. Nevertheless, he still had her loyal support. From their earliest days in America she had filled the essential role of secretary-protector, tactfully keeping unwanted visitors at bay, persuading publishers not to harry her husband with delivery-dates.

She was also quick to take up slurs, real or apparent, and early in 1943 wrote a strong letter to G. H. Hardy at Trinity protesting that the anti-Russell lobby in the United States was alleging that Trinity had "disowned" Russell. Hardy passed the letter to George Trevelyan, the Master, who replied that it was quite incorrect to say that Russell had been disowned. "There was trouble during the last war, but that hatchet was buried as long ago as 1920," he went on. "The last thing that had occurred between Trinity and your husband was that in 1925 the College appointed him to give the triennial Tarner Lectures on the Philosophy of the Sciences ... Nothing has since occurred to disturb our amicable relations." Trevelyan also enclosed a note: "If you and Bertie like to put this letter into the press, you are at liberty to do so. It is for you to decide."

Meanwhile, Russell remained unemployed. Much of the City College odium had by this time been washed away, his reputation in the academic world still glittered and, in his own opinion at least, his views on the war were now orthodox. Why, it may be asked, was he not therefore seized upon by the British authorities to present Britain's wartime case in the United States? He had supported the war with the resigned acceptance that matched the American stance. His political views, although well left of centre, were no more insupportable than those of many others brought into the wartime propaganda effort. He would, moreover, have had a ready-made audience far larger and more attentive than that of the hesitant amateur speakers sometimes launched across the States with little more than the hope that they would do no harm.

In fact, there were considerable and even respectable reasons for the British Embassy's failure to approach Russell. His pacifism of the First World War might have been more than balanced by his support for the Second. But his views on the future of India, then a bone of great controversy, were in direct conflict with those of Churchill, if not of the British Cabinet. Even more damning was his persistent and outspoken opposition to Communism, an attitude it was felt should be toned down rather than shouted from the rooftops when the Red Army, single-handed, was still engaging the overwhelming bulk of the *Wehrmacht.* If Russell's views on Socialism and sex had previously kept him from membership of the Establishment, he was as firmly kept from it now by his belief that the Soviet government was "even worse than Hitler's, and it will be a misfortune if it survives". He not only held embarrassing views; he both aired and embroidered them. Many Americans remember his convoluted after-dinner extravaganza, told in a precise high-pitched voice and asserting that the Marshal Timoshenko who held the Germans at bay was really a disguised Taffy Jenkins – the archetypical Welshman – from the Rhondda Valley of South Wales.

Nevertheless he was anxious to help the war effort and failure to find an outlet in America fed his urge to return to Britain. What he would do there was uncertain, but he felt the time had come to speak out on a number of political and social questions. So much so that he discussed with a highly placed visitor from Britain a scheme under which he would write a regular column for the *Manchester Guardian.* This might have been agreed at the highest level but for one thing: he insisted that he should have complete and absolute freedom to say whatever he wanted, a freedom that no editor could have guaranteed in wartime even had any editor been willing to take the risk.

In spite of the uncertainty, he pressed on with plans to get back to England, and in August was writing to Colette that Peter and Conrad would be returning in September and that he would be following in a month or two. Meanwhile, he wanted peace, time and quiet to complete the transformation of his Barnes lectures into his great *History.* He found it at Bryn Mawr. Here the library was put at his disposal and throughout the autumn he would often be seen sitting under the trees. He stayed with Lucy Donnelly and saw much of her friend Edith Finch, now teaching English at the college. The arrangement was a purely private one and he had been working there for some while when the Philosophy Department received an anonymous gift from a former pupil. With it went the proposal that it should be used to pay Russell for a series of lectures on the Postulates of Scientific Method. They were a tremendous success, wrote Professor Paul Weiss. "Despite torrential rains, students, faculty and others came from Swarthmore, Haverford and Philadelphia in considerable and increasing numbers."

The Bryn Mawr lectures marked a change in fortune. Russell was invited to lecture at Princeton where for some weeks, living in a pleasant house on the shore of Carnegie Lake, he had regular sessions with Einstein, Gödel and Pauli, three of the few living equals in his own intellectual fields. Then, with the enormous manuscript of the *History* ready for publication, he secured the substantial advance payment from Simon & Schuster.

Next, his claim against the Barnes Foundation was finally decided in his favour. Russell's case was the straightforward claim that the Foundation had broken its contract, and that Barnes's complaints against Lady Russell would have been irrelevant even had it been possible to substantiate them. The Foundation's allegation that Russell had skimped his lectures was not merely denied but looked ridiculous, since he by now had available as evidence two-thirds of *A History of Western Philosophy*. Barnes, going into the witness-box and giving his own version of the lectures, unwittingly helped to show that Russell had done his job properly. "If the case had been tried before twelve good men and true – the defence asked for a jury trial too late – they would probably have deduced from the parade of imposing exotic names that Russell had been underpaid," admits Barnes's biographer. "After the roll call of lectures was over, Judge Guy K. Bard ruled that it was irrelevant."

Barnes's defence was simply that by giving popular lectures Russell had broken his contract. At first glance it might have seemed that this was supported by Russell's own evidence. He admitted lecturing to a variety of bodies – earning a hundred dollars from a private group in Phoenixville, fifty dollars from another at the South Norwalk Foreign Policy Association, more than a thousand dollars for long articles in Haldeman-Julius's monthly, and other sums from publications ranging from *Free World* to *Vogue* and *Glamour*. It was an impressive tribute to his ability to deal with any job that came up, but it was irrelevant to the matter in issue, since the contract with the Foundation did not forbid outside work. There had, it is true, been the oral agreement, and it was not denied that as a result of it Russell was paid an additional 2,000 dollars a year. But no stipulation about extra-curricular work was written into the contract; and while Barnes took it that Russell would eschew such work, Russell stressed that he had no obligation to do so. The verdict awarded him 20,000 dollars – his expected salary of 24,000 dollars less the 4,000 dollars it was estimated he would earn in the unexpired period of his contract. Barnes appealed, and lost. He appealed a second time and lost a second time. After contemplating a third appeal, he contented himself with writing *The Case of Bertrand Russell versus Democracy and Education*, an ill-natured little pamphlet in which he summed up with the assertion that if his students at Merion had "learned anything whatever of democracy in education from [Russell], it was because he presented them with the perfect example of its antithesis".

The award of 20,000 dollars was welcome news. Better still arrived a few weeks later. This time it was Peter who had waved the magic wand. The letter which she had written to Hardy earlier in the year had not only been passed on to the Master, and replied to by him. It had also been read to members of Trinity Council. Nevertheless, it is by no means certain that this alone would have started the machinery which eventually brought Russell back to Trinity. Quite fortuitously, an appeal had also been made from a different quarter.

Two years earlier, while Russell had been questioning his own conscience about support for the war, he had been visited in California by Vera Brittain, pacifist and novelist, and her husband George Catlin, political scientist and philosopher. Back in England Catlin had remembered Russell's desperate financial situation and his equally desperate anxiety to return to Britain. Catlin, a man of many parts with fingers in innumerable pies, knew Professor H. H. Price, an Oxford philosopher with many Cambridge links. Catlin wrote to Price; Price wrote to his old Trinity friend C. D. Broad; and Broad thereupon began lobbying for Russell's return to Trinity. G. H. Hardy was at this time writing, and later had printed for private circulation, *Bertrand Russell and Trinity*, a full account of Russell's dismissal from his Lectureship in 1916. Hardy's story left little doubt that there was a wrong to be righted, and by 1943 the ground for Russell's return had therefore been well prepared.

No records exist of the happenings between spring and autumn, but after eight months of official silence the Council minutes recorded a proposal that Russell should be elected to a Fellowship under Title B; and, shortly afterwards, agreement to the election. The Council, it was added, would raise no objection to his doing other work, would not insist on residence – although it would be glad to offer rooms if wanted – and would not demand that he lecture, although everyone would be happy if he did. Admittedly, there is a lack of documentary evidence; nevertheless, there seems little doubt that it was Lady Russell's letter in combination with Hardy's book which started discussion among the Fellows, which led first to a tentative and then to a not-so-tentative proposal that "something should be done about Bertie", to a formal investigation of the possibility, and then to the offer which eventually brought him back to Cambridge. Peter's impetuosity had served her husband well.

Before he left America Russell wrote for the *Saturday Evening Post* a popular answer to the question "Can Americans and Britons be Friends?" It discussed the distorted image that each nation had of the other, but in a conciliatory way that Russell regarded as his "modest contribution towards Anglo-American co-operation". It evoked scores of letters, many of them confirming how ingrained the distortions were, but it had another unexpected effect. At the Foreign Office, where Russell's name had until recently tended to make blood-pressures rise, the reaction was all sweetness. "Very well done" and "certainly very good reading" were typical of the minuted comments. Lord Russell, the ex-jailbird author of "monstrous" articles, seemed to have changed his spots.

The author himself meanwhile was crossing the Atlantic in a liberty ship, carrying with him the manuscript of *A History of Western Philosophy*, already approved by the Censor as being of no use to the enemy. Once more there was the prospect of security and of Cambridge. Once more there would be the chance of getting down to philosophy in peace. There would also be the chance of deciding what should be done about his third marriage, already wearing a rather part-worn look.

18

A Member of the Establishment

Russell was seventy-two when he crossed the Atlantic as the Anglo-American invasion-force fought for its life on the Normandy beaches. Both physically and mentally he was not so much "well preserved" as in the state normally expected of much younger men. Physically he maintained this for another two decades with but few signs of wear and tear. Mentally, also, he had a unique reservoir on which to draw. Even in his bad moments – and like the rest of us he had them – he could make rings round most experts in his own special subjects.

Yet from this time onwards there are areas where his acute perception of events is interspersed with contrasting exhibitions of unawareness, there are disturbing events whose contradictions cannot be explained away by the stop-gap excuse of misreporting, and grotesque over-statements that did harm to the causes he had at heart. Just as there are "black holes" in the universe which astronomers are unable to explain or explain away, so does his last quarter-century present equally inexplicable areas where the writ of the natural law did not appear to run.

For Russell, most of the years ahead were to be dominated by the prospects held out by nuclear weapons, first the hope of world government, then the threat of world destruction. It was to be a period as tight-packed with excitement as any man could hope for even in his prime, and he sensed something of this future as the Liberty-ship convoy landed him back in Britain. The European war had another year to run. The euphoria that followed the Normandy landings dispersed, as another winter of fighting became inevitable. Nevertheless, Churchill's "light at the end of the tunnel" was at last growing brighter and the climate in which Russell settled down in Cambridge was already bubbling with the prospects of peace. It was England, moreover, the England of the Backs, of rooks in immemorial elms, of muddle and tolerance, of those inconsistencies and qualities which had made him kiss the earth when he returned from Paris almost exactly half a century earlier. "All this", he wrote of his new condition from Trinity to Lucy Silcox, "is such a change from the unspeakable misery we endured in America that one feels intoxicated."

Another cause for cheerfulness was that the family was once again reunited. Peter and Conrad had crossed the Atlantic by another route. John had joined the Royal Navy Volunteer Reserve and was in London, learning Japanese, expecting to be posted to the Far East. Kate, having ended her university career in what Russell rightly called "a blaze of glory" which had included one offer to join the Radcliffe teaching staff and another of a post at a Southern university, had returned to Britain and was working for the Ministry of Information.

The Russell who felt such inner satisfaction that all his children were in the same country as himself, was not yet, outside academic circles, the prestigious figure he was soon to become. Far from it, in fact. His change in status during the next few years was due to two contrasting factors. At the popular level, his voice and his aureole of white hair – the latter as much an asset as Einstein's – claimed an immediate audience. So did his obvious sincerity. Just as important was the fact that for once in his life he found himself swimming with the tide; the desire for change flowed as strongly in his veins as in those of the electorate which brought a Socialist government to power.

However, it was not only because of his radical views that Russell's influence began to grow. At a different level there was his unremitting anti-Communism. During the war it had been muted. In America, the influence that persisted after Roosevelt's death tended to throw a rosy glow over the most intransigent of Russian attitudes; at Yalta, and even under Truman at Potsdam, there was an American reluctance to face the facts about Russia. In Britain, scepticism about the mythology of Uncle Joe had always been greater, though muffled by the realities of the war and by genuine admiration for a Red Army that held the sky suspended. During the year that followed Russell's return to Britain, the scepticism grew as Stalin refused to release Poland, for whose liberty Britain had gone to war, and as the line from the Baltic to Trieste, first envisaged as a temporary post-war necessity, hardened into a barrier to be crossed at peril. Thus Russell, believing that Stalin's Russia was as bad as Hitler's Germany, represented a godsend to the permanent Establishment: a pillar of the B.B.C., which had discovered his value; a lecturer for the British Council in Berlin and in Norway; even a lecturer at the Imperial Defence College for five years in succession, and a speaker who urged elsewhere that the Russians should be brought into line. Lord John's grandson, the determined outsider, had been brought inside, and for a while it looked as though England had again dealt with a rebel in her customary way: by absorption.

The outcome was unexpected. The platforms to which Russell gained access during the later 1940s brought him again before the wider non-philosophical public which had known him mainly by his popular books of the inter-war years. Thus he had an army of devoted supporters when, after a decade of peace, he appeared to execute a smart U-turn and started to swim once more against the official stream.

His pleasure at being back home in 1944 was soon qualified by the trials of wartime England. At Trinity he had been given Newton's rooms. He was delighted with them, and he was thoroughly happy at his return to the academic ring he had known for more than half a century. "I dine in hall & enjoy seeing dons I used to know 30 years ago," he wrote to Colette. "George Trevy is much mellowed, very friendly, & nice. One can still play the game of great-uncles with him & his wife – his was Macaulay, hers Matthew Arnold, & the only subject they disagree about is which was the greater."

But finances were precarious. Cambridge was packed, and not until the 20,000 dollars from the Barnes Foundation were in hand could he buy his own house and resume family life with Peter and Conrad. He was also depressed by the losses and the changes which the war had exacted. "Almost every night before falling asleep I see the garden in which I passed my childhood, which has since been destroyed," he wrote to Gamel Brenan on Good Friday, 1945; "I mind its destruction quite as much as the deaths of people I have loved." To Peggy Kiskadden in America he wrote in the same vein a few months later.

> Everybody is utterly weary with years of overwork and suppressing fear. For 200 years we have been accustomed to be the dominant Power, & now victory has left us at the mercy of the U.S.A. and U.S.S.R., likely to be ground to powder when they come to blows. Much that one loved is destroyed – some of the best churches, the Temple, which had remained just as in Lamb's essay, & so on. Of my grandmother's house in Dover Street not a trace remains. What has survived, I fear, has survived only for a few years, as another war, worse than this, seems almost certain before very long.

But he managed to conceal his fears from all but closest friends. "If we met," he continued to Mrs Kiskadden, "you would find me full of laughter and jollity, apparently without a care in the world. My glands work so well that I can endure many pessimistic thoughts without ceasing to be cheerful."

There were soon a number of reasons for being cheerful. For one thing his finances, rehabilitated by the money from the Barnes Foundation, now began to experience a more permanent transformation. *A History of Western Philosophy*, the Barnes lectures in their new dress, was from the moment of publication a runaway bestseller on both sides of the Atlantic. His later claim that it earned more money than all the rest of his books put together may be an exaggeration; but its financial success was of that order. Sales in Britain would have been even higher but for the acute paper shortage which held up the English edition for a year after the American edition was in the shops.

It was not financial success alone which encouraged him. In his big *History* he had found a way of combining erudition and a flair for popular exposition on a new scale and with a success not previously achieved. The books of the inter-war years – *An Outline of Philosophy*, *The Scientific Outlook*, *Power* – might not be exactly pot-boilers, but after a glance back towards them the scope of the *History* becomes even more striking. The professional philosophers might criticize it in detail: but they read it, and not always without a touch of envy.

Thus encouraged, in his early seventies, he got down to work in the new home in Babraham Road, partly furnished by the unwieldy furniture he had acquired from Wittgenstein more than a quarter of a century earlier. Just as in his earlier and quasi-celibate years, he concentrated, and hard, putting his study out of bounds to everyone. "This rule was so sacred", his younger son has said, "that I did not venture to break in until I was eight. When I went in, with my heart in my mouth, my father was covering pages with an endless succession of mathematical symbols. When the door opened, he simply continued working and, after what seemed an age, I withdrew crestfallen wondering whether he had ever known I had been in the room."

Resuming his old habits, he also resumed his accustomed role in Cambridge. He kept his rooms in Trinity, where the only photograph on his desk was a framed portrait of Ottoline. He made no secret of his pleasure and pride that he had been invited back. Walking from his rooms to the library with a friend one day, past the marble busts on pedestals, he waved his hand as he passed the last one and said, "I shall be here one day."

Under the terms of his Fellowship there was no need for him either to teach or to give popular lectures. He did both. Notable among the lectures was the course on "An Introduction to Philosophy" in the autumn of 1947. The public expected something not too difficult to grasp, but Russell made few concessions; in the words of one listener he spoke as if he had been lecturing to an international congress. The tactics were surprisingly successful. The initial lectures were given in a small hall; the next in an Examination Hall that held five hundred. The last, delivered to the audience of five hundred, had to be relayed by a public-address system to overflow rooms. Russell took the reception for granted. "They come not so much to hear philosophy, as to hear me," he observed to more than one colleague.

What they saw, each Saturday morning, was impressive.

> The slim, erect figure, gown adjusted and manuscript in hand, would advance to the rostrum with a vigour and a resolution that

belied his years. Something of his age showed in the heavy wrinkles of his face, and in his habit of working the muscles of his jaw spasmodically. But his bearing was irresistibly youthful. The things you would remember after the lecture were the animated sparkle of his eyes and the quick, decisive movements that showed nothing of the palsy of old age; also, and chiefly, the virility of his mind and senses.

The public Russell, taking off his spectacles and leaning across the rostrum to confide to his audience: "You know, Euclid is a pleasant fairy tale, but you don't have to believe it;" the master speaker, hugely enjoying his mastery, was a phenomenon that pre-war Cambridge had not known. Yet the earlier Russell was still there. Since the days before the First World War he had been seeking the most philosophically feasible link between the world of common sense and the world of science that the physicists were revealing in constantly greater and more mysterious detail. Just as he had sought for unsophisticated certainty in his boyhood, so now was he still searching for some intellectually unassailable system to support both the nature of scientific knowledge and the experiences of everyday life. "I had become increasingly aware of the very limited scope of deductive inference as practised in logic and pure mathematics," he wrote later. "I realised that all the inferences used both in common-sense and in science are of a different sort from those in deductive logic, and are such that, when the premisses are true and the reasoning correct, the conclusion is only probable."

For a man seeking certainty this was not good enough, and as far back as 1943, outlining plans for future work, he had said that what he wanted to do next was "to attempt to systematize non-demonstrative inference". In an effort to find something better, he prepared his annual course on "Non-Demonstrative Inference", beginning with probability itself. This was to lead eventually to *Human Knowledge: Its Scope and Limits*, Russell's last testament on the problems associated with an empiricist philosophy. A long book, it would have been longer still had he not decided to publish separately the parts dealing with his theory of ethics. These appeared in *Human Society in Ethics and Politics*, reiterating the position he had maintained in ethics since Santayana had brought about his change of stance in 1913, and the views on politics he had first stated in *Principles of Social Reconstruction*. However, the central purpose of the book was to examine the relation between individual experience and the general body of scientific knowledge. Earlier in the century Russell's work on logic had centred on acquiring an understanding of demonstrative inference, in which there is a relation of certainty between premisses and conclusion. But with most inference about the world the premisses, at best, make the conclusion merely probable. Since Russell always regarded our knowledge of the world from an empirical viewpoint, powerful support would be given to his philosophy by a clear account of non-demonstrative inference. In *Human Knowledge*, he tackled one by one the problems raised, and by the end of the book had covered the whole field of epistemology. His answer was that the validity of non-demonstrative inference rested on five postulates which could neither be proved from any premisses more basic, nor established by an appeal to experience. Yet he believed that his postulates did have some kind of empiricist flavour since they yielded inferences which "are self-confirmatory and are not found to contradict experience". But if they could not be known in the way that facts were known one could simply accept them in order to work on in science. But this meant that as a philosophy empiricism had a limitation that Russell cheerfully admitted. "Indeed," he concluded, "such inadequacies as we have seemed to find in empiricism have been discovered by strict adherence to a doctrine by which empiricist philosophy has been inspired: that all human knowledge is uncertain, inexact, and partial. To this doctrine we have not found any limitation whatever."

The course on "Non-Demonstrative Inference" which led to this frustrating conclusion was only one part of his university work. There was also, as there had been thirty years previously, the week's court, open to all. "When you mounted the stairs and knocked on the door, you would get a cheery 'Come in'," one constant visitor has said. "On entering you would usually find him ensconced in the corner of a sofa, and invariably pulling on his pipe. If you were the first visitor of the day he would talk with you about any subject you might broach. As the others arrived one by one, the conversation would always shift to technical philosophy for a while, but no subject was taboo."

He retained his willingness to help anyone genuinely interested in mathematics. One Cambridge undergraduate, for instance, needed a particular edition of Frege which seemed to be unobtainable. "So he, a stranger, wrote to the expert of experts explaining his problem and asking for information," says Vincent Buranelli. "By return post he received Russell's personal copy of the book along with a note telling him to keep it until his work was finished." Above all, during this Indian summer of his academic life, there was what one listener has called the extreme democracy of his attitude and another has likened to a lift's ability to come to any required level. Russell never talked down to visitors, intuitively sensing what they could understand and phrasing his arguments accordingly. He never threw his weight about.

There was one exception: Wittgenstein. Following his examination by Russell and Moore in 1930 he had become a Fellow of Trinity and had then held a succession of lectureships throughout most of the following nine years. Shortly before the outbreak of war he was elected to the Chair of Philosophy in succession to Moore; but, taking up hospital-work, did not return to Cambridge until 1945. Throughout the previous decade he had gradually abandoned the ideas of the *Tractatus* with its basic assertion that language is a picture of reality depicting the logical structure of facts, and replaced it with a new linguistic philosophy to be outlined in his posthumous *Philosophical Investigations*. With the exception of one short paper, and a caustic review of a logic text, the *Tractatus* was the only work that Wittgenstein published in his lifetime. Yet, as Gilbert Ryle summed up,

> from his jealously preserved little pond there have spread waves over the philosophical thinking of much of the English-speaking world. Philosophers who never met him – and few of us did meet him – can be heard talking philosophy in the tones of his voice and students who can hardly spell his name now wrinkle up their noses at things which had a bad smell for him.

By the late 1940s Russell was allergic to Wittgenstein's new outlook. For his part, Wittgenstein had been heard to say disparagingly of Russell, "He isn't going to kill himself doing philosophy now," and to Moore he could write of Russell at the Moral Science Club as being "most disagreeable. Glib and superficial, though, as always, *astonishingly* quick."

Yet something of the old master–pupil relationship remained. It came to the surface in October 1946. Karl Popper had been invited by the Moral Science Club to read a paper on some "philosophical puzzle". Wittgenstein was in the chair, waiting for what the academic grapevine had correctly told him would be a provocation. Also present, the centre of an inner semi-circle, was Russell, upright in a high-backed rocking-chair. During the preliminaries, and after the meeting had broken up, he was particularly agreeable to Popper and went out of his way to show on which side his sympathies lay.

During Popper's discourse, Wittgenstein interrupted with almost off-hand casual arrogance. The questions under discussion, he said, were a great deal more complex and subtle than Popper had realized – in fact all the speaker had done was to confuse the real issues. Popper, retaliating, stressed that he had made use of the comparatively few writings in which either Wittgenstein or his pupils had explained their ideas.

Later Wittgenstein, casually picking up a poker to emphasize a point, asked: "Give me an example of a moral rule." Popper replied with: "Not to threaten visiting lecturers with pokers." Whereupon, Popper has written, "Wittgenstein, in a rage, threw the poker down and stormed out of the room, banging the door behind him." But not, according to some accounts, before Russell had pulled himself up in his chair and roared out: "Wittgenstein, it is you who is creating all the confusion."

Wittgenstein's discomfiture in such a way was a rarely known and even more rarely recorded event. As the club's minutes reported, "the meeting" had been "charged to an unusual degree with a spirit of controversy". An enriched version of the incident was soon circulating in Cambridge: three dons, including Russell, had quarrelled so violently that one had used a poker on another.

The speed with which Russelliana were passed on by word of mouth, and the size of his audiences, were not the result of professional standing alone; appearances on radio, and subsequently on television, contributed even more to make him a national figure after the Second World War. Just as the Brains Trust had transformed Julian Huxley and Joad into popular idols in the blacked-out homes of wartime England, so did Russell's crisp thought and shocking frankness – later supplemented by his photogenic figure on the TV screens – turn him into a Delphic oracle whose constantly expanding audience was prepared to listen to whatever he was talking about.

His induction into post-war broadcasting had been a curious story of near-missed opportunities. It began in February 1944 when an internal B.B.C. memo noted that Russell would soon be back in England, and asked whether there would be any objection to his speaking on a strictly academic philosophy-brief to India. Earlier, there had been an argument about engaging the astro-physicist Sir Arthur Eddington who, as a Quaker, had his own views on the war. The question of using Russell, it was pointed out, was not so clearly cut as the case of Eddington; it was easily possible to give someone like Eddington a purely scientific brief, but more difficult in the case of a general philosopher. The proposal to use Russell was not well received. It appeared to be a leap in the dark, and it was added that Russell had been long away and had no great reputation for reliability and stability. There were other queries and not until five months later, after Russell had settled into Trinity, was the prospect of using him again taken up.

The experiment finally began in the autumn when he was heard on the Brains Trust. Next he spoke on "The Future of Civilisation", a talk so successful that it was at once proposed he should give another. He debated with J. B. S. Haldane on "Should Scientists be Public Servants?", disagreeing with the proposition on the grounds that "public servants take their orders from the State, i.e. from eminent elderly gentlemen who either know no science, or at most that of the last generation". He accepted, but was later forced to abandon, due to pressure of work, a request to prepare six talks on mathematics for schools, a request "at first sight rather like asking a French chef (Cordon Bleu) to give a lesson in boiling an egg". A new Director-General, General Sir Ian Jacob, proposed that Russell should explain, on the European Service, the extent to which a philosophy based on logical analysis might influence events in non-philosophical fields; a project to which Russell happily agreed since he had, he said, observed since before the war that men of diverse and usually hostile nations, if they adopted this philosophy, could discuss the most controversial questions calmly and rationally.

He was one of three atheists or agnostics who spoke on "What I believe", a series only made possible by a change in policy which for the first time permitted controversial religious broadcasting, and by January 1947 he could write to a friend, "I am incredibly busy as the B.B.C. has developed a passion for me. I talk to all the countries of Europe and S. America."

Using Russell on what appeared to be an ever-expanding range of subjects was not only the result of his innate ability to talk entertainingly on almost anything. "Of all the many speakers I handled I would put Bertie among the most professional," says Ronald Lewin of the B.B.C. "His scripts were always immaculately composed to exactly the right length and written in a style which absolutely fitted his way of speaking. He was completely docile in rehearsal and never struck attitudes or made difficulties as many lesser individuals used to do. But then, his scripts were always so perfect that very little rehearsal was necessary."

But the prickliness had not been blunted. "I hardly think 'Science and the Christian Age' would be a suitable title," he replied to one proposal for a talk, "since from the frontiers of Poland to the shores of the Pacific the age is no longer Christian." Asked to define moral values in 1,100 words or 8½ minutes, he replied that he had a slight shrinking from the phrase "moral values" because he thought it would take him more than 8½ minutes to define the word "moral", and when he had done so the B.B.C. would be so shocked that it would not allow him to broadcast the definition. But he would like to deal with "Western values" – no doubt because he had things to say on the subject calculated to infuriate the users of the phrase. And when working on a talk dealing with punishment, he argued that the increase in juvenile crime was due to the war. If, for many years, almost all ministers of religion preach that killing is a young man's supreme duty, some may believe them, but it is unfair to attribute the result to the decay of religion, he argued.

Notwithstanding the regular pin-pricks, the Corporation continued to use Russell, a policy that led on to a major unscripted debate with Father Copleston on "The Existence of God". "Copleston is a find," the Director-General wrote the following day.

> He was the first man I had heard who could stand in the same ring as Russell on these matters and not seem out of place. Listening to him, particularly in the second half, I was more than once reminded of Bagehot's saying that "in true metaphysics unbelief seems to need a reason far oftener than belief" ... The outstanding success of the

broadcast was its temper. A feeling of intellectual integrity allied to a determination to examine any proposition the other man put forward has not come through so forcibly in any previous broadcast I have heard.

It could hardly have been otherwise in view of the mutual respect felt by the two men, exemplified by Copleston's summary of Russell in his *History of Philosophy* and by Russell's observation that "one can criticise [Copleston] for having become a Jesuit, but not for the detailed consequences of being one". After that, and until the issue of a directive limiting what could be said about nuclear weapons, Russell appeared regularly as a star performer, part of the process which during the later 1940s drew him with gathering momentum away from the academic world into public affairs.

The movement, partly due to the advent of nuclear weapons in 1945, partly to the coming of a Socialist government with its prospect of the millennium round the corner, was complete by 1952. It was carried out against a background of personal unhappiness and frustration which would have broken one less resilient and less philosophic. No doubt much of the trouble was of his own making, a reflection of his incorrigible belief that the next marriage would, at last, give him all he wanted. However, as one friend remarked, "Since he was seeking for an impossible combination of Cleopatra and Aspasia, Hypatia and St. Theresa, Boadicea and Joan of Arc and was also drawn to Quakers and other Puritan types as shown by his first and last choice of wives – his quest for enduring love was abortive." His work in philosophy, his broadcasts on whatever controversy appeared to offer most sport, his lecture-tours abroad, and his constant interventions in the nuclear debate had therefore all to be fitted into a life of frequent physical upheaval and almost constant emotional strain.

Years later he dictated to his fourth wife an account in which he tried to explain the failure of his relationships with women. It was distinctly subjective, and it criticized Peter – as well as Ottoline, Dora and Colette – for certain alleged actions. It also reveals that by 1945 any hope of keeping his current marriage in working order was slight. A chance of restoring the situation appeared to come when at the end of 1945 he and Peter spent some weeks at Portmeirion in North Wales – where they had collaborated on *The Amberley Papers* and *Freedom and Organization* a decade earlier – and considered settling in the area when his Cambridge lectures were finished the following year. On the face of it, and if he could spend in Cambridge whatever time he could spare, this might conceivably have been one way of keeping the marriage in being.

There was, in fact, more than one reason for this being unlikely. The first was Russell's continuing interest in Gamel Brenan. Even before the war he had written to her from America, "You know my affection for you. It was always warm, but leapt up to a much higher point when you and Gerald returned from Spain in the early days of the Civil War." Their correspondence was resumed after Russell's return to England in 1944 and they met occasionally in London. "Then she ceased to see him or to answer his letters," Gerald Brenan has written. "Although she never told me her reason for this, I imagine that he made some sort of a pass at her or even asked her to leave me and marry him."

It seems unlikely that marriage was what Russell had in mind, but his long series of letters to her more than justify Brenan's general suspicions. After one lengthy description of the things and people he had loved, he admits that "all the above is a long-winded way of saying that seeing you is important to me". But there are problems, as he explains a few weeks later. "For various rather complicated reasons it would not be wise for me to go to London merely for pleasure. This is a severe disappointment to me. When I do manage to see you I will tell you all about the ways in which I am not a free agent." The difficulties were eventually overcome, but two years afterwards he is pleading for further meetings. "I have a very ardent desire to see you," he says. "I have told Peter that this is so and she has acquiesced." When no meeting occurs he writes again. "I hate the way the months go by without our meeting, while the deserts of vast eternity draw nearer and nearer. I feel that what I miss now I may miss for ever, which I did not feel when I was younger. I have lived a great deal but am not yet sated. Goodbye dear Gamel. All my love."

Any doubt that his feelings were only those aroused by most intellectual and attractive women is removed by one sheet in his hand among Gamel Brenan's papers. "From the first I have loved your strange eyes, expressing a kind of gentle mockery and the wisdom of old pain assimilated," it begins.

> Then I noticed the loving kindness expressed in all your movements. Very soon I saw that, like me, you live in an alien world whose manners and customs and assumptions are not what seem deeply natural to you. This has caused us both to have a secret inner life of memory – memory of people and places we have loved, the people dead or estranged, the places deprived of their ancient beauty. Those with whom we are associated, even in apparent intimacy, cannot share the secret life and are even likely to be jealous of it. And so I came to look to you for a companionship I had no longer hoped to find. Your silences said more to me than the words of the most eloquent and explicit. Gradually your beauty invaded my inmost being. I feel it as I feel the night wind in the willows, or the note of distant curlews

on a lonely moor. I feel no longer alone, no longer dusty, for your existence sheds enchantment even over this arid world

While the relationship with Gamel Brenan was simmering away, Russell formed another emotional attachment. This was with the wife of a young Cambridge lecturer he had met soon after arriving back in Cambridge. Early in 1946, Peter had gone to hospital after an accident, and the young woman, her husband and her twin children had moved into Babraham Lodge, to relieve him of housekeeping as he explained to Gamel Brenan. Later in the year the family left Cambridge, but Russell kept up the friendship. "It would be a great joy to see you," he was soon writing to the young woman, "–I don't quite know whether you think of coming to Ruislip, or of meeting in London. I think it is only fair to warn you that there are risks, whichever we do–risks to you as well as me. But if you think them worth running I am willing." The friendship had a mixture of motives. But although she was still in her twenties and he in his seventies, she could later speak of "the peculiarly intense & complete nature of our very passionate feelings". The feelings waxed and waned, but three years later, when Russell's third marriage was finally breaking up and he was searching for another home, he could still write to her from Wales, "I am marooned here except for occasional nights in hotels, & then I feel I am probably being observed by detectives. I want to join with my son John & his family in a house; then I can be visited without providing evidence."

However, the affair, which mellowed into an almost father-and-daughter relationship lasting until Russell's death, did not have the depth of his feeling for Colette. She had returned to England from Scandinavia at the end of the war, but late in 1945 he learned that she planned to return to Finland. Horrified at the idea, since he saw that country as a potential battlefield again, he recommended Tierra del Fuego or the Antarctic as being safer. But he longed to see her. Shortly afterwards they met at her sister's flat where, he confessed, "It is like coming home." They met again, affectionately, and he confided to her that the years in America had poisoned his third marriage.

However, efforts to salvage it by moving base from Cambridge were by now under way, with a suitable house in North Wales being sought by a friend of Clough Williams-Ellis at whose Portmeirion hotel he and Peter had stayed. He was Rupert Crawshay-Williams, a great-grandson of T. H. Huxley and himself a philosopher, who with his wife was eventually to find Russell not one home in Wales but two. After some intelligent scouting around, the Crawshay-Williamses found an ideal house on the outskirts of Ffestiniog, a small village a few miles inland from Portmeirion, midway between the mountains and the sea. Once the village school, it lay in the grounds of a largish mansion which during the war had accommodated A. S. Neill's Summerhill. Outside, it had one of the finest views in North Wales, west to the massive contours of the Moelwyns and down the valley to the coast; inside, the school and the adjoining master's living-quarters could be transformed into a home fitting the Russells' requirements like a glove. Here Peter could get down to the enjoyable business of home-making at which she excelled; here, keeping his Fellowship as a link with the past, going to Cambridge or London only when professional or private engagements demanded, he could, at the age of seventy-three, settle down to hard work again.

Throughout the spring and summer of 1946 Russell thus spent a good deal of time in North Wales supervising the necessary alterations. Then, in midsummer, he learned that Colette had again left Britain for Scandinavia. The move distressed him, and he wrote that he had been thinking of her ceaselessly and wondering when they would meet again. She, for her part, replied that she might be coming to England in the autumn and could stay at a small country inn near Cambridge if that suited him.

In October, as the alterations at Ffestiniog neared completion, Russell gave up his rooms in Trinity and took instead a small flat in Dorset Square, London. But as he explained in a long and mournful letter to Colette, while Peter would not have been with him all the time in Cambridge she would usually be with him in London. If Colette came to England he would try to see her as often as possible; but it would no longer be easy. He goes on working, he adds, because that is what he has always done, but he would take to the bottle if it were not a stupid thing to do. And, as in earlier days, he recommends Arnold's "Dover Beach"–

> Ah, love, let us be true
> To one another! for the world, which seems
> To lie before us like a land of dreams,
> So various, so beautiful, so new,
> Hath really neither joy, nor love, nor light,
> Nor certitude, nor peace, nor help for pain;
> And we are here as on a darkling plain
> Swept with confused alarms of struggle and flight,
> Where ignorant armies clash by night.

Consolation could still be found in work, but it was in a mood of profound depression that he hung on, kept going by the prospect of seeing Colette once again. For much of 1947 his letters to her are spattered with ideas either for getting her to England or for a visit by him to Sweden. But the country was the most neutral of neutrals and the British government, willing to use Russell and his strong anti-Communist feelings in Berlin and in Norway, saw no reason for extending his services to Sweden. As a private individual, he was as hog-tied as the rest a quarter of a century ago by the red tape that covered permission to travel and money to spend. But there might be a way out. In 1948 *A History of Western Philosophy* was to be published in Sweden. Might not his Swedish publisher, he suggested to Colette, be persuaded to invite him to lecture? "In that case the atom bomb can explode immediately afterwards so far as I'm *personally* concerned," she replied.

Arrangements took time and it was not until 21 May 1948 that he finally arrived in Stockholm, the guest of "Natur och Kultur". It was eight in the evening before he reached the Reisen hotel where Colette had decked out his room with lilies-of-the-valley, violas and golden cowslips. He was wearing on his watch-chain the small gold coin she had given him after the Lulworth reunion of 1919. She was wearing the dress, trimmed with his mother's lace, which she had made for his return from China in 1921. Did his wife know, she asked, that she was not only in the same city, but in the same hotel and with a bedroom on the same floor? Russell, with a lifetime's experience of turning dangerous corners, was unperturbed. "I will make little of it," he replied.

He was to give four lectures, two in Stockholm, two in Uppsala. The first, on "Mind and Matter", was in Stockholm University. The following day he arrived in Uppsala, the guest of the Philosophical Faculty, repeating his Stockholm lecture in the afternoon and in the evening speaking on "Culture and the State". Here his emphasis was on the bureaucratic repression of the arts in Russia, with the tragic fate of the composer Prokofiev as the main example. Two days later he returned to Stockholm to complete his duty with a lecture on the international situation to a gathering of Swedish Members of Parliament.

That over, he travelled to Mariefred, thirty miles west of Stockholm, for a few more days with Colette. "The vivid interest he then took in everything – whether a Runic stone beside a Soedermanland castle – or the portrait of a Scandinavian writer who had died very young – or the precision-slicing of ham in a provincial shop – was a constant delight," she later wrote. "Of the precision-slicing he remarked: 'It's like a good literary style.'" They cruised on Maelaren, the long inland lake which stretches into the heart of Sweden, and anchored one evening below Stadhuset Castle. "The quay was deserted," wrote Colette, "the lamps were lit, Stadshuset's three golden crowns shone dimly above its copper dome. We stood on deck, gazing at the scene. At last he said slowly, 'I don't suppose I'll ever see this again'. I do not remember what I replied, but I remember very clearly what it was in my mind to reply: 'Oh yes you will. They'll be giving you the Nobel Prize.'" So they did – two years later.

During these few days together Russell repeatedly suggested that Colette should return to Britain, buy a small house or cottage, and settle down. She, for her part, asked whether she could do anything to make his life happier. In this atmosphere they returned to Stockholm, then he to London, taking a hamper of food she had packed for him to relieve the post-war austerities.

The next month she was back in Britain, searching for a suitably remote cottage. She had nearly settled for a croft in the Torridon highlands of north-west Scotland, one of the most lonely areas of the British mainland, when there came a telegram signed by Russell and Peter proposing she stay with them at Ffestiniog. On the back of the telegram she scribbled: "I don't think it'd answer, but it is nice of Peter, nevertheless." A letter from Russell followed; the invitation, he explained, had been prompted by Peter and both of them hoped that she might eventually settle in North Wales. But when Colette arrived in September 1948 Peter was ill in London.

"B and I had the whole of yesterday entirely to ourselves," Colette wrote to a friend on the 12th.

> Conrad was away for the night with friends. It was utter perfection; in some ways even more so than Stockholm; and I know that B felt that too. And as we walked up the hill in the darkness to the Pengwern [Arms] he said, very emphatically, "We should never have parted". The perfection was only broken into by B starting up (as if a tiger was in the next room), with a cry of "the telephone!" In fact it wasn't, but we dressed and went downstairs and, 15 minutes later, Peter did telephone from London. After which B remarked grimly, "Well, *that's* over."

As the stability of Russell's private affairs disintegrated during the later 1940s, his position as a public figure was reinforced. *Human Knowledge* appeared in 1948 and won considerable praise; requests for lectures, papers and articles were not only numerous but accompanied by fees so high they would have seemed ludicrous a few years before. Behind the scenes, preparations were already being made for bestowing on him the Nobel Prize for Literature and the Order of Merit, and he was soon to give the first of the B.B.C.'s enormously prestigious Reith Lectures.

He was also in demand by the British Council. In the summer of 1946 he had lectured for them in Switzerland on "Ethics and Power" and two years later had been flown into blockaded Berlin to speak to the troops. There was also a lecture-tour in Norway, proposed by Sir Laurence Collier, uncle of Crawshay-Williams and British Ambassador in Oslo, which nearly cost Russell his life. Sir Laurence was a fine non-conforming agnostic in the Huxley tradition whose father, John Collier, the Victorian portrait-painter, had married in succession two of T. H. Huxley's daughters – the second of them in Norway since this marriage contravened Britain's Deceased Wife's Sister Act. Collier believed, he wrote, that "it was time to introduce influential Norwegians to a vigorous and intelligent exponent of Western European ideals who was determinedly opposed to

Communism and, indeed, to any form of totalitarianism for reasons transcending either Conservative or Socialist politics". As a result Russell was booked through the British Council to deliver a series of lectures to the Anglo-Norse Society in Oslo and Trondheim, among them "Prevention of War", "Ideology and Commonsense", and those on "Culture and the State" and "Mind and Matter" which he had already given in Sweden. He liked Sir Laurence. "We had a polite discussion as to who should go through doors first", Russell wrote; "when we reached the Embassy he insisted on my going first, saying 'I don't believe in this Elevation of the Host'."

From Oslo, Russell flew up to Trondheim by flying-boat. The weather was stormy and as the craft touched down a gust of wind turned its wing into the water. "I found myself on the floor with some inches of water in which hats, coats, etc. were floating," Russell wrote.

> I exclaimed, "Well, well" and started looking for my hat, which I failed to find. At first I thought a wave had broken in at a window; it didn't occur to me that it was serious. I was in the very back of the plane, the only part where one could smoke; this turned out the best place to be. After a few minutes the crew opened a door and got the passengers from the back through to an open window, and shoved us one by one into the sea. By this time their haste had made me realize things were serious. I jumped clutching my attaché case, but had to let go of it to swim. When I got into the water I saw there was a boat close by. We swam to it and were pulled aboard. When I looked round nothing was visible except the tip of a wing.

All nineteen passengers in the non-smoking compartment had died.

Russell was taken to hospital, where to all press inquiries on how he felt in the water he replied, with one word: "Cold". He recovered without damage to wind or limb and, despite the cancellation of his official lecture, spoke informally to the students of Trondheim University before returning to Oslo. His only casualties were the paperback thrillers in his attaché case, his usual antidote against lonely evenings, and his trousers, ruined in the accident. When a replacement was ordered in London his tailor replied, "I am not surprised. I understand his Lordship has been *swimming* in them."

Back in Oslo, he spoke to the Anglo-Norse Society on "Prevention of War". His forecasts were gloomy as he stressed the menace from Russia and the chances of nuclear devastation. At the end of the lecture Sir Hughe Knatchbull-Hugessen, former British Ambassador to Turkey, turned to Sir Laurence. "Well, after that," he said, "the only thing to do is to go out, get drunk, and break some windows."

Russell himself claimed that the British government had "sent [him] to Norway in the hope of inducing Norwegians to join an alliance against

Russia". Although there is no evidence of this in the formal arrangements for the tour, there is a hint in Russell's private correspondence that at least some of his travels were more official than they appeared to be on the surface. Shortly before he lectured at the Sorbonne and to the Centre d'Études de Politiques Étrangères, he told a friend that his visit to Paris would be "for the Foreign Office", while in March 1950, before his visits to Australia and the United States, he described himself as "busy with articles & globe-trotting for the Foreign Office".

Movement into the Establishment made it less surprising that in 1948 he should be asked to give the first of the Reith Lectures, a decision which might well have made Reith himself wonder what the world was coming to. Speaking on "Authority and the Individual", he asked how it was possible to "combine that degree of individual initiative which is necessary for progress with the degree of social cohesion that is necessary for survival". The lectures were indicative of the new emphasis in Russell's interests, where philosophy was effectively giving way to human affairs, international relations and the future of the human race. "What the truth on logic is does not matter two pins if there is no-one alive to know it," he was to say a few years later. He held much the same view about philosophy from the early 1950s onwards and with the exception of *My Philosophical Development*, a long look back over more than half a century, *Human Knowledge* was to be his last serious philosophical writing.

With the Reith Lectures out of the way he turned again to the autobiography started twenty years previously in the tower of Telegraph House. He wanted to revise it, and bring it up to date. He earmarked March for the work, and planned to carry it out at Ffestiniog. Colette was still negotiating for her own cottage, and it was agreed that she should travel up in advance to the Russells' house where Russell and Peter would join her later in the month.

At first she camped out in Russell's small study, cleaning the house, weeding the garden, sweeping leaves from the stone-paved terrace and, with her experience of Finnish winters, organizing a huge stack of logs by the back door. He arrived on the 11th, with news that Peter was ill in the London Clinic. "He remarked", Colette wrote to a friend, "that Peter's last words to him were: 'If you want to make love to Colette, I shall ask no questions and I shall not mind'. It seems that she has been *unaware* of his relations with me; result, no doubt, of his 'I shall make little of it' after Stockholm."

This piece of news was only the beginning. "After they'd had two tremendous telephone rows here every single day, I got him to talk his troubles out," Colette continued. "He said he'd lately taken up with a young woman he'd known slightly long ago, ... by name. And when he got home from seeing her, Peter had chaffed him about her (at least so P. *now* says)."

Colette now became mother-confessor, once the role of Ottoline. As they untangled and discussed the situation there was no longer any doubt that Russell's third marriage was past saving. He did not yet know what to do about it, but his main worry was its effect on Conrad. His two older children had by this time returned to America; both had married and it was Conrad who now occupied the position so close to Russell's heart. A strong bond had grown up between father and son, remarkable in view of the age-gap but not surprising considering the interest and excitement with which Russell could invest everyday events and objects, explaining the different speeds of sound and light with the help of a blasting operation at the local slate quarries, and the pull of the moon on the oceans as they spent the day at Black Rock Sands on the edge of Snowdonia.

He still had, moreover, his infectious enthusiasm for the hills. He knew the exact height of all the main peaks of North Wales and would identify the tops from the summit of Snowdon with the same care and concentration he gave to the problems of mathematical logic. At Pen-y-Gwryd, the famous inn at the head of Nant Gwynant, he "signed the ceiling" with glee, climbing on a chair with great agility to do so and saying how flattered he was to be among the august company of mountaineers who had done the same. "I remember him reaching the top of Cnicht when he was 77 and I was 11 and our climbing powers were approximately equal," says Conrad, "and I remember him at 95, swinging over the steps to the balcony for the sheer delight of the view of Snowdon in the afternoon sun." All this generated an admiring response in the son. In one way at least the past decade had given Russell all he had hoped for.

The Ffestiniog house was another problem. To avoid estate-duty when he died, he had legally made this over to Peter, who could therefore put in a tenant or sell it. There was also the more general problem of finance. *A History of Western Philosophy* seemed likely to be a permanent source of income, and in his mid-seventies Russell was at the height of his earning capacity. Nevertheless, with the ghost of his divorce from Dora still lurking in the background, he shrank from entering that financial swamp a third time.

Worrying about the future, he had taken none of his usual hearty walks and had barely got down to the autobiography. Colette records a string of personal memories – "your 4½ minutes boiled egg in the dining room for breakfast (big side up); the post's arrival; your afternoon pot of Lapsang; the rising and the sinking of the sun with Moelwyn pricking the sky" – but he had not salvaged the undisturbed time he needed and on the 17th, six days after arriving in Ffestiniog, he left for London. Colette drove him to Bala across the seventeen miles of moorland with its splendid views of Snowdon. Russell, remarking on the sheep lying across the rain-sodden road, still maintained that he'd rather be intelligent and unhappy than stupid and happy. "But", wrote Colette, "my heart was wrung on seeing him standing, forlorn, in the beastly London train, holding the box of spring flowers I'd packed for Peter."

Within a few days he was to leave London for Aix-en-Provence, to receive an honorary degree from the Université d'Aix-Marseille; for Rome; and for a holiday in Taormina.

While he travelled down to London, Colette returned to the Ffestiniog cottage, scattered with the bric-à-brac from the Bury Street flat of thirty years ago. The following morning she devotedly wrote a letter to welcome him to Aix. "The sea, when I look westward, speaks always of my love for you, with the same fathomless depths, great breakers and infinite horizon; and the soaring wings of a gull are always to me the symbol of the pride of your mind and your spirit, and of whatever particle of eternity is embedded in our love." She concluded,

> But isn't it just another fleck of the irony which has always dogged our steps that what would have saved a number of shipwrecks in 1920 is out of place – or seems so – in 1949.
>
> I'll creep into your big bed tonight, to have the ghost of that kind of closeness as well as the "coldness of interstellar spaces". I expect that both will live on always in me, independent of everything.

A few days later a parcel arrived at Ffestiniog, addressed to Russell. Asked by telegram what was to be done with it, Russell replied that it was to be opened, the typescript inside put in his desk, and anything else destroyed. Colette did as instructed. The manuscript was a draft of his autobiography, describing in some detail his relations not only with Ottoline but with herself.

Russell now left London for Europe. He delivered his duty lectures, received his honorary degree, then moved on to Taormina. His hostess was Daphne Phelps, holding a house-party that included Julian Trevelyan, the son of his old friend Bob. Here, he anticipated, he would be able to enjoy a week or so away from it all, a haven in the turbulent seas through which he had been battling a way for too long. And here, after only a few days, Peter arrived with Conrad. At first, all went well. Then crisis dropped out of a peaceful sky. In any other context, Russell would have attributed the outcome to conspiracy. As it was, even he with his predilection for uncovering sinister motives to explain the disasters of history, had to admit that chance alone was the culprit.

The Russells had been in Taormina only a short while when a midnight picnic on a nearby island was proposed. Transport and victualling were to be in the hands of the local fishermen and there was no doubt that the local wine would be in good supply. The Russells were asked to join the party – with some hesitation since it would be unsociable for anyone to be too abstemious, and this type of midnight cavorting was considered slightly risky for a man only a few weeks off his seventy-sixth birthday. Nevertheless, Russell eagerly accepted, although Peter opted out.

The party went off hilariously. "It was in a most romantic setting," Julian Trevelyan has written. "Fishermen, who looked more like pirates, speared fish with acetylene flares as we approached the island. Once there, they built a fire over which they grilled the fish, while the bottles of wine stood cooling in the wet sand. The full moon cast strange shadows through the prickly pears. Bertie sat bolt upright in his neat dark suit on an upturned fishing basket saying: 'I thought that life had few new pleasures to offer me, but I find that I was wrong.'" Later, although opinions differ on just how much later, he commented, "I'm as drunk as a Lord, but then I am one, so what does it matter."

The following day Peter moved out of Russell's room. A few days later she left Taormina. Conrad went with her, aware only that some unbridgeable gulf appeared to have opened up between his parents. To Peter, Russell wrote a placatory letter saying she was making too much of his alleged affair with Colette. To Colette he wrote that he would be unable to see her for some months. But a few days later he cabled asking her to meet him in London and to bring the typescript of his autobiography from the desk of his Ffestiniog study.

Back in London he explained that Peter thought she could divorce him for adultery. But he added that she was mistaken, possibly believing that he could plead condonation. Nevertheless, he was on his way to the lawyers and, as a precaution, asked Colette whether she would mind if Peter cited her. "Not in the least," she replied.

He knew that she was returning to Sweden and asked when she would be coming back. "Never," she replied – "unless you ask me." He appeared astonished, repeating the one word, "Never." Then they went downstairs and out into the street together. More than twenty years later she could still describe to friends, in moving detail, how she had stood at the steps of her sister's house in Tavistock Square and watched him until he had walked the length of the square and turned the corner, out of her sight for the last time.

From London Russell went to North Wales, staying with the Crawshay-Williamses. But his luck had deserted him. Before leaving Taormina Peter had written to Colette. The reactions were subsequently described by Russell in a few sentences. "I had been seeing something of Colette in a friendly way and Peter imagined that Colette and I were plotting to live together," he said – an idea which demanded no huge feat of imagination. Distressing as all this was, he carried on with his work, writing confidently to a friend, "This summer I have been preparing an autobiography. In a few days I go to Paris for UNESCO. Next summer I go to Australia. In the interval I address the armed forces, working men at Oxford, earnest atheists, etc. When the time comes to die, I shall have to inform Death that I am too busy just now ..."

Then, in the middle of all the turmoil, admitting that he would have to jettison Peter, as ambivalent as ever about Colette, he received a note from Sir Alan Lascelles at Buckingham Palace. His Majesty, he was told, would be pleased to confer the Order of Merit on him. Was the suggestion agreeable?

The offer had been some time in coming. Whitehead had been made a member of the Order in 1945 even though he had emigrated to the United States two decades earlier; Eddington, whose strong pacifist feelings might have been considered a bar, in 1938. However, Russell had been consoled by the fact that most O.M.s were pillars of the Establishment and that many were what he described as "soupy". "We used the word 'soupy' to characterise people and temperaments which came down on the supernatural side," says Crawshay-Williams, "not merely in the religious field but in all fields: anti-determinist, for instance, in history and biography; believing in vitalism and Mind; in innate wickedness, in Absolute and eternal verities; and so on."

Nevertheless, the O.M. had been worth waiting for. Bestowing it the king, affable but slightly embarrassed at decorating an ex-jailbird, remarked, "You have sometimes behaved in a way which would not do if generally adopted." Russell kept back the reply that sprang to his mind: "Like your brother". Later in the afternoon, waiting on Paddington Station for the train to North Wales, he wrote a quick, pencilled note to Colette, now back in Scandinavia, saying what fun the ceremony had been.

The Order of Merit unexpectedly opened up the past. Alys had lived on in London throughout the war and the final stages of Logan's descent into senility, ended only by his death in 1946. Ever since her parting with Russell thirty-seven years earlier, she had maintained a secret and adoring surveillance of his activities equalled only by Colette's agonized and almost masochistic love. She had observed him occasionally from afar, at lectures and at concerts. In the 1920s she had looked through the uncurtained window of his Chelsea home and watched him reading to John and Kate, an experience which her Quaker stoicism alone made bearable. To Bernard Berenson she revealed in 1945, after the death of Mary, his wife and her sister, the love that kept her heart alive. She might at times begin "to think that I made a mistake in concentrating so exclusively on the memory of Bertie, when I might have been enjoying life with a fresh partner or partners!" But the exclamation mark always followed the phrase. More frequently she wrote of how she had always loved him and still did. To Berenson she relayed the post-war Cambridge gossip of his doings, the reports that "Bertie's wife has left him, & that he is greatly relieved", and the proud news that "Bertie's style & his clear thought are inimitable, but his Radio voice is not as good as mine, tho' his enunciation is perfect".

Now, in the summer of 1949, Alys wrote to congratulate him on his O.M., although only after she had heard that he was separated from Peter. "Dearest Bertie," she said, "I feel I must break the silence of all these years by sending thee a line of congratulation on thy OM. No one can rejoice in it more heartily than I do, just as no one was more sorry for the prison sentence & thy difficulties in America. Now I hope thee will have a peaceful old age, just as I am doing at 81, after a stormy time with Logan ..." He answered, suggesting an interview, she told Berenson, "& we had a long friendly talk about everything except his wives. He had just been to France for three days of lectures and receptions, sent by the Foreign Office to lecture on British Politics in French! Think of it – Bertie, the outlawed Jailbird!" Before they parted she asked him to come again as soon as he could spare the time. "I shall count the days till then," she added, "as I have so many questions I want to discuss with thee, & I hope it will be soon." On 18 May 1950, she arranged his seventy-eighth birthday-party, and recalled with pride that he talked for four hours as brilliantly as ever.

To mutual friends an air of tragi-comedy suffused this revelation of an adoration that neither age nor circumstance could erode. It was not only that Alys could write, "I am utterly devoted to thee, & have been for over 50 years. My friends have always known that I loved thee more than anyone else in the world, & they now rejoice with me that I am now able to see thee again." It was not only that in her early eighties she pinned a pink ribbon-bow in her hair for his visits, and so far abandoned her temperance scruples as to offer him dreaded drink. This was the comedy. But as his marriage with Peter drew to its expected end, a rumour sailed out among their friends: Bertie was at last to make an honest Countess of her. There is some evidence that Alys started it, and much evidence that she hoped it would come true.

There was nothing to justify her hopes. A friend, sent to Russell to discover tactfully whether he had really enjoyed the reunions, had it made evident in very frank words that Russell was ambivalent about the meetings. He had no objection to them, as such; but he did dislike the way in which Alys appeared to be taking up affairs where they had been dropped more than forty years previously.

Alys had, in fact, recently slipped on the stairs of her Chelsea home and broken some bones. Now she was told how delighted Russell had been to see her again; and within a few hours of her death a week or so later, she still doggedly tried to answer the telephone herself: after all, "it might be Bertie".

The Order of Merit which had given Alys the plausible excuse for meeting her Bertie once more was the latest of many signs that his position in the Establishment was firmly acknowledged. When his Fellowship had been about to end in 1948 the Council of Trinity extended it until Michaelmas 1949. Then, in September, he received the ultimate accolade: Fellowship under Title E which ensured that he would remain a Fellow for the rest of his life.

Later, in 1950, he flew out to Australia for a lecture-tour organized by the Australian Institute of International Affairs. World affairs, the subject of many of his lectures, was a delicate subject for Australia, made even more so by the outbreak of the Korean War, while even for a speaker in his prime the tour across the breadth of a continent would have been a gruelling test. For a man in his seventy-ninth year it was a Commando course, and the fact that Russell completed it successfully was a tribute to his physical as well as his intellectual stamina. Before leaving Britain he had made it clear that he would rather not be the guest of governors, abominated functions and liked a bathroom, but his only special request was for "two hours solitude every day where possible, preferably in the morning". Later, when his passion for detective novels was realized it was arranged for a supply to be sent to each hotel at which he stayed.

Within little more than two months he lectured in Sydney, Brisbane, Canberra, Melbourne and Adelaide, gave radio talks in all five cities, as well as attending university seminars, and wrote numerous articles for the Australian press. He also squeezed out time for a tour of Northern Queensland, saw the Great Barrier Reef, and later during the tour visited both Alice Springs and Kalgoorlie. At Alice Springs, returning to his hotel after a particularly gruelling function which could not be side-stepped, he found two elderly men from the outback – "sandgropers" in the untranslatable Australian term – who had walked miles into town in the hope of meeting him. He went down to see them, immediately struck up a lively conversation, and continued it until well after midnight.

The lectures ranged from "Obstacles to World Government", through "The Ferment in Asia" to "Living in the Atomic Age". The last was particularly important since Russell had been quick to see the industrial potential of nuclear energy and the change in the balance of power brought about by the explosion of the Russians' first nuclear weapon the previous year. He was still in his Establishment phase and his views, many of them worked into *New Hopes for a Changing World*, much of which had been drafted for the tour, were liberal rather than revolutionary, based on the potentials of the new technologies created during the war and warning, earlier than most preachers, that science might become man's master rather than his slave. Inevitably, he ran the usual gauntlet of criticism from both Right and Left: from the Catholic Archbishop Mannix of Melbourne, who was unwise enough to assert that the United States had refused to admit Russell, a mistake for which he had to apologize; and from the Communists, who dubbed him a "Man of War" since he preferred war to Russian control of the world.

Russell had barely returned from this exhausting tour – making radio broadcasts at Singapore, Karachi and Bombay *en route* – before starting off for yet another visit to America. This had begun with an invitation from Mount Holyoke College for Women in New England where he agreed to give a short course on philosophy. He crossed the Atlantic late in October and started the course as arranged. Before it was over he was invited to give the Matchette Foundation lectures at Columbia University later in November. Once again he accepted and decided to repeat the lectures on "The Impact of Science on Society" given earlier in the year at Ruskin College, Oxford.

After Holyoke, and before arriving in New York, he made a brief visit to Princeton, renewing his wartime acquaintance with Einstein and lecturing at the university about which he had been so scathing to Ottoline almost forty years previously. And while in Princeton he learned that he had been awarded the Nobel Prize for Literature, an event which quite fortuitously gave him added celebrity value when he arrived in New York.

Russell would in any case have drawn a crowd to the McMillan Theatre. With the aura of the Nobel Prize he attracted an audience which grew larger on each of three successive days, and two additional halls had to be wired for sound. "People were lined up 3 and 4 deep all the way around two blocks in the hope of getting in by some miracle, or at least hearing the piped voice, or catching a glimpse of Lord Russell in person," according to Julie Medlock, a New York literary agent assigned by the university to shepherd him through New York. "This crowd roundly cheered as we drove up ... [A reporter accompanying Russell] viewed the assemblage with considerable astonishment, 'Good Lord, Lord Russell,' he said, 'anybody would think it was JANE Russell they were here to see instead of just a philosopher.' "

With the Columbia lectures ending in a blaze of successful publicity, Russell visited Edith Finch, the friend of Lucy Donnelly who had died two years previously; travelled down to Washington to visit his daughter Kate; then returned across the Atlantic – but not before discussing with Miss Medlock plans for a future lecture-tour.

The next U.S. tour, made in 1951 when Russell was seventy-nine, would have been a testing enough obstacle course for a man half his age. It began with a three-day forum organized by the *New York Herald-Tribune*, at which Russell and other distinguished men sought out "the reasons for the present lack of balance between progress in science and the development of moral responsibility, and [tried to suggest] means of bringing the two fields into equilibrium". Russell's answer, as summarized by the *Herald-Tribune*, was that "men must learn to think of the human race as one family", a change of outlook which "could be brought about in a generation if educators cooperate in bringing up the young as citizens of the world instead of as predatory warriors".

That settled, he turned, as in 1950, to the McMillan Theatre and lectured to a capacity audience on "The Future of Happiness". Five days later he had to leave for a strenuous programme which was to take him to M.I.T. in Cambridge, Mass., to Washington, to the University of Virginia in Richmond, and after a quick return to Washington, to Indiana and Ohio. Nevertheless, before departure for what was almost an octogenarian whistle-stop tour, he found time in New York to lecture to the Young Men's and Young Women's Hebrew Association, tape five broadcasts for the C.B.S. and speak as the guest of honour at several receptions.

At Purdue University, Indiana, Russell had a stormy reception and, as he later wrote, remained in the State "just long enough to avoid getting lynched". The trouble had been caused by an article he had written for the *Manchester Guardian*. It had criticized the Indiana school system and it is possible now to see in it the first signs of Russell's later "anti-Americanism". Oberlin College, Ohio, was totally different. Here the hall was packed although the area was being battered by the worst snowstorm of the season. The audience waited for an hour after Russell was due to appear. Then another hour, then another. They hung on until midnight, some five hours after the lecture was due to begin. The sequel was recorded by Julie Medlock in describing a message she had received from the university president.

> The State Police had located the bus which had gone off the main road and become lost in the storm. He reported that Lord Russell himself had now arrived, in high good humour despite being half frozen. He had been thawed out, with brandy, hot coffee and food; the patient audience had been fortified with coffee and doughnuts, and at that hour, somewhat after midnight, the lecture was about to begin.

The following day he carried on as planned – to West Virginia and then to North Carolina, completing the schedule as laid down. But by 9 November, the tour completed, he was virtually all-in. As in wartime America, he had tended to polarize opinion; but whereas in the 1940s the controversy had been about morals, now it was about politics, American foreign policy and his acidulated criticisms of McCarthyism. There was one other difference from the 1940s. In 1944 he had returned to Britain virtually penniless. This time his three-week tour had earned £10,000.

As in 1950, some of the success sprang from the lustre of the Nobel Prize. This had been made for "philosophical works ... of service to moral civilisation", a wording which Russell rather curiously took to mean that the Prize was for *Marriage and Morals*. It was not only the honour that pleased him. Equally welcome was the tax-free cash-award of £11,000, a sum which gave him room for manœuvre in the divorce proceedings now rumbling nearer. By a singular coincidence Albert Einstein, on the point of divorce thirty years previously, had promised his wife the money from the Nobel award should he win it for physics – which he did, little more than a year later. Russell made no promise. But when Peter finally divorced him in 1952, £10,000 from the £11,000 Prize went to her.

He had flown to Stockholm to receive the award in December 1950, having turned down a suggestion from Sir Stanley Unwin that a lecture or two might help boost the sales of his books in Scandinavia. "I have had my fill of lecturing recently and one of the advantages of the Prize is that it will enable me to do less of it," he pleaded.

In Stockholm, as on all grand occasions, he sparkled, undazzled by the splendour of the ceremony and accepting the pomp and circumstance as part of a world with which Russells were familiar. The evening-dress habit helped. So did a family history in which consorting with kings and queens was not so very unusual. As one onlooker observed, "He came down to accept the award looking absolutely magnificent; and he immediately put the Royal Family at their ease."

Russell's aplomb in Stockholm was displayed against the subject of his Nobel Lecture, the price which Prize-winners pay for the award. Most devote it to an exposition of the work which has brought them to the ceremony; Russell chose to be different. His subject was "What Desires are Politically Important?" It was an impassioned plea for peace, coming a year after the Russians' successful test of their first nuclear weapon, and marking a change of tack in the policies which Russell had been advocating since 1945. "The atom bomb and the bacterial bomb, wielded by the wicked communist or the wicked capitalist as the case may be, makes Washington and the Kremlin tremble, and drives men further and further along the road to the abyss," he said. "If matters are to improve, the first and essential step is to find a way of diminishing fear. The world at present is obsessed by the conflict of rival ideologies, and one of the apparent causes of conflict is the desire for the victory of our own ideology and the defeat of the other."

The desire was, in fact, very like the policy which Russell himself had been advocating since the first nuclear weapons had exploded over Japan in August 1945.

The Last Attachment

19

Towards a Short War With Russia?

Russell was one of the comparatively few who quickly realized the full implications of the atomic bomb. To most, it was just an explosive of unprecedented power which had been added to the armoury. A few military men saw what it foreshadowed. A few scientists and a few bishops winced at the moral responsibilities, and were worried at the use which politicians might make of the horrific weapon which science had put into their hands. Few, however, had Russell's intuitive grasp of the difference between delivery of one 20,000-ton bomb and the delivery of 4,000 five-tonners. Few knew that the hydrogen bomb lay just over the horizon. Few, moreover, saw as clearly as he the possibility of peace through world government which nuclear weapons offered. The result was a realism that drove him into a succession of positions later swamped by the rising tide of nuclear protest. Together they make up what has been called his preventive-war phase, a phase which cannot be explained away by semantic excuses or honest disagreement as to what he really said or meant. Mention of it brings pained protest from his more woolly admirers, who prefer to brush it under the carpet, maintaining either that Russell never advocated preventive war – thus ignoring his own broadcast statement that he did: "and I don't repent of it" – or that if he did so it was merely a passing fancy not to be taken seriously, a curiously insulting conclusion when attributed to a man of Russell's calibre.

There is no doubt that the salvation of the human race from a nuclear holocaust was the last great attachment of Russell's life and at least two main questions therefore demand an answer: what policy did he actually support during the first years of the nuclear age? and what is to be made of the contradictory denials and avowals with which he spattered the 1950s? Both questions are resolved by a chronological account of events as they happened.

Russell's first public reaction to the news of Hiroshima was very different from Einstein's "Alas", even though he agreed that "the prospect of the human race is sombre beyond precedent". It was given a few days later in the Glasgow *Forward*, under the title "The Bomb and Civilisation". Russell first pointed out that neither the United States nor Russia was likely to agree to any pooling of armaments. He went on,

> If America were more imperialistic, there would be another possibility, less Utopian and less desirable, but still preferable to the total obliteration of civilised life. It would be possible for Americans to use their position of temporary superiority to insist upon disarmament, not only in Germany and Japan, but everywhere except in the United States, or at any rate in every country not prepared to enter into a close military alliance with the United States, involving compulsory sharing of military secrets.
>
> During the next few years this policy could be enforced; if one or two wars were necessary, they would be brief, and would soon end in decisive American victory. In this way a new League of Nations could be formed under American leadership, and the peace of the world could be securely established. But I fear that respect for international justice will prevent Washington from adopting this policy.

The last sentence was largely ironic. Russell's views were still crystallizing and as yet he had no time for big-stick diplomacy, as he made clear in a letter to Gamel Brenan in September. "There is no point in agreements not to use the atomic bomb as they would not be kept," he said.

> Russia is sure to learn soon how to make it. I think Stalin has inherited Hitler's ambition for world dictatorship. One must expect a war between U.S.A. and U.S.S.R. which will begin with the total destruction of London. I think the war will last 30 years, and leave a world without civilised people, from which everything will have to be built afresh – a process taking (say) 500 years ... There is one thing and one only which could save the world, and that is a thing which I should not dream of advocating. It is, that America should make war on Russia during the next two years, and establish a world empire by means of the atomic bomb. This will not be done.

The alternative, as he outlined it in a further article in *Forward*, later reprinted in the *Manchester Guardian*, was very similar to the policy of outlining new spheres of influence already agreed on at Yalta by Roosevelt, Churchill and Stalin. "Russia's immense military strength, as revealed by the war, is held in check for the moment by the atomic bomb," he said, "but before long Russia, no doubt, will have as good (or bad) a bomb as that of the Americans, & as soon as this has happened it will be possible to have a really serious war. Such madness must be prevented if possible but it is not easy to see how." His solution was that Britain should "concede a free hand to Russia in Eastern Europe (excluding Greece and Turkey) on the ground that in that region we cannot effectively intervene; but in return we should have an acknowledgement of our interest in the Mediterranean".

The first hint of change was apparently given in a letter to Kingsley Martin, editor of the *New Statesman*, towards the end of September. No copy of the letter appears to have survived,* but its tone can be judged from Martin's reply. "If you wish me to publish your letter on Russia as it stands, I will of course do so," it began.

> There are several reasons why I should be sorry if you do wish it. Your name stands for so much – it is one of the few which is not connected with some hate campaign or other – that I feel distressed when you use these highly provocative words. They would be taken up and quoted as proving that you are opening an anti-Bolshevik armada of the old type. I am myself very unhappy about much that Russia is doing, and I am expecting this week to criticise several aspects of the Soviet policy which you have in mind. On the substance of your letter, the most important point is that by the overwhelming testimony of those who have been to, or lived in, Russia recently – and I have seen a number of reliable witnesses – Russia shows everything, wants peace. Therefore to compare Russia with Nazi Germany is to my mind exceedingly harmful.
>
> One additional reason is that you are taking the chair at a meeting of Save Europe Now in which I and most of my friends are actively interested. The risk in any case is that this organisation will be regarded as "pro-German" and "anti-Soviet", though this is not its real intention. Your letter, appearing before the meeting, would certainly confirm these suspicions.
>
> I thought it best to state my views bluntly in this matter, and that your letter reads like the beginning of a war, even though you say that its intention is to stop one.

Martin passed on the letter to Victor Gollancz, leader of the Save Europe Now campaign, who immediately wrote to Russell in alarm at the impression of bellicosity it gave. "And," he went on, "if the letter appears on Friday, then it and your chairmanship on Monday [of the Save Europe Now meeting] will inevitably be linked together and the meeting may be given something of the character of an 'anti-Bolshevik crusade' in the bad sense. I am told that already, as a result of the things they have seen, a lot of soldiers in Bęrlin are saying 'Goebbels was right': we don't want *that* sort of development." The reasoning behind Russell's

*But see References for this page.

attitude was indicated at a later meeting of the Save Europe Now executive. "But for the fact that the United States had atomic weapons," he said to one of its members, "the Russians would be at the Channel ports within a few weeks."

His views, like those of many other men, were changing quickly as Russia's attitude became clearer during the first weeks of peace, and early in October he wrote to Gamel Brenan saying he was "glad that disagreements with Russia have come into the open, and relieved to find the present Government at least as anti-Russian as Churchill. The only hope is definiteness now."

Soon afterwards he was setting out his developing views in *Cavalcade* under the title of "Humanity's Last Chance". After describing the dangers of giving Russia the information needed to make nuclear weapons, he continued, "I should, for my part, prefer all the chaos and destruction of a war conducted by means of the atomic bomb to the universal domination of a government having the evil characteristics of the Nazis." He then outlined plans for a Confederation which would monopolize nuclear weapons and pointed out that the U.S.S.R. would be powerless as long as the U.S. retained its atomic lead. "There might be a period of hesitation followed by acquiescence," he went on, "but if the U.S.S.R. did not give way and join the confederation, after there had been time for mature consideration, the conditions for a justifiable war, which I enumerated a moment ago, would all be fulfilled. A *casus belli* would not be difficult to find."

Two points should be made. The first is that hope of Russian acquiescence in the face of a nuclear threat had little foundation in reality. As P. M. S. (later Lord) Blackett, one of Britain's leading nuclear physicists, wrote in a secret report to the new Labour government in November 1945: "That the U.S.S.R. would capitulate before a threat alone can be excluded as not remotely possible." On the contrary, he pointed out, the Russian reaction would be to speed up her nuclear research, consolidate her influence in the semi-satellite countries, and strengthen her air defence. Secondly, Russell's suggestion that it would not be too difficult to pick a quarrel with the Russians at a convenient moment was made more than five months before announcement of the Baruch proposals for international control of atomic energy. Their subsequent rejection by the Russians was often cited by him as justification for threatening Russia.

His attitude at the end of 1945 was given in the two-day debate on international affairs in the House of Lords in November. The debate ranged over the situation in Germany with its torrent of starving refugees; the future of the United Nations; and, above all, the consequences of Russia's steady retreat into the psychological fortress built up as much by Western hands as by Russian suspicions. But all revolved around the barely mentionable: the threat from the atomic bomb which many acknowledged but few understood. Lord Samuel, Lord Addison, Lord Jowitt, the Archbishop of York and Bishop Bell of Chichester all stood the problem firmly at the centre of their arguments. Would the Russians agree to international control? If not, how much of the alleged "secret" should be shared with them? And if the answer was "nothing at all", then surely the world would be set on the most disastrous of armament races.

Russell delivered the most potent of the arguments for forcing agreement on the Russians before they also had nuclear weapons. These were, he pointed out, still in their infancy. "The present atomic bomb in exploding produces temperatures which are thought to be about those in the inside of the sun," he said. "It is therefore possible that some mechanism, analogous to the present atomic bomb, could be used to set off [the] much more violent explosion which would be obtained if one could synthesize heavier elements out of hydrogen." The process would create "a very much greater release of energy than there is in the disintegration of uranium atoms"; in other words, the H-bomb, vastly more powerful than the weapons which destroyed Hiroshima and Nagasaki.

His proposals contrast with much of the mythology about his beliefs. "I do not see any advantage in the proposal which is before the world of making the United Nations the repository [of nuclear weapons]," he said. "I do not think that there is very much hope in that, because the United Nations, at any rate at present, are not a strong military body, capable of waging war against a great Power; and whoever is ultimately to be the possessor of the atomic bomb will have to be strong enough to fight a great Power." Neither did he believe that the process of manufacture should be unconditionally revealed to the Russians. If they were willing to co-operate in international control, then he thought "it would be right to let them know all about it as soon as possible, partly, of course, on the grounds that the secret is a short-term one . . . it is only a question of a very short time during which we have this bargaining point, if it is one". That time should be used to manœuvre the Russians into agreement; and if only the Western powers tackled the problem honestly, without question of national gain, then he thought the Russians would respond – "at least I hope so".

By this time the Russians had shown that they intended keeping Poland within their grasp. Eastern Europe was being digested piecemeal, Churchill had made his "Iron Curtain" speech in Fulton, Missouri, and Russian non-cooperation at the coming Foreign Ministers' Conference looked inevitable. Already, Russell's views were hardening. "I hate the Soviet Government too much for sanity," he admitted to Gamel Brenan.

Against this background, Russell stressed in "The Atomic Bomb and the Prevention of War" that what was most needed in dealing with the Russians was definiteness. "The American and British Governments should state what issues they consider vital, and on other issues they should allow Russia a free hand," he went on.

> Within this framework they should be as conciliatory as possible. They should make it clear that genuine international cooperation is what they most desire. But although peace should be their goal, they should not let it appear that they are for peace at any price. At a certain stage, when their plans for an international government are ripe, they should offer them to the world, and enlist the greatest possible amount of support; I think they should offer them through the medium of the United States. If Russia acquiesced willingly, all would be well. If not, it would be necessary to bring pressure to bear, even to the extent of risking war, for in that case it is pretty certain that Russia would agree.

These ideas, not uncommon at the time, were hardened up by Russian rejection of the Baruch proposals, an action which confirmed Russell's worst fears. "The next war will be between the Vatican and the Kremlin," he wrote despondently to Stanley Unwin; "in spite of 'The Tablet', I shall side (reluctantly) with the Vatican." To an old friend he was writing a few weeks later: "I am glad you are more anti-Russian than ever; so am I . . ." He also offered to write a foreword to "The Sign of the Hammer and Sickle", a manuscript about which the reader's report said that the author's answer to the Russian menace was "immediate war by Britain and America against Russia while we hold a monopoly of the atom bomb . . ." And to Einstein, whose pacifism had returned with the peace, he said that he saw no hope of reasonableness in the Soviet government. "I think the only hope of peace (and that a slender one) lies in frightening Russia," he went on. "I favoured appeasement before 1939, wrongly, as I now think; I do not want to repeat the same mistake . . . Generally, I think it useless to make any attempt whatsoever to conciliate Russia. The hope of achieving anything by this method seems to me 'wishful thinking'."

What he believed this meant in practice was soon revealed. Ten days after writing to Einstein, he addressed the Royal Empire Society on "The International Bearings of Atomic Warfare", a lunchtime talk in which he stated,

> I should like to see as soon as possible as close a union as possible of those countries who think it worth while to avoid atomic war. I think you could get so powerful an alliance that you could turn to Russia and say, "it is open to you to join this alliance if you will agree to the terms; if you will not join us we shall go to war with you". I am inclined to think that Russia would acquiesce; if not, provided this is done soon, the world might survive the resulting war and emerge with a single government such as the world needs.

The argument was repeated in "International Government", a paper which appeared in the January 1948 issue of the *New Commonwealth.* In it Russell gave a clue to the tenacity with which he propounded his point of view throughout the later 1940s. "The argument that I have been developing", he said, "is as simple and as unescapable as a mathematical demonstration."

It was soon to be qualified. The Imperial Defence College was about to reopen after its wartime closure, and Russell was invited to give the final talk of the annual course. A philosophical look into the medium- and long-term future, it was first given six days after the Royal Empire Society meeting, and was to be repeated in varying forms for a number of years. Eventually it developed into a discourse on short-term and medium-term strategy, not exactly the subject for which the College was paying its £10. 10*s.* 0*d.* honorarium.

Just how much secret material Russell was shown is not certain. But a highly secret report on new weapons, written by scientists in 1945, noted of the nuclear development: "Duelling was a recognised method of settling quarrels between men of high social standing so long as the duellists stood 20 paces apart and fired at each other with pistols of a primitive type. If the rule had been that they should stand a yard apart with pistols at each other's hearts we doubt whether it would long have remained a recognised method of settling affairs of honour." Russell's use of the simile in the 1950s does not prove that he had seen the report; but considered in context, and with other evidence, it makes this likely.

Certainly his close contact with senior Service officers qualified his belief that Russia should be threatened without delay. His modified views were set down in May 1948 to Dr Walter Marseille, a U.S. professor who had outlined his own scheme for compulsory inspection of Russian nuclear plants:

> I have read your paper with great interest. I agree entirely with all the underlying assumptions. As soon as Russia rejected the Baruch proposals, I urged that all nations favouring international control of atomic energy should form an Alliance, and threaten Russia with war unless Russia agreed to come in and permit inspection. Your proposal is, in effect, the same, for the compulsory inspection you advocate would be, legally, an act of war, and would be so viewed by the Soviet government.
>
> During the past year, conversations with professional strategists have slightly modified my views. They say that in a few years we shall be in a better position, and that Russia will not yet have atomic bombs; that the economic recovery and military integration of Western Europe should be carried further before war begins; that at present neither air power nor atomic bombs could prevent Russia

from over-running all Western Europe up to the Straits of Dover; and that the most dangerous period for us is the next two years. These views may or may not be correct, but at any rate they are those of the best experts.

There are some things of which Europeans are more vividly conscious than Americans. If Russia overruns W. Europe, the destruction will be such as no subsequent re-conquest can undo. Practically the whole educated population will be sent to Labour camps in N.E. Siberia or on the shores of the White Sea, where most will die of hardships and the survivors will be turned into animals. (Cf. what happened to Polish intellectuals). Atomic bombs, if used, will at first have to be dropped on W. Europe, since Russia will be out of reach. The Russians, even without atomic bombs, will be able to destroy all big towns in England, as the Germans would have done if the war had lasted a few months longer. I have no doubt that America would win in the end, but unless W. Europe can be preserved from invasion, it will be lost to civilisation for centuries.

Even at such a price, I think war would be worth while. Communism must be wiped out, and world government must be established. But if, by waiting, we could defend our present lines in Germany and Italy, it would be an immeasurable boon.

I do not think the Russians will yield without war. I think all (including Stalin) are fatuous and ignorant. But I hope I am wrong about this.

There is no doubt that Russell held these opinions strongly and sincerely. Just how much he was willing to admit openly is confused by his later evidence. A decade afterwards, writing to Eugene Rabinovitch, editor of the *Bulletin of the Atomic Scientists*, he said that the letter to Dr Marseille "was one which even at that time I should not have been prepared to see published". Yet a month after writing it he was calling in the *Dagens Nyheter* for an international inspectorate of nuclear energy and adding, "But should Russia refuse, which is all too likely, what would happen? Even were a precarious peace preserved for a time, one must – recalling the earlier history of human folly – expect that sooner or later war would break out. If it did, we should have a truly great cause to fight for: that of world government ..."

Nevertheless, in 1948 Russell was not too willing that the views he was expressing in private to Americans or in public to the Swedes should then be known to the British public: therefore the furore over "Atomic Energy and the Problem of Europe", an address which he gave in November to four hundred London students and schoolteachers at a New Commonwealth Schools Conference at Westminster School. Most of the address was no more than strongly anti-Communist. However, there was one key paragraph:

> The question is whether there is to be war or whether there is not; and there is only one course of action open to us. That is to strengthen the Western Alliance morally and physically as much and as quickly as possible, and hope it may become obvious to the Russians that they can't make war successfully. If there *is* war, it should be won as quickly as possible. That is the line of policy which the Western Nations are now pursuing. They are preparing for whatever the Russians may have in store. The time is not unlimited. Sooner or later the Russians will have atom bombs and when they have them, it will be a much tougher proposition. Everything must be done in a hurry, with the utmost celerity.

The paragraph – quoted here from what Russell later described as a verbatim transcript published in the *Nineteenth Century and After* – was taken up by questioners. His reply is given, third-person, in the same issue:

> As he saw it there were three alternatives *if the present aggressive Russian policy was persisted in*: (a) War with Russia before she has the atomic bombs, ending fairly swiftly and inevitably in a Western victory; (b) war with Russia after she has the atomic bombs, ending again in Western victory, but after frightful carnage, destruction and suffering; (c) submission. We could say to the Russians "Come in and govern us, establish your concentration camps, do what you like". This third alternative seemed to him so unutterably unthinkable that it could be dismissed; and as between the other two the choice to him, at least, seemed clear.

Nowhere in all this did Russell urge, in so many words, the starting of preventive war, while the qualifying "if" about Russian intentions added a conditional that many reports ignored; nevertheless, emphasis on the obvious fact that a war before Russia had nuclear weapons would be less disastrous than war afterwards was perilously close to it. Nevertheless, Russell was surprised by the reaction in the next day's papers. Typical was *Reynolds News*: "The distilled essence of all the wisdom he has accumulated in a long life is this message of death and despair," said a leading article. "Give up all faith in human reason, he tells us in effect. Resign yourselves to an endless orgy of killing, to the destruction of cities, to the poisoning of the fruitful earth by atomic radiation. Lord Russell, the famous philosopher, advances the oldest and most blood-drenched fallacy in History: 'the war to end wars'."

Not until the next week, back at Cambridge, did he feel that something should be done to counteract the reports of what he had said. Between lectures he telephoned Peter in London and asked her to tell the Prime Minister how sorry Lord Russell was if the current misrepresentations of his views had caused any embarrassment to him. Meanwhile, he wrote to *The Times*, denying that he had urged immediate war with Russia. "I did urge", he said,

> that the democracies should be *prepared* to use force if necessary, and that their readiness to do so should be made perfectly clear to Russia, for it has become obvious that the Communists, like the Nazis, can only be halted in their attempts to dominate Europe and Asia by determined and combined resistance by every means in our power, not excluding military means if Russia continues to refuse all compromise.

It was a clever letter, glossing over the meaning of "if necessary" and leaving unanswered the question of what should be considered a *casus belli*.

So far, Russell's statements had been all of a piece, simply summed up in an explanation in *How Near Is War?*

> I thought that while our side still had the monopoly of the bomb we could perhaps say to the Russians: "Now look here. Here is a proposal entirely in your interests. A proposal to internationalise the atom bomb. And if you really won't accept this proposal – well, we're almost compelled to draw the most sinister inferences from your refusal." I thought, at the time, there was something to be said for trying to bully the Russians into accepting the Baruch report.

The statement – which overlooked Russell's advocacy of finding a *casus belli* long before the Baruch proposals – was not formally a plea for preventive war; but complete dissociation from the policy demanded a considerable semantic wriggle.

When the acquisition by Russia of her own nuclear weapons made intimidation less attractive, Russell's views began to change. But they did not change quickly. In his article "Is a Third World War Inevitable?" published in *World Horizon* in 1950, he says,

> I do not agree with those who object to the manufacture of the hydrogen bomb. All arguments for a unilateral limitation of weapons of war are only logically defensible if carried to the length of absolute pacifism, for a war cannot be worth fighting unless it is worth winning. I think also, for the reasons given above, that every increase of Western strength makes war less likely. I do not think that, in the present temper of the world, an agreement to limit atomic warfare would do anything but harm, because each side would think that the other was evading it.

> The next war, if it comes, will be the greatest disaster that will have befallen the human race up to that moment. I can think of only one greater disaster: the extension of the Kremlin's power over the whole world.

Questioned in New York later in the year, he said that he approved America's decision to make the hydrogen bomb. He thought the West should undertake not to use this aggressively, but that the same undertaking should not be given about the atomic bomb, which might be the West's only chance of survival. He felt that two policies should be aimed at: "Rearmament as quickly as possible, including German rearmament, because the West cannot otherwise be defended." Secondly, the precise definition of an act by Russia that the West would consider a *casus belli*. This he offered as, "If they invaded Siam or Burma or West Berlin or re-imposed the blockade, or promoted a revolution as they had done in Czechoslovakia." Then, asked whether there was any circumstance in which the West might have to use the hydrogen bomb before the Russians did, he replied, "Yes, if the circumstances were clear about Russian intentions, whether the Russians used it first or not." And at the end of December 1950, he wrote, "When I compare the home Government of England and France with the home Government of Russia and when I reflect that the Russian system could easily spread over the whole world, I cannot but feel that a war would do less harm than world-wide tyranny."

As a result of this passage a resolution was passed by the Cambridge University Labour Club condemning the statement and considering it as incompatible with Russell's presidency of the club. Faced with the accusation, Russell replied, "I have never advocated a preventive war, as your members would know if they took any trouble to ascertain facts."

It was not only the Cambridge University Labour Club that was troubled. In the columns of the *New Statesman*, Kingsley Martin, no doubt remembering the letter he had decided not to print in 1945, reminded his readers, "After the last war, even more deeply troubled by the spread of Communism than he was by the power of Rome, which he had often denounced, [Russell] decided that it would be both good morals and good politics to start dropping bombs on Moscow." The outcome was that Russell compelled Martin to print what he described as "a long letter of refutation". The phrase is hardly accurate. At the end of the letter he admitted that he had once "thought it possible that the Russians might be induced by threats" to agree to the Baruch proposals; and, as he was later to say on exactly the same subject, "you can't threaten unless you're prepared to have your bluff called".

But he stuck to his denial for quite a while and in October 1953 embroidered it in a letter to the New York *Nation*. "The story that I supported a preventive war against Russia is a Communist invention." he protested.

> I once spoke at a meeting at which only one reporter was present and he was a Communist, though reporting for orthodox newspapers. He seized on his opportunity, and in spite of my utmost efforts I have never been able to undo the harm. Krishna Menon, with whom I had collaborated for years on Indian affairs, turned against me. "The New Statesman" in London wrote assuming the truth of the report, and it was only by visiting the editor in company with my lawyer that I induced "The New Statesman" to publish a long letter of refutation from me. You are at liberty to make any use you like of this letter, and I shall be glad if you can make its contents known to anybody who still believes the slanderous report.

The letter to the *Nation* was remarkable in two ways. It conveniently ignored his articles in *Cavalcade* and the *Dagens Nyheter*, his letter to Dr Marseille, his talks to the Royal Empire Society and the Imperial Defence College, and the private letters in which he had clarified his position.

In March 1959 he was interviewed by John Freeman on the B.B.C. After a detailed questioning about Russell's life, what he believed in, and the contemporary campaign for nuclear disarmament, Freeman asked, "Is it true or untrue that in recent years you advocated that a preventive war might be made against communism, against Soviet Russia?" Russell's reply was unequivocal. "It's entirely true, and I don't repent of it," he said.

> It was not inconsistent with what I think now. What I thought all along was that a nuclear war in which both sides had nuclear weapons would be an utter and absolute disaster. There was a time, just after the last war, when the Americans had a monopoly of nuclear weapons and offered to internationalize nuclear weapons by the Baruch proposal, and I thought this an extremely generous proposal on their part, one which it would be very desirable that the world should accept; not that I advocated a nuclear war, but I did think that great pressure should be put upon Russia to accept the Baruch proposal, and I did think that if they continued to refuse it might be necessary actually to go to war. At that time nuclear weapons existed only on one side, and therefore the odds were the Russians would have given way. I thought they would, and I think still that that could have prevented the existence of two equal powers with these means of destruction, which is what is causing the terrible risk now.

Russell was finally asked whether, if the Russians had not given way, he would have been prepared to face the consequences of using nuclear weapons on the Russians. "I should," he replied. "They were not, of course, nearly as bad as these modern weapons are. They hadn't yet got the hydrogen bomb, they had only the atom bomb (and that's bad enough, but it isn't anything like the hydrogen bomb). I thought then, and hoped, that the Russians would give way, but of course you can't threaten unless you're prepared to have your bluff called."

The discrepancy with Russell's earlier denials was soon pointed out. He blandly replied that his advocacy of nuclear war had slipped his memory. "I had, in fact", he confessed, "completely forgotten that I had ever thought a policy of threat involving possible war desirable."

Kingsley Martin, who in 1950 had written, "Bertrand Russell publicly advocated dropping atom bombs on Russia as a way of preventing another world war, both on the wireless and in a number of newspaper articles," has an explanation of this elephantine amnesia which does Russell less than justice. "I have no doubt that this lapse of memory was due to the intensity with which he now favoured the Soviet case," he wrote, a statement which side-steps Russell's undeviating detestation of the Soviet system.

Up to the date of the Freeman interview it is plausible, if barely so, to claim that in the new situation of the later 1950s, where mutual nuclear annihilation was at least a possibility, Russell had simply forgotten what he had been preaching a decade or more earlier. After all, he was by now well into his eighties and the forgetfulness of old age could well have been taking its toll. Yet this explanation will hardly do. In 1962, three years after being driven into an admission that his earlier denials had been completely unjustified, he wrote to a correspondent, "I should be in your debt if you could contribute towards putting the lie to the fiction that I have advocated war against the Soviet Union." But in 1969, a few years on, he is once again agreeing that he had suggested that an arms race might be avoided by the threat of immediate war.

The criticism often made against Russell in this episode, and one which was to prove a millstone round his neck in later and equally genuine efforts to avert a nuclear holocaust, is not that of inconsistency – a red herring with which he sometimes drew off his attackers. It is not, necessarily, the assertion that a policy of bullying Russia with the bomb before she had her own was a policy of gargantuan immorality: a case could perhaps be made for defending a war for world government as "a truly great cause to fight for". The real point is simply that Russell denied making certain statements he had certainly made, and accused his accusers of lies and distortions.

His explanation that he had simply forgotten what he had said, given in the *Listener* after the Freeman interview, and later in his autobiography, would be more acceptable if applied to one speech rather than to a long series of articles and statements, the first made months before the appearance of the Baruch proposals. It might be possible to argue that his disavowal of advocating preventive war was based on the most academic interpretation of the term: that advocating the threat of war unless a potential enemy submitted, even though being prepared to have your bluff called, was not advocacy of preventive war. But even this questionable escape-route is blocked by Russell's own statement to Freeman and by his earlier suggestion that "a *casus belli* would not be difficult to find".

The truth seems simpler. By the middle 1950s, when the forces on both sides of the Iron Curtain had deployed thermo-nuclear weapons, Russell believed that he could help keep the peace of the world. If his earlier statements had to be brushed under the carpet, the risk to his reputation was justifiable for such high stakes.

But one danger of such jiggery-pokery was that even his colleagues and advisers might begin to believe the truth of the cover-up, as is shown by an undated eight-page summary of "Bertrand Russell's Work for Peace, 1945–50", among his papers. "When Russia refused to adhere to [the Baruch] Plan," it says, "he thought that the United States could compel adherence, if necessary by the threat of war (this was never urged publicly, but only stated in private correspondence – since published – and conversation)."

There were times when a diligent questioner such as Freeman might squeeze the truth from him. At others he had, for the good of the cause, to tell another story. If the suggestion that he deliberately tried to conceal his earlier views is repugnant, the record does not really allow any other conclusion to be drawn.

20

Into the New World

The news that the Russians had exploded an atomic bomb in August 1949 caused Russell to change tactics with the realism of a good military commander who learns of a new weapon in his opponent's armoury. But it made no difference to the end for which he was willing to drive himself as hard as mind and matter allowed: an international authority with overwhelming military power. From the start of the nuclear age, four years previously, he had seen the new weapons as a means of forcing world government and world peace down the throat of nations still attracted by the juicier tit-bits of aggression. But no one had listened, and the situation was now being dramatically changed. With both sides armed, if not equally at least well enough for each to wreak massive destruction on the other, nuclear sabre-rattling could no longer be expected to usher in the millennium. The coming of the hydrogen bomb in the early 1950s ruled out what vestigial hope remained.

The radical change in the balance of power and possibilities began as Russell was reaching his peak of respectability. So far his post-war views had run along lines very similar, if not parallel, to those of the British and U.S. governments. Now came the parting of the ways, and his growing opposition to the official line. Future progress into what for long looked like the wilderness continued for the last two decades of his life and fell into three over-lapping stages. The first included "Man's Peril", his dramatic Christmas broadcast appeal in 1954, the Russell–Einstein Manifesto, and the foundation of the Pugwash movement; the second found him supporting, then disillusioned with, the Campaign for Nuclear Disarmament; the third, which developed under the controversial and encroaching influence of his secretary, Ralph Schoenman, witnessed the start of the Committee of 100, his eventual disillusion with that too, and the development of a plethora of allied but peripheral activities which gained more importance as the nuclear threat slowly began to appear less dangerous.

These preoccupations, more than enough for most men half his age, did not entirely fill his time, although for the last twenty years of his life they were given top priority. But his restless mind was still constantly lured out on to academic sorties which produced books, lectures and papers on philosophy, on science and its impact on society, and on a profusion of other subjects. "Six days in the week I dictate to secretaries, and on Sunday I speak somewhere," he wrote to Elizabeth Trevelyan. "I wish Stalin would disarm & then I would have leisure." In 1954 the output contained more than forty items, ranging from a paper on J. S. Mill for the British Academy to a series of popular articles for *Everybody's* describing "You and Your Work" and "You and Your Leisure", and a brief article on "Birth Control and World Problems" for *Crux*, the magazine of the Union of Catholic Students. Nevertheless, the balance perceptibly changed. From 1950 onwards, Russell emerges as the world's most persistent propagandist for peace, devoting more and more time and effort to the cause and rather naively surprised that he was not always listened to.

Much of his activity was carried on against a personal background that was at first both untidy and unhappy. In 1949 Peter formally left him and took Conrad with her. The Ffestiniog house was abandoned, but his attempts to buy back what had once been his own home were unsuccessful and he reluctantly decided to move into quarters near London.

Meanwhile, Colette had gone to Sweden for the summer. Russell did not write. Not until her return to England in the autumn did he suggest a meeting towards the end of the year, but he concluded somewhat brusquely that the meeting must not cause scandal. Even from Russell, this was too much. "I am very sorry that I cannot meet you as we'd planned," she wrote to him,

> – because there is nothing I can say or do to help you in your troubles, or help me in mine; so I'd rather keep silent.
>
> I see everything quite clear now, and it seems a dreary end to all our years. I see now that your inability to care for anybody, with the whole of you, for longer than a rather short time, must be more painful to you than it is to those who are able to continue caring in spite of everything.
>
> Your life is a complicated cocoon, getting more and more involved always. Three times I've been drawn into its centre and three times thrown aside.
>
> If there is anything not clear to you in all this, you need only read my letters written since I saw you into the train at Bala on 17 March. All the answers are there. Goodnight now and goodbye. It is at least a clean break.

She was near collapse and a friend personally delivered her letter to Russell. He replied soon afterwards to the go-between, appearing puzzled at the suggestion that he had treated her badly. A few months later, he wrote again, inquiring of her health. This time he asked for a photograph: he needed it for his autobiography.

He had now moved south. His elder son John had come earlier to England from the United States and was living with his wife and young daughters in Richmond, Surrey. He toyed with the idea of renting nearby Pembroke Lodge and moving with son and family into the house he had known as a boy. It would have been a prodigal's return, satisfying his sense of history and his persisting desire for a home with a view. However, Pembroke Lodge had fallen on hard times. A private house until the outbreak of the Second World War, it had later become the headquarters of "Phantom", the reconnaissance regiment. Then, the war over, it descended into the hands of the Civil Service. "When they discovered, what they did not know until they were told, that it had been the home of famous people, they decided that everything possible must be done to destroy its historic interest," Russell wrote bitterly. Part of it was turned into a café, part into flats for park-keepers. The chances of restoring it to domestic use were nil and he had reluctantly to take a largish house near the Park.

The two lower floors of the new home were occupied by John Russell and his family, the top two by his father. Here, in the most domestic of surroundings, Russell settled down to work once more. Apart from a bedroom he had a small, book-lined study and a book-lined living-room beyond whose huge window there spread out gardens, trees, lawns and a great expanse of sky. A desk was stacked with papers, a day-bed with books to be read; tea-table, and deep armchairs and sofa for visitors completed the furniture. It was by no means ideal; but it would do.

Family incursions from below might have worried one less able to ride the breakers philosophically, less delighted with children in general and his own grandchildren in particular. One visitor wrote,

> There is the happy clamor of voices, far downstairs, with the usual bumps, bangs, and noise-making of childish play, and then the sound of tears and muffled wails and sobs. "My, my", says Lord Russell, puffing calmly on his pipe, "what a terrible lot of sorrowing is going on down there". Next, the sound of small feet racing up the stairs, followed by the cautious opening of the door. Three heads, in stair-step formation, with three pairs of sparkling eyes, peek into the room. "Come in" says Lord Russell politely, putting down his teacup. At this, pandemonium breaks loose. They run to embrace "Diddy", as they call him, full of downstairs news and chatter. Then they climb the high-backed sofa before the fire, and, at the risk of life and limb, they bounce up and down, up and down, reciting sing-song jingles which they make up as they go along – sort of a nursery calypso. When interest in this performance finally lags, they try diving off

headlong into the couch seat, arms and legs flying. Lord Russell maintains a cool and smiling placidity through all of this, and sometimes interrupts to offer them a tea cake, or to tell them a story. They are particularly fond of Hilaire Belloc's "Cautionary Tales", which has forced Russell to memorise them all, with appropriate gestures.

When they had gone, I asked him, nodding towards the long rows of books bearing Bertrand Russell's name: Do they interrupt or disturb your work? "O, nothing interrupts that", he said. "I have always loved having children around me – students, my own children, and now these grandchildren. I even like to hear their noise; it cheers rather than disturbs me, and hearing their voices around as I work makes me happy. I feel that this world is a very different one from the one I was brought up in, and young people help me to feel at home in it. They give me hope for this world, after all!"

There were soon other grounds for hope. Before the end of 1952, Peter had divorced him for desertion, and on 15 December he married Edith Finch: teacher from Bryn Mawr; earlier a friend of both Lucy Donnelly and Alys; and the biographer of both Dr Carey Thomas and Wilfrid Scawen Blunt, who with his aristocratic independence, support for the weak, and ability to shock, had much in common with Bertrand Russell. Colette, returned from Scandinavia, read the news in Moorfields Eye Hospital, awaiting an operation and expecting to go blind from glaucoma. "Fortunately the glaucoma proved a scare," she later wrote. "But that day was one of the worst in my life."

Russell had known Edith since 1925 when they had been introduced by Lucy Donnelly. They had met several times during his subsequent visits to America and seen a good deal of one another when he was completing *A History of Western Philosophy* at Bryn Mawr in 1943. They had met again during his visit to New York in 1950, and their friendship had ripened so quickly that, as he wrote, "soon we could no longer bear to be parted by the Atlantic". Nevertheless, their marriage was a surprise, even to close friends, one of whom wrote to congratulate Russell not only with enormous affection but with delighted laughter and adding, "well I'm damned – I bet sixpence you will marry the holy virgin when you get that far".

The marriage was a success. Whatever else may be uncertain about Russell's later years, there is no doubt that at the age of eighty he had found the ideal companion. There is one ghost to be laid. The fourth marriage took place as the prospects of forcing the Russians into acceptance of international nuclear control faded into the past and as the price of another world war appeared to be a nuclear holocaust which would engulf both victor and vanquished. It was easy to see Russell's new ideas of what should be done as a "softening" in his attitude to the Russians, a construction often applauded by the Left Wing but demolished by even the briefest look at the facts. The presence of a fresh and highly literate Lady Russell of liberal views fitted into an easily conceived framework, and during the next few years observers linked the alleged change of tack in Russell's attitude towards Communism with the influence of his wife. Freda Utley, arguing with all the passion of those who had moved to the Right, added the acid comment on Lady Russell, "A woman of Bryn Mawr who has no more understanding or knowledge of Communism than a nun in a convent insulated against evil has about the world, the flesh and the devil."

The truth is more complex but more human. Russell's attitude to the practical workings of Communism was certainly affected by the death of Stalin in 1953 and the hope that the major barbarities of the police state might wither away under a new regime. He had a ruthlessly realistic view of how relations with Russia must be handled now that both she and the West possessed hydrogen bombs. But his judgment of Communism as the rule of "a minority resting its power upon the activities of a secret police ... cruel, oppressive and obscurantist" remained. As late as 1959 he was telling the World Council of Churches that "the greatest contribution that could be made towards ending the Cold War would be the abandonment of militaristic imperialism by Russia and China".

Russell was among the first to emphasize that, with the coming of the hydrogen bomb, war between nuclear powers was no longer Clausewitz's continuation of politics by other means, but a recipe for mutual destruction. Liddell Hart, the distinguished military historian, had written as early as 1946 that "where both sides possess atomic power, '*total* warfare' makes nonsense", while immediately after the Second World War a formidable case was put forward for Britain remaining a non-nuclear power. It is now known that not only Professor P. M. S. Blackett but also such responsible defence-advisers as Sir Henry Tizard did not wish Britain to build her own nuclear weapons. Churchill himself, assuming that U.S. bombs would be available, wrote, "I have never wished since our decision during the war that England should start the manufacture of atomic bombs. Research however must be energetically pursued. We should have the art rather than the article."

By the mid-1950s a further factor had dramatically undermined Britain's ability to survive another world war. This was the setting-up in Central Europe of Russian-controlled rocket-batteries whose nuclear-tipped missiles could destroy civilized life in an island whose fifty million inhabitants were packed into 93,000 square miles.

A few years later the Secretary of State for Defence, Duncan Sandys, admitted the fact in his famous White Paper statement: "It must be frankly recognised that there is at present no means of providing adequate protection for the people of this country against the consequences of an attack with nuclear weapons." The so-called nuclear deterrent of the manned V-bomber force, which had to fly comparatively huge distances to reach essential targets, had a plausibility which could bear little critical inspection, and as Richard Crossman neatly put it in a Defence debate, "The trouble about the nuclear deterrent is that if we have one big enough to be militarily significant, we ruin the country, and if we have one within the economic resources of the country, then it is so trivial that it impresses no Great Power."

In this situation, Russell's position was unequivocal:

> The situation now is that we cannot defeat Russia except by defeating ourselves. Those who still advocate war seem to me to be living in a fool's paradise. I must add, however, that I do not now, any more than at an earlier time, advocate either appeasement or a slackening in rearmament, since either might encourage the Communist powers in aggressive designs and would therefore make war more likely. The problem for statesmanship in the present situation, as I see it, is to avoid war without surrender on our part or the expectation of surrender on the other.

Unemotional as the stance might be, it could hardly be expected that either politicians or the Services would be equally willing to admit that Britain was indefensible. Sandys's honest statement, if it did not entirely sink him, hardly furthered his onward and upward political career. Russell realized all this well enough. He realized also that it was the appeal to the emotions that moved men. He might distrust the policy, but this was an example of ends justifying means, and in mid-June 1954 he wrote to the B.B.C. "In common with everybody else," he said, "I am deeply troubled about the prospects for mankind in view of the H-bomb. I have a profound desire to do whatever lies in my power to awake people to the gravity of the issue." Would it be possible, he wondered, for him to broadcast the final chapter of *Human Society in Ethics and Politics*, adding to it if necessary? "I do not like suggesting anything that may seem pushing," he concluded, "but I feel that this is the best that I can do on this stupendous issue."

The idea was basically unadventurous, but it was transformed by the proposal of a talk in the Home Service one Sunday evening about the turn of the year, after the 9 o'clock news. Almost unbelievably, although offered this peak listening-time on a psychologically significant date, Russell was unimpressed. He doubted whether he could produce anything as useful as the chapter in his book; but he would try. He was formally signed up, but not until the end of November did he receive details of how his talk was to be used. His warning on the perils of nuclear annihilation, he learned, was to be broadcast under the omnibus title of "Three Generations" and sandwiched between two other talks. One by a journalist, Sally Graves, would describe her view of the world in 1935; the other would be by the runner, Roger Bannister.

"I find your letter very disquieting," Russell replied by return. "What I had in mind, as I explained quite clearly, was an exceedingly solemn appeal to mankind to turn back from universal suicide before it is too late. Various foreign countries have allowed me opportunities for such an appeal and I had hoped that my own country might do likewise. Such as appeal would be quite impossible as part of a stunt about three generations and I am not willing to fall in with the frivolous suggestion conveyed by your letter." The Corporation capitulated. The concluding sentence of Russell's letter may have shamed them: "I am sure you will have no difficulty in finding some old man who will do."

The result was "Man's Peril", a strikingly successful broadcast on 23 December. Its effect was intensified by the fact that its warning of universal death came at the height of the pre-Christmas jollifications, and that scientists in the United States and Japan, in Italy, India and Russia, as well as in Britain and other European countries, were having worried after-thoughts about the problems they had let out of Pandora's box. Few laymen knew enough to understand the full implications, and fewer still felt that anything could be done about it, but the shadow of a doubt had begun to form at the back of the public conscience, no longer entirely unresponsive to the kind of appeal that Russell made: obviously sincere and obviously well informed.

What the B.B.C. had thought of as the sandwich-filling between a journalistic reminiscence and an athletic look forward had become vintage Russell. Its effect was achieved by calm understatement, an appeal to both reason and emotion, with support not from pacifists or left-wingers but from the "soundest" of military men, all carried along on the emotional current of human survival. He was speaking, Russell began, not as a Briton or a European, nor even as a member of a Western democracy, but as a member of the human species. The question which man had to ask did not concern the road to military victory for any particular group but the way of avoiding a military contest of which the issue must be disastrous to all sides. In support of his contention that this would be inevitable, he quoted not only Lord Adrian, the President of the British Association, but Marshal of the Royal Air Force Sir John Slessor – "A world war in this day and age would be general suicide" – and the even more scaring conclusion of Air Chief Marshal Sir Philip Joubert: "With the advent of the hydrogen bomb, it would appear that the human race has arrived at a point where it must abandon war as a continuation of policy or accept the possibility of total destruction."

Comparing the world situation to that of duellists in early times, Russell saw the only hope in a move by neutral countries. "I should like to see one or more neutral powers appoint a commission of experts, who should all be neutrals, to draw up a report on the destructive effects to be expected in a war with hydrogen bombs, not only among the belligerents but also among neutrals," he said. "I should wish this report presented to the Governments of all the Great Powers with an invitation to express their agreement or disagreement with its findings. I think it possible that in this way all the Great Powers could be led to agree that a world war can no longer serve the purposes of any of them, since it is likely to exterminate friend and foe equally and neutrals likewise."

A final masterly touch pointed out that it was not only humans who would perish "but also the animals, whom no one can accuse of Communism or anti-Communism". The conclusion was the moving and much-quoted peroration. "I appeal as a human being to human beings: remember your humanity, and forget the rest. If you can do so, the way lies open to a new Paradise; if you cannot, nothing lies before you but universal death."

"Man's Peril" marked something more than the point beyond which Russell's involvement in the great debate swiftly accelerated. All before had been preparation for the task that now opened out. Dealing with the correspondence that poured in by the bagful, he might almost have felt with Montgomery, flying up from Cairo to take over the Eighth Army after "Strafer" Gott's death, the "kind of inward feeling that the call *would* come": quite convinced that all his long experience had been but preparation for the task ahead.

The basic question asked in the broadcast was whether the human race was "so destitute of wisdom, so incapable of impartial love, so blind even to the simplest dictates of self-preservation, that the last proof of its silly cleverness is to be the extermination of all life on our planet". The torrent of letters from listeners was evidence of widespread fear that the answer was "yes". Few had a solution to offer, but Russell had certainly aroused large numbers of ordinary people as well as officials and scientists in all continents.

A year previously he had suggested to Mrs Pandit, the Indian High Commissioner in London, that her country might intervene in the nuclear debate. Now, early in 1955, he seized the opportunity of meeting Jawaharlal Nehru, the Indian Prime Minister, on his visit to London. Nehru's sympathy was confirmed by Sir Russell Brain, the neurologist, who reported to Russell, "[Nehru] said that they were prepared to do 'something on the lines' of your suggestion. It would have been better if several neutrals could have combined for this, but that would take time and there would be obstacles, so India would go on alone." But when Russell shortly afterwards met Dr Bahba, India's leading physicist, he found a lack of enthusiasm for either statement or conference. If India's help were to be obtained it would only be after an uphill fight.

However, another promising line had now opened up. Among the letters which had poured in during the first weeks of the New Year, the encouragements, the cries of "scaremonger" and the inevitable correspondents who blamed the situation on the Pyramids, there was one from Frédéric Joliot-Curie, the French physicist who sixteen years earlier had shown that a nuclear chain-reaction was possible. Joliot-Curie, an ardent Communist, had fought in the French Resistance during the German Occupation, had helped after the war to plan the first French nuclear reactor and had then been sacked for his Communist sympathies. By 1955 he was President of the World Federation of Scientific Workers, which had already tried unsuccessfully to convene an international meeting on the threat of nuclear weapons. "The danger that faces humanity", he wrote to Russell, "appears so terribly real that I believe it essential for scientists whom people respect for their eminence to come together to prepare an objective statement on the matter." In addition, he went on, there should be a conference at which scientists should stress not only the dangers facing humanity but the potential benefits of scientific discovery. The Federation had in fact already approached a number of scientists. "While the response to these approaches has been very encouraging it must be admitted that there are in some quarters lingering reservations and suspicions, and the removal of these may take some time. Such doubts would vanish if some great, universally respected figures, such as yourself, gave the support of their great authority to the idea of a conference."

Russell well knew the Federation's reputation for being Communist-dominated and his reply was cautious. While he agreed that scientists should be induced to make a declaration stating the peril to mankind, he did not think that a conference should be the first step. However, he was weighing carefully the dangers of supping with a long spoon, and he thought it could be done. "We all have our prejudices in favour of one side or the other," he wrote, "but in view of the common peril it seems to me that men capable of scientific detachment ought to be able to achieve an intellectual neutrality, however little they may be neutral emotionally."

Without waiting for Joliot-Curie's reply, Russell wrote to Einstein. Joliot-Curie would, he imagined, be able to get support from Communist scientists: did Einstein know of any Americans who would help? In the United States, movements were already under way, notably that led by Eugene Rabinovitch, editor of the *Bulletin of the Atomic Scientists.* Einstein replied enthusiastically. Russell now redrafted the Christmas broadcast into the Russell–Einstein Manifesto which gave chapter and verse for the appalling consequences of a nuclear war, called for a meeting of scientists from both sides of the Iron Curtain, and proposed that these scientists should then urge all governments to admit that it was no longer possible to further their purposes by war.

At this point control of events was slipping fast from the hands of the

Federation, and Joliot-Curie urged Professor Burhop, head of its activities in Britain, to see Russell. The result was that the statement was amended by what Russell called "important changes with a view to conciliating Communist opinion". But he could not be persuaded to consider seriously either a new draft drawn up by Burhop or another from Professor Bernal, a former President of the Federation. "Of course he remains a convinced advocate of World Government," Burhop wrote to Dr Pierre Biquard. "But he has carefully refrained from referring to that in the document. On our part we believe that peace can only be secure when capitalism and imperialism have been eliminated. But we also do not insist on saying this in the document. That is as it should be."

From this letter, and others like it, it might seem that Russell and his reputation were being used by the Communists whose policies he detested. It was in fact about this time that one of his acquaintances, Lancelot Law Whyte, was approached by a member of the British government: he should warn Russell, he was told, that his circle was being infiltrated by Party members. Whyte, a physicist and philosopher who had undertaken many unexpected jobs in a varied life – including that of finding cash for the development of Whittle's pre-war jet-engine – declined on the ground that he did not know Russell well enough for such a delicate task. However, it is unlikely that much was lost: with rare exceptions, Russell knew, to a nicety and better than his opponents, the state of play in any undercover attempt to use his name and influence. Typically, if unfairly, he once noted to Lord Simon, "My own feeling is that I should be rather wary of any organisation in which Bernal is important." And his unrelenting feelings about the Russians were shown a few years later when he advised, "One of the most effective things we could do as propaganda would be to drop millions of leaflets all over Asia with just three words: Russians are whites." This was frequently proposed by Russell from 1950 onwards, notably in an N.B.C. television interview with Romney Wheeler.

But now Russell sent his revised statement to Einstein. Then he left England to attend in Rome a conference of the World Association of Parliamentarians for World Government. The British branch of the Association had from the first favoured the plan outlined in "Man's Peril", and Russell had discussed with its members his scheme for India to carry out alone the role of neutral assessor. In Rome he elaborated his plans before leaving for Paris. Crossing the Alps, the pilot broke into the usual description of weather and places with an item of world news: Albert Einstein had died in Princeton.

"I felt shattered," Russell later said, "not only for the obvious reasons, but because I saw my plan falling through without his support." He was probably unduly pessimistic; nevertheless, Einstein's name would give, to any statement intended to catch the eye of the masses, a cachet that nothing else could give. Russell was justifiably worried as he was driven from the airport into Paris. There, waiting for him, was a letter from Einstein agreeing to sign the amended document.

Russell now had available, for circulation to the chosen list of men on either side of the Iron Curtain, a declaration of intent agreed to not only by himself but by the most famous scientist in the world. However, Einstein's death had uncomfortably tied his hands. For while the Russell–Einstein Manifesto had been drawn up to show how the nuclear peril overrode the ideological split between Communism and the West, many scientists had their own personal reservations on how the statement of aims should be phrased. If any alterations were made it was obvious that Einstein's agreement, as much a cornerstone of the enterprise as Russell's, would have to be cancelled.

The issue arose when Russell saw Joliot-Curie soon after his arrival in Paris. The two men went through the manifesto sentence by sentence. "I accepted every amendment suggested by you, and ... at the end you said, 'these alterations are so slight that you can retain Einstein's signature', and I agreed," Russell later wrote. However, back in England, Russell received a letter from Joliot-Curie implying that what they had discussed was merely a draft, and enclosing a further modified version which he was prepared to sign. Russell pointed out that he had already obtained further signatures to the statement agreed to by Einstein. "I think that if it is really impossible for us to agree on a joint statement," he replied, "the publication of yours and mine simultaneously would perhaps be the best course. I continue to think, however, that failure to agree is exceedingly regrettable. I had hoped to build a bridge between opposing camps and if this proves impossible, a large part of the purpose of the statement is lost."

Eventually the problem was solved with honour on both sides. Joliot-Curie agreed through an emissary to add his signature to the Russell–Einstein Manifesto on condition that his qualifications were added as footnotes. One of these excised the statement that a limitation of national sovereignty was necessary: another implied that the Communists refused to renounce the principle of class warfare, of violent revolution or of "just wars of liberation". Nevertheless, scientists from both sides of the Iron Curtain had at least subscribed to some common principles. To many it must have seemed that the untouchables had at last been touched, even if cautiously and fearfully.

By the end of May Russell had signatures from Percy W. Bridgman and Hermann J. Muller of the United States; Cecil F. Powell and Joseph Rotblat from England; Leopold Infeld from Poland; Hideki Yukawa from Japan, and Max Born from Germany. Linus Pauling signed shortly afterwards. All except Infeld and Rotblat were Nobel Prize-winners.

But although the list of names was impressive, the roll-call was shorter than Russell had expected. Furthermore, it lacked some important signatures he had hoped to get. One reason was that preparations were already under way for the issue of a statement signed by the Nobel Prize-winners who met every year at Lindau on Lake Constance. Their declaration appeared, in fact, only six days after the Russell–Einstein Manifesto was made public. But, similar in tone and in content though it was, it lacked the glamour of the Russell and Einstein names and it passed comparatively unnoticed.

A more telling reason for the shortness of Russell's list of signatures was the common belief that anything signed by Communists must inevitably be furthering Communist aims. Max Born had in fact begun his reply of acceptance with such a strong anti-Communist protest that on reading it Russell mistakenly thought the letter was a refusal and omitted Born's name as a supporter when the Manifesto was announced. Otto Hahn and Manne Siegbahn were two Nobel Prize-winners who did refuse to sign on similar grounds. Such feelings, which would have been even stronger had the World Federation's part in guiding the emergence of the Russell–Einstein Manifesto been known, were natural if short-sighted. It is true that agreed nuclear disarmament by the super-powers would in 1955 have benefited Russia more than the West, a point that cannot have entirely escaped even the most humanitarian Communist. Yet this in itself was no reason for refusing to open a dialogue. The Russians themselves had good reason for caution, although, as Burhop wrote to Joliot-Curie, "whatever [Russell] may have done in the past I feel he is being frank and sincere on this issue".

Two footnotes to the question of signatures, typical of Born and of Niels Bohr, were added later. Born, with a magnanimity that merits the word noble, refused to criticize Russell for the appalling blunder of saying he had refused to sign the Manifesto. And Bohr, meeting Russell in Denmark a few years later, took literally hours trying to explain why he had not signed.

With nearly a dozen signatures, Russell had to ensure maximum publicity, and a room in Caxton Hall, Westminster, was hired for 9 July. There remained the problem of finding a chairman. He had to be a scientist with sufficient knowledge to field the technical questions. He had also to be of independent character, unafraid of the scorn which might be poured on the enterprise. Joseph Rotblat, Professor of Physics at St Bartholomew's Hospital Medical College, filled the bill. Rotblat had worked on nuclear fission with Sir James Chadwick in Liverpool University, had become a member of the British nuclear-weapon team in Los Alamos, and on returning to England in 1945 had switched from defence to medical work. Russell had been impressed when he first met Rotblat the previous year on a B.B.C. programme dealing with hydrogen weapons. On holiday in Southern Ireland, Rotblat now received a call from the local policeman whose house boasted the only telephone in the village. At the other end of the line was Russell, asking whether he would chair a meeting to launch the Russell–Einstein Manifesto. Rotblat accepted.

The Caxton Hall meeting was an unexpected success. The scores of journalists and television and radio reporters had been invited to hear an unspecified announcement of whose nature they had been given no clue. Russell justifiably wondered what their reactions would be. He frequently over-estimated, or imagined, the hostility of the press, discounting the demands of news-value and attributing to conspiracy, or personal bias, attempts to present his case with less than the importance he felt it deserved. On this occasion one more statement of the nuclear peril, discussed at great length ever since 1945, was not a subject which necessarily demanded front-page treatment, even when under-written by nearly a dozen eminent scientists, most of whose names were in any case unknown to the general public.

Yet the meeting got exceedingly good coverage. Russell himself was largely responsible, taming an initially sceptical audience as he had tamed the unruly audiences of Oxfordshire on behalf of Philip Morrell all those years ago. Einstein's eve-of-death signature and the circumstances in which Russell heard of the event were usefully dramatic. But it was Russell's obvious sincerity, as well as Rotblat's, that convinced all except the unconvincible that it might, after all, be worth an effort to halt the roll down the precipice. Even more important was the feeling among many journalists, Left, Right and Centre, that many ordinary readers had, beneath their jokey exteriors, a common-sense intuition, if no factual knowledge, of the dangers ahead.

In 1955 the idea that scientists should concern themselves with world affairs was still discussed seriously only within a very small circle; outside it, such a breakthrough was considered certainly presumptuous, possibly ill-informed and probably Communist-inspired. Yet in spite of a background of non-interested semi-disapproval, the suggestion of a major meeting between scientists from East and West now won much approval. On the far Right Wing, those who might have been expected to douche the idea with cold water tended to be non-committal; those in the political centre began, for the first time, to admit the possibilities. Thus a scientific trans-Iron Curtain meeting became a respectable proposition, if not overnight at least in the weeks that followed the Caxton Hall meeting. Even so, the prospects of its translation into reality still remained slim. Those who had signed the Manifesto did their best. Lobbying groups tried to maintain the momentum of what was seen, if distantly seen, as a chance of pushing the mushroom cloud back into the genie's lamp. Nevertheless, it is difficult to believe that events would have continued moving forward but for Russell's almost demonic personal energy. He was now eighty-three and still churning out a constant flow of articles, letters, exhortations and ideas. Months earlier Einstein had implored him, "Regard yourself as the dictator of the project and give orders." Now he was doing so.

At first, India offered the best prospect of a meeting-ground, and Russell's earlier contact with Nehru was followed up by C. F. Powell, who left with Nehru an aide-mémoire beginning: "Proposal to secure an independent and authoritative appraisal by an international group of scientists of the consequences for the future of mankind of hydrogen-bomb tests and of their use in war." Reporting on the Indian Prime Minister's reaction, Powell wrote, "He was very sympathetic to the whole question and anxious to help if a satisfactory form could be found. He readily agreed that if it was so desired, the meeting of an initiating committee could take place in India and said that the scientists attending it could receive hospitality from the Indian Government."

Plans now went ahead for a meeting in New Delhi the following January. They were halted by the Anglo-French invasion of Suez and the closing of the Canal in November. Travel round the Cape would be too expensive, while the Suez operation and the Russian invasion of Hungary each put its own separate spoke into East–West co-operation.

In his autobiography Russell says that he "did not at the time fulminate against the Russian suppression of the Hungarian Revolt ... because there was no need. Most of the so-called Western World was fulminating." However, on 29 November he answered with his usual dispatch a request received the day before from the government's Central Office of Information for which he had already contributed short pieces on such subjects as "The Marxist Fraud", and "Are Human Beings Necessary?" The C.O.I. wanted a thousand words on "a personal assessment of the impact of the Soviet action in Hungary on British intellectuals". In it he dealt also with Suez. "If you do feel that this is objectionable," he said in his reply to the C.O.I., "I should wish you not to publish any part of what I enclose. I should feel guilty of 'nauseating hypocrisy' if I denounced the one crime without mentioning the other." The Paris Embassy, which had requested the article, did not circulate it, thus confirming Russell's suspicions.

As far as Suez was concerned he had two months earlier written an unconsciously prophetic letter to Patrick Armstrong, Clerk of the Parliamentary Group for World Government. After saying that any international system must have the support of Russia if it were to work, he added, "If universal chaos is to be avoided, it will be necessary for Russia and the United States to form an alliance against little countries, such as England and Egypt, to keep them in their place and prevent them from indulging in nationalistic adventures." Just such an unexpected alliance brought a sudden end to the Anglo-French operation.

The Hungarian and Suez invasions appeared to have killed before birth any child of the Russell–Einstein Manifesto. But a rescuing hand now reached out from Russell's past. At the University of Chicago nearly twenty years previously he had been warmly welcomed by the wealthy industrialist Cyrus Eaton, a Trustee who had been partly responsible for his appointment. One of those rare men who prove that power does not necessarily corrupt, Eaton had been born in Canada, had made one fortune in the United States, lost it in the Great Depression, then made another. His home was at Pugwash, a small village on Northumberland Strait, the arm of the St Lawrence separating Prince Edward Island from the mainland, and to Pugwash he regularly invited scientists, statesmen and intellectuals, for informal conferences at which they discussed the world's problems. A man of liberal views, collecting thinkers as others collect postage-stamps or coins, Eaton had made a preliminary attempt to draw Russell to Pugwash soon after announcement of the Russell–Einstein Manifesto, but Nova Scotia had then seemed too remote. Now Russell asked Eaton precisely what help he was prepared to give.

Eaton replied with a generous offer, and by the first weeks of 1957 Russell was deep in preparations for the first meeting of scientists at Pugwash – a name which he would always drop privately for "Houndsditch". An initial problem was raised by the inclusion of scientists from Communist countries, and at an early stage he had to ensure that the Canadian government would allow them in. With Eaton pulling the necessary strings, this was accomplished without difficulty, and in July 1957 a mixed bag of twenty-two physicists, biologists and chemists met for five days' discussions. At the end of it they issued a statement, dealing in some detail with the most controversial issues of the day and setting out the role and responsibility of scientists. This was a remarkable document in that it gained support from both sides of the Iron Curtain. More was to follow. From 1957 onwards the number of scientists attending the conferences increased. So did their status. At first, a residual suspicion that the organization was a propagandist body tended to keep away those who had official links with governments. As this suspicion evaporated, men with more power to influence events joined them. Sometimes they found that their selection for official duties forced them out, as when Edward Bullard became involved in the Geneva disarmament talks and had to resign.

The gradual evolution into respectability was due partly to the care with which Russell held the scales in the early days. He himself attended only two of the conferences, but he nevertheless supplied an invisible but ever-present moral backbone. In 1940 he had been accused by the American press of rabid pro-Communism. In 1947 he had advocated war, if necessary, against Soviet Russia. In 1954 "Man's Peril" laid him open to accusations, however ill founded, that he was fast slipping down the hill from his anti-Communist position. Now he had not only to hold the balance but be seen to be holding it, a tricky operation which only the aristocrat would have attempted with equanimity and which Russell, almost alone among living men, had the background and the resolution to carry out with some chance of success.

The delicacy of his position became apparent when in November 1957 his name was put forward for the International Peace Prize sponsored by the World Council of Peace. He replied,

> As you know, I have been endeavouring throughout recent years to remain in all my public actions strictly impartial as between East and West. The World Council of Peace is regarded, I do not know with what justice, as a pro-Communist organisation. I feel that if I accepted money from an organisation which was either definitely Right or definitely Left, I should lose in the eyes of the public the position of impartiality at which I have been aiming. In the case of this particular prize, more especially, I should, if I accepted it, very much diminish my chance of influencing American opinion, and American opinion must be influenced if disaster is to be averted.

To Powell, still a pillar of Pugwash, although a Left-Wing pillar, he wrote that he and other non-Communists certainly deplored many actions of the West. But, he went on,

> we find that our Communist colleagues are not equally willing to criticize Communist Governments. We think the subjection of Eastern Germany and Hungary to an alien military tyranny quite as bad as what the English and French intended to do in the Suez campaign. We think the same of Chinese action in Tibet. When we hear from Communists denunciations of Western Imperialism, we cannot but reflect that all successful imperialism in our day is Russian or Chinese.

For a philosopher, an academic who had spent most of his life in the intellectual stratosphere, Russell now began to exhibit a political awareness that increases the nearer one gets to his activities. Thus in the early autumn of 1959 when Kruschev appealed to the United Nations for universal disarmament, Russell – with Rotblat and others – resisted a suggestion from Cyrus Eaton that the Pugwash organization should issue a statement supporting it. Russell continued to regard Eaton with a cool objectivity which gave credit where it was due but was hardly blind to what he saw as faults. "I have been wondering", he wrote to Rotblat, "what your emotions are on the occasion of Cyrus Eaton's being awarded the Lenin Peace Prize. I hope they are thoroughly Christian."

The Third Pugwash Conference, held in Kitzbühel and Vienna, brought forth a statement on "Dangers of the Atomic Age and what Scientists Can Do about Them", and was remembered for Russell's formal address at which he recalled how his grandfather had attended a diplomatic conference in Vienna 103 years previously. "He favoured terms which the Russian Government was willing to accept," he noted, "but Napoleon III, envious of his uncle's military fame, insisted upon another twelve months of senseless slaughter. I, alas, cannot speak for the British Government, but I equally stand for peace." He also noted, *sotto voce*, as one speaker's allotted ten minutes stretched to forty, "now is the time to drop the bomb"; and, more openly, "that the only war that intelligent men would consider justified was the Trojan War since it was fought on behalf of a beautiful woman".

Russell's personal contacts with Pugwash tended to diminish after he had set it on its feet, but he did not lose interest in its activities. He chaired a meeting of the organization's Continuing Committee, made an important speech at the Tenth Conference in London, and regularly heard progress reports from Professor Rotblat, the Secretary-General. There was, however, a change of emphasis in his views of what he believed it could do. As it gained the confidence of governments, East and West, as it drew in for its annual conferences scientists who could influence events from inside rather than from outside the Establishment, his enthusiasm became more qualified. He might later agree that the Pugwash Conferences had helped to make possible the nuclear test-ban, the nuclear non-proliferation agreements, and the negotiations which eventually led to the SALT talks. As *Nature* later pronounced, "the organisation is no doubt regarded by all Governments as a valuable listening post, to say nothing more of it". But Russell had a constitutional distrust of governments and by the early 1960s he was, in any case, devoting his energies to more controversial operations.

As he allocated more of his time to the campaign to avoid nuclear war, he began to regard his earlier accomplishments in a new light. He would, and did, still say, "My most important work is my share of 'Principia Mathematica'." But he would add "If mankind survives, my work on behalf of this will be the most important thing I have done. What is the truth on logic does not matter two pins if there is no-one alive to know it." The *Principia* had had a chequered career on its path to becoming a classic. It had survived, criticized but comparatively unscathed, for two decades. Then had come Kurt Gödel, the Austrian who had shown that any axiomatic system strong enough to prove the truths of elementary arithmetic could be either consistent or complete, but not both. The *Principia*, he showed, was the first but not the second. The implication was that the great work had not done all that its authors had expected. It also suggested that certainty, that Holy Grail which Russell had followed throughout his adult life, was as much a chimera in mathematics as Heisenberg had shown it to be in physics.

Even so, the *Principia* remained more than a heroic failure. It was read and studied as a unique attempt to logicize mathematics, and although it had sold only about 1,600 copies before going out of print in 1947, more than three times as many were sold during the 1950s and 1960s – as well as over 10,000 copies of a paperback edition of the first half of the first volume. It had, moreover, a number of unexpected uses, as Russell learned in 1956, after Professor Simon of the Carnegie Institute of Technology produced the first computer-programme for discovering proofs of mathematical theorems, and tested the programme with the theorems in the first chapters of *Principia*. Success was so considerable that Simon, writing to Russell, wondered whether the facts should be made known to schoolboys. "I am delighted by your example of the superiority of your machine to Whitehead and me," Russell replied. "I quite appreciate your reasons for thinking that the facts should be concealed from schoolboys. How can one expect them to learn to do sums when they know that machines can do them better?" And in a subsequent letter he added, "I wish Whitehead and I had known of this possibility before we both wasted ten years doing it by hand. I am quite willing to believe that everything in deductive logic can be done by a machine."

Although Russell now dedicated more time to the nuclear debate, less to philosophy, this was a change of emphasis rather than abandonment of what had been, until Hiroshima, the central issue of his life. With an almost maddening energy, he continued to sandwich in, between his support for world government, Pugwash, and a miscellany of pacifist and similar organizations, philosophical work that ranged from the popular *Wisdom of the West*, through his autobiographical *My Philosophical Development* to an article in *Mind* in which he strenuously defended his fifty-year-old Theory of Descriptions.

His professional interest in philosophy was now concentrated on attacking the linguistic school which had grown up, centred on Oxford, during the post-war decade. Many of its beliefs could be traced back to Wittgenstein and the predominance he gave to language in the solution of philosophical problems; most of its variants took it for granted that nothing more was needed than ordinary language. Then, correctly handled, the problems would disappear and metaphysics itself fade like the morning mist. Russell believed that "this view ignores the fact that ordinary language is shot through with the fading hues of past philosophic theories." He was confident that philosophy demanded modifications of both vocabulary and syntax, and that philosophy and real life spoke different languages. "I detest linguistic philosophy more and more as time goes on and I am sorry that at one time I thought well of Wittgenstein," he wrote to one correspondent. And commenting on a leading exponent he noted, "I find Ryle's work always repulsive, in the sort of way in which a bad smell is repulsive. I looked him up in connection with your paper but my disgust became so strong that I had to put him down ..."

Any member of the new school brave enough to tackle Russell was asking for trouble. Thus Peter Strawson, who strongly criticized the Theory of Descriptions in *Mind*, was answered with a glittering, if not entirely satisfactory, reply which demonstrated the meaning of "here" with an account of a walk in the dark, and compared the meaning of the word "day" in the first chapter of Genesis with the true solar day, the mean solar day and the sidereal day of the astronomers. "Suppose (which God forbid) Mr. Strawson were so rash as to accuse his charlady of thieving:" he continued; "she would reply indignantly, 'I ain't never done no harm to no one'. Assuming her a pattern of virtue, I should say that she was making a true assertion, although, according to the rules of syntax which Mr. Strawson would adopt in his own speech, what she said should have meant: 'there was at least one moment when I was injuring the whole human race.' "

In his eighties he could not only defend himself with wit but could handle technical mathematics with devastating precision. Three mathematicians, Robin Gandy, Martin Löb and Georg Kreisel, who visited him in 1960 were enormously impressed. "Kreisel had said it was astonishing how acute Russell's understanding had seemed to be even though he had not done any work on mathematical logic for about thirty years," Crawshay-Williams recorded in his diary. "It was not merely that his brain was beautifully clear for somebody of 87; it was beautifully clear for anybody of any age."

Like Einstein, who always declared that with pencil and paper he could work anywhere, Russell could work on his philosophical problems wherever he happened to be. The same was true of the purely literary work with which he filled in the odd nooks and crannies of his time. His reminiscences of Whitehead, of the Webbs, Maynard Keynes, Lawrence and Strachey, published in *Portraits from Memory*, were drawn from his mind, not his archives, and his excursions into fiction, beginning with *Satan in the Suburbs*, could have been written in a deckchair anywhere in the world.

So could much of *My Philosophical Development*, his distillation of a lifetime's reflections on philosophical problems. One great theme, the "gradual retreat from Pythagoras", ran through them all. Like Pythagoras, Russell had found mathematics, and mathematical logic in particular, emotionally satisfying; as evidence accumulated to undermine the central position he had accorded them, he felt the changed situation deeply. Lesser men might have tried to will away the evidence. Russell faced it and found that some things remained. "I still think that truth depends upon a relation to fact, and that facts are non-human," he declared; "I still think that man is cosmically unimportant, and that a Being, if there were one, who could view the universe impartially, without the bias of *here* and *now*, would hardly mention man, except perhaps in a footnote near the end of the volume; but I no longer have the wish to thrust out human elements from regions where they belong; I have no longer the feeling that intellect is superior to sense, and that only Plato's world of ideas gives access to the 'real' world." It would forever be impossible for man to achieve the impartiality which some attributed to the Deity, but he could at least make the effort. "To show the road to this end", he concluded, "is the supreme duty of the philosopher."

However, by now his interest was centred firmly on the nuclear dilemma. Achievement here demanded contacts at the centre of the political web, and as he was drawn more closely into the ramifications of the nuclear-protest movement, the demand grew greater. Thus there remained a good case for staying close to the centre of power, a case that grew stronger as his activities expanded, with the greater need to keep tabs on his organization and those who ran it. It is true that the concept of a Russell taken over in old age and run by a group of Young Turks is in large part myth. His follies as well as his farsightedness were usually his own. Nevertheless, had he remained in London his last decade and a half would have told another story. Moving to a remote Welsh eyrie kept away the idolators and other unwanted callers, but it meant also that a good deal of his political work was handled by remote control. Neither the telephone nor the devotion of a secretary-wife made up for that. Once again, therefore, his political life was influenced by the hazards of personal affairs: for the move from London, with its conflicting advantages and disadvantages, was largely the result of the break-up of the Richmond household.

Russell's marriage to Edith Finch had worked out well and did much to compensate for the loss of Conrad's companionship which had followed the divorce from Peter – a sad development for a man of Russell's highly developed family instincts. There were of course his two elder children; but his relationship with both was qualified by circumstance. Kate's husband had left the State Department to become a minister in the Episcopal Church and had drawn his wife into a similar state of religious enthusiasm. "I myself," Russell later remarked, "naturally, had little sympathy with either of them on this score." Nevertheless it was not only family affection that bound him: both Kate and her husband were, judged by most standards, liberal in thought and outlook; they subsequently settled with their children for two years in England, preparing for missionary work in Africa, and after their summer visits to him, Russell could write, "I loved my daughter dearly and was fond of her family."

While Russell deplored what he regarded as his daughter's theological falling from grace, he at first had nothing to regret about his son's ambitions. John wanted to write and if there seemed small likelihood that he could support his wife and the three children that made up their family, that was no more than the hazard of the profession. However, that was not all. There were already signs of trouble ahead.

Life in Richmond became more disordered and reached its climax at

Christmas, 1953. Earlier in the year Russell had fought his way through a nearly lethal bout of pneumonia. Now he was preparing to enter hospital for a prostate operation. And now, after Christmas dinner, John and his wife decided that they were "tired of children" and walked out. There are at least two conflicting eye-witness accounts of the affair. However, John's health deteriorated and he was eventually taken by his mother, Dora Russell, to be nursed in the Porthcurno house where he had been brought up three decades previously. It was all hideously harrowing for Russell, Edith wrote to a friend.

Eventually it became obvious that Russell would have to make long-term arrangements for his grandchildren's care and upbringing. The solution lay in finding a largish house in the country and he once again turned to North Wales. The grandchildren had been taken to Portmeirion a few years earlier by their parents and already had friends in the Williams-Ellis family, a fact which gave the area a head-start over any others. Once again the Crawshay-Williamses were asked to keep eyes open for suitable properties. Eventually they reported that an ideal home was coming vacant.

This was Plas Penrhyn, a Regency house on the Portmeirion peninsula, and only a few hundred yards from Deudraeth Castle where Russell had stayed twenty years previously. The house had two distinctive advantages.

One was the view. In the foreground lay the Glaslyn estuary on the last stretch of its run to the open sea. Sixty years earlier Russell had written of his "tremendous romantic passion for [the sea which] satisfies all my love of boundlessness and change & vast regularity, & has an extraordinarily exhilarating & yet calming effect on all my thoughts and feelings". Here there were also the mountains, the horseshoe peaks of Snowdon, the Moelwyns and the unlikely and dramatic peak of Cnicht, "the Matterhorn of North Wales". On certain days of the year, moreover, the setting sun appeared to roll down the hills beyond the estuary, a natural phenomenon that delighted him. With the light fading and the mountains darkening, he told a visiting friend, he had to fight down his "absurd mystical impulses".

Then, too, there was Tan-y-Rallt, on the other side of the estuary, the cottage where Shelley was attacked after being sent down from Oxford. Russell had always been intrigued by the Tan-y-Rallt episode and the sight of its white walls shining in the evening sun removed any last doubts. Fellow feeling played its part. "I think perhaps, even now, the neighbouring gentry might have some difficulty in welcoming an ardent young Communist who had been sent down from Oxford for atheism and excluded from decent society for preaching free love," he wrote years later after being accepted by the people of the area. "But in our degenerate days the gentry are not quite what they were and the doctrine that virtue is proportional to income has become unfashionable."

Late in 1955 the Russells moved to Plas Penrhyn. For the next fifteen years it was to be both home and headquarters.

21

The Genesis of Protest

There is a myth, more widespread than it deserves to be, that the Campaign for Nuclear Disarmament sprang fully formed from Russell's keen brain. Another, equally misleading, maintains that once he had called the organization into being, his influence sank to that of the aged academic, bungling practical affairs which the hard men would have handled more efficiently. These legends have arisen partly through distortion by interested parties, partly through muddle. A further, and more respectable, reason is that C.N.D. evolved from the merger of two different groups moving on parallel lines but for some while only vaguely aware of each other's movements. In such cases stories naturally differ, even without failing memories and human vanity. However, Russell's real place in the movement – that of a figurehead giving academic respectability and white-headed publicity, but also of a tactician making common-sense policy-amendments which often prevented demonstrators making fools of themselves – emerges clearly from the documents.

The first rumblings of popular nuclear protest, as distinct from political discussion on international control, military talks about Russia's potential, and the disillusion of many scientists with what they had done, came early in 1952 when ten members of the Peace Pledge Union organized a demonstration outside the War Office in London. In June, Michael Randle led a demonstration at the U.S. Air Base at Mildenhall, protesting against the presence in Britain of U.S. nuclear-armed bombers – and unaware that he had an ally in the British Chief of Air Staff who had complained to the Cabinet that the situation was "intolerable". The following year minor demonstrations were organized outside the British nuclear-weapons research-station at Aldermaston, and in 1954 the growing, but still small, handful of protesters coalesced into two groups: the Hydrogen Bomb National Campaign and the Emergency Committee for Direct Action. Canon Collins, a wartime chaplain in the R.A.F. and now Precentor of St Paul's, tried unsuccessfully to inaugurate in Christian Action, of which he was chairman, a national campaign for Britain's unilateral nuclear disarmament. Next came the Council for the Abolition of Nuclear

Weapon Tests; at first a purely local group in Hampstead, later a national organization.

In the first half of the 1950s, before the birth of C.N.D., three distinct proposals were being made by these various groups in the nuclear protest movement. The first was that "the West" should abolish nuclear weapons and that every effort should be made to persuade the Russians to do the same. The second was that nuclear-weapon tests should be stopped; the third, that Britain should herself renounce nuclear weapons whatever the Americans or the Russians chose to do.

On the first of these issues Russell was adamant. Asked at the time of the Russell–Einstein Manifesto whether he favoured the renunciation of nuclear weapons by the West on moral grounds, he replied,

> No, most emphatically not. I do not think that is the right way to go about it . . . If you can induce the Communist world to reduce its armaments to a degree that is as important for us as would be the renunciation of thermo-nuclear weapons, then you have got a real step forward. But I do not want to see thermo-nuclear weapons abolished if you are not going to get from the other side a *quid pro quo* which is really of equal military importance.

He emphasized this attitude on other occasions. Asked on television by Aidan Crawley whether he thought it practical to try and abolish the use of nuclear weapons, he replied, "No, I don't think it's possible. I think it's a perfectly futile thing to attempt." On the same lines was the reply sent to the British Peace Committee and to the organizers of a Brains Trust on Nuclear Warfare whose appeal he declined, saying, "I think that since nuclear weapons have been invented the disasters that they threaten can only be avoided by avoiding war and that we ought to concentrate our efforts on this, rather than on banning the bomb."

He still held that view as late as 1957 when in an interview he said of the hydrogen bomb, "I'm not in favour of its abolition, as I've so often been assumed to be. Fear is a great and effective force in human nature. The H-bomb is a real deterrent in three ways not possessed by any previous weapons. It gives equal power to each side; the leaders are no safer than the rest of the population; and the devastation would be on such a scale as to make any victory very problematical indeed." Mis-reporting, the apologist's favourite explanation of uncomfortable truths, cannot be pleaded here. When the interview was printed shortly afterwards in *Le Soir* Russell complained to the editor that a mistake in translation inferred that he no longer believed in world government, which was not the case; but he asked for no alteration to his statement that the deterrent deterred. He retained his belief at least until October 1958. Then, in a private letter to Lord Simon of Wythenshawe, he discussed the view that America would not go to war with Russia to defend Western Europe or

Britain. "I do not myself believe that the American Government would fail to fulfil its obligations," he said. "It is obvious that the Soviet Government, also, does not believe this. Consider the question: Why does Russia not occupy Western Berlin? I see no answer except fear of America."

That Russell did not feel this to be an entirely unhappy situation is shown by his disavowal of anti-Americanism in a letter to the *New York Times* in 1957. "America has become the torch-bearer for the West," he stated, "and it is the duty of all of us to do what we can to keep the torch burning brightly."

On nuclear testing, also, his views were in the early days a good deal more pragmatic than is usually appreciated. Asked in April 1954, for instance, whether there was any virtue in stopping H-bomb testing, he replied, "None whatever, unless we have found a way of causing the Russian experiments to be stopped too." Going on to say that international inspection was the only answer, he continued, "The Russians have a morbid fear of being inspected. We shall have to help them to overcome it. For until they are agreeable to it nothing can be effectively done. The H-bomb tests must be helping to persuade them. Hence to put off the tests would simply be to put off the day of agreement." Nevertheless, he eventually came round to the orthodox protest view, influenced largely, he said, by the after-effects of the Bikini Atoll tests of 1954 which showed the dangers from fall-out to be far greater than estimated.

However, it was the third question that finally set the C.N.D. tinder ablaze. On the question of Britain's own nuclear weapons and their significance in the world of the mid-1950s, Russell held unequivocal views: they would be no real deterrent and they might, through Britain's links with America, draw her into war just as, he believed, Grey's talks with the French had paved the way for 1914. Only this time Armageddon would be no fancy name.

"Man's Peril", the Russell–Einstein Manifesto, the moves leading up to the Pugwash Conferences, and Russell's other writings and lectures on the nuclear threat, would almost inevitably have made him a key figure of the nuclear-disarmament movement as it emerged at the end of 1957. However, another development had quite fortuitously made this even more certain.

In November he had become more than usually despondent about the international situation. Russia and America appeared to be set firm on a collision-course and, unless one or both changed tack, the chances of war would increase to what he believed to be mathematical certainty. In this ominous situation he remembered Lord John, the grandfather who always dealt with the man at the top and who could address even the queen on friendly terms. Early in the month Russell sat down at his desk on the first floor of Plas Penrhyn and dictated a letter to Premier Kruschev and President Eisenhower. It began "Most Potent Sirs", and reminded the recipients that what they and their two countries had in common was far more important than their differences. Surely, therefore, they should be able to reconcile their disagreements without the disaster of nuclear war.

Russell sent the letters to Moscow and Washington, copies to Kingsley Martin at the *New Statesman*, which published them in the next issue. So far so good. But in the eyes of many, including Martin, this was no more than a typically Russellian gesture. Then came the surprise. A letter, at first thought to be a hoax, was brought into Martin's office. On closer examination it was found to be a genuine and lengthy reply to Russell from Mr Kruschev. There was no response from Eisenhower, but two months later Mr Dulles, the U.S. Secretary of State, replied on his behalf–in a letter which after publication brought an answer from Mr Kruschev to the points made by Mr Dulles. Russell rounded off the exchange in a concluding letter to both men. But he was not optimistic, noting in his covering letter to the journal that it was "awful that the continued existence of the human race should be dependent upon the whims of a pair of nincompoops". The correspondence was published in the *New Statesman*, a world-scoop for the journal that also brought Russell considerable publicity.

This was the situation as the two separate forces which generated C.N.D. began to converge. At the Labour Party's annual conference at Brighton in September 1957, the Party Leader, Hugh Gaitskell, reiterated his belief that Britain should have nuclear weapons and be prepared to use them if necessary. He was supported by Aneurin Bevan, the Shadow Foreign Secretary, who helped defeat a motion for Britain's renunciation of nuclear weapons; that would mean, he argued, that a Foreign Secretary would be going "naked in the international conference chamber". The statement, Max Born maintained to Russell, showed "that not only power corrupts but even the prospect of power".

Only a few weeks later the first Russian sputnik was launched into the Asian skies: a harbinger of the nuclear-tipped intercontinental ballistic missile. The event, seen by many as making a dangerous situation even more menacing, sent a shiver down the spine which only the most complacent sections of the public could entirely ignore. At this point, and almost inevitably, the figure of Victor Gollancz appeared on the scene. The eminent left-wing publisher had been a leading light in the post-war campaign to save Europe from starvation and in the later campaign for ending the death-penalty. In both he had been helped by Peggy Duff, an able and born organizer of dissent who was now the secretary of the National Committee for the Abolition of Nuclear Weapon Tests. Mrs Duff advised Gollancz to divert some of his energies to a movement protesting against Britain's nuclear weapons; Gollancz spoke to Kingsley Martin, and Martin appealed to J. B. Priestley, one of his regular contributors.

The outcome was "Britain and the Nuclear Bombs", the article which later caused Martin to write that "the founder of the C.N.D. was really J. B. Priestley". A proof of the article was sent to Russell, who replied that he disagreed with it only on minor points, and added a few fresh ones in support of the policy Priestley advocated. It was a simple one. "Now that Britain has told the world she has the H-bomb, she should announce as early as possible that she has done with it, that she proposes to reject, in all circumstances, nuclear warfare."

Priestley's article brought such a flood of letters that the *New Statesman* could not cope with them. In desperation Martin turned for advice to the Canon Collins who a year or so earlier had failed to start a nuclear-protest campaign within Christian Action. "He asked me if I knew of any organisation that could handle [the correspondence]," says Collins. "We agreed that the N[ational] C[ouncil] for A[bolition] of N[uclear] W[eapon] T[ests], though limited to opposing the testing of nuclear weapons, was the only body then in existence that might be capable of handling it; and it was to that body that he sent it."

But both Priestley and Martin felt that something more should be done, and on 3 December Priestley wrote to Martin. "I have just written to Pat Blackett – as a test-case, so to speak – to see if he would join a sort of arts–science–etc. non-political group to denounce nuclear warfare," he said. "Let us see how this develops. I am not strong on generals. I have exchanged letters with Horrocks, who seems a nice civilised chap, but his position as Black Rod would probably prevent his joining anything even if he agreed ..."

Blackett, who years earlier had stated firmly that it would not be in Britain's interest to build her own nuclear weapons, agreed to attend a meeting in Martin's flat. So did George Kennan, former U.S. Ambassador to Moscow, who had been delivering the current Reith lectures on "Russia, the Atom and the West", in which he questioned the Dulles idea of world peace as dependent on nuclear deterrents. Russell was also present; "an imposing, somewhat stern gentleman ... on that occasion somewhat taciturn", as Kennan describes him.

The object of the meeting was, according to Martin, "to discuss the possibility of a national organisation which would supersede the National Committee for the Abolition of Nuclear Weapon Tests", but no one from that group was invited to be present and commit hara-kiri. However, many of its members had in fact been considering the need to change the nature of the campaign now that Britain had joined the nuclear club. The Committee's sponsors, it was suggested, should cease merely lending their names and become active participants. Eric Tucker, Secretary of the Friends' Peace Committee, crystallized the new feelings in a letter written early in December to Rex Phillips, a member of the committee campaigning against nuclear tests. He had, he said, just returned from a meeting of the Peace Committee at which recent developments in public reaction to nuclear weapons had been discussed; he continued,

> One of the suggestions that we have now been asked to follow up is that some of the leaders of public opinion who have been expressing themselves forcibly on nuclear policy should be brought together to consider what are the next steps to be taken in an effort to make the British Government change its policy, and lead it to an acceptance of the rightness of the unilateral abandonment of nuclear weapons. We have in mind trying to bring together people like Commander Sir Stephen King-Hall, J. B. Priestley, Bertrand Russell, Victor Gollancz and the Bishop of Manchester.

Preparations for such a meeting were started by Dr Sheila Jones of the anti-testing committee, and it was arranged to book a room at a London hotel where the sponsors could comment on the proposed new organization. At this point Peggy Duff announced that she had been able to arrange for the use of a large room in Canon Collins's Amen Court home. Most of the sponsors of the anti-testing committee arrived on 16 January, and so, of course, did the majority of those who had met earlier in Kingsley Martin's flat. At this meeting, attended by between fifty and sixty people, including Russell, a small *ad hoc* committee under Kingsley Martin's chairmanship was set up to prepare a basic policy-statement, and Arthur Goss said he felt confident that if his committee was satisfied with this it would disband and hand over its bank balance, its new office in Fleet Street, and its booking of the Central Hall, Westminster, for a public meeting of the anti-testing committee in February to the new organization.

On the 27th they met again. "Arthur Goss opened the meeting by stating his readiness to amalgamate and I took over the Chair and simply asked the company whether they were prepared to accept Bertrand Russell as President and Canon Collins as Chairman," Martin has said. "There was no rival motion. I thought that for the time being, at any rate, it would save trouble if I put forward names as members of the committee. They were all accepted and Mrs. Peggy Duff became organising secretary . . ."

Goss had suggested as a name for the new organization founded on the 27th, the Campaign for Sane Nuclear Policy; Priestley, the League Against Atomic Warfare; Kingsley Martin, the Council for Nuclear Disarmament, the title finally agreed upon with the substitution of "Campaign" for "Council". Plans were decided for the Central Hall meeting in February at which the new movement was to be presented to the public and it was agreed that while a collection should be held, "No cheques should be 'planted' in the audience beforehand."

One other ticklish point had to be settled. Whatever the impact so far made on the public by those who objected to Britain's bomb, it had been made by those willing to defy the law on moral grounds. What should be done about them? The answer came in a resolution of beatific English compromise.

> The secretary reported on plans for Direct Action proposed by the Emergency Committee for Direct Action, and the Labour H-Bomb Committee. It was agreed that the Executive Committee should give its blessing to the Emergency Committee's plans, and should publicise them, but should make it clear that at this stage of the campaign they could not be very closely involved, and that the H-Bomb Campaign Committee should be informed on similar lines.

The decision was certainly a sensible one, and got the new-born C.N.D. off an embarrassing hook, leaving in doubt only how close was "close". Even so, the situation was odd. Russell had for long supported the Direct Action Committee financially; he continued to do so, although president of an organization which even in private did not wish to be "very closely" involved with it and in public took considerable care to steer clear of its activities. In 1958 the situation was merely anomalous; later it was disastrous.

The organization of which Russell now became president, and which he was to support for at least a few years as the best of its kind in the anti-nuclear field, bore no comparison with Pugwash. Whereas Pugwash was powered by a small number of like-minded scientists of comparable background and calibre, the nuclear disarmers soon numbered men and women whose minds ranged along the whole intellectual scale from woolly to pin-sharp. It included those who opposed British nuclear weapons on Christian grounds and those – like Russell – whose moral concern was buttressed by a sense of practical military realities. It included those who – again like Russell – believed that Britain's security would be strengthened rather than weakened by nuclear disarmament, and those who believed that nothing less than nuclear disarmament all round was essential. It included men of strong conscience and a few of no conscience at all; Communist Party members who devoutly believed that their ends justified any means; egocentric hangers-on, and the constitutional protesters. Its Aldermaston marches, taken over, after some initial misgivings, from the Direct Action group, attracted a fair sprinkling of extrovert showoffs, nattily exploited by some of the press to introduce an air of burlesque. But the hard core of its members were sincere men and women who honestly believed that their efforts might help avert a nuclear holocaust. While they had little discernible effect on policy, in Britain or elsewhere, they did gradually, over a decade and more, bring at least a partial awareness of what the nuclear age meant to a reluctant proletariat more interested in bingo and the pools.

The movement thus had some similarities with the No-Conscription movement of forty years earlier. There were the disparate qualities of the men and women it attracted; their mixture of hopeless optimism and practical realism – the latter frequently injected by Russell – and their success not in guiding events but in changing the climate of public opinion. In a comparable way, Russell's own impact on both movements was strikingly similar. To both he was welcomed principally as a moral figurehead and in both he demonstrated that the academic can also be a successful, and if needs be ruthless, political tactician. As a speaker for the No-Conscription Fellowship he had what even his enemies admitted was "a good deal of misguided cleverness"; as the Cassandra of nuclear disaster he left following speakers, as Alistair Cooke once put in, "in the uncomfortable spot of following a sermon on the Resurrection with a vestryman's search for the boy who had broken the parsonage window".

In the No-Conscription Fellowship he had swum against the stream by maintaining that he was not a fully fledged pacifist, and that some wars were justified; in the nuclear-disarmament movement he was soon to offend by proclaiming that when talk alone was shown to be ineffective, courageous men should take up the weapon of civil disobedience – a reaction easy enough for those born into the aristocratic tradition but slightly shocking to the respectable middle classes who supplied the cannon-fodder of the movement. In both cases resignation from the movement was eventually demanded by his own stern discipline of principle and in both it was accomplished with a minimum of ill-will, although in the early 1960s he could not prevent an internecine conflict that at times had all the restraint of a beer-house brawl.

There was also a debit side to his involvement. In a subject as convoluted and changeable as nuclear policy, attitudes and opinions developed quickly and what might seem right or expedient in one set of circumstances could be wrong or damaging a few months later. The very complexity of the subject, requiring that almost every statement should be hedged round with qualifications if it were to be accurate, meant that opinions could easily be matched against each other to suggest conflicts that did not really exist. Even so, none of this entirely accounted for the contradictions and wild phrases to be found in some of Russell's statements and often used against him. His constitutional weakness for the colourful exaggeration often backfired. His assurance in 1961 that everyone in the world would be dead in a year's time was, as he admitted later, just a rhetorical flourish; but it tended to devalue the currency of his more sober judgments: and the fact that he was using rhetoric for the old demagogic purpose of moving the mob disillusioned at least some of his listeners. On his own confession, he was also no less human than the rest of us. "I know from experience that in careless talk I am apt to say things which are not exactly what I think and which I should not wish to have broadcast," he wrote to one correspondent. "... One also sometimes says things which one believes to be wholly true but which it might be injudicious to say publicly." Both common traits, but for a public figure the first was a dangerous one.

There was also the extent, far greater than most people realized, to which his intellectual judgment could be falsified by perverseness or by surrender to the mood of the moment. His views on the chances of avoiding an atomic holocaust reveal an attitude not always appreciated by those who drank in every word of his messianic speeches. "He answered that it all depended on how he felt," stated one interviewer. "When he felt well, then he believed that man could save himself from such a holocaust, but when he was not up to snuff he had no hope at all for man and his chances of survival." Switchbacks of feeling are part of the human make-up and Russell in such a mood need not be taken too literally; nevertheless, the trail of the nuclear movement was to be blazed across hostile territory, and on more than one occasion he laid its flanks dangerously open to attack.

In the background, moreover, there was the shadow of his preventive-war period and the cool way in which he had described nuclear weapons before the advent of the hydrogen bomb. Thus in 1952 he had been asked if he thought that use of the atomic bomb would be justified should the American army invade China and get bogged down there. His answer was given in the pamphlet *How Near Is War?*:

> You know, I'm sorry, but speaking of it as a weapon, pure and simple, I think there's far too much fuss about this atom bomb. There is always a fuss about a new weapon of war. You remember when Nobel invented dynamite he thought it would abolish war because it would make war so dreadful that nobody would fight. But it didn't work out that way. As a matter of fact the destruction of life through the atom bomb would probably be no greater than the destruction of life by older methods. Indeed, in the old days when they had the oldest imaginable weapons of war mortality was greater than it is now. It was mortality through plague, not through weapons, but whole armies just melted away, over and over again. Mortality in war was greater in the Middle Ages and in antiquity than it is now. The atom bomb doesn't increase the mortality, and I think it is sentimental, and a little absurd, this aspect of the fuss that's made about it.

A lot had of course happened in the five years that followed this statement and it was possible to maintain both that too much fuss had been made about the atomic bomb and that not enough could ever be made about the hydrogen bomb. Nevertheless, Russell's presidency of the movement had its dangers as well as its value.

From the spring of 1958 he gave top priority to work for the Campaign for Nuclear Disarmament. He spoke at meetings and rallies throughout Britain, broadcast frequently and wrote extensively – as easily for the popular press as for the most erudite journals. For *Maclean's Magazine* he could produce "How to Diminish the Risk of Nuclear War": for *John Bull*, "Disarmament: Is It Practicable?" and for the *Sunday Dispatch*, "Four Minute Madness". At a different level there was "Mankind versus the H-Bomb" for Canada's *International Affairs*, and contributions to the *Radical Humanist*, an Indian journal; *Science and Religion*, a Russian publication; and the *New Statesman*. In all this, and in the prefaces, introductions and forewords to other people's books, he hammered away at the basic proposition he had put forward in *The Times* on 18 March. He started with a rash over-statement of the kind that did the cause little good, asserting that "as things stand, H-bombs will soon be possessed by all and sundry, Communist, anti-Communist, Middle Eastern Powers and the rest". Then he went on:

> The greater the number of Governments possessing this weapon, the greater is the likelihood that at least one will prefer the extermination of the human race to the victory of its enemies – a point of view already expressed by many Americans and some western Europeans. For this reason, it is important that H-bombs should be possessed by as few Powers as possible. America and Russia already provide a deterrent which sane men should find adequate, and what Britain can add is negligible. British renunciation of the bomb would make it more possible for America and Russia to agree, as they easily could, that no other Power should possess the bomb. This, in itself, would be a useful step and would make more possible the ultimate renunciation of the bomb throughout the world.

The proposal that "no other Power should possess the bomb" gave America and Russia, by implication at least, the right that Russell had been willing to give to America alone in 1945: the right to impose peace by force, an implication largely overlooked since the chances of such agreement then seemed nonexistent.

But it was as a speaker, armed at all points and virtually uninterruptable, that Russell was of greatest use to the movement. He could deal devastatingly with a heckler as he demonstrated during a Manchester meeting early in the campaign. Lord Simon, Canon Collins and A. J. P. Taylor were among the speakers, but Russell was the star. At one point he was interrupted by a young man who shouted, "Bertrand Russell, you are a traitor. The League of Empire Loyalists denounce you as a traitor, for your subservience to atheistic bolshevism." Russell did not refer to his well-known and life-long hatred of bolshevism, or its denunciation in the book he had written before the interrupter was born. "Instead," says one of his audience, "he responded in kind and in his wrath was terrible to behold. Drawing himself up to his full height he extended a skinny finger in the direction of the heckler and said, very loudly and very crossly indeed, 'You silly young man! Which of us, I ask you, is the greater traitor: you, who apparently wish everybody in the world to die, or I, whose only desire is that *some* people should remain alive?' " There was no reply.

He was full of bright ideas, some of them too near the knuckle to be practicable. Thus, at the height of discussion about the genetic perils of nuclear fall-out, he proposed using a poster which would show mother, father and three children. Each of the children would be two-headed, the parents would be saying, "Perhaps we should have voted differently?" and the caption would be, "Are two heads better than one?" Of more value was *Common Sense and Nuclear Warfare*, a short book written in his best persuasive style and setting out the logical justification for Britain's renunciation of the bomb. It had the cachet of Russell's name and it did for the careful thinker what the Aldermaston Marches did for the populace at large: drew attention to a problem which most people preferred to ignore.

In 1959 he turned his hand to another method. The House of Lords had never been high on his list of respected institutions, but he was not yet entirely disillusioned and he now collaborated with Lord Simon to stage a Lords debate on a motion urging Britain to persuade the non-nuclear powers to renounce the manufacture, ownership and use of nuclear weapons; she herself should, as part of the persuasion, offer to renounce them; and she should try to persuade Russia and the United States to accept United Nations enforcement of such an agreement. Before the resolution was finally worked out, Simon discussed it in great detail with Russell. Physicists, politicians, economists, ministers of religion and social workers were all drawn into discussions. "I must have had at least 50 lunches at Marsham Court in connection with this debate," Simon recorded in his diary. "All begin with smoked salmon and sherry; all end in the friendliest possible talk. A most effective way of spending money."

"At the age of 80 Simon organised everything with almost unbelievable courtesy coupled with efficiency," says Arthur Goss. "So many minutes only of social chat, and then he used to produce a slip of paper on which he had already prepared a list of items about which he wished to ask or on which he had something to say. Having ticked off all the items, the final few minutes of social chat, and then goodbye."

Hugh Gaitskell, Leader of the Opposition, and Lord Henderson, the Labour Front Bench speaker for foreign affairs in the Lords, were implacably against the motion and neither would agree that any Labour Front Bencher should support it. "Gaitskell has, of course, thought a great deal about it," Simon informed Russell, "and, up to a point, was very impressive." Lord Rea, the Liberal Leader, was found to know a great deal about nuclear warfare, and was sympathetic. There was even the hope that Montgomery might be willing to support the motion, although Russell feared that they "would only secure his support by weakening [their] contentions".

The debate, planned for the last weeks of 1958, was postponed under pressure from the Foreign Office, which through Lord Home reported real hope of getting agreement with the Russians on the cessation of tests: anything said in Parliament might result in delay. "Home was reasonable and friendly, but firm," Simon added. "He made it quite clear that if we went ahead now he would have to do what he could to make the debate unimportant."

It was finally held on 11 February. The outcome was virtually inevitable. Russell and Lord Adrian supported the motion on scientific grounds and the Bishops of Manchester, Portsmouth and Chichester did so for moral reasons. But the science was above the heads of Their Lordships, and Christian morals got a rating lower than the practicalities of the situation. The motion was, by leave, withdrawn, a necessary action reinforcing Russell's opinion that "nobody takes the House of Lords seriously, and there is no particular reason why any-one should: they have never shown themselves very willing to earn the respect of the nation with courageous action".

From the early days of C.N.D., the movement fought a constant battle against the accusation that it was being used, even if unknowingly, to further Communist aims. To a public unable or unwilling to accept the fact that Britain's nuclear weapons were irrelevant in a world context, the allegation was understandable. But as a consequence C.N.D. organizers had the difficult task of balancing offers of Communist help against the odium that acceptance was likely to bring. In this delicate situation Russell was of great use. After the first test-explosion of the H-bomb, he believed that agreement with the Russians would have to come if nuclear disaster was to be avoided, and the death of Stalin seemed to make that agreement less impossible. Nevertheless, his detestation of Communism remained adamantine – a fact not unnaturally soft-pedalled by Communists themselves, always anxious for support from a Nobel Prize Medallist, a Fellow of the Royal Society or a member of the Order of Merit, and especially eager to win the three trophies in one man.

Yet Russell's attitude was left in no doubt in the late summer of 1958 when it was pointed out that his name was being given as a sponsor to the forthcoming Stockholm Peace Congress. He wrote to Lord Halsbury, who had asked what his position was,

> My only connection with its activities has been a refusal to all requests to take this or that action. I do not know how it came about that I appear as a Sponsor, but I suppose I must have given permis-

> sion at some time. At one time there seemed more hope of a limited co-operation with Communists and I sent an address to the Congress at Helsinki, though I refused to go myself and made it clear in the address that I was opposed to Communism. Since that time things have been reverting towards Stalinism and hopes of co-operation are fading.

To the organizers of the congress he was obligingly outspoken. "I am writing to withdraw my name as one of the Sponsors of the forthcoming Congress in Stockholm and generally as a supporter of the World Council of Peace," he said.

> The policy of this Body is more pro-Communist than I can agree with. Those in the West who think as I do are always willing to condemn what we consider bad actions by Western Governments, but I do not observe that the World Council for Peace is prepared to condemn actions by Communist States which all non-Communists consider worthy of condemnation. I should like to see the Congress at Stockholm pass a resolution to the effect that men who have been given safe-conducts should not be treacherously executed by those who had granted them safe-conduct. Failing this kind of action, I cannot regard your organisation as impartial, and I must therefore sever all connection with it.

His reference to the murder of those who had led the Hungarian uprising two years previously was an accurate index of his feelings. Yet within a few months he was involved in a project which might have struck dismay into more timid C.N.D. leaders had they known of it: nothing less than a proposal to Mr Kruschev, the Russian Premier, that he, Kruschev, should write an autobiographical book for publication in America, explaining the Soviet point of view in human and personal terms, and that he should accept, if necessary, the help of a Western journalist. Russell was, in fact, putting up an idea for what finally became the famous Kruschev *Memoirs*.

The project originated during a visit to Plas Penrhyn of Wolfgang Foges from Aldus Books. Foges mentioned that Douglas Black, president of Doubleday's, the American firm which owned Aldus Books, had recently published Eisenhower's *Memoirs* and he discussed with Russell the Russell–Kruschev correspondence published by the *New Statesman*.

A few weeks later, on 29 January 1959, Russell wrote to Kruschev:

> May I put before you a suggestion of a very practical kind which I think might aid the cause of peace and understanding between East and West? The proposal is that a book written by yourself should be published in the United States explaining the Soviet point of view in personal and human terms; and that this should be done in condi-

tions that render impossible the distortions and misunderstandings that so often accompany the publication of official documents and the reports of official speeches . . . I must emphasise that the success of such a book, which I think could have an unprecedented sale, would depend very much on its having a personal character. People are conditioned against the stock phrases of diplomacy and propaganda. They would be intensely interested in an account by the Head of the Soviet Union of his experiences through revolution and war and of the faith that he still holds and the practical programme he advances to save the world from destruction.

I am well aware that it would be absurd to ask the Head of the Soviet Union, encompassed with responsibilities, to sit down and write an autobiography. But there may be ways, I suggest, in which this object can be obtained, without any excessive demands on your time. A Western and a Soviet journalist, for instance, might together submit to you a series of questions or headings for comment, inviting you to reply through a tape-recorder. They could then work on the recording, and you, of course, would do what you like with the result. There are other techniques which could be suggested. Any of them would provide you with an opportunity to talk in a direct way to the Western world and to make sure that your message would reach the Western public without distortion.

As a first step, he asked, would it be possible for Douglas Black and Wolfgang Foges to visit Kruschev in Moscow to discuss the proposal? It might also be well for an English journalist to accompany them and Kingsley Martin would seem to be an admirable choice. "He has wide experience of journalism and would do all in his power to forward such a project," Russell concluded.

He then signed two copies of the letter. One he posted in the ordinary mail to Moscow; the other he sent to Mr Malik, the Soviet Ambassador in London, asking him to ensure that it went to Moscow in the diplomatic bag.

For five weeks nothing happened. Then Foges and Kingsley Martin were invited to the Russian Embassy, to which they took a further letter from Russell. Malik, Foges reported to Russell, "promised to let us have an answer to your letter to Mr. Kruschev about the book as soon as possible." Russell remained sceptical, although Foges told Kingsley Martin that he still hoped "to put salt on Mr. K's tail". However, in April, Malik told Russell that his proposal had "met with a positive response on the part of Mr. N. S. Kruschev [who would] think over the plan of his book after which you will be informed about the material appertaining to its contents".

Events began to chug forward. In May Foges called at the Russian

Embassy with Douglas Black. "It seems," he told Russell, "that Mr. Kruschev is working on the synopsis of his book and will send you an outline of it for comment." The following month Lord Boyd Orr, to whom Russell had earlier confided the proposal, discussed the situation with two members of the Politburo while in Moscow. "They realised [the project's] importance for World Peace especially when the USSR and USA are getting together in trade with an American industrial[ist] in Moscow and a Russian one in America. The difficulty is to get Mr. K. to write the book." Why did Russell not write again to Mr K.?

In London, Kingsley Martin drafted a hastener which was signed by Russell and passed on to Moscow through the London Embassy. "Today," it said, "it seems to me even more important than ever that some of the nonsense believed about you in the west should be dispersed and I am sure you will agree with me that this object is most likely to be achieved not by anything which looks like propaganda but by what everyone will realise is a sincere and personal book."

Shortly afterwards Russell was visited in North Wales by Foges, Kingsley Martin and the latter's friend Dorothy Woodman. They brought a verbal message from the Soviet government inviting Russell to Russia.

At this stage in the game he might well have accepted. A pacifist Mr Standfast, he had so far thrown himself without reservation into the battle, even though this had laid him open to the wildest possible accusations of being a Communist supporter. But now the Russell who had once told his friend Crawshay-Williams that *all* Russians would crawl on their bellies to betray their friends drew the line at visiting the Union of Soviet Socialist Republics. Memories of 1920, of Allen, of the Volga and post-war chaos – possibly of what had happened to Colette's Finland – were together too strong. So was Russell's common-sense unwillingness to hand himself over as a hostage to fortune. "I sent back a verbal message by them saying that I regretted that I could not accept an invitation to visit Russia," he told Stanley Unwin, a slightly worried publisher when he heard that Russell was contemplating such a journey.

Despite Russell's uncompromising "no", the project went on, and in December 1959, Douglas Black, Lord Boyd Orr and Wolfgang Foges arrived in Moscow with hopes of signing a contract. They met a succession of officials. They tried to negotiate, although stone-walling was obviously the order of the day, and they were interminably passed along one corridor to the next. Finally, after eighteen days, they left Moscow: empty-handed. However, Mr Kruschev was still apparently willing to collaborate.

A few months later, in a climate in which official opposition to the personality cult made success even less likely, one event stopped progress completely: the U2 incident, and the consequent breakdown of the Russo-American talks in Paris following the revelation that America was spying on Russia from the air. For some years nothing happened. Then

Kruschev's *Memoirs* appeared. In content, and in style, they followed the lines proposed by Russell seven years previously.

The U2 incident, which brusquely ended the dialogue between Russell and Mr Kruschev, killed off the newly sprouted relationship between America and Russia and brought the threat of nuclear war back towards the centre of the stage. But it was only one incident among many which during 1959 and 1960 began to convince Russell that the activities of C.N.D. were not sufficiently effective. In a television programme with Lord Boothby, Mr Gaitskell and Mrs Roosevelt, he heard Mrs Roosevelt declare that she would prefer to have the human race destroyed rather than let it succumb to Communism. The same unequivocal support for the policy of "better dead than Red" came in a debate Russell conducted with Sidney Hook, a well-known American philosopher.

The revelation that influential Americans could seriously consider the extinction of the human race as preferable to Communist rule caused Russell to reconsider his own position. Immediately after the Russian Revolution he had believed that Communism could be successfully opposed with little more than resolution and the economic barriers of a stable Western Europe. After the Second World War, with the Red Army on the Elbe – and across it in the strategic bridgehead which the West had been forced to evacuate before being allowed into Berlin – the price would be higher. But only when the two great powers could boast of atomic weapons did the price of war with Russia seem likely to be mutual extinction; with the coming of the H-bomb it seemed a near-certainty. This was a different sort of counter in the scales. There might be little chance for human freedom under Communism, but there would be none if the human race ceased to exist. The inference was clear.

In this situation what had C.N.D. achieved? It had certainly made an apathetic public slightly less unaware of what nuclear war would mean. More important, it had educated many M.P.s, some ministers and some Civil Servants, to an understanding of the nuclear threat, and made them realize how necessary it was to keep an East–West conversation going. However, the main purpose of the organization had been to persuade a Labour government to renounce nuclear weapons if it came to power, and the crucial question was how effective it had been. Considerable impact had been made on the Labour Party, but those who were likely to wield power in a Labour government still showed little inclination to abandon the weapons which, they were convinced, would alone give them a place at the high table where international affairs were debated. Nevertheless, a powerful group within the Party, led by Frank Cousins, General Secretary of the Transport and General Workers' Union, had been won over by the argument that Britain would be safer without the bomb. There was at least a chance that this faction would swing the vote at the Party Conference in the autumn of 1960 and a possibility, small but by no means remote, that a Conference resolution calling for renunciation of the bomb might force a Labour Cabinet to act against its better judgment and to send their Foreign Secretary into the conference chamber lacking even a nuclear fig-leaf. To have brought the Party so far in such a little while was no mean achievement. The image of "Jolly Jack" Priestley and of Canon Collins's gaunt figure, Russell's white halo and commanding tones, the skilled advocacy from such masters of the media as Michael Foot and James Cameron, had combined to bring success within grasp. This was one view of the situation: that the early battles had been won and that one more push would send the Campaign through the enemy's final defences.

Contrariwise, it was felt by others – although rarely admitted openly – that the Campaign for Nuclear Disarmament had achieved what it had achieved only by deploying all the forces and the arguments of which it was capable; that it had shot its bolt and that no further success could reasonably be expected.

Russell took the second view. He knew the comparatively slim hold that C.N.D. had on the electorate's interest and, rejecting the idea that the Campaign should promote parliamentary candidates, had written in the autumn of 1959, "I am afraid that at present a non-Party candidate standing on our programme would get so few votes that the propaganda effect would be unfortunate." By the following summer his views had hardened, and it seemed to him "as if Pugwash and C.N.D. and the other methods that we had tried of informing the public had reached the limit of their effectiveness".

Approaching his ninetieth year, he was determined to use a new method. He did so, and split the movement down the middle.

22

The Rise of Ralph Schoenman

By the summer of 1960 Russell had been settled in North Wales for five years. He kept a small home in London, first on Millbank, then in Hasker Street, Chelsea, and when necessary made the journey south. But he was always glad to return to Plas Penrhyn, with a mountain and an estuary within sight once more. Many visitors came to him, although he appreciated the usefully insulating effects of his move and would often deter unwanted callers with a casual, "I do not know whether you would think the long journey worthwhile. It takes seven and a half hours by train . . ." However, it was a social life, with a fine clutch of interesting personalities living nearby and a constant stream of others, attracted to Clough Williams-Ellis's Portmeirion Hotel on the peninsula. Russell himself frequently remarked that it was just like the Place de l'Opéra: all you had to do was sit in Portmeirion, or the nearby Croesor Valley, and in time everyone would pass by.

He had come through a variety of illnesses – pneumonia, removal of the prostate, and trouble with the muscular reflexes of his throat which forced him to live on liquids – and yet in his eighties he showed few signs of limiting his arguments or his output. In 1959 he had written the opening address for the Nuclear Disarmament Congress in Germany, broadcast on G. E. Moore who had died a few months earlier, and written for *The Times of India* on Nehru's foreign policy. He continued to contribute to the *New Statesman*, produced prefaces and introductions to other people's books and saw through the press three of his own: *Common Sense and Nuclear Warfare*, *Wisdom of the West* and *My Philosophical Development*. In 1958 he was in Paris to receive UNESCO's Kalinga Prize for "distinguished popular writing in science", and in 1960 he had travelled to Denmark to accept the Sonning Prize of 100,000 Danish kroner for "meritorious work for the advancement of European civilisation". He was still attacked frequently, although this no longer worried him. "I agree with you that being thrown to the wolves is tedious," he wrote to one correspondent, "but after 87 years of it my reactions are no longer so vehement as they once were."

Apart from professional contacts with philosophers, a large correspondence about nuclear weapons, and much personal mail, there was a lot else to keep the postman cycling up the quarter-mile beech avenue to Plas Penrhyn. Some of the burden was eased by printed cards saying he was unable to read manuscripts, or to do various other tasks that were regularly asked of him. But these did not help with the one-off requests, like that from the elderly lady who wrote, "I am desperately in need of a loan of £6,000 for which I can guarantee you a return in two years with interest," a letter on which Russell pencilled a note, "No. Total capital is £300 in unrealisable securities." His post included scripts of plays, poems galore, letters of praise, and the inevitable gentleman convinced that Russell was the agent of the Devil. Ideas for holding congresses, founding movements, and starting new and sometimes esoteric appeals were numerous, and the assortment included a fair sprinkling of off-beats like the Australian whose wife had become a lesbian. Since Russell was presumed to approve of this, what advice did he give? Russell neatly side-stepped, "It all depends."

One unexpected correspondent was Sir Oswald Mosley, to whom Russell sent a vintage reply:

> Thank you for your letter and for your enclosures. I have given some thought to our recent correspondence. It is always difficult to decide on how to respond to people whose ethos is so alien and, in fact, repellent to one's own. It is not that I take exception to the general points made by you but that every ounce of my energy has been devoted to an active opposition to cruel bigotry, compulsive violence, and the sadistic persecution which has characterised the philosophy and practice of fascism.
>
> I feel obliged to say that the emotional universes we inhabit are so distinct, and in deepest ways opposed, that nothing fruitful or sincere could ever emerge from association between us.
>
> I should like you to understand the intensity of this conviction on my part. It is not out of any attempt to be rude that I say this but because of all that I value in human experience and human achievement.

He gave help wherever he could, as when he passed on a manuscript to Philip Noel-Baker, saying of its author, "He is very ill, very sincere, and very earnest, and therefore I did not feel that I could refuse his request to send his typescript to you. But, as far as I am concerned, I shall not be surprised if you are too busy to reach an opinion on his theory."

To students sending theses for comment he devoted an astonishingly large amount of his time and, approaching ninety, still kept his light touch. He wrote to one young man,

> I suppose that you are really denying indeterminacy and suggesting that what appears to the physicist indeterminate is really determined by mental causes. There is no empirical justification for such a view, which would imply that radium has a peculiarly high-brow intelligence ... I cannot understand why freewill is thought so important and I cannot but think that misapprehensions are involved. It would be difficult to run a household if nobody could predict that people want food at meal-times and I do not shed tears over the fact that my cook can predict this.

Often he pulled out from his nonagenarian memory just the right phrase or allusion. Thus in refusing an invitation to give the Romanes Lectures at Oxford he pleaded pressure of work in preventing nuclear war and added, "As it is, I am compelled to echo the sad words of Lady Jingly Jones: 'Your proposal came too late.'"

Aided only by the secretarial help of his wife, he managed to answer most of his mail within twenty-four hours, helped by a set routine which had much similarity with that of his Fernhurst days more than sixty years earlier. He wrote in the morning. A walk, or sometimes a drive with his wife, took the place of the after-lunch croquet with Logan; frequently there were visitors for tea. Another stint of writing or reading in the evening was followed by a final bout of reading from the long shelf of thrillers – eventually in the special large-type print for which he became increasingly grateful as his eyesight worsened in his mid-nineties.

Russell's consumption of thrillers was enormous, and a regular supply was fetched from the local library by his neighbour Crawshay-Williams. Traditionally, three of his four County Library tickets were available for fiction, with the fourth ear-marked for non-fiction. But Russell wanted four detective stories each time. "I was granted a special dispensation," Crawshay-Williams has written. "The County Council felt that Bertrand Russell was probably sufficiently cultured already."

It was at this point that Russell, still mentally pin-sharp, disillusioned with what he regarded as the failure of C.N.D., an intellectual juggler still keeping half a dozen activities on the go at the same time, received out of the blue a letter from Ralph Benedek Schoenman, a young American living in London. Schoenman was twenty-four. He had studied philosophy at Princeton and shortly afterwards had come to London for post-graduate studies at the London School of Economics and had joined C.N.D. in 1958. From the first he had gravitated towards the more militant wing.

These facts are among the few known without doubt about the man who within a few months was to become a feature of the Russell household at Plas Penrhyn and within only a few more to become what Bernard Levin has called Russell's left-hand man.

Schoenman's letter, written on 21 July 1960, explained that he had taken part in the nuclear-disarmament campaign, but felt a disparity between the argument for urgency and the fact that the Campaign was to hold a C.N.D. summer holiday in France and was forming a Campaign cricket team. He went on to say that many people in the movement were willing to undertake a demonstration of civil disobedience and that he was trying to organize one. Schoenman had in fact already moved a resolution at the annual conference of the youth group within C.N.D. in favour of mass civil disobedience. It had been only narrowly defeated.

Russell replied by return, and encouragingly. But he thought that his correspondent "should be able to work as part of the Direct Action Movement which has shown itself vigorous and courageous". Since Schoenman had said in his letter that the members of the Direct Action Committee commanded a kind of nervous respect, but not emulation, Russell's reaction was unexpected. However, Schoenman was not a man to let grass grow under his feet. He telephoned Plas Penrhyn, fixed an appointment, and hitchhiked to North Wales. Some persuasion may have been necessary on the telephone; Russell had by this time been warned that his visitor was a nuisance.

Far from being a nuisance, Schoenman turned out to be a charmer. A stocky youth with a neat brown beard like the strap of a military helmet, he exuded a mixture of confidence and naivety. He had limitless energy, a refreshing inability to worry about what anyone thought of him, and an alarming ignorance of the damage he could cause. A prickly customer in the protest movement, he had already caused members to echo Ernest Bevin's comment on hearing Aneurin Bevan described as his own worst enemy: "Not while I'm alive."

Announcing that he did not know whether to say Lord or Earl, Schoenman quickly won his host's confidence. "I had the same problem with the Aga Khan," Russell admitted. However, although he found his visitor anything but a nuisance, he was still cautious and brought his wife into the interview on the principle of using an American to catch an American. She too was charmed.

Schoenman put forward ambitious plans for an organization which would carry out major demonstrations of civil disobedience; not such a startling suggestion as he imagined it to be.

Russell himself had been a supporter of the Direct Action group since its foundation in the mid-1950s, although he, better than many members, appreciated its implications. "I know well that this is a dangerous doctrine," he had once written of civil disobedience, "and that the claim to set up one's own individual judgement in defiance of legally constituted authority leads logically to anarchy. At the same time almost all great advances have involved illegality. The early Christians broke the law;

Galileo broke the law; the French revolutionaries broke the law; early trade unionists broke the law. The instances are so numerous and so important that no one can maintain as an absolute principle obedience to constituted authority." John Stuart Mill was sent to prison for advocating birth control. In 1878 Bradlaugh went to prison for the same thing. Fear of revolt forced Parliament to pass the Reform Bills of 1832 and of 1867. Disobedience often worked.

There was another reason in its favour which Russell later explained to an interviewer who asked why he had chosen a policy of civil disobedience. "Purely to get attention," he replied. "All the major organs of publicity are against us. It was extremely difficult to get any attention at all until we resorted to it. I have no views in principle either for or against civil disobedience. It has always been practised at different times and places. With me, it is purely a practical question of whether to do it or not, a method of propaganda." Nevertheless, it had certain difficulties if presented by the president of the C.N.D. since, as the *Guardian* neatly put it, breaking the law would "alienate the British public, especially the sweet young suburban wives who form an important part of the movement".

However, Russell felt that he, at least, could ride both horses, as he indicated to Peggy Duff in a letter discussing the respective roles of C.N.D. and Direct Action. "I incline to think that complete independence is the only feasible policy," he said.

> They will do what they think right, whatever we may think, and I do not see that one can blame them for this. I am convinced that they are doing very useful work and that their methods are more successful than ours in securing desirable publicity ...
>
> I am constantly reminded of the agitation in favour of votes for women in which I was active 50 years ago. I disliked the unconstitutional methods of the Suffragettes, but in the end one had to confess that it was they who had secured votes for women.
>
> Recollections of that campaign make me hesitate to condemn direct action. For these reasons, I think that our movement and theirs will have to pursue their independent courses, and that the attempt to integrate the two will have to be abandoned.
>
> Each seems to me to have its separate utility which will be diminished by an attempt at too close co-operation.

To Mrs Priestley he made the point that there had to be a sphere for the individual conscience. Russell's enabled him to send a £50 subscription to the C.N.D. in January 1960 and the same amount to the Direct Action Committee to be spent in whatever manner was thought most desirable. A few months later £200 went to Mrs Duff for the C.N.D., and £100 to Direct Action. Hunting with both packs was defensible as long as both organizations seemed to be doing equally valuable work. But by the summer of 1960 he was beginning to feel that the voice of the Church militant, epitomized by Collins's chairmanship of C.N.D., was becoming little more than a whisper in the parish magazine.

Schoenman's proposals therefore arrived, quite fortuitously, at a moment when Russell was particularly susceptible. It is thus unfair to heap on to Schoenman's shoulders all the blame for developments which marked the beginning of the end of C.N.D. as a voice that was listened to.

Nevertheless, Russell's response was cautious. He wrote to Schoenman on 16 August,

> I feel that the question as to what form civil disobedience should take is somewhat delicate and, moreover, one the answer to which must vary with circumstances. I have thought about it a good deal since our talk together and I am still convinced, perhaps even more firmly than when we talked, that we should begin by only obstructing activities which, in themselves, we find objectionable, i.e. launching sites, etc. I think this for various reasons. One is that it would be very much easier to get massive support for this form of civil disobedience. Another is that, although the authorities could not tolerate it, the general public would not be antagonised by it. A third is that our action would not appear to ordinary people to be subversive or anarchical or such as to cause serious inconvenience to average unpolitical people. I think that the other project which we discussed should for the present be kept in reserve. I discussed the matter yesterday with [a C.N.D. official] who is quite willing to give his platonic blessing to such action as obstructing work at nuclear and launching bases and sites. He is quite willing to contemplate more general obstructive action at some later stage or at some moment of crisis, e.g. if America resumes tests. I think that a considerable proportion of the members of C.N.D. would agree with this point of view.

He was not anxious to affront the main body of C.N.D. members, however much he might feel that stiffer action was demanded, and he underlined the point a few days later in another letter to Schoenman. "I am not prepared to say the time for marching is past," he said. "There are those who will march but will not practise civil disobedience, and we ought to do nothing to alienate them." Schoenman, on the contrary, had a tendency to thrust ahead, alienation or not, and it is easy to understand why, more than a decade later, "a faint chill tends to come over the conversation of nuclear disarmers when Schoenman's name is mentioned". Nevertheless, Russell, his wife and a majority of his helpers accepted Schoenman for some years, a period during which his influence steadily increased and the seriousness with which Russell was taken as steadily declined.

During August, Russell held a number of meetings in London with Schoenman and the Rev. Michael Scott, for long one of the more militant supporters of the anti-nuclear movement. The uniqueness of the proposed new organization soon became obvious. The Direct Action group had been an élitist body whose aspirations, in Russell's words, "were too often concerned with individual testimony by way of salving individual consciences". The Campaign for Nuclear Disarmament, on the other hand, had been a mass movement.

The new proposal was for a body which would try to grab the best of both worlds: dedicated to the use of civil disobedience but aspiring to the influence of a mass movement. Its character would be indicated by its title, The Committee of 100, first put forward when the Guelphs and the Ghibellines with their Council of 100 cropped up in conversation between Schoenman and a colleague. The new body, if it came into existence, would inevitably attract the more militant C.N.D. supporters. Russell was the C.N.D. president and Schoenman was a member. In the circumstances Russell, who planned to announce the new body when he welcomed C.N.D.'s Edinburgh-to-London marchers on 24 September, might have been expected to give the C.N.D. Executive Committee details of what was afoot. Instead, he wrote on 4 September to Canon Collins. "When I speak in Trafalgar Square on September 24th," he said, "I plan to say something in support of those who practise direct action. I believe that they play an essential part in the progress of our campaign. I hope you will not mind my doing this."

Collins replied on the 9th saying that it was not for him to limit Russell in saying anything he wished at any Campaign meeting. "But", he went on, "on this occasion, for reasons of general tactics (particularly with the Labour Party Conference coming a week later) . . . I would like to take advantage of your generously asking me whether I would mind your saying something in support of those who practise direct action, and beg you not to do so. I make this as a purely personal appeal to you, and would sympathise and understand if, despite it, you should feel you must still do so."

The letter was followed by a telephone call and Russell agreed to meet Collins at his London house on the 16th. By this time, however, he was about to press the button.

On 11 September he drafted letters announcing that a group of a hundred people called "The Committee of 100 for Civil Disobedience against Nuclear Warfare" was being formed. By the 16th, he was sending letters to the potential hundred. The intention was to launch the new Committee after what it was hoped would be a unilateralist victory at the Labour Party's Scarborough Conference. It would then become neces-

51 Russell in London, October 1958: a portrait by Phillipe Halsman

52 (*left*) Russell being interviewed in 1959 by John Freeman for the B.B.C. television programme "Face to Face"

53 (*below, left*) Russell with Peter Sellers

54 (*right*) Russell with the Rev. Michael Scott outside the Soviet Embassy in London in 1961, protesting against Russian nuclear tests

55 (*below*) Russell with the Committee of 100 demonstrating outside the Ministry of Defence, London, 1961

56 Russell and Ralph Schoenman at a Hyde Park demonstration on Hiroshima Day, August 1961

57 Earl and Countess Russell arriving at Bow Street in 1961

sary to convince more of the public that nuclear weapons should be abolished, even if this meant unilateral action on Britain's part and the Committee of 100 was to undertake this job. "It has been fairly obvious", Russell said in his letter inviting support, "that it is impossible to get this feeling and reasoning to the majority of people by any means of communication, such as the Press or the Wireless or the T.V., unless it is shown by some dramatic means ..."

The means were already being prepared when Russell met Collins on 16 September. The accounts of their meeting differ. According to Russell, Collins "did not dispute the possible efficiency of civil disobedience or oppose my upholding such a new movement". According to Collins, Russell "throughout the conversation ... never said anything about a plan to start a new mass organization for civil disobedience". The statements are not, necessarily, contradictory; matters which were not discussed were obviously not disputed.

The talk had been amicable and it was agreed that Collins should ask Frank Cousins what effect a statement by Russell in support of direct action would have on the Scarborough Conference where the Transport and General Workers' Union was on 5 October to move a resolution calling for Britain's unilateral nuclear disarmament. Cousins's reply left no doubt. Russell agreed to postpone his Trafalgar Square statement on the 24th.

All was apparently well. But Collins was then perturbed to receive a telephone call from Victor Gollancz, one of the chosen hundred. Gollancz, among the most peaceful of men, had received a letter from Russell and Scott asking him to join a Committee of 100 to organize civil disobedience on a mass scale. What, he asked in some dismay, was happening? "I could only answer that I knew nothing whatsoever about it and had never set eyes on any such letter," Collins replied. Then he rang Russell, who in reply to his misgivings assured him that nothing would be made public until after the Scarborough Conference.

As promised, Russell kept off the forbidden topic in Trafalgar Square and Collins wrote thanking him for doing so. One of his major concerns was that the Campaign as a whole stuck together as much as possible. At the last annual conference, he pointed out, the movement had provided a large majority vote in favour of sticking to legal demonstrations until the next conference – when the matter could be re-discussed. There had been no vote against illegal action on principle but only on grounds of tactics for the ensuing year. He repeated an earlier claim that there was no need for any fresh group within the movement, and ended with an appeal that Russell should hold matters up till they had had an opportunity for another talk.

From this comparatively unworried letter it seems that Gollancz's few words on the telephone had given little idea of the determination with which the Committee of 100 campaign was being launched. However, even had the situation been different, even had Collins now successfully appealed to Russell to hold his hand, the outcome would have been the same. For chance had now let the cat out of the bag.

Russell and Scott had written to a fair cross-section of those with left-wing views and the ability to influence opinion. John Osborne, Arnold Wesker, Herbert Read, Ethel Mannin and John Braine had responded with varying degrees of enthusiasm. A young cartoonist pointed out that imprisonment would probably mean a lost job and quoted his accountant as saying "you can either be a revolutionary or a member of the affluent society". Miles Malleson, an echo from the past, accepted and sent his congratulations "for all your efforts to avoid an overwhelming horror & calamity". One authoress was enthusiastic although warning that "if it doesn't look as if we can carry on a fairly large, energetic and sustained campaign, then I'm against starting at all". Compton Mackenzie was glad to join and suggested a bunch of alleged "possibles" including James Robertson Justice, John Betjeman, Lord Boothby, Lord Boyd Orr and Group-Captain Cheshire. He also suggested "John Connell". Here, unexpectedly, was the crack through which the story spilt out.

It is not certain whether the sequel was the result of a monumental misjudgment on Compton Mackenzie's part or of mismanagement in the Committee of 100 office. The prevailing theory is that the "John Connell" proposed by Compton Mackenzie was the publicist best-known for his presidency of the Noise Abatement Society, an able propagandist for unpopular causes and a man who might well have bright ideas for nuclear protest. Nevertheless, after mentioning Connell's name Mackenzie went on to suggest an approach to Field Marshal Sir Claude Auchinleck, a wartime commander whose biography had been written by another John Connell, a former Chief Military Press Censor in India, author of a book on Churchill, member of the Special Forces and Beefsteak Clubs, and whose papers, by a strange coincidence, are now filed opposite Russell's in McMaster University Library. And it was this John Connell who was now invited to support a programme of civil disobedience. He would, indeed, have been a formidable recruit to the Committee of 100. He was, however, among the men in Britain least likely to support it. It is of course just possible that the "wrong" John Connell was deliberately approached to ensure that the operation would not be aborted at the last minute; although a Byzantine operation, this would not have been untypical of the events which coloured Russell's last decade.

So strongly did John Connell the author feel about the invitation that he passed it on to George Hutchinson, a member of the London *Evening Standard*'s staff. The paper's own cartoonist, Vicky, had in fact already been approached by Russell; but Vicky, being sympathetic, kept quiet.

The Committee of 100 story was disclosed by the *Evening Standard* on

Wednesday 28 September. The revelation that a group of individuals was seriously planning a campaign of civil disobedience would have been headlineable at any time; it was far more so in the atmosphere of political and moral turmoil created by the debate about nuclear weapons. But it was Russell's personal reputation and standing which gave the story a particular quality, a touch of the incredible being made credible, which accounted at least in part for the disgruntlement of the C.N.D. establishment. For it was not necessary to agree with Russell's tactics – or even with his basic belief in the need for civil disobedience – to see that in the appeal for public attention he had out-distanced everyone else in the nuclear protest movement.

On the day the news was published he refused to comment, beyond agreeing that he had sent out the letters. Canon Collins, feeling it necessary to prevent enlargement of the damage that had been done, issued a formal statement that was a minor masterpiece. "The C.N.D. is bound by conference decision to use legal and democratic methods of argument, persuasion and demonstration to achieve its aims, though, of course, we have sympathy and respect for individuals who feel bound by conscience to use illegal means and undergo imprisonment," it said, before adding: "This is not to say that if we felt that a minority was holding down a majority, I would be opposed to the organising of civil disobedience."

Reaction the following day went according to expectations, although condemnation even in such places as *The Times* was rather more muted than it might have been. Those who had wished to condemn C.N.D. out of hand now preferred to drop a few crocodile tears at the thought that Russell's letters would do the movement no good. Collins was seriously embarrassed. Stephen King-Hall described Russell's proposals as "both improper and futile".

The events of the next ten days, and the statements and communiqués which ensued, must be considered with the scepticism needed to understand the story of a wartime battle in progress. Russell in particular, like Reynard on the run, knew that a minimum of foxiness was necessary for survival. It is not that those involved necessarily lie or falsify the story; but each side naturally makes the best of its case and each, when forced to retreat, speaks of taking up fresh positions. This is particularly so when the situation approaches Hegel's definition of tragedy – "the conflict not between Right and Wrong but between Right and Right". And here Russell firmly believed that C.N.D. needed to be jerked out of what he saw as its apathy; Collins, quite as sincerely, believed that the situation should stay as it was.

The following day, 29 September, Collins called an emergency meeting of the C.N.D. Executive Committee. "Only a few were able to be present at such short notice, but those who came, and others with whom we were able to keep in contact by phone, insisted upon a further Press statement being issued ..." Russell's account was that the meeting consisted only of Collins himself and two members of the executive, one of whom arrived late. "Few of the 27 members of the Executive were informed, except through the following day's press, as to what went on in that gathering," he added. The two accounts are of course not incompatible; but they serve to illustrate the diverse ways in which the same facts can be presented.

Whatever the status of the tête-à-tête in 2 Amen Court, the outcome was a quasi-official statement which not only widened the gulf between Russell and the rest of the movement but gave him the quality of a pariah who should not be approached too closely. "Individuals who advocate methods of civil disobedience, whatever their standing, do so without having consulted either the Executive Committee or the rank and file of the Campaign," it was emphasized. This was of course just what Russell had been saying from the start. The difference was that he was now being singled out and reprimanded. In defence, he and Scott now issued their own statement, announcing that they had always believed individual members of C.N.D. to be free to support civil disobedience if they wished. Moreover, they would like some evidence that the majority of C.N.D. members did disagree with them, as implied. This was a studied backhander at Collins, who later described the statement as one "which, unfortunately, was at variance with the facts as I and others had supposed them to be, and in which my own good faith was questioned".

At this stage the controversy had taken on an almost theological character, in which the degree of freedom of members to do what they wanted assumed all the importance of how many angels could dance on the head of a pin. But there were two other aspects of the affair which raised it above the importance of a parochial squabble. The first was its effect on the vote at Scarborough; the second, its effect on the C.N.D. movement. Together, they made it as clear to Collins as it was to Russell that there must be efforts to paper over what was quickly widening from crack to chasm. It would not be easy since neither believed that the other had shown any particular readiness to put his cards on the table, an attitude which created a distinct lack of mutual trust.

The air was by now thick with rumours that Russell had either been threatened with expulsion from C.N.D. or was threatening to resign. To many outside London the fragmentary details that filtered through were as confusing as the vignettes of Waterloo which Tolstoy descried through the smoke of battle. For some, the threat of direct action brought the terrifying realization that they might be associated with events outside the law. Those of stouter heart were typified by the Hampstead C.N.D. group which sent a message of support to Russell and Scott. Then, as the rumours of resignation grew stronger, Edward Carter, the group's chairman, wrote to Russell again. "Our Hampstead's very sincere plea", he said, "is that *you should not do so* ... We think that Canon Collins's precipitous disclaimer was uncalled for. No one has pretended before this that the committee could so literally speak *ex cathedra* on questions of method. Next, perhaps, he will issue an edict to stop young enthusiasts writing 'ban the bomb' on railway walls because that sort of thing is not respectable in Amen Court."

In this atmosphere of claim and counter-claim, Collins suggested that he and Russell should meet and resolve their problems. Russell at first refused, then agreed on condition that Scott was present as a witness. Collins pointed out that Scott was *parti pris*, and suggested having two independent witnesses. He at first proposed Kingsley Martin, but Russell refused to accept him as a "second". Finally Arthur Goss and Michael Howard were agreed upon, and on Monday 3 October Collins, Goss and Howard called on Russell in Hasker Street. Awaiting them was not only Russell but a tape-recorder. Collins reluctantly agreed to its use, although thinking "that human understanding and reconciliation were hardly likely to be helped by all this paraphernalia of mistrust in the shape of witnesses and tape-recorders". Perhaps mistrust was an understatement. Russell, asked later what he thought of Collins, said that he had put on record all he wanted to say that was not libellous. "The atmosphere in that part of the movement affected by this quarrel", says one of those closely involved, "was quite poisonous, and it was impossible to know the truth about anything."

Meetings between Russell, Collins, the respective seconds brought in to see fair play, and the tape-recorder brought in to prevent unilateral forgetfulness, began on a Monday and were repeated nightly until Friday. They were, Canon Collins has reported, unhappy and unsatisfactory.

> We struggled to find a formula to which we could both subscribe, and so enable [Russell] to remain as president, but without much success. The nearest we got to an agreed statement was on the Wednesday, the day of the Scarborough vote; that evening we broke off discussion to listen to the wireless and heard the news that the vote on the motion to commit the Labour Party to a policy of unilateral nuclear disarmament had been won. By the end, however, it was not until the Friday evening that we reached an understanding. We agreed that, as he and I were both going away and I would not be back until the end of the month, we would let matters rest as they were till our return.

However, the meetings brought forth a diminutive mouse, the anodyne statement expressing hope that those who believed in direct action and those who did not would nevertheless continue to work together.

Russell had thus been saved for the movement. At least, that was the way it looked at first. But after a fortnight he sent in his resignation as president. "My reason for doing so", he said, "is that I find it impossible to work with the present National Chairman of the Campaign. Nonetheless, I profoundly believe that the Campaign is doing good and most important work and I shall continue to do my best to support it."

Here, it might have been thought, was the end of the matter. However, Russell, expecting the same precision in the cut-and-thrust of a political battle as in a philosophical paper, regarded Collins's statements as unfairly accusing him of acting beyond the lines of policy laid down by the Executive Committee. He considered he had been unjustifiably smeared and he drew up a short statement that the *Observer* agreed to publish. It was withdrawn after he had been told falsely – not by Collins or the *Observer* – that Collins would sue for libel, and the argument subsided as both men got back to work on more urgent matters.

Russell's resignation brought a bombardment of letters. Some writers upheld his action, others accused him of splitting the nuclear-disarmament movement, an understandable accusation in view of the contradictory claims, counter-claims and counter-counter-claims.

It is certainly true that from the birth of the Committee of 100 in the autumn of 1960 the influence of C.N.D. began to decline. It is true, also, that the activities of the new movement made considerable impact, aroused enthusiasm – particularly among the young and active – and gained enough coverage in the newspapers and on the radio and TV to justify Russell's defence of civil disobedience as a method of propaganda. And as the new and more energetic movement got under way with its sit-down protests, the nuclear disarmers began to coalesce into two groups; those who "marched with Collins" and those who "sat with Russell", although this division was more marked among the leadership than among the rank and file. However, the vote at Scarborough in September might well have marked the high tide of C.N.D., and been reversed at Blackpool, even had the Committee of 100 not stemmed it.

The new movement, whose inaugural meeting was held the day after Russell resigned from the presidency, owed a great deal to Ralph Schoenman with his luck of descending upon Russell at a psychologically fortuitous moment. It was thus not surprising that a great many people should be allergic to this brisk if brusque American: movers and shakers are rarely popular. However, behind this expected reaction to a young man intent on getting things done, whomever he upset, there was soon to spring up a phalanx of theories and speculations. For the next six years Schoenman was seen to be exercising a growing influence over Russell's activities, and two questions were repeatedly asked: what was the real motive behind his influence? and how great was it? On motive, theories covered the complete spectrum, with Schoenman cast as everything from Trotskyist operator to dedicated and carefully planted agent of the C.I.A., briefed to do Russell the maximum harm. There is in fact no evidence for either theory and a good deal of internal evidence against both.

The truth is simpler. Schoenman was a young left-winger with a genuine horror for the evils of the world, what many believed was a greatly inflated sense of his own importance and what was felt to be, according to viewpoint, great persuasive powers or the gift of the gab. He also had a facility for kicking in doors that others could not open and a lack of worldly wisdom that some felt helped reduce Russell's credibility to near-vanishing point in the Western world. A well-intentioned bull charging round the china-shop, breaking up a good deal of worthless bits and pieces, and quite unaware of the Wedgwood, is not a totally fair analogy: but it is fairer and more accurate than many.

If Schoenman's motives were less complicated than is sometimes believed, and his technique more counter-productive, his influence on Russell was more complex than popular legend usually asserts. For almost half a century Russell had encouraged young men along his own path, bolstered them up with aid of various kinds, then diverged in disagreement. Wittgenstein, Lawrence, Eliot are only the most prominent examples. More than one friend noted this tendency, and in *The Coming Back* Colette has one of her characters seeing Gregory/Russell with a flash of insight as "a man exhausting other men by his intellect; exhausting women by his intensity; wearing out his friends; sucking them dry, passing from person to person, never giving any real happiness – or finding any".

Had this ever been a balanced verdict on Russell, it was no longer so now that he was approaching his nineties. Nevertheless, there is more than an echo of the earlier relationships in the vigour with which Schoenman was brought into the Russell menage, first as secretary then, as age began to tie Russell more securely to North Wales, as his spokesman in London. For Russell the advantages of the situation were obvious; even when it became difficult to run Schoenman on a tight rein, he still had his uses. On the debit side there was Schoenman's immature cops-and-robbers approach to affairs – what one commentator has called a "sort of adventure story tempo" – which made it no easy task for Russell to gain serious attention for his peace activities.

For his part, Schoenman was to make two claims: that "every major political initiative that has borne the name of Bertrand Russell since 1960 has been my work in thought and deed"; and that the theory of a Russell "taken over by a sinister young revolutionary ... touched a partial truth".

There is a good deal of justification for the first of these claims. According to Russell himself the Committee of 100 certainly originated with Schoenman. The idea of the Bertrand Russell Peace Foundation was, according to Russell, hatched, "I think, by the fertile brain of Ralph Schoenman", who himself says, "By creating a Russell Foundation, I was able to deploy this influence to campaign in forty countries for the release of political prisoners ..." As for the International War Crimes Tribunal, an idea initially rejected by Russell, its inception bore all the hallmarks of Schoenman, who was, from the first, its Director-General. These three operations at least, launched under Russell's name, all had Schoenman as their driving force, just as all were hampered by the regularity with which his inexperience showed through.

On Schoenman's second claim, in effect his conversion of Russell to the revolutionary New Left, the evidence is less conclusive. Most of the operations started by Schoenman had objectives which were certainly Russell's. The paths down which he led his master were often those chosen by the master himself, and there is more than a hint that when Schoenman met Russell Greek met Greek. However, the question is one of balance. Russell never became senile, but in the nature of things he allowed more and more of his affairs to be handled by the thrusting young American. Eventually, he disowned him. But this was only at the last minute of the last hour, and however many articles of the new faith he had adopted was irrelevant by comparison.

All this lay some years ahead when the Committee of 100 was inaugurated in the Friends' House, Euston Road, in October 1960. Russell was president, but there were no office-holders or other key figures. He had remembered the confusion caused in the First World War when leaders of the No-Conscription Fellowship had been picked off for prison one by one, and he hoped to avoid this happening again. From the start he aimed at the maximum publicity, and judging by the roll-call of apparent supporters, he seemed likely to get it. Lindsay Anderson, Reg Butler, Doris Lessing, John Osborne and Arnold Wesker were among those present at the inaugural meeting, while the names of Robert Bolt, John Berger, John Braine, Augustus John, Sir Compton Mackenzie and Sir Herbert Read were read out as being supporters. The high concentration of playwrights and literary intellectuals had considerable value, but the Committee was weak on the cool-headed organization necessary if it was to make much impact. The weakness eventually turned out to be crippling and was not entirely counteracted by Russell's own calm assessment of what was needed, useful though this was.

His approach was shown early on when he replied to a correspondent who inquired how the Committee would work. "I think the question of openness with the authorities is a purely tactical one," he said.

> You can appreciate that it is not possible to organise the participation of fifty thousand people for civil disobedience without it coming to the attention of the police. Since that is the case we make the best of it by announcing these plans to the press so that at least we will gain publicity where we are unable to gain the benefits of police

ignorance. With respect to the placing of Committee members' names on leaflets, I think there are strong practical arguments for and against. The argument against is clear enough, there is no point making the charge of incitement an easy one for the police to bring through the publication of names on leaflets. On the other hand, the publication of those names does spread the responsibility and does give heart to our supporters who see us willing to take the public responsibility for a particular demonstration through the publication of our names. As things hot up, we shall no doubt have to weigh the former argument more heavily than the latter. Where information to the police compromises the efficacy of either our organisation or our demonstration, it simply should not be available to them. It is my belief that on this question the Committee will have to avoid inflexibility and to judge very carefully how to most intelligently advance the growth of our resistance.

Quite so. But with such a disparate body of individualists on the bridge, neither secrecy nor efficiency was easy to ensure. The *Guardian*–formerly the *Manchester Guardian*–was able to publish a coloured but reasonably accurate forecast that the Committee's first demonstration was to be a four-hour sit-down outside the Air Ministry, planned for 18 February, the day on which the U.S. *Proteus*, a submarine tender, was due in Holy Loch, Scotland, to help service America's Polaris-carrying submarine fleet.

Announcing plans in mid-December for the demonstration, Russell said it would be abandoned unless two thousand people pledged themselves to take part. He himself would demonstrate and, if arrested, would go to prison rather than pay a fine. Nearly half a century earlier, he added, he had refused to pay a fine and the authorities had sold his Bible to get it.

Russell knew perfectly well what he was doing, and underlined the fact in "Civil Disobedience", printed in the *New Statesman* below Kingsley Martin's editorial notice: "We do not believe that either his assumptions or the tactics he advocates are correct in present circumstances, but we believe that he should have a full opportunity to explain his position." Civil disobedience, Russell said, could be against a law that people thought wicked. "The second kind of disobedience, which is the one that I wish to consider, is its employment with a view to causing a change in the law or in public policy. In this aspect, it is a means of propaganda, and there are those who consider it an undesirable kind. Many, however, of whom I am one, think it to be now necessary."

Whether it would be effective was another matter. A month later, only five hundred pledges to demonstrate had been obtained, although 34,000 leaflets had been distributed; many felt that only cancellation of the demonstration could prevent a fiasco. Nevertheless, it was decided to continue.

On the afternoon of Saturday 18 February an orderly crowd, estimated at about 6,000 by the demonstrators and at about 1,000 by the police, marched down Whitehall. As planned, they sat for more than two hours outside the Air Ministry.

Worried government forecasts of chaos and disorder proved wrong. Reporters squatting beside Russell were friendly, and when Russell and Scott began to fix to the Ministry doors a demand that the government should scrap the Polaris agreement, a Ministry official stepped forward with sticky tape to replace Russell's nail.

However, in spite of considerable coverage in the Sunday papers the following day, results were hardly what the Committee had hoped for. "We do not want for ever to be tolerated by the police," Russell commented. "We want", Schoenman added with typical bombast, "to put the Government in the position of either jailing thousands of people or abdicating."

Russell well knew that there was not the slightest chance of either possibility, but he still pinned his faith on passive resistance, writing to a correspondent in the United States,

> I feel that you should consider very carefully the possibility of organising a mass civil disobedience action. If you were able to get 8,000 students to Washington, you should be able to get at least 1,000 to take part in civil disobedience. I suggest that you should decide where and when to hold your demonstration (the next opening session of Congress?) and then pledge people to take part, making it quite clear that you will not go ahead until 1,000 people have promised to take part. An action of this sort would achieve worldwide publicity, and have a marked effect on American public opinion.

As far as Britain was concerned, he felt that the authorities would not tolerate peaceful protest for ever; eventually they would put a foot wrong. Eventually they did, but not before he had done the same.

He continued to speak at C.N.D. rallies, and in mid-March, then again in mid-April, addressed meetings in Birmingham. On the second occasion he outlined the nuclear threat in familiar but sober terms, reading from the script he had prepared in advance. For the peroration he had notes only, and according to these should have continued: "If the foregoing remarks are true, and I believe that they are, then Macmillan and Kennedy, through misguided ignorance and deliberate blindness, are pursuing policies which are likely to lead to the extermination of the whole human race. Hitler set out to exterminate the Jews. On a purely statistical basis, Macmillan and Kennedy are about fifty times as wicked as Hitler."

There might be a broken link in the logic, but the phrases "statistical basis" and "fifty times" gave a cloak of respectability to the statement. But according to the Campaign's tape-recorder what Russell actually said was,

> We used to think that Hitler was wicked when he wanted to kill all the Jews. But Kennedy and Macmillan want to kill not only all the Jews but all the rest of us too. They're much more wicked than Hitler and this idea of weapons of mass extermination is utterly and absolutely horrible, and it's a thing which no man with one spark of humanity can tolerate and I will not pretend to obey a Government which is organising the massacre of the whole of mankind. I will do anything I can to oppose the government in every way that seems likely to be fruitful and I should exhort all of you to feel the same way. We cannot obey these murderers. They are wicked and abominable. They are the wickedest people that ever lived in the history of man, and it is our duty to do what we can.

The difference was significant. It was inevitable that the press should seize on the "much more wicked than Hitler" phrase, and according to one close friend, Russell "knew the words to be a mistake the moment they were on the air". Two years later the papers would probably have fathered the phrase on Ralph Schoenman. On this occasion it was Russell's. The press naturally made the most of the Birmingham speech. Russell, no doubt checking with his notes rather than with what he had actually said, claimed that he had been quoted out of context and those who wished ill of the protest movement hoped only that he would go on talking.

When, some while later, the speech came to be printed, his attention was drawn to the discrepancy between notes and tape-recorder. He amended the criticized paragraph and inserted a phrase which would at least have reduced the size of the headlines. "But Kennedy and Macmillan and others both in the East and in the West", he now wrote, "pursue policies which will probably lead to killing not only all the Jews but all the rest of us too. They are much more wicked than Hitler ..." Still an inflammable statement, but sharing the wickedness with Mr Kruschev.

Russell himself has admitted that he would sometimes present facts in their most sensational form to create the maximum effect, his own variant of the urge to *épater les bourgeois*. He usually did the trick well, but the Birmingham incident was an occasion on which a spate of emotion blew a carefully prepared speech off course. At times, however, a policy would be pursued in the face of the evidence with disconcerting enthusiasm. This was so when Russell dealt with the threat of war by accident, based on the theory that a flight of birds, mistaken on radar screens for enemy rockets, could trigger off nuclear war. This was of course a possibility in the sense that even the most unlikely event in the universe could still be technically a possibility. But there had, in fact, been many occasions on which birds, friendly planes and other objects had triggered off radar warnings and then been correctly identified by the existing mechanisms designed to do this.

Having long declaimed against the dangers of war by accident, Russell made an effort to discover the facts. In the belief that the U.S. authorities would fail to come up with the answers, he wrote to Sir Bernard Lovell, the wartime radar expert become master of the huge Jodrell Bank radio-telescope, asking him how reliable he thought the American radar-systems were. "I am afraid that I cannot do this," Sir Bernard replied, "neither do I think that it would be possible for anyone else to sustain the case you require in a scientific sense unless there was complete access to the details of the systems in question." However, the requirement was support in a propaganda rather than a scientific sense and Russell's warnings of war by accident continued as before.

On the credit side, Russell accomplished much to compensate for such attitudes and for such gaffes of enthusiasm as the Birmingham speech. During the summer he wrote *Has Man a Future?*, a follow-up to *Common Sense and Nuclear Warfare*, and exercised a practical and restraining influence over the Committee of 100's activities.

His large fund of common sense was also applied to details that others overlooked. Thus he agreed with the Committee's plan to mount an all-night vigil outside the War Office but pointed out, "It would have been better to have 'watches' so that some people take (say) the hours from midnight to 4 am and others the hours from 4 am to 8 am. There may be practical difficulties in arranging this, but I do not think they could be as great as the practical difficulties which would face an individual who intended to stay at one outdoor spot for twelve hours." When Russell protest-sat, he ensured that there was an ingenious air cushion in his trousers. When withholding of taxes was proposed as a method of civil disobedience, he damped down the idea with the advice that "they could sell up one's goods and make one's work impossible, and I am afraid that in the end, the interference with work would do more harm than is done by paying taxes".

Other curious ideas were abroad, and one lady proposed a boycott of every product and service which brought the government revenue, and that "a chosen demonstrator should take a purificatory bath and starve to death, hugging a hot water-bottle by the side of a large portrait of Lord Russell". Another group planned to stop the Ebor Handicap which was being run on a date close to Hiroshima Day. Russell refused to support it, fearing that someone might be killed, and probably having a shrewd idea that interference with an Englishman's racing would be counter-productive. He was in favour of occupying Parliament Square. "But I do not think that the idea of a People's Parliament, with burning of passports, etc. is wise at present," he went on. "I am afraid that we are not yet sufficiently numerous to make such a move without appearing somewhat ridiculous."

From the first he realized that supporters of civil disobedience would include those who would, for personal reasons, be unwilling to go to prison. "I do not think that those who join our proposed Committee undertake to practise civil disobedience themselves," he wrote to one correspondent.

> There are a great many people who, like you, have private reasons of a valid kind for not themselves practising civil disobedience. I think that all that is demanded of a member of the Committee is support and approval for those who are free to risk imprisonment itself in our cause. I have heard it suggested that joining our Committee may be, in itself, illegal, but certainly no further illegality is to be considered as a condition of membership.

He was in favour of starting underground newspapers. "The 'private' wireless is more difficult because of the ease with which it can be blocked if and when it becomes a serious threat to accepted transmission and the views of Authority," he wrote. "Nevertheless, it is a suggestion which has been and is still being explored." The need was greater than he knew. As far back as the summer of 1955 there had been a directive from the Director-General of the B.B.C. forbidding negotiations for broadcasts about nuclear weapons without prior approval by him of a general outline of both programme and speakers.

During 1961 the Committee successfully got off the ground. As Russell had forecast, its activities received more press coverage than the middle-aged and respectable C.N.D., and it was attracting younger, tougher, supporters who were more ready and more able to risk imprisonment. It caused people in Britain to think about the menace of nuclear weapons and with a stiffening of discipline, and the help of a few good staff-officers under Russell's command, it might have done even more.

On 6 August, Hiroshima Day, the Committee laid a wreath on the Cenotaph. To many this linking of Japanese victims with those who died fighting the Japanese was blasphemous although "It is doubtful", Russell observed, "if many of these same people object to the statue of General Washington or of General Smuts being given places of public honour." There had earlier the same day been a meeting in Hyde Park at which Russell began to speak through a microphone before being stopped by the police, who pointed out that it was against Park regulations. The meeting was adjourned and Russell then led a march down Oxford Street to

Trafalgar Square where the meeting was resumed. Marchers and police behaved with equal decorum, and it seemed that the Committee was already being threatened by the respectability which had had its effect on C.N.D.

The situation was soon to be dramatically altered. Early in September Russell and his wife were presented in North Wales with a summons to appear at Bow Street on the 12th of the month. They were to be charged, under an Act of 1361, with inciting the public to civil disobedience, as were thirty-six other members of the Committee of 100. Someone in Whitehall had decided to give Russell a martyr's crown.

He was as quick as he had been in 1916 to see that the authorities had made an error in tactics by charging him. "We were not so innocent as to fail to see that our imprisonment would cause a certain stir," he later wrote. An interview with their barrister suggested that he might be able to prevent a prison sentence, but this was not at all what was wanted. "We instructed him", Russell said, "to try to prevent our being let off scot-free, but, equally, to try to have us sentenced to not longer than a fortnight in prison."

The trial went as expected. In the dock, Russell made one of the best short speeches of his life, cogently pointing out that civil disobedience had been started with great reluctance and only as a last resort. "Patriotism and humanity alike urged us to see some way of saving our country and the world," he argued. "No-one can desire the slaughter of our families, friends, our compatriots, and a majority of the human race, in a contest in which there will be only vanquished and no victors." This was mitigation rather than denial. Nevertheless, the sentence of two months' imprisonment handed down by the magistrate to both Russell and his wife brought cries of surprise from the court. Regarding the whole campaign, in Russell's words, as a method of propaganda, the sentence was a gift from the magisterial gods.

More than half a century earlier he had written, "Prosecutions are helpful to us, & would be especially so if they ended in imprisonment without the option of a fine." On this occasion he had taken care to have less than 10*s*. in his pocket at the trial, thus blocking one escape-route for any who felt that a prison sentence would make the government look ridiculous rather than wicked. There were representations from Russell's doctors, the sentences on him and Lady Russell were reduced to a week, and both were served in prison hospitals, with Russell getting through a number of detective stories and the life of Madame de Staël which he had long wanted to read.

The prosecutions were certainly counter-productive. The sentences on the other members of the Committee who were charged, including Ralph Schoenman, would have aroused little remark. Russell's was different, obviously something that should have been avoided by any government not entirely ignorant of what moves public opinion. Abroad, the fact that the British appeared to regard as dangerous a member of their own Order of Merit now in his ninetieth year proved the well-known point that they were an eccentric race. But the pictures of Russell's arrest, and the news of his sentence, drew massive attention to the nuclear-disarmament movement, and one is reminded of how members of the No-Conscription movement reacted to the threat of his prosecution in 1916–"they were all delighted and hoping that I should get a savage sentence. It is all great fun, as well as a magnificent opportunity. The sort of opportunity I have longed for ..." At nearly ninety the fun might be modified but the principle was the same. Just as the Lord Mayor in 1916 had no alternative but to make an ass of himself, so the unfortunate magistrate in 1961 had none but to follow the procedure laid down. Thus it was almost unfair for the *New Statesman* to claim that the authorities had "behaved with a unique, one might say almost inspired, blend of stupidity and panic".

One of the things which raised Russell many notches in the estimation of those constitutionally allergic to his views was the calmness with which he took the affair. In spite of the occasional wild over-statement when carried away by emotion, his outpourings on the threat of nuclear war had usually been a good deal more balanced than many from the movement, and his unruffled acceptance of arrest, prosecution and prison maintained the same philosophic standard.

Some of the goodwill was dissipated by a leaflet written by Russell and issued while he was still in prison. Its opening sentence – "Along with valued colleagues I am to be silenced for a time – perhaps for ever, for who can tell how soon the great massacre will take place?" – typified the high hysteria with which it presented common-sense facts and did much to repel many who were beginning to take the movement seriously. From Eccleshall Prison Schoenman wrote to the Russells. The Government had closed all of central London, assumed powers to shut tubes and to arrest anyone in the Central London area on suspicion, he claimed before adding that a meeting protesting against the prison sentences was to be held in Trafalgar Square. The atmosphere in London was electric, he added, while on buses and tubes people were talking as if it were war time. A demonstration was certainly being planned for Trafalgar Square on 17 September: but the comparison with wartime came from a youth who had then been a boy.

On the 17th, the sit-down took place. The police lost their tempers, as expected, many arrests were made during what Russell called the general scrum, and the Committee reaped a propaganda harvest. In the mêlée, many who had come to watch rather than sit were bundled into Black Marias; television films of police lashing out on all sides provided useful publicity.

Russell and his wife were released the following day. The Duke of

Bedford, the cousin whom Russell barely knew, invited them to Woburn Abbey, hoping that they would be the first guests ever to come direct from Brixton Prison. Instead, they returned to North Wales.

He and Edith coped as best they could at Plas Penrhyn with the sackfuls of letters – deprived as they were of the secretarial services of Schoenman – and discussed plans for the future. At first it seemed that nothing but good would come of the prosecution, the imprisonment, the 17 September demonstration and its aftermath. Certainly the authorities had by their wholesale prosecutions cut down the leadership in a way that Russell had wanted to avoid. Nevertheless, regarded as a whole the operation seemed to have unleashed a good deal of unsuspected support.

All went well to begin with. He spoke to large and enthusiastic audiences in Trafalgar Square in October, and at Cardiff in November. Even those who disagreed with his views, and those who agreed but saw little chance of civil disobedience being effective, found it difficult not to admire his attack and his tenacity. He was of course fair game for the critics, for the opposition cartoonists, and for those who made the best use of the weapons he would often hand them with his exaggerations and over-statements.

By this time, moreover, he was becoming slightly too sensitive for a self-appointed public figure. If his statements were reported too critically it was a deep-laid plot rather than honest disagreement, and if they were not reported at all it was a conspiracy of silence. This was not the real Russell and it was not entirely the result of old age. It was partly the natural reaction of a determined, single-minded man with only a few years left who wanted the maximum publicity for what he had to say. But it is difficult to discount the influence exercised by Ralph Schoenman. When he left prison in November his visa had only a short while to run and at first an extension was refused. Russell then formally appointed him his secretary, and an appeal to the Home Office finally brought an extension, granted after Schoenman had given an undertaking not to break the law in future or actively to help its breach by others. The Committee of 100 announced that he had resigned. Schoenman confirmed that he was nevertheless still a supporter. As Russell's factotum, moreover, he had stepped a number of rungs up the ladder.

In 1961, Russell still criticized the Russians as well as the West, and in October delivered to the Soviet Embassy in London a protest signed by himself and Michael Scott against Russia's testing of the fifty-megaton bomb. Surprisingly, Kruschev sent a long reply. "The statement to me contains the usual mixture of the truth and falsehood which we have learnt to expect from statements of either side," said Russell. "Its criticisms of the West are, to a considerable extent, justified. Its defence of the Soviet Government is almost entirely unjustified."

Later in the autumn ambitious plans were made for December demonstrations outside a number of U.S. air-bases in Britain. The key operation was to be at Wethersfield, but the plans were announced so well in advance that the authorities had no difficulty in taking effective counter-measures. The Committee had also totally under-estimated the difficulties of marshalling a sufficient number of demonstrators to an isolated area of East Anglia, and they ingenuously believed that since the drivers of the buses they hired were well disposed, the bus company would allow their vehicles to be used. At the last minute they refused. The result was a flop. A flop, however, which still allowed the government to prosecute five carefully selected Committee members under the Official Secrets Act.

One of those prosecuted decided to evade arrest by going underground, and there was much discussion within the Committee on the propriety of the move. Russell had no doubt and on 15 December signed a memorandum containing his views. After stressing that every member of the movement was free to make up his own mind how to support it, he went on,

> We have said as a Committee that we defy the law on grounds of conscience and as a contribution to human survival. We have said we are prepared to take the consequences of that violation. That we have done, and [this member] more so than most. His decision now not to give himself up to the Government is one I personally believe to be the right one in the interest of our movement as a whole, and in his circumstances I should do as he has done.

Russell's attitude was unequivocal, but for reasons which are understandable he marked his memorandum "not for publication"; less understandably, he failed even to mention the man's name when he later wrote of the Committee's work.

The September arrests had already weakened the Committee, and those in December removed more of its administrative muscle. Had Russell been fifty years younger – or even twenty – the situation would have been different. As it was, he could only deplore the shambles brought about by the loss of many able members, and the eagerness of some Committee members to oppose not only the government's nuclear policies but also many others with which they disagreed.

The main aim of the Committee was to get publicity for what Russell sincerely believed to be the growing threat of nuclear calamity. Why, therefore, did he not make his case in the House of Lords? However useless he may have considered its normal activities, however strong his fear that the press would ignore him, surely it would have been worth the effort? Russell himself eloquently explained why he thought otherwise after Lord Hailsham wrote to congratulate him on his ninetieth birthday, noted that he accused the Establishment of wishing to prevent his views becoming known, and invited him to speak in a debate on disarmament to be held in June 1962. Russell's presence, he went on, would be a pleasure even for those – possibly a majority – who would not agree with what he said.

"The House of Lords, you must admit, is not a body whose deliberations affect events," Russell replied.

> I cannot feel that this issue can be politely discussed on a fixed date, and then forgotten by the next day, until, perhaps, the next polite occasion.
>
> I spoke in 1945 in the House of Lords, to warn against the atomic arms race and the development of fusion bombs, which was then only theoretically possible. It has been my experience that this issue requires a degree of dedication and an intensity of commitment far beyond anything which can be provided in a debate according to the rules in the House of Lords. When I speak of the Establishment, I am not engaging in clever political debate; I am referring to the entire institutional weight of a society which is organised to launch and to participate in nuclear war. I refer to the systematic preparation of the public mind for such a possibility; I refer to the use of the means of communication and the sources of public entertainment to lull people into a belief that such a thing is not possible and that such a danger is not imminent.
>
> It requires a colossal failure of imagination for men to acquiesce daily and weekly in a policy, the implications of which are so staggering and so profane ...
>
> I have spent my life in mathematics and science, and if I were capable of detachment about the state of our fellow men I could not allow any conclusion to arise from the evidence before us but that accidental nuclear war is a matter of statistical near-certainty. With every day that passes, the variables and the additional instances make more probable this event.
>
> I cannot play politics with this issue; I cannot engage in the enjoyable debate I have engaged in in years past in the House of Lords and on the B.B.C. I mean no disrespect, but I am unable to go about my daily affairs and calmly contemplate the enormity of the policies of governments, without feeling that I would not be fit to live if I did not struggle in serious ways and with all the energy at my command in opposition to an evil against which my whole being cries out.
>
> Perhaps you will be kind enough to explain to those leading members of Church, Government and polite Opposition, that if a policy involving such weapons is to be conducted, then I for one would prefer to be in your prisons while you do it.

Please accept the sincerity of my appreciation to you for writing to me now, and the reasons for which I cannot feel it worthwhile to speak any longer in the House of Lords.

Russell's ninetieth birthday was celebrated by a private dinner, a luncheon in his honour organized by Fenner Brockway in the House of Commons and a concert in London's Festival Hall. Congratulations arrived from all over the world. Salvador de Madariaga pointed out that Russell was "perhaps today the outstanding figure in the intellectual world". Wolf Mankowitz praised his embodiment of "the wisdom of non-conformism" and Lord Rothschild contributed the commendation that he had "influenced the way thoughtful people think all over the world". Contrasting with these tributes to intellect, there came a moving message from Colette. "Russell, to some of us who were young in 1916," she wrote, "was the sun which lit our world. His spirit appeared indestructible; and today, after the long years, we know that it is ..."

As the Russells returned to Wales, events were already moving towards the Cuba crisis and Russell's controversial pronouncements on it. Until the American and Russian archives are accessible, his influence on the crisis, if any, is a matter for speculation. The choice is between a wide range of options, running from Russell's own assessment that his influence had been nonexistent, to claims that his actions had been a determining factor in stopping World War Three. Even if Russell is nearer the mark than his admirers, which seems distinctly likely, the events of October 1962 were of significance in one way that is not generally appreciated: they turned the spotlight of newspapers and radio on to the figure of Ralph Schoenman, obstreperously stage-managing the master's appearances and statements.

The progress of events deserves a brief recapitulation. The overthrow of the Batista government in 1958 by Fidel Castro, and its supersession by a regime which leaned ideologically on Communism and economically on Soviet Russia, was followed by threats of invasion by American-based exiles, supported in greater or lesser degree, overtly or covertly, by the U.S. authorities. In 1961 the threats culminated in the American-sponsored attack by Florida-based exiles on the Bay of Pigs, a disastrous failure which lost the recently elected President Kennedy much prestige. Little more than a year later American aircraft identified the construction of nuclear-missile bases on the island, and evidence then showed that these were being established and were to be serviced by Russia. America, reacting vigorously to the idea that the southern States might in the near future be within range of nuclear-tipped missiles, declared a blockade of Cuba, late on 22 October, well aware that Russian vessels were already approaching the island.

It was at this stage that Russell, the "nonagenarian intellectual in carpet slippers in his cottage in North Wales", stepped openly on to the international stage. He had, in fact, made a preliminary move some weeks previously, issuing the following statement to the press:

> The situation of Cuba involves a serious threat to the peace of the world. The Cubans have every right to the Government they wish, and if it is a Communist government it in no way justifies American intervention. If the United States invades Cuba, it may provoke dangerous warlike action from the Soviet Union. If Russia supplies arms and troops to Cuba, the danger of unwise and warlike action by the Americans will be increased, with the imminent risk of world war. The situation demands a definite undertaking by the Government of the United States not to invade Cuba and by the Soviet Union not to give armed support to Cuba. Precipitate action by either may provoke world-wide disaster.

Very little notice was taken of the statement, partly because it tended towards the obvious, partly because it was equally critical of both parties in the developing confrontation. However, one point demands attention: in this opening shot in the war of words, Russell acknowledged that Russian supply of arms to Cuba would increase the danger of action by the Americans and "the imminent risk of world war".

Shortly before America's announcement of the blockade, and responding to the news that President Kennedy had called the Ambassadors of all NATO and Latin American countries to a conference in Washington, Russell issued the first of what was to be a series of statements to the press. As typed, it began, "Mankind is faced tonight with a grave crisis." This sentence was then crossed through and Schoenman wrote, in his own hand, "It seems likely that within a week you will all be dead to please American madmen." Russell suggested that the opening phrase should read "... a week or two ...", and wrote in the amendment. But the statement as issued contained the opening as Schoenman had written it.

Following Kennedy's midnight announcement that the blockade had started Russell dispatched five telegrams. To Kennedy and to Kruschev he sent appeals for caution, but it was later noted that while he denounced Kennedy's action as having "no conceivable justification" he made no criticism in his cable to Kruschev of the "armed support to Cuba" which had provoked the blockade and against which he himself had warned a few weeks earlier. Here, as on other occasions, there is both a conflict between Russell's detestation of Communism and his wish to balance the scales impartially, and a hint of Schoenman's finger on the scales.

To U Thant Russell appealed for "swift condemnation of tragic U.S. action", an appeal which in view of the good relations between the two men was sensible if probably unnecessary. To Mr Macmillan, the British Prime Minister, and to Mr Gaitskell, Leader of the British Opposition, he sent appeals for action, although it is difficult to conceive that either the Conservative or the Labour Leader would have risked a second snub from America only six years after Suez.

Later on the 23rd three more statements, this time to the press, were issued from Plas Penrhyn over Russell's signature. Like the earlier ones, they contained a good deal of common sense, counter-balanced by a note of stridency as though Christ had begun to speak with the voice of Billy Graham. The press took little notice.

The situation was dramatically altered the following day. On the afternoon of the 24th, Moscow Radio began to broadcast the text of a letter in which Mr Kruschev replied to Russell's cable of the 22nd. The text was being issued through Tass, the official Russian news agency, and it was immediately clear that Mr Kruschev's reaction would bring Russell on to the centre of the stage. Within a few hours, press and radio correspondents were arriving in North Wales, anxious to interview him and to get the background details of what appeared on the surface to be an extraordinary state of affairs: the head of a powerful state making use of a nonagenarian philosopher in the power game.

Russell later described the next moves in what quickly became known, as more correspondents and television teams arrived in the small Welsh village, as the Battle of Penrhyndeudraeth.

> I answered the questions of these journalists and radio reporters to the best of my ability, and bore with the television lights and their wires which, for some days, made moving about in my house a hazard, because I hoped that, in view of the serious danger through which we had all lived and which was not yet altogether passed, a few facts that had not been published in our country might be presented to the public. But the expense of energy and time was almost entirely wasted. Some papers asked for special interviews of considerable length. The reporters for the most part seemed friendly and to have a fairly just estimate of what was going on. But when I looked at and heard the reports published in their papers and on the wireless, I found that each newspaper published only that part of their reporter's interview with me that fitted with what they had already published, and coloured what they did publish according to their already determined view of what had taken place and their own advertised political bias.

No doubt. But it was a little late in life for Russell to show surprise at this. There were also very genuine grounds for being cautious about his enthusiastic reception of Mr Kruschev's clever reply.

The Russian letter ignored the installation of missiles in Cuba – which was in fact still being denied by the Russian delegate to the United Nations – and merely condemned the American action in operating a blockade to prevent the missiles from being brought into operational service. The Russians, Mr Kruschev said, would "do everything possible to prevent" a military catastrophe. What this "everything" was still remained uncertain, since it was clear from the context of the letter that the Russians were determined to push on with their plans and to challenge the blockade. The only hint of compromise came in the penultimate paragraph: "The question of war and peace is so vital", said the Russian Premier, "that we should consider a top-level meeting in order to discuss all the problems which have arisen, to do everything to remove the danger of unleashing a thermonuclear war."

From the Russians' point of view, Russell's letter had had its use, since they could reiterate in public their intentions to push on while at the same time preparing to pull back if necessary. This could be done, furthermore, without involving themselves in direct diplomatic negotiations with the Americans, who showed a marked reluctance to consider any form of compromise. Russell had followed up receipt of Kruschev's letter by a further cable to President Kennedy, urging him "to make a conciliatory reply to Kruschev's vital overture", an awkward request since the overture had been made to Russell and not to Kennedy, who now cabled to Penrhyndeudraeth criticizing the lop-sidedness of Russell's messages: "I think your attention might well be directed to the burglars rather than to those who have caught the burglars."

Russell has given two versions of what happened next. In *Unarmed Victory*, he says that he replied to Kennedy "at once", and "at the same time, 3.30 in the morning of 26 October, I telegraphed to Premier Kruschev ... also, at this time, I cabled to Dr. Fidel Castro". The cable to Castro asked him to "accept dismantling of any missiles, even if only defensive, in exchange for a solemn pledge that Cuba will not be invaded", and does something to qualify the impression that throughout the operation Russell's attitude was alarmingly pro-Soviet.

However, seven years later, Russell gave a different account in a 7,000-word memorandum, written after he had sacked Schoenman. This version deals with the early hours of 26 October and says,

> By well after midnight I had become very tired by the stress of the day. I went to bed after a long discussion with Ralph and after arranging what might be done in various eventualities. I exacted a promise from him that he would wake me if anything further transpired before breakfast. He did not wake me, but woke my wife to obtain her backing in sending a further telegram to Kruschev, the possibility of which we had discussed. It was sent and, when I woke, I approved of its having been sent. It did not occur to me that Ralph did more than a good secretary should have been expected to do in the circumstances.

The account is both charitable and plausible, as far as it goes. What it fails to reveal is whether the good secretary at the same time, and off his own bat, cabled Castro and replied to Kennedy and whether he or Russell composed the cables as distinct from signing them. Russell goes on to say, "I did not know until considerably later that [Schoenman] was most indiscreetly and inaccurately putting it about, or perhaps allowing it to be put about, that the correspondence at that time was all initiated and accomplished by him." Russell's 1969 memorandum does only a little to damp down the suspicion.

Later, on the 26th, he sent a long letter to Kruschev. On the 27th he proposed that U Thant should visit Cuba as arbitrator and on the 28th he made a final appeal to Castro, asking him to "make a great gesture for humanity and agree to dismantle the bases", and a similar appeal to Kruschev. Within twenty-four hours Kruschev announced that Russia was willing to remove all nuclear missiles from Cuba.

From the first Russell had seen, like everyone else, the danger of stumbling into nuclear war. The vision had, however, blinded him to the nature of the Russians' initial action – the very kind against which he had warned in September. He had been reluctant to admit that the Russians had done what they had done; when the facts could no longer be evaded he had stressed the undoubted legality of the Russian move and the equally undoubted illegality of the American action – conveniently forgetting his own frequent statements that situations sometimes did justify illegal acts. Thus his attitude was neither as impartial as his more uncritical supporters claimed nor as totally biased as his detractors maintained. As far as action was concerned he was sternly realistic and when Pat Arrowsmith, a veteran protester, wrote to him of plans to fly a plane-load of supporters to the Russian bases in Cuba and/or the U.S. base at Guantanamo, he drily observed that the ideas seemed very ambitious. "I should wish that such things be undertaken only if there is the realistic possibility of organising them in a serious way, otherwise they will only serve to embarrass the peace movement."

Among impartial summings-up perhaps the most balanced came from Max Born, to whom Russell sent copies of his letters later in the year. "I admire very much your energy," Born wrote, "but again I am not very happy about some of your wording. It seems to me that right from the beginning you have shown an inclination to put the blame upon Kennedy, and I cannot share your admiration of Kruschev, still less of Castro."

A more relevant question is whether Russell's actions and private lobbying did anything at all to change the course of history. So far there is no evidence either way. There had in fact been a private exchange of letters between Kennedy and Kruschev, of which Russell naturally knew nothing. Common sense suggests that the Russians were swayed by this if they were swayed by anything more than their normal cool calculation of how far the enemy could be pressed. Russell himself seemed clear enough. To one friend in Penrhyndeudraeth he said when the crisis was past, "I do not consider that I have altered the course of history by one hair's-breadth;" to another, "I don't suppose I have altered the course of events by a fraction of an inch." And writing to Lord Dundee at the Foreign Office a few weeks later he said, "Probably Kruschev only does what I ask if he has decided to do it anyhow."

But in Penrhyndeudraeth Russell's supporters had been much impressed by the scurry of unusual activity which the corps of press and radio correspondents had brought to the quiet little village. Nothing like it had been known before, and it was exciting to believe that the fate of the world was being decided not in Moscow or Washington but behind the grey stone walls of Plas Penrhyn.

Schoenman, who had confidently played ring-master throughout the proceedings, succumbed to the euphoria that followed the Russian decision not to challenge the blockade. He encouraged the wish of local people to thank Russell for what he had done, and helped in organizing the ceremony which took place on 10 November when a procession, complete with small boy carrying a banner saying, "Thanks to Bert, We're still unhurt," marched from the village to the field behind Plas Penrhyn. What followed, with speeches all round, was a sincere and touching illustration of affection. Many might dislike Russell's views and some might detest them, but few could withhold admiration and personal liking for an old man who battled on with such vigour.

A more partisan view was given in *Unarmed Victory*, a Penguin Special tailored together by Russell and his helpers out of the Cuba messages and those which he sent to the Chinese and Indian leaders during the Sino-Indian dispute. Russell did not make in it any specific claim to have influenced events. Yet the overwhelming impression created is that the end of the crisis followed Russell's cables as effect follows cause – an impression hardly less damaging to Russell than the partisanship which shows through the wording of his letters and cables.

Inevitably, speculation arose about Schoenman's part in writing the book. "He was out of the country at the time of its writing," Russell has said, "and, when he returned to London I asked him to verify and supply certain facts that I needed. In reply he sent me a long account of the whole affair from his point of view, a book, which he had written. My wife and I spent a day in concentrated search for the few facts that I needed. It was the culmination of his tendency to write full-length reports of his impressions instead of the factual notes required of him."

There was one minor footnote to the Cuban crisis, unimportant in itself but significant of the way things were going at Plas Penrhyn. At the public thank-you meeting on 10 November the start of a local Peace Fund was announced. Many people in the district had realized that Russell had been paying out considerable sums to keep the Cuban campaign going – his telephone bill alone being £400 for the quarter – and the fund was proposed as a friendly gesture from those who admired him even though they did not necessarily agree with his political views in general or his actions about Cuba in particular. Among the supporters was Clough Williams-Ellis, a tower of goodwill who had known Russell for three decades, and it was he who towards the end of the occasion brandished an old leather fire-bucket and called for donations with the exhortation that Russell had prevented the fire starting.

Shortly afterwards, Schoenman was co-opted into the fund as joint treasurer with a local bank-manager. The chances of misunderstanding were considerable. For, while the fund had been started on a strictly non-political basis, its supporters soon found themselves in the position of underwriting the claim that Russell's actions had prevented the outbreak of the Third World War. More than one friend was offended. One who sent cash had the money returned by Schoenman with a brusque letter. Relations between Russell's secretary and Russell's local friends sank to the point where the secretary was telling the friends that they were banned from Plas Penrhyn.

Eventually, a meeting was arranged at which Schoenman stated that the original organizers of the fund had misunderstood the purpose, the spirit and the propriety of contributions to the fund. By now there existed the same mutual distrust as had existed a year previously between Russell and Canon Collins. This time, also, a tape-recorder was on hand to prevent unilateral misunderstanding. The highlight of the meeting was a stand-up confrontation between Schoenman and Williams-Ellis, who took the brunt of the attack but refused to rise to the bait. As Schoenman's voice rose, Williams-Ellis became calmer, a fitting display of self-control under fire from a man who in the First World War had won the Military Cross, and after it written a history of the Tank Corps.

Ultimately the argument about the Peace Fund sank into oblivion. The incident, however, was an omen. "It was after the Cuban crisis", Russell has put on record, "that I began to see more clearly than I had done the effect of the reverse side of Ralph's good qualities."

23

The Enigmatic Friendship

The autumn crisis gave a new urgency to Russell's activities. Although he was sceptical of his influence on the outcome, there was nevertheless an outside chance that his letters to Kruschev had helped tip the scales. Furthermore, even if the cables and *pronunciamentos* from North Wales had in fact been used by the Russians, as they had been brushed aside by the Americans, they had captured the imagination of many people, made the headlines and gained for Russell's views more attention than they usually gained.

This was one reason, and a strong one, for carrying on with a policy of lordly intervention in international affairs. There were others. Russell was approaching his ninety-first birthday; he knew he had little time left and he intended to make the most of it. Moreover, he had one great advantage: he could afford to fail. Just as Einstein, his reputation firmly based on Relativity, could mortgage the second half of his life on a desperate search for a viable Unified Field Theory, so could Russell, already among the greatest philosophers of the century, afford to spend his last few years hammering on the world's chancellery doors with the demand that men should behave rationally.

Even before the Cuba crisis his activities had begun to range beyond the purely nuclear debate. Now they were to spread further and now they turned more directly against American policies: a change of direction usually laid at Ralph Schoenman's door. In fact the reason lay elsewhere. As Russell saw it, the world after the crisis differed in two subtle ways from the world before. Nuclear war had been avoided. He was not yet an optimist, but the world had drawn back from the brink, and it was possible to believe that the threat of nuclear war had diminished. However small the improvement might be, it did allow him to redeploy his forces and turn to other parts of the international scene where he felt he could set the world on the path he believed it should go.

Quite as important, the balance of danger from East and West appeared to have shifted. Russell still despised the theory and detested the practice of Communism as much as ever; but after Cuba he believed that the

United States presented a greater threat to the peace of the world than did the Union of Soviet Socialist Republics, a belief soon reinforced by the war in Vietnam. To these views Schoenman might add a shrill touch, but this was often no more than an echo of his master's voice.

Russell turned to the extension of his work with all the vigour he had devoted to symbolic logic sixty years previously, and with good reason. "If you want to be happy you must first have enough money and good health, and secondly, in old age, you must have an impersonal job which you care about and which largely fills your life," he had written to Lord Simon on his eightieth birthday.

In this frame of mind he cleared the decks for action. First he resigned from the Committee of 100. It was probably inevitable and not only because of the fissiparous tendencies as natural to protest-organizations as disintegration to a radio-active nucleus. He had helped found the Committee and had then brought it to the top of its form; judging by past experience, that was the time to move on to something else – a pattern that in philosophy had already earned him Broad's famous comment: "Mr. Russell produces a different system of philosophy every few years," and in the protest-movement had brought a reputation for abandoning campaigns when they reached the crest of the wave.

With the Committee of 100, the normal urge was reinforced by circumstance. In the aftermath of the Cuba crisis he had felt "tried by the folly of some of the leading members of the Committee ... during the events of September and by the growing dissipation of the Committee's policies". He can hardly have relished the news that two women members of the Committee had fled to Western Ireland when they expected the holocaust; or, even less, the statement implying that they had been kidnapped, issued by some members of the Committee shortly before the women turned up safe and sound in London. By February 1963 less than forty of the original members of the Committee remained active, the rest having faded away as their colleagues looked round for non-nuclear grievances which might be given publicity by civil-disobedience techniques. This in particular irked Russell, appreciative as he was of the good military maxim of concentrating force. The organization had, after all, been founded to combat the threat of nuclear war, not to attack the government's policies on employment, housing, pensions or subsidized milk. In addition, he had become increasingly alarmed at wild proposals with their negative hope of success; and with a good sense of the counter-productive, he feared that they might harm the work of Pugwash, an organization he had not yet written off as being too respectable to be worth while.

Nevertheless, he had no wish to hamper the Committee. He was still a believer in mass civil disobedience, and in announcing his resignation gave two plausible and innocuous reasons: he had become involved in work which was slightly different though having the same ends; and as he was now spending most of his time in Wales, it was difficult to influence decisions for which he would nominally be responsible.

That done, he pressed on with the creation of a new organization through which his work could be carried out. He had been considering this even before the Cuba crisis. In 1962 he had sent a letter to prominent men and women throughout the world outlining his plan. The letter to Dr Schweitzer was typical. It pointed out that if the public was to be made aware of the dangers of nuclear war, the propaganda would have to be carried out on a far larger scale than had so far been attempted. "I have become convinced, therefore, of the need to have a great Peace Foundation which would be capable of receiving very large sums which could be tax-free," Russell went on. "Such a Foundation could reasonably attract substantial financial support from all parts of the world and could undertake the co-ordination of efforts on behalf of peace internationally. The means wherein this might be achieved would be the sponsoring of diverse means of communication: journals, press, films to educate the public and create the conditions for resistance."

The plan had much potential advantage. While Russell's personal income had been sufficient to fund routine activities, it could not cope with the bigger enterprises he was considering even before Cuba. A Foundation might conceivably bring in the large sums needed.

Nearly a year was spent in working out details, and not until September 1963 was the formation of the Bertrand Russell Peace Foundation officially announced. Its main object – "to oppose institutionalized violence and cruelty, to identify the obstacles to world community and campaign against them, and to further the cause of peace with freedom and justice" – excluded it from charitable status. A second organization, the Atlantic Peace Foundation, devoted exclusively to education, was therefore set up and it was planned that the two should be run on complementary lines. Methods were outlined in an announcement that said,

> The anti-war movements have lived from hand to mouth. They have gone begging to the press and film media for a crumb of publicity. That publicity which has been achieved concerning the danger of nuclear war and the necessity of disarmament has been distorted, inadequate and sporadic. We intend to develop our own media of communication – radio, press, films, journals – a community of discussion which will not depend upon the establishment-controlled or government-intimidated press.

If plans were to become more than dreams, a great deal of money would be required, and with this in mind an impressive roll-call of sponsors was persuaded to support the aims of the organization. They included the

Duke of Bedford, Max Born, Lord Boyd Orr and Linus Pauling. Nine heads of state backed the enterprise – one of its aims being "to oppose institutionalized violence and cruelty" – and as Georg Kreisel said in his Royal Society obituary notice of Russell, the Foundation was memorable in uniting among its sponsors Nehru of India, Ayub Khan of Pakistan and Kwame Nkrumah of Ghana. The list was completed with a sprinkling of famous names such as Pablo Casals, Danilo Dolci, Vanessa Redgrave and others all equally on the side of the angels. It was a news-worthy list; nevertheless, the money failed to roll in fast enough. The government of Pakistan donated £4,000. Saudi Arabia, whose Emir Faisal noted that "with the help of God we shall not delay in assisting the Bertrand Russell Peace Foundation", gave £1,000. President Ho Chi Minh of North Vietnam gave money. Yet many potential supporters did not appreciate that the Foundation would attack Russian cruelties as outspokenly as it attacked Greek or American, and feared that their money would be helping only left-wing causes. Left-wingers, on the other hand, tended to remember Russell's admission that he had advocated preventive war against Russia and saw no reason to repent of it. If these little difficulties made the path of the Foundation uphill and stony, there was also the presence of Ralph Schoenman, making transatlantic telephone calls for money that one potential helper described as "high-pressure tactics in money-raising that I do not like", directing the Foundation's activities from a London office, issuing press statements, and giving the impression that he was the voice either of Bertrand Russell or, if not of him, at least of God.

As early as January 1964, only some four months after the setting-up of the Peace Foundation, two of Schoenman's colleagues arrived at Plas Penrhyn. They spoke, they said, for themselves and for three other members of the Foundation, and they begged Russell to get rid of Schoenman. Although faced with criticisms, Schoenman was nevertheless able to persuade Russell to take no action. In any case, Russell admitted, there was no one else who could take his place and carry on his work.

Schoenman remained, effectively the chief executive of an organization which continued many of the campaigns Russell had started as an individual. Russell's intervention in the Arab–Israeli confrontation and in the Sino–Indian dispute were two examples. On the first he had at the start been resolutely impartial, warning that both sides were playing with the idea of arming their forces with nuclear weapons, an idea that looked fanciful enough at the time but could not be entirely ruled out. With no sign of a change in attitude on either side, Russell then wrote to the heads of nine Middle East states, appealing for an agreement for inspected disarmament of all delivery systems and nuclear plant in the area by any agreed authority outside the Israeli and Arab world. His appeal, whose net would apparently have caught only the single Israeli nuclear reactor, brought no response, and a few months later Schoenman and Pat Pottle were dispatched to the Middle East to argue Russell's case with whoever would listen. They had little success, either then or later; which was hardly surprising, since Schoenman had accepted a prize on Russell's behalf in Israel and been hailed by papers there as "Lord Russell's Jewish secretary".

If Middle East statesmen tended to ignore Russell's efforts as those of an uninformed outsider, his old friend Nehru, and the Chinese who had not forgotten his visit of forty years earlier, gave him a hearing. Both Nehru and Chou En-lai had earlier answered his personal appeals to settle the Sino–Indian border dispute without recourse to all-out war. Both had received his representatives, Schoenman and Pottle, and an accommodation between the two parties had eventually been arrived at. Reading the thick file of correspondence it is difficult not to feel that Russell's intervention played at least some part in the arrival.

Here, as elsewhere, he had paid a stiff price for Schoenman's help. In Russell's words, it was the latter's "infamous folly" in taking it upon himself, during his visit,

> to teach the Chinese whom he met the folly, as he considered it, of the moralities and customs inculcated by their Government. At the first interview given to him and his companion by Premier Chou En Lai they were received most courteously and the Premier was friendly and helpful. At their second interview, they were received coldly and severely chided for their behaviour and tactless indiscretions while in China. As their sponsor, naturally, I was rendered suspect. To my distress and to the grave embarrassment of our work, I have never been able to recover the warmth and friendliness formerly accorded me by the Chinese Government.

Attempted intervention in wars which threatened to break out, or had already broken out, was but one of the tasks to which Russell now turned his hand. His attitude may suggest a touch of the presumptuous or the ridiculous, but it should be remembered that the family had for long helped run Britain as other people run the local tennis-club. As a boy, he had played in the room where Lord John and the other members of the Cabinet had decided on the Crimean War. Writing to presidents, premiers and other elected leaders came easily to him while his independence, only slowly eroded by the ultra-Socialist, anti-American tinge which came over it, kept him free in personal diplomacy from the fetters that hampered many men. "I can understand your envying me," he once wrote to Nehru, "because a private person is not obliged to bear in mind the very complex considerations which beset a head of state."

From this privileged position he now began to lobby heads of state for a multiplicity of good causes, appealing for the release of political prisoners, politely excoriating regimes in Brazil, Burma, the Congo, Greece, the Philippines, Russia and Iraq. He laid about with devastating impartiality, writing in friendly terms to President Soekarno of Indonesia in one year, but accusing him a year later of "an appalling betrayal of the Indonesian Revolution" by slaughtering members of the Left. He pleaded again with Mr Kruschev for political co-existence and the release of political prisoners; warned Archbishop Makarios about the dangers of allowing a NATO force into Cyprus, and proposed that the United Nations should do the job. He corresponded with Haile Sellassie on the treatment of the Rwanda-Burundi, with President Ho Chi Minh on what was really happening in North Vietnam. Throughout the 1960s his own personal files, and then those of the Peace Foundation, take on the air of the *Statesman's Yearbook* index. At times, however, the atmosphere suggests that of a political Peyton Place in which all the characters are convinced of their own importance and unaware that their impact is often that of a feather on a stone.

With activities so numerous, the law of diminishing returns soon began to operate. It was also asked whether Russell was wavering in his opposition to Communism. The answer was an unequivocal "No", his attitude being epitomized when he refused to raise the subject of democratic world government with the Russians: "I do not feel willing to give in to the Russian usage according to which the word 'democratic' means a military tyranny imposed by alien forces – as in East Germany and Hungary."

But there were now two provisos. "If it can be secured that only U.S. and U.S.S.R. have nuclear weapons I favour negotiations between them for abolition of nuclear weapons by both sides." On the face of it, this was a complete *volte-face* from his earlier position when he had declared, in 1954, after the advent of the H-bomb, "I do not want to see thermonuclear weapons abolished if you are not going to get from the other side a *quid pro quo* which is really of equal military importance." However, the *quid pro quo* which would reduce Russia's natural superiority of force in a non-nuclear world, was still considered an essential to the negotiations, although Russell now failed to dot the 'i's' in his statement. The second proviso was perhaps more important, since he did believe that if all negotiations proved futile and no alternatives remained except Communist domination or extinction of the human race, the former alternative was the lesser of the two evils. In contrast to Mrs Roosevelt's better dead than Red.

It can also be asked whether the work of Russell's later years was success or failure; whether he exercised any influence at all or was just a man of high ideals shouting into the wind. There were some obvious, if minor, successes. The East Germans released Heinz Brandt after Russell's personal appeal to the East German president, Herr Ulbricht, and his much-publicized return of the Ossietsky Medal which the East Germans had awarded him a few years earlier. The Austrian Chancellor, Herr Gobach, responded to an appeal for the release of nine Iranian students. The Bolivian and Peruvian authorities eventually did the same with a group of political prisoners. All small stuff, of course – except to those concerned. At the other end of the scale there was Vietnam; what Plas Penrhyn thought about that particular war, the world in general tended to think a few years later, while on to the Labour Party's attitude Russell was able to pin a "guilty" tag which not even the most Wilsonian wriggle could remove.

Yet if it is impossible to claim more than irregular and sporadic successes for the huge wash of paperwork which poured from Plas Penrhyn or the Peace Foundation's office in London, it is parochial to claim that the outpouring represented no more than the good-intentioned but sometimes badly informed efforts of a professional philosopher turned amateur diplomat. There is certainly no indication that Russell was taken seriously by those who made policy in Britain, in the United States or in Russia. Yet the same was not true elsewhere. Nehru and Chou En-lai agreed with only a small part of what Russell said and did; yet the tone and context of their letters, and that of the minor walking-on characters with whom he corresponded, shows that he was listened to in the Third World with respect, notwithstanding differences of political views.

Nehru reported to the Indian Parliament on his talks with Schoenman and Pottle. His successor, Lal Bahadur Shastri, made a special journey to North Wales to discuss Sino–Indian and Indo–Pakistani relations with the ninety-three-year-old Russell. There was a cordial correspondence between Marshal Tito and Russell in which the two men discussed a wide range of international moves, while correspondence with Archbishop Makarios suggests that Russell may well have tilted the scales at a crucial point when the future of Cyprus was under examination. Among the neutrals, Russell had a status, justified or not, more important than that accorded him in Washington or Whitehall.

However, as Russell's credibility in the Third World increased, so did it decline in the United States and in Britain. The reaction in America is understandable. Russell's reputation as a philosopher was counterbalanced, outside academic circles, by the residual mud of the New York City College affair; his opposition to Communism had never been fully appreciated and it was easy to misinterpret, deliberately or otherwise, his pronouncements about nuclear disarmament. There were, moreover, his steadily growing attacks on U.S. policy; the decidedly anti-American note of the Cuban affair; and the attitude to the war in Vietnam which he was maintaining years ahead of its adoption by a fair-sized segment

58 Earl and Countess Russell and Ralph Schoenman arriving at the House of Commons at the time of Russell's ninetieth birthday, 1962

59 Russell speaking in the East End of London in 1962 on behalf of the Committee of 100

60 Russell with Schoenman (*bottom, right*) at an anti-nuclear demonstration

61 Russell in discussion with James Baldwin

62 Russell speaking at an Anti-Apartheid rally in Trafalgar Square, 1964

63 Russell tears up his Labour Party card, resigning as a protest against the Labour Government's Vietnam policy in 1965

of the American public. By the early 1960s it was explicable enough that the average American should be allergic to Bertrand Russell.

In Britain, proud of its great men but prouder still of its amiable eccentrics, Russell had offended by refusing to retire into silence. But much goodwill remained, and it was only gradually that it began to seep away as month by month it seemed more likely that he had abdicated from personal control of his own political affairs in favour of Ralph Schoenman.

It was not entirely so. Just as, in Russell's words to Lord Dundee, Kruschev only did what Russell asked if he had decided to do it anyway, so did Schoenman often do what Russell wanted him to do anyway.

But this was not always the case. Schoenman himself – stating that by setting up the Foundation he "was able to deploy [Russell's] influence" – spoke of Russell's hesitation about "the aid provided to armed revolutionary struggles by the Russell Foundation or the financial and other support received by us from governments and revolutionary movements. In weighing these decisions, which were so removed from the political choices facing him in tamer times, he counted upon and trusted my judgment."

Although Schoenman's influence on Russell's developing political attitude is susceptible to no simple clear-cut analysis; although each may at times have led the other one particular way the impact of Schoenman on the statements issued by Russell is easier to assess. From the foundation of the Committee of 100, as it has rightly been written, "Russell no longer spoke simply as an individual but as the head of a movement, and his thoughts and writing, although in many cases still his own, were the inevitable product of a collegial enterprise." Russell himself has dealt with this situation by pointing out that government officials and business executives sign letters and make speeches that are prepared by secretaries, and that he did no more. But a good many people had considered Russell as on a higher level. The practice led, moreover, to such statements as

> The Profumo affair is most grave, not because of the fact that the Cabinet consists of voyeurs, homosexuals or street walkers. It is grave because those in power have totally destroyed the integrity of the Judiciary, faked evidence, intimidated witnesses, colluded with the police in the destruction of evidence and have even allowed the police to murder a man because he was a material witness in the Ward case. This is the extent of the damage – that power has been shamelessly abused to protect privilege.

As the Duke of Wellington said when addressed as "Mr Smith", if one believes that one can believe anything – whatever misgivings there may be about the Profumo case.

It was not only in public and political pronouncements that Schoenman's influence began to make people wonder what had happened to Russell. The secretary's personal feelings often came through, as when he wrote "Insufferable pig" across a personal letter to Russell from the great geneticist J. B. S. Haldane – who had reneged on the Communists when no longer able to stomach the prostitution of science to Soviet doctrine. David Astor, editor of the *Observer*, writing to Russell about the way a book of his had been handled, felt forced to comment, "I certainly never said that your book or that of Mr. Fred Cook were 'Lousy, not worth a damn, nor meriting a sentence' or anything of that sort. These are Ralph's phrases, not mine, and reflect his state of excitement when telephoning me." The same excitement made it necessary for Russell to write to his old friend Sir Stanley Unwin after Schoenman had protested about the handling of one book. "It was only yesterday that I saw Schoenman's letter to you of January 12," Russell wrote. "I do not wonder that the tone of it shocked you, and I wish to express my regret on this account."

With such an over-enthusiastic advocate handling much of his correspondence, it was not always easy for Russell to know what was going on. Evidence of this is given by a small printed slip put into his outgoing letters. "If you believe that Bertrand Russell's work for peace is valuable, perhaps you would care to help to support it financially," it said. "Its continuation depends on such support. Kindly send your contribution, large or small, to ......, Treasurer, The Bertrand Russell Peace Fund. This note is inserted quite unknown to Lord Russell by his secretary." At times the method backfired and on one occasion the Treasurer had to admit to a correspondent that it was a disastrous error that such a slip was inserted.

Such fund-raising efforts were, however, merely a beginning and one correspondent, asking for Russell's signature, was told in writing by Schoenman that Russell was overwhelmed by such requests "and, for that reason, I am obliged to ask a charge of £3, which amount is put towards the furtherance of his peace work". Two years later the sum demanded was down to £2. There were other efforts to get money for the Foundation. The C.O.I., for whom Russell had been glad to provide 1,000 words for 30 guineas, asked if he would give a young Ceylonese journalist a short interview on the nuclear test-ban and world peace. It was told by Schoenman that a fee of £150, to be used to promote Lord Russell's peace efforts, would be necessary.

Yet Russell himself was well aware, if not of the details of Schoenman's actions, at least of the strong criticisms of his influence that were being made. Early in 1964 Pat Pottle and Tom Kinsey resigned from the Foundation, a clear warning of trouble ahead. On one occasion Russell was visited by Professor Rotblat, who protested about the harm he claimed

Schoenman was doing to Russell's reputation. "He tended to agree," says Rotblat. "But, he went on, he could find no-one else who had the tireless energy of Schoenman or who would do all that he was doing without demanding a salary he was unable to pay. If I could find someone else, he would be glad to sack Schoenman." In London, Rotblat did eventually find two men who together would be a substitute for Schoenman. But when it came to the crunch, Russell would have none of it. Schoenman stayed. On the profit-and-loss account he was still in credit. But by this time Russell appreciated, even if Schoenman did not, that the credit was running out.

The effect of Schoenman's influence can be judged from the reaction of one typical supporter of the Peace Foundation: Elias Bredsdorff, the Dane who had invited Russell to Denmark a quarter of a century earlier, and who had offered his services with the creation of the Peace Foundation. He has said,

> I met Ralph Schoenman several times in London, and I became more and more sceptical of him; he was so full of wild and completely unrealistic ideas that I failed to see how he could be a useful director of the Bertrand Russell Peace Foundation. We usually met at the office of the Peace Foundation in Shavers Place, Haymarket, and then we often went to a nearby café or restaurant, and he would entertain me with stories in which he himself appeared as a kind of Red Pimpernel. He spoke about his visits to Nehru and Chou En-Lai when he acted as Russell's personal messenger during the Sino–Indian Border Conflict, and it was only much later that I heard that in Peking he had behaved so badly that Chou En-Lai had to tell him that if he had not come as Lord Russell's personal ambassador he would have been thrown out of the country.
>
> But what worried me most of all was Schoenman's utterly unrealistic ideas about what the Bertrand Russell Foundation could achieve. He seemed convinced that the Foundation might soon be able to start a daily paper which would take over all the best journalists from "The Times" and "The Guardian" and steal all their readers, and that the Foundation would soon be able to open up its own radio and television station to serve as an international voice for nuclear disarmament; also that the Foundation would produce its own films to be shown all over the world on a commercial basis.

All this could perhaps be dismissed as nothing more harmful than the wild imaginings of an over-enthusiastic and under-experienced young man. When the question of finance had earlier been raised, the Krupp millions came somewhere into the story. So did the Swedish millionaire, Axel Wenner-Gren who, Schoenman later stated, had approached them together with a group of industrialists. But the outcome must have seemed inevitable, and Schoenman later spoke of "the clandestine murder of Wenner-Gren".

Schoenman travelled extensively, either for the Peace Foundation or as Russell's personal representative, to any gathering where he believed he could get a hearing for his views, and in the summer of 1965 attended the World Congress for Peace, National Independence and General Disarmament in Helsinki. In mid-July Russell received a telegram from the delegation of the Federal Republic of Germany. "Speech of your personal representative caused uproar," this said. "Strongly rejected by audience. Tremendous provocation of Peace Congress. Bertrand Russell Peace Foundation discredited. Essential you dissociate yourself from Schoenman and his speech. Friendly greetings."

Schoenman had in fact persuaded the organizers of a public meeting in the city to let him read a "Statement from Bertrand Russell". According to members of the audience who knew Russell well, the statement was extremely un-Russellian. However, it was not this that caused the trouble. With the "Statement" finished, and the chairman preparing to call the next speaker, Schoenman announced that he wished to read a statement by the Peace Foundation on the report by the American delegation. As the report had only been read the previous evening, Schoenman obviously intended to give an early airing of his own views. He at once launched into the most provocative speech heard in Helsinki. The chairman, at first too amazed to do anything, became restless, then called on the speaker to stop. Schoenman went on. The chairman banged his gavel but to no effect. The audience grew critical, but Schoenman had the microphone and continued through the hubbub. Finally the chairman vaulted over a table, strode along the platform and forcibly snatched away the microphone. Schoenman, faced with reports of the incident, "promised again to be less violent and ill-mannered in future".

The effect of such tactics was not limited to Peace Congresses. More unfortunately for Russell, Schoenman's unstoppable enthusiasm had much the same result when he tried to gain the Foundation publicity in Britain. This would have been difficult enough had the task been approached with the sober caution it warranted; as it was, the credibility of material coming from the Foundation steadily diminished. A typical reaction came from *The Economist*, reporting a speech read by Russell at the London School of Economics early in 1965.

> It was painful on Monday to see him slowly stumbling his way through a prepared text that ignored vital evidence, slid over the true and suggested the false, and fell back on innuendo instead of direct accusation. Sitting beside him was Mr. Ralph Schoenman, the anti-American American who is now Lord Russell's secretary and

who, until he proves the contrary, will be presumed to produce the stuff the old man takes responsibility for. "I am quite willing to suppose", Lord Russell once wrote in another book, "that my views, like other men's, are influenced by social environment." His present environment does not become him. There are many people who respect Bertrand Russell enough to believe that he could, if he wanted, show a glint of the cutting edge of his mind to all this nonsense; and dearly wish he would.

According to Russell's entourage all such reports were of course the biased indictments of the capitalist press. Few looked beyond their own blinkered line of sight to see how some of the many statements being made on Russell's behalf could not fail to reduce his credibility. Yet it was the satirical weekly *Private Eye* which caught exactly the atmosphere in which Russell was trying to make himself heard when it printed the news, "Bertrand Russell Swims Atlantic".

In an amazing feat unparalleled in the history of the world, Bertrand Russell the 94 year old philosopher and "Happy Pilgrim of Peace" yesterday swam the Atlantic Ocean in two hours. The news was revealed in a special dispatch from the Ralph Schoenman Press Bureau, at Penrhyndeudraeth, Merionethshire.

According to the dispatch, Earl Russell ("our respected and beloved leader") entered the chilly waters of the Atlantic Sea at 6.00 p.m. yesterday morning.

"The Atlantic" says the report "was raging in a violent tempest of wind and rain. Giant waves, many of them a million feet high, crashed in anger on the rocky coast."

But Lord Russell was not to be deterred by the elements. "Looking ruddy and cheerful, his muscles shining with youthful vigour, he leapt into the swirling waters and within minutes was well out to sea."

With him were the local secretary of The Committee of 100, the Organising Chairman of Bombs for the Viet Cong (Wales) Association and Mr. Schoenman himself.

"As Earl Russell breasted the mighty billows of the deep" the report continues, "he chatted jokingly with his companions, only pausing to kill marauding sharks with a savage blow from his virile fist or tear off slabs of whalemeat to relieve the hunger of his comrades."

Within two hours the party had landed in America and were taking part in a sit-down demonstration outside the White House.

Reporters were not allowed to witness the actual swimming but later photographs were issued (one of which we reprint above). "These" the report states, "will put paid to the lying and slanderous smears on the part of the capitalist lackeys and hacks of the war-mongering British Press as to the alleged senility or even death of the righteous warrior of peace."

The tone was just right, even to the slip of timing "morning" as 6 p.m.

There was, however, profit as well as loss in Schoenman's methods and without them the Foundation might not have got off the ground at all. In addition, it must be admitted that at times Russell himself, in contrast to the practical sense he had often displayed in his C.N.D. and Committee of 100 activities, showed an ignorance of what was possible. Thus in 1964 he seriously believed that the Foundation might sponsor research into the transformation of Gaza into a modern port and into making the Jordan Valley arable. "I believe that the Bertrand Russell Peace Foundation will be acceptable to the Arabs as an agency for conducting research and promoting construction of a modern port in Gaza and have received a welcoming response from the Egyptians about this," he wrote to U Thant of the United Nations. U Thant, friendly as he was, had to reply that "there may be a slight misunderstanding on your part", before pointing out that it would be impossible for the United Nations to give either financial or moral support to such a project.

The problem of securing a permanent peace in the Middle East, in the forefront of Russell's mind when the Foundation was started, was soon overshadowed by the war in Vietnam, a development which quickly convinced him that first the Kennedy and then the Johnson administration was hell-bent on imperial expansion as dangerous as that of the Russians. His belief, founded first on the public statements of the Americans themselves and later on the reports which Schoenman and his successor, Christopher Farley, brought back from North Vietnam, was simple enough: that the Americans had no justification except that of self-interest for being in Vietnam, and that they were waging a barbaric war by barbaric methods.

The belief was symptomatic of a further leftward swing in Russell's sympathies and is usually attributed entirely to Schoenman's influence; no doubt partly true, it is nevertheless an over-simplification. The constant influence of the young man working his way up the ladder had its effect on an old one whose best friends had to admit that he was beginning to tire. But Russell maintained his critical faculties to the end. When he felt it worth while he could still make rings round Schoenman, as he was to show in the apocalyptic Memorandum of his final months. And there is considerable evidence to suggest that his political beliefs were both his own and the result of a natural evolution from his Victorian liberalism. "My views", he wrote in April 1966, "have changed slightly in response to the overwhelming exploitive power exercised by American capitalism in the world. This reality has led me to the conclusion that, where a revolution against foreign domination takes place, humane men have a responsibility to support the oppressed. The route to peace can only be found through effective opposition to U.S. militarism, both internationally and within the U.S.A."

Yet this was a special case and the operative word is "slightly". Just as he had always been unwilling to make a blanket judgment which condemned all war, so was he unwilling to be led up the garden-path of universal revolution. He made mistakes, but not of that order. Schoenman himself lamented the fact, noting his employer's hesitations about "the aid provided to armed revolutionary struggles by the Russell Foundation" and explaining the situation in two perceptive paragraphs:

> There were, however, serious intellectual doubts which inhibited him from engaging wholeheartedly in mass movements with revolutionary aims. He felt that cultural excellence and unique achievement were the product of favoured circumstance. The tutoring, élite schooling and other accountrements of class privilege seemed to him responsible for outstanding achievement and, although he disliked the undemocratic, he distrusted the assumption that its removal would have no detrimental consequences. Russell had many aristocratic attributes which infused his entire sensibility. It provided him with strength when standing out against orthodoxy but it sapped his confidence in the outcome of dramatic change. He was influenced by bourgeois trepidations which dissolved revolutionary transformation into categories like "mass society". He felt that excellence came from the special nurturing of individual talent and that mediocrity or cultural decline would follow the overthrow of privilege. He desired its overthrow but he mourned in advance some of the consequences as he saw them. Russell knew that oppressed peoples harboured talented women and men denied the opportunity to grow. But he did not believe in the creative energy and untapped possibilities in great masses of ordinary men and women, except perhaps as an abstract hope for a distant future.
>
> Great evils, such as nuclear war or the genocidal conflict inflicted on the Vietnamese, moved him to place these reservations far behind the moral imperative of action against barbarity. If social upheaval set back cultural advance for a time, it was a lesser price to pay than acquiescence in butchery. But this very formulation expressed his scepticism regarding the liberation assumed by revolutionaries for society at large.

In the early 1960s, when the American presence in South Vietnam was 16,600 para-military "advisers", Russell was almost alone in warning of what was to come. As civilian advisers were first replaced by troops and then supported by area-bombing and any other horror that might help the free world, a reluctant public was slowly educated by articles, letters, speeches, and creation of the Vietnam Solidarity Committee, into an awareness of what was happening. The Communists were of course front-runners in the process, and for many people it was difficult to understand that Russell, taking the Communist line over Vietnam, was at the same time protesting to the Russians about the imprisonment of Russian writers, the treatment of Russian Jews, and the detention of political prisoners.

The simplest course, that of writing off Russell as a fellow-traveller, was followed by much of the Labour Party, which in power was as pusillanimously subservient to the Americans as their predecessors had been. Russell, who had spent almost half a century pleading the general line of the Labour cause, was as a result involved in two famous incidents. In the first, Mr Wilson approached Russell and thrust out his right hand with the words "Lord Russell". Russell thrust both hands into his pockets. In the second, Russell concluded a long speech condemning Labour Party policy on Vietnam by announcing his resignation from the Party and then dramatically taking his membership card from his pocket and tearing it up. Canon Collins, also on the platform, remarked to the press that Russell had stage-managed the affair. "If I had been able to do so, I do not know why I should not have done so," Russell later said, "but, in actual fact, all the management was in the hands of the Youth C.N.D. under whose auspices the meeting was held" – which was not a denial that the incident had been stage-managed. Before leaving for the meeting Russell had in fact asked a friend to collect his card as it would be specially needed.

Russell's campaign against the Vietnam war was the best-known of his attacks on American policy. But there were others, ranging from his plea for a re-trial of Morton Sobell, jailed for thirty years in the trial of the Rosenbergs, to his prolonged attack on the Warren Commission and his founding of the Who Killed Kennedy? Committee. So far, no decisive evidence to support his views has come to light in either case; but his contentions – that Sobell was "framed" and that the Warren Commission concealed rather than discovered the truth about the assassination of President Kennedy – look slightly less bizarre today than they did a decade ago. They might have looked even less bizarre in the 1960s had they been presented less wildly.

According to Russell, his suspicions about the Kennedy killing were aroused by the early press-reports of the assassination and it seemed to him "that there had been an appalling miscarriage of justice and that probably something very nasty was being covered up". He was therefore in a receptive mood when Mark Lane – originally briefed by the mother of Oswald, arrested for the assassination and himself soon afterwards killed – visited Britain. There were certainly curious features in the case, but any inclination to look at the evidence before coming to a decision was quickly swamped by Russell's conspiracy view of history. Since the Peace Foundation's aims would have to be abnormally elastic to include this subject, the British Who Killed Kennedy? Committee was created, although eventually the Committee was brought under the Foundation's wing.

Late in September 1964 the Warren Commission's report was issued. On the same day Russell issued a strongly worded denunciation, calling it a sorrily incompetent document which covered its authors in shame. At first it was unwisely stated that Russell himself had not read the report when he made the statement, but he subsequently followed up by saying that it had been based on the summary and conclusions of the Warren Commission report – roughly 3½ per cent of the text. Only later was it stated that he had in fact been sent an early copy of the report and had thus had time to consider it. This administrative shambles brought the newspaper comment that "it is a pity that the 92-year-old Lord Russell does not apply to politics the rigorous standards of inquiry and proof that made his great reputation as a logician", and it brought also a letter from some members of the British Who Killed Kennedy? Committee, who dissociated themselves from what they called the wild condemnation of the Warren report.

There were other proposals for criticism of American affairs which, luckily enough, did not get off the ground. One was an attempt to whip up opposition to Senator Goldwater's candidacy for president. The method was to canvass among prominent men for signatures to a letter outlining the dangers to world peace should Goldwater be elected. Kingsley Martin, former editor of the *New Statesman* and a man who certainly detested Goldwater's policies, refused. So did the then editor, John Freeman. So did numerous other men and women of enlightened outlook. Many warned that the idea was potentially disastrous, since it not only interfered in the policies of another country but could well strengthen Goldwater's views at a time when there were signs that they were weakening. Nothing could do more to enhance Goldwater's chances than the action Russell proposed, wrote Attlee in declining. Americans, he went on, before warning Russell to think again, intensely resented intrusion from outside into their domestic affairs.

The aborted anti-Goldwater campaign was typical of the ideas which frightened away potential support. Money was not being subscribed in anything like the hoped-for amounts and the Foundation would have gone under completely but for the £3,000 a year which Russell contributed on an *ad hoc* basis. However, it was soon obvious that money in much more substantial amounts would be needed if work was to go on.

Russell had been fighting this particular good fight at least since 1954 when his "Man's Peril" broadcast had first awakened people to the dangers of the times. Now he could honourably have retired from the scene. Many men would have done so. Instead, aided once again by Schoenman, he began to search for fresh ways of keeping the Foundation afloat.

For a while he toyed with the idea of selling outright the copyrights of his sixty or seventy books still in print. However, someone luckily remembered that when Sir Compton Mackenzie had done the same thing a few years previously, the capital sum received had been taxed as income, with disastrous financial consequences. The idea was dropped.

But Russell still had two shots in his locker. The first to hand was his autobiography, dictated in the tower of Telegraph House more than thirty years previously, and intermittently brought up to date. "I have now finished my autobiography as far as it can be finished while I still do not know what events lie ahead," he had written to Stanley Unwin in 1952. "As you know, I do not wish it to be published until I am dead, and there are a few other people as old as me, who had better be dead before it is published. I do not know what is the best way of keeping the MS safe. I do not think it would be safe anywhere in London, or New York or Washington, as all these cities are quite likely to be radio-actively disintegrated before long ..." To Max Lincoln Schuster, his American publisher, he said roughly the same, adding, "I do not wish to enter into any binding agreement with any publisher about it. There are very solid reasons for this, connected with English death duties."

Until the end of the 1950s he was still saying that the autobiography could not be published until after his death. Now, encouraged by Schoenman, he began to have second thoughts. It was, after all, natural enough that Russell should be anxious to cash in on the book on behalf of the Foundation. But some indication of the pressures needed to make him change his mind is given by a letter written some years earlier to Robert Gathorne-Hardy, known to be editing Lady Ottoline's journals. In it, Russell sent a shot across Gathorne-Hardy's bows and effectively silenced any mention of his *affaire* with Lady Ottoline. However, having effectively spiked Ottoline's account, he now agreed to publish his own: no doubt fortified by Voltaire – "One owes respect to the living. To the dead one owes nothing but the truth."

At this point Russell was introduced to the man who was to put in order his somewhat haphazard financial affairs. A few years earlier he had met Lloyd Chandler, a rich Canadian who had supported his peace activities. Chandler was an acquaintance of Anton Felton, an able accountant and literary administrator who was now introduced to Russell by Ralph Schoenman. Felton himself had for long admired Russell's work and after a visit to Plas Penrhyn became not only his literary agent but responsible for having catalogued, and subsequently sold, his unique archive of papers as well as for successfully putting his financial affairs on a business-like basis.

The manuscript of the autobiography had matured like port and was now a literary property worth very much more than when written; but certain problems remained, notably the fact that Russell had last worked on it during the era of the Westminster School speech he made in November 1948. The epoch during which the Russians had produced their own nuclear weapons, the epoch of the Russell–Einstein Manifesto, of C.N.D. and the Committee of 100, would all have to be painted in as far as the laws of libel allowed, a formidable task however much help he could call upon from others.

The first move was to discuss the project with Sir Stanley Unwin, who was now invited to Plas Penrhyn. Russell's relations with his publisher had always been strangely formal; they had rarely dined together, and even more rarely visited each other's home. "Sir Stanley", says a close friend, "knew his place. He was a good tradesman. Russell was the aristocrat, and although each trusted and respected the other professionally, they kept socially aloof." However, it was with great expectations that Sir Stanley arrived at the Russell home. He was both surprised and delighted that his customer had changed his mind, being under no illusion about the possibilities of the autobiography – or about the careful legal vetting and editorial tidying-up which would be required.

All went well, although Sir Stanley was irked by one thing: the intervention of Ralph Schoenman. For some while Allen & Unwin had been receiving caustic criticism of their promotion of Russell's books. Some letters came from Schoenman. Others, signed by Russell, used phrases and expressions which suggested that they had been neither written nor dictated by him. However, if Schoenman's ideas were expressed in rather peremptory fashion they were sometimes extremely sound. They proved so on this occasion.

Sir Stanley bought not only the English but also the foreign rights in the book and proceeded to offer the U.S. rights to Simon & Schuster, now Russell's regular publishers in America. Schoenman intervened, protesting that the 30,000 dollars offered on account of royalties was quite inadequate and that the rights should be auctioned. Sir Stanley agreed, but under protest, later expressing the hope that he would never be forced to do such a thing again. But the rights were bought by Little, Brown for more than 200,000 dollars, a sale which gave game and set but not match to Schoenman. For in one respect the result of over-selling volume one was crippling; when the third volume was available Little, Brown declined and Simon & Schuster were left to pick up the bits.

Once the financial hurdles had been overcome, Russell's manuscript was prepared for the press. The original was on the short side and on the publisher's request he supplied a large number of letters, some of them previously earmarked for possible use in the autobiography. The work also had to be brought up to date by adding the story of the last decade and a half, and when this was finished the original two volumes had expanded to three.

However, the autobiography was not the only potential source of cash for his activities. There were also his private papers. For almost eighty years he had kept correspondence from philosophers and politicians, from Cantor and Frege who belonged to the prehistory of mathematical logic, from Whitehead and Wittgenstein who had helped build the structure of contemporary thought, and from many others. This huge mass of correspondence was only a small part of the rich hoard of material in Plas Penrhyn. There were the Amberley papers which had come to him on the death of his brother in 1931, a collection whose hundreds of letters gave a vivid portrait of the dominant Russells of mid-Victorian England. There were many scores of letters from Alys and her contemporaries, many hundreds from Ottoline, from Colette, and from the other women in Russell's life. Some of the correspondence was filed in six tall cabinets, but much more lay in nearly a dozen tin boxes, a large wooden packing-case that had once held the Russell silver, and a variety of other files and containers. In all, there were nearly a quarter of a million documents forming the most important single archive of its kind in Britain. In addition there was Russell's library of 5,000 volumes, many of them containing his invaluable annotations.

In the summer of 1963 Russell had received a letter from Lord Adrian, Master of Trinity, suggesting that the College Library "would be a good place for any papers of yours which you might be disposed to leave us for future generations to study ... " He replied cautiously, saying that he would consider the idea and adding, "I should be proud to be in the neighbourhood of Lycidas." This, however, was not to be allowed him. "We now", says Schoenman, "made a decision to create an archive of Russell's letters and documents," which "brought the prospect of very large sums". The first task was to put them into order and catalogue them, a task quite fortuitously started by a young Canadian then preparing a Russell bibliography. Kenneth Blackwell, ending a year's travel in Europe, arrived in Penrhyndeudraeth, and rang Plas Penrhyn for an appointment. The interview was brief. "But as I left the house I chatted with [Russell's] young American secretary," he says. "When he found I knew something about Russell's writings, and had checked with Russell, he asked me to tea that afternoon. The tea lasted three incredibly short hours. Russell was witty, lucid and enquiring. For example I asked him what he thought of De Gaulle, who had just visited Russia. He said: 'Well, I don't know. What do *you* think of him?' "

A few days later Blackwell was hired for a three-week initial sorting of the papers which were to be sold by a special company formed for the purpose by Russell's literary agents. Next the papers were taken from Plas Penrhyn to London – in two vehicles which were first described as armoured cars, and which later achieved the status of a fleet of armoured trucks. In London a team which Blackwell subsequently joined was formed to catalogue the papers and to edit the 340-page description of them which was expected to help their sale.

However, it was soon apparent that the sale would not be easy, at least for the price it was hoped to obtain. The British Museum, so hard-pressed for funds that it could barely keep the world-famous Reading Room properly staffed, was out of the running. The Royal Society, which might have been attracted by some portions of the Archive, was in much the same state. So was Trinity. The University of Texas, which was later to acquire Russell's 1,900 letters to Ottoline from her daughter, may have been doubtful about pouring funds into an organization which spent a good deal of its time condemning President Johnson as a war criminal. Even had it been otherwise, Russell himself was not particularly anxious for his papers to go to the United States. A number of other American universities were tentatively interested but, apart from Russell's attitude, they tended to rule themselves out for other reasons. Thus the University of Chicago and the Massachusetts Institute of Technology put forward a plan under which Chicago would receive the mathematical papers and M.I.T. those dealing with philosophy, a splitting-up of related material which only those at M.I.T. and Chicago really favoured.

At this point there appeared on the scene an unlikely figure representing an even more unlikely buyer. Professor William Ready, librarian of McMaster University, Hamilton, Ontario, had during the previous decade built up an international reputation as an extraordinarily determined buyer of literary material, a man who, starting off with comparatively small funds, had already built up an important group of specialist collections at McMaster. The university's origins lay far back in a Christian school of learning which had come to Hamilton with the help of Baptist funds. Until 1957, when it became a public non-denominational institution, the Governors had been elected by the Baptist Convention of Ontario and Quebec – a curious background for the last resting-place of Russelliana. In addition, Ready himself was a good Roman Catholic, a fact which added an ironic touch to the battle for the papers which now began.

"I wrote to Lord Russell advising him of our interest and beseeching him that whatever happened to the archives they should finally be deposited in a place where they were secure, intact, and available for scholars of all creeds, nationalities, colour or condition," Ready later said. "I described McMaster as well as I could, pointing out its high scientific stature, as well as its record in the arts." He also pointed out that the principal of their University College was a distinguished Cambridge scholar and that their then president, Harry Thode, was a Fellow of the Royal Society. Not unnaturally, he did not mention that President Thode had worked on the bomb at Chalk River during the Second World War and had later become a member of Canada's Defence Research Board. The softening-up process worked successfully and Russell replied cordially.

But Ready still had to find the money. First he persuaded the provincial university librarians that the acquisition would not only add a feather to Ontario's bibliographical cap but would attract a constant stream of visitors. The Ontario librarians in turn advised the Canada Council to support the attempt, while the University of Toronto, which had been eyeing the Archives but was unable to raise the money, agreed to support McMaster's effort. Cyrus Eaton, a student at McMaster in the early years of the century, sent a cheque for 25,000 dollars, Canadian foundations and institutions rallied round, but Ready was still short of the required amount as other contenders in the market began to appear. "*Time* magazine had a story of twelve or more representatives of great institutions, of wealthy individuals bidding against one another in a closed room, and how all eyes widened when, the bids being opened, McMaster University had been given the nod," says Ready. "There were tales of an Arabian sheikh who had been anxious to buy the collection. Meetings around the Mandelbaum Gate; tracks of camel pads in the snow of Snowdonia."

It was clear that if the reserve-price could be paid by McMaster, Russell would be happy to see the Archives end up in Hamilton. But the sellers would be unlikely to wait much longer and Ready was on the verge of co-opting other universities. He still held off, since this would mean breaking up the collection. Then he was visited by the secretary of the Atkinson Foundation. "He asked me how much money I needed to enter the ring with any chance of success," he has said. "I replied 'two hundred and fifty thousand dollars'. He produced a guarantee letter from the trustees, said 'American or Canadian?' and filled in the amount of $250,000 U.S."

Within two months a contract had been signed and the papers were being flown to Canada. In London, more than one learned society protested that they should have been kept in Britain. There were questions in the House of Commons and letters to *The Times*. The unfortunate booksellers whom Ready had used as export agents were fined for breaking the regulations by exporting without a licence letters from Lord John Russell to his son Lord Amberley which were more than a hundred years old. Ready, back in Canada, was questioned about his plans if the British government demanded the return of the papers.

Nothing happened. The papers had arrived at McMaster and were soon being put into order under the devoted control of Kenneth Blackwell, the man who by this time knew more about the papers than Russell himself.

The influx of cash from the publication of Russell's autobiography and the sale of his papers was badly needed since in 1966 he had launched his ill-fated International War Crimes Tribunal. It was to drain funds from the Peace Foundation with impressive speed.

Even before the revelations which came during the last year of the fighting, the idea of investigating alleged American atrocities in Vietnam had become steadily more plausible; handled impartially it could, as events were later to show, have given a damning indictment which all but the most rhinoceros-skinned would have been forced to consider. What happened was that the Tribunal achieved a record of another kind: condemnation from such rare bedfellows as the *New York Times* and the *New Leader* in the United States, and from *Peace News* and the *Daily Mail* in Britain. The condemnation was all the more remarkable since although many of the individual allegations of atrocities made in Russell's name were not proven, his general argument that the Americans were conducting the war with atrocious means did prove to be justified.

In 1959 Norman Birnbaum, then of the London School of Economics, had put forward the idea of a different kind of war-crimes trial. Birnbaum pointed out that John Dewey had before the Second World War, during the Moscow treason trials, been chairman of an investigating commission which showed that the allegations against Trotsky had been fictitious. This had included what was, in effect, a mock trial. "Would you think much of the idea of a mock trial of Messrs. Eisenhower, Kruschev, Macmillan *et al.*?" he went on.

> An indictment could be drawn up on the basis of the Four Power Declaration at the Nuremburg trials: under Nuremburg law, the present chiefs of state are clearly guilty of planning crimes against humanity. They could be invited to defend themselves, either personally or through authorised representatives; in any case, perhaps some will be found who are willing to undertake the defence – authorised or not.

The idea raised doubts. "The example of John Dewey on Trotsky was scarcely a precedent, since he could invoke anti-Soviet feeling and was not concerned to point out sins on the part of the West," Russell replied.

> Almost everybody that I know is prepared to admit faults on one side, not on the other: Suez was wicked, but Hungary was not – or *vice versa*. I am afraid that, if a committee were formed to point out faults on both sides, it would quickly divide into two factions, each critical of only one side, and that any debate between them would only exacerbate differences. I do not think that the example of the Nuremberg trials is any more to the purpose than the example of

Dewey on Trotsky. Only *German* war criminals were tried. It was probably the Russians who committed the Katyn massacre, but no investigation was permitted. I think you show an optimism which I cannot share in supposing that genuinely impartial people could be found to conduct your suggested trial. I think, further, that the way to get Governments to reform is not only to point out sinfulness of past actions but also to point out the possibility of different policies and the imperative necessity of avoiding disaster. I do not mean that Governments are undeserving of censure. I mean only that censure is not the most likely way to induce them to change, and censure alone is likely to be only one-sidedly admitted and therefore to harden existing opposition.

Six years later M. S. Arnoni, editor of the radical U.S. journal, the *Minority of One*, proposed a war-crimes trial specifically dealing with events in Vietnam. "I was interested in your suggestion of an international tribunal to pass judgment on Johnson for his murder of North Vietnamese civilians," Russell replied. "The idea is attractive but it has been our experience that to organise effective international actions involving the sort of people who might be asked to take part in such a tribunal, requires about three months' preparation. Because the situation in Vietnam is changing rapidly and also because our resources are already stretched to the limit, I fear that it will not be possible for me to take up your suggestion."

By the early months of 1966 Russell had changed his tune. Ralph Schoenman had been sent to North Vietnam to collect evidence, and Russell himself was sounding out potential members of a Tribunal which would hear evidence, and adjudicate on, American activities in Vietnam. There is considerable circumstantial evidence that Schoenman was largely responsible for Russell's changed view. But, as in other spheres, he reinforced tendencies already present, while Russell himself had been influenced during the last months of 1965 by the mounting evidence of atrocities in Vietnam, and by the growth of unrest with the war in America itself. He was also – a fact which his enemies were reluctant to concede – a patriot seriously perturbed by the supine attitude of the British government and its reluctance to make any statement which could possibly be construed as critical of American policy. "My belief that Mr. Gladstone was the greatest Prime Minister is equalled only by my certainty that Mr. Wilson is the most despicable," he wrote. "If I were to meet him in Hell, I should have the greatest difficulty in shaking his hand." Thus an inner urging that someone should speak up for Britain had drawn Russell forward almost as much as the voice of Ralph Schoenman.

Preparations went ahead throughout the summer. To start with,

Russell threw overboard what he had previously considered essential: a Tribunal of "genuinely impartial people". Vladimir Dedijer, the author who had been Marshal Tito's delegate to the Paris Peace Conference of 1945, and who was to become the Tribunal's chairman, Jean-Paul Sartre, Isaac Deutscher, were all eminent men in their own specialities; but if their impartiality was to be even faintly credible they would all have to renounce their known political persuasions. The same was true of the supporting team which included Laurence Daly, future General Secretary of Britain's National Union of Mineworkers; Lazaro Cardenas, former president of Mexico; Simone de Beauvoir; and Amado Hernandez, Poet Laureate of the Philippines.

Any lingering belief in the impartiality of the Tribunal's members has been dispelled by Schoenman. He was to be Secretary-General. And he has described them as "a partial body of committed men", the test of the Tribunal's proceedings as "the data and their verifiability ... not a fake impartiality which no judge in any trial has ever possessed". The idea that the Tribunal might take a more unbiased attitude than the legendary French headline, "Assassin to be tried", was removed by a statement issued in Russell's name, calling for the investigation of individual crimes, and demanding the trial of "the war-criminals – Johnson, Rusk, McNamara, Lodge, and their fellow-criminals". The language was not only stupidly emotive; it went on to speak of those who "send American soldiers to Vietnam as company cops", words that came strangely from a Fellow of Trinity and a master of English prose. The assumption of guilt before trial, and the extension of the Tribunal's activities to cover not only specific alleged atrocities about which evidence could be gathered, but also high policies of state about which little could be known, were alarming signs that what could have been a courageous and impartial investigation was sinking to the level of a propaganda exercise. The Tribunal in fact became a powerful weapon in the hands of those who claimed that Schoenman had really taken over from Russell.

Worse was to come. For it was soon obvious that Russell had abandoned any belief that the Tribunal should concern itself with the alleged crimes of both sides; alleged American and South Vietnamese atrocities would be investigated but not those of the North Vietnamese or the Vietcong. Many potential supporters were disillusioned and one long letter of protest summed up the objections in a sentence: "But is it the position of the Tribunal that the N[ational] L[iberation] F[ront] is completely innocent? that when a little child is killed by American napalm it is clearly a crime, but that if that same child were killed by an N.L.F. terrorist it would be no crime at all?"

The question, sent to Russell, was answered by Schoenman. Those who had joined the Tribunal, he replied, did not consider the National

Liberation Front's resistance to the United States as terror any more than they would have regarded the resistance of the Jews against Nazism.

A declaration that violence was not necessarily a crime could easily be justified by the secretary of a man who had contemplated finding a *casus belli* with the Russians and who could see a war with them for world government as "a truly great cause to fight for". Nevertheless, it added to the difficulty of claiming that the Tribunal should be taken seriously.

By November 1966, Russell was ready to announce its setting-up. This he did in London, at a press conference stage-managed by Schoenman. It was not a happy occasion. Russell had already had a heavy day, was tired, and arrived half an hour late, giving Schoenman a chance to deny some earlier statements that he himself had made. When Russell arrived he walked slowly up a crowded aisle, picking his way over the TV wires and greeting journalists he knew. He then read a short statement about not committing "the crime of silence" over Vietnam, and left as he had entered. "The journalists were very disappointed that he did not stay to answer questions," says one observer, "and they surmised it was because, as Schoenman's puppet, he was too senile but to repeat a prepared script. I was angered by the comments to this effect around me as I had talked to Russell for hours only some weeks earlier and knew that he could have been adequate to the occasion if it had not been so poorly managed; a man of 94 should not be submitted to the glare and heat of up to half a dozen sets of TV spotlights in a crowded room." Even as sympathetic an observer as David Horowitz, a director of the Peace Foundation for some years, was forced to admit that time was taking its toll. "Between [1961] and the Tribunal the body had begun to give up," he wrote.

> No longer could he speak extemporaneously before the public; the eyes had weakened, and he read only with immense effort under the television lights; the voice was thinner and seemed at times ready to disappear forever; the dignified stride had collapsed into an unseemly shuffle; and the face often became slack, giving a false impression of vacuity that the incomparably quick mind still burning inside must have found especially painful to bear.

The Tribunal was now set up as an independent body. The Bertrand Russell Peace Foundation was transformed into a limited company which lent the Tribunal the necessary funds to start work. Schoenman formally became Secretary-General of the Tribunal while Russell himself understood that he "would not be expected to take part in the administration of the Tribunal's affairs". Instead he devoted himself to raising money, public support, and resolving internecine grievances.

Troubles quickly arose and before the end of the year Schoenman was complaining to Sartre in Paris that the Tribunal's executive committee had met and discussed the rules under which the Tribunal was to operate, but that he, the Secretary-General, had not even been told of this. Sartre, for his part, later told Schoenman, "You can't hide behind Russell and keep him in your pocket at the same time." Shortly afterwards, Schoenman was apologizing to Dedijer, also in Paris, for the failure to send documents and other material.

Soon there was more trouble, following Schoenman's tour in North Vietnam, and he now met with serious difficulty in travelling about Europe in search of a site where the Tribunal could begin its hearings. Britain was ruled out, since the Labour government had already stated that it would not allow entry into the country by the North Vietnamese who were willing to give evidence. However, Russell's plans still remained optimistic, not to say grandiose. "The proposal is for a session in New York in July, in Japan in August and in Auschwitz in September," he wrote to Dedijer, who was later to arouse Russell's wrath by declaring that the next session would be held in the Vatican.

Finally, Switzerland was chosen for the first session, but after a hall had been booked the Swiss government banned the Tribunal from the country. Next came France, but the chosen hotel cancelled the booking. Finally, on 23 April, de Gaulle announced that the government opposed the Tribunal being held anywhere in France.

In desperation the Tribunal turned to Sweden, and took evidence in Stockholm. Then they turned south to Denmark. Their judgment was a foregone conclusion. By this time it was more widely suspected that the war in Vietnam was being waged by methods even more dubious than those used in the incineration of Lübeck in 1942, of Hamburg in 1943 and of Dresden in 1945. Moreover there was creeping into American opinion a growing doubt about the need for the war anyway. However, it was neither of these factors, nor even public apathy, which resulted in the Tribunal's verdict being accepted only by dedicated members of the Left. More important was the uncomfortable feeling that the verdict would have been the same whatever the evidence.

If this made the issue of the Tribunal's judgment an anticlimax, there was something else which disturbed those among the Left who, with ears closer to the ground, heard the chaos behind the scenes.

Even before the Tribunal had got properly under way, its members had moved the executive base across the Channel to Paris although their Secretary-General, Ralph Schoenman, remained in England. The rest followed on. Thus on 19 May 1967 Schoenman received a cable from his Tribunal in Paris telling him to release their verdict in London. This was not possible since he had not yet received the text. The request, he cabled back, could not be implemented because of this neglect.

The confusion was symptomatic of much more. Early in May Russell had sent a long letter to members of the Tribunal protesting against proposals that they should not honour their financial debt to the Peace Foundation. "I have spent nearly all my time since our November session in writing and broadcasting about the Tribunal and helping to raise money through my writing," he said.

> This money has been made available as it arrived, though on several occasions the Foundation was in severe financial difficulties. But by earning advances on future work, by spending money due for future taxation and by the entire Board of Directors of the Foundation taking personal liability for the loans of the Foundation to the Tribunal, we have somehow managed. I have to admit quite frankly that I was never anxious to lend too much money to the Tribunal because I saw little evidence that it was raising money energetically and I feared that an easy income from the Foundation would only confirm the Tribunal in this pattern. The Tribunal and its working committee, however, took a series of decisions without stating how these would be financed, and left the Foundation in the position of having to find the money for them or see the Tribunal collapse in public ridicule.

Ten days later he was complaining to another member of the Tribunal that he could "no longer tolerate remaining silent". There were complaints of an attempt to strangle Schoenman, of threats to other associates of Russell, and of statements to the press that Russell's own remarks were discrediting the Tribunal. "These unauthorised statements", Russell went on, "have brought the Tribunal to ridicule and have called in question the association I have with a Tribunal which I inaugurated, supported in all ways, and of which I am an Honorary President." What Schoenman called a very sordid and vindictive internal struggle, during which the Tribunal members in Paris had tried to carry on without intervention from their Secretary-General, was now coming to an end.

Before the year was out, internal reorganization had given the Tribunal a new lease of life and it was soon embarking on investigation of alleged crimes outside Vietnam. It had been a plausible idea, but if it was to be taken seriously by any but the already converted it needed a ballast of objectivity and a stiffening of competent organization which it palpably lacked. Moreover it had quickly bored a large monetary hole in Russell's Peace Foundation when this was poorly equipped to deal with the problem of staying financially afloat.

24

Once More His Own Man

When the Tribunal delivered its judgment, Russell was ninety-five. "As regards health," he had written a decade earlier, "I have nothing useful to say since I have little experience of illness. I eat and drink whatever I like, and sleep when I cannot keep awake. I never do anything whatever on the ground that it is good for health, though in actual fact the things I like doing are mostly wholesome." Age eventually began to qualify that statement, but when he began to complain that it was more difficult to get over gates, he still remained remarkably fit. He continued to smoke the "Golden Mixture" he had bought from the same London suppliers for seventy years and told an inquirer that he had smoked a pipe for seventy-five years, adding, "I do not expect to stop until everything stops for me." Even with strong glasses, he was no longer able to read many ordinary books. But he had an insatiable appetite for the large-print volumes, three rows of which, mainly detective stories, stood by his bed near the "Observer" series on birds, flowers and shells, looking across to the portraits of Leibniz and Frege he had known for three-quarters of a century. He was visited regularly by the local G.P., and occasionally by a masseur, but his approach was expressed in a letter asking Lord Amulree to accept him as an occasional patient. "I am now in my ninety-fifth year and am fortunate to enjoy good health," this said. "I am, naturally, anxious to obtain the best possible advice on continuing this situation."

It was not to go on much longer. Shortly before Christmas 1967, he went down with a bad bout of pneumonia. For a fortnight it was touch and go. Then, in the New Year, he began to recover slowly, pulling himself back to what he hoped would be his previous invigorating form. It was not to be quite like that. Until this attack he had always taken in his stride the two steps which led from the sitting-room on to the balcony from which the view of the Snowdon peaks spread out eastwards. Now he went carefully, and with a stick. Now, moreover, he took to a wheelchair.

At last he had to resign himself to old age. Lady Russell helped a lot, almost persuading him that he was really only taking a holiday. He knew better, and reluctantly admitted that he would at last have to give up a full-time working life; there would be no more books, no more campaigns, no more projects. "From his childhood onwards he had learned to find his safety, and his sense of permanence, in his work and in the world out-of-doors," says his son Conrad, with whom he had by now become reconciled. "In his last two years, after he had finished his *Autobiography*, and when he could no longer walk more than a few yards from the front door, he had to learn what was in many respects a new way of living. It was perhaps the greatest triumph of his mental resilience that he learnt it, and in his last year was perhaps happier than he had ever been before."

His happiness was not entirely due to the wife whose devotion enabled her to surmount the problems of nursing a very old and fragile husband. In his last two years, and even more forcefully during his last few months, his mental independence erupted in a succession of actions and statements that would have been remarkable at any age. At last he realized that the stories of his conversion to Communism, of his becoming a puppet in the hands of his staff, really must be proclaimed as the distortions they were. The main course of his actions, the misjudgments as well as the triumphs, had been his own more often than not. Thus the record of his last two years is a strangely contrasting patchwork of cosy family parties, of carefully cosseted excursions around the neighbourhood, of last visits and goodbyes, yet of letters and statements setting down his unshakeable convictions. At sunset there was still lightning about.

One regularly repeated tale had it that he had changed his mind about religion. "Thank you for bringing to my attention these continuing rumours of my imminent conversion to Christianity," he wrote to the American Humanist Association. "Evidently there is a lie factory at work on behalf of the after-life. How often must I continue to deny that I have become religious. There is no basis whatsoever for these rumours. My views on religion remain those which I acquired at the age of sixteen. I consider all forms of religion not only false but harmful. My published works record my views." Nevertheless, his earlier indifference to upsetting people had mellowed. In his nineties he had toyed with the idea of writing an illustrated joke-book about the Bible. But he realized that it would have to cover the New Testament as well as the Old, and would inevitably cause offence. He dropped the idea.

On mathematics, the dominating intellectual love, he could admit only failure to find exact truth. He had been led to think of mathematical exactness as a human dream but had long ago dropped that article of faith. "I try to console myself", he had written a few years earlier, "with the knowledge that mathematics is still the necessary implement for the manipulation of nature." The consolation was comparatively slight. "I set out", he had said a decade or so earlier, "with a more or less religious belief in a Platonic eternal world, in which mathematics shone with a beauty like that of the last Cantos of the Paradiso. I came to the conclusion that the eternal world is trivial, and that mathematics is only the art of saying the same thing in different words."

When it came to the problems of philosophy, his position resembled that of Einstein who in physics had let loose the avalanche of indeterminacy but, with his avowal that "God does not play dice with the world," had refused to admit the implications. Russell, under whose tutelage Wittgenstein had helped found linguistic philosophy, could now only see "behind all the minute argumentation ... a curious kind of arid mysticism".

As for humanity, he had a great love of it. But in the first decade of the century he had written that "no one could pretend that a workingman has as a rule the same equipment for forming sound political opinions as a professional man or a man of leisure". Half a century later he told one interviewer that his attitude to the common man had always been on the verge of contempt, although he tried to judge people kindly. In his eighties he noted that it was a dreadful thing to lay claim to any kind of superiority except in athletics, movies and money-making. And to Gilbert Murray he admitted, "Where democracy and civilisation conflict, I am for civilisation." Once it is admitted, as it must be, that women were as necessary to him as air and sustenance, one fact of Russell's life becomes significant: that the two women for whom he had the greatest love for the greatest time, Lady Ottoline and Lady Constance, both gave him, as he said specifically of Lady Ottoline, "a kind of restfulness and sense of home-coming", when he "came in contact with [her] aristocratic habits of mind". And he later confessed, "My ideal age was 18th-century France just before the Revolution. I should like to have been a French aristocrat shortly before the storming of the Bastille. Eighteenth-century rationalism was delightful and humane. Oppression was real but not sufficiently severe to prevent inspired rebellion from the thinkers of the time."

He still enjoyed life, particularly Christmas, when he would appear in the full-length red-silk robe which an admirer had sent him from China, and with Lord John's gold watch splendidly decorating his chest. He also enjoyed the birthdays on which, year after year, there still arrived a bunch of red roses from Colette. "I am enjoying [them] both in themselves & as symbols," he wrote in May 1967. "They are still blossoming cheerfully, & there are still buds for the future." In May the following year he was recovering from flu so there was no party; only Edith, his son Conrad, his friends the Crawshay-Williamses and his new secretary, Christopher Farley. On the birthday-cake Edith had arranged one row of nine candles and another of six; he succeeded in snuffing them in about three puffs. Then, after his health had been drunk in champagne, he replied, "I am pleased and gratified that you have so generously drunk my health in my champagne. And I am convinced that I shall feel a great deal better for it ... I shall henceforth recommend this treatment to all doctors." Then he proposed that they should drink "To the Silent Ones" – those in Eastern Europe, or behind the walls of Pentonville or Brixton, who no longer had the freedom to speak aloud.

He still dealt personally with much correspondence and he still received visitors. To an inquiry about a letter from Tagore quoted in his *Autobiography* he replied that he could not agree with that philosopher: "His talk about the infinite is vague nonsense. The sort of language that is admired by many Indians unfortunately does not, in fact, mean anything at all." To Hugh Scanlon, he wrote of his enthusiasm for Scanlon's support of Workers' Control, adding, "I am delighted that there is a resurgence for the Movement for Industrial Democracy which is so necessary if we are to create a socialist opposition in this country." His contempt for what he believed to be wrong still burned brightly, and his secretary has described how one day Russell received a letter which he felt contained a dishonest proposition. "At once he dictated a brief reply and having signed it immediately, he instructed me to take it straight to the post office," Farley has said. "Unaccustomed to such a practice, I hesitated in the doorway. Russell became visibly distressed. It was clear that he did not think his house quite clean until the offending correspondence had been answered and filed away."

He was quick to condemn publicly the Soviet invasion of Czechoslovakia, and finding that the American *Dialog*, a journal he sponsored, was taking a pro-Soviet line, wrote briskly to withdraw support, declaring that he did not "wish to be associated with what you are publishing, in particular the attack on Mr. Louis Aragon for his stand on Czechoslovakia and the denial of anti-Semitism in the Soviet Union". Independence had its disadvantages. On being asked to intercede for the release of two specific Jews from Russia, since Russell's appeared to be "the only voice outside its frontiers which seems able to reach and influence the Soviet Government", he said he was not optimistic of being able to help. "The situation of Soviet Jews has deteriorated considerably," his secretary replied, "while Lord Russell has made so many criticisms of the Soviet Union that the authorities may no longer heed them."

He still managed to keep abreast not only of politics but of new books on his own subject and one visitor found him checking, in a new book on mathematical logic, the translation of his correspondence with Frege of sixty years earlier. He continued to tell good stories, and was fond of describing his meeting with Zena Dare, the great beauty of the English stage between the wars. Neither had recognized the other. "She seems quite beautiful," Russell had remarked to a friend afterwards, only to learn that Miss Dare had observed, "He seems quite intelligent."

His memory was still exceptional, and Christopher Farley remembers that in the course of conversation Russell mentioned how the existence of *pi*, the constant ratio between the circumference and the diameter of a circle, had been known in Biblical times. But they had got it wrong, he said, and went on to quote chapter and verse. When Farley discovered that the quotation was word-perfect he asked when Russell had last read that particular book of the Bible. "Oh, thirty or forty years ago," replied the man who believed in knowing his enemies.

For his ninety-seventh birthday he held two celebrations. One day was reserved for younger friends, to whom he recounted his favourite stories. On the other, there was the family birthday-party which included Conrad and his wife, their young son, and Franz Hampl, a Czech mathematician who was doubling the roles of male nurse and general helper.

The red roses arrived from Colette, and his neighbours, Michael Burn and his wife, brought a large and curiously elegant sheet of parchment. It had, they assured Russell, been left on the lawn of Plas Penrhyn that very morning by a dove and a golden eagle. The document was studded with flowers, wished Russell the best of birthday wishes, and was signed by a distinguished company that included Hume, Plato, Voltaire, Spinoza, Beethoven, John the Baptist, Descartes and St Francis of Assisi, Shakespeare, Queen Elizabeth and the Peterloo martyrs. Michael Burn had added the collective signature of the Battle of Britain pilots because, he said, "they had risked and lost their brief lives in causes for which Russell had spent his long one". Someone had added Nell Gwyn. Edith had added the Queen of Sheba, and others whose good wishes she knew Russell would appreciate – the architects of Chartres Cathedral, the sculptors of certain Buddhas and the unknown author of "O western wind, when wilt thou blow".

It was an imaginative touch which Russell thoroughly appreciated. He needed the uplift. For now, in his ninety-eighth year, he was at last to be driven towards an irreparable breach with Ralph Schoenman. During the previous two years he had become progressively disillusioned with the young man's achievements, increasingly aware that although his former secretary was an independent director of the Peace Foundation, an independent Secretary-General of the War Crimes Tribunal, he was still looked upon as Russell's mouth-piece. Still Russell did nothing – "a grave tactical mistake", as he admitted, made partly out of respect for the young man's energy, partly out of loyalty to a former employee, partly because he found it difficult really to believe that anyone could seriously assume that a Russell did not make up his own mind.

However, a decided change in his attitude had taken place by the summer of 1969. On 9 July he revoked Schoenman's appointment in his will as one of his Trustees and Executors. Ten days later he wrote formally breaking off relations. And on 6 September, Schoenman was removed from the board of the Bertrand Russell Peace Foundation by a vote taken at an Extraordinary General Meeting. Then Russell tried to obtain from Schoenman an undertaking that he would not use his name "in any way whatsoever" to suggest that their activities were linked. Schoenman has another story. "The convergence of Russell's incapacity, my inability to return to the country and the sudden advent of substantial funds made things easier for hangers-on who preferred that the organisation concentrate on British questions, foregoing the risks attendant upon involvement with revolutions abroad," he later countered. "Russell's wife was well-disposed to this point of view."

Before the summer was over Russell had a touch of bronchitis, and was still working off its side-effects when at the end of August Crawshay-Williams took him and Edith for a drive up the Ffestiniog Valley. The car was open and although it was a hot summer's day Russell, still very tottery, kept his coat on. It was to be his last sight of the mountains except from the grounds of his home. "When we got him out of the car on returning to Plas Penrhyn, with his feet on the ground and standing up with his back to the wheel-chair," Crawshay-Williams noted in his diary," he wanted to turn round so as to see the chair before getting into it. Franz Hampl said: 'The chair's just behind you; all you've got to do is to sit in it'. We held Bertie's shoulders. Sceptical, reluctant, he began to sit. 'You expect me to sit down on thin air, do you?' he said."

Throughout the next few weeks, as autumn began to close in, he still made no public statement about Schoenman. In 1966, when he had cut the painter, he had failed to declare openly that the young man was henceforth sailing under his own flag. Now, once again, he kept quiet, apparently ready to compound the tactical mistake. This state of affairs might have continued had he not now been shown a three-page, closely typed letter which Schoenman had written to two co-directors of the Peace Foundation some months earlier. In this document Schoenman attacked Russell's description of him in the autobiography, and claimed, among other things, that Lady Russell had gone out of her way to set her husband against him.

Yet from the evidence it seems more likely that if any criticism is to be made of Lady Russell, it is that at every stage of the relationship her Quaker background induced her to give Schoenman the benefit of the doubt, to plead extenuating circumstances, and to hope, with Russell, that he would change his ways. So much so that in one discussion Russell said to her, almost in exasperation, "We must say 'No' to Ralph sometime."

Russell was shown the revealing statement from Schoenman late in November. He discussed the situation with his wife. There was now the possibility that Schoenman would attempt to make public his own version of events and it was therefore considered essential to record the facts while they could still be told by Russell himself.

Consequently on Monday 8 December he told Edith that he wanted to put on record the details of his relationship with Schoenman since the day he had arrived dripping wet in Plas Penrhyn more than nine years earlier. He dictated and Edith typed. He initialled each sheet of the memorandum and a few days later signed a note, typed on a different machine, which said, "This is *my* memorandum. I told my wife what I wished her to type and she has typed it. I have read it over to myself twice carefully and she has read it aloud to me once. I entirely endorse it as being mine and what I wished to say."

The nub of Russell's verdict was given in a few lines:

> I early recognised [Schoenman's] lively instinct for self-dramatization, his swash-buckling assumption of the importance of his own role in the centre of the stage. His conviction of his unshakeable belief in the penetration and breadth of his understanding were obvious. I did not for some time, however, grasp the closely related characteristic of his utter incapability of imparting reliable information. His reports of people's reactions and his observations were – and unfortunately, I fear, still are – very often excessively and misleadingly incorrect and his quotations must always be verified. I was impressed by his courage, both moral and physical, although it too often flouted necessary caution and resulted in unnecessary provocation. And I was impressed by his generosity in helping anyone of whom he thought well or thought to be suffering injustice, although it often led to useless waste of effort and money, both of which might have been far more advantageously spent.

He might have left it at that. Most men would, especially in Russell's situation, knowing the damage done and with little time left to put it right. But instead he paid a tribute to Schoenman's *joie de vivre*. "In fact," he added, "in a world made up largely of people who act, if at all, only upon second or more thoughts, and guard themselves well with subsidiary clauses, his companionship was as welcome as a delicious fresh breeze on a muggy day."

This was the introduction to a detailed record of Schoenman's impact on the peace movement. "The balance of his accomplishments over his drawbacks has only gradually been reversed," Russell said towards the end of the 7,000-word document.

The "Private Memorandum concerning Ralph Schoenman" was intended for publication only if Schoenman gave his own version of the story. For public consumption Russell released a brief notice announcing that Schoenman had not been his secretary for some three and a half years, and that for considerably more than three months he had had no contact with him and no knowledge of his activities.

Some of Russell's supporters hoped for something more. Among them was Michael Scott, who felt strongly that Russell should give himself additional protection. Russell wrote to Scott telling him of the Memorandum, and shortly afterwards sent him a copy. As events turned out, it was not kept as a counterblast to whatever Ralph Schoenman might publish. Seven months after Russell's death Michael Scott, believing that Russell's account of the Russell–Schoenman relationship should be made public, took his copy to *Black Dwarf*, a British underground newspaper, which immediately published it. The *New Statesman* did the same a week later. On publication of the Memorandum in the *New Statesman*, some 5,000 of whose 100,000 copies were distributed in the United States, Schoenman stated that it was a "ludicrous concoction by those who seized control of the Bertrand Russell Peace Foundation". Lady Russell and two of the directors of the Foundation, Christopher Farley and Ken Coates, stated it was authentic. Before the end of the year the Memorandum had been produced as a pamphlet by the Queensland, Australia, branch of the Foundation. Its existence was recorded in such standard reference works as the National Union Catalog, the British Humanities Index and the Social Sciences and Humanities Index, and a copy of the pamphlet lodged in the Library of Congress, Washington.

Publication of the document cleared the air. But it left two important questions unanswered. Why had Russell, who now stated that he had dispensed with Schoenman's services as secretary in 1966, kept the fact secret? How much that was issued under Russell's name was in fact written by Russell?

The answer to the first question is simple enough. In 1966 Russell had not "sacked" Schoenman, as could be implied by his 1969 statement. He had already by that time grave suspicions about his efficiency: now he would see how he worked on his own. It was of course giving a hostage to fortune; but Russell had never been one to avoid risks and he was unlikely to change tack in his nineties. Schoenman may have "taken the bit in his teeth and careered away unrestrained as Secretary-General of the War Crimes Tribunal". But it was Russell who had voluntarily dropped the reins. One writer has asked why Russell could not then have "published a simple letter explaining that Schoenman was still working for the Bertrand Russell Peace Foundation, but was not his personal secretary any more". The answer is that Russell, ninety-four, and still engaged on a multitude of activities, just failed to see the necessity.

As to how far he was responsible for what was issued over his name, the position as he described it in his autobiography is correct as far as it goes: "In point of fact, what goes out over my name is usually composed by me. When it is not, it still presents my opinion and thought. I sign nothing – letters or more formal documents – that I have not discussed, read and approved."

To this admission of collegiate authorship, three riders should be added. That at times, in the press of circumstance, trying to cope with more than he could properly handle, Russell almost certainly signed statements that he would, with more time and thought, have altered into less wild language; that he might well forget the odd occasion when he had signed without reading; and that in London an eye-witness has reported seeing sheets of letterhead with Russell's signature two-thirds of the way down an empty page.

These qualifications should be kept in proportion. Schoenman, and at times others, no doubt, added their own fancy touches to the output; at times these caught the eye. But the basic beliefs which were reiterated again and again from Plas Penrhyn, and from the Peace Foundation, were with comparatively few exceptions those of Bertrand Russell.

The Memorandum was a remarkable document, marshalling the complicated facts of the previous seven years with exceptional lucidity. Whatever help came from Edith in the checking of facts, or in the confirmation of dates, the impartial weighing of for's and against's, the illuminating phrase, and the invigorating professionalism were Russell's own.

As in previous decades, he went from the crest to the trough, physically now as he had once gone mentally. A fortnight later, a few days before Christmas, the bronchial troubles returned and he was again given massive doses of antibiotics. The few personal friends invited for Christmas Day could not be put off, and it was a dispiriting occasion.

When the effects of the drugs dispersed, he sprang back quickly. Within a few days his mind was in working order again. His normal delight in the world was still there, and one morning he cried out with joy at a sudden and unexpected gleam of sun on the snowslopes beyond the estuary. Nevertheless, each day he was getting more tired. To Edith he reflected, "I do so hate to leave this world."

Early in January there arrived a letter from the Sixth Form Society of Wolstanton Grammar School. Years ago they had created the post of Rector for "a distinguished person whom the Society admired". Its only incumbent had been Einstein, and after his death the appointment had lapsed. Now it was to be revived. Would Russell accept? Russell agreed, happy that once again, at this penultimate stage, his name should be linked with Einstein's.

A few days later he renewed his annual subscription for the *Large Type Weekly* of the *New York Times*, with which he had fought so many battles during the last decade.

And on the afternoon of 31 January he called Christopher Farley to his study. He had a message he wished to dictate, to be read to the International Conference of Parliamentarians at Cairo in three days' time. This in itself was unexpected. The message was even more so.

From the closing stages of the Second World War, Russell had argued for the creation of a Jewish State, but since the start of the Israeli–Arab wars with the Arab invasion of Israel in 1948, he had taken a strictly impartial view. Believing there was right on both sides, he had from the first argued for negotiations, however tortuous they might be and for however long they might be necessary. Now he came off the fence, condemning the latest Israeli air-raids on Egypt, and lambasting the Israelis for their treatment of the Palestine refugees. The last political statement that he was to make, it was one of the most controversial:

> The aggression committed by Israel must be condemned, not only because no State has the right to annex foreign territory, but because every expansion is also an experiment to discover how much more aggression the world will tolerate ... We are frequently told that we must sympathise with Israel because of the suffering of the Jews in Europe at the hands of the Nazis. I see in this suggestion no reason to perpetuate any suffering. What Israel is doing today cannot be condoned, and to invoke the horrors of the past to justify those of the present is gross hypocrisy.

Farley typed the statement and brought it back. Russell read it carefully, then signed it in a shaky but legible hand.

The "Message from Bertrand Russell to the International Conference of Parliamentarians in Cairo, February 1970" was in some ways the most remarkable of his many statements. It can well be argued that it showed faulty judgment; that it condemned the Israelis for doing no more than they were forced to do by the realities of life. It can be pointed out, by those with suspicious minds, that Russia was by this time espousing the Arab cause and equipping the Arab armies. Here, it can also be claimed, was a case comparable to that made for bludgeoning Russia into acceptance of post-war nuclear control; a case where logical argument, applied to illogical human affairs, loses both force and sense. To those who see in Israel the heroic figure of one man fighting against five, the message can most easily be written off as one of those inexplicable black holes in Russell's later years. Yet the message itself is quintessential Russell: condemning what he believed to be wrong, equally unperturbed by the protestations of friends or the wrath of foes, overturning the apple-cart in a good cause without the slightest thought of the consequences.

The next day, Sunday, he spent quietly. He seemed to have recovered from the last attack and it was only on the evening of Monday, 2 February, at 7 o'clock, that he felt rather ill. He was dead within the hour.

On 6 February the body was taken from Plas Penrhyn to the Colwyn Bay crematorium in an unadorned oak coffin. There were only some twenty people outside the small red-brick building, but five men instead of four carried the coffin: Brendan Lynch, an earlier C.N.D. supporter, had arrived unexpectedly, and with the family's consent was added to the bearers. There had been a request for no flowers: but on the coffin lay a single bunch of daffodils and irises, with an unsigned message: "In affectionate remembrance".

From Plas Penrhyn, Edith wrote Colette a long, detailed letter and a few weeks later, in mid-May, when the eulogies had been printed and put in the files, the usual bunch of red birthday roses arrived. Edith put them in the usual place, on Russell's desk.

The cool clinical monster of popular fallacy would have liked that.

Appendix

Private Memorandum concerning Ralph Schoenman

[Russell dictated the following memorandum at Plas Penrhyn on 8 December 1969. Four days later he pinned to it a signed note saying: "This is *my* memorandum. I told my wife what I wished her to type and she has typed it. I have read it over to myself twice carefully and she has read it aloud to me once. I entirely endorse it as being mine and what I wished to say."]

I am writing this memorandum concerning Ralph Schoenman, not necessarily for publication, but for reference in case any of my actions in relation to him should be called in question by him or, possibly, by his friends or by anyone else. In part, I am writing it for my own satisfaction since I have been told that he "has it in writing that I am senile" – the implication being that whatever I now do or say in regard to him is said or done, in reality, by someone else using my name. This is not true. My relations to him have been mine from our first meeting when he came to see me at Plas Penrhyn towards the end of July, 1960, to the time of my letter breaking off relations dated 19 July, 1969.

My general analysis of his character is given on page 109ff. of the Allen and Unwin edition of the third volume of my autobiography. In it I tried to give my first impressions of him, both *pro* and *con*, and to indicate what I later discovered. In the first draft of this analysis I was somewhat more adversely outspoken than in the published version, which I toned down partly to avoid both the possibility of libel and the difficulties of recriminations and long-winded "evidence" and "defence", and partly because I did not wish to injure him in any way or his position in working for causes that seem to me to be just.

I had said in the first draft that I found him "surprisingly unlicked". I found him not only impetuous but "aggressive and entirely undisciplined and I realised that these characteristics might well make him seem a 'dangerous young man' ", as I had been warned that he was, "to anyone of whom he did not approve." I early recognized his lively instinct for self-dramatization, his swash-buckling assumption of the importance of his own role in the centre of the stage. His conviction of his unshakable belief in the penetration and breadth of his understanding were obvious. I did not for some time, however, grasp the closely related characteristic of his utter incapability of imparting reliable information. His reports of people's reactions and his observations were – and unfortunately, I fear, still are – very often excessively and misleadingly incorrect and his quotations must always be verified. I was impressed by his courage, both moral and physical, although it too often flouted necessary caution and resulted in unnecessary provocation. And I was impressed by his generosity in helping anyone of whom he thought well or thought to be suffering injustice, although it often led to useless waste of effort and money, both of which might have been far more advantageously spent.

Were I to list his kindnesses to me, the list would be very long and would include many generous deeds that must have cost him dear in worry and work. I found the quickness of his mind, although it made for considerable superficiality and glibness, immensely refreshing as I did his sense of fun and absurdity and irony, although this often created difficulty, unrestrained as it was by any sense of decorum. In fact, in a world made up largely of people who act, if at all, only upon second or more thoughts and guard themselves well with subsidiary clauses, his companionship was as welcome as a delicious fresh breeze on a muggy day. The drawbacks and faults that I found were, I both hoped and thought, such as would be tempered, even erased, by time and experience. They seemed to me to be the outcome of his prodigious driving energy. I underestimated, because, certainly in the early years of our acquaintance, it was rarely shown in my presence, the extreme irritability that sometimes accompanies such quick energy. Only after considerable time did I come to appreciate, as I said in the first draft of my autobiography, "the essential intolerance of opposition and the ruthlessness of his rush towards whatever happened to be his immediate objective." I did not understand in him at first "the ascendancy of the ego over intelligence" which has prevented him from profiting by his experience or his recognised mistakes. He has not grown up – only grown older and more rigidly confirmed in all his characteristics. He has amassed a great deal of experience, but it remains a mass of experience. The pattern of his thought and attitude and action remains the same. I have had occasion to call his attention to this fact increasingly often. He himself sometimes alluded to it in deference to my criticisms.

To the admirable obverse of Ralph's characteristics there is always the reverse to be feared. His optimism, for instance, is invaluable. It permits him to see the practicability of ideas that anyone less hopeful would not even attempt to carry out and to inspire others to work for these ideas. His persistent determination to justify his optimism supports him through set-backs that would discourage most people. But these qualities, so admirable in some respects, are disastrous in other ways. They are in large part responsible for his marked tendency to act as if gestures of support and half-hearted promises of financial help are firm promises which will be confirmed and to count upon them as if they were already confirmed. They are also in large part responsible for his firm belief that if he but tries long and hard enough he can extract support from even the most reluctant target. This, in turn, led to his prolonging the many travels and visits that he made on my behalf or on that of the Foundation to twice, or much more, the length that they had been planned to take. And, in its turn, this extension of his term of absence from my or the Foundation's daily work has left his colleagues to carry on activities that he began but of which he had not fully informed them because he expected to return in time to deal with them himself. Moreover, as he moved about with speed and often with no prior notification to his colleagues, it was impossible to obtain information from him quickly, if at all. As his journeys became more and more frequent during the years that he was working for the Foundation he became more and more difficult to work with. And the fact that the "promises" and "important things" that he was accomplishing so seldom bore observable fruit, tended to bewilder and dismay and ultimately discourage his colleagues.

Linked to, and perhaps causing, this failure to bring promises and schemes to fruition is his failure to retain the respect or liking of most of those with whom he has had any sort of protracted relationship. He has drawn many people into the work of the Foundation. He has inspired many others, some of them of public distinction, to see the work of the Foundation, as I do, as potentially important to the world. But those who have been drawn in gradually drop out or, because they are led to emulate his extravagances, have had to be sacked. Often after several meetings with those who at first were ready to help us he has lost their sympathy by his importunities and exaggerations, arrogance and bad manners.

His self-assurance, which enabled him to carry through actions that would have been impossible without it, also permitted disastrous displays of tactlessness and offensive importunities. These displays were increased by the limelight shed upon our part in the Cuban affair. It inflated his ego more than I at the time realized. When, for instance, he went to China on my behalf at the end of 1962, or the beginning of 1963, he took it upon himself to teach the Chinese whom he met the folly, as he considered it, of the moralities and customs inculcated by their Government. At the first interview given to him and his companion by Premier Chou En lai they were received most courteously and the Premier was friendly and helpful. At their second interview, they were received coldly and severely chided for their behaviour and tactless indiscretions while in China. As their sponsor, naturally, I was rendered suspect. To my distress and to the grave embarrassment of our work, I have never been able to recover the warmth and friendliness formerly accorded me by the Chinese Government.

On the other hand, it was necessary to balance against Ralph's infamous folly in China the fact that he had gone there bearing a message from Nehru which might have provided a way out of the entanglements of the Sino-Indian Border Dispute. Against great odds, he and his companion had managed to reach Nehru and obtain this message from him. And they had also obtained the backing of Mme. Bandaranaike, then Prime Minister of Ceylon. No-one else, I believe, would have done this. No-one else would have believed in the possibility of doing it or had the persistence and hardihood to achieve it. It provides an obvious example of the dichotomy of Ralph's work, admirable up to a point, but finally ruined by impetuous egoistical folly.

Again, I remember that on one of his visits to Israel for me he was given an interview by the Prime Minister, Ben Gurion. He took it upon himself to lecture the Prime Minister on his and the Israel government's shortcomings, a lecture naturally resented by its recipient. He told me of this, as he told me of the Chinese episode, upon his return and I pointed out that I thought that he had been greatly at fault. He agreed with me. I optimistically believed that he would not repeat these quite uncalled-for rude provocations.

The lack of good manners was obvious both in very important matters such as I have just recounted and in the small daily give and take. Discipline was abhorrent to Ralph and he revolted from it instinctively, whether it was administered from without or was recognisably called for from within. No rudeness to someone of whom he disapproved was flinched from by him. No engagement for a fixed time, whether made with an elderly or a distinguished pundit or one of his friends, could be kept on time. He was unable to restrain himself from taking over the conversation if it seemed to be going as he did not wish. Sometimes this was extremely unfortunate. I remember two occasions in particular when this happened. Once when an old friend, with whom I had worked closely and had had many vehement discussions, came to see me concerning our joint work and disagreed with me, Ralph drew the unhappy impression that I was being brow-beaten and not being treated with due deference. Finally, my friend remarked angrily that he had come to see me and not to see Ralph. In the end, I had to ask Ralph to leave us. On another occasion, Ralph believed that I did not hear correctly what was being said by an American acquaintance. He undertook to reply, himself, to all questions put to me until my acquaintance, like my friend, pointed out that the questions were addressed to me. Both these unwarranted intrusions caused considerable trouble. In spite of my remonstrances, I do not think Ralph ever understood the discourteous stupidities of which he had been guilty. The basis of them was perhaps the amiable one, from my point of view, of a wish to protect me, a wish that sometimes led him into fulsome follies or worse, as it did at the end of my speech at the London School of Economics in February, 1965. The wish sprang, I still think, at least in part from a genuine affection for me, and, possibly, admiration, as did his rather fulsome flatteries. I am by no means immune to flattery. It is so rare as to be sweet in my ears. But, if it is very obvious, it can only be irritating and embarrassing. And his was too often so obvious as to make me feel a fool. At first I thought that this was the result of sincere feeling and of his desire to please me, but later I realized that it was also an indirect way of inflating his own ego. On all occasions he used my reputation and any weight that my name might carry to support his own views. And he had a vastly inflated opinion of my importance.

Ralph could not, of course, resist the limelight, even in small and silly ways and even against my expressed wishes. Towards the end of June, 1965, a Lobby against our Government's support of U.S. policy in Vietnam was held at the House of Commons. Ralph wished me to attend it. I did not want to do so as it seemed to me that my views on the Vietnamese War were very well known and that there were plenty of others who would attend the lobby. Finally, however, I gave way to his pleas on condition that, since it was a very serious occasion, I should go quietly and as one of many. Ralph acceeded to this condition. When, however, we reached the House of Commons he produced a large sign that he insisted my being photographed holding. He then proceeded, like a monkey on a stick, to climb all over the motor car in which we had driven up in order to flout the police – I forget now how and why. It was all quite foolish and undignified, and I was ashamed. Again, after his ostracism by the British Government, he appeared here – his last visit – done up in a preposterous "disguise" late one evening. It did not occur to him that in doing so he was exposing me to the charge and penalties of harbouring someone forbidden entry to Britain. He simply could not resist flamboyant showing off.

It was after the Cuban crisis that I began to see more clearly than I had done the effect of the reverse side of Ralph's good qualities. He found himself at that time at the centre of the events in which I took part and have related in my book *Unarmed Victory* and came to regard himself as having been indispensable to me at the time. Perhaps he was. Perhaps I should never have sent the telegrams that gave Khrushchev an opportunity to send his open letter of withdrawal had it not been for Ralph's encouragement and work or for the telegram that he sent to Khrushchev for me in the early hours of 26 October, 1962. By well after midnight I had become very tired by the stress of the day. I went to bed after a long discussion with Ralph and after arranging what might be done in various eventualities. I exacted a promise from him that he would wake me if anything further transpired before breakfast. He did not wake me, but woke my wife to obtain her backing in sending a further telegram to Khrushchev, the possibility of which we had discussed. It was sent and, when I woke, I approved of its having been sent. It did not occur to me that Ralph did more than a good secretary should have been expected to do in the circumstances. I did not know until considerably later that he was most indiscreetly and inaccurately putting it about, or perhaps allowing it to be put about, that the correspondence at that time was all initiated and accomplished by him. At first I did not believe this of him, but reports coming in through the years giving chapter and verse concerning this and similar indiscretions have convinced me that he is not to be trusted where his ego is concerned. I am now forced to believe that he has made it incorrectly evident that he or, to a lesser extent, others have been entirely responsible for various writings and statements published by me since our acquaintance began. Whether he has ever claimed to have written *Unarmed Victory* or not, I do not know. He was out of the country at the time of its writing and, when he returned to London, I asked him to verify and to supply certain facts that I needed. In reply he sent me a long account of the whole affair from his point of view, a book, which he had written. My wife and I spent a day in concentrated search for the few facts that I needed. It was the culmination of his tendency to write full length reports of his impressions instead of the factual notes required of him. Since that egregious performance, he has improved in this respect, in regard to my work at any rate. For my answer to the charge that anyone else, other than I, has written my letters or publications or opened and replied to letters from my correspondents see page 164 of the Allen and Unwin edition of Volume III of my autobiography.

Complaints, all couched as jokes, came to me in the early days as often as might be expected from the people upholding our civil disobedience work. Ralph would, they said, try to bully them into doing what he thought right by saying that he was speaking as my secretary and voicing my wishes. This, I gathered, moved them less than he thought it should. Not till the year following the establishment of the Foundation did I receive serious complaints of him save from people who did not in any case like what we were trying to do. Always, when any complaints of him came to my notice, I discussed them with him and more often than not he admitted them, promising reform and thereafter often referring to my criticisms and his determination to defer to them.

After the establishment of the Foundation in September, 1963, however, the unfortunate traits of which I have spoken became steadily more marked. I began to receive serious complaints from his colleagues and others who were sympathetic to our work. At the end of January, 1964, two of his colleagues called upon me at Plas Penrhyn to beg me to expel him from his position in the Foundation and as my secretary. They spoke for themselves and three other colleagues. Their charges had three main bases: (1) that Ralph was ruining my reputation by telling people that he was responsible for what purported to be my work; (2) that he was playing fast and loose with funds obtained on the ground that they were to be used for my work for peace; (3) that his attitude was dictatorial and his intolerance of opposition intolerable. For these charges they presented chapter and verse. I asked the two who had come to see me and the other three colleagues to put their charges in writing. They did so, and with their letters gave me some precise knowledge that I had not before possessed. I was grateful to them for troubling to do this. Neither they nor any of Ralph's other associates in the work had, up to this time, made to me any serious or precise complaints. When asked why not, they all said, in various ways, that they had not wished to distress me. They did not seem to realize that by delaying they had put me into a very false position and one that would inevitably harm our work if and when I tried to extricate myself from it. They had hinted at dissatisfactions, but had never given me any information with which to face Ralph. I could now, and did, tackle Ralph about the matters that they had brought up. He either denied the charges and the evidence for them *in toto* or explained what the "evidence really sprang from". In view of his rebuttal of the charges, his promise to reform in one case (the charge of wasting money and energy on ill-planned journeys) and, especially, the fact admitted by all his colleagues, that there was no-one else who could take his place and carry on his work, I did not repudiate him. Moreover, I had strong reasons to doubt the reliability and even the capability of most of the complainers. I now suspect that these "reasons" may have been carefully provided by Ralph himself. The most reliable and capable of Ralph's colleagues were unwilling at that time to bear the unpleasant consequences of plain speaking, although later they were driven to do so. Their reluctance has done great harm both to me and, what is worse, to our work.

Among the first serious complaints that I received from anyone not working with us followed the Peace Conference at Helsinki in July, 1965. On 15 July I received a telegram signed by the "Delegation of Federal Republique of Germany" saying: "Speech of your personal representative caused uproar. Strongly rejected by audience. Tremendous provocation of Peace Congress. Bertrand Russell Peace Foundation discredited. Essential you dissociate yourself from Schoenman and his speech. Friendly greetings." (The stops, absent in the telegram, are added by me.) Needless to say, I was exceedingly disturbed by this. As I knew nothing of what had gone on at the Congress, however, I felt that I must await further news and, especially, Ralph's version of the matter, before taking any action. Following the Conference, I received many conflicting reports. Towards the end of July, I replied to one correspondent:

> Thank you for your letter of 26 July and its enclosure. It was kind of you to write expostulating with me directly about the difficulties at Helsinki. As I was not there, I find it hard to straighten out the conflicting reports which have come to me. The statement that you enclose [which she said in her letter "was the speech which caused a great deal of disturbance"] was a message from me. From all that I can gather I make out that it was not this message but a later speech by Mr. Schoenman that caused the difficulty. At any rate, the final resolution adopted by the Congress seems to me admirable – but not the first that they adopted, after the first meeting. It seems to me just possible that strong, obstructionist methods were needed to make the change between the first and the final resolution possible. If so, I am glad that they were taken, though I am sorry that the Foundation has to bear the burden of the disapproval of some of the delegates. As to whether the same end could have been achieved by another and more acceptable manner, I should think probably it could have been, but I was not there, I repeat, in the heat of conflicting points of view. I am glad that you found the Conference a success from many points of view.

From this reply, it may be understood how tangled, apparently prejudiced, and often mistaken, the criticisms were. Those who upheld Ralph's action were hardly clearer. What I made of it all at the time, the above letter indicates. Moreover, as I have said above, the resolution of which I approved was adopted by the Conference after, and not before, Ralph's uproar and was probably owing to it.

A month later, a woman scientist, who had done very commendable work in Britain for international peace, wrote to my wife criticising Ralph's actions at the Conference very severely. She had not herself been present and based her remarks upon those of a delegate who did not himself complain to me.

All these criticisms I took up with Ralph when he returned. He replied that he had gone to Helsinki not only as my representative but, also, as an appointed delegate in his own right. He said that, apart from reading my message, he had made it clear that he was acting and speaking not as my representative but as himself. He was "convinced" – a favourite word of his – that had he not acted and spoken as he did, the Chinese delegates would have had short shrift. He was convinced that the Conference had been rigged by the Americans against the Chinese. It seemed to me, as I told him, that, even if this were so, he might have achieved his end by restraining his temper and being very much more tactful and quiet. He agreed reluctantly that possibly this was so and that he would try not to commit such impetuous and provocative errors again.

A few weeks later, I received a long letter from a friend, who had also been a delegate to Helsinki, describing Ralph's actions and describing how fantastic and fanatical they had appeared to be and, consequently, how harmful to our work. They destroyed, she said, much goodwill towards it and achieved only an immediate and Pyrrhic victory for Ralph's point of view. Again I discussed these matters with Ralph, pointing out clearly that, while the end that he had wished to achieve might have been praiseworthy, his methods of achieving it had been altogether deplorable. He countered by saying that no other methods would have been effective. I disagreed. He promised again to be less violent and ill-mannered in future.

I received a long letter from this same friend a year later. She had been in London for six weeks, during which time, she said, not fewer than twenty-six people, all of whom were sympathetic to my own work, had remarked on the way in which my "image was being tarnished" and my friends alienated by "Ralph's unfortunately arrogant personality plus attitudes and methods which are all too often open to question, I am told, from the standpoint of ethics." These people had asked: "What is the hold this man has over Russell? Is Russell now senile and unable to make his own decisions and so is accepting whatever is put before him? How is it Ralph seems to overrule Russell to continue doing the things Russell himself has personally repudiated?" To my request for specific facts backing up these charges, I received no reply, and they continued to seem quite unreal to me.

A month or two later in this same year, I received a letter of resignation from one of the Directors of the Foundation. In it he said:

> My sympathies and engagement in your work and the aims of the Foundation are what they always were. I feel as strongly about the war in Vietnam as ever. I think that the Bertrand Russell Peace Foundation – with the extra-

ordinary example of your life and work – could become the most important independent intellectual force in the world today.

The reason for my resignation is personal. I feel that Ralph Schoenman has captured the Foundation and turned it into a monolithic expression of his own limited interests and abilities.

Before my resignation becomes official, I would strongly urge that an independent group examine Mr. Schoenman's competence to continue further his sole leadership of the Foundation. I also feel that an independent group of accountants should make a report to the board of directors concerning both income and disbursement over the last three years.

Believe me, Lord and Lady Russell, that resigning at this moment is painful. I also find it painful to be unable to conclude the film about you which I have begun. I have notified Schoenman of this on four separate occasions in writing; I believe that the raw materials of the film, as now unedited, is of great value. As of today, Schoenman has not answered any of my letters concerning its disposition. I feel that it is improper for me to continue physical ownership of the negative and film. Will you be kind enough to let me know what should be done with it.

I should at that time willingly have consulted accountants and an independent group of individuals as to Ralph's administration of funds and general competence. But where could I find such a group? As to the matter of the film, Ralph and his colleagues told quite a different story from that told above. We were finding it difficult to extract the film from its maker in spite of many letters to him asking to have it sent to the Foundation. I made clear my belief that it was necessary to have accountants audit the accounts of the Foundation.

Until that time, though I had received other complaints, few had given me precise information that could not, and was not, explained away by Ralph. A good example, and a very nice letter, of this sort of vague accusation, came to me from a young man unknown to me in May, 1967:

I have an unusual letter to write, so may I in advance beg your patience and forgiveness.

I have been engaged in the activities of the Hampstead C.N.D. and the Camden Committee for Peace in Vietnam during the past two years, and, more recently, Hampstead Labour Party.

Inside and outside the committees I have met a great many people holding a great many views, although naturally almost all fall within that part of the spectrum called the Left. I have found however two things that almost everybody has in common, one is a profound respect for you, the other is dislike of Ralph Schoenman.

I certainly have no doubts concerning his dedication to your work, it is his public presentation that is in question. I wish I could give you specific examples of what I mean, but this is very difficult. There is a certain conceit, a certain unwarranted hostility towards people that goes ill with his position. My impression of Mr. Schoenman is general, as are the impressions of most people, but such as it is it is a bad one. I would not presume to write to you thus were I alone in this feeling.

I am vague on the cause, perhaps I can better illustrate the effect. I have a friend who holds a very responsible position, has a most pleasant disposition, and excellent opinions. I remarked to him on the photograph of you on your verandah in the Observer earlier this year. He agreed with me, an excellent picture, but added that Ralph Schoenman was probably just out of sight propping you up. He was half in jest, but others make similar remarks and are serious. The spite, or cynicism, of such remarks is not directed at you but at Mr. Schoenman.

My purpose is to bring to your attention something that I find very disheartening. Had I not met many other people who share my opinion I would not presume to write to you.

I must say I intend no harm or calumny to Mr. Schoenman, but knowing how widespread my feeling is I think it has to be of some importance.

I hope you will not think me impertinent, for I am sir, with the greatest respect, yours most faithfully.

Such generous and obviously sincere criticisms as the foregoing were extremely disturbing and carried entire conviction. But it was quite impossible to make Ralph understand them. His reply was to the effect that anyone who worked with energy for the ends that I desired would be more than likely to incur such criticism. And it seemed to me that there was a great deal of truth in this reply. I could only beg Ralph to be gentler and more tolerant in his presentation of our views and beliefs.

As I watched the development of the War Crimes Tribunal in 1967 doubt became even stronger in my mind. Ralph was appointed the Secretary General of this Tribunal. I watched his doings with greater objectivity than I had been able to do formerly since he was acting, not as my secretary or representative, but as an executive of an organization which I entirely supported though in the running of which I took no active part. I had been increasingly aware for some time that, though Ralph was invaluable in developing an idea to the point of practicability, he was disastrous to that idea when he attempted, himself, to carry it out. This belief was confirmed by his actions as Secretary General and by the unnecessary quarrels and muddles largely created, I understood, by him. Again, the dichotomy was visible: it is quite possible that the Tribunal would never have got off the ground had it not been for his intense efforts; but had his efforts been accompanied by even a little restraint and considered planning and with less provocation to those who did not approve of his methods or of the Tribunal itself, the latter might have accomplished as great – and it was great – a work as it did with far less cost in human frustration and futile work as well as in money.

I felt that his display of egoism and flouting of advice, especially of advice given by his colleagues, at this time and in the following months when he flew about the world, as it seemed to me, heedlessly, rendered him only a liability to the Foundation. But the Foundation had become, in November, 1966, a limited company. The change had my entire approval. The company was administered by directors of whom I was not one. I had no executive position in it. It was, consequently, no part of my business to retain or to dismiss Ralph except as my secretary. And he ceased to be my secretary in 1966.

I felt that Ralph should be dismissed from the Foundation. I had for some time insisted that he should not speak either as my secretary or my representative except on such occasions as we had specifically agreed that he should do so. I reiterated this in a letter in 1966. He assured me that he honoured this decision of mine. I constantly, however, heard and read of his having made pronouncements as my secretary or representative. He pointed out that this was not his fault, that, in spite of his denials, others took it for granted that he was still my secretary. Perhaps this was true. In any case, I could do no more than urge him to make it very clear that he was not speaking or acting for me. I felt that I might or might not agree with what he said or did. I wrote to him in 1967 on this subject in categorical terms, such as I had used only in speech theretofore.

The Directors of the Foundation company were not even yet fully convinced that he could no longer be useful to the work and was harming it. I had frequent discussions with some of them about the matter. They appeared to feel that it would make their position as colleagues of Ralph more difficult were. I myself to break with him. They feared also, I learned, that if I did so, he would retaliate in ways that would not only hurt my feelings but would harm my work. I did not know at this time that this was one, and perhaps the chief, of their reasons for their cooler than luke-warm reception to my wish to break with him. Nevertheless, I now think I should have broken with him several years ago. Instead, I temporised. I made a grave tactical mistake: in my desire to put my attitude towards him and my criticisms quite clearly before him and yet in no way harm the efficiency of his work as the directors had made me feel I might do, I agreed with my wife that she should make the criticisms to him in my presence and that I would merely agree with them. It was a foolish plan. Unfortunately, his assurance was such that he took refuge in the belief that my wife was persuading me to oppose and mistrust him. I soon realized that all I was doing by this roundabout method was confirming in him the very characteristics that I most deplored. When, in 1969, I learned of what I had not suspected hitherto, that, consciously or, again, through over-optimism, he was indulging on behalf of the Foundation in what can only be termed dishonest means of accumulating funds for his work, I could no longer continue to support him in any way. He was, without authority, selling the rights of books, refusing to send on funds owing to the Foundation in London, attempting to divert funds payable to it from the sale of my archives, insisting that English tax laws be flouted, and employing other such discreditable means. Perhaps I should have recognized this tendency towards financial unscrupulousness in Ralph earlier, for I had had occasion to remonstrate with him a number of times when it seemed to me that he was sailing very close to the wind. For instance, he arranged with the editor of one journal to pay a certain sum for the right to publish statements and articles by me hitherto unpublished. He then sent these articles and we received the money for them. But he sent them to other journals which occasionally, owing to their dates of appearance, published them before the editor with whom he had made the original contract could get them out. Naturally, this editor was angry. And so was I. I quarrelled with Ralph about it, but failed to convince him. At the time I felt that I had to support Ralph. I now believe I was mistaken in this.

During the past two years, since he has been forbidden entrance to Britain, he seems to have been attempting to carry out his ideas without reference to the advice and needs of his colleagues in the Foundation. Certainly, he has flouted my criticisms, paying no attention to them save to pronounce them ill-based. His actions have reenforced the confirmation that the War Crimes Tribunal has given to my belief as to where his value lay when he was still valuable. But his actions since 1967 have become so egregious that he appears to me no longer to have any value in carrying on the work that I believe the Foundation to be engaged in and which I think should be done. It is for his colleagues to give the facts of their difficulties in working with him. My own reasons for breaking with him I have tried to make clear in this memorandum and to indicate to a slight degree in my autobiography. I have given them directly to Ralph himself in the past, especially on the few occasions when he has visited me here in the last three or four years. I have referred to them in my last letters to him, copies of which I think are in my files along with other correspondence addressed to me by him and others. I am particularly sorry to have had to make this open breach with Ralph because I fear that it will distress his parents whom I both like and respect – unless, of course, they can take refuge in the belief that I have been persuaded, or even forced, to make it by my wife and the other wicked people who surround me.

The question of cardinal importance that has been put to me is why did I not break with him earlier. I did not do so because, until the last few years he was the only person who could and would carry out the work that I thought should be done. The balance of his accomplishments over his drawbacks has only gradually been reversed. His faults and mistakes were of less importance than his ability to turn vision to practicable effect and his courage and optimism in carrying out our ideas. When, sometime after the Cuban debacle, he finally took the bit in his teeth and later careered away unrestrained as Secretary General of the War Crimes Tribunal, I became increasingly doubtful of his usefulness to the work and remonstrated with him both frequently and severely. Since his methods, however, have become importunately open to question and, consequently, intolerable, during the last two years, and during the last year can only be termed dishonest, I have felt it necessary to make a definitive break with him.

I did this in my letter to him of July, 1969, to which I received no reply. Towards the end of November, 1969, I was obliged to write again in an endeavour to extract an undertaking that he would cease using either my name or my wife's as he has been doing to support his own work. And in the past few days, I have found it necessary to prepare a public statement of repudiation, since I must, if possible, dissociate myself and my wife from all Ralph's actions in the minds of all men who will listen.

Russell

Postscript:

Had I seen the letter which Ralph wrote to two of his co-directors on 29 June, 1968, earlier I would have unhesitatingly broken definitively with him at once. But I was not shown this until late in November, 1969. It is a preposterous document. But in it he presents his point of view on our association at length. It therefore deserves examination. In it he objects to what I said of him in my autobiography on the ground that it is "a betrayal of all the years I have devoted to the Foundation and to Bertie, years in which I have worked flat out and at the risk of life for twenty hours a day." Possibly he is referring to the first draft of my autobiography. I was, and still am unaware of any occasion upon which he risked his life either for my sake or that of the Foundation. If he is referring to his travels in Africa, the dangerous part of those were made without authorization from either me or the Foundation. The same is true if he is referring to his second journey to Bolivia when he got himself imprisoned and shot at. In both cases he was begged to return to London or to stay in London as he had been away many weeks longer than had been intended and all the work of the Foundation was held up by efforts to straighten out what he had begun and abandoned. Much of the rest of his letter, three closely typed pages, is a diatribe against my wife who, he states, has been waging a campaign against him. In the course of this he utters nonsense, saying that "she has tried to deny me help of the Foundation when I have been in prison or in need of assistance to recover my passport. She has manoeuvred to prevent my return to Britain and when I did return she put out a vicious Press statement dissociating Bertie from me which only a miracle prevented the bourgeois press from blowing up into a major scandal." All this is, of course, untrue. She has often helped Ralph, and would have helped him in prison had there been anything that she could have done for him. She has never put out a Press statement of any sort, vicious or otherwise. Moreover, he says that "she has harassed and bullied and tormented Bertie to secure his acquiescence in her efforts." I have never been harassed or bullied or tormented by her. The idea is ludicrous. And in point of fact, she felt optimistic about Ralph for a longer time than I did. Ralph thinks that it was she who made me demand that he should not be my secretary. "The muted and scarcely existent public support of Bertie for me when I have been in grave danger and now banned from Britain" is owing to her. And her nefarious actions culminate in "harmful" remarks that I make about him in my autobiography. I had been under the impression that I had helped Ralph as much as I could, and I do not think that I have been ungenerous to him in my autobiography.

There follows in this letter a long, very revealing paragraph. He sums it up in the introductory sentence: "the truth is that every major political initiative that has borne the name of Bertrand Russell since 1960 has been my work in thought and deed." He continues, naming what he considers these major political initiatives. To all this he says that I have agreed enthusiastically. I have referred to my wife's evil campaign against him "with anguish", apologising, assuring, even crying. This is entirely the figment of his imagination. He himself, he says, has been "trapped in the dilemma of not tearing him (that is me) apart by fighting Edith."

I should ask Ralph to reflect on his own past speeches concerning the duties of a good secretary. And also upon the number of times that I have urged him to work and publish in his own name. Further, I should ask him to compare the paragraph about my wife on page 5 (Allen and Unwin edition) in the Preface written by himself to the book which he edited entitled *Philosopher of the Century*. It was first published in 1967. I entirely subscribe to what he says in that paragraph, as does my wife. But I should think that the change that he finds to have taken place in one year, 1967–68, would seem even to Ralph to be unlikely. I suppose that he has invented my wife's campaign as a face saving device against my criticisms. There is no slightest danger, and never has been, of my being torn apart by conflicts between my wife and Ralph.

This letter leaves me with the impression that Ralph must be well established in megalomania. The truth is, I suppose, that I have never taken Ralph as seriously as he liked to think I did. I was fond of him in the early years. But I never looked upon him as a man of parts and weight and much individual importance.

Russell

Sources and Bibliography

The Russell Archives of McMaster University, Hamilton, Ontario, are today by far the most important source of material on the life and work of Bertrand Russell. Their papers include not only the huge collection sold to the University by Russell himself but many hundreds of other items. In addition the Archives contain photostats of much original material held by other libraries and individuals throughout the world.

The most important of these other collections is held by the Humanities Research Center, University of Texas, at Austin, which owns more than 1,900 letters written by Russell to Lady Ottoline Morrell between 1911 and her death in 1938, and the later portion of a private and intimate journal kept intermittently by him between 1888 and 1905. Trinity College Library, Cambridge, owns interesting material, including the correspondence between Russell and Mrs Robert Trevelyan. The Passfield Papers at the London School of Economics contain Beatrice Webb's unpublished comments on Russell, while official sources in England include the Public Record Office, which contains unexpected delights in the official view of Russell during the First World War, and the B.B.C. archives which hold material almost as intriguing. The Strachey archives, in private hands, the papers of J. M. Keynes at King's College, Cambridge, and of Kingsley Martin and Leonard Woolf at the University of Sussex, also include material which fills in the background of Russell's life. Numerous collections of papers concerning the history of the Campaign for Nuclear Disarmament and the Committee of 100 supplement the considerable and official material at McMaster, and I am indebted to many individuals, notably Mr Arthur Goss, for making them available to me.

Russell's own works range in scale from the three-volume *Principia Mathematica*, written with A. N. Whitehead, to "My Own Philosophy", a thirty-page essay written in 1946 and published in 1972; in time, from the *German Social Democracy* of 1896 to the third volume of his autobiography in 1969. The number of his books depends on where the line is drawn between book and extended pamphlet, but more than sixty were in print when he died. Papers, studies, monographs and newspaper articles by Russell on philosophy, pacifism, world affairs and social questions are numbered quite literally by the thousand. Bibliographies include that by Lester Denonn in *The Philosophy of Bertrand Russell*, 1944; and by Harry Ruja in Pears's *Bertrand Russell: A Collection of Critical Essays*. The latest, now in preparation by Kenneth Blackwell and Harry Ruja, will contain more than 2,600 items. An abridgement will appear this year in a new edition of *The Philosophy of Bertrand Russell*.

Selections from Russell's works include *The Basic Writings of Bertrand Russell*, edited by Robert E. Egner and Lester E. Denonn; *Logic and Knowledge*, edited by Robert C. Marsh; *Essays in Analysis*, edited by Douglas Lackey, and numerous volumes of essays published in the United States and Britain under different titles and including different selections. *Festschriften* include *The Philosopher of the Century*, edited by Ralph Schoenman; *Bertrand Russell's Philosophy*, edited by George Nakhnikian; and *Russell in Review*, edited by J. E. Thomas and Kenneth Blackwell. Biographical material of varying value is found in G. H. Hardy's *Bertrand Russell and Trinity*; Rupert Crawshay-Williams's *Russell Remembered*; Alan Wood's *Bertrand Russell: The Passionate Sceptic*; occasional pieces which Russell himself contributed to the *Rationalist Annual*, *The Philosophy of Bertrand Russell* and *Portraits from Memory*, as well as the autobiography published when Russell was in his nineties. G. Kreisel's biographical memoir for the Royal Society and those in the *Bulletin of the London Mathematical Society* by C. D. Broad and R. O. Gandy are particularly valuable.

Dissertations on Russell's philosophy are as numerous as their quality is varied and can be found liberally scattered through the journals of the last seventy years. Books include A. J. Ayer's *Russell and Moore: The Analytical Heritage*, the same author's *Russell* in the Fontana Modern Masters series and Ronald Jager's *The Development of Bertrand Russell's Philosophy* in the Muirhead Library of Philosophy.

Bibliography

(Place of publication is London except where otherwise indicated.)

Armstrong, William M.: "Bertrand Russell Comes to America, 1896", *Studies in History and Society*, vol. 2 (1969–70), 29–39.

Ayer, A. J.: Obituary of Russell in the *New Statesman*, 6 Feb. 1970.

—— *Russell*, Fontana Modern Masters, 1972.

—— *Russell and Moore: The Analytical Heritage*, 1970.

Bagnold, Enid: *Autobiography*, 1969.

Beloff, Max: *Imperial Sunset*, 1969.

Berenson, Bernard: *Sunset and Twilight: From the Diaries of 1947–1958*, 1964.

Blackwell, Kenneth M.: "Wittgenstein's Impact on Russell's Theory of Belief" (unpublished thesis, M.A., McMaster University, 1974).

—— "The Importance to Philosophers of the Bertrand Russell Archive", *Dialogue*, vol. VII, no. 4 (1969), pp. 608–15.

Blanshard, Brand: "Eliot in Memory", *Yale Review* (summer 1965).

Bordessa, Ronald, and **Silzer, Vykki J.:** "Bertrand Russell's Response to Environment", *Places*, vol. 1, no. 2 (July 1974), pp. 37–42 (Indiana, Penn.).

Boulton, David: *Objection Overruled*, 1967.

Braithwaite, R. B. (and others) (eds): *The Foundations of Mathematics, and other logical essays*, by Frank Plumpton Ramsey, 1931.

Bredsdorff, Dr Elias: "Some Personal Reminiscences of Bertrand Russell" (unpublished).

Broad, C. D.: "Bertrand Russell as Philosopher", *Bull. London Mathematical Society*, vol. 5 (1973), pp. 328–41.

Brockway, Fenner: *Inside the Left: Thirty Years of Platform, Press, Prison and Parliament*, 1942.

Brookfield, Frances M.: *The Cambridge "Apostles"*, 1906.

Brown, W. J.: *I Meet America*, 1942.

Buranelli, Vincent: "Bertrand Russell: An Impression", *Prairie Schooner*, vol. 29 (1955), 44–8.

Bynner, Witter: *Journey with Genius*, 1953.

Carnap, Rudolf: *Introduction to Symbolic Logic and Its Applications*, New York, 1958.

Carrington, Noel (ed.): *Mark Gertler: Selected Letters*, 1965.

Cavitch, David: *D. H. Lawrence and The New World*, 1969.

Charms, Leslie de: *Elizabeth of The German Garden*, 1958.

Chow Tse-tsung: *The May Fourth Movement*, Cambridge, Mass., 1960.
Collins, Canon L. John: *Faith Under Fire*, 1966.
Copi, Irving M.: *The Theory of Logical Types*, 1971.
Cory, Daniel (ed.): *The Letters of George Santayana*, 1956.
Coulton, C. G.: *The Main Illusions of Pacifism: A Criticism of Mr. Norman Angell and of the Union of Democratic Control*, 1916.
Crawshay-Williams, Rupert: *Russell Remembered*, 1970.
Dewey, J., and **Kallen, H. M.** (eds): *The Bertrand Russell Case*, New York, 1941.
Dorward, A. J.: *Russell: A Short Guide to His Philosophy*, 1951.
Driver, Christopher: *The Disarmers: A Study in Protest*, 1964.
Duffett, John (ed.): *Against the Crime of Silence*, 1968.
Dutt, R. Palme: "Bertrand Russell, 1872–1970", *Labour Monthly*, vol. 52 (Mar. 1970), pp. 97–110.
Eames, E. R.: "Contemporary British Criticism of Russell", *Jnl of Southern Philosophy*, vol. 6 (1968), pp. 45–51.
Eastman, Max: *Great Companions*, 1959.
Edwards, Paul (ed.): *Encyclopaedia of Philosophy*, 1967.
Engelmann, Paul: *Letters from Ludwig Wittgenstein, with a Memoir*, 1967.
Feinberg, Barry (ed.): *The Archives of Bertrand Russell*, 1967.
Ferguson, C. L.: *A History of the Magpie and Stump Debating Society, 1866–1926*, Cambridge, 1931.
Fremantle, Anne: *Three-Cornered Heart*, 1971.
Gandy, R. O.: "Russell as a Mathematician", *Bull. London Mathematical Society*, vol. 5 (1973), pp. 342–8.
Gathorne-Hardy, Robert (ed.): *Recollections of Logan Pearsall Smith*, 1949.
—— *Ottoline: The Early Memoirs of Lady Ottoline Morrell*, 1963.
—— *Ottoline at Garsington*, 1974.
Gerhardi, William: *Memoirs of a Polyglot*, 1931.
Gilbert, Martin: *Plough My Own Furrow: The Story of Lord Allen of Hurtwood*, 1965.
Goldman, Emma: *Living My Life*, 1932.
Gowing, Margaret: "Independence and Deterrence", *Policy Making*, vol. 1 (1974).
Graves, Robert: *Goodbye to All That*, 1929.
Hapgood, Hutchins: *A Victorian in the Modern World*, New York, 1939.
Hardy, G. H.: *Bertrand Russell and Trinity*, 1970.
Harrod, R. F.: *The Life of John Maynard Keynes*, 1951.
Hart, B. H. Liddell: *The Revolution in Warfare*, 1946.
Hassall, Christopher: *Edward Marsh: Patron of the Arts*, 1959.
Hazelhurst, Cameron: *Politicians at War: July 1914 to May 1915*, 1971.
Heijenoort, Jean van: *From Frege to Gödel: A Source Book in Mathematical Logic, 1879–1931*, Cambridge, Mass., 1967.

Hemmings, Ray: *Fifty Years of Freedom: A Study of the Development of the Ideas of A. S. Neill*, 1972.

Hobhouse, Stephen, and **Brockway, Fenner** (eds): *English Prisons Today*, 1922.

Hobson, J. A.: *Confessions of an Economic Heretic*, 1938.

Holroyd, Michael: *Lytton Strachey: A Critical Biography*, vol. I (1967); vol. II (1968).

Howgate, George W.: *George Santayana*, University of Pennsylvania Press, Philadelphia, Pa., 1938.

Huxley, Aldous: *Crome Yellow*, 1921.

Huxley, Julian: *Religion Without Revelation*, 1967.

Jager, Ronald: *The Development of Bertrand Russell's Philosophy*, 1972.

Jørgensen, Jørgen: *A Treatise of Formal Logic*, 1931.

Jourdain, P. E. B.: *The Philosophy of Mr. B*rtr*nd R*ss*ll*, 1918.

Keynes, John Maynard: *Two Memoirs: Dr. Melchior: A Defeated Enemy and My Early Beliefs*, 1949.

Kreisel, Georg: "Bertrand Russell, F.R.S.", *Biographical Memoirs of Fellows of the Royal Society*, vol. 19 (1973), 583–620.

Laurence, Dan H. (ed.): *Bernard Shaw: Collected Letters 1874–1897*, 1965.

Lowe, Victor: *Understanding Whitehead*, Johns Hopkins University Press, Baltimore, Md, 1966.

McComb, A. K. (ed.): *The Selected Letters of Bernard Berenson*, 1965.

Magee, Bryan: *Modern British Philosophy*, 1971.

Malcolm, Norman: *Ludwig Wittgenstein: A Memoir*, 1967.

Malleson, Constance: *After Ten Years: A Personal Record*, 1936.

—— *The Coming Back*, 1933.

—— *In the North*, 1947.

Mariano, Nicky: *Forty Years with Berenson*, 1966.

Marquand, David: "Bombs and Scapegoats", *Encounter*, vol. 16 (Jan. 1961), 43–8.

Marsh, Edward: *A Number of People*, 1939.

Marsh, Robert C. (ed.): *Logic and Knowledge*, by Bertrand Russell, 1956.

Martin, Kingsley: *Father Figures*, 1966.

—— *Editor*, 1968.

Marwick, Arthur: *Clifford Allen: The Open Conspirator*, 1964.

Matthews, W. R.: *Memories and Meanings*, 1969.

Meynell, Sir Francis: *My Lives*, 1971.

Mirsky, Dmitri: *The Intelligentsia of Great Britain*, 1935.

Moore, Harry T. (ed.): *D. H. Lawrence's Letters to Bertrand Russell*, New York, 1948.

—— *A D. H. Lawrence Miscellany*, 1961.

Morley, John: *Memorandum on Resignation*, 1914.

Murray, Gilbert: *An Unfinished Autobiography*, 1960.

Nakhnikian, George (ed.): *Bertrand Russell's Philosophy*, 1974.

Nehls, Edward (ed.): *D. H. Lawrence: A Composite Biography*, University of Wisconsin Press, Madison, Wis., 3 vols., 1957–9.

Nicolson, Harold: *Diaries and Letters, 1945–1962* (ed. Nigel Nicolson), 1968.

Packe, Michael St John: *The Life of John Stuart Mill*, 1954.

Park, Joe: *Bertrand Russell on Education*, Columbus, Ohio, 1963.

Parker, R. A.: *The Transatlantic Smiths*, New York, 1960.

Parris, Henry: "The Political Thought of Bertrand Russell", *Durham University Journal*, vol. 58 (1965–6), pp. 86–94.

Patmore, Derek (ed.): *My Friends When Young: The Memoirs of Brigit Patmore*, 1968.

Pears, D. F.: *Russell and the British Tradition in Philosophy*, 1967.

—— (ed.): *Bertrand Russell: A Collection of Critical Essays*, New York, 1972.

Pinto, Vivian de Sola: *The City that Shone: An Autobiography (1895–1922)*, 1969.

Popper, Karl R.: *Conjectures and Refutations*, 1963.

Prest, John: *Lord John Russell*, 1972.

Price, Lucien: *Dialogues with Alfred North Whitehead*, 1956.

Ready, W.: *Necessary Russell*, Toronto, 1969.

Rolph, C. H.: *Kingsley: The Life, Letters and Diaries of Kingsley Martin*, 1973.

Rosenbaum, S. P.: "Bertrand Russell: The Logic of a Literary Symbol", in *Russell in Review*.

Rotblat, Joseph: *Pugwash: A History of the Conferences on Science and World Affairs*, 1967.

Rothenstein, William: *Men and Memories*, vol. II, 1932.

Russell: The Journal of the Bertrand Russell Archives (spring 1971–), Hamilton, Ontario.

Russell, Bertrand: Russell's books and principal pamphlets are followed here by a selection of the more significant of the more than 2,000 papers and articles written by him between 1895 and 1970.

German Social Democracy, 1896.

An Essay on the Foundations of Geometry, 1897.

A Critical Exposition of the Philosophy of Leibniz, 1900, 2nd edn 1937.

The Principles of Mathematics, 1903, 2nd edn 1937.

(with A. N. Whitehead) *Principia Mathematica*, 3 vols, 1910, 1912 and 1913; 2nd edn 1925 and 1927.

Philosophical Essays, 1910.

Anti-Suffragist Anxieties, 1910.

The Problems of Philosophy, 1912.

Our Knowledge of the External World, 1914.

War, the Offspring of Fear, [1914].
Justice in War-Time, 1916.
The Policy of the Entente: A Reply to Professor Gilbert Murray, [1916].
Principles of Social Reconstruction, 1916.
Political Ideals, New York, 1917.
Roads to Freedom, 1918.
Mysticism and Logic, 1918.
Introduction to Mathematical Philosophy, 1919.
The Practice and Theory of Bolshevism, 1920.
The Analysis of Mind, 1921.
The Problem of China, 1922.
Free Thought and Official Propaganda, 1922.
(with Dora Russell) *The Prospects of Industrial Civilization*, 1923.
The ABC of Atoms, 1923.
Icarus, or the Future of Science, 1924.
(with Scott Nearing) *Bolshevism and the West*, 1924.
What I Believe, 1925.
The ABC of Relativity, 1925.
On Education, especially in Early Childhood, 1926.
Selected Papers of Bertrand Russell, New York, 1927.
An Outline of Philosophy, 1927.
The Analysis of Matter, 1927.
Sceptical Essays, 1928.
Marriage and Morals, 1929.
The Conquest of Happiness, 1930.
The Scientific Outlook, 1931.
Education and the Social Order, 1932.
Freedom and Organization, 1814–1914, 1934.
In Praise of Idleness, 1935.
Religion and Science, 1935.
Which Way to Peace?, 1936.
(with Patricia Russell) *The Amberley Papers*, 2 vols, 1937.
Power; A New Social Analysis, 1938.
An Inquiry into Meaning and Truth, New York, 1940.
Let the People Think, 1941.
A History of Western Philosophy, New York, 1945.
Physics and Experience, 1946.
Human Knowledge, Its Scope and Limits, 1948.
Authority and the Individual, 1949.
Unpopular Essays, 1950.
The Impact of Science on Society, New York, 1951.
New Hopes for a Changing World, 1951.
The Good Citizen's Alphabet, 1953.
Satan in the Suburbs, 1953.

Human Society in Ethics and Politics, 1954.
Nightmares of Eminent Persons, 1954.
History as an Art, 1954.
Portraits from Memory, 1956.
Logic and Knowledge (ed. R. C. Marsh), 1956.
Why I Am Not a Christian (ed. Paul Edwards), 1957.
Understanding History, 1957.
Bertrand Russell's Best (ed. R. E. Egner), 1958.
The Vital Letters of Russell, Kruschev, Dulles, 1958.
Common Sense and Nuclear Warfare, 1959.
Wisdom of the West, 1959.
My Philosophical Development, 1959.
Bertrand Russell Speaks His Mind, 1960.
Fact and Fiction, 1961.
Has Man a Future?, 1961.
The Basic Writings of Bertrand Russell (ed. L. E. Denonn and R. E. Egner), 1961.
History of the World in Epitome, 1962.
Unarmed Victory, 1963.
The Labour Party's Foreign Policy, 1965.
War Crimes in Vietnam, 1967.
The Autobiography of Bertrand Russell, 3 vols, 1967, 1968 and 1969.
The Art of Philosophizing, 1968.
Dear Bertrand Russell, 1969.
Atheism: Collected Essays, 1943–1949, 1972.
The Collected Stories of Bertrand Russell (ed. B. Feinberg), 1972.
My Own Philosophy, Hamilton, Ontario, 1972.
Bertrand Russell's America, vol. 1, 1896–1945 (ed. B. Feinberg and R. Kasrils), 1973.
Essays in Analysis (ed. D. P. Lackey), 1973.

1903 "The Free Man's Worship", *Independent Review*, vol. 1 (Dec.), pp. 415–24.
1905 "On Denoting", *Mind*, n.s., vol. 14 (Oct.), pp. 479–93.
1906 "The Nature of Truth", *Mind*, n.s., vol. 15 (Oct.), pp. 528–33.
1908 "Mathematical Logic as Based on the Theory of Types", *American Journal of Mathematics*, vol. 30 (May), pp. 222–62.
1909 "Pragmatism", *Edinburgh Review*, vol. 209 (Apr.), pp. 363–88.
1910 "Ethics", *New Quarterly*, vol. 3 (Feb.), pp. 21–34; (May), pp. 131–143.
1911 Review of William James's *Memories and Studies*, *Cambridge Review*, vol. 33 (16 Nov.), p. 118.
1911 "Knowledge by Acquaintance and Knowledge by Description", *Proceedings of the Aristotelian Society*, n.s., vol. 11 (1910–11), pp. 108–128.

1912 "On the Relations of Universals and Particulars", *Proceedings of the Aristotelian Society*, n.s., vol. 12 (1911–12), pp. 1–24.
1912 "The Essence of Religion", *Hibbert Journal*, vol. 11 (Oct.), pp. 46–62.
1912 "The Philosophy of Bergson", *Monist*, vol. 22 (July), pp. 321–47.
1913 "The Philosophical Importance of Mathematical Logic", *Monist*, vol. 23 (Oct.), pp. 481–93.
1914 "Mr. Balfour's Natural Theology", *Cambridge Review*, vol. 35 (4 Mar.), pp. 338–9.
1914 "On the Nature of Acquaintance", *Monist*, vol. 24 (Jan.), pp. 1–16; (Apr.), 160–87; (July), pp. 435–53.
1914 "Mysticism and Logic", *Hibbert Journal*, vol. 12 (July), pp. 780–803.
1914 "The Relation of Sense-Data to Physics", *Scientia*, vol. 16 (July), pp. 1–27.
1915 "The Ethics of War", *International Journal of Ethics*, vol. 25 (Jan.), pp. 127–42.
1915 "The Ultimate Constituents of Matter", *Monist*, vol. 25 (July), pp. 399–417.
1916 "Rex vs. Bertrand Russell. Report of the Proceedings before the Lord Mayor at the Mansion House Justice Room 5 June 1916."
1916 "Open Letter to President Wilson", *Survey*, vol. 37 (30 Dec.), pp. 372–3.
1918 "The German Peace Offer", *Tribunal*, no. 90 (3 Jan.), p. 1.
1918 "The Philosophy of Logical Atomism", *Monist*, vol. 28 (Oct.), pp. 495–527; vol. 29 (Jan. 1919), pp. 33–63; (Apr. 1919), pp. 190–222; (July 1919), pp. 344–80.
1919 "Democracy and Direct Action", *English Review*, vol. 28 (May), pp. 396–403.
1920 "Democracy and Revolution", *Liberator*, vol. 3 (May), pp. 10–13; (June), pp. 23–5.
1924 "Logical Atomism", in *Contemporary British Philosophy: Personal Statements*, First Series, ed. J. H. Muirhead.
1924 "Philosophy in the Twentieth Century", *Dial*, vol. 77 (Oct.), pp. 271–90.
1926 "What Shall We Educate For? An Inquiry into Fundamentals", *Harper's Monthly Magazine*, vol. 152 (Apr.), pp. 586–97.
1928 "Science and Education", *St. Louis Post-Dispatch*, 9 Dec., pp. 4–5.
1936 "The Limits of Empiricism", *Proceedings of the Aristotelian Society*, n.s., vol. 36 (1935–6), pp. 131–50.
1936 "Auto-Obituary – 'The Last Survivor of a Dead Epoch' ", *Listener*, vol. 16 (12 Aug.), p. 289.
1938 "My Religious Reminiscences", *Rationalist Annual*, pp. 3–8.

1946 "The Atomic Bomb and the Prevention of War", *Polemic*, no. 4 (July–Aug.), pp. 15–22.
1947 "The Faith of a Rationalist", *Listener*, vol. 37 (29 May), pp. 826, 828.
1949 "Atomic Energy and the Problems of Europe", *Nineteenth Century and After*, vol. 145 (Jan.), pp. 39–43.
1952 "The Next Eighty Years", *Observer*, 18 May, p. 4.
1952 "How Near is War?", *Fleet Street Forum*.
1954 "Man's Peril from the Hydrogen Bomb", *Listener*, vol. 52 (30 Dec.), pp. 1135–6.
1957 "Mr. Strawson on Referring", *Mind*, n.s., vol. 66 (July), pp. 385–389.
1958 "Let's Stay Off the Moon", *Maclean's Magazine*, vol. 71 (30 Aug.), pp. 7, 45–6. Reprinted in 1969 in *The Times* and the *Wall Street Journal*, without change.
1960 "The Case for Neutralism", *New York Times Magazine*, 24 July, pp. 10, 35–6. Debate with Gaitskell.
1962 "For and Against Being 90", *Observer*, 13 May, p. 10.
1964 "Semantics and the Cold War", *Playboy*, vol. 11 (Dec.), pp. 175, 206, 251.
1966 "An Appeal to the American Conscience", *The Minority of One*, vol. 8 (Sept.), pp. 12–14.
1969 "Labour's Goldwater", *Tribune*, 28 Nov., p. 1.
1970 "On American Violence", *Ramparts*, vol. 8 (Mar.), pp. 55–7.
1970 "Private Memorandum concerning Ralph Schoenman", *Black Dwarf*, vol. 14 (5 Sept.), pp. 7–10; *New Statesman*, vol. 80 (11 Sept.), pp. 292–6. Later published by the Queensland, Australia, branch of the Bertrand Russell Peace Foundation.

Russell, Dora: *The Tamarisk Tree: My Quest for Liberty and Love*, 1975.

Russell, J. F. S.: *My Life and Adventures*, 1923.

Russell, John: *A Portrait of Logan Pearsall Smith*, New York, 1950.

Ryle, Gilbert: *Collected Papers*, vol. 1, *Critical Essays*, 1971.

Santayana, George: *Winds of Doctrine*, 1913.

—— *My Host the World*, 1953.

—— *The Middle Span*, 1947.

—— *The Birth of Reason and Other Essays*, Columbia University Press, New York, 1968.

Sassoon, Siegfried: *Memoirs of an Infantry Officer*, 1930.

Schack, William: *Art and Argyrol: The Life and Career of Dr. Albert C. Barnes*, New York, 1960.

Schilpp, Paul A. (ed.): *The Philosophy of Bertrand Russell*, Northwestern University, Evanston and Chicago, 1944.

—— *The Philosophy of G. E. Moore*, 1942.

—— *The Philosophy of Alfred North Whitehead*, 1941.

Schoenman, Ralph (ed.): *Bertrand Russell: Philosopher of the Century*, 1967.

Sencourt, Robert: *T. S. Eliot: A Memoir*, 1971.

Shulman, Milton: *How to be a Celebrity*, 1950.

Smillie, Robert: *My Life for Labour*, 1924.

Smith, Grover (ed.): *Letters of Aldous Huxley*, 1969.

—— *Josiah Royce's Seminar as Recorded in the Notebooks of Harry T. Costello*, Rutgers University Press, New Brunswick, 1965.

Sprigge, Sylvia: *Berenson*, 1960.

Stewart, Jessie: *Jane Ellen Harrison: A Portrait from Letters*, 1959.

Stone, I. F.: "Bertrand Russell as a Moral Force in World Politics" (unpublished McMaster Russell Centenary Paper, 1972).

Stocks, Mary: *Ernest Simon of Manchester*, Manchester, 1963.

Swartz, Marvin J.: *The Union of Democratic Control in British Politics during the First World War*, 1971.

Swinnerton, Frank: *Figures in the Foreground*, 1963.

Taylor, Robert: "The Campaign for Nuclear Disarmament", in *The Age of Affluence, 1951–1964* (ed. Vernon Bogdanor and Robert Skidelsky), 1970.

Tedlock, E. W. Jnr (ed.): *Frieda Lawrence: The Memoirs and Correspondence*, New York, 1964.

—— *D. H. Lawrence: Artist & Rebel; A Study of Lawrence's Fiction*, Albuquerque, N.M., 1965.

Thomas, J. E., and **Blackwell, Kenneth** (eds): *Russell in Review, The McMaster Russell Centenary Celebrations, 1972*, Toronto, 1975.

Unwin, Stanley: *The Truth about a Publisher*, 1960.

Utley, Freda: *Odyssey of a Liberal*, Washington, D.C., 1969.

Webb, Beatrice: *Our Partnership*, 1948.

Wells, H. G.: *Experiment in Autobiography*, 1934.

Whitehead, A. N.: *Process and Reality, An Essay in Cosmology*, 1929.

Wiener, Norbert: *Ex-Prodigy*, New York, 1953.

—— *I Am a Mathematician*, 1956.

Wiffen, J. H.: *Historical Memoirs of the House of Russell from the Time of the Norman Conquest*, 1833.

Wilson, Trevor (ed.): *The Political Diaries of C. P. Scott*, Cornell University Press, Ithaca, N.Y., 1970.

Wittgenstein, L.: *Letters to Russell, Keynes and Moore*, ed. G. H. von Wright, 1974.

Wood, Alan: *Bertrand Russell: The Passionate Sceptic*, 1957.

Woolf, Leonard: *Sowing: An Autobiography of the Years 1880–1904*, 1967.

Wright, G. H. von (ed.): *Letters to C. K. Ogden, with Comments on the English Translation of the Tractatus Logico-Philosophicus*, 1973.

—— *Wittgenstein's Letters to Bertrand Russell, Maynard Keynes and G. E. Moore*, 1974.

Younghusband, Francis: *The Light of Experience*, 1927.

Notes and References

Full details of the sources quoted, manuscript and printed, are given with bibliographical information in the "Sources and Bibliography", pages 654–62.

page

19 "the true spirit of delight": Russell, "The Study of Mathematics", in *Mysticism and Logic*, 60.

22 "... the best English tradition": Frank Russell, *My Life and Adventures*, 11.

22 "as in many Russells": Russell and Patricia Russell, *The Amberley Papers*, II, 250 (afterwards referred to as "*Amberley*").

22 "A good house": Lady Amberley's Journal, 14 Apr. 1870, Russell Archives, McMaster University (afterwards referred to as "R.A.").

22 For the contemporary state of Ravenscroft, see Dorinda Taylor, "Restoring Ravenscroft", *Russell*, no. 7 (Autumn 1972), 9.

22 "I was quite enchanted": Lady Amberley's Journal, 20 July 1870, R.A.

22 a misadventure in ... birth-control: "I believe I am myself accidental. My Parents did not intend to have me ... I didn't know anything about it till I grew up": Russell interviewed in *Sunday Dispatch*, 31 Aug. 1958.

23 "At about 3.30": Lord Amberley's Journal, 18 May 1872, R.A.

23 "The boy vigorous and strong": Lord Amberley's Journal, 19 May 1872, R.A.

23 The naming of Russell: *Amberley*, II, 490–95.

23 "We hesitated to ask": quoted Michael St John Packe, *The Life of John Stuart Mill*, 439.

23 John Stuart Mill: Ann Robson, "Bertrand Russell and his godless Parents", *Russell*, no. 7 (Autumn 1972), 3–9, gives further details of the association between the Amberleys and Helen Taylor.

24 "of admirable taste": *Dictionary of National Biography, 1922–1930*, 193.

24 "at the door of the house": Queen Victoria's Journal, entry on 25 Apr. 1874, Royal Library, Windsor.

24 "made a nice little bow": Agatha Russell–Lady Amberley, 27 Apr. 1874, R.A.

24 "In getting out of a carriage": Russell, *The Autobiography of Bertrand Russell*, I, 202 (afterwards referred to as "*Auto.*").

24 "failed totally": Entry for 8 Apr. 1903 in private journal kept intermittently by Russell from the mid-1890s until the mid-1900s. Earlier parts in private hands: later parts from November 1902 are in the Humanities Research Center, the University of Texas at Austin (afterwards referred to as "Journal").

page

24 "dubious of ever begetting a child": Dora Russell, *The Tamarisk Tree* 208.

24 "Gossip has put": Dora Russell, *The Tamarisk Tree*, 208.

25 "Of all the children": Lord Amberley–Lady Russell, 3 July 1874, R.A.

25 "Frank remained sobbing": Maude Stanley–Lady Russell, quoted *Amberley*, II, 576.

25 "but he seems to have grown": Russell–Elizabeth Russell, 9 Apr. 1937, photocopy, R.A., of original in Henry E. Huntington Library, Pasadena, California.

25 "Apparently upon grounds of pure theory": *Auto.*, I, 17.

25 Spalding: for a note by J. B. S. Haldane, see "Introducing Douglas Spalding", *The British Journal of Animal Behaviour*, vol. 2 (Jan. 1954), 7.

26 still destroying Amberley correspondence: Note by Russell on Agatha Russell–Russell, 7 Nov. 1913, R.A.

26 "vaguely sensed a dark mystery": Russell, "My Mental Development", in Paul Arthur Schilpp (ed.), *The Philosophy of Bertrand Russell*, 3 (afterwards referred to as "'Mental Dev.'").

26 "The garden was neglected": Russell–the Lady Ottoline Morrell, postmarked 12 Apr. 1911, courtesy of the Humanities Research Center, the University of Texas at Austin (afterwards referred to as "T" followed by the number of the letter – here T. 26. Many letters are undated and in some cases successive letters are given a single number. Some letters are accompanied by envelopes and, where this helps in dating, the postmark dates are given).

27 "After the dreadful experience": George Santayana, *My Host the World*, 36.

28 inside the flyleaf: "Mental Dev.", 5.

28 Russell always said "we": Freda Utley, *Odyssey of a Liberal*, 168 (afterwards referred to as "Utley").

29 "There were three huge folio volumes": "Mental Dev.", 6.

29 his bedroom: T. 432, n.d.

30 "I am quite sure": W. M. Mee–Russell, 24 Oct. 1888, R.A.

30 unendurable little prig: Frank Russell, *My Life and Adventures*, 38.

30 "I was a solitary, shy": Russell, "An Autobiographical Epitome", *Portraits from Memory*, 9 (afterwards referred to as "*Portraits*").

30 "What do you think of Auntie's engagement": Russell–Frank Russell, 14 Sept. 1884, R.A.

30 "And I am left again": entry for 3 May 1888, in Russell's private diary, written in Greek characters and disguised as "Greek Exercises", R.A. (afterwards referred to as "'Greek Exercises'").

30 "with the more intensity": Journal, 14 Jan. 1905.

30 "I read an article": "Greek Exercises", 9 Mar. 1888.

30 an article in the *Nineteenth Century*: "Genius and Insanity" by James Sully, *Nineteenth Century*, vol. 17 (June 1885), 948–69.

31 "I gave Bertie": Frank Russell, *My Life and Adventures*, 101.

31 "At these words": Russell, "Why I Took to Philosophy", *Portraits*, 19.

31 "It turned out that while not without aptitude": Russell, "Things That Have Moulded Me", *Dial*, vol. 83 (Sept. 1927), 181, reprinted as Introduction to *Selected Papers of Bertrand Russell* (New York, 1927), ix.

page

31 "partly mere pleasure in discovering": "Mental Dev.", 5.

32 "They [had] told me when I was an infant": Russell, interviewed by John Freeman, B.B.C., 4 Mar. 1959, *Listener*, 19 Mar. 1959.

32 "poor Ewen": "Greek Exercises", 29 Apr. 1888.

32 "it has taken away cheerfulness": "Greek Exercises", 3 June 1888.

32 "I should like to believe": "Greek Exercises", 20 May 1888.

33 "My childhood was, on the whole, happy": *Auto.*, 1, 38.

33 "From adolescence onwards": Russell, "Private Memoirs", unpublished, private source (afterwards referred to as "'Memoirs'").

33 "Don't do it": quoted Anne Fremantle, *A Three-Cornered Heart*, 123.

33 "My attitude to my grandmother": T. 529, pmk. 6 Aug. 1912.

34 "I feel being where there is some life": "Greek Exercises", 25 Apr. 1888.

34 "No mind": "Greek Exercises", 20 May 1888.

34 "Yes, he's getting on": *Auto.*, 1, 36.

34 "As soon as I realised": *Auto.*, 1, 36.

35 "Bertie came to claim": The references to Russell's visits to John Tyndall are contained in Tyndall's diaries in the Royal Institution, London.

35 "laboratories & experiments": T. 972, pmk. 18 Jan. 1914.

36 "Thee can get on relying on thy charm": quoted Nicky Mariano, *Forty Years with Berenson*, 64.

36 "funny grammar": Edward Marsh–Russell, 25 Mar. 1894, R.A.

36 "To me, as to Goethe": *Auto.*, 1, 76.

36 "if I *lived* in England": quoted Robert Allerton Parker, *The Transatlantic Smiths*, 123.

36 "It was strange to see Bertie": Santayana, *The Middle Span*, 45.

37 "aristocratic, anarchic and artistic": quoted Margaret Cole, *Beatrice Webb* (1945), 66.

37 "Do you see that young man over there": quoted Robert Gathorne-Hardy (ed.), *Ottoline at Garsington*, 265 (afterwards referred to as "*Garsington*").

38 "a little like cultivating tropical flowers": Santayana, *My Host the World*, 36.

38 "There was a footpath": *Auto.*, 1, 43.

39 "I like mathematics": T. 373, pmk. Mar. 1912.

39 "Long afterwards": Note by Russell on letter W. D. Bushell–Russell, 15 Oct. 1895, R.A.

40 "the bumbling McTaggart": R. Palme Dutt, "Bertrand Russell, 1872–1970", *Labour Monthly*, vol. 52 (Mar. 1970), 97–110.

40 "with the tenacity of a bulldog": Leonard Woolf, *Sowing*, 134.

40 "I have made, however, so many corrections": Russell–G. E. Moore, 9 May 1900, R.A.

40 "on fundamental questions of philosophy": Russell, *The Principles of Mathematics*, preface.

40 transparent and crystal: T. no number, n.d.

40 "do you *always* speak the truth": *Auto.*, 1, 64.

40 "You don't like me": quoted Alan Wood, *Bertrand Russell: The Passionate Sceptic*, 87 (afterwards referred to as "Wood").

41 "I love to think of the bright shining passionless creation": T. 951, n.d.

page

41 "McTaggart, in the course of conversation": Moore, autobiography in Schilpp (ed.), *The Philosophy of G. E. Moore*, 13.

41 the 533rd meeting: *Cambridge Review*, 11 June 1891, 389.

41 twenty meetings on: *Cambridge Review*, 12 May 1892, 302.

42 "Nothing that might influence": C. L. Ferguson, *A History of the Magpie and Stump Debating Society, 1886–1926*, 30.

42 "a common craving": Frances M. Brookfield, *The Cambridge "Apostles"*, 3.

43 "The coercion": Einstein, autobiography in Schilpp (ed.), *Albert Einstein: Philosopher-Scientist*, 17.

43 "The attempt to acquire examination technique": Russell, "Why I Took to Philosophy", *Portraits*, 20.

43 "Those who taught me": Russell, *My Philosophical Development*, 35 (afterwards referred to as "*Phil. Dev.*").

43 "presented as a set of clever tricks": *Phil. Dev.*, 38.

43 "some reason": *Auto.*, I, 67.

43 "Philosophy, as I shall understand the word": Russell, *History of Western Philosophy*, 10 (in America, *A History of Western Philosophy*).

44 "all the delight of a new landscape": Russell, "Why I Took to Philosophy", *Portraits*, 20.

44 "In Britain rain comes from Ireland": Russell, *Wisdom of the West*, 290.

44 "the most egregious example": Stephen D. Crites, "Hegelianism", in Paul Edwards (ed.), *Encyclopedia of Philosophy*, III, 457.

45 "like a jelly": Russell, "Why I Took to Philosophy", *Portraits*, 21.

45 "In this philosophy I found comfort": Russell, "Why I Took to Philosophy", *Portraits*, 21.

45 "He and McTaggart between them": "Mental. Dev.", 10.

45 "Great God in boots! . . .": for the American public the phrase was altered to "Great Scott".

45 "the best of all possible worlds" and ". . . everything in it is a necessary evil": quoted Russell, *History of Western Philosophy*, 604.

45 "My intellectual pleasures": Russell–Alys Russell, 4 Nov. 1894, R.A.

46 "The chief need of English philosophy": F. H. Bradley, *Appearance and Reality*, xii.

46 "We are always bad at choosing wives": quoted T. 1016, 13 Apr. 1914.

47 "Some hours later": T. 103, 6 June 1911.

47 "They said she was no lady": *Auto.*, I, 82.

47 "I hope this is not so": Maude Stanley–Russell, 11 May 1894, R.A.

47 "solemn and reiterated warnings": Journal, 20–21 July 1894.

48 "But he will find himself among friends": Lord Dufferin–Lady Russell, 4 Sept. 1894, R.A.

48 "I am sure you will like it": Lord Dufferin–Russell, n.d., R.A.

48 "the great interest I take in you": Lord Dufferin–Russell, 6 Sept. 1894, R.A.

48 "I am deeply obliged to you": Russell–Lord Dufferin, 11 Sept. 1894, R.A.

49 "I am not sure, but it might be worthwhile for Bertram [*sic*]": John Morley–Lady Russell, 9 Sept. 1894, R.A.

49 "I think it a great pity": Lady Russell–Russell, 13 Sept. 1894, R.A.

page

50 "Last night, I counted the letters": Russell–Alys, 30 Oct. 1894, R.A.
50 "I saw thee worshipped brains": Russell–Alys, 29 Oct. 1894, R.A.
50 "My intellect is drying up": Russell–Alys, 21 Oct. 1894, R.A.
50 "I had much rather not": Russell–Alys, 8 Sept. 1894, R.A.
50 "long dispatches": "Mental. Dev.", 10.
51 "I lay awake a long time": Russell–Alys, 1 Nov. 1894, R.A.
51 "Coming back": Russell–Alys, 31 Oct. 1894, R.A.
51 "As to seeing the world": Russell–Alys, 27 Oct. 1894, R.A.
51 "blind fear of the aristocracy": Russell–Alys, 30 Aug. 1894, R.A.
51 "aristocratic acquaintance": Russell–Alys, 12 Oct. 1894, R.A.
51 "might, if things didn't improve extraordinarily": Russell–Alys, n.d., R.A.
52 "The inspiration": Russell–Alys, 28 Oct. 1894, R.A.
52 "it seems to me much too hard to be understood": Russell–Alys, 29 Oct. 1894, R.A.
52 "He gives me a sense of perpetual discomfort": Russell–Alys, 16 Oct. 1894, R.A.
52 "falling in love with different people": Russell–Alys, 1 Nov. 1894, R.A.
52 "everybody is wicked": Russell–Alys, 4 Nov. 1894, R.A.
53 "full of very severe criticism": T. 529, pmk. 6 Aug. 1912.
53 "thee is fat": Russell–Alys, 12 Oct. 1894, R.A.
53 "'I didn't use'": Russell–Alys, 25 Oct. 1894, R.A.
53 "Logan once told me": Russell–Alys, 22 Oct. 1894, R.A.
53 "The whole fuss of a wedding": Russell–Alys, 8 Oct. 1894, R.A.
53 "Don't imagine that I really seriously mind": Russell–Alys, 2 Nov. 1894, R.A.
53 "It is sad that my Grandma": Russell–Alys, 31 Oct. 1894, R.A.
54 "on English ground once more": Russell–Alys, 3 Nov. 1894, R.A.
54 "My visit ... has put me": Russell–Alys, 4 Nov. 1894, R.A.
54 "How strange thee should write": Russell–Alys, 30 Oct. 1894, R.A.
54 "never had complete relations": *Auto.*, I, 203.
55 "She seems anxious to be 'stimulated'": Russell–Alys, 5 Nov. 1894, R.A.
55 "been making me talk about sexual morality": Russell–Alys, 10 Nov. 1894, R.A.
55 "She seems to be enjoying herself": Russell–Alys, 12 Nov. 1894, R.A.
55 "we repeated the ceremony": Russell–Alys, 12 Nov. 1894, R.A.
55 "been such a fool": Russell–Alys, 15 Nov. 1894, R.A.
56 "A Psychological Explanation": Russell–Alys, 15 or 16 Nov. 1894, R.A.
57 "whether she deliberately and consciously": Parker, *The Transatlantic Smiths*, 42.
57 "one of the results of illness": Mary Berenson–Russell, 28 July 1936, R.A.
57 "I will make little of it": Russell quoted "Letters to Bertrand Russell from Constance Malleson: 1916–1969", II, 103, unpublished two volumes. Lady Constance appears in this, as in most other Russell correspondence, under the "Colette" of her stage-name of Colette O'Niel (afterwards referred to as "Colette").
58 "How thankfully I remember": Lady Russell–Russell, 10 Dec. 1894, R.A.

page

58 a variant of Quakerism: Russell, *History of Western Philosophy*, 18.
58 "I can't read on practical things": Russell-Moore, 31 Jan. 1897, R.A.
59 "a feeling of intense mental life": Hutchins Hapgood, *A Victorian in the Modern World*, 113.
59 "I remember a spring morning": "Mental Dev.", 11.
59 "If you're to do anything reasonable": Aldous Huxley, *Crome Yellow*, 106.
59 For a study of Russell in fiction see S. P. Rosenbaum, "Bertrand Russell: The Logic of a Literary Symbol", read McMaster Centenary Celebrations, 13 Oct. 1972, printed in *University of Toronto Quarterly*, vol. 42 (Summer 1973), 301–27, and Thomas and Blackwell (eds), *Russell in Review*.
60 "The runaway couple": Sylvia Sprigge, *Bernard Berenson*, 114 (afterwards referred to as "Sprigge").
60 "Bertie I have been seeing a great deal": Berenson–R. C. Trevelyan, 6 Nov. 1896, quoted A. K. McComb (ed.), *The Selected Letters of Bernard Berenson*, 65.
60 "I used to listen with rapture": quoted Wood, 80.
60 "The atmosphere of Art and luxury": Journal, 14 Jan. 1903.
60 "I've looked at everything": Miss Lucy Norton–author, Nov. 1973.
60 "But this is out and out mysticism": quoted Wood, 80.
60 "I . . . felt he was under a misapprehension": quoted Sprigge, 140.
61 "about as enjoyable as any travelling": Russell–Moore, 14 Oct. 1898, R.A.
61 "It is perfectly divine here": Russell–Moore, 19 Oct. 1897, R.A.
61 "mothers-in-law": T. 506, pmk. 20 July 1912.
61 "I remember my difficulties at Friday's Hill": T. 308, pmk. 1 Jan. 1912.
62 "solved all philosophical questions": *Auto.*, 1, 125.
62 "an object whose properties": Russell, *Essay on the Foundations of Geometry*, 147.
62 "Einstein's revolution": *Phil. Dev.*, 40.
62 "My darling Rosebud": Russell–Alys, 9 Oct. 1895, R.A.
63 "There is no fear": Rollo Russell–Russell, 12 Oct. 1895, R.A.
63 "magnificent work": Russell, *German Social Democracy*, 10.
63 "This haughty claim": Russell, *German Social Democracy*, 1.
64 "I oppose him": *Yorkshire Post*, 18 Apr. 1962.
64 "Called on . . . a seamstress": Entry for 15 Nov. 1895, in diary kept by Alys Russell, photocopy in R.A., original in London School of Economics.
64 "in a fairly respectable house": Alys's diary, 18 Nov. 1895, R.A.
65 "We know no Prussian Officers": Russell–Lady Russell, 2 Dec. 1895, R.A.
65 "as he is a rising man": Dr Carey Thomas–Daniel Gilman, 7 July 1896, quoted William M. Armstrong, "Bertrand Russell Comes to America, 1896", *Studies in History and Society*, vol. 2 (1969), 29–39 (afterwards referred to as "Armstrong").
66 "I never heard of Mr. Bertrand Russell": Simon Newcomb–Gilman, 26 Aug. 1896, quoted Armstrong.
66 "a dozen mathematicians": Thomas Craig-Gilman, 31 Aug. 1896, quoted Armstrong.
66 "This College is a very nice place": Russell–Rollo Russell, 20 Nov. 1896, R.A.

page

66 "I do most sincerely hope": Alys Russell–Dr Carey Thomas, 26 Nov. 1896, R.A.

67 "I was very fond of her": *Auto.*, I, 132.

67 "I went to the Cavendish Lab": Russell–Philip Jourdain, 10 Apr. 1910, courtesy Ivor Grattan-Guinness, original in Institut Mittag-Leffler, Stockholm, copy in R.A.

67 "it seems the greatest sign of friendship": Russell–Alys, 22 Dec. 1895, R.A.

67 "a black-bearded man": Journal, 1 Dec. 1902.

68 "I enjoyed my stay there": Russell–Moore, 9 May 1900, R.A.

68 "The contrast between the two men": Woolf, *Sowing*, 134.

68 "a rather scratch sort of paper": Russell-Moore, 7 Dec. 1897, R.A.

69 "whereas most great philosophers": Bryan Magee, *Modern British Philosophy*, 31.

69 "certitude was gone": Whitehead, quoted Lucien Price, *Dialogues of Alfred North Whitehead*, 12.

69 "Three theoretical constructions": Minutes of Moral Science Club, 25 Feb. 1898.

69 "started gaily on the philosophy of matter": T. 695, pmk. 8 Feb. 1913.

70 "They differ as man and boy": Russell, *Introduction to Mathematical Philosophy*, 194.

70 "every relation is grounded": Russell, review of Joachim's *The Nature of Truth*, *Mind*, n.s. vol. 15 (Oct. 1906), 528–33.

70 "by skating over the difficulties": Russell–Moore, 20 July 1898, R.A.

71 "in the sense that God has so ordained": Russell, *Wisdom of the West*, 203.

71 "I felt ... as if I had escaped from a hot-house": *Phil. Dev.*, 61.

72 "I don't know how other people philosophise": Russell–F. H. Bradley, 30 Jan. 1914, R.A.

72 "the definition of truth": Russell, "The Nature of Truth", read to Jowett Society, Oxford, June 1905, unpublished, quoted Kenneth Blackwell, "Wittgenstein's Impact on Russell's Theory of Belief", 20.

73 "My marriage checked growth": T. 347, 18 Feb. 1912.

73 "It wasn't Alys that spoilt me": T. 669, pmk. 12 Jan. 1913.

74 "the first five years": T. 287, 14 Dec. 1911.

74 "I had been brought up": "Memoirs".

75 "From you and Alys": Frank Russell–Russell, 12 June 1900, R.A.

75 "Your suggestion": Frank Russell–Russell, 19 June 1900, R.A.

75 "Mrs. Whitehead dislikes [Alys]": T. 20, n.d.

75 "My wife's background": Whitehead, autobiographical notes in Schilpp (ed.), *The Philosophy of A. N. Whitehead*, 6.

75 "By myself": Price, *Dialogues of Alfred North Whitehead*, 15.

76 "In discussions at the Congress": *Auto.*, I, 144.

76 "I wish to read all your works": *Phil. Dev.*, 65.

77 "Always a step ahead of me": Anonymous, "The Forerunner", in *Fear No More, a Book of Poems for the Present Time*, 35.

77 "The Congress was admirable": Russell–Moore, 16 Aug. 1900, R.A.

77 "extended the region of mathematical precision": "Mental Dev.", 44.

77 "as much as a naked woman": Jacques Boell, *High Heaven*, 51.

page

77 "Nature is my inspiration": Journal, 12 Nov. 1902.
78 "Every evening": *Auto.*, I, 145.
78 "It was an exquisite moment": Journal, 12 Nov. 1902.
78 "She said she would not like to live": Journal, 13 Nov. 1902.
78 "But he is too democratic for me": Russell–Gilbert Murray, 12 Dec. 1902, R.A.
79 "He seemed quite the fool": Journal, 13 Nov. 1902.
79 "The talk, the atmosphere": Journal, 20 Nov. 1902.
79 "she begins at once talking of real things": Journal, 1 Dec. 1902.
79 "she is extraordinarily sympathetic": Journal, 4–7 Feb. 1903.
79 "sentimental and fluffy-headed old Hegelian": Russell, quoted Alys, private note, 1 Dec. 1900, R.A.
79 "a subject on which he knows little": Russell–Ivy Pretious, 27 Oct. 1907, Sir Charles Tennyson, copy in R.A.
79 Russell's review of Haldane's address: *Mind*, vol. 17 (1908), 238–42.
79 "It is an ancient puzzle": Russell, "The Philosophy of Logical Atomism", *Monist*, vol. 28 (Oct. 1918) and vol. 29 (Jan.–Apr.–July 1919), reprinted in Russell, *Logic and Knowledge*, ed. R. C. Marsh, 262 (afterwards referred to as "Marsh").
80 "This process led me": *Phil. Dev.*, 75–6.
80 "Never glad confident morning again": Robert Browning, "The Lost Leader".
81 "there is just one point": Russell–Frege, 16 June 1902, quoted Jean van Heijenoort (ed.), *From Frege to Gödel: A Source Book in Mathematical Logic, 1879–1931*, 124 (letter translated Beverly Woodward).
81 "Your discovery of the contradiction": Frege–Russell, 22 June 1902, quoted Jean van Heijenoort (ed.), *From Frege to Gödel*, 127 (letter translated Beverly Woodward).
81 "As I think about acts of integrity and grace": Russell–Professor Jean van Heijenoort, 23 Nov. 1962, *From Frege to Gödel*, 127.
82 "I am very deep in proofs": Russell–Murray, 16 Sept. 1902, R.A.
82 "For my part, I am very dissatisfied with it": Russell–Elie Halévy, 19 July 1903, R.A.
82 "In the book": Russell–Bradley, 11 Feb. 1904, R.A.
82 "to say the last word on any subject": review by R. W. H. T. Hudson, *Nature*, vol. 68 (1903), 412.
84 "killed passion": T. 451, 14 May 1912.
84 "died a gradual death": T. 46, pmk. 29 Apr. 1911.
84 "Much my strongest affection": T. 150, 17 July 1911.
85 "The moment of my first conversion": T. 154, n.d.
86 "I saw that pain of such intensity": Russell–Dr Ernest Jones, 28 Jan. 1957, R.A.
86 "I got on with Alys very well": T. 49, 2 May 1911.
86 "Last night": Sidney Webb–Beatrice Webb, 7 Mar. 1900, Passfield Papers, London School of Economics.
87 "Evelyn and I had an exceedingly frank talk": Russell–Alys, 13 July 1901, R.A.
87 "All goes well": Russell–Alys, 14 July 1901, R.A.
87 "Mrs. Whitehead was in perpetual fear": *Auto.*, I, 150.

page

87 surreptitious financial support: In an unpublished draft of his autobiography (R.A.), Russell gave the figure, which he subsequently deleted, as £8,000. At early twentieth-century values, the sum looks too large and the possibility of a typing error which added a nought to £800 cannot be ruled out.

87 "What I have been able to do": T. 327, 29 Jan. 1912.

87 "the scheme of their joint life": Beatrice Webb, *Our Partnership*, 215.

88 "I had had no idea": *Auto.*, I, 147.

88 "not to be indiscreet": Journal, 9 Feb. 1902.

88 "I now believe": unpublished draft of autobiography, R.A.

88 "Again I loved": T. 407, pmk. 4 Apr. 1912.

89 "something was amiss": *Auto.*, I, 148.

89 "Poor Alys has been too unwell": Beatrice Webb, *Our Partnership*, 242.

89 "act as a good companion": Beatrice Webb, diary, 21 July 1902, Passfield Papers, London School of Economics.

89 "I shall always remember your great kindness": Alys Russell–Beatrice Webb, 3 June 1911, Passfield Papers, London School of Economics.

89 "I was inspired": Journal, 18 May 1903.

89 "I finished it in a hurry": T. 463, 23 May 1912.

90 "a thousand times more experience in pain than in pleasure": Russell–Lucy Donnelly, 23 May 1902, R.A.

90 "And I too felt a great joy": Journal, 18 May 1903.

90 "the answer that love was dead": Journal, 18 May 1903.

90 "Alys never at any time stirred my depths": T. 425, pmk. 27 Apr. 1912.

90 "I sat alone": Journal, 18 May 1903.

91 "in a glass bowl": Journal, 18 May 1903.

91 "Happy lady in your play": Russell–Robert Trevelyan, 1 Aug. 1902, R.A.

91 never leave her for long: Journal, 18 May 1903.

91 "is hell": Journal, 8 Mar. 1903.

91 "At night, from my study": Journal, 29 Sept. 1902.

91 "strange months in town": Journal, 18 May 1903.

91 "London grows more and more odious": Journal, 25 Nov. 1902.

91 "The river is becoming to me a passionate, absorbing love": Journal, 11 Feb. 1903.

92 "The river shines": Russell–Murray, 4 Dec. 1902, R.A.

92 "Only the river": Russell–Murray, 12 Dec. 1902, R.A.

92 "Tiny and North": Journal, 20 Nov. 1902.

92 "As like as a gibbering spectre": Journal, 20 Nov. 1902.

92 "When I got home": Journal, 21 Nov. 1902.

92 "At night, I didn't kiss Alys": Journal, 25 Nov. 1902.

92 "she cried visibly": Journal, 13 Dec. 1902.

92 "after the light was out": Journal, 13 Dec. 1902.

92 "At luncheon ... just come from seeing the Kinsellas": Journal, 28 Nov. 1902.

93 "I have been making myself a shrine": Russell–Murray, 16 Dec. 1902, R.A.

93 "I urged her being mostly in town": Journal, 17 Dec. 1902.

93 a stroke of great good luck: quoted Sprigge, 163.

page

93 "in my heart": Russell–Berenson, 28 Feb. 1903, R.A.
93 "Just behind the house": Russell–Murray, 28 Dec. 1902, R.A.
94 "where Alys was very unhappy": Journal, 14 Jan. 1903.
94 "the total result": Journal, 10 Feb. 1903.
94 "The human surroundings": T. 548, 24 Aug. 1912.
94 "suddenly and vividly aware": Russell, "From Logic to Politics", *Portraits*, 35.
94 "only for people in great unhappiness": T. 20, n.d.
94 "That Man is the product": Russell, "The Free Man's Worship", originally published in the *Independent Review*, vol. 1 (Dec. 1903), 415–24.
95 "It was written as an exhortation": Journal, 4–7 Feb. 1903.
95 "students of English": R. K. DasGupta, "Russell as a Man of Letters", *Russell*, no. 9 (Spring 1973), 3–14.
95 "Perhaps the most flattering appreciation": Berenson–Russell, 22 Mar. 1903, R.A.
95 "I wrote with passion & force": T. 462, pmk. 23 May 1912.
95 "Fundamentally, my view of man's place in the cosmos": Russell, *Why I Am Not a Christian* (New York, 1957), 104.
96 "I am unhappy": Journal, 27 Jan. 1903.
96 "horribly painful": T. 114, July 1911.
96 "spent the first evening": Journal, 2 Feb. 1903.
96 "I am learning not to feel tragic": Journal, 4–7 Feb. 1903.
96 "Yesterday the Whiteheads came": Journal, 8 Mar. 1903.
96 "who said it was my duty to run the risk": Journal, 13 Mar. 1903.
97 "Last night for the first time": Journal, 18 Mar. 1903.
97 "The last sacrifice to A.": Journal, 8 Apr. 1903.
97 "Moore ... wrote curtly": Journal, 8 Apr. 1903.
97 "About the reading party": Moore–Russell, 20 Mar. 1903, quoted Moore–Desmond MacCarthy, 20 Mar. 1903, Mrs Dorothy Moore.
97 "Of course, I can't be sure": Moore–Desmond MacCarthy, 25 Mar. 1903, Mrs Dorothy Moore.
98 "[Alys] is still miserable": Journal, 26 July 1903.
98 a good eye for scenery: see Ronald Bordessa and Vykki J. Silzer, "Bertrand Russell's Response to Environment", *Places*, vol. 1 (July 1974), 37–42.
98 "I came here along the coast": Russell–Murray, 24 Mar. 1904, R.A.
99 "I suppose she will never learn": Journal, 26 July 1903.
99 "I know I am deeply the worse": T. 275, 10 Mar. 1912.
99 "a tragic austerity": Beatrice Webb, *Our Partnership*, 274.
99 "They have a competent way of sizing up a Cathedral": Russell–Murray, 26 Sept. 1903, R.A.
99 "I have got over my chief sorrow": Journal, 14 Jan. 1905.
99 "It seems odd to be writing to thee": Alys–Russell, 13 Nov. 1905, R.A.
100 "I cannot agree with you": Maude Burdett–Russell, 11 Dec. 1905, R.A.
100 "philosophy in modern times": Russell reviewing *Studies in Humanism* by F. C. S. Schiller, *Nation*, 2 Mar. 1907.
100 "I got on very well without any money": Russell–Alys, n.d., R.A.
100 For history of Lower Copse, see I. Grattan-Guinness, "Russell's Home at Bagley Wood", *Russell*, no. 13 (Spring 1974), 24–6.
101 "(1) it is interest": Russell–Ivy Pretious, 27 Oct. 1907, Tennyson.

page

101 "The habit of not speaking to Alys": Journal, 9 Mar. 1905.

102 "Hardly a week goes by": Russell–Hallam Tennyson, 1956 (in conversation).

102 "My wife has decided": Russell–Ivy Pretious, n.d., Sir Charles Tennyson.

102 "I am now ... horribly anxious about a girl": Russell–Lucy Donnelly, 19 Sept. 1904, R.A.

102 "They ... agreed that Janet": Note by Mary Moorman on "Bertrand Russell's Friendship with Ivy Pretious", Tennyson.

103 "I begin to see possibilities of emancipation": Russell–Ivy Pretious, n.d., Tennyson.

104 "I am very sorry to say": Russell–Ivy Pretious, 6 July 1905, Tennyson.

104 "the same kind of thing": Russell–Ivy Pretious, 11 Jan. 1907, Tennyson.

104 "I fear that if I go to Argyll Mansions": Russell–Ivy Pretious, 18 Dec. 1906, Tennyson.

104 "luckily there was nothing": Russell–Ivy Pretious, 2 Dec. 1907, Tennyson.

105 "I am even being contended for": Russell–Alys, 11 Apr. 1908, R.A.

105 "Bradshaw consists ...": Russell, "Determinism and Morals", *Hibbert Journal*, vol. 7 (Oct. 1908), 113–21.

105 "The reader who will": Russell, "Pragmatism", *Edinburgh Review*, vol. 209 (Apr. 1909), 363–88.

105 "preserved a discreet and continuous": Russell, *The Principles of Mathematics*, 287.

105 "Walk with Russell": Moore, diary entry 30 Aug.–2 Sept. 1909, Mrs Dorothy Moore.

106 "The pragmatic difference": Russell–James, 22 July 1909, copy in R.A., original in Houghton Library, Harvard University.

106 "... pragmatism appeals": Russell, "Pragmatism", *Edinburgh Review*, vol. 209 (Apr. 1909), 363–88.

106 "But for one who does not believe": Russell, draft article dated "Jan. 1907", the Humanities Research Center, the University of Texas at Austin, copy in R.A.

107 "that all pure mathematics": Russell, *The Principles of Mathematics*, v.

107 "The project of deducing mathematics from logic": Russell, "Whitehead and *Principia Mathematica*", *Mind*, vol. 57 (Apr. 1948), 137.

107 "We ... discovered that our projected volumes": Whitehead, autobiography in Schilpp (ed.), *The Philosophy of A. N. Whitehead*, 10.

108 "Although it may seem strange": Russell–Professor G. Revesz, 6 Dec. 1932, R.A.

108 "Broadly speaking": *Phil. Dev.*, 74.

109 "hardly a page": Russell, review of Keynes's *Treatise on Probability*, *Mathematical Gazette*, vol. 11 (July 1922), 124n.

109 "frequently a draft of some portion": Russell–Professor Revesz, 6 Dec. 1932, R.A.

109 "practically due to Russell": Whitehead, *Process and Reality*, 10.

109 "Everything ... sacrificed to making proofs look short and neat": Whitehead–Russell, undated note marked "1902", R.A.

109 "more like a pot of treacle": Russell, "Beliefs: Discarded and Retained", *Portraits*, 40.

page

109 "You think the world is what it looks like": quoted Russell, "Beliefs: Discarded and Retained", *Portraits*, 41.

109 The scope of *Principia Mathematica* was outlined most succinctly in the document which the authors drew up on applying to the Royal Society for a publication grant, and to which each contributed separate pages of argument. Whitehead began by stating that the object was "a complete investigation of the foundations of every branch of mathematical thought. The book commences by stating the logical principles and ideas which govern the course of all demonstrative reasoning. Then all the fundamental ideas which occur in pure mathematics are considered in detail. Each idea is stated in its most general form and is shown to be definable in terms of the fundamental logical notions which are considered at the commencement of the book. It is also proved by exact reasoning that the fundamental propositions from which the various branches of pure mathematics start, are deducible from the logical principles stated in the book, without the aid of any other undemonstrated axioms. Thus the definitions form an analysis of all mathematical ideas, and the demonstrations are (1) proofs of the 'axioms' from which the various branches of mathematics start, (2) guarantees of the adequacy of the analysis of ideas effected in the definitions by exhibiting the ways in which the ideas as thus analysed occur in reasoning."

At this point Russell took over. "We have", he says, "in each case sought the utmost generalization of the various mathematical ideas involved which is compatible with the truth of the properties usually assumed in their mathematical treatment. Thus for example in Cardinal Arithmetic we seek the most general definitions of cardinal numbers, and of the addition and multiplication of cardinal numbers, which secure the truth of the associative laws of addition and multiplication and of the distributive law, and we then show that these laws are applicable without distinction to the infinite and to the finite, and are themselves capable of generalized forms which include their usual forms as special cases. Similarly, in dealing with limits of functions and the continuity of functions, we so generalize the usual definitions as to make them independent of number, thereby greatly extending their scope. In short, given the usual 'axioms' of any subject, our problem is to find the most general hypotheses from which these axioms follow, in other words, the largest set of objects to which they are applicable.

"The proofs are so arranged that it is possible to trace through the whole work the occurrences of any idea or any proposition."

110 "At the time I often wondered": *Auto.*, I, 152.

110 "Neither of us alone": Russell, *Mind*, vol. 57 (1948), 137.

110 "What makes it vital": T. 429, pmk. 30 Apr. 1912.

110 "describing things ... in such a repulsive manner": *Auto.*, I, 65.

110 "Dear Bertie, The following": Whitehead–Russell, 18 June 1908, R.A.

110 "I am *sure* there can be no really great achievement": T. 426, pmk. 28 Apr. 1912.

111 "the contradictions were trivial": *Auto.*, I, 152.

111 Whitehead's telegram: 21 July 1903, R.A.

111 "On Denoting": *Mind*, n.s., vol. 14 (1905), 479–93.

page

112 "a kind of morning innocence": *Phil. Dev.*, 158.

112 For influence of Meinong, see Elizabeth R. Eames, "Russell's Study of Meinong", *Russell*, no. 4 (Winter 1971–2), 3.

112 "two millenia of muddle-headedness": Russell, *History of Western Philosophy*, 860.

113 "Russell found a patch": Gilbert Ryle, "Ludwig Wittgenstein", *Analysis*, vol. 12 (1951–2), 1–9.

113 a paper to the London Mathematical Society: "On Some Difficulties in the Theory of Transfinite Numbers and Order Types", *Proceedings of the London Mathematical Society*, 2nd ser., vol. 4, 7 Mar. 1906, 29–53, reprinted in Russell, *Essays in Analysis*, ed. Douglas Lackey, 135–64.

113 this second paper: "On the Substitutional Theory of Classes and Relations", printed in Russell, *Essays in Analysis*, 165–89.

114 "I work 9 or 10 hours": Russell–Ivy Pretious, 25 Dec. 1907, Tennyson.

114 "When I got unstuck": quoted Constance Malleson, *After Ten Years*, 241.

114 "I have been studying you on Types": Whitehead–Russell, 6 Jan. 1908, R.A.

115 "The manuscript became more and more vast": *Auto.*, I, 152.

115 "It is easy to picture the dismay": *Spectator*, 22 July 1911.

115 "Bertie informs me": Lytton Strachey–"Pippa" Strachey, 9 July 1906, quoted Michael Holroyd, *Lytton Strachey*, I, 290.

116 "Russell is writing a chapter on the Improper Infinitive": Lytton Strachey–his mother, 16 June 1904, quoted Holroyd, *Lytton Strachey*, I, 193.

116 many articles and reviews: See Russell, *Essays in Analysis*, 17.

116 "In the train": Russell–Ivy Pretious, 25 May 1908, Tennyson.

116 "That was the only time": T. 412, 9 Apr. 1912.

117 "All the spectres": T. 396, 21 Mar. 1912.

117 "As long as I live": T. 1606, 17 July 1922.

117 "Now I am in sight of Boar's Hill": T. 454, 17 May 1912.

117 "Land in sight": Whitehead–Russell, 12 Oct. 1909, R.A.

117 "As to cutting down": Whitehead–Russell, 31 Oct. 1909, R.A.

118 "the record of 'Paradise Lost' ": *Auto.*, I, 152. Milton sold the copyright for £5.

118 "arrived at a great moment": Russell–Lucy Donnelly, 18 Oct. 1909, R.A.

118 "feel such a sense of lightness & freedom": Russell–Ivy Pretious, 2 Dec. 1907, Tennyson.

118 "I have made a mess of my private life": Russell–Lucy Donnelly, 18 Oct. 1909, R.A.

119 "felt an inclination": *Auto.*, I, 201.

120 "because the Empire has come to seem": Journal, 26 July 1903.

120 "flung out of the club": H. G. Wells, *Experiment in Autobiography*, II, 765.

120 "I stated my objections": *Auto.*, I, 153.

120 "I went to Bertie's lecture": quoted John Russell, *A Portrait of Logan Pearsall Smith*, 80.

121 "I remember when Tariff Reform began": T. 169, 11 Aug. 1911.

121 "Stout's expectation": Russell–Halévy, 19 July 1903, R.A.

page

121 "It is a great comfort to me": Russell–Halévy, 22 Nov. 1904, R.A.

121 "I have to tell you a queer piece of news": Russell–Ivy Pretious, 1 May 1907, Tennyson.

122 "The mere fact": *Daily Chronicle*, 4 May 1907.

122 "This campaign is very educating": Alys Russell–Mrs Hannah Pearsall Smith, 7 May 1907, R.A.

123 "I look as handsome as I can": Alys Russell–Mrs Pearsall Smith, 8 May 1907, R.A.

123 "I am afraid it will swell up": Alys Russell–Mrs Pearsall Smith, 9 May 1907, R.A.

123 "I was very dignified": Alys Russell–Mrs Pearsall Smith, 10 May 1907, R.A.

123 "Ten days of standing for Parliament": Russell–Professor James, 6 Nov. 1908, copy in R.A., original in Houghton Library, Harvard University.

123 "I think I *can* go on seeing you": quoted Robert Gathorne-Hardy, *Recollections of Logan Pearsall Smith*, 151.

124 "I sat looking at this little mathematical wonder": Robert Gathorne-Hardy, *Ottoline: The Early Memoirs of Ottoline Morrell*, 96 (afterwards referred to as "*Ottoline*").

124 "I began to wish": T. 2, n.d.

124 "Bertrand Russell is most fascinating": *Ottoline*, 183.

124 "the beginning": T. 3, pmk. 21 Mar. 1911.

124 "She said that Bertie had enjoyed our visit": *Ottoline*, 183.

125 "I felt somewhat at a loose end": *Auto.*, I, 201.

129 "At some places we were stoned and booed at": *Ottoline*, 192.

130 "I have never thrown away any letters": T. 1606, 27 July 1922.

130 "no implication that the lectureship": Whitehead–Russell, 27 May 1910, R.A.

130 "a fairly large room": Russell–Lucy Donnelly, 20 Aug. 1911, R.A.

130 "When I argued with him": *Auto.*, I, 72.

130 "Obviously a nice man": quoted Nigel Nicolson (ed.), Harold Nicolson, *Diaries and Letters, 1945–1962*, 202.

130 "This morning I went to hear [him]": T. 221, 16 Oct. 1911.

131 "One hundred per cent": quoted Wood, 86.

131 "The old logic put thought in fetters": Russell, *Our Knowledge of the External World*, 59.

131 "Unless you have all the answers": Whitehead–Russell, 20 Jan. 1911, R.A.

131 For details of the fundamental mistake, see Ivor Grattan-Guinness, "The Russell Archives; some new light on Russell's logicism", *Annals of Science*, vol. 31 (1974), 387–406.

132 "Bertie Russell attracted": *Ottoline*, 193.

132 "I was wildly excited": T. 21, 7 Apr. 1911.

133 "I did not know I loved you": T. 11, 31 Mar. 1911.

133 "I was utterly unprepared": *Garsington*, 267.

133 "For external and accidental reasons": *Auto.*, I, 203.

133 "Bob Trevy babbled on": T. 2, n.d.

133 "All my life": T. 4, pmk. 22 Mar. 1911.

page

133 "I don't at the moment see how things will work out": T. 5, pmk. 23 Mar. 1911.
134 "all the eminent Frenchmen": T. 5, pmk. 23 Mar. 1911.
134 "It is horrible here": T. 6, pmk. 26 Mar. 1911.
134 "I don't quite know": T. 6, pmk. 26 Mar. 1911.
134 "Heaven knows how I shall manage": T. 6, pmk. 26 Mar. 1911.
134 "If I were less tired": T. 6, pmk. 26 Mar. 1911.
134 "took it very well": T. 7, pmk. 28 Mar. 1911.
134 "I do not think she is suffering very much": T. 14, pmk. 2 Apr. 1911.
135 "I do not know what he thought": *Garsington*, 269.
135 "Goodbye": T. 10, pmk. 29 Mar. 1911.
135 "I had another interview with Bertie": *Garsington*, 269.
135 "the dear letter": T. 11, pmk. 31 Mar. 1911.
135 letters ... during the last days of March: Ottoline–Russell, 25, 26, 27, 29 Mar. 1911, R.A.
135 "I have been cunning": T. 37, pmk. Apr. 1911.
136 "She was such an awful liar": Whitehead quoted C. D. Broad, "Bertrand Russell's First 42 Years in Self-portraiture", *Phil. Review*, vol. 77 (1968), 455.
136 "I think it is better to avoid places": T. 17, n.d.
136 "Providence has been very kind": T. 105, pmk. 9 June 1911.
137 "I can come day or night": T. 107, pmk. 10 June 1911.
137 "I could get a room": T. 45, pmk. 27 Apr. 1911.
137 "Your economical soul": T. 71, 18 May 1911.
137 "I find the Whiteheads are coming": T. 48, pmk. 30 Apr. 1911.
137 "I have never missed a train": T. 244, 4 Nov. 1911.
137 "It is obvious my bedmaker is quite unsuspicious": T. 62, 11 May 1911.
137 "This place ... where the civilised half of me belongs": T. 37, 28 Apr. 1911.
138 meeting Clive Bell: Russell–Clive Bell, 6 May 1910, Charleston Papers, University of Sussex.
138 "It would be absolutely useless": T. 22, pmk. 7 Apr. 1911.
138 "I have just had a thoroughly satisfactory talk with Alys": T. 22, pmk. 7 Apr. 1911.
138 confirmed their earlier arrangements: Ottoline–Russell, 9–10, 11, 13–14 Apr. 1911, R.A.
138 "Do you want to go?": *Garsington*, 267.
139 "He assumed at once": *Garsington*, 272.
139 "What Philip might think or feel": *Auto.*, I, 203.
139 "among the few moments": *Auto.*, I, 204.
139 "absurd": T. 35, pmk. 21 Apr. 1911.
139 "I have a perfectly cold intellect": T. 46, 29 Apr. 1911.
140 Alys "very wild and very miserable": T. 76, pmk. 21 May 1911.
141 "I gather it is all right": T. 88, 29 May 1911.
141 "We are safer now": T. 89, pmk. 29 May 1911.
141 What had happened: Ottoline–Russell, 25, 27, 28 May 1911, R.A.
141 "I imagine what Logan said": T. 113, 14 June 1911.
141 "prudent to appear unhappy": T. 308, 1 Jan. 1912.
141 "I hate this injured-martyr business": T. 113, 14 June 1911.

page

142 "If you want to see me elsewhere": T. 215, 11 Oct. 1911.
142 "I long to get right away": T. 140, 8 July 1911.
142 "It passed away peacefully": T. 287, 14 Dec. 1911.
143 "It will be very nice": T. 199, 28 Sept. 1911.
143 "Mrs. W. undertook": T. 195, pmk. 26 Sept. 1911.
143 "you could come there very early": T. 225, 18 Oct. 1911.
143 "I found a charming apartment": T. 228, 20 Oct. 1911.
143 "He says the Stephens know": T. 123, 21 June 1911.
143 "while I am writing": Alys Russell–Moore, 18 June 1911, Mrs Dorothy Moore.
144 "I am sorry to hear about your friend": quoted Julian Trevelyan–Russell, 9 Mar. 1967, R.A.
144 "The whole post was handed to Mrs. Bob": T. 305, pmk. 31 Dec. 1911.
144 "divided by the bells": Russell, *My Own Philosophy*, 11.
144 "Envied for her power of enduring excess": Journal, 13 Nov. 1902.
144 "heard, on very reliable authority": T. 106, pmk. 10 June 1911.
144 "We had, as you say, an idea": Frank Russell–Russell, 6 June 1911, R.A.
144 "I have been feeling": Alys Russell–Beatrice Webb, 21 Sept. 1911, Passfield Papers, London School of Economics.
145 "continued friendliness and good wishes": Mary Berenson–Russell, 17 June 1911, R.A.
145 a "cutting letter": *Auto.*, III, 74.
145 "did Russell from the beginning": Bernard Berenson, diary, 26 July 1952, *Sunset and Twilight: From the Diaries of 1947–1958*, 269.
145 "It was during this stay in London": Mariano, *Forty Years with Berenson*, 228.
145 "Her feelings were romantic and sentimental": "Memoirs".
146 "Nowadays, I long to have beautiful things about me": T. 74, 19 May 1911.
146 "I don't think he ever felt an active need": Rupert Crawshay-Williams, *Russell Remembered*, 55.
146 "It is so nice hearing it in a Cathedral": T. 366, pmk. 4 Mar. 1912.
146 "I find it so hard to concentrate": T. 112, June 1911.
147 "I try to think there will be many years ahead": T. 97, pmk. June 1911.
147 "Dearest, you *have* liberated something very important in me": T. 992, pmk. 23 Feb. 1914.
148 "to get the best minds in the country": Murray–Russell, 12 Sept. 1910, R.A.
148 "Tell me of another philosopher": Murray–Russell, 19 Sept. 1910, R.A.
149 "I must try to find more things to say": T. 105, pmk. 9 June 1911.
149 "Leibniz and Spinoza on my mantelpiece": T. 107, pmk. 10 June 1911.
149 "I wrote the stuff such ages ago": T. 243, Nov. 1911.
149 regular and detailed instructions: Ottoline–Russell, 28 June 1911, R.A.
149 "It was exhausting but delightful": *Garsington*, 278.
150 "It was delicious in the woods": T. 138, pmk. 8 July 1911.
150 first raised in April: T. 30, pmk. 15 Apr. 1911.
150 "You needn't be afraid of being sentimental": T. 138, pmk. 8 July 1911.
150 "If I were in the country": T. 139, pmk. 8 July 1911.

page

151 "without very great inconvenience": Russell–Professor Ralph Barton Perry, n.d., R.A.
151 dreadful to be parted: Ottoline–Russell, 4 June 1911, R.A.
151 "I found my friendship with Bertie Russell": *Ottoline*, 213.
151 "I remember now the exact spot": T. 428, Apr. 1912.
151 "loved once again": T. 46, pmk. 29 Apr. 1911.
151 "Thrice have I loved": included in T. 407, pmk. 4 Apr. 1912.
152 "the one thing I absolutely must not tell about": T. 147, 14 July 1911.
152 "First, you must not wish me to make friendships with women": T. 149, pmk. July 1911.
152 [Ottoline] had been interested in philosophy: *Ottoline*, 102.
152 "considered that the ultimate value of religion": *Dictionary of National Biography, 1901–1911*, 209.
152 "explain obversion, inversion": T. 122, pmk. 20 June 1911.
152 "Axiom I. The attraction between": T. 121, pmk. 19 July 1911.
153 For Whitehead's comments on manuscript, see Victor Lowe, "Whitehead's 1911 Criticism of *The Problems of Philosophy*", *Russell*, no. 13 (Spring 1974), 3–10.
153 "I arrived without having seen a soul": T. 180, pmk. 15 Sept. 1911.
153 "Alys had guessed": T. 195, pmk. 26 Sept. 1911.
153 "[It] caused me some perplexity": T. 181, n.d.
153 "I have the energy of 20 steam-engines": T. 181, n.d.
153 "Doing this book has given me": T. 146, 12 July 1911.
153 "I am surprised to find": T. 243, 4 Nov. 1911.
154 "The distinction is quite simple": Russell–Miss Bransby, 18 June 1960, R.A.
155 "wants to know what things seem to be": Russell, *The Problems of Philosophy*, 12.
155 "to keep alive that speculative interest": Russell, *The Problems of Philosophy*, 241.
155 "The life of the instinctive man": Russell, *The Problems of Philosophy*, 244.
156 "It is a distinction which divorces the being ... ": Bernard Bosanquet, *Mind*, vol. 21 (1912), 556.
156 "What *is* one to do": T. 602, pmk. 13 Oct. 1912.
156 "being very impressed by the intensity": Fr D'Arcy–Russell, 31 Oct. 1967, R.A.
156 "a saint and a mystic": Dean Matthews–author, 1 May 1972.
156 "When we first found each other": T. 493, 10 July 1912.
157 "In very early days": T. 1053, pmk. 16 July 1914.
157 "It is funny about religion": T. no number, n.d.
157 "I want to get free from business": T. 74, 19 May 1911.
157 "She read all Wells's novels as they came out": *Ottoline*, 97.
158 "More than 20 years ago": T. 270, pmk. 29 Nov. 1911.
158 "Your belief only survives": T. 270, pmk. 29 Nov. 1911.
158 "It is true that I shall sometimes publicly attack things": T. 25, pmk. 10 Apr. 1911.
159 "You with your God": T. 187, 21 Sept. 1911.
159 "To give religion to those who cannot believe in God": T. 170, pmk. 12 Aug. 1911.

page

159 "The world's a prison": T. 120, pmk. July 1911.
159 "I feel like Napoleon": T. 161, 30 July 1911.
159 "If they will let me have a key": T. 158, pmk. 24 July 1911.
159 "I have no skill in that sort of thing": T. 163, pmk. 31 July 1911.
160 "provides worship, acquiescence, love": T. 183, pmk. Aug. 1911.
160 "[Alfred] has not read it yet": T. 224, pmk. 18 Oct. 1911.
161 " 'Prisons' has the dullness that comes to middle-aged men": T. 416, pmk. 15 Apr. 1912.
161 "One of his chapters": T. 216, pmk. 13 Oct. 1911.
161 "merely traditional mysticism": Russell, "Philosophy in the Twentieth Century", *Sceptical Essays*, 65.
161 "that of the company-promoter": Russell, "Philosophy in the Twentieth Century", *Sceptical Essays*, 65.
161 "felt like a gourmet": T. 235, pmk. 28 Oct. 1911.
161 "Shaw explained Bergson's philosophy lucidly": T. 236, pmk. 29 Oct. 1911.
162 "While I am in the midst of the Whiteheads": T. 297, 25 Dec. 1911.
162 their first serious row: Ottoline–Russell, 27 Dec. 1911, R.A.
162 "What you call God": T. 301, 29 Dec. 1911.
163 "I think Christ was right": T. 303, 30 Dec. 1911.
163 she cancelled the meeting: Ottoline–Russell, 29 Dec. 1911, R.A.
163 "I was much amused by it": T. 414, pmk. 13 Apr. 1912.
164 "only my own": Russell–Murray, 7 Aug. 1912, R.A.
164 "During this past year I have written": T. 286, pmk. 13 Dec. 1911.
166 "right ... about chastity": Russell–Irina Wragge-Morley, 5 Mar. 1947, private source.
167 "I do not come in contact": Russell–Lucy Donnelly, 21 Jan. 1912, R.A.
167 "In my lecture yesterday I changed my mind in the middle": T. 363, 1 Mar. 1912.
167 "I have grown more and more careful": T. 41, Apr. 1911.
168 "I dined at an inn": T. 155, n.d.
168 "Here I have the sort of love": T. 290, pmk. 22 Dec. 1911.
169 "First McTaggart came before the official time": T. 216, pmk. 13 Oct. 1911.
169 "After dinner I got entangled": T. 358, pmk. 25 Feb. 1912.
169 "to be kind enough to act as the Director": J. N. Keynes–Dr W. M. Fletcher, 5 June 1912, quoted G. H. von Wright (ed.), Ludwig Wittgenstein, *Letters to Russell, Keynes and Moore*, 1 (afterwards referred to as "Wittgenstein, *Letters*").
170 "He turned out to be a man": T. 225, 18 Oct. 1911.
170 "perhaps the most perfect example": *Auto.*, II, 98.
170 "My German friend threatens to be an infliction": T. 227, 19 Oct. 1911.
170 "My German engineer very argumentative": T. 238, pmk. 1 Nov. 1911.
170 "My lecture went off all right": T. 254, 13 Nov. 1911.
170 "My German engineer, I think, is a fool": T. 241, 2 Nov. 1911.
170 "looked under all the desks": Russell, "Ludwig Wittgenstein", *Mind*, vol. 60 (1951), 297.
170 "My ferocious German came": T. 259, 16 Nov. 1911.
170 "I am getting to like him": T. 271, pmk. 29 Nov. 1911.

page

171 "My German is hesitating": T. 268, pmk. 27 Nov. 1911.

171 "Very good, much better than my English pupils do": T. 320, pmk. 23 Jan. 1912.

171 "a very good original suggestion": T. 360, 27 Feb. 1912.

171 "Moore thinks enormously highly of [his] brains": T. 368, pmk. 5 Mar. 1912.

171 "I like Wittgenstein more and more": T. 373, pmk. 8 Mar. 1912.

171 "never believes what I say": Russell–Lucy Donnelly, 26 Mar. 1912, R.A.

171 "He has more passion about philosophy": T. 385, 16 Mar. 1912.

172 "I have the most perfect intellectual sympathy with him": T. 388, 17 Mar. 1912.

172 "In discussion with him": T. 388, 17 Mar. 1912.

172 "Wittgenstein . . . a homosexual": Irina Stickland, letter to ed., *The Times Literary Supplement*, 22 Feb. 1974, 186.

172 "When he left I was strangely excited by him": T. 388, 17 Mar. 1912.

172 "I love him & feel he will solve": T. 397, pmk. 22 Mar. 1912.

173 "It was incredibly beautiful": T. 395, pmk. 21 Mar. 1912.

173 "a splendid walk": T. 396, pmk. 21 Mar. 1912.

173 "I have found a sheltered spot in the sun": T. 397, pmk. 22 Mar. 1912.

174 "I *longed* to go & demand his gospel": T. 397, pmk. 22 Mar. 1912.

174 "It was raining a great part of the time": T. 400, pmk. 24 Mar. 1912.

174 "I do wish I could get inside your skin": T. 400, pmk. 24 Mar. 1912.

175 "When physical pain flares up": T. 403, pmk. 26 Mar. 1912.

175 "He sits inside the car": T. 409, pmk. 5 Apr. 1912.

175 "wanted a wife and a cat": T. 323, 24 Jan. 1912.

175 "[She] began at once on sex questions": T. 409, pmk. 5 Apr. 1912.

175 "but rather to my relief": T. 411, pmk. 6 Apr. 1912.

175 "moment of heaven": T. 417, 16 Apr. 1912.

176 "I have got a number of new technical ideas from him": T. 422, pmk. 23 Apr. 1912.

176 "everybody has just begun to discover [him]": T. 435, pmk. 2 May 1912.

176 "On reflection": T. 435, pmk. 2 May 1912.

176 "There is one great question": T. 286, 13 Dec. 1911.

177 "a model of cold passionate analysis": T. 423, pmk. 24 Apr. 1912.

177 "It will shock people": T. 426, 28 Apr. 1912.

177 "It is not as clear as it ought to be": T. 449, pmk. 13 May 1912.

177 "*He* thinks my paper on Matter the best thing I have done": T. 460, pmk. 22 May 1912.

177 "It is really amazing": T. 510, 24 July 1912.

178 "I think if I ever publish that autobiography": T. 423, 25 Apr. 1912.

178 "It worries me rather": T. 459, pmk. 21 May 1912.

178 "but I will put the bulk of it": T. 459, pmk. 21 May 1912.

179 "I copied out for 'Forstice' ": T. 1090, n.d.

179 "It wants changes": T. 485, 2 July 1912.

179 "It wants to be approached": T. 498, pmk. 14 July 1912.

180 "I found myself alone with her": T. 521, n.d.

180 "[She] thought the nun quite unreal": T. 523, pmk. 3 Aug. 1912.

page

180 "About the nun, it really is *only* the inappropriateness": T. 532, pmk. 8 Aug. 1912.

180 "I do really think it has the quality": Lowes Dickinson–Russell, 21 July 1912, R.A.

180 "I wish I knew more of the world": T. 527, Aug. 1912.

180 "What I should like to do": T. 570, n.d.

181 "I feel so hampered": T. 563, pmk. 3 Sept. 1912.

181 "I do *wish* I were more creative": T. 569, pmk. 7 Sept. 1912.

181 "I was wrong in thinking": T. 552, pmk. 26 Aug. 1912.

181 "another dialogue for Forstice": T. 563, pmk. 3 Sept. 1912.

182 "His view is that I might leave": T. 1055, pmk. 22 July 1914.

182 Russell gave the manuscript of *Forstice* to Lucy Donnelly. It was kept in the Library of Bryn Mawr until returned to Russell in 1959.

182 "Whilst I am satisfied with the first part of the work": Russell–Anton Felton, 6 Apr. 1968, R.A. It has been suggested that when writing in 1968 Russell wrote "second" when he meant "third". This is possible, and it is certainly true that the nun was partly Ottoline's conception. Just as interesting is the fact that Tristram Forstice's unrequited love for the nun mirrors Russell's feelings for the woman he loved in 1902.

183 "Seeing that you, who have the whole of two men": T. 423, pmk. 25 Apr. 1912.

183 "The thing I was thinking of": T. 428, Apr. 1912.

183 "I must try to make my passion less": T. 456, May 1912.

184 Philip welcomed the idea: Ottoline–Russell, 25 May 1912, R.A.

184 "*Of course*, I shouldn't dream of letting anyone know": T. 467, pmk. 26 May 1912.

184 "Would you not, as far as your own happiness is concerned": T. 471, pmk. 30 May 1912.

184 "I ought not to come": T. 477, 3 June 1912.

184 "You say you know what I feel": T. 475, 1 June 1912.

185 "The afternoons we spent together": *Ottoline*, 226.

185 "I remember all the changing moods": T. 1006, 19 Mar. 1914.

185 "the extraordinary beauty of the evg.": T. 784, pmk. 23 May 1913.

186 "Fate and chance seem to draw one": *Ottoline*, 226.

186 "There's Karin": T. 520, pmk. 1 Aug. 1912.

186 "I turned and fled": T. 520, pmk. 1 Aug. 1912.

186 "I didn't see her till we were passing": T. 520, pmk. 1 Aug. 1912.

186 "was inexpressibly painful to me": Russell–Lucy Donnelly, 3 Sept. 1912, R.A.

186 "On reflection I think her look at me was not all tragedy": T. 519, 1 Aug. 1912.

187 "Let us go to Putney": T. 500, July 1912.

187 "I had just begun to feel really alive": T. 580, 18 Sept. 1912.

187 "I went into the village": T. 580, 18 Sept. 1912.

188 "While we were sitting": *Garsington*, 281.

188 "That means 3 days quite clear": T. 598, 9 Oct. 1912.

188 "Last Sunday, the 'Heretics' here had a paper": T. 608, n.d.

188 "He looks the ideal picture of a logician": T. 547, pmk. 22 Aug. 1912.

188 "I have an odd sense of treachery": T. 547, pmk. 22 Aug. 1912.

page

188 "I find it excites me": T. 546, 21 Aug. 1912.

189 "I slipped away from all the math'ns. one moment & found your letter": T. 547, pmk. 22 Aug. 1912.

189 "From 9.30 to 1": T. 549, pmk. 23 Aug. 1912.

189 "In the evening there was a party": T. 547, pmk. 22 Aug. 1912.

190 "particular, finite, self-centred": Russell, "The Essence of Religion", *Hibbert Journal*, vol. 11 (Oct. 1912), 46–62.

190 "had been a traitor to the gospel of exactness": T. 600, pmk. 11 Oct. 1912.

190 "because I half agree with him": T. 600, pmk. 11 Oct. 1912.

190 "atheism implanted by a motor-car": T. 601, pmk. 12 Oct. 1912.

190 "A more brilliant intellect I never met": Sir Francis Younghusband, *The Light of Experience*, 219.

191 "I love him": T. 889, 7 Oct. 1913.

191 "What is important, I wonder?": Russell–Lowes Dickinson, 13 Feb. 1913, R.A.

191 "We talk about music, morals": T. 564, pmk. 4 Sept. 1912.

191 "He is *very* fussy": T. 566, pmk. 5 Sept. 1912.

192 "He is on the verge of a nervous breakdown": T. 617, pmk. 31 Oct. 1912.

192 "Thank you very much for the cocoa": T. 621, 4 Nov. 1912.

192 "I was cross because North had been beaten": T. 629, pmk. 9 Nov. 1912.

193 "The poor man [Russell] is in a sad state": Lytton Strachey–Saxon Sydney-Turner, 20 Nov. 1912, quoted Holroyd, *Lytton Strachey*, II, 71.

193 "I knew nothing at the time": Russell–Michael Holroyd, 14 Sept. 1966, quoted Holroyd, *Lytton Strachey*, II, 71.

193 "to warn them of dangers about Wittgenstein": T. 632, pmk. 10 Nov. 1912.

193 "All the difficulties I anticipated have arisen": Russell–Maynard Keynes, 11 Nov. 1912, Keynes Papers, King's College, Cambridge.

194 "Wittgenstein has left the Society": T. 950, n.d.

194 "The paper lasted only about four minutes": Minutes of the Moral Science Club, 29 Nov. 1912.

194 "It *is* true": T. 605, 15 Oct. 1912.

195 "As regards Matter, I have got into deep water": T. 626, pmk. 7 Nov. 1912.

195 "It is a vast & very difficult subject": T. 627, pmk. 8 Nov. 1912.

195 "At present it is appallingly difficult": T. 628, pmk. 9 Nov. 1912.

195 "No good argument for or against the existence of matter": Minutes, Moral Science Club, Nov. 1912.

196 "a serious attempt at a unified and systematic Philosophy of Nature": *Mind*, n.s., vol. 5 (1896), 410–17.

196 "I am going on reading popular books": T. 639, pmk. 17 Nov. 1912.

197 "From my experience": Russell–Professor Perry, 19 Dec. 1912, R.A.

197 "be quite dreadful when the time comes": T. 638, pmk. 16 Nov. 1912.

197 "America contains a number of people who are ready": T. 628, pmk. 9 Nov. 1912.

197 "go to Harvard permanently": T. 693, pmk. 6 Feb. 1913.

page

199 "Ever since you went": T. 1412, Aug. 1916.

200 "He only feels life through his brain": *Garsington*, 47.

200 "the problems which Moore and I have been agitating lately": Santayana, *Winds of Doctrine*, 113.

200 "that the mind or soul is an entity": Santayana, *Winds of Doctrine*, 113.

200 "Thus *good* and *bad* are qualities": Russell, "The Elements of Ethics", in *Philosophical Essays*, 21.

201 "Driven from the particular sciences": Russell, "Mysticism and Logic", in *Mysticism and Logic*, 29.

201 "But he is a *scoundrel*": Russell–Lowes Dickinson, quoted Wood, 61.

201 "where ethics is concerned": Russell, "Reply to Criticisms", in Schilpp (ed.), *The Philosophy of Bertrand Russell*, 719.

201 "not a very trustworthy thinker": Santayana–B. A. G. Fuller, 10 Nov. 1913, Daniel Cory (ed.), *The Letters of George Santayana*, 129.

201 "There is a strange mixture in him": Santayana–B. A. G. Fuller, 7 Feb. 1914, Daniel Cory (ed.), *The Letters of George Santayana*, 137.

202 "I can give them the same stuff": T. 808, pmk. 15 June 1913.

202 "The excitement of philosophical construction": T. 755, pmk. 26 Apr. 1913.

202 "Winston monopolised Venetia": T. 765, pmk. 6 May 1913.

203 "I can't think who buys it": T. 748, pmk. 19 Apr. 1913.

203 "I feel so bursting with work": T. 779, 18 May 1913.

203 "Work is a desperate business": T. 996, 3 June 1913.

203 "[Causality] depends on induction": T. 747, pmk. 18 Apr. 1913.

203 "The night is hot & delicious": T. 784, pmk. 23 May 1913.

203 "Oddly enough [Wittgenstein] makes me less anxious to live": T. 475, 1 June 1912.

204 "I had a terrific contest with [him]": T. 717, 6 Mar. 1913.

204 "Poor wretch! I know his feelings so well": T. 729, 29 Mar. 1913.

204 "I think there is a danger of it": T. 762, 2 May 1913.

204 "We were both cross from the heat": T. 787, 28 May 1913.

205 "an event of first-rate importance in my life": Russell–Ottoline, 1916, *Auto.*, II, 57.

205 "I think in all likelihood they are just": T. 792, n.d.

205 "a sort of inner voice": T. 793, 1 June 1913.

205 "He came analysing all that goes wrong": T. 798, 5 June 1913.

206 "I am very sorry": Wittgenstein–Russell, 22 July 1913, R.A.

206 Blackwell ... points out: Kenneth Milton Blackwell, "Wittgenstein's Impact on Russell's Theory of Belief", 74, which gives a detailed analysis of the highly technical arguments involved, of Russell's partially published manuscript and of Wittgenstein's attitude. Professor Elizabeth Ramsdon Eames was the first to reconstruct the original manuscript.

206 "But Wittgenstein's objection": Kenneth Blackwell–author, 30 Oct. 1974.

206 "It was very difficult": T. 811, pmk. 20 June 1913.

207 "It seems to me today that we ought to part": T. 819, 28 June 1913.

208 "I have never known any place": T. 827, n.d.

208 "It seems a sin": T. 840, pmk. 5 Aug. 1913.

208 "It has that strange sense of peace": T. 847, 14 Aug. 1913.

209 It ... ran to 16 pages: Ottoline–Russell, 14–15–16 Aug. 1913, R.A.

page

209 "I am utterly and absolutely miserable": T. 848, n.d.

209 "I feel even more hopeless": T. 850, pmk. 19 Aug. 1913.

211 "curious sudden adventure": T. 857, pmk. 29 Aug. 1913.

212 "civilized and morally tolerable human life": *Auto.*, I, 208.

212 "It was *wonderful*": T. 865, 11 Sept. 1913.

212 "I think I have always felt": Russell–Watts-Armstrong, 3 Oct. 1961, R.A.

213 British Association Birmingham meeting: For account of Section A (Mathematics and Physics) meetings attended by Niels Bohr, Madame Curie, Hendrijk Lorentz and other foreign scientists, see *Nature*, vol. 92, 6 Nov. 1913, 304–9.

213 "It seems one of the Danes": T. 870, 16 Sept. 1913.

213 "I have been hearing more about the new physics": T. 873, pmk. 20 Sept. 1913.

214 "I am sure it is *far* the most useful thing": T. 902, 8 Oct. 1913.

214 "On the Nature of Acquaintance": This is a portion of the "Theory of Knowledge" book, the part missing in manuscript.

214 "the things commonly regarded as mental": Russell, "On the Nature of Acquaintance", *Monist*, vol. 24 (Jan.–July 1914), reprinted Marsh, 139.

214 "if physics is to be verifiable": Russell, "The Relation of Sense-Data to Physics", *Scientia*, vol. 16 (July 1914), reprinted *Mysticism and Logic*, 146.

214 "those objects which have the same metaphysical": Russell, "The Relation of Sense-Data to Physics", *Mysticism and Logic*, 148.

214 "Thus the relation of a *sensibile*": Russell, "The Relation of Sense-Data to Physics", *Mysticism and Logic*, 148.

215 "Said Lord Russell": variants of the limerick abound; this one was found on a sheet slipped into Russell's Journal at the Humanities Research Center, the University of Texas at Austin.

215 "in philosophy he has pursued studies": Leo Wiener–Russell, 15 June 1913, R.A.

215 "Nevertheless, he turned out well": *Auto.*, I, 223.

215 "While this information was being poured out": T. 877, pmk. 26 Sept. 1913.

216 "Yes, the infant phenomenon is staying here": T. 879, pmk. 29 Sept. 1913.

216 "his Dr.'s thesis": see Ivor Grattan-Guinness, "Wiener on the Logics of Russell and Schröder. An Account of his Doctoral Thesis, and of his Discussion of it with Russell", *Annals of Science*, vol. 32 (1975), 103–32.

216 "the youth has been flattered": Russell–Lucy Donnelly, 19 Oct. 1913, R.A.

216 "Wiener good at mathematics": quoted T. 976, n.d.

216 "McTaggart, a Hegelian and the Dr. Codger": Norbert Wiener, *Ex-Prodigy*, 194.

216 "The third, Dr. G. E. Moore": Norbert Wiener, *Ex-Prodigy*, 196.

216 "My New England puritanism": Norbert Wiener, *Ex-Prodigy*, 192.

217 "I said it would be dark": Russell–Lucy Donnelly, 19 Oct. 1913, R.A.

217 "could only just understand": T. 886, 6 Oct. 1913.

217 "Well, that is true, anyway": quoted Russell–James Griffin, 19 May 1958, R.A.

page

217 "After much groaning": T. 891, pmk. 9 Oct. 1913.

218 *Notes on Logic*: For discussion of the text, see B. F. McGuinness, "Bertrand Russell and Ludwig Wittgenstein's 'Notes on Logic' ", *Revue Internationale de Philosophie*, vol. 26 (Mar. 1973), 444–60.

218 "I have been translating": T. 997, 28 Feb. 1914.

218 "Even Russell – who is of course most extraordinarily fresh": Wittgenstein–Moore, 19 Nov. 1913, quoted G. H. von Wright (ed.), Wittgenstein, *Letters*, 145.

218 "I should never have believed": Wittgenstein–Russell, 12 June 1919, R.A.

218 "They will all have to be re-written": T. 869, pmk. 15 Sept. 1913.

219 "worked for 3 hours": T. 904, pmk. 2 Nov. 1913.

219 "I shall be thankful when I have done with them": T. 904, pmk. 2 Nov. 1913.

219 "I shall be free to go on preparing": T. 905, pmk. 5 Nov. 1913.

219 "which will be a relief": T. 908, pmk. 8 Nov. 1913.

219 "Now I am free from that weight": T. 919, pmk. 23 Nov. 1913.

219 Lowell Lectures: A detailed account of Russell's contradictory explanations of how the Lowell Lectures came to be written is given in "Our Knowledge of *Our Knowledge*", by Kenneth Blackwell, *Russell*, no. 12 (Winter 1973–4), 11–13.

219 "Chicago University wants me": T. 914, pmk. 17 Nov. 1913.

219 "She has just now answered": T. 894, pmk. 14 Oct. 1913.

220 "There is a thing I have it on my conscience to say": T. 920, pmk. 26 Nov. 1913.

220 unselfishly willing to let him go: Ottoline–Russell, 21 and 22 Dec. 1913, R.A.

220 "You need not be afraid": T. 939, pmk. 22 Dec. 1913.

220 "I know that whatever happens": T. 939, 22 Dec. 1913.

221 "The situation perplexes my instinct": T. 943, n.d.

221 "You have reduced to order": Joseph Conrad–Russell, 22 Dec. 1913, R.A.

221 "[It] has somehow brought me a flash of insight": T. 955, pmk. Dec. 1913/Jan. 1914.

222 "My rooms looked very friendly": T. 956, pmk. 4 Jan. 1914.

223 "Talking to her was very soothing": T. 965, n.d.

224 "I am very sorry indeed": T. 984, n.d.

224 "I had no anger": T. 986, pmk. 13 Feb. 1914.

224 "sudden outburst ... asking me not to give you up altogether": T. 989, pmk. 17 Feb. 1914.

225 "Since I came back": T. 960, 8 Jan. 1914.

225 "Don't tell them": Russell–Lucy Donnelly, 20 Feb. 1914, R.A.

225 "It cost me a frightful lot of time": T. 972, pmk. 18 Jan. 1914.

225 "From the time I came here": T. 972, pmk. 18 Jan. 1914.

226 "I don't at all discard": T. 426, 28 Apr. 1912.

226 "I know now what I really believe": T. 961, 9 Jan. 1914.

226 "an intense exercise": Ronald Jager, *The Development of Bertrand Russell's Philosophy*, 495.

226 "aim at eloquence": T. 968, n.d.

page

226 "Perhaps [the visit] will give you": Wittgenstein–Russell, Jan. 1914, R.A.

226 "I dare say his mood will change": T. 989, pmk. 17 Feb. 1914.

226 "Now I'll make a proposal to you": Wittgenstein–Russell, 3 Mar. 1914, R.A.

227 "I haven't been living within my £20 a month": T. 895, pmk. 15 Oct. 1913.

227 "Will America be shocked": Russell–Lucy Donnelly, 14 Nov. 1913, R.A.

227 "I have tried to get help from my brother": T. 961, 9 Jan. 1914.

227 "It is awful to have to leave you": T. 998, 1 Mar. 1914.

228 "[Russell] is a socialist": Younghusband, *The Light of Experience*, 220.

228 "It is a comfort reading some philosophy": T. 591, 28 Sept. 1912.

229 "This is a regular American place": T. 1006, 19 Mar. 1914.

229 "the one I have most to do with": T. 1004, 14 Mar. 1914.

229 "it only leaves dinner": T. 1010, 26 Mar. 1914.

229 "as we walked back": Professor H. A. Hollond–Russell, 26 May 1964, Trinity College Library.

229 "My first Lowell lecture": T. 1005, 19 Mar. 1914.

229 "it seems to me futile": T. 1010, 28 Mar. 1914.

230 "to show, by means of examples": Russell, *Our Knowledge of the External World*, v.

230 "the American tendency": T. 1004, 14 Mar. 1914.

230 "America produces a type of bore": T. 1005, 19 Mar. 1914.

230 "Boston prides itself": Russell–Margaret Llewelyn Davies, 12 Apr. 1914, R.A.

230 "Nobody here broods": T. 1006, 19 Mar. 1914.

230 "they were the kind of people": T. 1010, 26 Mar. 1914.

231 "its mere name is romantic to me": T. 1008, n.d.

231 "When we who were trained": Costello, quoted Grover Smith (ed.), *Josiah Royce's Seminar as recorded in the notebooks of Harry T. Costello*, 190.

231 "In teaching able men": T. 1028, 8 May 1914.

231 "This morning two of my pupils came": T. 1010, 26 Mar. 1914.

231 "proficient in Plato": Russell–Lucy Donnelly, 11 May 1914, R.A.

231 "But it gave me a sense of pleasure": T. S. Eliot, quoted Brand Blanshard, "Eliot in Memory", *Yale Review*, vol. 54 (Summer 1965), 635–40.

232 "To my surprise I liked him very much": T. 1008, 22 Mar. 1914.

232 "a view which is really marvellous": T. 1016, n.d.

232 "I am afraid it made me more affectionate to Helen Flexner": T. 1030, 15 May 1914.

232 "of Fragilion, that shy figure": T. S. Eliot, "Mr. Appollinax", in *Prufrock*, 1917, reprinted in Eliot's *Collected Poems, 1909–1962*.

232 "Your very dear letter": T. 1017, 15 Apr. 1914.

232 "On Friday, I spoke on suffrage": T. 1020, 20 Apr. 1914.

233 "I do not like to have Bryn Mawr students": Lucy Donnelly–Dr Carey Thomas, 8 Mar. 1914, R.A.

233 "Miss Thomas might just as well have let you speak": Lucy Donnelly–Russell, 24 Apr. 1914, R.A.

233 "full of new Gothic": T. 1022, 24 Apr. 1914.

page

233 "suitable for an audience": Russell–Professor Gardiner, 18 Apr. 1914, Smith College, Northampton, Mass.
233 "You can't think the happiness it is": T. 1031, 23 May 1914.
234 "I stay with some people named Dudley": T. 1031, 23 May 1914.
234 "terrific sexual urges": Utley, 72.
234 "I half think if women were free": T. 1023, 27 Apr. 1914.
234 " ... This is the last letter before I sail": T. 1034, 1 June 1914.
236 "was beautiful beyond belief": T. 1035, n.d.
236 "sticking up in a conical shape": Russell–Margaret Llewelyn Davies, 9 June 1914, R.A.
236 "the well-to-do unintellectual graduate": Russell, review of Santayana, *Soliloquies in England*, *Dial*, vol. 73 (1922), 559.
236 "Ah God! to see the branches stir": Rupert Brooke, "The Old Vicarage, Grantchester".
236 "stayed with Helen Dudley's people": Russell–Lucy Donnelly, 6 June 1914, R.A.
237 "practical problems – when & how to leave Trinity": T. 1035, n.d.
237 "Cambridge holds a great part of my affections": T. 1056, pmk. 24 July 1914.
237 "It happens that tonight I am unusually clear-sighted": T. 1042, pmk. 23 June 1914.
238 "the lonely nights grow unbearable": T. 1042, pmk. 23 June 1914.
238 "The chief thing": T. 1044, pmk. 24 June 1914.
239 "But I feel no passion": T. 1051, pmk. 12 July 1914.
239 "I don't think H.D. will do any harm": T. 1059, pmk. 29 July 1914.
239 Ottoline's references to the Dudleys, written in her Memoirs in 1931 and published in 1974, conceal the name of Helen Dudley under the guise of "Hilda Ward", whose father is described not as a doctor but as a well-known Chicago lawyer.
239 "I feel now an absolute blank indifference": T. 1065, pmk. 2 Aug. 1914.
239 "Unless captured by Germans": T. 1068, pmk. 7 Aug. 1914.
239 "I have had a postcard from my German lady": T. 1053, pmk. 16 July 1914.
240 "When I saw with what hopes": *Garsington*, 287.
240 "I don't think she realises": T. 1081, n.d.
240 "I am very very sorry": T. 1093, pmk. 29 Aug. 1914.
240 "I couldn't understand your saying": T. 1090, n.d.
240 "Yesterday morning, I had a letter from Helen": T. 1078, n.d.
241 Helen to the Bury Street flat: T. 1085, 26 Aug. 1914.
241 "It was *wonderfully* happy today": T. 1085, pmk. 25 Aug. 1914.
241 "Nothing on earth": T. 1093, pmk. 29 Aug. 1914.
241 "I was sorry not to see you tonight": T. 1100, pmk. 4 Sept. 1914.
241 "amused & pleased to hear": T. 1124, n.d.
241 "I wouldn't let her in": T. 1137, n.d.
241 "queer talk we had about Miss C. W.": T. 1178, n.d.
242 "She was beautiful": Enid Bagnold–author, 30 July 1974.
242 "He was, as Margot Oxford said": Enid Bagnold–author, 30 July 1974.
242 "I think I may easily come to have a *very* great affection": T. 1189, pmk. 8 Jan. 1915.

page

243 she reacted generously: Ottoline–Russell, 7 Jan. 1915, R.A.

243 Ottoline was forced to deny: Ottoline–Russell, 9 Jan. 1915, R.A.

243 go away with Russell: Ottoline–Russell, 20 Jan. 1915, R.A.

243 "I have written to her": T. 1204, pmk. 20 Jan. 1915.

243 "I have a real and great affection for her": T. 1217, n.d.

243 "It worries me": T. 1147, pmk. 11 Nov. 1914.

244 "Insufferable race": Russell–Lucy Donnelly, 25 June 1914, R.A.

244 "We help in the perpetration of a crime against liberty": T. 272, n.d.

244 "... I have always regarded Grey": Russell–C. P. Sanger, 7 Aug. 1914, R.A.

244 "If we succeed": Russell–Lucy Donnelly, 22 Aug. 1914, R.A.

244 "I don't know how sincere": T. 1045, pmk. 3 July 1914.

245 "I can see no mortal reason": Lord Fitzmaurice–J. A. Spender, 31 July 1914, Spender Papers, B.M. Add. 46392, quoted Max Beloff, *Imperial Sunset*, 177.

245 "I have not found a *single* person": T. 1064, pmk. 1 Aug. 1914.

245 "when they try to protect their homes": T. 1064, pmk. 1 Aug. 1914.

245 "War upon [Germany]": *Cambridge Daily News*, 1 Aug. 1914.

245 "the supreme conviction": *Cambridge Daily News*, 3 Aug. 1914.

245 "to the effect that if Germany had delayed her violation": C. P. Scott, quoted Trevor Wilson (ed.), *The Political Diaries of C. P. Scott, 1911–1928*, 115.

246 "I seem to feel all the weight of Europe's passion": T. 1063, pmk. 1 Aug. 1914.

246 "I am fixing some things in my mind": T. 1065, pmk. 2 Aug. 1914.

246 "told Philip he was to make": unpublished draft of *Auto.*, R.A.

246 "never pass the empty region": T. 1690, 12 Oct. 1931.

246 "After about three years of war": Russell–Prof. Alfred Havighurst, 9 Mar. 1965, R.A.

247 "We are terribly alone": T. 1066, pmk. 5 Aug. 1914.

247 "The prize bore": T. 1067, pmk. 6 Aug. 1914.

247 "the Socialist firebrand": T. 1083, pmk. 22 Aug. 1914.

247 "immaculate in evening dress": T. 1083, pmk. 22 Aug. 1914.

247 "... we couldn't have the Germans": Edward Marsh, *A Number of People*, 47.

247 "the kind of obscene philosophic insect": Russell–Ottoline, 27 Aug. 1918, private source, copy in R.A.

247 "Wells ... 'enthusiastic' for this war": Russell–Lucy Donnelly, 22 Aug. 1914, R.A.

247 "Clearly the Germans are the worst": Russell–Lucy Donnelly, 21 Oct. 1914, R.A.

247 "I do see the point": T. 1066, pmk. 5 Aug. 1914.

248 "We are all patriots in one sense": Russell–Lucy Donnelly, 23 Feb. 1915, R.A.

248 "I take it for granted": T. 1095, 30 Aug. 1914.

248 "I agreed with thee": Alys–Russell, 24 Sept. 1914, R.A.

248 "ashamed of ever having liked him": T. 1110, pmk. 18 Sept. 1914.

248 "as squashy as a slug": T. 1149, pmk. 18 Nov. 1914.

248 "... let this dark shadow": Agatha Russell–Russell, 27 Feb. 1916, R.A.

page

248 "When I got here": T. 1070, pmk. 14 Aug. 1914.
249 "I hope it will answer": T. 1074, pmk. 15 Aug. 1914.
249 "I am miserable": Whitehead–Russell, 28 Aug. 1914, R.A.
249 "meeting Belgian refugees": T. 1104, pmk. 11 Sept. 1914.
249 "It is perfectly awful here": T. 1105, n.d.
249 "I dread the Whiteheads": T. 1244, pmk. 3 Apr. 1915.
249 "more or less sane": T. 1279, pmk. 22 May 1915.
249 "something that if I had been religious": Russell, "An Autobiographical Epitome", *Portraits*, 11.
250 "I had meant to avoid discussion with you": Whitehead–Russell, 16 Apr. 1916, R.A.
250 "on the whole, men who refuse military service": Whitehead–Russell, 16 Apr. 1916, R.A.
250 "the bully must be stopped": Evelyn Whitehead–Russell, 4 Aug. 1914, R.A.
250 "hated challenging": Evelyn Whitehead–Russell, 16 Feb. 1916, R.A.
250 "if ... not made myself clear": Evelyn Whitehead–Russell, 24 Feb. 1916, R.A.
250 "... Try and think out a place of work": Evelyn Whitehead–Russell, 9 Feb. 1918, R.A.
251 "It seems strange that of all the people in the war": T. 1148, pmk. 12 Nov. 1914.
251 "I never knew till the war came": T. 1236, pmk. Mar. 1915.
251 "If I should perish in this war": Wittgenstein, quoted T. 1199, 15 Jan. 1915, also Wittgenstein, *Letters*, 59–60.
252 "The evening was dreadful": T. 1069, 11 Aug. 1914.
252 real parliamentary control: Circular letter, dated Aug. 1914, signed Ramsay MacDonald, Charles Trevelyan, E. D. Morel.
252 "It would be unwise": Russell–Charles Trevelyan, 2 Oct. 1914, University of Newcastle.
253 "every student of strategy": Russell, *War: The Offspring of Fear*, 10.
253 "The present is not the time to discuss peace": William Phillips–Elizabeth Perkins, 2 Nov. 1914, R.A.
253 "No solution will be possible": Russell, "The Future of Anglo-German Rivalry", *Atlantic Monthly*, vol. 116 (July 1915), 127.
254 "... the use of force is justifiable": Russell, "The War and Non-Resistance", *Atlantic Monthly*, vol. 116 (Aug. 1915), 266.
254 "able and willing to secure obedience by force": Russell, "The War and Non-Resistance", *Atlantic Monthly*, vol. 116 (Aug. 1915), 266.
254 "If it were adopted deliberately": Russell, "The War and Non-Resistance", *Atlantic Monthly*, vol. 116 (Aug. 1915), 266.
254 "Men have learned gradually": Russell, "War As An Institution", *Atlantic Monthly*, vol. 117 (May 1916), 603.
255 "I can make a terrific piece of invective": T. 1171, Christmas Eve 1914.
255 "The Ethics of War": *International Journal of Ethics*, vol. 25 (Jan. 1915), 127–42, reprinted in *Justice in Wartime*, 20–39.
256 "One of my chief reasons": Russell–George Turner, 26 Apr. 1915, R.A.
256 "I have been for some time in two minds": Russell–Herbert Bryan, 6 July

page

1915, quoted Marvin Schwartz, *The Union of Democratic Control in British Politics during the First World War*, 99.

256 "What I can do further in philosophy": T. 1147, Nov. 1914.

257 "All the white men are gone": Russell–C. D. Broad, 4 Dec. 1914, R.A.

257 "These fussy bloodthirsty old men": T. 1317, dated by Ottoline "Summer 1915".

257 "One of the divinity professors": A. J. Dorward–Russell, 31 May 1915, R.A.

257 "All that one has cared for is dead ...": T. 1361, 19 Mar. 1916.

258 "the same impression as the letters of Apollinaris Sidonius": T. 1381, May/June 1916.

258 "If I accept it": T. 1222, pmk. 13 Feb. 1914.

258 members "would consider favourably": Council Minutes, 21 May 1915, quoted G. H. Hardy, *Bertrand Russell and Trinity*, 27 (afterwards referred to as "Hardy").

258 "improved by occasional excursions into other fields": Russell–H. McLeod Innes, 21 May 1915, Trinity College Library.

258 "The College has been rent into violent factions": T. 1269, n.d.

259 "I lose £140": T. 1279, pmk. 27 May 1916.

259 "Fancy Helen being back": T. 1208, pmk. 22 Jan. 1915.

259 "these two passionate men": *Ottoline*, 273.

260 "Have you seen him": quoted Witter Bynner, *Journey with Genius*, 116.

260 "Your letter was very kind to me": Lawrence–Russell, 26 Feb. 1915, Harry T. Moore (ed.), *The Collected Letters of D. H. Lawrence*, 323 (afterwards referred to as "Moore").

260 "I don't want to be horribly impressed": Lawrence–Russell, 2 Mar. 1915, Moore, 328.

260 "was morose from the outset": J. M. Keynes, *Two Memoirs*, 78.

261 "was *at* Lawrence": Keynes, *Two Memoirs*, 79.

261 "Lawrence had rather liked him": T. 1234, pmk. 8 Mar. 1915.

261 "Keynes was hard": T. 1234, pmk. 8 Mar. 1915.

261 "It is true Cambridge": Lawrence–Russell, 19 Mar. 1915, Moore, 330.

261 "We talked of a plan for lecturing": T. 1306, pmk. 19 July 1915.

261 "Bertie Russell is here": Lawrence–Lady Ottoline Morrell (20 ?June 1915), Moore, 349.

262 "vitally, emotionally, much too inexperienced": Lawrence–Lady Ottoline Morrell (?5 July 1915), Moore, 351.

262 "Don't be angry": Lawrence–Russell, 15 July 1915, R.A.

263 "Lawrence . . . is disgusted with my lecture-syllabus": T. 1302, pmk. 8 July 1915.

263 "I am depressed": T. 1302, pmk. 8 July 1915.

263 "There must be a revolution": Lawrence–Russell, 12 Feb. 1915, Moore, 317.

264 "The enemy of all mankind": Lawrence–Russell, 14 Sept. 1915, Moore, 367.

264 "I was inclined to believe": *Auto.*, II, 22.

264 "The idea of suicide": T. 1333, n.d.

264 "I've got a real bitterness in my soul": Lawrence–Lady Cynthia Asquith, 16 Aug. 1915, Moore, 362.

page

264 "It is rather uneducated stuff": T. 1287, pmk. 12 July 1915.

265 "frankly rubbish": *Auto.*, II, 22.

265 "They may have come through": Mrs Igor Vinogradoff–author, also *Garsington*, 94.

265 "Lawrence . . . one of a long line of people": T. 1757, 15 Feb. 1937.

265 "the harshest words": James L. Jarrett, "D. H. Lawrence and Bertrand Russell", in H. T. Moore (ed.), *A D. H. Lawrence Miscellany*, 173.

265 "As to the effect of Lawrence on me": Russell–E. Jones, 28 Jan. 1957, R.A.

266 "he gets dreadfully on my nerves": *Garsington*, 45.

266 "The result was that the impulse stopped dead": T. 1455, n.d.

266 ". . . to write about the wickedness of the Germans": *Auto.*, II, 17.

266 "a snivelling sentimental ass": Russell–Lucy Donnelly, 14 Dec. 1914, R.A.

266 "We had a very painful conversation": T. 1312, 8 Aug. 1915.

267 "If you are writing anything": C. Delisle Burns–Russell, 15 Oct. 1915, R.A.

267 "On the way back, Bertrand Russell told me": quoted Martin Gilbert, *Plough My Own Furrow*, 133.

268 "I feel our friendship still lives": Russell–Murray, 28 Dec. 1915, R.A.

268 "I wonder if you or Bessie": Russell–Robert Trevelyan, n.d., R.A.

268 "They must have hated it": T. 1343, n.d.

268 "Bertie's lectures help one": Lytton Strachey, quoted Holroyd, *Lytton Strachey*, II, 173.

269 "the nearest things": Kingsley Martin, *Father Figures*, 100.

269 "His lectures are all right in themselves": Lawrence–Lady Ottoline Morrell, 15 Feb. 1916, Moore, 427.

269 "I don't believe your lectures *are* good": Lawrence–Russell, 19 Feb. 1916, Moore, 423.

269 "They unhesitatingly agreed": Stanley Unwin, *The Truth about a Publisher*, 152.

270 "to suggest a philosophy of politics": Russell, *Principles of Social Reconstruction*, 5–6.

270 "The logical meaning": Russell–W. V. Brigstocke, 14 Sept. 1917, R.A. The passage referred to is from "Men fear thought", 165, line 21, to "chief glory of man", 166, line 4, of the first edition.

270 "at every moment during the war": Russell, *Principles of Social Reconstruction*, 127.

271 "I have not read Bertrand Russell's book": Lawrence–Barbara Low, 11 Dec. 1916, quoted Edward Nehls (ed.), *D. H. Lawrence: A Composite Biography*, I, 407.

271 "the monastic detachment": *Athenaeum*, no. 4612 (Dec. 1916), 577.

271 "thoroughly mischievous book": *Spectator*, 6 Dec. 1916.

272 "Power over people's minds": Russell–Lucy Donnelly, 10 Feb. 1916, R.A.

273 "Bertie was most sympathetic": Lytton Strachey–Ottoline, 31 Dec. 1915, quoted Holroyd, *Lytton Strachey*, II, 171.

274 "joining at the rate of thousands a day": T. 1240, pmk. 18 Mar. 1915.

page

274 "But I have a good deal to do for my lectures": T. 1326, pmk. 29 Oct. 1915.

274 "The non-resistance people I know": T. 1286, pmk. 11 June 1915.

274 "Very able as an organiser & leader": T. 1352, pmk. 5 Feb. 1916.

275 "A Superior View of the War": *The Times Literary Supplement*, 6 Apr. 1916.

275 "I hold that the State has the right": Whitehead–Russell, 16 Apr. 1916, R.A.

275 "might have been delivered at any gathering of persons dissenting": Beatrice Webb, diary, 8 Apr. 1916, Passfield Papers, London School of Economics.

275 "You are satisfying": Lawrence–Russell, 14 Sept. 1915, Moore, 367.

276 "working day and night": Lytton Strachey–Vanessa Bell, 17 Apr. 1916, quoted Holroyd, *Lytton Strachey*, II, 174.

276 "I have these two Huns": quoted Victor Lenzen, "Bertrand Russell at Harvard, 1914", *Russell*, no. 3 (Autumn 1971), 4.

276 "My two men": Elizabeth Russell, diary entry 1 Nov. 1917, quoted Leslie de Charms, *Elizabeth of the German Garden*, 196.

276 "the most inspiring and happy thing": T. 1364, pmk. 10 Apr. 1916.

277 "I hope it will last": *Garsington*, 103.

277 "He was very unsatisfactory": T. 1364, pmk. 10 Apr. 1916.

277 "At the end, as we were leaving": *Auto.*, II, 24.

278 "Let all the Great Powers of Europe": *Labour Leader*, 13 (16), 20 Apr. 1916, reprinted *Russell*, no. 2 (Summer 1971), 10–11. For Brockway's confirmation of Russell's authorship, see *Russell*, no. 6 (Summer 1972), 5.

278 "He writes and speaks with a good deal of misguided cleverness": E. Troup–C. W. Mathews, 25 Aug. 1916, Public Record Office (afterwards referred to as "P.R.O.") H.O.45/11012/314670/6213.

278 "For my part, I get so much fun out of it": T. 1421, pmk. 7 Sept. 1916.

279 "In 1915 I was wandering about London": Miles Malleson, broadcast talk, 19 May 1964.

279 "There is a man in Wandsworth": H.Q. of N.-C.F.–Russell, n.d., R.A.

279 "I don't think I shall ever forget": Clifford Allen–Russell, n.d., quoted Gilbert, *Plough My Own Furrow*, 75.

279 "I am living all against impulse": T. 1514, n.d.

279 risk . . . of being shot: Russell–Murray, 17 Apr. 1916, R.A.

279 teetotalism . . . killing Germans: *Auto.*, I, 126.

280 "You can't be meaning to suggest": A. E. Taylor–Russell, 19 Sept. 1915, R.A.

280 "This has been a glorious and beautiful weekend": Keynes–Mrs John Neville Keynes, 27 May 1916, quoted R. F. Harrod, *The Life of John Maynard Keynes*, 212.

280 "brilliant colours everywhere": Naomi Bentwich–Marjorie Mace, 17 Apr. 1916, Mrs Naomi Birnburg (née Bentwich).

280 Maria and Mlle: Maria Nys, later to become Mrs Aldous Huxley, and Mlle Juliette Baillot, later to become Mrs Julian (later Lady) Huxley.

282 "she gave me less and less": "Memoirs".

282 "Why do they leave me alone": T. 1383, May 1916.

283 "Prosecutions are helpful to us": Russell–Allen, 18 May 1916, R.A.

page

283 "This prosecution is the very thing": T. 1401, n.d.

283 "Don't you make any admission": Frank Russell–Russell, 31 May 1916, R.A.

283 "Let me know if and how I can help": Whitehead–Russell, 4 June 1916, R.A.

283 "I am not anxious to secure an acquittal": T. 1402, 1 June 1916.

283 "If not, it was a serious omission": Russell–Allen, 6 June 1916, R.A.

284 "what Englishmen admire": *Dictionary of National Biography, 1941–1950*, 826.

284 "took a very energetic part": *Dictionary of National Biography, 1941–1950*, 914.

284 "a verbatim report": Hardy, 35.

284 "One thing which is perfectly certain": A. H. Bodkin, quoted Hardy, 35.

284 "I agree with Mr. Herbert Samuel": quoted from draft of Russell's speech, R.A. For verbatim account, see *Rex vs. Bertrand Russell. Report of the Proceedings before the Lord Mayor at the Mansion House Justice Room 5 June 1916*, 13.

285 "put in a way more likely": Hardy, 38.

285 "I would say, my Lord": Draft of Russell's speech, R.A. For verbatim account, see *Rex vs. Bertrand Russell*, 23.

285 "quite well – but simply a propaganda speech": Lytton Strachey, quoted Holroyd, *Lytton Strachey*, II, 174.

285 "I have allowed you a great deal of latitude": mimeographed typescript of Russell's defence, 7, R.A. For a slightly different report, see *Rex vs. Bertrand Russell*, 23.

285 "I have learned how to speak now": T. 1399, 9 June 1916.

285 "what I want permanently": T. 1421, 7 Sept. 1916.

286 "This country ... perfectly heavenly": T. 1397, n.d.

286 "upwards of 100 ozs. of PLATE": Printed sale list of Messrs Catling & Son, Trinity College Library.

286 "Some disappointment": *Cambridge Daily News*, 27 July 1916.

286 "The £125 was subscribed": H. T. J. Norton–Russell, Aug. 1916, R.A.

287 "regarded in Washington": T. 1297, pmk. 28 June 1915.

287 "it doesn't seem now": T. 1219, 3 Feb. 1915.

287 "*Against*, there is, first": T. 1346, 17 Jan. 1916.

288 "He quite agrees with me": Professor James Woods–Russell, 21 Mar. 1916, R.A.

288 "I think I ought to warn you": Russell–Woods, 25 Apr. 1916, R.A.

288 "owing to the strong local feeling": Woods–Russell, 26 May 1916, R.A.

288 "It is to be given": T. 1268, 18 May 1915.

288 "President of Harvard": Cipher, 28 May 1916, P.R.O., H.O.45/11012/314670.

288 "[Russell] ought by all means": Minute, 29 May 1916, P.R.O., H.O.45/11012/314670.

289 "I think his effect would be disastrous": Minute, 29 May 1916, P.R.O., H.O.45/11012/314670.

289 "First let us ask the Home Office": Note to Private Secretary, Treaty Department, 29 May 1916, P.R.O., H.O.45/11012/314670.

page

289 "I submit that it would be folly to let him go to America": Minute, 31 May 1916, P.R.O., H.O.45/11012/314670.

289 "Mr. Russell has been convicted": Foreign Office–Spring-Rice, 7 June 1916, P.R.O., H.O.45/11012/314670.

289 "Personally I am relieved": T. 1395, n.d.

290 "been convicted": Hardy, 41.

290 "not satisfied with the action of the College": Hardy, 42.

290 "If I were The Prince of Peace": quoted Wood, 103.

290 "I don't know how one *can* advocate": T. 1547, n.d.

290 "the important question": Hardy, 45.

290 "My first impression": Gilbert Murray, *Cambridge Magazine*, 14 Oct. 1916.

290 "Their refusal to draw such a distinction": *Nation*, 16 Sept. 1916.

290 "Mr. Russell suffers penalties for his opinion": *Manchester Guardian*, 20 July 1916.

290 "Love your enemies": G. E. Moore, *Cambridge Magazine*, 27 Nov. 1915, 143.

290 "something seemed to go out of Cambridge": Lawrence–Brewster Ghiselin, n.d., quoted Edward Nehls (ed.), *D. H. Lawrence: A Composite Biography*, 286.

290 "Have you seen my pamphlet on you": Whitehead–Russell, 14 Sept. 1916, R.A.

291 "The words were on my lips": quoted Jessie Stewart, *Jane Ellen Harrison: A Portrait from Letters*, 152.

291 "What brings me here": quoted Hardy, 41.

291 "The opinion of the academic world": *Manchester Guardian*, 15 July 1916.

291 "About Russell": McTaggart–Hilton Young, 7 Jan. 1917, Kennet Papers, University of Cambridge Library.

292 "Yes, I am delighted": T. 1387, n.d.

292 "If they hound you out of Trinity": Lawrence–Russell, 29 May 1915, Moore, 346.

292 "Some of the most prominent students": C. D. Broad–Russell, 16 Aug. 1916, R.A.

292 "great fun": T. 1414, n.d.

293 "The war, it seemed to me, was folly": Russell, *Which Way to Peace?*, 209.

293 "I like you, Meynell": Sir Francis Meynell, *My Lives*, 89.

293 "although an heir to an earldom": Fenner Brockway, *Inside the Left*, 68.

293 "Bertrand gleefully wondering": Brockway, *Inside the Left*, 71.

293 "Well, I move that we adjourn to Scotland Yard": Brockway, *Inside the Left*, 72.

294 "liberation of pent-up passion": T. 1394, 9 July 1916.

294 "But I had said all that mattered": T. 1391, n.d.

295 "a really *wonderful* meeting": T. 1392, n.d.

295 "The police took down every word": T. 1395, n.d.

295 "I personally shall go down in this fight": T. 1395, n.d.

295 "I enjoy it all": T. 1387, n.d.

295 "all the working-men who are hungry": T. 1387, n.d.

296 "I see my career": T. 1391, n.d.

296 "seeing all sorts of people": T. 1387, n.d.

page

296 "Mugwumpery": Undated War Office article and comments on, P.R.O., H.O.45/11012/314670/6213.

297 "was to throw a blaze of limelight": Sir Charles Mathews–Sir Ernley Blackwell, 28 Aug. 1916, P.R.O., H.O.45/11012/314670/6213.

297 "We cannot dismiss [his] remarks": Edward Troup–Sir Charles Mathews, 25 Aug. 1916, P.R.O., H.O.45/11012/314670/6213.

297 "Since then the same offence": Russell–Professor Woods, 30 July 1916, P.R.O., H.O.45/11012/314670/6213.

297 "Lord Robert Cecil said in the House": Minute by General George Cockerill, 13 Aug. 1916, P.R.O., H.O.45/11012/314670/6213.

298 "with the papers relating to Mr. Russell": Home Office–General Cockerill, 15 Aug. 1916, P.R.O., H.O.45/11012/314670/6213.

298 considerable strain: Sir Charles Mathews–Sir Ernley Blackwell, 28 Aug. 1916, P.R.O., H.O.45/11012/314670/6213.

298 "to harangue them": Report Samuel–Prime Minister, 20 Sept. 1916, P.R.O., H.O.45/11012/314670/6213.

298 "I am quite sure that it is important to see the men there individually": T. 1416, 1 Sept. 1916.

299 "I think it will be difficult to defend": Home Secretary, 1 Sept. 1916, P.R.O., H.O.45/11012/314670/6213.

299 "I have no notion": T. 1418, 1 Sept. 1916.

299 "The whole thing cheers me up": T. 1414, n.d.

299 "I begin to feel any day wasted": T. 1421, pmk. 7 Sept. 1916.

300 "There is no reason to be miserable": T. 1421, pmk. 7 Sept. 1916.

300 "Allen has a scheme": T. 1387, June 1916.

300 "preferred to treat an Englishman": *Daily News*, 2 Sept. 1916, quoted *Bertrand Russell and the War Office: A Personal Statement*, R.A.

300 "Providence would favour the War Office": *Manchester Guardian*, 2 Sept. 1916.

300 "Proceed to Glasgow": Russell–Lt-Col the Hon. A. V. F. Russell, 8 Sept. 1916, R.A.

301 "held to be a person likely to communicate": General H. H. Brade–Russell, 11 Sept. 1916, R.A.

301 "The subjects on which you wished to speak": General Cockerill–Russell, 13 Sept. 1916, R.A.

301 "May I say that I consider homicide usually regrettable": *Bertrand Russell and the War Office: A Personal Statement*, R.A.

302 "I think it quite likely": Russell–Elizabeth Trevelyan, 5 Sept. 1916, Trinity College Library.

302 "Dearest Bertie, I have felt most indignant": Alys–Russell, 11 Sept. 1916, R.A.

302 "a man of transparent integrity": *Dictionary of National Biography, 1931–1940*, 814.

302 "On dark days": Robert Smillie, *My Life for Labour*, 236.

303 "When I finished the lecture": Smillie, *My Life for Labour*, 237.

303 "had information from a very reliable source": *Hansard*, Commons, 18 Oct. 1916, col. 539.

303 "ridiculous to pretend": *Daily News*, 16 Sept. 1916, quoted *Bertrand Russell and the War Office, A Personal Statement*, R.A.

page

303 "A man who goes about preaching": M.I.5–Home Office, 3 Sept. 1916, P.R.O., H.O.45/11012/314670/6213.

303 "[The War Office] charged me": Russell, *Political Ideals* (1963), foreword.

304 "If you have not already": Walker M. Bailey–Russell, 20 Oct. 1916, R.A.

304 "been persecuted and pursued": *Hansard*, Commons, 19 Oct. 1916, col. 826.

304 "could undoubtedly have been made": *Hansard*, Commons, 19 Oct. 1916, col. 880.

304 "I do not advocate the prosecution": Sir Charles Mathews–Sir Ernley Blackwell, 28 Aug. 1916, P.R.O., H.O.45/11012/314670/6213.

304 "I should be sorry to repeat them": *Hansard*, Commons, 19 Oct. 1916, col. 881.

305 "a small man": Malleson, *After Ten Years*, 104.

306 "I never cease being glad and grateful": Colette–Russell, 12 Mar. 1917, Colette, I, 74.

306 "we found ourselves placed side by side": Constance Malleson, "Fifty Years, 1916–1966", in Ralph Schoenman (ed.), *Bertrand Russell: Philosopher of the Century*, 17.

306 "Cannan was stopping": Malleson, *After Ten Years*, 106.

307 "woke up one fine morning": Malleson, *After Ten Years*, 91.

307 "should never have parted": Colette, II, 109.

307 "Nothing on this earth": Colette–Russell, 24 Dec. 1968, Colette, II, 158.

307 "I woke to the dim fog": Colette–Russell, 25 Sept. 1916, Colette, I, 1.

307 "I remember her splendid bearing": Colette–Russell, 2 Oct. 1916, Colette, I, 6.

308 "Having daily work": Colette–Russell, 3 Oct. 1916, Colette, I, 8.

308 "I've sent you the Hoppé": Colette–Russell, 2 Oct. 1916, Colette, I, 6.

308 "He was so gentle": Colette–Russell, 28 Oct. 1916, Colette, I, 31.

308 "I cannot tell you": Katherine Mansfield–Russell, n.d., R.A.

308 "I have just re-read your letter": Mansfield–Russell, Dec. 1916, R.A.

309 "I am 25": Mansfield–Russell, pmk. 25 Jan. 1917, R.A.

309 "They read as if we were having an affair": Note by Russell, 1949, R.A.

310 "I loved him": T. 388, 17 Mar. 1912.

310 "slim and rather small": Derek Patmore (ed.), *My Friends When Young: Memoirs of Brigit Patmore*, 84 ("Vivien" as spelt by Eliot and Russell: sometimes spelt "Vivienne").

310 "I expected her to be terrible": T. 1301, n.d.

310 "used her for the purpose": T. 1416, pmk. 28 Aug. 1916.

311 "I never contemplated risking my reputation": T. 1416, 1 Sept. 1916.

311 "I am worried about those Eliots": draft letter Russell–Ottoline, dated "1916", private source.

311 "As to your coming to stay the night": T. S. Eliot–Russell, 11 Sept. 1915, R.A.

312 "There is no occasion for your fears": T. 1319, pmk. 10 Sept. 1915.

312 "I am getting very fond of Mrs. Eliot": T. 1323, n.d.

page

312 "a very great affection": T. 1323, n.d.
312 "I shall be seeing a great deal of her": T. 1337, pmk. 24 Nov. 1915.
312 "I have found out what it is": T. no number, n.d.
313 "I don't know what I want": T. 1408, n.d.
313 "I had a long talk with Bertie": *Ottoline*, 120.
313 "fragile grasp on sanity": Robert Sencourt, *T. S. Eliot: A Memoir*, 57.
313 "her taking of drugs": Russell–Sencourt, 28 May 1968, R.A.
314 "She wants to learn logic": T. 1119, 3 Oct. 1914.
314 "some very considerable time": Colette, I, 50.
314 "I want to get to know [her] really well": T. 1439, n.d.
315 "It was amazingly fine": T. 1214, 30 Jan. 1915.
315 "You have an opportunity of performing a signal service": Russell (open letter)–President Wilson, 4 Dec. 1916, R.A.
316 "Mysterious Girl": *New York Times*, 23 Dec. 1916.
316 "It has been brought to the President's knowledge": Spring-Rice–Balfour, 26 Dec. 1916, R.A.
316 "Mr. Russell cannot have it both ways": *Morning Post*, 15 Jan. 1917.
316 "Having pursued quiet enquiries": Inspector Buckley–Home Office, 6 Feb. 1917, P.R.O., H.O.45/11012/314670/6213.
317 "I don't want my ideas propagated": Whitehead–Russell, 8 Jan. 1917, R.A.
317 "As the result of damping down": Whitehead–Russell, 8 Jan. 1917, R.A.
318 "Every person there": T. 1459, n.d.
318 "who spent the time telling long stories": *Auto.*, II, 31.
318 "Snowden & MacDonald & Anderson": T. 1460, 5 June 1917.
319 "It was a good beginning": T. 1460, 5 June 1917.
319 "The thousand or more delegates": Beatrice Webb, diary, 7 June 1917, Passfield Papers, London School of Economics.
319 "be at least as much concerned": Russell, "The Impact of the Russian Revolution on the N.-C.F.", undated draft to Branch Secretaries, R.A.
320 he had only read the foreword: Siegfried Sassoon–Russell, 23 Apr. 1917, R.A.
320 "publish something outspoken": Siegfried Sassoon, *Memoirs of an Infantry Officer*, 274 (afterwards referred to as "*Infantry Officer*").
320 "My first impression": *Infantry Officer*, 283.
321 "a strong liking for Tyrrell": *Infantry Officer*, 285.
321 "He is altogether splendid": Russell–Mrs Swanwick, 20 July 1917, R.A.
321 "I am making [it] as an act of wilful defiance": draft of Sassoon's Statement, with Russell's revisions, R.A.
322 "You are quite wrong": T. 1462, 7 July 1917.
322 "I talked to Massingham": T. 1462, 7 July 1917.
322 "There was nothing for it": *Infantry Officer*, 307.
322 "hating the prospect of painful interviews": T. 1463, 15 July 1917.
322 There was at first no response: Sassoon–Russell, n.d., R.A.
323 "I knew, too, that as a gesture it was inadequate": Robert Graves, *Goodbye to All That*, 322.
323 "He said, that the Colonel at Litherland had told him": *Infantry Officer*, 331.
323 "So far so good": Graves, *Goodbye to All That*, 324.

page

323 "I expect you can help me": Graves–Evan Morgan, 19 July 1917, R.A.

324 "It is just what was to be expected": T. 1463, 21 July 1917.

324 "I do not think even my hon. Friends opposite": Ian Macpherson, *Hansard*, Commons, 30 July 1917, col. 1805.

324 "... Sassoon has been forced": Graves–Russell, 19 July 1917, R.A.

325 "A vast crowd of roughs and criminals": T. 1468, 28 July 1917.

326 "when the war is over": Russell–Lucy Donnelly, 23 Mar. 1917, R.A.

326 "For a long time, I have been burdened": Agatha Russell–Russell, n.d., R.A.

327 "In a gay boyish mood": T. 1436, n.d.

327 "only now and then": T. 1453, pmk. 5 May 1917.

327 "I asked him about Lady Constance": *Garsington*, 178.

327 "... I began to know her well in the autumn": T. 1455, June 1917.

328 "You speak of being shut out": T. 1525, n.d.

328 "You'll read to me out in the woods": Colette–Russell, 21 July 1917, Colette, I, 117.

328 "We walked enormously": Malleson, "Fifty Years: 1916–1966", in Schoenman (ed.), *Bertrand Russell: Philosopher of the Century*, 20.

329 "would not be quite genuine": T. 1465, n.d.

330 "I did not want to do": T. 1512, n.d.

330 "This morning I read a paper": T. 1302, n.d.

330 "very difficult – bullying everyone": T. 1452, Good Friday 1917.

330 "The thing to remember": Russell–Catherine Marshall, 1 Jan. 1917, R.A.

331 "For goodness sake": Marshall–Russell, n.d., R.A.

331 "I am sorry that I have to write you": Marshall–Russell, 7 Mar. 1917, R.A.

331 "If I did not realise": Russell–Marshall, 8 Mar. 1917, R.A.

331 For a full account of Russell's collaboration with Mrs Hobhouse, see Jo Newberry, "Russell as Ghost-Writer", *Russell*, no. 15 (Autumn 1974), 19–23.

331 "Full of petty quarrels": T. 1444, n.d.

332 "It seems to me clear": Russell–Members of the National Committee, 18 May 1917, R.A.

332 "the divergence of view": Edmund J. Ford–Russell, 5 Nov. 1916, R.A.

332 "fearful rumpus": Russell–Marshall, n.d., R.A.

332 "I am a conscientious objector": Russell–Members of the National Committee, 18 May 1917, R.A.

333 "The world grows more full of hope": Russell–Allen, 2 Feb. 1918, R.A.

333 "it was very largely for his sake": T. 1477, 18 Dec. 1917.

333 "He is getting tired": Leslie de Charms, *Elizabeth of the German Garden*, 196.

333 "My interest in philosophy": Russell–Jourdain, 5 Sept. 1917, R.A.

333 "I long to be back at philosophy": T. 1444, n.d.

333 "solely for the sake of filthy lucre": Russell–Leonard Woolf, 6 Sept. 1917, R.A.

334 "of a kind with which": *The Times Literary Supplement*, 12 Dec. 1918.

334 For a contemporary assessment of *Roads to Freedom*, see Vivian Harper, "Bertrand Russell and the Anarchists", *Anarchy*, no. 109 (Mar. 1970), 68–71, which reprints a review from *Freedom* (Mar. 1919).

page

334 "Pacifist work": T. 1476, n.d.

334 600-word analysis of her character: Colette, I, 158.

334 "are exactly like everybody": Russell–Gerald Brenan, n.d. (*c.* 1954), quoted in Sotheby's Auction *Catalogue*, 3 Dec. 1974, 44.

334 "I'll be waiting on the doorstep": Colette, I, 177.

335 "I enjoy immensely doing work": T. 1477, 23 Dec. 1917.

335 "very largely concerned": Russell's prefatory note to *The Philosophy of Logical Atomism*, reprinted Marsh, 177.

336 "adopted the philosophy of logical atomism": *Phil. Dev.*, 11.

336 "all things are discrete and atomic": Russell–Lady Welby, 26 Mar. 1905, photocopy, R.A., original, York University, Toronto.

336 "in the course of thinking": Russell, *The Philosophy of Logical Atomism*, Marsh, 178.

336 "When I say that my logic is atomistic": Marsh, 178.

336 "The reason I call my doctrine": Marsh, 179.

337 Russell's latest book: Russell's book was in fact his *Introduction to Mathematical Philosophy*.

337 "I hope it was not Jourdain": Russell–Unwin, 30 Mar. 1919, R.A.

337 "It is practically asking me to bother": Jourdain–Russell, 24 May 1919, quoted I. Grattan-Guinness, "Russell and Philip Jourdain", *Russell*, no. 8 (Winter 1972–3), 7–11.

337 Christmassing at Garsington: Aldous Huxley–Julian Huxley, 3 Mar. 1918, Grover Smith (ed.), *Letters of Aldous Huxley*, 146.

338 "The American garrison": *Tribunal*, no. 90, 3 Jan. 1918.

338 "a foolish and reckless sentence": Hardy, 47.

338 "Of course if I had known the blaze of publicity": Russell–Murray, 15 Feb. 1918, R.A.

338 "we may hope to have an American garrison": Russell, "Imperialist Anxieties", *Tribunal*, no. 72, 30 Aug. 1917, 2.

338 "Two detectives visited me": Russell–Allen, 2 Feb. 1918, R.A.

339 "It is very annoying": T. 1488, n.d.

339 "It would be a pitiable thing": *The Times Literary Supplement*, 7 Feb. 1918.

339 done . . . his duty: John Dickinson–T. J. Cobden-Sanderson, 11 Feb. 1918, R.A.

340 "I had completely withdrawn": Russell–E. S. P. Haynes, 18 Feb. 1918, Mrs Renée Tickell.

340 "It is the fortune of war": T. 1480, 9 Feb. 1918.

340 "I am writing to tell you how sorry": North Whitehead–Russell, 2 Apr. 1918, R.A.

340 ". . . how you would have loved one another": Cobden-Sanderson–Russell, 16 Apr. 1918, R.A.

341 "which concedes what is valid": Russell, *Roads to Freedom*, 13.

341 "I think there is practically no chance": Russell–Murray, 7 Mar. 1918, R.A.

341 "I would certainly employ counsel": Russell–E. S. P. Haynes, 18 Feb. 1918, Mrs Renée Tickell.

341 "I have become gradually more satisfied": T. 1444, n.d.

341 "It seems decided that the military age is to be raised": Russell–Murray, 2 Apr. 1918, R.A.

page

342 "It seems to me very improbable": Russell–Wildon Carr, Good Friday 1918, R.A.

343 "I do not share his present views": Alys Russell–Lord Haldane, 3 Mar. 1918, R.A.

343 "My brother knew everybody": Russell interviewed by John Freeman, B.B.C., 4 Mar. 1959, *Listener*, 19 Mar. 1959.

343 "huge blustering pink-cheeked schoolboy": Colette, I, 24.

343 "The rules affecting them": Stephen Hobhouse and Fenner Brockway (eds), *English Prisons Today*, 221.

344 "I am sure I shan't mind the time in prison": T. 1483, 16 Apr. 1918.

344 "Don't think your reason going": Evelyn Whitehead–Russell, 1 Apr. 1918, R.A.

344 "All goes well with me": Russell–Frank Russell, 6 May 1918, R.A.

344 "Days here succeed each other": Russell–Frank Russell, 16 May 1918, R.A.

345 "one lives here in constant irritation": Russell–Frank Russell, 27 May 1918, R.A.

345 "Personally I think this prisoner should have little or no consideration": Note by Bowater, Home Office, P.R.O., H.O.45/11012/314670/6213.

345 "The only real hardship": Russell–Frank Russell, 6 May 1918, quoted Gilbert, *Plough My Own Furrow*, 114, original in R.A.

347 "I have nearly finished an 'Introduction to Mathematical Philosophy' ": Russell–Frank Russell, 27 May 1918, R.A.

347 "Lord Russell is desired": Frank Russell–C. D. Broad, 11 July 1918, R.A.

348 "very like trying to swallow a whale": Colette, I, 237.

348 "I have lived on charity": Russell–Frank Russell, 3 June 1918, R.A.

348 "My principal reason": Russell–Frank Russell, 12 Aug. 1918, R.A.

349 "My instinctive belief": Russell–W. G. Rinder, 16 June 1918, R.A.

349 "Were you in for several years": Colette, I, 243.

350 "I'm so glad you are glad": Colette–Russell, 4 Aug. 1918, Colette, I, 262.

350 "anointed with Madame Helena Rubinstein's face cream": Colette, I, 256.

350 "It is terrible when I come to see you": Colette, I, 239.

350 "I must, I *must*, before I die": quoted Malleson, "Fifty Years, 1916–1966", in Schoenman (ed.), *Bertrand Russell: Philosopher of the Century*, 21.

351 "with a most touching physiognomy": Colette–Russell, 18 July 1918, Colette, I, 253.

352 "If you possibly can, write me longer letters": Russell–Colette, 16 Aug. 1918, private source.

352 a singularly moving letter: Helen Dudley–Russell, 19 Aug. 1918, R.A.

352 "It does sound as though you had really reached harbour": Helen Dudley–Russell, 17 Nov. 1920, R.A.

352 "Then he asked me if I could explain": Helen Dudley–Russell, 8 Jan. 1922, R.A.

352 "I keep thinking of the moment": Colette, I, 284.

353 "I walk fr. room to room": Colette, I, 290.

353 "I am thankful that thee is free again": Alys–Russell, 29 Sept. 1918, R.A.

page

353 "BR arrives": quoted Gilbert, *Plough My Own Furrow*, 125.
353 "Now, I enjoy getting back to work": T. 1497, 30 Oct. 1918.
353 "It will be a *great* disappointment": Russell–Ottoline, 4 Sept. 1918, private source, copy in R.A.
354 "The way it developed": T. 1493, 25 Sept. 1918.
354 "I see CM at her place": T. 1495, 30 Oct. 1918.
354 "talked much with BR": Allen, diary entry 15 Oct. 1918, quoted Gilbert, *Plough My Own Furrow*, 126.
354 "B.R. sat by the fire": Allen, diary entry 28 Oct. 1918, quoted Gilbert, *Plough My Own Furrow*, 126.
355 "Mr. Bertrand Russell has now been released": Murray's Memorandum, R.A.
355 "I hope Murray's lectureship scheme": T. 1495, 30 Oct. 1918.
355 "It was grand seeing all those pages": Colette, 1, 297.
356 "It is very difficult to adjust oneself": T. 1495, 10 Nov. 1918.
356 "This letter is a cry of distress": T. 1497, 20 Nov. 1918.
357 "The crowd rejoiced": Russell, "Experiences of a Pacifist", *Portraits*, 34.
358 "I profoundly hate the social upheavals": Russell–Murray, 14 Oct. 1919, R.A.
358 "When I examine my own conception": Russell, "Things that Have Moulded Me", *Dial*, vol. 83 (Sept. 1927), 181, reprinted *Selected Papers of Bertrand Russell*.
359 "She was dressed in a bright scarlet frock": Vivian de Sola Pinto, *The City that Shone*, 254.
359 Russell ... again at Garsington: Ottoline–Mark Gertler, n.d., Mrs Igor Vinogradoff.
359 "You are sitting puffing at your pipe": Colette–Russell, 11 Jan. 1919, Colette, 1, 303.
360 "in a spacious upper chamber": Santayana, *My Host the World*, 120.
360 "Direct Action has its dangers": *English Review*, vol. 28 (May 1919), 403.
361 "I think you are really trying for two birds": Colette–Russell, 7 Feb. 1919, Colette, 1, 318.
361 "Whoever reads": Russell, *Analysis of Mind*, 5.
362 "If you have a nightmare": Russell, "Mind and Matter", *Portraits*, 136.
362 "Would you have a picture of a living skeleton": Russell–Unwin, 29 Dec. 1955, R.A.
362 from meeting Peano: Colette, 1, 374.
362 " 'Do Men Think' ": Russell–Unwin, 15 Oct. 1921, R.A.
362 "Physics and psychology": Russell, *Analysis of Mind*, 307.
363 "an habitation of great charm": Conrad–Russell, 2 Nov. 1921, R.A.
363 "I am glad to be no longer worried about money": T. 1535, 12 June 1919.
363 "the big simple eternal things": T. 1541, 27 Sept. 1919.
363 "All the large and simple beauty of this place": T. 1538, 14 Aug. 1919.
363 "in time get a daily companionship": Colette, 1, 325.
364 "Will be with you ten o'clock tonight": Colette, 1, 327.
364 "The parting with Colette": T. 1536, 2 July 1919.
364 "to think I've spent my life on *muck*": quoted Professor John E. Littlewood–author, 4 Apr. 1972.

page

364 "I believe I've solved our problems finally": Wittgenstein–Russell, 10 Mar. 1919, R.A., also Wittgenstein, *Letters*, 67.

365 "I wish I could see [Russell]": Wittgenstein–Keynes, n.d., Keynes Papers, King's College, Cambridge, printed Wittgenstein, *Letters*, 112.

365 "Heaven give me escape from this Paris nightmare": Keynes–Russell, 12 Apr. 1919, R.A.

365 "I should never have believed": Wittgenstein–Russell, 12 June 1919, R.A., printed Wittgenstein, *Letters*, 69–70.

366 "I said that a new point was involved": Littlewood–Dr J. M. Rollett, 20 Nov. 1969, quoted I. Grattan-Guinness, "Russell and Jourdain: an exchange", *Russell*, no. 9 (Spring 1973), 20–21.

366 "Your telegram came just too late": Laura Jourdain–Russell, 26 Sept. 1919, quoted Grattan-Guinness, "Russell and Philip Jourdain", *Russell*, no. 8 (Winter 1972–3), 7–11.

367 the day when she had first met Russell: Dora Russell–Elizabeth Trevelyan, 12 Nov. 1932, Trinity College Library.

367 "We have here Nicod and his wife": T. 1540, 4 Sept. 1919.

367 "Dora and I became lovers": *Auto.*, II, 97.

367 "More intellectual 'ticking-off' ": Allen, diary entry 11 Aug. 1919, quoted Gilbert, *Plough My Own Furrow*, 134.

367 "A dull, provocative spirit": Allen, diary entry 21 Aug. 1919, quoted Gilbert, *Plough My Own Furrow*, 134.

367 "Car, chaque jour je t'aime d'avantage": Colette, I, 331.

367 "He wrote to me a week ago": Wittgenstein–Russell, 19 Aug. 1919, R.A.

368 "I can remember our committee meeting to decide who next": Stark Murray–author, 28 May 1972.

368 "Alas, No time": quoted Stark Murray–author, 28 May 1972.

368 "to consider the desirability": Petition dated 13 Mar. 1919, Trinity College Library.

369 "I cannot remember how it came about": Hollond, "Bertrand Russell and Trinity", *Trinity Review* (Easter 1972), 5.

369 "He [had] found himself": Hardy, 55.

370 "I came to think even better of it": T. 1542, 20 Dec. 1919.

370 "All logic and all philosophy": Gilbert Ryle, *Analysis*, vol. 12 (1951).

370 "All mathematical proof": Russell, "Is Mathematics Purely Linguistic?", *Essays in Analysis*, 304–5.

370 "I found Wittgenstein's 'Tractatus' very earnest": Russell–Professor C. W. K. Mundle, 20 Dec. 1968, R.A.

371 "My book will probably not be printed": Wittgenstein–Engelmann, 8 May 1920, quoted Paul Engelmann, *Letters from Ludwig Wittgenstein, with a Memoir*, 31.

371 "All the refinement of your English style": Wittgenstein–Russell, 6 May 1920, R.A.

371 A detailed account of the negotiations for publication, and Russell's part in them, is given in the historical introduction by G. H. von Wright to Wittgenstein's *Prototractatus*, 1971.

371 "There is eagerness for your lectures": Hollond–Russell, 17 Dec. 1919, R.A.

371 "The present intention": T. 1542, 20 Dec. 1919.

page

371 "We both thought that marriage": "Memoirs".

372 "Beloved, I'm wanting to stroke your heathery head": Colette–Russell, 20 Dec. 1919, Colette, I, 339.

372 "As for divorce": T. 1543, 27 Dec. 1919.

372 "I don't think I can avoid going to Cambridge": T. no number, n.d.

372 " . . . I forgot to say in so many words": T. 1553, 1 Jan. 1920.

373 "His mind is rather wearing him out": Ottoline–Mark Gertler, 1 June 1920, in Noel Carrington (ed.), *Mark Gertler, Selected Letters*, 163.

373 "I'm alone": Colette, I, 365.

373 "still floating like a flag": Max Eastman, *Great Companions*, 144.

374 "I suppose you wouldn't come to Russia?": Malleson, *After Ten Years*, 141.

374 "I feel sure I shall have": T. 1566, 6 May 1920.

374 "I am infinitely unhappy in this atmosphere": Russell–Colette, 13 May 1920, quoted *Auto.*, II, 107.

375 "Most members of the mission": Emma Goldman, *Living My Life*, 792.

375 "In spite of his profession of Socialism": Marguerite E. Harrison, *Born for Trouble*, 210.

375 "View over Neva": Russell's Russian journal, entry 12 May 1920, R.A.

376 "None like the Communists": Russian journal, 13 May 1920, R.A.

376 "I am a democrat, but . . . ": Russell–William B. Curry, 5 Nov. 1936, R.A.

376 "Actually, he was revolted": Harrison, *Born for Trouble*, 210.

377 "He said he was more international": Russian journal, 15 May 1920, R.A.

377 "I feel that all": Russian journal, 16 May 1920, R.A.

377 "Very Napoleonic impression": Russian journal, 17 May 1920, R.A.

377 "Almost exactly as in England": Russian journal, 25 May 1920, R.A.

377 "Good law, bad tribunals": Russian journal, 25 May 1920, R.A.

378 "His room is very bare": Russian journal, 19 May 1920, R.A.

379 "It seemed to me possible": Russian journal, 20 May 1920, R.A.

380 "more like hell": *Auto.*, II, 103.

380 "Partly owing to [Allen's] illness": T. 1566, 25 June 1920.

380 "the best of all his worlds": Leonard Woolf, *Political Quarterly*, vol. 39 (1968), 347.

380 "Miss Black, against my wishes": Russell–Allen, 26 June 1920, R.A.

381 "for the first time in [their] lives": Allen–Elizabeth Russell, 19 July 1920, quoted Gilbert, *Plough My Own Furrow*, 145.

381 "I shall come back from the other side of the world": T. 1572, 14 Aug. 1920.

382 "competitors who would probably not have considered your work": Unwin–Russell, 7 July 1920, R.A.

382 now prepared for the *Lancet*: "The Illness of Mr. Clifford Allen", *Lancet*, vol. 199, 17 July 1920, 159.

382 "to be back among people who are sane and kindly": T. 1567, 5 July 1920.

382 "Every moment together": Colette–Russell, 17 July 1920, Colette, I, 373.

382 "He has half forgotten what he felt about the Bolshies": T. 1568, 17 July 1920.

page

382 "loved the Bolshies": Russell–Colette, 22 July 1920, Colette, I, 375.
383 "a world of dying beauty and harsh life": T. 1565, 13 May 1920.
383 "But an uneasy doubt remains": Russell–Colette, 13 May 1920, *Auto.*, II, 107.
383 "A divorce will be a relief": Russell–Murray, 2 Aug. 1920, R.A.
383 "I have always felt it would be better": Alys, quoted C. P. Sanger–Russell, 28 July 1920, R.A.
383 "I haven't seen her for so long": T. 1569, n.d.
384 "I am very happy": T. 1572, 14 Aug. 1920.
384 "I should be very grateful": Russell–Unwin, 25 Aug. 1920, R.A.
384 "I expect universal abuse": Russell–Unwin, 29 Aug. 1920, R.A.
384 "involved being quarrelled with": Russell–Elizabeth Russell, 16 Feb. 1921, R.A.
384 "The book deals with a situation": Russell–Unwin, 14 Oct. 1923, R.A.
384 "are coming to the station to see us off": T. 1572, 14 Aug. 1920.
384 "My heart is gone to you": Colette–Russell, 14 Aug. 1920, Colette, I, 381.
385 "There will be a letter for you at every port of call": telegram Colette–Russell, 14 Aug. 1920, Colette, I, 382.
385 "I am quite extraordinarily happy": T. 1572, 14 Aug. 1920.
385 "One who believes, as I do": Russell, *The Practice and Theory of Bolshevism*, 16.
385 "In view of the sort of people": *Auto.*, II, 125.
385 "I was sensitive": *Auto.*, II, 124.
386 "[Saigon] is a nightmare place": T. 1574, 11 Oct. 1920.
386 "No one seems to mind our relations": T. 1574, 11 Oct. 1920.
386 "It is not literally true": private source.
386 "The Legation people are tumbling over": T. 1578, 17 Nov. 1920.
386 "He is stated to have expressed pro-Bolshevik ... sentiments": Clive–Foreign Office, 22 Oct. 1920, P.R.O., F.O. 371.5347–F2568/2568/10.
386 "though discredited in this country": Minute signed E. A. Walker, 26 Oct. 1920, P.R.O., F.O.371.5347–F2568/2568/10.
387 "But Bertrand Russell returned from Russia": Ashton–Gwatkin, Foreign Office minute, 9 Nov. 1920, P.R.O., F.O.371.5347–F2568/2568/10.
387 "Would it not be possible": Peking–Clive, P.R.O. F.O.371.5347–F2568/2568/10.
387 "Stayed at Changsha": Director of Military Intelligence, Secret Abstract for January 1921, P.R.O., F.O.371.5347–F2568/2568/10.
387 "Very nice and good": T. 1578, 17 Nov. 1920.
387 "very much what I had expected": Yuen Ren Chao, "With Bertrand Russell in China", *Russell*, no. 7 (Autumn 1972), 14.
387 "This place is wonderfully beautiful": T. 1574, 18 Oct. 1920.
388 "The Americans sprawl": T. 1583, 21 Feb. 1921.
388 "Dewey's feelings about Russell": quoted William Schack, *Art and Argyrol: The Life and Career of Dr. Albert C. Barnes*, 323.
388 "He can print extracts": T. 1574. 28 Oct. 1920.
388 "We have 3 rickshaw boys": T. 1578, 17 Nov. 1920.
389 "I resigned": Note by Russell on letter Littlewood–Russell, 30 Jan. 1921, R.A.

page

389 "The party members' political views": Chow Tse-tsung, *The May Fourth Movement: Intellectual Revolution in Modern China*, 232.
389 "We have settled down to a regular life": T. 1579, 17 Dec. 1920.
389 "There being different words in Chinese": Yuen Ren Chao, "With Bertrand Russell in China", *Russell*, no. 7 (Autumn 1972), 14–17.
390 "China did one thing for me": "Mental. Dev.", 17.
390 "People seem good": T. 1579, 17 Dec. 1920.
391 "We are both very happy here": T. 1583, 21 Feb. 1921.
391 "It was still wintry and windy": Yuen Ren Chao, "With Bertrand Russell in China", *Russell*, no. 7 (Autumn 1972), 14–17.
391 "Prof. Dewey made out form": Yuen Ren Chao, diary entry 26 Mar. 1921, *Russell*, no. 7 (Autumn 1972), 14–17.
391 "At last, she became a little curt with them": *Auto.*, II, 132.
391 "I told them I thought it was very improbable": Frank Russell–Russell, 29 Apr. 1921, R.A.
392 "That news broke me": Malleson, *After Ten Years*, 155.
392 "[She] says my recovery is literally a miracle": T. 1586, 11 May 1921.
392 "She was a deeply religious woman": *Auto.*, II, 131.
392 "I have missed much by not dying here": T. 1586, 11 May 1921.
392 " ... I am just able to write again": T. 1584, 28 Apr. 1921.
394 "I am astonished to find how much I love life": T. 1586, 11 May 1921.
394 "I mildly regret": Russell–Allen, 2 June 1921, R.A.
394 "we are both overjoyed": T. 1586, 17 June 1921.
394 "We both long for home": T. 1587, 25 June 1921.
395 "I would do anything in the world to help the Chinese": T. 1596, 31 Jan. 1922.
395 "Regret to advise": CPO Services Ltd.–Russell, 16 June 1921, R.A.
395 "You will have to pass through a stage": quoted *Peking Leader*, 7 July 1921, R.A.
395 "I hope furthermore": Russell, quoted Chow Tse-tsung, *The May Fourth Movement: Intellectual Revolution in Modern China*, 234.
396 "I memorise the Chinese saying": Colette, II, 151.
396 "Miss Black is going to marry him": quoted Colette, I, 471.
396 "My Beloved, I don't know how to wait": Colette, I, 483.
396 "On my return from China": "Memoirs".
397 "In the autumn of 1921": Malleson, *After Ten Years*, 161.
397 "There's no new pain left": Colette–Russell, 30 Aug. 1920, Colette, I, 490.
397 "by Almighty God": *Auto.*, II, 136.
397 wrote Russell's lawyer: Withers–Russell, 28 Sept. 1921, R.A.
397 Nobody was more disappointed: Dora Russell–Rachel Brooks, 12 May 1922, R.A.
397 "that wife who libels me": quoted Elizabeth Russell–Katherine Mansfield, 5 Oct. 1921, Alexander Turnbull Library, Wellington, N.Z.
401 "He is now so busy": Russell–Jean Nicod, 13 Sept. 1923, R.A.
402 "You, Beatrice, only like the Japanese": quoted Martin, *Father Figures*, 115.

page

402 "Physically aged with an impaired vitality": Beatrice Webb, diary 16 Feb. 1922, Passfield Papers, London School of Economics.

403 "Side by side": *London Mercury*, vol. 4 (June 1921), 164.

404 "objected to by landlords": Russell–Unwin, 23 Oct. 1921, R.A.

404 "Tom says he is quite sure": Vivien Eliot–Russell, 1 Nov. 1921, R.A.

404 "The night seemed just like Tristram Shandy": T. 1594, 16 Nov. 1921.

404 "Does the world have some little problems": James L. Jarrett, "D. H. Lawrence and Bertrand Russell", in Moore (ed.), *A D. H. Lawrence Miscellany*, 185.

405 "Broad himself is very anxious": Moore–Russell, 12 July 1925, R.A.

405 "must write 50,000 words": T. 1640, 17 Mar. 1925.

405 "Gradually, as a result of a complex development": Russell–Josephine K. Piercy, 6 Aug. 1925, R.A.

407 "I will try to get it finished": Russell–Unwin, 30 Nov. 1921, R.A.

407 "The main things which seem to me important": Russell, *The Problem of China*, 11–12.

408 "One, Two, Three–Bang": Russell–Warder Norton, 16 Feb. 1932, R.A.

408 "I have known Mr. Russell": Minute from Sidney Waterlow, 29 Sept. 1924, P.R.O., F.O.371/10244–F3166/19/10.

408 "a monstrous article": Foreign Office files, P.R.O., F.O.371/10244–F3166/19/10.

409 "the use of lighted candles": *Dictionary of National Biography, 1922–1930*, 677.

409 "Lord Phillimore's embarrassment": Sir Eyre Crowe minute, 3 June 1924, P.R.O., F.O.371/10244–F3166/19/10.

410 "I am not disposed to yield": Ramsay MacDonald–Phillimore, 4 June 1924, P.R.O., F.O.371/10244–F3166/19/10.

410 "Moreover there exists": Sir Eric Geddes–Foreign Office, 2 Dec. 1924, P.R.O., F.O.371/10244–F3166/19/10.

410 "Beyond circulating the [Boxer Indemnity] Bill": Minute by Sidney Waterlow, 3 Dec. 1924, P.R.O., F.O.371/10244–F3166/19/10.

410 "Like Tweedledee": J. Ashton-Gwatkin, minute, 5 Feb. 1925, P.R.O., F.O.371/10244–F3166/19/10.

410 "I am sorry but I do not wish to do a book on Confucius": Russell–Unwin, 18 Mar. 1929, R.A.

410 "I am compelled to fear that science": Russell, *Icarus, or the Future of Science*, 5.

411 "ultimately be used for making more deadly explosives": Russell, *The ABC of Atoms*, 11.

411 "most men of science": Russell–Warder Norton, 31 Jan. 1931, R.A.

411 "I think this chapter": Russell–The Syndics (C.U.P.), 20 Mar. 1923, Cambridge University Press.

412 "the authors" ... were "under great obligations": *Principia Mathematica*, vol. 1 (1925), Introduction to Second Edition, xiii.

412 "To some extent, its author's standing": Victor Lowe, *Understanding Whitehead*, 150.

page

412 "be compared to attending a Rugby football match": Broad, *Mind*, vol. 37 (1928), 88.

412 "every few days Americans descend on me": T. 1654, 23 July 1927.

413 "On Wife-Beating", "The Back to Nature Movement" and "Furniture and the Ego": Printed in *Sunday Referee*, 15 Dec. 1935, and *New York American*, 30 Apr. 1934 and 20 Apr. 1932.

413 "On Tuesday, the critical day": T. 1667, 17 Feb. 1929.

413 "the sheer intellectual perversity": Julian Huxley, *Religion without Revelation*, 35.

413 "curious and pathetic document": *Monthly Criterion*, vol. 6 (Aug. 1927), 177.

414 "the things which had worried Russell": *The Times*, 10 Oct. 1957.

414 "Whereupon, R. C. Tawney resigns": Beatrice Webb, diary, 10 July 1922, Passfield Papers, London School of Economics.

414 "I never wanted to get in": T. 1610, 17 Nov. 1922.

414 "I don't like him": quoted Wood, 142.

414 "Vote for my mummy": T. 1633, 10 Nov. 1924.

415 "I think if [the Government] wins": T. 1648, 10 May 1926.

415 "In this process, America will play the chief role": Russell, quoted *New York Times*, 4 Apr. 1924.

416 "Bertrand Russell Sees Dark Future": *New York Times*, 4 Apr. 1924.

416 "general feeling that socialism": Russell, "Impressions of America", *New Leader*, London, 22 Aug. 1924.

416 "But this is not the worst": *Unity*, Chicago, 19 June 1924.

417 "I preached leisure": Russell–Lucy Donnelly, 3 June 1924, R.A.

417 "[She] is entirely rational": T. 1629, 2 June 1924.

417 "Most of my time, we spent travelling": T. 1629, 2 June 1924.

418 "He was delicious when I arrived": T. 1629, 2 June 1924.

418 "I've seen Bertie several times": Elizabeth Russell–Katherine Mansfield, 7 Nov. 1921, Alexander Turnbull Library, Wellington, N.Z.

418 "I like [Dora] very much": Elizabeth Russell–Katherine Mansfield, 28 Aug. 1922, Alexander Turnbull Library, Wellington, N.Z.

418 "He is so happy now": Elizabeth Russell–Katherine Mansfield, Oct. 1922, Alexander Turnbull Library, Wellington, N.Z.

418 "It is so lovely here": T. 1601, 11 May 1922.

419 "playing on the sands": T. 1606, 17 July 1922.

419 "When I have any time to spare": T. 1616, 12 May 1923.

419 "he has not quite grasped": T. 1643, 17 Oct. 1925.

419 "In spite of my efforts": Russell–Lucy Silcox, 27 Aug. 1928, Trinity College Library.

420 "If there's a current": quoted Conrad Russell, "Memories of My Father", *Sunday Times*, 14 May 1972.

420 "Bertie would say": Crawshay-Williams, *Russell Remembered*, 151.

420 "It had been raining all day": Utley, 70.

421 "somewhat unduly optimistic": *Auto.*, II, 151.

421 "It is an amateurish and in some ways ignorant book": Russell–Dewey, 15 June 1926, R.A., original at Southern Illinois University.

421 "A great deal of needless pain and friction": Russell, *Education and the Social Order*, 171.

page

421 "It seemed to me, and still seems": Russell, "An Autobiographical Epitome", *Portraits*, 14.

421 "to consider whether human development": *New Republic*, 9 Sept. 1931, 92.

422 "It seemed as though not enough thought": Dora Russell, quoted Terry Philpot, "The Russells and Beacon Hill", *Humanist* (June 1969), 173.

422 "Our school opens on September 22": T. 1655, 16 Apr. 1927.

423 "Whatever good it did to the children": E. Boris Uvarov–author, 11 Apr. 1972.

423 "I am afraid that education": Russell–Sixth Formers, Warwick Public School.

423 "With regard to religion": Russell–Sydney Carton, 6 Feb. 1928, R.A.

424 "Even small children of 3": Dora Russell, "Beacon Hill", *Modern Schools Handbook*, 31.

424 "this Council disapproves of sloshing": Dora Russell, "Beacon Hill", *Modern Schools Handbook*, 30.

424 "I'll teach you mathematics": Russell, quoted Mrs Beatrix Dennis–author, June 1972.

425 "All goes well here": T. 1662, 12 Nov. 1928.

425 "Those who know English country society": Russell, "Education without Sex Taboos", *New Republic*, 16 Nov. 1927, 346.

425 "allowed to remove all their clothes": Dora Russell, "What Beacon Hill Stood For", *Anarchy*, no. 71 (Jan. 1967), 11–16.

425 "The children wandered quite freely": quoted Rev. P. H. Francis–A. J. Ayer, 19 June 1972.

426 "absolutely insist": Russell–A. S. Neill, 31 Jan. 1931, R.A.

426 "I wish I had only nuns for staff": Russell, quoted Mrs N. Musgrave–author, 31 May 1972.

426 "We both thought that marriage": "Memoirs".

426 "his inability to restrain": Utley, 68.

426 "As we both have to go to London": Russell, quoted Mrs N. Musgrave–author, 31 May 1972.

426 "had been guilty of numerous acts of adultery": *Times Law Reports*, vol. 2 (1 Feb. 1935), 179.

427 "one of the most personally unhappy": Russell–Joe Park, 1 Feb. 1961, R.A.

427 "We find that in the first twelve months": Russell–Celeste Holden, 28 Nov. 1928, R.A.

427 "a school is an administrative enterprise": Russell, "An Autobiographical Epitome", *Portraits*, 14.

428 "I regard with horror": Russell, "If I Were a Preacher: The Grave Mistake of Inculcating Fear", *Daily Telegraph*, 4 Jan. 1929, 8.

428 "Anyone with an idea": Russell, quoted E. Boris Uvarov–author, 11 Apr. 1972.

429 "I like most about myself": Answers to questionnaire appearing last number *Little Review* and sent to contributors before publication ceased in 1929; printed *Little Review* (May 1929).

429 "Anyone who takes these debates": Max Eastman, *Great Companions*, 139.

430 "but if I had the devising": Russell–Ivy Pretious, 2 Dec. 1907, Tennyson.

page

430 "I hope and believe": Russell, *Forum* (July 1928).

430 "As you know, I believe in the fullest discussion": Frederick Robinson–Bishop Manning, 19 Aug. 1929, R.A., original in Manning Papers, General Theological Seminary, New York.

431 "He often delivers": *New York Times*, 26 Mar. 1928.

431 "Helen herself I did not see": T. 1658, 17 Dec. 1927.

431 "It has been drawn to my attention": Russell–Unwin, 23 Apr, 1963, R.A.

431 "The first thing to be secured": Russell, *Marriage and Morals*, 246.

432 "It should serve instead of vibro-massage": Russell–Elizabeth Russell, n.d., R.A.

432 did not believe ... Butler would allow: Manning–Dr Butler, 30 Aug. 1929, R.A., original in Manning Papers, General Theological Seminary, New York.

432 Russell would not lecture: Butler–Manning, 4 Sept. 1929, R.A., original in Manning Papers, General Theological Seminary, New York.

432 "Hither flock all the crowd": Roy Campbell, *The Georgiad.*

433 "The Mormons tried to convert me": Russell–C. P. Sanger, 23 Dec. 1929, R.A.

433 "I have been North, South, East & West": T. 1670, 19 Dec. 1929.

434 "Who May Use Lipstick", "On the Fierceness of Vegetarians", "Love and Money" and "Should Socialists Smoke Cigars?": Printed *New York American*, 14 Sept. 1931, 13 Apr. 1932, 14 Dec. 1932 and 30 Nov. 1932.

435 "... you and I are shipwrecked mariners": T. 1658, 17 Dec. 1927.

436 "It was very horrible": T. 1690, 9 Mar. 1931.

436 "lost him every penny": Russell–Unwin, 8 Mar. 1931, R.A.

436 "I always call him 'Bertie' ": Private source.

436 "A title is a great nuisance": Russell–Warder Norton, 11 Mar. 1931, R.A.

436 "And now I won't be a Countess": Private source.

437 "I hope to take my seat": Russell–Lord Marley, 29 Mar. 1931, R.A.

437 "It seems that Marley is a very vigorous Whip": Russell–Fenner Brockway, 29 Mar. 1931, R.A.

437 "You have more courage than I": Murray–Russell, 5 Mar. 1931, R.A.

437 "I shrink from the thought": Russell–Murray, 8 Mar. 1931, R.A.

438 "I think ... that unless Wittgenstein has changed his opinions": Russell–Moore, 27 May 1929, R.A.

438 "Go on, you've got to ask him": Russell, quoted Wood, 156.

438 "Don't worry, I know you'll *never* understand it": Wittgenstein, quoted Wood, 156.

438 "At the same time, since it involves arguing with him": Russell–Moore, 11 Mar. 1930, R.A.

438 "Of course we couldn't get very far": Wittgenstein–Moore (Mar. or Apr. 1930), Wittgenstein, *Letters*, 155.

438 "I have at the moment so much to do": Russell–Moore, 7 May 1930, R.A.

439 "The theories contained in this new work": Russell–Council of Trinity, 8 May 1930, R.A.

439 "the whole of this effort": *Auto.*, II, 160.

439 "While there I had a brief and unimportant affair": "Memoirs".

page

440 "My family gave him hospitality": tape-recording, Mrs Joan O'Mara (née Follwell) interviewed by Harry J. Pollock, Oct. 1970, R.A.
440 "I should awfully like to know": Russell–Joan Follwell, 29 July 1927, R.A.
440 "I do not in the least mind": Russell–Joan Follwell, 11 Aug. 1927, R.A.
440 "The advantages of [a hotel]": Russell–Joan Follwell, 10 Sept. 1927, R.A.
441 "Remember that I am very fond of you": Russell–Joan Follwell, 15 July 1928, R.A.
441 "It is true that I am by no means completely free": Russell–Joan Follwell, 29 May 1929, R.A.
441 "The second time": Joan Follwell, tape-recording, Oct. 1970, R.A.
441 "... Only a moment remains": Russell–Joan Follwell, n.d., R.A.
441 "I think myself": Joan Follwell, tape-recording, Oct. 1970. R.A.
442 "tramping home on winter evenings": Colette–Russell, 20 Jan. 1926, Colette, II, 7.
443 "On my side of course there isn't": Colette–Russell, n.d., Colette, II, 15.
443 seemed "unable": Dora Russell, *The Tamarisk Tree*, 222.
443 "Since I cannot do my part": Russell–Dora Russell, 14 Nov. 1929, quoted Dora Russell, *The Tamarisk Tree*, 222.
443 "So I tried to endure the new child": "Memoirs".
444 "She and I were left *tête-à-tête*": "Memoirs".
444 "There's a nursery-governess": Colette–Lady Annesley, 29 July 1930, Colette, II, 17.
444 "The children were the children of one's dreams": Malleson, *After Ten Years*, 311.
444 "his wiry leanness ... gone": Colette–Lady Annesley, n.d., Colette, II, 16.
444 "B has told her": Colette–Lady Annesley, n.d., Colette, II, 19.
444 " 'What keeps you going?' ": Colette–Lady Annesley, Colette, II, 18.
444 "anyone would think": "Memoirs".
445 "to work out a *modus vivendi*": "Memoirs".
445 "There were various reasons": "Memoirs".
445 as dear as he always was: Dora Russell–Lady Ottoline Morrell, T. 1686, 19 Dec. 1930.
445 "Dora and I remain": T. 1694, 12 Oct. 1931.
445 "I returned from America": "Memoirs".
446 "It suffices to say": Sir Boyd Merriman, President of the Court, 25 Jan. 1935.
446 saying she had not neglected: Dora Russell–Sir Francis Meynell, 10 May 1935, Meynell.
446 "It was so with Bertrand Russell": Sir Francis Meynell, *My Lives*, 189.
447 "At the appointed hour the lady arrived": Elias Bredsdorff, "Bertrand Russell: Some Personal Reminiscences" (unpublished).
448 "a great deal of the motherless small boy": Peter Spence–Lady Ottoline Morrell, T. 1703, 1 Feb. 1933.
448 "I am anxious to write a book": Russell–Unwin, 22 Feb. 1932, R.A.
448 "I do not want to write an ordinary history": Russell–Unwin, 8 Nov. 1932, R.A.

page

449 "half the research": Russell, *Freedom and Organization, 1814–1914*, 8.
449 "I enjoy writing history": Russell–Norton, 31 Mar. 1933, R.A.
449 "I have in mind another big book": Russell–Unwin, 16 Dec. 1933, R.A.
450 "I am very keen on it myself": Russell–Unwin, 10 July 1937, R.A.
450 "Secondly, – and this is more important": Russell–Murray, 15 Jan. 1939, R.A.
450 "I fully intend to write it before long": Russell–Unwin, 22 Nov. 1930, R.A.
451 begged him to leave them out: Ottoline–Russell, undated draft, Mrs Igor Vinogradoff.
451 "What you said about my autobiography": T. 1703, n.d.
451 arouse a great deal of interest: Peter Spence–Lady Ottoline Morrell, T. 1719, 2 Mar. 1933.
452 "I cannot imagine any point in going on living": T. 1736, 29 Jan. 1935.
452 "though sane": *Auto.*, II, 191.
452 "the pro's and con's are fairly balanced": T. 1743, 3 Nov. 1935.
452 "Do you think he will perhaps come back": Colette–Elizabeth Russell, 2 Feb. 1936, private source.
452 "In one sense my ship had gone down": Malleson, *In the North*, 186.
453 "Modesty forbids": Russell, quoted Wood, 200.
453 "I have observed in former books of yours": Russell–C. E. M. Joad, draft dated 14 Dec. 1935, R.A.
454 "Joad had no influence upon me": Russell–Clemens, 23 Dec. 1953, R.A.
454 "Like one of those extinct bird-lizards": Aldous Huxley, *Crome Yellow*, 21.
454 "You could always tell by his conversation": Russell–author, 8 July 1965.
454 "merely an expansion": Russell–Unwin, 22 Feb. 1932, R.A.
454 "But I am in the unfortunate position": Russell–Moore, 8 Feb. 1937, R.A.
455 "I gather that there is a university": Russell–Warder Norton, 30 Nov. 1936, R.A.
455 "haven where scholars and scientists": Alexander Flexner, *I Remember*, 382.
455 "I have been pulling wires": Norton–Russell, 4 Jan. 1937, R.A.
456 "I should *very much* like to succeed Whitehead": Russell–Norton, 18 Feb. 1937, R.A.
456 "Do you think Santayana would mind": T. 1764, 6 July 1937.
456 "I got a letter this morning": T. 1767, 2 Sept. 1937.
456 "I have gone back to philosophy": T. 1769, 25 Sept. 1937.
456 "a first sketch of serious philosophical work": Russell–Unwin, 10 July 1937, R.A., original with George Allen & Unwin Ltd.
457 "much more linguistic": Russell, *The Principles of Mathematics*, Introduction to Second Edition, 1937, xi.
457 "seemed inclined to treat the realm of language": *Auto.*, II, 194.
457 "The best hope for the world": Russell, "The Case for U.S. Neutrality", *Common Sense* (Mar. 1939).
457 "My feelings are three-fold": Russell–Norton, 28 Dec. 1936, R.A.

page

457 "We should expect you": Richard P. McKeon–Russell, 15 Mar. 1938, R.A.

458 "I have very little hope": T. 1775, 10 Apr. 1938.

458 " . . . The news is a terrible blow": Russell–Philip Morrell, 22 Apr. 1938, Mrs Igor Vinogradoff.

459 "The living image of my Grandmother Stanley": quoted Colette, II, 33.

459 "wondering about the marriage": Colette–Lady Annesley, July 1938, Colette, II, 34.

459 "He stood at the open window": Colette–Lady Annesley, Colette, II, 35.

460 "Yesterday, I was in despair": Russell–Gamel Brenan, 15 Sept. 1938, the Henry W. and Albert A. Berg Collection, New York Public Library, the Astor Lenox and Tilden Foundations (afterwards referred to as "Berg").

460 "The University, so far as philosophy is concerned": Russell–Murray, 15 Jan. 1939, R.A.

460 "Everything possible is being done by Stalin": Russell, *Which Way to Peace?*, 189.

461 "Your advice to individual pacifists": Gerald Brenan–Russell, 18 Nov. 1936, R.A.

462 "Spain has turned away from pacifism": Russell–Murray, 3 Mar. 1937, R.A.

462 "I am afraid war would do an extraordinary amount of harm": Russell, quoted *New York Times*, 26 Sept. 1938.

462 "I was glad of the settlement": Russell–Gamel Brenan, 23 Nov. 1938, Berg.

463 "been swimming upstream against the current": Walter Johnson (ed.), *The Papers of Adlai E. Stevenson*, I, 406.

463 "foremost on the side of peace": *Daily Maroon*, 30 Sept. 1938.

463 "I have some remarkably able pupils": Russell–Lucy Donnelly, 31 Jan. 1939, R.A.

463 "something like the Correlation": *Auto.*, II, 217.

463 "It was an extraordinarily delightful Seminar": *Auto.*, II, 217.

463 "We had tea at the Ritz": quoted *New Yorker*, 21 Feb. 1970.

464 "Even if there is no war": Russell–Curry, Apr.–May 1939, R.A., original at Dartington Hall School.

465 "I supported the policy of conciliation": Russell, *New York Times*, 16 Feb. 1941.

465 "My dear Mr. President": Russell–Roosevelt, 15 Apr. 1939, R.A., original in Roosevelt Presidential Library, Hyde Park, N.Y.

465 "I remained in favour of peace": Russell–Unwin, 7 Aug. 1960, R.A.

466 when "Stalin's Russia turned against us": Russell–Murray, Sept. 1940, R.A.

466 Since Thermopylae: Russell–Colette, 21 Apr. 1940, Colette, II, 39.

466 "The Bolsheviks have at last shown themselves": Russell–Lucy Silcox, 22 Dec. 1939, Trinity College Library.

466 "I share your gloom": Russell–Norton, 14 Sept. 1939, R.A., original in W. W. Norton Papers, Columbia University.

466 "we and Russell": Alvin Hunter–author, Nov. 1974.

466 "I have so far abstained": Russell–Unwin, 21 Jan. 1940, R.A.

466 "To me, love of England": Russell–Gamel Brenan, 1 Feb. 1939, Berg.

page

467 "Ever since the war began": Russell–Kingsley Martin, June 1940, quoted Martin, *Father Figures*, 194.

467 "I am still a pacifist": Russell–Elizabeth Trevelyan, 29 July 1940, Trinity College Library.

467 "I am not a pacifist this time": Russell–Elizabeth Trevelyan, 19 Jan. 1941, Trinity College Library.

467 "I don't think anything so important": Russell–Robert Trevelyan, 19 May 1940, R.A.

467 a brief statement: *New York Times*, 11 June 1940.

467 "the United States can better serve suffering humanity": Russell, *New York Times*, 16 Feb. 1941.

467 "objections to the war that was coming": *New York Times*, 16 Feb. 1941.

468 "On the whole, I no longer believe": Russell–Emily G. Balch, 6 June 1940, R.A. original in Pattee Library, Pennsylvania State University.

468 "[His] old pacifism is completely gone": W. J. Brown, *I Meet America*, 116.

468 "When Tis and Ben went over to the Russells": Peggy Kiskadden–Edith Russell, 29 Feb. 1972, private source.

469 "I shall never forget watching": Peggy Kiskadden–Edith Russell, 29 Feb. 1972, private source.

469 "He couldn't bring himself to enter": Peggy Kiskadden–Edith Russell, 29 Feb. 1972, private source.

469 "struck at the security and intellectual independence": *New York Times*, 20 Apr. 1940.

470 "recognised propagandist against religion": quoted John Dewey and Horace M. Kallen (eds), *The Bertrand Russell Case*, 19.

470 "sinister ..." support: Circular letter from Manning, 12 Mar. 1940, R.A.

470 "In one of his books": H. L. Mencken, "On Academic Freedom", *Baltimore Sun*, *c.* May 1940, clipping, R.A.

470 "the philosophical anarchist": *The Tablet*, quoted Paul Edwards, "How Bertrand Russell was Prevented from Teaching at the College of the City of New York", in Russell, *Why I Am Not a Christian* (New York, 1957), 210.

470 "desiccated, divorced, and decadent": *America*, quoted Paul Edwards, 210.

471 "Quicksands threaten": Telegram to La Guardia, quoted Paul Edwards, 210.

471 "The issue now passes": quoted Dewey and Kallen (eds), *The Bertrand Russell Case*, 5.

471 "lecherous, libidinous, lustful": Goldstein, quoted Horace M. Kallen, "Behind the Bertrand Russell Case", in Dewey and Kallen (eds), *The Bertrand Russell Case*, 20.

471 "I cannot think of any predecessors": Russell–Murray, 5 June 1955, R.A.

471 "Russell conducted a nudist colony": Goldstein, quoted Paul Edwards, 219.

472 "He is not a philosopher": Goldstein, quoted Horace M. Kallen, "Behind the Bertrand Russell Case", in Dewey and Kallen (eds), *The Bertrand Russell Case*, 20.

page

472 "in effect establishing a chair of indecency": Justice McGeehan, quoted Dewey and Kallen (eds), *The Bertrand Russell Case*, 225.

473 "As Americans we can only blush": John Dewey, "Social Realities *versus* Public Court Fictions", in Dewey and Kallen (eds), *The Bertrand Russell Case*, 60.

473 "however wise such action might have been": Russell, *New York Times*, 26 Apr. 1940.

473 "You must forgive me": Russell–Norton, 11 May 1940, R.A.

474 "In these days I am almost afraid": Russell–Lucy Silcox, 20 July 1940, Trinity College Library.

475 "When a sentence or belief is 'true'": *Phil. Dev.*, 189.

476 "A hen, terrified by a motor-car": Russell, "British and American Nationalism", *Horizon* (London, Jan. 1945).

476 "It is impossible to say how overjoyed": Russell–Colette, quoted Malleson, *In the North*, 184.

476 "been greatly excited by the attack": Randall–Peter Russell, 24 May 1940, R.A.

477 "I cannot tell you what an immense boon": Russell–Barnes, 18 June 1940, quoted Schack, *Art and Argyrol: The Life and Career of Dr. Albert C. Barnes*, 324.

477 "I do not know whether you want me to lecture on philosophy": Russell–Barnes, 20 July 1940, quoted Schack, *Art and Argyrol: The Life and Career of Dr. Albert C. Barnes*, 324.

477 "It is, I think, rather essential": Russell–Barnes, 17 Aug. 1940, quoted Schack, *Art and Argyrol: The Life and Career of Dr. Albert C. Barnes*, 325.

478 "In the first place": Russell–Barnes, 24 Aug. 1940, quoted Schack, *Art and Argyrol: The Life and Career of Dr. Albert C. Barnes*, 326.

478 "The programme of the meeting": Arnold Lunn, *And the Floods Came*, 162.

479 "I said 'No'": quoted Arnold Lunn, *And the Floods Came*, 163.

479 "Learning things [he had] always wanted to know": Russell–Lucy Silcox, 9 May 1941, Trinity College Library.

479 "Sometimes the longing for home": Russell–Elizabeth Trevelyan, 29 July 1940, Trinity College Library.

479 "Are all the trees": Russell–Elizabeth Trevelyan, 6 Apr. 1941, Trinity College Library.

479 "subsidise Russell so that a controversy": *Time*, 1 Feb. 1943.

480 an infraction of the Foundation's regulations: Miss M. Mullen–Peter Russell, 3 Mar. 1941, R.A.

480 "Many [English people in the United States]": Russell–Lord Halifax, 10 May 1941, R.A.

480 "orally, without formality": Russell–Trustees, Barnes Foundation, 1 Nov. 1941, R.A.

480 "been officially informed that": Peter Russell–Angelo Pinto, 28 Nov. 1941, R.A.

480 "one hour of knitting": Dr Barnes' lecture, 4 Dec. 1941.

481 "did not obligate [themselves]": Dr Barnes–Russell, 4 Dec. 1941, R.A.

481 "breach of contract": Barnes, quoted Schack, *Art and Argyrol: The Life and Career of Dr. Albert C. Barnes*, 347.

page

481 "Judging from the letters": Press statement by Dr Barnes, 16 Jan. 1943.

481 "With this gross breach of contract": Barnes, quoted Schack, *Art and Argyrol: The Life and Career of Dr. Albert C. Barnes*, 347.

481 "whole income (illegally)": Russell–Unwin, 13 June 1940, R.A.

481 "financial stringency [was] not so much": *Auto.*, II, 222.

482 "One was to warm the place": *Auto.*, II, 222.

482 "I realised by now": Utley, 171.

483 "There was trouble during the last war": George Trevelyan–Peter Russell, 12 Mar. 1943, Trinity College Library.

484 "even worse than Hitler's": Russell–Murray, 18 Jan. 1941, R.A.

484 "Despite torrential rains": Professor Paul Weiss, *Bryn Mawr Alumnae Bulletin* (Dec. 1943).

485 "If the case had been tried": quoted Schack, *Art and Argyrol: The Life and Career of Dr. Albert C. Barnes*, 349.

485 "learned anything whatever of democracy": Barnes, *The Case of Bertrand Russell versus Democracy and Education.*

485 machinery which eventually brought Russell back to Trinity: Sir George Catlin–author, and Trinity Council Minutes.

486 "modest contribution towards Anglo-American co-operation": Russell, "British and American Nationalism", *Horizon* (London, Jan. 1945), reprinted *Bertrand Russell's America*, I, 341.

486 "Very well done": Foreign Office, minuted comments, P.R.O., F.O.371. 1944–File 6/38510.

488 "All this is such a change": Russell–Lucy Silcox, 8 Dec. 1944, Trinity College Library.

490 "I dine in hall": Russell–Colette, 20 Sept. 1944, R.A.

490 "Almost every night": Russell–Gamel Brenan, Good Friday 1945, Berg.

490 "Everybody is utterly weary": Russell–Peggy Kiskadden, 14 June 1945, R.A.

491 "This rule was so sacred": Conrad Russell, "Memories of My Father", *Sunday Times*, 14 May 1972.

491 "I shall be here one day": quoted Irina Stickland–author, 26 Jan. 1974.

491 "The slim, erect figure": Vincent Buranelli, "Bertrand Russell, An Impression", *Prairie Schooner* vol. 29 (1955), 44.

492 "You know, Euclid is a pleasant fairy tale": Buranelli, "Bertrand Russell, An Impression", *Prairie Schooner*, vol. 29 (1955), 44.

492 "I had become increasingly aware": *Phil. Dev.*, 190.

492 "to attempt to systematize non-demonstrative inference": Russell, "Project of Future Work", unpublished typescript, Feb. 1943, R.A.

493 "are self-confirmatory": Russell, *Human Knowledge, Its Scope and Limits*, 515.

493 "Indeed, such inadequacies": Russell, *Human Knowledge, Its Scope and Limits*, 527.

493 "When you mounted the stairs": Buranelli, "Bertrand Russell, An Impression", *Prairie Schooner*, vol. 29 (1955), 46.

493 "So he, a stranger, wrote to the expert of experts": Buranelli, "Bertrand Russell, An Impression", *Prairie Schooner*, vol. 29 (1955), 46.

page

494 a caustic review: Ludwig Wittgenstein, "On Logic and How Not to Do It", reviewing P. Coffey, *The Science of Logic*, *Cambridge Review*, 6 Mar. 1913, reprinted in Homberger *et al.*, *The Cambridge Mind.*

494 "from his jealously preserved little pond": Gilbert Ryle, *Analysis*, vol. 12 (1951).

494 " 'He isn't going to kill himself' "; Wittgenstein, quoted Norman Malcolm, *Ludwig Wittgenstein: A Memoir*, 68.

494 "most disagreeable": Wittgenstein–Moore, 3 Dec. 1946, Wittgenstein, *Letters*, 186.

494 "give me an example": quoted Popper, *The Philosophy of Karl Popper* (ed. Schilpp), I, 98. Popper gives a full account of the incident on pp. 97–8 of the volume.

495 "the meeting" had been "charged to an unusual degree": Minutes, Moral Science Club, Oct. 1946.

495 question of using Russell: Internal B.B.C. Memoranda, 10 Feb. 1944, 7 Mar. 1944, B.B.C. Archives.

495 "at first sight rather like": Mary Somerville, Memo. 6 Nov. 1944, B.B.C. Archives.

496 "I am incredibly busy": Russell–Irina Wragge-Morley, 23 Jan. 1947, private source.

496 "Of all the many speakers I handled": Ronald Lewin–author, 25 July 1974.

496 "I hardly think 'Science and the Christian Age' ": Russell–D. J. G. Holroyde, 30 July 1951.

496 "Copleston is a find": Sir William Haley, 29 Jan. 1948, B.B.C. Archives.

497 "one can criticise [Copleston]": Russell–Paul Edwards, 3 July 1956, R.A.

497 "Since he was seeking for an impossible combination": Utley, 68.

498 "You know my affection for you": Russell–Gamel Brenan, 1 Apr. 1939, Berg.

498 "Then she ceased to see him": Gerald Brenan, *Personal Record, 1920–1972*, 271.

498 "all the above": Russell–Gamel Brenan, Good Friday 1945, Berg.

498 "For various rather complicated reasons": Russell–Gamel Brenan, 10 May 1945, Berg.

498 "I have a very ardent desire to see you": Russell–Gamel Brenan, 22 Jan. 1947, Berg.

498 "I hate the way the months go by": Russell-Gamel Brenan, 5 Mar. 1947, Berg.

498 "From the first": Russell–Gamel Brenan, undated note, Berg.

499 "It would be a great joy to see you": Russell–Irina Wragge-Morley, 7 Oct. 1946, private source.

499 "the peculiarly intense & complete": Irina Stickland–author, 26 Jan. 1974.

499 "I am marooned here": Russell–Irina Wragge-Morley, 25 Oct. 1949, private source.

499 "It is like coming home": Colette, II, 83.

500 " 'Ah, love, let us be true' ": Matthew Arnold, "Dover Beach", quoted Colette, II, 91.

page

501 "In that case the atom bomb can explode": Colette–Russell, 15 Dec. 1947, Colette, II, 96.

501 "I will make little of it": quoted Colette, II, 103.

501 "The vivid interest he then took": Malleson, "Fifty Years, 1916–1966", in Schoenman (ed.), *Bertrand Russell: Philosopher of the Century*, 24.

501 "The quay was deserted": Malleson, "Fifty Years, 1916–1966", in Schoenman (ed.), *Bertrand Russell: Philosopher of the Century*, 24.

502 "I don't think it'd answer": Colette, II, 107.

502 "B and I had the whole of yesterday": Colette, II, 109.

502 "it was time to introduce influential Norwegians": Sir Laurence Collier, quoted Crawshay-Williams, *Russell Remembered*, 51.

503 "We had a polite discussion": Russell, quoted Crawshay-Williams, *Russell Remembered*, 53.

503 "I found myself on the floor": Russell-Crawshay-Williams, 1948, quoted Crawshay-Williams, *Russell Remembered*, 52.

503 "I am not surprised": quoted Crawshay-Williams, *Russell Remembered*, 53.

503 "Well, after that": Sir Hughe Knatchbull-Hugessen, quoted Sir Laurence Collier–author, 6 Dec. 1973.

503 "sent [him] to Norway": *Auto.*, III, 21.

504 "for the Foreign Office": Russell–Irina Wragge-Morley, 28 Dec. 1949, private source.

504 "busy with articles": Russell–Irina Wragge-Morley, 25 Mar. 1950, private source.

504 "combine that degree of individual initiative": Russell, *Authority and the Individual*, 11.

504 "What the truth of logic is": Russell interviewed *Compass and Fleet* (L.S.E. student journal) (Dec. 1964).

504 "He remarked ... Peter's last words": Colette, 17 Mar. 1949, Colette, II, 113.

504 "After they'd had two tremendous telephone rows": Colette, II, 113.

505 "I remember him": Conrad Russell, "Memories of my Father", *Sunday Times*, 14 May 1972.

505 "your 4½ minutes boiled egg": Colette, II, 13.

506 "But my heart was wrung": Colette, II, 116.

506 "The sea, when I look westward": Colette, II, 118.

507 "It was in a most romantic setting": Julian Trevelyan, "An Old Friendship", in Schoenman (ed.), *Bertrand Russell: Philosopher of the Century*, 30.

507 "I'm as drunk as a Lord": quoted Julian Trevelyan, "An Old Friendship", in Schoenman (ed.), *Bertrand Russell: Philosopher of the Century*, 30.

507 "Not in the least": Colette, II, 123.

507 "Never": Colette, II, 123.

507 "I had been seeing something of Colette": "Memoirs".

507 "This summer I have been preparing an autobiography": Russell–Miriam Reich, 24 Apr. 1949, R.A.

508 "We used the word 'soupy'": Crawshay-Williams, *Russell Remembered*, 55.

page

508 "You have sometimes behaved": King George VI–Russell, quoted *Auto.*, III, 26.

508 "Like your brother": *Auto.*, III, 26.

508 "to think that I made a mistake": Alys Russell–Berenson, 28 Jan. 1949, R.A.

508 "Bertie's wife has left him": Alys Russell–Berenson, 3 July 1949, R.A.

508 "Bertie's style & his clear thought": Alys Russell–Berenson, 6 Feb. 1949, R.A.

509 "Dearest Bertie, I feel I must break the silence": Alys–Russell, 9 June 1949, R.A.

509 "& we had a long friendly talk": Alys Russell–Berenson, 6 Feb. 1950, R.A.

509 "I shall count the days": Alys–Russell, 9 Mar. 1950, R.A.

509 "I am utterly devoted to thee": Alys–Russell, 14 Apr. 1950, R.A.

510 Russell in Australia: See Francis Keighley, "Left-wing Liberal: Bertrand Russell in Australia, 1950", unpublished research essay, Australian National University 1973; and Nicolas Griffin, "Russell in Australia", *Russell*, no. 16 (Winter 1974–5), 3–15.

511 "People were lined up 3 and 4 deep": Julie Medlock, unpublished manuscript on Russell, R.A.

512 "The State Police had located the bus": Julie Medlock, unpublished manuscript, R.A.

513 "I have had my fill of lecturing": Russell–Unwin, 23 Nov. 1950, R.A.

513 "He came down to accept the award": Kathleen Nott–author, Sept. 1973.

513 "The atom bomb and the bacterial bomb": Russell, "What Desires Are Politically Important?", Nobel Lecture, 11 Dec. 1950, reprinted as pt II, ch. 2, *Human Society in Ethics and Politics* (1954).

517 "and I don't repent of it": Russell, interviewed by John Freeman, B.B.C., 4 Mar. 1959, *Listener*, 19 March 1959.

518 "If America were more imperialistic": *Forward*, 18 Aug. 1945.

518 "There is no point in agreements": Russell–Gamel Brenan, 1 Sept. 1945, Berg.

518 "Russia's immense military strength": Russell, *Manchester Guardian*, 2 Oct. 1945.

519 a letter to Kingsley Martin: Although Russell's original letter to Kingsley Martin cannot be traced either in Martin's archives or in those of Victor Gollancz, to whom Martin sent it, the Russell Archives contain an undated letter in Russell's hand whose contents suggest that it is the draft of the letter eventually sent. It runs as follows:

Sir,

We of the Western democracies, who have profited by Russian help in winning the war, & who have acquiesced in Russian occupation of all Germany east of the Elbe (with the exception of a part of Berlin), have to face a very grave responsibility – as grave as any that has ever confronted human beings in the whole history of the world. By the unanimous testimony of all who have knowledge of the facts, the Russians, & the Poles with Russian acquiescence, are perpetrating a vast atrocity larger in scale,

page

& scarcely less horrible in detail, than those perpetrated by the Nazis in concentration camps. They have adopted a policy which must result, & evidently is intended to result, in the extermination of a very large proportion of the Germans who have hitherto lived east of the Elbe. In the Russian zone machinery, live stock, stores of food, etc., have been confiscated, nominally as reparations, but often only to be wantonly destroyed. The harvest has rotted for want of labour. Nothing whatever has been done to avert the consequent widespread starvation. Raping of women, on a scale hitherto unknown, has proceeded unchecked in circumstances of unspeakable cruelty, sometimes by large numbers in the presence of the children or mothers of the women. As a result, in some districts as many as fifty per cent of the women have become infected with venereal disease.

An even more direct responsibility lies on the governments of Russia, Poland, & Czechoslovakia for the expulsion of Germans from the territories annexed in what used to be parts of Germany. These expulsions have been carried out with utter barbarity: at a few minutes' notice, women, children, & old men have been herded into trains where they were kept for days without food, so that many died on the journey & many were [sic] shortly after their arrival in Berlin. From Berlin, after days & nights in queues, still starving, they were packed into other trains & taken to the western edge of the Russian zone, where no means of keeping them alive had been prepared, & where the existing population was already on the verge of starvation. It is universally agreed that during the coming winter many millions will die unless Russian policy is changed.

Friendly representations, both by the British Government & by that of the United States, have been tried without avail. It is clear that there will be no improvement unless & until the Russian Government has reason to fear that its brutality, with the problems which it raises for us through the influx of millions of destitute refugees in the zones of the Western Powers, will give rise, if continued, to active hostility on the part of Britain & America.

Only great firmness *now* can prevent the world from marching towards another world war. Acquiescence at this stage is bound to lead, as it did in the case of the Nazis, to continually fresh offences, until at last, perhaps in very unfavourable circumstances, the Western Powers find themselves compelled to resist.

However that may be, it is the duty of every humane individual to do all that is possible to mitigate a vast disaster which we unavoidably have helped, by our alliance with Russia, to bring about.

Yrs

BERTRAND RUSSELL.

519 "If you wish me to publish your letter": Kingsley Martin–Russell, 1 Oct. 1945, R.A.

519 "And, if the letter appears on Friday": Victor Gollancz–Russell, 1 Oct. 1945, R.A.

520 "But for the fact that the United States": Russell, quoted Peggy Duff–author, 24 July 1974.

page

520 "glad that disagreements with Russia": Russell–Gamel Brenan, 6 Oct. 1945, Berg.

520 "I should, for my part": Russell, *Cavalcade*, 20 Oct. 1945.

520 "That the U.S.S.R. would capitulate": P. M. S. Blackett, "Atomic Energy: An Immediate Policy for Great Britain", quoted Margaret Gowing, *Independence and Deterrence*, I, 198.

520 Baruch's proposals for international control of atomic energy were put forward on behalf of the American Government at the first meeting of the Atomic Energy Commission in New York, 13 June 1946.

521 "The present atomic bomb": Russell, *Hansard*, Lords, 28 Nov. 1945, cols. 87–92.

521 "I hate the Soviet Government": Russell–Gamel Brenan, 15 Jan. 1946, Berg.

521 "The American and British Governments should state": Russell, "The Atomic Bomb and the Prevention of War", *Polemic*, no. 4 (July–Aug. 1946), 15–22.

522 "The next war will be between": Russell–Unwin, 15 Nov. 1946, R.A.

522 "I am glad you are more anti-Russian": Russell–Irina Wragge-Morley, 23 Jan. 1947, private source.

522 "I think the only hope of peace": Russell–Einstein, 24 Nov. 1947, R.A.

522 "I should like to see": Russell, at Royal Empire Society, 3 Dec. 1947, printed *United Empire*, vol. 39 (Jan.–Feb. 1948), 18–21.

523 "Duelling was a recognised method": Report on new weapons to Chiefs of Staff, quoted Gowing, *Independence and Deterrence*, I, 163.

523 "I have read your paper": Russell–Dr Walter Marseille, 5 May 1948, R.A.

524 "was one which even at that time": Russell–Rabinovitch, 4 Feb. 1958, R.A.

524 "But should Russia refuse": Russell, "Prevention of War", *Dagens Nyheter*, 1 June 1948.

525 "The question is whether": Russell, *Nineteenth Century and After*, vol. 145 (Jan. 1949), 43.

525 "As he saw it there were three alternatives": Russell, *Nineteenth Century and After*, vol. 145 (Jan. 1949), 43.

525 "The distilled essence": editorial, *Reynolds News*, 21 Nov. 1948.

526 "I did urge that the democracies should be *prepared*": Russell, *The Times*, 30 Nov. 1948.

526 "I thought that while our side": Russell, "How Near Is War?", *Fleet Street Forum*, 1952.

526 "I do not agree with those": Russell, *World Horizon* (Mar. 1950).

527 "Rearmament as quickly as possible": Russell quoted *Manchester Guardian*, 16 Nov. 1950

527 "When I compare the Home Government of England and France": Russell–Anna Melissa Graves, 28 Dec. 1950, R.A.

527 "I have never advocated a preventive war": Russell–Harvey Cole, 30 Nov. 1950, R.A.

527 "After the last war": *New Statesman*, 18 Nov. 1950.

527 "a long letter of refutation": *New Statesman*, 21 Apr. 1951.

527 "The story that I supported": Russell, *Nation*, 29 Oct. 1953.

page

528 "Is it true that in recent years": John Freeman–Russell in B.B.C. interview, 4 Mar. 1959, *Listener*, 19 Mar. 1959.

528 "I should": Russell–Freeman in B.B.C. interview, 4 Mar. 1959, *Listener*, 19 Mar. 1959.

529 "I had in fact completely forgotten": Russell, *Listener*, 28 May, 1959.

529 "Bertrand Russell publicly advocated": Kingsley Martin–F. Din, 23 Nov. 1950, R.A.

529 "I have no doubt that": Kingsley Martin, *New Statesman*, 1 Mar. 1967.

529 "I should be in your debt": Russell–Miriam Dyer-Bennett, 21 Oct. 1962, R.A.

532 "Six days in the week": Russell–Elizabeth Trevelyan, 8 July 1951, Trinity College Library.

532 "I am very sorry": Colette, II, 139.

533 "When they discovered": *Auto.*, III, 69.

533 "There is the happy clamor": Julie Medlock, unpublished manuscript, R.A.

534 "Fortunately the glaucoma proved a scare": Colette, II, 149.

534 "soon we could no longer bear to be parted": *Auto.*, III, 64.

534 "well I'm damned": Elizabeth Crawshay-Williams–Russell, n.d., R.A.

535 "A woman of Bryn Mawr": Utley, 68.

535 "a minority resting its power": Russell, "Why I Am Not a Communist", *Portraits*, 212–13.

535 "the greatest contribution": Russell–E. Cotton, 24 Apr. 1959, R.A.

535 "where both sides possess atomic power": Liddell Hart, *The Revolution in Warfare*, 85.

535 "I have never wished": Churchill–Cherwell minute, quoted Gowing, *Independence and Deterrence*, I, 406.

536 "The situation now": Russell, "1948 Russell vs. 1954 Russell", *Saturday Review*, 16 Oct. 1954.

536 "In common with everybody else": Russell–Ronald Lewin, 17 July 1954, R.A.

537 "I find your letter very disquieting": Russell–Eileen Molony, 24 Nov. 1954, R.A.

537 "Man's Peril": Russell, "Man's Peril from the Hydrogen Bomb", *Listener*, vol. 52, 30 Dec. 1954, reprinted *Portraits.*

538 "[Nehru] said that they were prepared": Sir Russell Brain–Russell, 15 Feb. 1955, R.A.

539 "The danger that faces humanity": Frédéric Joliot-Curie–Russell, 31 Jan. 1955, Professor E. S. H. Burhop.

539 "We all have our prejudices": Russell–Joliot-Curie, 4 Feb. 1955, Burhop.

540 "important changes": Russell–Joliot-Curie, 17 June 1955, Burhop.

540 "Of course he remains a convinced advocate": Professor Burhop–Pierre Biquard, 8 Apr. 1955, Burhop.

540 Lancelot Law Whyte, was approached: Whyte–author, Aug. 1972.

540 "My own feeling is": Russell–Lord Simon of Wythenshawe, 19 Nov. 1959, R.A.

page

540 "I felt shattered": *Auto.*, III, 74.

541 "I accepted every amendment": Russell–Joliot-Curie, 17 June 1955, Burhop.

541 "I think that if it is really impossible": Russell–Joliot-Curie, 17 June 1955, Burhop.

542 "whatever [Russell] may have done": Burhop–Joliot-Curie, 25 July 1955, Burhop.

543 "Regard yourself as the dictator": Einstein–Russell, 4 Mar. 1955, R.A.

544 "Proposal to secure an independent": quoted C. F. Powell–Russell, 18 Feb. 1956, R.A.

544 "He was very sympathetic": C. F. Powell–Russell, 18 Feb. 1956, R.A.

544 "did not at the time": *Auto.*, III, 83n.

544 "a personal assessment": J. M. Spey–Russell, 28 Nov. 1956, R.A.

544 "If you do feel that this is objectionable": Russell–Central Office of Information, 29 Nov. 1956, R.A.

544 "If universal chaos is to be avoided": Russell–Patrick Armstrong, 6 Sept. 1956, R.A.

546 "As you know": Russell–Burhop, 30 Nov. 1957, R.A.

546 But . . . "we find that our Communist colleagues": Russell–C. F. Powell, 17 Nov. 1959, R.A.

546 "I have been wondering": Russell–Professor Joseph Rotblat, 5 May 1960, R.A.

546 "He favoured terms": Russell, Address at Vienna Pugwash Conference, 20 Sept. 1958.

547 "now is the time to drop the bomb": Russell, quoted Cyrus Eaton, McMaster Centenary Celebrations, Oct. 1972, printed *Russell in Review*.

547 "that the only war": Russell, quoted Cyrus Eaton, McMaster Centenary Celebrations, Oct. 1972, printed *Russell in Review*.

547 "the organisation is no doubt regarded": *Nature*, 24 Sept. 1971.

547 "My most important work": Russell, interviewed *Compass and Fleet* (Dec. 1964).

547 "If mankind survives": Russell, interviewed *Compass and Fleet* (Dec. 1964).

547 Gödel's Proof: "Uber formal unentschiedbare Sätze der Principia Mathematica und verwandter Systeme" (On Formally Undecidable Sentences of 'Principia Mathematica' and Related Systems), *Monatshefte für Mathematik und Physik*, vol. 38 (1931), 173–98.

548 "I am delighted by your example": Russell–Professor Herbert A. Simon, Carnegie Institute of Technology, 2 Nov. 1956, Professor Simon.

548 "this view ignores the fact": Russell, *Wisdom of the West*, 309.

548 "I detest linguistic philosophy": Russell–Professor C. W. K. Mundle, 10 Dec. 1968, R.A.

548 "I find Ryle's work always repulsive": Russell–Professor Mundle, 19 June 1967, R.A.

549 "Suppose (which God forbid)": *Phil. Dev.*, 243.

549 "Kreisel had said it was astonishing": Crawshay-Williams, *Russell Remembered*, 129.

page

549 "I still think that truth depends": *Phil. Dev.*, 213.

550 "I myself, naturally, had little sympathy": *Auto.*, III, 109.

550 "I loved my daughter dearly": *Auto.*, III, 109.

551 "tired of children": *Auto.*, III, 70.

551 all hideously harrowing: Edith Russell–Elizabeth Trevelyan, 18 Oct. 1955, Trinity College Library.

551 "tremendous romantic passion": Russell–Alys, Sept. 1894, R.A.

551 "I think perhaps, even now": Russell–H. M. Dowling, n.d., R.A.

553 "intolerable": quoted Gowing, *Independence and Deterrence*, I, 315.

554 "No, most emphatically not": Russell at Press Conference, Caxton Hall, London, 9 July 1955.

554 "No, I don't think it's possible": Russell, TV interview, 16 Mar. 1955.

554 "I think that since nuclear weapons ... invented": Russell–Ianthe Carswell, 17 Apr. 1956, R.A.

554 "I'm not in favour of its abolition": Interview, *Daily Mail*, 15 May 1957.

555 "I do not myself believe": Russell–Simon, 17 Oct. 1958, R.A.

555 "America has become the torch-bearer for the West": *New York Times*, 8 Sept. 1957.

555 "None whatever": *News Chronicle*, 1 Apr. 1954.

555 "Most Potent Sirs": Russell, *The Vital Letters of Russell, Kruschev, Dulles*, 15.

556 "awful that the continued existence of the human race": Russell–Freeman, 24 Mar. 1958, R.A.

556 "not only power corrupts": Max Born–Russell, 23 Nov. 1957, R.A.

557 "Britain and the Nuclear Bombs": J. B. Priestley, *New Statesman*, 2 Nov. 1957, 554–6.

557 "the founder of the C.N.D.": Kingsley Martin, undated manuscript "The C.N.D.", Martin Papers, University of Sussex.

557 "Now that Britain has told the world": Priestley, "Britain and the Nuclear Bombs", *New Statesman*, 2 Nov. 1957, 554–6.

557 "He asked me if I knew of any organisation": Canon L. John Collins, *Faith Under Fire*, 302.

557 "I have just written to Pat Blackett": J. B. Priestley–Kingsley Martin, 3 Dec. 1957, Martin Papers, University of Sussex.

557 "an imposing, somewhat stern gentleman": George Kennan–author, 12 July 1974.

557 "to discuss the possibility": Martin, undated manuscript, "The C.N.D.", Martin Papers, University of Sussex.

558 "One of the suggestions": Eric Tucker–Rex G. Phillips, 9 Dec. 1957, Arthur Goss.

558 In view of the convoluted claims and counter-claims that have been made about the birth of C.N.D., a statement to the author from Arthur Goss, 30 Aug. 1974, is significant. "It was only after most of the people had actually arrived that I knew for the first time that something else was afoot," he says of this 16 Jan. meeting. "Since what had been planned, so to speak behind our backs, was exactly what I wanted to propose to the meeting, I accepted the situation quite readily. I suppose the only difficulty at that meeting was that others had decided that Kingsley Martin should take the

page

Chair – and this he did. Had these 'Outside' moves not been made, the outcome would have been the same because my intention was to speak for 10 or 15 minutes and if my proposals were acceptable, to ask the gathering there and then to appoint a Chairman to take over the meeting and to put into effect the proposals I had outlined. As this would almost certainly have been Kingsley Martin, the meeting in fact followed the lines that we had intended all along, the difficulty only being that a small group decided that they wanted it to go that way without prior consultation with us. So here is a classic case of two groups having a slightly different idea of events. Kingsley Martin, Priestley, etc. wanted to speak with a group of influential people and start some sort of campaign against nuclear weapons and Peggy Duff, in effect, handed them one on a plate ready-made."

558 "Arthur Goss opened the meeting": Martin, undated manuscript "The C.N.D.", Martin Papers, University of Sussex.

558 "There was no rival motion": Martin, undated manuscript, "The C.N.D.", Martin Papers, University of Sussex.

559 "The secretary reported": C.N.D. Minutes, private source.

560 "In the uncomfortable spot": *Manchester Guardian*, 24 May 1955.

560 "I know from experience": Russell–Mrs S. M. May, 27 Apr. 1960, R.A.

561 "He answered that it all depended on how he felt": Russell, quoted Dr Martin Garstens–McMaster University, 29 Feb. 1972, R.A.

561 "You know, I'm sorry": Russell, *How Near is War?*, 1952.

562 "... he responded in kind": Alan Smith–author, 28 Apr. 1972.

563 "Perhaps we should have voted differently": Russell–Pat Arrowsmith, 24 May 1959, R.A.

563 "I must have had at least 50 lunches": quoted Mary Stocks, *Ernest Simon of Manchester*, 148.

563 "At the age of 80": Arthur Goss–author, 23 Sept. 1974.

563 "Gaitskell has, of course, thought a great deal": Simon–Russell, 30 Sept. 1958, R.A.

564 "would only secure his support": Russell–Simon, 30 Oct. 1958, R.A.

564 "Home was reasonable": Simon–Russell, 4 Dec. 1958, R.A.

564 "nobody takes the House of Lords seriously": Russell interviewed *Yorkshire Post*, 18 Apr. 1962.

564 "My only connection with its activities": Russell–Lord Halsbury, 4 July 1958, R.A.

565 "I am writing to withdraw my name": Russell–Stockholm Peace Congress, 4 July 1958, R.A.

565 "May I put before you": Russell–Kruschev, 29 Jan. 1959, R.A.

566 "promised to let us have": Wolfgang Foges–Russell, 10 Mar. 1959, R.A.

566 "to put salt on Mr. K's tail": quoted Martin–Russell, 2 Apr. 1959, R.A.

566 "met with a positive response": Y. Malik–Russell, 9 Apr. 1959, R.A.

567 "It seems that Mr. Kruschev": Foges–Russell, 14 May 1959, R.A.

567 "They realised [the project's] importance": Lord Boyd Orr–Russell, 22 July 1959, R.A.

567 "Today, it seems to me": Russell–Kruschev, 27 July 1959, R.A.

567 "I sent back a verbal message": Russell–Unwin, 10 Sept. 1959, R.A.

569 "I am afraid that at present": Russell–Walker, 18 Sept. 1959, R.A.

569 "as if Pugwash and C.N.D.": *Auto.*, III, 109.

page

570 "I agree with you": Russell–Patrick Corbett, 26 Nov. 1959, R.A.

571 "I am desperately in need of a loan": Begging letter–Russell, 12 Nov. 1958, R.A.

571 "Thank you for your letter": Russell–Sir Oswald Mosley, 22 Jan. 1962, R.A.

571 "He is very ill": Russell–Philip Noel-Baker, 9 Sept. 1960, R.A.

572 "I suppose that you are really denying indeterminacy": Russell–C. McCarthy, 16 June 1960, R.A.

572 "As it is, I am compelled": Russell–W. Oakeshott, 7 Feb. 1964, R.A.

572 "I was granted a special dispensation": Crawshay-Williams, *Russell Remembered*, 150.

573 "should be able to work": Russell–Schoenman, 21 July 1960, R.A.

573 "I had the same problem": Russell, quoted Schoenman (ed.), *Bertrand Russell: Philosopher of the Century*, 3.

573 "I know well that this is a dangerous doctrine": Russell, *Which Way to Peace?*, 207.

574 "Purely to get attention": Russell, interview, *Playboy* (Mar. 1963).

574 "alienate the British public": *Manchester Guardian*, 25 Oct. 1960.

574 "I incline to think that complete independence": Russell–Mrs Peggy Duff, 11 Jan. 1959, R.A.

575 "I feel that the question": Russell–Schoenman, 16 Aug. 1960, R.A.

575 "I am not prepared to say the time for marching is past": Russell–Schoenman, 29 Aug. 1960, R.A.

575 "a faint chill": Christopher Driver, *The Disarmers: A Study in Protest*, 112.

576 "were too often concerned": *Auto.*, III, 110.

576 "When I speak in Trafalgar Square": Russell–Collins, 3 Sept. 1961, private source.

576 "But on this occasion": Collins–Russell, 9 Sept. 1961, quoted *Faith Under Fire*, 320.

577 "It has been fairly obvious": Russell–potential supporters, Sept. 1960, R.A.

577 "did not dispute the possible efficiency": *Auto.*, III, 110.

577 "throughout the conversation": Collins, *Faith Under Fire*, 320.

577 Cousins's reply: Frank Cousins–Russell, 22 Sept. 1960, R.A.

577 "I could only answer": Collins, *Faith Under Fire*, 319.

577 Collins wrote thanking him: Collins–Russell, 25 Sept. 1960, R.A.

578 "for all your efforts": Miles Malleson–Russell, 19 Sept. 1960, R.A.

579 "The C.N.D. is bound by conference decision": quoted Driver, *The Disarmers: A Study in Protest*, 113.

579 "Only a few were able to be present": Collins, *Faith Under Fire*, 322.

580 "Few of the 27 members": Russell statement, 21 Oct. 1960, R.A.

580 "Individuals who advocate methods of civil disobedience": Press statement, 29 Sept. 1960.

580 "which, unfortunately, was at variance": Collins, *Faith Under Fire*, 322.

580 "Our Hampstead's very sincere plea": Edward Carter–Russell, 3 Oct. 1960, R.A.

page

581 "that human understanding and reconciliation": Collins, *Faith Under Fire*, 323.

581 all ... that was not libellous: Russell–Michael Scott, 15 May 1968, R.A.

581 "The atmosphere in that part of the movement": unattributable statement to author.

581 "We struggled to find a formula": Collins, *Faith Under Fire*, 323.

581 anodyne statement: signed Russell and Collins, 6 Oct. 1960.

581 "My reason for doing so": Russell–C.N.D. Chairman and Executive Members, 21 Oct. 1960, R.A.

583 "a man exhausting other men": Malleson, *The Coming Back*, 307.

583 "sort of adventure story tempo": Edward F. Sherman, "Bertrand Russell and the Peace Movement: Liberal Consistency or Radical Change?", read at Symposium, University of Indiana, Bloomington, March 1972, and printed in George Nakhnikian (ed.), *Bertrand Russell's Philosophy*, 260 (afterwards referred to as "Nakhnikian").

583 "every major political initiative": Russell, "Private Memorandum concerning Ralph Schoenman", dictated 8 Dec. 1969, published *Black Dwarf*, 6 Sept. 1970, *New Statesman*, 11 Sept. 1970, and as pamphlet by Bertrand Russell Peace Foundation, Queensland, Australia, Branch, Dec. 1970 (afterwards referred to as "'Memorandum'").

583 "taken over by a sinister young revolutionary": Ralph Schoenman, "Bertrand Russell and the Peace Movement", read at Symposium, University of Indiana, Bloomington, March 1972, and printed in Nakhnikian, 241.

583 hatched "I think": *Auto.*, III, 158.

583 "By creating a Russell Foundation": Schoenman, "Bertrand Russell and the Peace Movement", Nakhnikian, 248.

584 "I think the question of openness": Russell–David Markham, 3 Dec. 1961, R.A.

584 "We do not believe": Russell, *New Statesman*, 17 Feb. 1961.

586 "We do not want for ever": Driver, *The Disarmers: A Study in Protest*, 118.

586 "I feel that you should consider very carefully": Russell–Philip Altbach, 18 Apr. 1962, R.A.

586 "If the foregoing remarks are true": Russell, pamphlet, *On Civil Disobedience*, First Annual Conference of the Midlands Region, Youth Campaign for Nuclear Disarmament, in Birmingham, 15 Apr. 1961.

587 "We used to think that Hitler was wicked": Russell, tape-recorded speech, quoted Y.C.N.D., R.A.

587 "knew the words to be a mistake": Michael Burn, "Bertrand Russell: St. George and the Dogma", *The Times*, 18 May 1972.

587 "But Kennedy and Macmillan and others ...": record of telephone conversation with Y.C.N.D., R.A.

588 "I am afraid that I cannot do this": Sir Bernard Lovell–Russell, 8 Feb. 1962, R.A.

588 "It would have been better to have 'watches'": Russell–Michael Randle, 1 Dec. 1960, R.A.

588 "they could sell up one's goods": Russell–Pat Arrowsmith, 31 Mar. 1960, R.A.

588 "a chosen demonstrator should take a purificatory bath": *Guardian*, 9 Oct. 1961.

page

589 "But I do not think that the idea": Russell–Michael Randle, 23 Mar. 1961, R.A.

589 "I do not think that those who join": Russell–Mr Milligan, 26 Sept. 1960.

589 "The 'private' wireless is more difficult": Russell–Mr Wentworth, 12 Nov. 1960, R.A.

589 "It is doubtful if many of these same people": *Auto.*, III, 115.

590 "We were not so innocent": *Auto.*, III, 115.

590 "We instructed him to try to prevent": *Auto.*, III, 116.

590 "Patriotism and humanity alike urged us": Russell in the dock at Bow Street, 12 Sept. 1961.

590 "Prosecutions are helpful to us": Russell–Clifford Allen, 18 May 1916, R.A.

591 "they were all delighted": T. 1401, June 1916..

591 "behaved with a unique": *New Statesman*, 15 Sept. 1961.

591 "Along with valued colleagues": Russell, leaflet issued when in prison, R.A.

591 The Government had closed all of central London: Schoenman–Russell and Edith Russell, 17 Sept. 1961, R.A.

592 "The statement to me contains": Russell, "Thoughts on the 50-Megaton Bomb", *New Statesman*, 3 Nov. 1961.

594 invited him to speak: Lord Hailsham–Russell, 21 May 1962, R.A.

594 "The House of Lords, you must admit": Russell–Lord Hailsham, 28 May 1962, R.A.

595 "Russell, to some of us who were young in 1916": Colette–organizers 90th Birthday celebrations, printed programme, *Into the Tenth Decade: Tribute to Bertrand Russell.*

595 "nonagenarian intellectual in carpet slippers": "Cuba: Troubled Island", undated mimeographed pamphlet, R.A.

596 "The situation of Cuba involves a serious threat": Russell Press statement, 4 Sept. 1962, quoted letter A. Yule–Dr Alfredo Cordoba, Cuban Embassy, 5 Sept. 1962, R.A.

596 "Mankind is faced tonight": Original manuscript document, R.A.

596 "no conceivable justification": Cable, Russell–Kennedy, 23 Oct. 1962, R.A.

596 "swift condemnation": Cable, Russell–U Thant, 23 Oct. 1962, R.A.

597 "I answered the questions": Russell, *Unarmed Victory*, 35.

598 would "do everything possible": Kruschev, quoted Russell, *Unarmed Victory*, 36.

598 "The question of war and peace": Kruschev, quoted Russell, *Unarmed Victory*, 37.

598 "to make a conciliatory reply": Russell, *Unarmed Victory*, 38.

598 "I think your attention": Kennedy, quoted Russell, *Unarmed Victory*, 45.

598 "at the same time": Russell, *Unarmed Victory*, 46.

598 "accept dismantling of any missiles": Russell, *Unarmed Victory*, 46.

598 "By well after midnight": "Memorandum".

599 "make a great gesture for humanity": Russell, *Unarmed Victory*, 50.

599 "I should wish that such things be undertaken": Russell–Pat Arrowsmith, 1 Nov. 1962, R.A.

page

599 "I admire very much your energy": Max Born–Russell, 5 Dec. 1962, R.A.

600 "I do not consider that I have altered": Russell, quoted Michael Burn–Edith Russell, 11 Feb. 1963, R.A.

600 "I don't suppose I have altered": Russell, quoted Crawshay-Williams, *Russell Remembered*, 141.

600 "Probably Kruschev only does what I ask": Russell–Lord Dundee, 28 Dec. 1962, R.A.

600 "He was out of the country": "Memorandum".

601 "It was after the Cuban crisis": "Memorandum".

603 "If you want to be happy": Russell, quoted Stocks, *Ernest Simon of Manchester*, 155.

603 "Mr. Russell produces a different system": Broad, "Critical and Speculative Philosophy", in J. H. Muirhead (ed.), *Contemporary British Philosophy*, 1st ser. 79.

603 "tried by the folly of some of the leading members": *Auto.*, III, 125.

604 "I have become convinced, therefore": Russell–Dr A. Schweitzer, 11 Oct. 1962, R.A.

604 "to oppose institutionalised violence and cruelty": Bertrand Russell Peace Foundation, Press statement, 29 Sept. 1963

604 "The anti-war movements": Press statement, 29 Sept. 1963.

606 "infamous folly ... to teach the Chinese": "Memorandum".

606 "I can understand your envying me": Russell–Nehru, 30 Sept. 1961, R.A.

607 "an appalling betrayal": Russell–Soekarno, 27 Jan. 1966, R.A.

607 "I do not feel willing to give in": Russell–L. D. Oxley, 28 June 1961, R.A.

607 "If it can be secured": Russell–Alfred Kohlberg, 8 Mar. 1958, R.A.

607 "I do not want to see": Russell at Press Conference, Caxton Hall, London, 9 July 1955.

609 "was able to deploy": Schoenman, "Bertrand Russell and the Peace Movement", Nakhnikian, 249.

609 "the aid provided to armed revolutionary struggles": Schoenman, "Bertrand Russell and the Peace Movement", Nakhnikian, 242.

609 "Russell no longer spoke": Sherman, "Bertrand Russell and the Peace Movement: Liberal Consistency or Radical Change?", Nakhnikian, 259.

609 "The Profumo affair is most grave": undated statement, R.A.

610 "Insufferable pig": Schoenman, comment written on Haldane–Russell, 21 May 1962, R.A.

610 "I certainly never said": The Hon. David Astor–Russell, 16 Apr. 1963, R.A.

610 "It was only yesterday": Russell–Unwin, 19 Jan. 1967, R.A.

610 "If you believe that Bertrand Russell's work for peace": undated printed slip, R.A.

610 "and, for that reason, I am obliged to ask a charge": Schoenman–Elizabeth Jordan, 26 Mar. 1963, R.A.

611 "He tended to agree": Rotblat–author, 6 Aug. 1974.

page

611 "I met Ralph Schoenman": Elias Bredsdorff, "Bertrand Russell: Some Personal Reminiscences" (unpublished).

612 "Speech of your personal representative caused uproar": Telegram, quoted "Memorandum".

612 "promised again to be less violent": "Memorandum".

612 "It was painful on Monday": *The Economist*, 20 Feb. 1965.

613 "'Bertrand Russell Swims Atlantic'": *Private Eye*, 5 Aug. 1966, 121.

614 "I believe that the Bertrand Russell Peace Foundation": Russell–U Thant, 23 Sept. 1964, R.A.

614 "there may be a slight misunderstanding": U Thant–Russell, 5 Oct. 1964, R.A.

614 "My views have changed slightly": Russell–Professor Murti, 21 Apr. 1966, R.A.

615 "the aid provided to armed revolutionary struggles": Schoenman, "Bertrand Russell and the Peace Movement", Nakhnikian, 242.

615 "There were, however, serious intellectual doubts": Schoenman, "Bertrand Russell and the Peace Movement", Nakhnikian, 233.

616 "If I had been able to do so": *Auto.*, III, 163.

616 "that there had been an appalling miscarriage": *Auto.*, III, 165.

617 "it is a pity": *Evening Standard*, 28 Sept. 1964.

617 Nothing could do more to enhance: Attlee–Russell, 10 Sept. 1964, R.A.

618 "I have now finished my autobiography": Russell–Unwin, 29 Mar. 1952, R.A.

618 "I do not wish to enter into": Russell–Lincoln Schuster, 23 Jan. 1951, R.A.

619 "Sir Stanley knew his place": Private source.

620 "would be a good place for any papers of yours": Lord Adrian–Russell, 13 June 1963, R.A.

620 "I should be proud to be in the neighbourhood of Lycidas": Russell–Adrian, 21 June 1963, R.A.

620 "We now made a decision": Schoenman, "Bertrand Russell and the Peace Movement", Nakhnikian, 251.

620 "But as I left the house": Kenneth Blackwell, "Becoming an Archivist", *University of Victoria Alumni Quarterly*, vol. 4 (Winter 1969), 8–9.

621 "I wrote to Lord Russell": Professor William Ready, "How the Russell Papers Got to Hamilton", *Spectator* (Hamilton, Ontario), 12 Oct. 1972.

622 "There were tales of an Arabian sheikh": Ready, *Spectator* (Hamilton, Ontario), 12 Oct. 1972.

622 "He asked me how much money": Ready, *Spectator* (Hamilton, Ontario), 12 Oct. 1972.

623 "Would you think much of the idea of a mock trial": Norman Birnbaum–Russell, 2 Mar. 1959, R.A.

623 "The example of John Dewey": Russell–Birnbaum, 6 Mar. 1959, R.A.

624 "I was interested in your suggestion": Russell–M. S. Arnoni, 12 Mar. 1965, *The Minority of One*, R.A.

624 "My belief that Mr. Gladstone": Russell–Stephen Bagnall, 21 Mar. 1967, R.A.

625 "a partial body of committed men": Schoenman, "Bertrand Russell and the Peace Movement", Nakhnikian, 250.

page

625 "the data and their verifiability": Schoenman, "Bertrand Russell and the Peace Movement", Nakhnikian, 250.

625 "But is it the position of the Tribunal": Staughton Lynd–Russell, 13 Jan. 1967, R.A.

626 "The journalists were very disappointed": Private source.

626 "Between [1961] and the Tribunal": David Horowitz, "Bertrand Russell: the Final Passion", *Ramparts*, vol. 8 (Apr. 1970), 38–49, reprinted Horowitz, *The Fate of Midas and Other Essays* (1972).

626 "would not be expected to take part": Russell–Vladimir Dedijer, 14 Feb. 1967, R.A.

627 "You can't hide behind Russell": Private source.

627 "The proposal is for a session in New York": Russell–Dedijer, 23 Mar. 1967, R.A.

628 "I have spent nearly all my time": Russell–Members of Tribunal, 4 May 1967, R.A.

628 "no longer tolerate": Russell, 14 May 1967, R.A.

628 very sordid and vindictive: Schoenman–Gunther Anders, 19 May 1967, R.A.

629 "As regards health": Russell, "How to Grow Old", *Portraits*, 51.

629 "I do not expect to stop": Russell–Countess von Zeppelin, 30 June 1966, R.A.

629 "I am now in my ninety-fifth year": Russell–Lord Amulree, 7 Oct. 1966, R.A.

630 "From his childhood onwards": Conrad Russell, "My Father – Bertrand Russell", *Illustrated London News*, 14 Feb. 1970.

630 "Thank you for bringing to my attention": Russell–American Humanist Association, 21 June 1968, R.A., printed as "Bertrand Russell on the Afterlife", *Humanist*, vol. 28 (Sept.–Oct. 1968), 29.

630 "I try to console myself": Russell, "Beliefs: Discarded and Retained", *Portraits*, 42.

630 "I set out": Russell, "Reflections on My Eightieth Birthday", *Portraits*, 56.

631 "behind all the minute argumentation": Russell, intro. to E. A. Gellner, *Words and Things*, 14.

631 "no one could pretend that": undated manuscript on the status of women written by Russell *c.* 1907, possibly for Miss Ivy Pretious, Tennyson, printed *Russell*, no. 14 (Summer 1974), 3–12.

631 "Where democracy and civilisation conflict": Russell–Murray, 27 Apr. 1949, R.A.

631 "a kind of restfulness": "Memoirs".

631 "My ideal age was 18th-century France": Russell, interviewed *Compass and Fleet* (Dec. 1964).

631 "I am enjoying [them]": Russell–Colette, 22 May 1967, private source.

631 "I am pleased and gratified": Russell, quoted Crawshay-Williams, *Russell Remembered*, 153.

632 "His talk about the infinite": Russell–N. Chatterji, 26 Apr. 1967, R.A.

632 "I am delighted that there is a resurgence": Russell–Hugh Scanlon, 8 May 1968, R.A.

page

632 "At once he dictated a brief reply": Christopher Farley at McMaster Centenary Celebrations, reprinted *Humanist in Canada*, vol. 4 (Nov. 1972), 5–10.

632 did not "wish to be associated with": Russell, quoted Farley–*American Dialog*, 25 Nov. 1969, R.A.

632 "the only voice outside its frontiers": ... –Russell, 31 Jan. 1969, R.A.

632 "The situation of Soviet Jews": Farley– ..., 25 Feb. 1969, R.A.

632 "She seems quite beautiful": quoted Crawshay-Williams, *Russell Remembered*, 155.

633 "a grave tactical mistake": "Memorandum".

634 "in any way whatsoever": Russell statement, quoted *Guardian*, 10 Dec. 1969.

634 "The convergence of Russell's incapacity": Schoenman, "Bertrand Russell and the Peace Movement", Nakhnikian, 251.

634 "When we got him out of the car": Crawshay-Williams, *Russell Remembered*, 156.

634 "We must say 'No'": Private source.

635 "I early recognised": "Memorandum".

636 could not then have "published a simple letter": Adam Roberts, *New Statesman*, 18 Sept. 1970.

636 "In point of fact, what goes out over my name": *Auto.*, III, 164.

637 "I do so hate to leave this world": Russell–Edith Russell, private source.

637 "a distinguished person": A. J. Bearsted–Russell, 1 Jan. 1970, R.A.

638 "The aggression committed by Israel": Russell, "Message from Bertrand Russell to the International Conference of Parliamentarians in Cairo" (Feb. 1970). Widespread publication, e.g. *Spokesman*, no. 2 (Apr. 1970), 5.

Index

Throughout the index, Bertrand Russell *is noted as* B.R.